# OCEANS, COASTS AND LAW

*Holdings of eighteen Libraries with Union List, plus selected additional Books, Papers, Foreign and U.S. Articles categorized by Topic*

by
**HELENA P. von PFEIL, B.A., B.S., M.L.S.**
*Assistant Librarian
University of Puget Sound Law School*

## VOLUME II
Union List, keywords/descriptors,
legal and related articles

*Foreword by*
**MYRON NORDQUIST**
*Attorney, United States Department of State
Alternate Representative, U.S. Delegation
to the Third United Nations Conference on
the Law of the Sea*

*Preface by*
**H. GARY KNIGHT**
*Campanile Charities Professor of Marine Resources,
Louisiana State University*

1976 OCEANA PUBLICATIONS, INC. DOBBS FERRY, N.Y.

Library of Congress Cataloging in Publication Data

Von Pfeil, Helena P.
  Oceans, coasts, and law.

  CONTENTS: v. 1. Holdings of eighteen libraries. — v. 2. Union list, keywords/descriptors, legal and related articles.
  1. Maritime law—Bibliography. 2. Territorial waters—Bibliography. 3. Maritime law—United States—Bibliography. I. Title.
  Z6464.M2V65   [JX4411]   016.34144'8   76-28310
  ISBN 0-379-00586-7

© Copyright 1976 by Oceana Publications, Inc.

All rights reserved. No part of this publication may be reproduced or transmitted in any form or by any means, electronic or mechanical, including photocopy, recording, xerography, or any information storage and retrieval system, without permission in writing from the publisher.

Manufactured in the United States of America

A portion of the initial research was funded by the Oregon State Sea Grant Program. The major part of the work was undertaken at the University of Puget Sound Law School, Tacoma, Washington, and this institution provided a portion of the financial support.

CONTENTS

VOLUME II

| | page |
|---|---|
| How to use the topic categories/reference symbols for books and articles | 427 |
| Union List plus selected additional books, papers and articles | 430 |
| Reference materials | 683 |
| Skeleton list of keywords/descriptors | 703 |
| Legal and related articles | 724 |

UNION LIST OF MONOGRAPHS AND PAPERS
INCLUDING LIBRARY NUMBER, AND BROAD TOPIC CATEGORY

Explanation of breakdown:

A number has been assigned to each of the eighteen participating libraries, and to the Law of the Sea Institute publications. (Two library holdings were submitted late and therefore appear out of sequence.) The library numbers are shown above the entries.

Additional selected recent publications which do not appear in the individual library holdings are labelled ***.

Selected papers presented at conferences, etc., are labelled ART, and are not included in the separate section of periodical articles.

Each item has been slotted under a broad topic category appearing to the left of the entry. These categories may serve as call numbers in a special collection - e.g., publications dealing mainly with Coastal matters could be shelved under II, Marine Resources (Living) III, Marine Resources (Non-living) IV, and General V. Because of the overlapping which occurs in selected publications dealing with admiralty and maritime law, these items are categorized as VMLAD. Researchers who want materials dealing with boundaries, jurisdiction, contiguous zones, continental shelf, and the economic/exclusive zone are advised to consult categories IIB, IIIB, IVB, VB; IVCS, VCS; and IIIEZ, IVEZ, VEZ. It was also difficult to separate law of the sea and international law, and both categories should be checked. CAVEAT, this is not the only subject covered in the particular publication. A further breakdown by subject will be found in the library catalog.

A special section is entitled KEYWORD MASTER LIST. It is intended to serve as a beginning list of direct terms. These keywords could be used to index, and as an aid in compiling special collections. The terms may later be developed into a thesaurus to provide access to a computer data bank. (p.703)

Reference tools such as bibliographies, dictionaries, atlases, etc., appear as a separate section between the Union List and the selected periodical articles. (p.653)

An attempt was made to include materials through May, 1976.

## LIBRARY NUMBERS

1  American Society of International Law Library, Washington, D.C.
2  Cornell University Law Library, Ithaca, N.Y.
3  Fordham University School of Law Library, New York, N.Y.
4  Law of the Sea Institute, Kingston, R.I.
5  Louisiana State University School of Law Library, Baton Rouge, La.
6  Tulane University School of Law Library, New Orleans, La.
7  United Nations, Legal Library, New York, N.Y.
8  U.S. Department of Commerce, NOAA, Library, Rockville, Md.
9  U.S. Department of State Law Library, Washington, D.C.
10 University of California Law Library, Los Angeles, Calif.
11 University of Houston Law Library, Houston, Texas
12 University of Miami Law Library, Coral Gables, Fla.
13 University of Oregon Law Library, Eugene, Or.

14   University of Puget Sound Law Library, Tacoma, Wash.
14a  University of Puget Sound, Collins Memorial Library, Tacoma, Wash.
15   University of Rhode Island, Marine Affairs Program Library, Kingston, R.I.
16   University of Washington Law Library, Seattle, Wash.
17   Woodrow Wilson International Center for Scholars Library, Washington, D.C.
18   Massachusetts Institute of Technology Library, Cambridge, Mass.

## TOPIC CATEGORIES

II   COAST

    IIB..............................Boundaries
    IICONS...........................Conservation
    IICR.............................Coastal Resources
    IICZM............................Coastal Zone Management
    IIDR.............................Dredging
    IIE..............................Estuaries
    IIENE............................Energy
    IIENV............................Environment
    IIINTL...........................International Law
    IIOCET...........................Oceanography, Oceanology, Engineering,
                                     Marine Archaeology, Biology, Chemistry,
                                     Science and Technology
    IIOD.............................Ocean Dumping
    IIODAS...........................Ocean Data Acquisition Systems
    IIOL.............................Offshore Leasing
    IIORM............................Ocean Related Matters
    IIOSTR...........................Offshore Structures
    IIP..............................Pollution
    IIP&H............................Ports and Harbors
    IIREC............................Recreation
    IIREFS...........................Reference materials (bibliographies, etc.)
    IISL.............................Submerged Land, Tidelands, Wetlands,
                                     Marshes
    IIT&L............................Treaties and Legislation
    IIWQ.............................Water Quality

III  LIVING RESOURCES

    IIIAFF...........................Aquaculture and Fish Farming
    IIIB.............................Boundaries
    IIIBIO...........................Biology
    IIICONS..........................Conservation
    IIIENV...........................Environment
    IIIEZ............................Exclusive Economic Zone
    IIIF.............................Fish and Fisheries
    IIIFP............................Fishery Products
    IIIFV&G..........................Fishing Vessels and Gear
    IIIINTL..........................International Law
    IIILOS...........................Law of the Sea
    IIIMM............................Marine Mammals
    IIIOCET..........................Oceanography, Oceanology, Engineering,
                                     Marine Archaeology, Biology, Chemistry,
                                     Science and Technology
    IIIOD............................Ocean Dumping
    IIIOI............................Ocean Industry
    IIIOL............................Offshore Leasing
    IIIOR............................Ocean Resources
    IIIORM...........................Ocean Related Matters

| | | |
|---|---|---|
| | IIIOSTR | Offshore Structures |
| | IIIP | Pollution |
| | IIIREFS | Reference materials (Bibliographies, etc.) |
| | IIISF | Sea Food |
| | IIIT&L | Treaties and Legislation |

IV    NON-LIVING RESOURCES

| | | |
|---|---|---|
| | IVB | Boundaries |
| | IVCONS | Conservation |
| | IVCS | Continental Shelf |
| | IVDRIL | Drilling |
| | IVENV | Environment |
| | IVEZ | Exclusive Economic Zone |
| | IVLOS | Law of the Sea |
| | IVM | Mining |
| | IVMMR | Marine Mineral Resources |
| | IVMT | Marine Transportation, Maritime Transit |
| | IVOCET | Oceanography, Oceanology, Engineering, Marine Archaeology, Biology, Chemistry, Science and Technology |
| | IVOD | Ocean Dumping |
| | IVODAS | Ocean Data Acquisition Systems |
| | IVOI | Ocean Industry |
| | IVOL | Offshore Leasing |
| | IVORM | Ocean Related Matters |
| | IVOSTR | Offshore Structures |
| | IVP | Pollution |
| | IVREFS | Reference materials (bibliographies, etc.) |
| | IVT&L | Treaties and Legislation |

V    GENERAL

| | | |
|---|---|---|
| | VAC | Arms Control |
| | VB | Boundaries |
| | VC | Canals |
| | VCONS | Conservation |
| | VCS | Continental Shelf |
| | VENE | Energy |
| | VENV | Environment |
| | VEZ | Exclusive Economic Zone |
| | VINTL | International Law |
| | VLOS | Law of the Sea |
| | VMLAD | Maritime Law and Admiralty |
| | VMT | Marine Transportation, Maritime Transit |
| | VOCET | Oceanography, Oceanology, Engineering, Marine Archaeology, Biology, Chemistry, Science and Technology |
| | VOD | Ocean Dumping |
| | VODAS | Ocean Data Acquisition Systems |
| | VOI | Ocean Industry |
| | VOR | Ocean Resources |
| | VORM | Ocean Related Matters |
| | VOS | Ocean Study |
| | VOSTR | Offshore Structures |
| | VP | Pollution |
| | VREFS | Reference materials (bibliographies, etc.) |
| | VSG | Sea Grant |
| | VSUB | Submersibles |
| | VT&L | Treaties and Legislation |

VINTL   Abbott, Richard D., ed. ARCTIC SOVEREIGNTY AND EXTRATERRITORIAL JURISDICTION. Montreal, Canadian Council of Resource Ministers, 1971. 2 Vols.

***

VENV    _____  _____  READINGS ON THE LAW OF ENVIRONMENTAL QUALITY. Montreal, Canadian Council of Resource Ministers, 1971. 851p. 2 Vols.

14

VENE    Abelson, Philip, ed. ENERGY: USE, CONSERVATION, AND SUPPLY: A SPECIAL SCIENCE COMPENDIUM. Washington, American Association for the Advancement of Science, 1974. 154p.

7

VLOS    ABIDJAN WORLD CONFERENCE ON WORLD PEACE THROUGH LAW, AUGUST 26-31, 1973. Session on Law of the Sea; Regulation and Control of the Seas: The United Nations Proposed Conference: An Opportunity or a Trap: African View by E.O.A. Idowu, Nigeria.

14

IVORM   Abir, Mordechai. OIL, POWER, AND POLITICS: CONFLICT IN ARABIA, THE RED SEA AND THE GULF. London: Cass, 1974. xiii, 221p.

1

VINTL   Académie Bulgare des Sciences. Institut des Sciences Juridiques. LE RÉGIME INTERNATIONAL DU DANUBE: RECUEIL. Sofia, Editions de l'Academie Bulgare des Sciences, 1964. In Bulgarian, with French summaries.

***

VOD     Achrem, T.J. OCEAN WASTE DISPOSAL IN THE NEW YORK BIGHT. Anaheim, Cal., Interstate Electronics Corporation, Oceanics Division, 1973. 129p.

***

VENV    Ackerman, B.A., et al. THE UNCERTAIN SEARCH FOR ENVIRONMENTAL QUALITY. New York, MacMillan Publishing Company, Free Press, 1974. 389p.

***

VSUB    Ackerman, B.F. THE USE OF SUBMERSIBLES FOR GEOPHYSICAL SURVEYS UNDER THE ARCTIC ICE. In Oceans Ontario. Technical Symposium held April 22, 1972. Toronto, Canada, James McAllister MacInnis Foundation, 1972?

7

VP      ACTE FINAL DE LA CONVENTION SUR LA PRÉVENTION DE LA POLLUTION MARINE RESULTANT DE L'IMMERSION DE DECHETS. London, 13 November, 1972.

1,13

VP      Acuff, A. Dewey, et al. REPORT OF THE WORK GROUP ON OCS SAFETY AND POLLUTION CONTROL, U.S. GEOLOGICAL SURVEY. n.p., 1973. ii, 33p.

ART

IIIB    Adam, P. ECONOMIC CONSEQUENCES OF EXTENDING FISHERIES JURISDICTION. In G. Pontecorvo, Fisheries Conflicts in the North Atlantic. Cambridge, Mass., 1974. pp. 135-146.

IIILOS    Adam, Paul. NOTES ON THE MANAGEMENT OF NORTH SEA FISHERIES. ART In Alexander, Lewis M., ed.: Law of the Sea; the United Nations and Ocean Management. Proceedings of the Fifth Annual Conference of the Law of the Sea Institute, Kingston, R.I., 1970. Kingston, University of Rhode Island, 1971. pp. 256-263.

\*\*\*

IVMMR    Adams, M.V., et al. MINERAL RESOURCE MANAGEMENT OF OUTER CONTINENTAL SHELF (WITH LIST OF REFERENCES). Reston, Va., Geological Survey, Interior Department, 1975. iv, 32p.

ART

IVMMR    Adams, W.M. OIL FINDS ACCELERATE SCOTTISH R AND D. In Ocean Industry 8:79-82, February 1973.

14

IVORM    Adie, W.A.C. OIL, POLITICS, AND SEAPOWER: THE INDIAN OCEAN VORTEX. Strategy paper no. 24. New York, Crane, Russak, 1975. vi, 98p.

\*\*\*

IVOSTR    ADMIRALTY INLET OIL PIPELINE CROSSING: FEASIBLE? In Pacific Northwest Sea 8(1):3, 13 (1975).

\*\*\*

IIIP    Advisory Committee on Oil Pollution of the Sea. RECOMMENDED TREATMENT OF OILED SEABIRDS. Report of the Research Unit on the Rehabilitation of Oiled Seabirds. England, University of Newcastle upon Tyne, Department of Zoology, 1972. 11p.

\*\*\*

IIIP    Advisory Committee on Oil Pollution of the Sea. SECOND ANNUAL REPORT OF THE ADVISORY COMMITTEE ON OIL POLLUTION OF THE SEA. Research Unit on the Rehabilitation of Oiled Seabirds. England, University of Newcastle upon Tyne, Department of Zoology, 1972. 38p.

14

VENV    AEC Environmental Protection Conference. PROCEEDINGS OF THE SECOND AEC ENVIRONMENTAL PROTECTION CONFERENCE, HELD AT ALBUQUERQUE, NEW MEXICO, APRIL 16-19, 1974. Sponsored by Division of Operational Safety, U.S. Atomic Energy Commission. Washington, U.S.G.P.O., 1974. 2 Vols.

14

VCZM    AESTHETIC RESOURCES OF THE COASTAL ZONE. Prepared for the Office of Coastal Zone Management, National Oceanic and Atmospheric Administration. Cambridge, Mass., Roy Mann Asoociates, Inc., 1975. vi, 199p.

14a

IIIF    Aflalo, Frederick G. THE SEA-FISHING INDUSTRY OF ENGLAND AND WALES; A POPULAR ACCOUNT OF THE SEA FISHERIES AND FISHING PORTS OF THOSE COUNTRIES. With a sea fisheries map and numerous photographs by the author and others. London, E. Stanford, 1904. xx, 386p.

\*\*\*

IIIF    Agnello, Richard J., and Lawrence P. Donnelley. THE INTERACTION OF ECONOMIC, BIOLOGICAL, AND LEGAL FORCES IN THE MIDDLE ATLANTIC OYSTER INDUSTRY. Reprinted from Fishery Bulletin 73:(2)256-261(1975). Newark, College of Marine Studies, University of Delaware.

|  |  |
|---|---|
| | 13 |
| VLOS | Aguilar, Andres. THE PATRIMONIAL SEA - PRESENTATION BY DR. ANDRES AGUILAR M., AMBASSADOR OF VENEZUELA TO THE UNITED STATES OF AMERICA, BEFORE THE SEVENTH ANNUAL SUMMER CONFERENCE OF THE LAW OF THE SEA INSTITUTE AT THE UNIVERSITY OF RHODE ISLAND. Mimeo. Kingston, University of Rhode Island, 1972. 20p. |
| | 13 |
| IIIMM | Aharkov, H.B., et al. IMPLANTATION OF TELEMETERING DEVICES IN THE SKIN OF SEA ANIMALS. Arlington, Va., Joint Publications Research Service. 20 December, 1972. 9p. |
| | 1,5,14,15,16 |
| IVMMR | Ahern, William R., Jr. OIL AND THE OUTER COASTAL SHELF; THE GEORGES BANK CASE. Cambridge, Mass., Ballinger Publishing Company, 1973. xiv, 133p. |
| | *** |
| IICR | Ahr, Wayne M., et al. RESOURCE EVALUATION STUDIES ON THE MATAGORDA BAY AREA, TEXAS. TAMU-SG-74-204. College Station, Texas A&M University, 1973. 161p. |
| | 13 |
| IIIF | Ahsan, Abu E., et al. COSTS AND EARNINGS OF TUNA VESSELS IN HAWAII. Sea Grant report no. UNIHI-SEAGRANT-AR-72-01. Honolulu, University of Hawaii, 1972. 22p. |
| | *** |
| VLOS | Aja Espil, J.A. EL DERECHO DEL MAR. Bogotá, TEMIS, 1973. 122p. |
| | *** |
| VINTL | Akademiia nauk SSSR. Institut gosudarstva i prava. THE LEGAL REGIME OF THE WORLD. Moscow, Social Sciences Today, 1973. 181p. |
| | *** |
| IISL | Akins, Glenn J. COASTAL WETLANDS OF OREGON; A NATURAL RESOURCE INVENTORY REPORT. Florence, Oregon Coastal Conservation and Development Commission, 1975. 190p. |
| | 16 |
| IICZM | ALABAMA GOVERNOR'S CONFERENCE ON COASTAL ZONE MANAGEMENT. Proceedings, Gulf Shores, Alabama: 1974. MASGP-74-042. Ocean Springs, Mississippi-Alabama Sea Grant Consortium, 1974. |
| | *** |
| IICZM | Alabama. State Planning Division. PROCEEDINGS OF THE ALABAMA COASTAL LEADERS CONFERENCE ON COASTAL ZONE MANAGEMENT. MASGP-75-012. Mobile, Office of Governor, Alabama Development Office, 1975. i, 71p. |
| | 14 |
| IVMMR | Alaska. Department of Natural Resources. Division of Oil and Gas. STATISTICAL REPORT ON OIL AND GAS ACITVITY. Anchorage, 1969- |
| | 14 |
| VOR | Alaska. Joint Federal-State Land Use Planning Commission for Alaska. RESOURCES OF ALASKA, A REGIONAL SUMMARY. rev. June, 1975. Anchorage, 1975. 618p. |

                                                                    ***
IIIF    Alaska. Legislative Affairs Agency. REPORT ON THE MEETINGS OF THE
        HOUSE INTERIM COMMITTEE ON FISHERIES AND THE SENATE SPECIAL COMMIT-
        TEE ON FISHERIES, SEPTEMBER-DECEMBER, 1973. Juneau, Alaska Legisla-
        tive Council, Legislative Affairs Agency, 1974. 37p.
                                                                    ***
IICZM   Alaska. Office of the Governor. Coastal Management Program. WHAT'S
        HAPPENING ON ALASKA'S COAST? Juneau, n.d. 2p.

                                                                    16
IIIF    ALASKA FISHERIES: HEARINGS, MESSAGES AND SPEECHES. Washington,
        U.S.G.P.O., 1923. 463p.

                                                                    14
VSG     Alaska Sea Grant Program. A REPORT ON THE UNIVERSITY OF ALASKA SEA
        GRANT PROGRAM FOR 1971-1972. Alaska sea grant report no. 73-8.
        Fairbanks, University of Alaska, 1973. 16p.

                                                                    13
VOR     Alaska. University. Alaska Sea Grant Program. UNDERSTANDING ALAS-
        KA'S MARINE AND COASTAL RESOURCES. Anchorage, Alaska, n.d. 4p.

                                                                    2
VP      Albertson, Rachel, ed. URGAN ENVIRONMENTAL PROBLEMS; A GRADUATE
        INTERDISCIPLINARY SEMINAR. Organized by Edwin E. Pyatt. Water Re-
        sources Research Center publication no. 2. Florida Engineering and
        Industrial Experiment Center Bulletin series no. 128. Gainesville,
        University of Florida, 1967. 98p.

                                                                    13
IIIP    Aldrich, John W. REVIEW OF THE PROBLEM OF BIRDS CONTAMINATED BY
        OIL AND THEIR REHABILITATION. U.S. Department of the Interior,
        Resource Publication 87. Washington, U.S.G.P.O., May, 1970. iv,
        23p.

                                                                    ART
VLOS    Alejo, F.J., et al. ASPECTOS ECONÓMICOS DE LA POSICIÓN DE MEXICO
        SOBRE EL MAR PATRIMONIAL. In Mexico y el regimen del mar, 1974.
        n.p. pp. 187-216 (1974).

                                                                    ***
IIIAFF  Alexander, Barbara A., ed. PROGRESSIVE FISH-CULTURIST. Washington,
        Bureau of Sport Fisheries and Wildlife, Fish and Wildlife Service,
        Interior Department, 1974-

                                                                    16
VB      Alexander, Lewis M. ALTERNATIVE METHODS FOR DELIMITING THE OUTER
        BOUNDARY OF THE CONTINENTAL SHELF. Washington, U.S. Department of
        State, 1970. 56p.

                                                                    16
VB      _____  _____  A COMPARATIVE STUDY OF OFFSHORE CLAIMS IN NORTHWESTERN
        EUROPE. Albany, State University of New York, 1960. 239p.

                                                                    15
IICZM   _____  _____  NARRAGANSETT BAY: A MARINE USE PROFILE. Kingston,
        University of Rhode Island, n.d.

|      | 1,5,15,16 |
|------|-----------|
| VB   | Alexander, Lewis M. OFFSHORE GEOGRAPHY OF NORTHWESTERN EUROPE: THE POLITICAL AND ECONOMIC PROBLEMS OF DELIMITATION AND CONTROL. Chicago, Rand McNally, for the Association of American Geographers, 1963. |

VLOS    13
\_\_\_\_\_ \_\_\_\_\_ SEMI-ENCLOSED SEAS. Draft copy, for distribution at the Law of the Sea Institute Eighth Annual Conference, June 18, 1973. Mimeo. 1973. n.p. 9p.

VLOS    1,4,5,7,13,14,15,16,18
Alexander, Lewis M., ed. GULF AND CARIBBEAN MARITIME PROBLEMS. Law of the Sea Workshop, February 1972. Kingston, University of Rhode Island, 1973. 107p.

VLOS    1,3,4,5,7,8,10,11,13,14,15,16,18
\_\_\_\_\_ \_\_\_\_\_ THE LAW OF THE SEA: A NEW GENEVA CONFERENCE. Proceedings of the Sixth Annual Conference of the Law of the Sea Institute, June 21-24, 1971. Kingston, University of Rhode Island, 1972. v, 231p.

VLOS    1,3,4,5,7,8,10,11,13,14,15,16,18
\_\_\_\_\_ \_\_\_\_\_ THE LAW OF THE SEA: INTERNATIONAL RULES AND ORGANIZATION FOR THE SEA. Proceedings of the Third Annual Conference of the Law of the Sea Institute, June 24-27, 1968. Kingston, University of Rhode Island, 1969. v, 464p.

VLOS    4,8,10,11,13,14,15,16,18
\_\_\_\_\_ \_\_\_\_\_ THE LAW OF THE SEA: NATIONAL POLICY RECOMMENDATIONS. Proceedings of the Fourth Annual Conference of the Law of the Sea Institute, June 23-26, 1969. Kingston, University of Rhode Island, 1970. vi, 533p.

VLOS    3,4,5,6,8,9,10,11,13,14,15,16,18
\_\_\_\_\_ \_\_\_\_\_ THE LAW OF THE SEA: OFFSHORE BOUNDARIES AND ZONES. Columbus, Ohio State University Press, 1967. xv, 321p.

VLOS    1,2,4,5,7,9,10,13,14,15,16,18
\_\_\_\_\_ \_\_\_\_\_ THE LAW OF THE SEA: THE FUTURE OF THE SEA'S RESOURCES. Proceedings of the Second Annual Conference of the Law of the Sea Institute, June 26-29, 1967. Kingston, University of Rhode Island, 1968. v, 155p.

VLOS    1,3,4,5,7,8,10,13,14,15,16,18
\_\_\_\_\_ \_\_\_\_\_ THE LAW OF THE SEA: THE NEEDS AND INTERESTS OF THE DEVELOPING COUNTRIES. Proceedings of the Seventh Annual Conference of the Law of the Sea Institute, June 26-29, 1972. Kingston, University of Rhode Island, 1973. 238p.

VLOS    1,2,3,4,5,7,8,10,11,13,14,15,16,18
\_\_\_\_\_ \_\_\_\_\_ THE LAW OF THE SEA: THE UNITED NATIONS AND OCEAN MANAGEMENT. Proceedings of the Fifth Annual Conference of the Law of the Sea Institute, June 15-19, 1970. Kingston, University of Rhode Island, 1971. vi, 390p.

VLOS    1,4,5,7,11,13,14,16
Alexander, Lewis M., and Gordon R.S. Hawkins, eds. CANADIAN-U.S. MARITIME PROBLEMS. Law of the Sea Workshop, June 1971. Kingston, University of Rhode Island, 1972. 88p.

IIE  Alexander, V., et al. ENVIRONMENTAL STUDIES OF AN ARCTIC ESTUARINE SYSTEM, FINAL REPORT. R-74-1. Fairbanks, University of Alaska, Institute of Marine Science, 1975. vi, 539p.

VINTL  Allen, Donald R., and Patrick H. Mitchell. THE LEGAL STATUS OF THE CONTINENTAL SHELF OF THE EAST CHINA SEA. Photocopy. n.p., 1971.
*** 13

IIIINTL  Allen, Edward W. BRISTOL BAY PRESENTS ISSUES BETWEEN AMERICAN SYSTEM OF FISHERY CONSERVATION AND FOREIGN SYSTEM OF UNRESTRICTED EXPLOITATION. Address given before the Commonwealth Club of California, San Francisco, March 3, 1939.
16

IIIF  _____ _____ NORTH PACIFIC: JAPAN, SIBERIA, ALASKA, CANADA. New York, Professional and Technical Press, 1936. vii, xvi, 282p.
14a,16

VINTL  _____ _____ TURMOIL IN THE NORTH PACIFIC. Paper delivered at Northwest Pacific regional conference on international law, University of British Columbia, April 6, 1963.
1

IVOSTR  Allmendinger, E. Eugene. A SEAFLOOR BASED SYSTEM FOR SURVEYING AND MAINTAINING SUBSEA OIL-GAS PRODUCTION COMPLEXES. Durham, University of New Hampshire, 1975. 23p.

VP  Altouney, E.G., and Charles G. Gunnerson. INDUSTRIAL WASTES. Albany, New York Sea Grant Institute, 1975.
***

VLOS  Alvarado Garaicca, Teodoro. EL DOMINIO DEL MAR. Guayaquil, Universidad de Guayaquil, Departamento de Publicaciones, 1968. 200p.
1,15

VOR  Alverson, Dayton L. EXAMPLES OF NATIONAL CONTRIBUTIONS TO THE DEVELOPMENT AND MANAGEMENT OF THE OCEANS' LIVING RESOURCES. In Marine Technology Society. Ninth Annual Conference, Washington, D.C., September 10-12, 1973. Washington, D.C., 1973. pp. 191-208.
ART

VLOS  _____ _____ FISHERIES USES OF THE SEA; GOVERNMENT APPROACHES. In Conference on Local Impacts of the Law of the Sea, Seattle, Wash., 1972. Local impacts of the law of the sea; proceedings of a conference held in Seattle, October 10-12, 1972. Seattle, Wash., Division of Marine Resources, University of Washington, 1973. pp. 75-80.
ART

IIIAFF  _____ _____ MARICULTURE AND THE INTERNATIONAL LAW OF THE SEA. In Northwest Mariculture Laws - papers and presentations from a symposium held at the law center, University of Oregon, Eugene, June 7, 1974. Corvallis, Oregon State University, 1975.
ART

IVMMR  Amann, H., H. Backer, and E. Blissenbach. METALLIFEROUS MUDS OF THE MARINE ENVIRONMENT. In Offshore Technology Conference, 5th, Houston, Tex., 1973. Dallas, Tex., 1973. Vol. 2, pp. 345-358.
ART

|       |       |
|-------|-------|
| VLOS | Amerasinghe, H. REPORT ON THE FINDINGS OF THE U.N. AD HOC COMMITTEE OF THE SEABEDS. THE SEA AND THE STATES: MUTUAL PROBLEMS AND THEIR SOLUTIONS. Miami, Florida, 1968. pp. 156-167. [16] |
| VLOS | American Assembly. USES OF THE SEAS. Report of the 33d American Assembly, May 2-5, 1968, Arden House, Harriman, N.Y. New York, Columbia University, 1968? 15p. [2,5,7] |
| VOR | AMERICAN BAR ASSOCIATION NATIONAL INSTITUTE: MARINE RESOURCES; SUMMARY OF PROCEEDINGS. n.p., 1967. 102p. [15,16] |
| VLOS | American Bar Association. Section of International and Comparative Law. INFORMATION REPORT ON THE LAW OF THE SEA. Chicago, American Bar Association, 1974. ii, 51p. [16] |
| IVMMR | _____ NON-LIVING RESOURCES OF THE SEA; A SUMMARY AND CRITIQUE OF CHAPTER 4, PART III, OF THE REPORT OF THE MARINE SCIENCE COMMISSION. Joint report of the Section of International and Comparative Law, the Section of Natural Resources Law, and the Standing Committee on World Order under Law of the American Bar Association. Revised draft. Chicago? 1969. ii, 56p. [6,9,13,16] |
| VOCET | _____ Committee on Oceanography. SUMMARY OF REPORT OF THE PRESIDENT'S COMMISSION ON MARINE SCIENCE, ENGINEERING AND RESOURCES WITH SUGGESTED COMMENT IN THE LIGHT OF THE RECOMMENDATIONS OF THE AMERICAN BAR ASSOCIATION. Prepared by members of the Committee on Oceanography ... n.p., 1969. 47p. [8] |
| VP | American Chemical Society. Committee on Chemistry and Public Affairs. Subcommittee on Environmental Improvement. CLEANING OUR ENVIRONMENT, THE CHEMICAL BASIS FOR ACTION; A REPORT. Washington, American Chemical Society, 1969. ix, 249p. [2] |
| IVOCET | American Mining Congress. STATEMENTS OF T.S. ARY, UNION CARBIDE EXPLORATION CORPORATION, AND C.H. BURGESS, KENNECOTT COPPER CORPORATION, BEFORE THE SUBCOMMITTEE ON OCEANOGRAPHY OF THE COMMITTEE ON MERCHANT MARINE AND FISHERIES, U.S. HOUSE OF REPRESENTATIVES, MAY 16, 1972. 17, 19p. [1] |
| VP | American Petroleum Institute. 1975 CONFERENCE ON PREVENTION AND CONTROL OF OIL POLLUTION. Washington, D.C., 1975. 569p. [***] |
| IVENV | _____ OIL AND THE CHALLENGE OF ALASKA - THE PETROLEUM INDUSTRY'S CONCERN FOR THE ENVIRONMENT. A staff paper by the Committee on Public Affairs of the American Petroleum Institute. Washington, D.C., American Petroleum Institute, 1971. 15p. [13] |
| VP | _____ PROCEEDINGS OF JOINT CONFERENCE ON PREVENTION AND CONTROL OF OIL SPILLS, JUNE 15-17, 1971. Washington, D.C. vii,544p. [13] |

                                                            \*\*\*

VOR      American Society for Oceanography. THE OCEAN AND THE INVESTOR: papers presented at the April 1968 annual conference ... held at Los Angeles, California. San Francisco, Dean Witter and Company, 1969. 132p.

                                                            13

VLOS     American Society of International Law. DEVELOPMENTS IN THE LAW OF THE SEA. A regional meeting of the American Society of International Law. Sponsored by Northwestern School of Law of Lewis and Clark College and the American Society of International Law. Working papers. Portland, Or., 1973.

                                                         9,13

VLOS     _____ _____ PACIFIC NORTHWEST REGIONAL MEETING, 1956. PROCEEDINGS. Institute of International Affairs bulletin no. 12. Seattle, University of Washington, 1956. 4 parts in 1 Vol.

                                                           18

VENV     _____ _____ Joint Working Group on Ocean Environment. WHO PROTECTS THE OCEAN? THE ENVIRONMENT ISSUE IN THE DEVELOPMENT OF THE LAW OF THE SEA. Study. Washington, American Society of International Law, 1971. 5 Vols. in 1.

                                                            1

VOCET    American Society of International Law. REGIONAL MEETING, UNIVERSITY OF MIAMI LAW CENTER. FREEDOM OF RESEARCH. COASTAL ZONE AND OCEAN LAW: PROBLEMS OF THE USER. Program and outlines. Miami, Fla., December, 1969.

                                                         1,16

IIIF      _____ _____ REGIONAL MEETING, UNIVERSITY OF WASHINGTON, 1956. MARGINAL SEAS AND PACIFIC FISHERIES. University of Washington, Institute of International Affairs bulletin no. 12, part 2. Seattle, 1956.

                                                        1,5,7

VOD       _____ _____ THE QUESTION OF AN OCEAN DUMPING CONVENTION. CONCLUSIONS OF THE WORKING GROUP ON AN OCEAN DUMPING CONVENTION JOINTLY FORMED BY THE AMERICAN SOCIETY OF INTERNATIONAL LAW AND THE COMMITTEE ON INTERNATIONAL MARINE SCIENCE AFFAIRS POLICY OF THE NATIONAL ACADEMY OF SCIENCES. Background paper by Lawson A.W. Hunter. Studies in transnational legal policy no. 2. Washington, August 1972. 53p.

                                                         \*\*\*

VINTL    AMERICAN SOCIETY OF INTERNATIONAL LAW STUDIES IN TRANSNATIONAL LEGAL POLICY. St. Paul, Minn., West Publishing Company, 1975. 189p.

                                                        1,7,14

IIILOS    American Society of International Law. Working Group on Living Marine Resources, panel on the law of the sea. PRINCIPLES FOR A GLOBAL FISHERIES MANAGEMENT REGIME. Studies in transnational legal policy no. 4. Washington, D.C., May, 1974. vii, 20p.

                                                            1

IIIF      American Tunaboat Association. STATEMENT BEFORE SUBCOMMITTEE ON FISHERIES AND WILDLIFE CONSERVATION ON H.R.10607, A BILL TO AMEND THE ACT OF AUGUST 27, 1954, CITED AS THE "FISHERMEN'S PROTECTIVE ACT OF 1967." 91st Congr., 1st sess. Mimeo. June 4-5, 1969. 20p.

                                                                        ***
VP         Amphlett, C.B., TREATMENT AND DISPOSAL OF RADIOACTIVE WASTES. New
           York, Pergamon, 1961. 289p.

                                                                        ART
IIP&H      Amundson, Paul A. WHO SHOULD OPERATE THE OFFSHORE TERMINALS: WHAT
           ARE THE OPTIONS? In Proceedings of the Fifth National Sea Grant
           Conference held in Houston, Texas, 1972. Sea Grant Publication no.
           TAMU-SG-73-101. College Station, Texas A&M University, 1973?

                                                                         13
VINTL      Anand, R.P. "EQUITABLE USE AND SHARING OF THE COMMON HERITAGE OF
           MANKIND." Delhi, India, Department of International Law, School of
           International Studies, Jawaharlal Nehru University, n.d. 44, viip.

                                                                        ***
IIOSTR     Anderson, J.H. RESEARCH APPLIED TO OCEAN SITED POWER PLANTS. Semi-
           annual Progress Report NSF-RA/N-72-056. Washington, U.S. National
           Science Foundation, 1973. 66p.

                                                                        ART
VENE       Anderson, J.H., and J.H. Anderson, Jr. THERMAL POWER FROM SEAWATER.
           In Mechanical Engineering Vol. 88, April, 1966. pp. 41-46.

                                                                        ***
IIWQ       Anderson, Peter W., and Richard T. Dewling. WATER QUALITY. Albany,
           State University of New York, New York Sea Grant Institute, 1975.

                                                                         16
IIIF       Andersen, Raoul, and Cato Wadel, eds. NORTH ATLANTIC FISHERMEN;
           ANTHROPOLOGICAL ESSAYS ON MODERN FISHING. St. Johns, Institute of
           Social and Economic Research, Memorial University of Newfoundland,
           1972. 175p.

                                                                        ART
IVM        Anderson, Richard J. RECENT DEVELOPMENTS IN OFFSHORE MINING. In
           Offshore Technology Conference, 4th, Houston, Tex., 1972. Dallas,
           Tex., 1972. Vol. 1, pp. 703-710.

                                                                        ***
IISL       Anderson, Roger D., et al. LEGAL SYMPOSIUM ON WETLANDS: AN EXECU-
           TIVE SUMMARY. Gloucester Point, Virginia Institute of Marine Sci-
           ence, 1974. 8p.

                                                                         16
VINTL      Andrassy, Juraj. IMPLICATIONS OF THE JUDGMENT OF THE INTERNATIONAL
           COURT OF JUSTICE ON THE NORTH SEA CASE. Paper at Pacem in Maribus
           Preparatory Conference on the Legal Framework and the Continental
           Shelf. January 30-February 1, 1970. Kingston, University of Rhode
           Island, 1970?

                                              1,2,5,7,9,10,11,12,14,15,16,18
VINTL      _____ INTERNATIONAL LAW AND THE RESOURCES OF THE SEA. New
           York, Columbia University Press, 1970. xviii, 191p.

                                                                         16
VAC        _____ THE PRESENT REGIME OF THE MILITARY USES OF THE SEA-BED.
           POSSIBLE REGIMES TO BE ENVISAGED. Paper at Symposium on the Inter-
           national Regime of the Sea-bed. Rome, 1969.

                                                                                                  ***

IVMMR     Andrews, J.E., et al. FERROMANGANESE DEPOSITS OF THE OCEAN FLOOR. Cruise report Mn-74-01, R/V Moana Wave, Honolulu to San Diego, 17 July-10 August, 1974. Honolulu, University of Hawaii, Institute of Geophysics, 1974. 194p.

                                                                                               ART

IVMMR     Andrews, W.P., Jr. MANGANESE NODULES AND INTERNATIONAL LAW. In S.W. Wurfel, Emerging Ocean Oil and Mining Law. Sea Grant Publication UNC-SG-74-02. Chapel Hill, University of North Carolina School of Law, 1974. pp. 30-39.

                                                                                ***

IIIF      Andrews, William P., Jr. NORTH CAROLINA FISHERY LAW: ITS RELATIONSHIP TO INTERNATIONAL, FEDERAL AND SISTER STATE LAW. UNC-SG-75-10. Raleigh, North Carolina State University, 1975. 24p.

                                                                                ***

IIE       Angel, H. THE WORLD OF AN ESTUARY. London, Faber and Faber, 1974. 125p.

                                                                                ***

IIIOR     Angot, Michel. VIE ET ÉCONOMIE DES MERS TROPICALES. Paris, Payot, Bibliothèque scientifique, 1961. 326p.

                                                                          5,7,16

VCS       Anninos, Peter C. THE CONTINENTAL SHELF AND PUBLIC INTERNATIONAL LAW. The Hague, H.P. deSwart and Fils S.A., 1953. 167p.

                                                                             ***

VSG       ANNUAL PROGRESS REPORT OF SEA GRANT ACTIVITIES. Technical Report no. 8. Madison, University of Wisconsin, Sea Grant Program 1971. 221p.

                                                                             ***

VINTL     ANNUAL REPORT OF THE INTER-GOVERNMENTAL MARITIME CONSULTATIVE ORGANIZATION 1972/1973. IMCO. n.p. 1973. 45p.

                                                                           15

IIIF      Anson, Peter F. BRITISH SEA-FISHERMEN. London, W. Collins, 1944.

                                                                           7

VT&L      THE ANTARCTIC TREATY. Signed at Washington, 1 December 1959. 12 UST 794; TIAS 4780; 402 UNTS 71; Cmnd. 5502.

                                                                           1

VB        Aoussat, Claude A. THE CONTINENTAL MARGIN AND THE BOUNDARIES OF THE SEA BED. Master dissertation. Mimeo., Washington, D.C., Catholic University of America, 1972. 88p.

                                                                            ***

VB        Aramburu Menchaca, A.A. HISTORIA DE LAS 200 MILLAS DE MAR TERRITORIAL. Piura, Universidad de Piura, 1973. 117p.

                                                                        ART

VOR      Arangio-Ruiz, Gaetano. POLITICAL ACTION SO FAR TAKEN TO SOLVE THE PROBLEMS OF UTILIZING THE OCEAN DEPTHS. In Symposium on the Exploration and Exploitation of the Sea-bed and its Subsoil, held in Strasbourg, France, December 3-5, 1970. New York, U.S. and World Publications Inc., Manhattan Publishing Company, 1971?

VLOS      Arangio-Ruiz, G. REFLECTIONS ON THE PRESENT AND FUTURE REGIME OF THE SEA-BED OF THE OCEANS. Paper at Symposium on the International Regime of the Sea-bed. Rome, 1969.

VB        Arbuet Vignaly, H. LA SOBERANÍA URUGUAYA EN LOS ESPACIOS MARÍTIMOS. In Revista Uruguaya de Derecho Internacional, Vol. 2, 1973. pp. 127-155.

IIOSTR    Arciniega, J.R., and P.D. Komar. SHORELINE CHANGES DUE TO JETTY CONSTRUCTION ON THE OREGON COAST. Corvallis, Oregon State University, Sea Grant College Program, 1975. 85p.

VENV      Arctic Institute of North America. ANNUAL REPORT, 1973. Washington, 1973. 14p.

IICZM     Armstrong, John M. THE STRUCTURE OF MANAGEMENT AND PLANNING FOR THE COASTAL ZONE; TALK DELIVERED TO THE WOODS HOLE NATIONAL WORKSHOP ON CRITICAL PROBLEMS OF THE COASTAL ZONE, WOODS HOLE OCEANOGRAPHIC INSTITUTION, 2 JUNE 1972. Woods Hole, Mass., 1972. 24p.

IIENV     Arnal, Robert E. A SHORT SURVEY OF THE ENVIRONMENT AT THE DUMPING SITE FOR SANTA CRUZ HARBOR DREDGING. Moss Landing, California State University, 1972. 18p.

VENV      Arthur, Donald R. MAN AND HIS ENVIRONMENT. New York, American Elsevier Publishing Company, 1969. 218p.

IIIOSTR   ARTIFICIAL REEFS FOR TEXAS. Sea Grant Publication TAMU-SG-73-214. College Station, Texas A&M University, 1974. 42p.

VP        ASSESSING POTENTIAL OCEAN POLLUTANTS. Washington, D.C., National Academy of Sciences, 1975. 465p.

VP        Association Nationale de la Recherche Technique. Commission "Lutte contre la Pollution des Eaux." LUTTE CONTRE LA POLLUTION DES EAUX; RECHERCHES ACTUELLES. Réalisé par Mme. Leygue, et al. Paris, Editions Eyrolles, 1970. 182p.

VOD       Atomic Energy Agency, Vienna. DISPOSAL OF RADIOACTIVE WASTES INTO SEAS, OCEANS, AND SURFACE WATERS. Symposium proceedings. New York, National Agency for International Publications, 1966. 898p.

VLOS      ATTITUDES REGARDING A LAW OF THE SEA CONVENTION TO ESTABLISH AN INTERNATIONAL SEABED REGIME. Chapel Hill, University of North Carolina School of Law. n.d.

                                                                                           ***

VP        Aubert, M., and J. Aubert. POLLUTIONS MARINES ET AMENAGEMENT DES RIVAGES. REVUE INTERNATIONALE D'OCEANOGRAPHIE MEDICALE. Nice, France, C.E.R.B.O.M., Groupe de Recherches de l'I.N.S.E.R.M., 1973. 299p.
                \_\_\_\_\_ \_\_\_\_\_ SUPPLEMENT, 1973.

                                                                                             1,5,7,16
VCS      Auguste, Barry B.L. THE CONTINENTAL SHELF: THE PRACTICE AND POLICY OF THE LATIN AMERICAN STATES WITH SPECIAL REFERENCE TO CHILE, ECUADOR AND PERU; A STUDY IN INTERNATIONAL RELATIONS. Geneva, E. Droz, 1960. 408p.

                                                                                             ART
IVMMR    Auldridge, Larry. SURGING WORLD OIL FLOW TO HIT 56 MILLION B/D IN '73. In Oil and Gas Journal, 18 June, 1973.

                                                                                              13
IIIAFF   Avault, James W., Jr., and Kenneth O. Allen. MARICULTURE IN THE UNITED STATES - AN OVERVIEW. Louisiana State University, Coastal Studies Bulletin no. 5. Special Sea Grant Issue. February, 1970. Baton Rouge, Louisiana State University, 1970.

                                                                                              16
VC       Avram, Benno. THE EVOLUTION OF THE SUEZ CANAL STATUS FROM 1869 TO 1956. Geneva, E. Droz, 1958. 170p.

                                                                                             ***
IIIF     Azbelev, V.V. EXPERIENCE IN REGULATING SALMON FISHERY IN THE WATERS OF THE KOLA PENINSULA. Montreal, Canada, Fisheries Research Board, 1971. 7p.

                                                                                             ART
VCS      Azcárraga Bustamante, José Luis de. EL CONCEPTO DE PLATAFORMA CONTINENTAL ANTE EL DERECHO TRIBUTARIO. In Mulvalidad Benefíca del Cuerpo de Inspectores Técnicos Fiscales. Semana de Estudios de Derecho Financiero, 1973. pp. 777-791.

                                                                                              7
VCS      \_\_\_\_\_ \_\_\_\_\_ LA PLATAFORMA SUBMARINA Y EL DERECHO INTERNACIONAL. n.p. 1952.

                                                                                              7
VINTL    \_\_\_\_\_ \_\_\_\_\_ REGIMEN JURIDICO DE LOS ESPACIOS MARITIMOS. n.p. 1953.

                                                                                             ART
VOCET    Azhazha, V.G. ON THE HISTORY OF INVESTIGATION AND DEVELOPMENT OF THE OCEAN WITH SUBMARINE VEHICLES. In Proceedings of the 2d International Congress on the History of Oceanography, held in Edinburgh, Scotland, September 12-20, 1972.

                                                                                             ***
VOCET    \_\_\_\_\_ \_\_\_\_\_ THE POTENTIAL OF A SUBMARINE RESEARCH VESSEL. Washington, National Marine Fisheries Service. Division of Foreign Fisheries, 1971? 4p.

|         |                                                                                                                                                                                                                                                                                   |
|---------|---------------------------------------------------------------------------------------------------------------------------------------------------------------------------------------------------------------------------------------------------------------------------------------------------|
| VOCET   | Azhazha, V.G., ed. SOME RESULTS AND PROSPECTS FOR THE USE OF UNDERWATER HABITATS IN MARINE INVESTIGATIONS. In Nekotoryye Rezutaly i Perspektivy Primeneniya Podvodnykh Domov v Morskikh Issledovaniyakh. Moscow, June, 18, 1973. pp. 1-148. [ART] |
| VMLAD   | Azuni, Domenico A. THE MARITIME LAW OF EUROPE. Tr. from the French by William Johnson. New York, Printed by G. Forman for I. Riley and Company, 1806. 2 Vols. [1,6] |
| IIIINTL | Bacon, R., and J. Scott, eds. NORTH ATLANTIC COAST FISHERIES ARBITRATION AT THE HAGUE. Cambridge, Harvard University Press, 1917. 445p. [16] |
| VOCET   | Badgley, Peter, Leatha Miloy, and Leo Childs, eds. SYMPOSIUM ON THE STATUS OF KNOWLEDGE, CRITICAL RESEARCH NEEDS, AND POTENTIAL RESEARCH FACILITIES RELATING TO THE STUDY OF THE OCEANS FROM SPACE, Houston, Tex., 1969? OCEANS FROM SPACE; PROCEEDINGS. Houston, Gulf Publishing Company, 1969. ix, 234p. [16] |
| IICONS  | Bailery, Gilbert E., and Paul S. Thayer. CALIFORNIA'S DISAPPEARING COAST: A LEGISLATIVE CHALLENGE. Berkeley, Institute of Governmental Studies, University of California, 1971. xi, 99p. [13] |
| IIIF    | Bailey, Jack E. ALASKA'S FISHERY RESOURCES: THE PINK SALMON. U.S. Department of the Interior. U.S. Fish and Wildlife Service. Bureau of Commercial Fisheries. Fishery Leaflet 619. Washington, 1969. iv, 8p. [13] |
| VLOS    | Bailey, Kenneth H. AUSTRALIA AND THE LAW OF THE SEA. Melbourne, Australian Institute of International Affairs, 1959. 31p. [16] |
| VSUB    | Bailey, Vincent R., et al. DIVER LOCKOUT AND OBSERVATION SUBMERSIBLES: A PERSPECTIVE OF PARTICIPATION IN OFFSHORE OPERATIONS. In Offshore Technology Conference, 4th, Houston, Tex., 1972: Preprints. Dallas, Tex., 1972. Vol. 1, pp. 547-556. [ART] |
| IIP     | Baker, H. THE DELAWARE ESTUARY SYSTEM, ENVIRONMENTAL IMPACTS AND SOCIO-ECONOMIC EFFECTS: UPPER ESTUARY POLLUTION AND TRANSFER RELATIONSHIPS. n.p. September, 1973. 53p. [***] |
| IIIMM   | Baker, Ralph C., et al. THE NORTHERN FUR SEAL. Fish and Wildlife Service Circular 336. Washington, D.C., 1970. iii, 19p. [13] |
| IIENV   | Baker, Simon, ed. COASTAL DEVELOPMENT AND AREAS OF ENVIRONMENTAL CONCERN; PROCEEDINGS OF A SYMPOSIUM HELD MARCH 5, 1975, SPONSORED BY THE U.S. OFFICE OF SEA GRANT AND THE NORTH CAROLINA DEPARTMENT OF ADMINISTRATION. UNC-SG-75-18. Raleigh, University of North Carolina, 1975. 99p. [***] |

|  |  |
|---|---|
| | *** |
| VOR | Bakish, R., ed. PRACTICE OF DESALINATION. Park Ridge, N.J., Noyes Data Corporation, 1973. 278p. |
| | 16 |
| IVP | Baldwin, Malcolm F. THE SANTA BARBARA OIL SPILL -- A DISCUSSION PAPER. Photocopy. Washington, Conservation Foundation, 1969. 81p. |
| | 16 |
| VP | Baldwin, Malcolm F., ed. LEGAL CONTROL OF WATER POLLUTION. Davis, University of California, 1969. 273p. |
| | 14 |
| IVMMR | Baldwin, Pamela L., and Malcolm F. ONSHORE PLANNING FOR OFFSHORE OIL: LESSONS FROM SCOTLAND. Washington, D.C., Conservation Foundation, 1975. 183p. |
| | *** |
| VMT | Balfe, Margaret, et al. ANALYSIS OF INTERNATIONAL GREAT LAKES SHIPPING AND HINTERLAND. Special report no. 23. Milwaukee, University of Wisconsin, 1975. 300p. |
| | 13 |
| IIIF | Ball, John L., Jr. FINANCIAL ASSISTANCE PROGRAMS FOR HAWAII'S COMMERCIAL FISHERMEN. Sea Grant Advisory Report, UNIHI-SEAGRANT-AR-75-01. Honolulu, University of Hawaii, 1974. iii, 16p. |
| | *** |
| IIIF | _____ FISHERIES AND THE STATE OF HAWAII INPUT TO THE NATIONAL FISHERIES PLAN. Working Paper no. 4. Honolulu, University of Hawaii, 1975. 80p. |
| | *** |
| VP | Ballenegger, Jacques. LA POLLUTION EN DROIT INTERNATIONAL. Geneva, Librairie Droz, 1975. 268p. |
| | 1,5,8,13 |
| VMLAD | Barabolya, P.D., et al. MANUAL OF INTERNATIONAL MARITIME LAW. (Voennomorskoy mezhdunarodno-pravovoy spravochnik. Moscow, Military Publishing House of the Ministry of Defense of the USSR, 1966). Translated and published by the Department of the Navy, Washington, D.C., 1968. 475p. II Parts. |
| | 5,17 |
| IIIOR | Bardach, John E. HARVEST OF THE SEA. London, George Allen and Unwin; New York, Harper and Row, 1968. viii, 301p. |
| | 13 |
| IIIAFF | Bardach, John E., et al. AQUACULTURE: THE FARMING AND HUSBANDRY OF FRESH WATER AND MARINE ORGANISMS. New York, Wiley-Interscience, 1972. xii, 868p. |
| | 12 |
| IIIAFF | Bardach, John E. THE STATUS AND POTENTIAL OF AQUACULTURE. Washington, D.C., American Institute of Biological Sciences, 1968. |
| | *** |
| VP | Bardin, D.J., and P. Mandelbaum. CONTROL OF POLLUTION IN THE MEDITERRANEAN SEA. Mimeo. Jerusalem, State of Israel Environmental Protection Service, 1974. 14p. |

|         |          ART |
|---|---|

VINTL    Bardonnet, D.  LA DÉNONCIATION PAR LE GOUVERNEMENT SÉNÉGALAIS DE LA CONVENTION SUR LA MER TERRITORIALE ET LA ZONE CONTIGUË ET DE LA CONVENTION SUR LA PÊCHE ET LA CONSERVATION DES RESSOURCES BIOLOGIQUES DE LA HAUTE MER, EN DATE DU 29 AVRIL 1958 À GÉNÈVE.  In Annuare Français de Droit International, Vol. 18, 1972.  pp. 123-180.

16

IVORL    Barker, Lucius J.  OFFSHORE OIL POLITICS:  A STUDY IN PUBLIC POLICY MAKING.  Photocopy.  Urbana, Ill., 1954.  243p.

ART

VOR      Barlet, Alain.  PRODUCTIONS MARITIMES ET PROBLÈMES ALIMENTAIRES DU TIERS MONDE.  In Tiers Monde, Vol. 12, October-December, 1971.  pp. 825-842.

\*\*\*

IIE      Barnes, R.S.K., and J. Green, eds.  THE ESTUARINE ENVIRONMENT.  Barking, Essex, England, Applied Science Publishers, 1972.  148p.

2

VP       Barr, John.  THE ASSAULTS ON OUR SENSES.  London, Methuen, 1970.  218p.

7,13,16

VP       Barros, James, and Douglas M. Johnston, eds.  THE INTERNATIONAL LAW OF POLLUTION.  New York, Free Press, 1974.  xvii, 476p.

13

IVLOS    Barry, Frank J.  ADMINISTRATION OF LAWS FOR THE EXPLOITATION OF OFFSHORE MINERALS IN THE UNITED STATES AND ABROAD.  Remarks at American Bar Association National Institute on Marine Resources.  Long Beach, California.  June 9, 1967.  14p.

ART

VOSTR    Bascom, Willard and Mansfield Bascom.  TENSION-LEG BRIDGE COULD SPAN STRAIT OF GIBRALTER.  In Undersea Technology, Vol. 11, June, 1970.  pp. 22-24.

\*\*\*

VOCET    Bass, George F.  ARCHEOLOGY BENEATH THE SEA.  New York, Walker and Company, 1975.  238p.

13

VMT      Bates, Charles C., and Paul Yost.  WHERE TRENDS THE FLOW OF MERCHANT SHIPS?  For inclusion in the proceedings of the Eighth Annual Conference, Law of the Sea Institute, 18-21 June, 1973.  Kingston, University of Rhode Island, 1973.  40p.

5,13

VP       Bates, Martha.  WATER POLLUTION BY OIL SPILLAGE.  Industrial Information Services Search No. 696.  Dallas, Southern Methodist University, 1969.  2 Vols.

13

VCS      Battelle Memorial Institute, Columbus, Ohio.  DEVELOPMENT POTENTIAL OF U.S. CONTINENTAL SHELVES.  A report by the Battelle Memorial Institute on its study of the Coast and Geodetic Survey's products and services as related to economic activity in the U.S. continental shelf regions.  Washington, U.S. Department of Commerce, Coast and

Geodetic Survey, 1966. 1 Vol.

14a
IIE    Battelle Memorial Institute, Columbus, Ohio. THE ECONOMIC AND SOCIAL IMPORTANCE OF ESTUARIES. David C. Sweet, project director. Environmental Protection Agency, Water Quality Office, Technical Support Division. Washington, U.S.G.P.O., 1971.

***
VP    _____ Pacific Northwest Laboratory, Richland, Washington. REVIEW OF SANTA BARBARA CHANNEL OIL POLLUTION INCIDENT TO DEPARTMENT OF INTERIOR FEDERAL WATER POLLUTION CONTROL ADMINISTRATION AND DEPARTMENT OF TRANSPORTATION, U.S. COAST GUARD, WASHINGTON, D.C.; RICHLAND. Washington, National Technical Information Service, 1969.

1
VMLAD    Baty, Thomas. BRITAIN AND SEA LAW. London, G. Bell, 1911.

***
VP    Bauer, W.H., et al. CHEMICAL ADDITIVES FOR IMPROVEMENT OF OIL SPILL CONTROL; FINAL REPORT. U.S. Department of Transportation, U.S. Coast Guard. Springfield, Va., National Technical Information Service, 1974. 198p.

***
IIP    Baumgartner, D.J. A BRIEF OUTLINE OF A STUDY OF SEWAGE SLUDGE DUMPING IN THE NEW YORK BIGHT. Working paper no. 5. Corvallis, Or., Pacific Northwest Environmental Research Laboratory, 1972? 11p.

1,5,12,14,16
VC    Baxter, Richard R. THE LAW OF INTERNATIONAL WATERWAYS, WITH PARTICULAR REGARD TO INTEROCEANIC CANALS. Cambridge, Mass., Harvard University Press, 1964. vii, 371p.

***
VLOS    Baxter, R.R. THE LAW OF THE SEA CONFERENCE: WHERE WE STAND NOW. Third annual Sea grant lecture and symposium. MITSG 75-3(1974). Cambridge, Massachusetts Institute of Technology, 1974. 10p.

***
VLOS    _____ SEMINAR ON THE LAW OF THE SEA, 1972-1973. Cambridge, Mass., 1972.

1,5,7,9,12,16
IIIINTL    Bayitch, S.A. INTERAMERICAN LAW OF FISHERIES; AN INTRODUCTION WITH DOCUMENTS. Dobbs Ferry, N.Y., Oceana Publications, Inc., 1957.

***
VENE    Beane, Marjorie, and John E. Ross. THE ROLE OF NUCLEAR POWER PLANTS. Sea Grant publication. Madison, University of Wisconsin, 1974. 154p.

***
IIIFP    Beard, Harry R. NEFCO FROM SEA TO WORLD MARKETS. Seattle, Wash., New England Fish Company, 1953.

15
IIB    Beazley, Jon S. WHAT THE MEAN HIGH WATER LINE MEANS. Florida Department of Transportation, October 6, 1972.

                                                                    ***
VENE       Bebout, D.G., et al. GEOTHERMAL RESOURCES, FRIO FORMATION, MIDDLE
           TEXAS GULF COAST. Austin, University of Texas, 1975. 43p.

                                                                    ***
VOR        Becht, J. Edwin, and L.D. Belzung. WORLD RESOURCE MANAGEMENT: KEY
           TO CIVILIZATION AND SOCIAL ACHIEVEMENT. Englewood Cliffs, Prentice-
           Hall, 1975. xii, 329p.

                                                                    ***
IVP        Becker, Mary. SUPERSPILL: AN ACCOUNT OF THE 1978 GROUNDING AT BIRD
           ROCKS. Austin, Texas, Madrona Press, 1971. 161p.

                                                                    17
VOCET      Bedford Institute. BIENNIAL REVIEW. 1967/68-    Dartmouth, N.H.


                                                                    17
VOCET      Behrman, Daniel. EXPLORING THE OCEAN. UNESCO document COM.70/11.30/A.
           Paris, UNESCO, 1970. 89p.

                                                                    16
VOCET      _____ _____ THE NEW WORLD OF THE OCEANS; MEN AND OCEANOGRAPHY.
           Boston, Little, Brown, 1969. xii, 436p.

                                                                    1,5,13
IIIF       Bell, Frederick H. ESTIMATION OF THE ECONOMIC BENEFITS TO FISHERMEN,
           VESSELS AND SOCIETY FROM LIMITED ENTRY TO THE INSHORE U.S. NORTHERN
           LOBSTER FISHERY. U.S. Bureau of Commercial Fisheries, Division of
           Economic Research working paper no. 36, March, 1970.

                                                                    5,12
IIIINTL    Bell, F. Heward. AGREEMENTS, CONVENTIONS AND TREATIES BETWEEN CANA-
           DA AND THE UNITED STATES OF AMERICA WITH RESPECT TO THE PACIFIC HALI-
           BUT FISHERY. Seattle, Wash., report of the International Pacific
           Halibut Commission, 1969. 102p.

                                                                    5,16
IIIF       Bell, Frederick W., and Jared E. Hazelton, eds. CONFERENCE ON FISH-
           ERIES ECONOMICS, BOSTON, 1965. RECENT DEVELOPMENTS AND RESEARCH IN
           FISHERIES ECONOMICS: PAPERS. Dobbs Ferry, N.Y., Oceana Publica-
           tions, Inc., 1967. xv, 233p.

                                                                    ART
IIIOR      Bell, Frederick, W., et al. THE FUTURE OF THE WORLD'S FISHERY RE-
           SOURCES TO THE YEAR 2000. In Marine Technology Society. Seventh
           Annual Conference, Washington, D.C., August 16-18, 1971. Washington,
           D.C., 1971. pp. 541-554.

                                                                    ***
IVM        Bell, M. MINERAL RESOURCE DEVELOPMENT OFF CANADA'S EAST COAST. Pa-
           per presented at Marine Resource Exploitation in the Northwest At-
           lantic Region Seminar, May 3, 1973, at Halifax, Nova Scotia. Mimeo.
           Ottawa, Canada, Department of Energy, Mines and Resources, 1973.
           26p.

                                                                    ***
IIE        Bella, D.A., and P.C. Klingeman. GENERAL PLANNING METHODOLOGY FOR
           OREGON'S ESTUARINE NATURAL RESOURCES. Corvallis, Oregon State Uni-
           versity, 1973. 117p.

|        |     |
|--------|-----|
| VOR | Bellanger, Francois. LEGAL PROBLEMS OF EXPLORING AND EXPLOITING THE RESOURCES OF THE SEA-BED AND ITS SUBSOIL. In Symposium on the Exploration and Exploitation of the Sea-bed and its Subsoil, held in Strasbourg, France, December 3-5, 1970. New York, U.S. and World Publications Inc., Manhattan Publishing Company, 1971? [ART] |

ART
VP     Belyashova, M.A. DISTRIBUTION OF AEROSOLS OVER SEAS. In M.E. Berlyand, ed., Air Pollution and Atmospheric Diffusion. New York, John Wiley and Sons, Halsted Press; Jerusalem, Israel Program for Scientific Translations, 1974. pp. 134-150.

***
VENV     BENEFICIAL MODIFICATIONS OF THE MARINE ENVIRONMENT. Washington, D.C., National Academy of Sciences, 1972. 122p.

13
IICONS     Bennett, D.W. 202 QUESTIONS FOR THE ENDANGERED COASTAL ZONE. Highlands, N.J., American Littoral Society special bulletin no. 6. 1970. 28p.

ART
IVM     Bennett, E. LEGAL CLIMATE FOR UNDERSEAS MINING. In Marine Technology Society, Exploiting the Ocean. Washington, D.C., 1966. pp. 204-210.

14a
IIIF     Bennett, George W. MANAGEMENT OF LAKES AND PONDS. 2d ed. New York, Van Nostrand Reinhold Company, 1971. xx, 375p.

***
VOCET     Benson, Richard C. THE MARINE TECHNICIAN - PAST, PRESENT AND FUTURE. Sea Grant special bulletin no. 10. Florida, University of Miami, 1973. 17p.

1,9
VINTL     Berber, Friedrich J. RIVERS IN INTERNATIONAL LAW. London; New York, 1959.

1
VINTL     _____ _____ SOME METHODOLOGICAL CONSIDERATIONS CONCERNING THE STUDY ON THE USES OF THE WATERS OF INTERNATIONAL RIVERS. Munich, Institut für völkerrecht, 1957.

14a
IIIF     Berger, Josef. IN GREAT WATERS: THE STORY OF THE PORTUGUESE FISHERMEN, by Jeremiah Digges (pseud.) New York, The Macmillan Company, 1941. xix, 282p.

ART
VLOS     Bergs, Helgi, et al. AN INTERNATIONAL REGIME FOR THE SEA BED. In Symposium on the Exploration and Exploitation of the Sea-Bed and its Subsoil, held in Strasbourg, France, December 3-5, 1970. New York, U.S. and World Publications, Inc., Manhattan Publishing Company, 1971.

13
IIIFP     Berk, Zeki. PROCESSING SQUID FOR FOOD. MIT Sea Grant Report MITSG 74-13. Cambridge, Massachusetts Institute of Technology, 1974. iii, 39p.

                                                  \*\*\*

IIICONS   Berkson, Harold. MARINE SANCTUARIES IN CALIFORNIA. Prepared at the request of Senator Henry M. Jackson, Chairman, Senate Committee on the Interior, pursuant to S.Res.45. A National Fuels and Energy Policy Study. Serial no. 92-95. Washington, U.S.G.P.O., 1972. 21p.

                                                  ART

VLOS     Berlin, Michael J. U.N. DEBATE ON OCEAN CONTROL MOVES INTO CHOPPY SEAS. In War and Peace Report, May-June, 1973. Vol. 12, pp. 18-21.

                                                  ART

VP       Bernard, Harold and Kurt Jakobson. EFFECTIVENESS OF DEVICES FOR THE CONTROL AND CLEANUP OF OIL SPILLS. In Offshore Technology Conference. 4th, Houston, Tex., 1972: Preprints. Dallas, Tex., 1972. Vol. 1, pp. 171-182.

                                                 16

IVINTL    Bernfeld, S. EXPLOITATION OF MINERALS IN AND UNDER THE SEAS UNDER SANCTION OF LAW: THE GENEVA CONVENTIONS OF 1958 AND BEYOND. Paper at Symposium on Private Investors Abroad. Dallas, Texas, 1967. pp. 337-390.

                                                 1

VCS      Bernfeld, Seymour S. THE CONTINENTAL SHELF AND THE LAW OF THE SEA. A SERIES OF PAPERS. n.p. 1967-?

                                               13

IIIOR     Berrill, N.J. THE LIFE OF THE OCEAN. N.Y., McGraw-Hill, 1969. 232p.

                                               14

IVMMR    Berry, Mary Clay. THE ALASKA PIPELINE - THE POLITICS OF OIL AND NATIVE LAND CLAIMS. Bloomington, Indiana University Press, 1975. 302p.

                                              \*\*\*

IIP       Bertges, W.C. RECREATIONAL VESSEL WASTE POLLUTION. Washington, U.S. Coast Guard, 1974. 147p.

                                               ART

VLOS     Bettini, E. POSSIBLE FUTURE REGIMES OF THE SEA-BED RESOURCES. Paper at Symposium on the International Regime of the Sea-bed. Rome, 1969.

                                             ART

VOR      Bezard, P. LES PROBLÈMES POSÉS PAR L'EXPLORATION ET L'EXPLOITATION DES FONDS SOUS-MARINS. In Fourth Conference on World Peace through Law, Bangkok, 1969. Proceedings. Genève, 1971. pp. 436-454.

                                             13

IIIFP     Bhongsvej, Nophorn, and Frederick J. Smith. FISHERMEN/PROCESSOR ARRANGEMENTS IN FISH MEAL PRODUCTION. Corvallis, Oregon State University, n.d. 16p.

                                           13

IVP      Bianchi, Ralph A. THE DEVELOPMENT AND DEMONSTRATION OF AN UNDERWATER OIL HARVESTING TECHNIQUE. Environmental protection technology series. EPA-R2-73-205. Washington, D.C., Office of Research and Monitoring, U.S. Environmental Protection Agency, 1973. viii, 86p.

						3,9
VINTL	Bijnkershoek, Cornelis van. DE DOMINIO MARIS DISSERTATIO; a photographic reproduction of the second edition (1744) with an English translation by Ralph van Deman Magoffin. New York, Oxford University Press, 1923. 107p.

						ART
IIIINTL	Bilder, Richard B. THE ANGLO-ICELANDIC FISHERIES DISPUTE. Reprinted from the Wisconsin Law Review, Vol. 37, no. 1, 1973.

						ART
VP	_____ THE CANADIAN ARCTIC WATERS POLLUTION PREVENTION ACT: NEW STRESSES ON THE LAW OF THE SEA. A reprint from the Michigan Law Review, Vol. 69, no. 1, November 1970. University of Wisconsin Sea Grant reprint WIS-SG-71-305. 1971. 54p.

						13
VP	_____ CONTROLLING GREAT LAKES POLLUTION: A STUDY IN UNITED STATES-CANADIAN ENVIRONMENTAL COOPERATION. University of Wisconsin Sea Grant Program WIS-SG-72-325. Reprinted from Michigan Law Review, Vol. 70, January, 1972. pp. 469-556.

						13,18
IIIB	_____ THE EMERGING RIGHT OF PHYSICAL ENFORCEMENT OF FISHERIES IN AND BEYOND TERRITORIAL LIMITS. University of Wisconsin Sea Grant Program. WIS-SG-74-222. Technical report no. 222. Madison, July, 1974. 28p.

						13,18
IVENV	_____ THE ROLE OF UNILATERAL STATE ACTION IN PREVENTING INTERNATIONAL ENVIRONMENTAL INJURY. University of Wisconsin Sea Grant Program WIS-SG-73-219. Madison, 1973. v, 59p.

						***
VOCET	Billaud, V., and D.W. Hood. AN APPROACH TO MARINE RESEARCH DEVELOPMENT IN ALASKA. Fairbanks, University of Alaska, Institute of Marine Science, 1975. 6p.

						ART
VINTL	Bingham, Joseph W. CHANGING CONCEPTS OF INTERNATIONAL LAW: MARITIME JURISDICTION IN TIME OF PEACE. In Proceedings of the American Society of International Law, 1940. pp. 54-62.

						ART
IIIF	_____ PACIFIC COASTAL FISHERIES. In American Bar Association, Section on International and Comparative Law, Selected Papers and Reports. Chicago, 1940. pp. 46-48.

						1,3,5,14a,16
IIIINTL	_____ REPORT ON THE INTERNATIONAL LAW OF PACIFIC COASTAL FISHERIES. Calif., Stanford University Press; London, H. Milford, Oxford University Press, 1938. vii, 75p.

						***
IIIP	BIOLOGICAL ASPECTS OF THERMAL POLLUTION. PROCEEDINGS OF THE NATIONAL SYMPOSIUM ON THERMAL POLLUTION. Nashville, Tenn., Vanderbilt University Press, 1969. 407p.

                                                                    ***
IICR    Bird, Marsha.  1974 LEGISLATION RELATING TO NEW YORK STATE'S COASTAL
        AND MARINE RESOURCES.  Albany, State University of New York, Sea
        Grant Institute, 1974.  12p.

                                                                    16
VLOS    Birnie, Patricia.  A ROLE IN SEARCH OF AN ORGANIZATION.  New York,
        Sierra Club Office of International Environment Affairs, 1975.  45p.

                                                                    13
IICR    Bish, Robert L.  AN ECONOMIC APPROACH TO LAND AND WATER RESOURCE
        MANAGEMENT:  A REPORT ON THE PUGET SOUND STUDY.  University of Wash-
        ington, Institute for Economic Research, Department of Economics.
        Seattle, 1972.  18p.

                                                                    14
IICR    Bish, Robert L., et al.  COASTAL RESOURCE USE: DECISIONS ON PUGET
        SOUND.  Seattle, University of Washington Press, 1975.  vii, 206p.

                                                                    ART
IIP&H   Black, R.W.  CURRENT STATUS OF ALTERNATIVE DEEPWATER TERMINAL FEASI-
        BILITY STUDIES.  In Proceedings of the Fifth National Sea Grant Con-
        ference held in Houston, Texas, 1972.  Publication no. TAMU-SG-73-
        101.  College Station, Texas A&M University, 1973.

                                                                    13
IIP&H   Black, Richard W.  OFFSHORE TERMINAL DESIGN CONSIDERATIONS FOR UNI-
        TED STATES WATERS.  Presented to the Chesapeake section of the So-
        ciety of Naval Architects and Marine Engineers.  Washington, D.C.,
        U.S. Department of Commerce, Maritime Administration, January 7,
        1974.  14p.

                                                                    13,15
IIIFV&G Blair, Carvel H., and Willits D. Ansel.  A GUIDE TO FISHING BOATS
        AND THEIR GEAR.  Cambridge, Md., Cornell Maritime Press, 1968.
        xii, 142p.

                                                                    14
VENE    Blanc, Gene A.  THE STATE ROLE IN THERMAL POWER PLANT SITING:  A
        REPORT TO THE STATE OF WASHINGTON.  San Francisco, Reid, Batchelor
        and Associates, Inc., 1969.  36p.

                                                                    ***
VP      Blockwick, Thomas N., et al.  AT-SEA TESTING OF HIGH SEAS OIL RE-
        COVERY SYSTEM, FINAL REPORT.  Washington, U.S. Department of Trans-
        portation, 1974.  iii, 95, 28p.

                                                                    1,5,16
VINTL   Bloomfield, L.M.  EGYPT, ISRAEL AND THE GULF OF AQABA IN INTERNATION-
        AL LAW.  Toronto, Carswell, 1957.  240p.

                                                                    1,9,16
VB      Bloomfield, L.M., and G.F. Fitzgerald.  BOUNDARY WATERS PROBLEMS OF
        CANADA AND THE UNITED STATES.  The International Joint Commission
        1912-1958.  Toronto, Carswell, 1958.

                                                                    ART
IVOSTR  Blumberg, R., and S.A. Taher.  ANALYSIS OF OFFSHORE PIPELINE RISERS
        AND UNDERWATER TIE-INS.  In Petroleum Mechanical Engineering Con-
        ference.  ASME publication 73-Pet-25.  Houston, Texas, 1973?  14p.

|       | 1,5,11 |
|-------|--------|

VINTL    Boczek, Boleslaw A. FLAGS OF CONVENIENCE: AN INTERNATIONAL LEGAL STUDY. Cambridge, Mass., Harvard University Press, 1962.

\*\*\*

IICZM    Bode, Robert V., and W.P. Farthing, Jr. COASTAL AREA MANAGEMENT IN NORTH CAROLINA: PROBLEMS AND ALTERNATIVES. Raleigh, University of North Carolina, 1974. 24p.

\*\*\*

VP       Boehme, Eckart. TANKER UNFAELLE AUF DEM HOHEN MEER: DIE ZULAESSIGKEIT STAATLICHER MASSNAHMEN ZUR GEFAHRENABWEHR. Hamburg, In Kommission beim Alfred Metzner Verlag Frankfurt am Main und Berlin, 1970. 92p.

1,3,5,7,10,12,14,16

VLOS     Boehme, Eckart, and Max I. Kehden, eds. FROM THE LAW OF THE SEA TOWARDS AN OCEAN SPACE REGIME. PRACTICAL AND LEGAL IMPLICATIONS OF THE MARINE REVOLUTION. Werkhefte no. 19. Hamburg, Forschungsstelle für Völkerrecht und ausländisches öffentliches Recht der Universität Hamburg, 1972. 174p.

5,13

VP       Boesch, Donald F., et al. OIL SPILLS AND THE MARINE ENVIRONMENT. A REPORT TO THE ENERGY POLICY PROJECT OF THE FORD FOUNDATION. Cambridge, Mass., Ballinger Publishing Company, 1974. xv, 114p.

8

VB       Boggs, S. Whittemore. DELIMITATION OF THE TERRITORIAL SEA. Reprinted from the American Journal of International Law, Vol. 24, no. 3, July, 1930. pp. 541-555.

1,5

VINTL    _____ _____ NATIONAL CLAIMS IN ADJACENT SEAS. Reprinted from The Geographical Review, Vol. XLI, no. 2, 1951.

\*\*\*

VP       Boley, Scott L., and Larry S. Slotta. RELEVANT DATA CONCERNING PROPOSED DISCHARGES OF DOMESTIC WASTES INTO NETARTS BAY. ORESU-T-74-002. Corvallis, Oregon State University, Sea Grant College Program, 1975.

17

VOR      Bollow, George E. ECONOMIC EFFECTS OF DEEP OCEAN MINERALS EXPLOITATION. Monterey, Calif., Naval Postgraduate School, 1971.

ART

IVMMR    Bolton, Frank C., Jr. NATURAL GAS IN THE OFFSHORE. In Slovenko, Ralph, ed., Oil and Gas Operations. Baton Rouge, Claitor's, 1963. pp. 315-321.

1

IIIB     Borchardt, Edwin M., comp. COASTAL WATERS. ENGLISH TRANSLATIONS OF EXTRACTS FROM WORKS OF FRENCH, GERMAN, AUSTRIAN, ARGENTINIAN, SPANISH, SWISS, RUSSIAN, ITALIAN, AND BELGIAN PUBLICISTS ... FOR USE BEFORE THE PERMANENT COURT OF ARBITRATION AT THE HAGUE ASSEMBLED UNDER THE PROVISIONS OF THE SPECIAL AGREEMENT BETWEEN THE UNITED STATES OF AMERICA AND GREAT BRITAIN CONCLUDED JANUARY 27, 1909. Washington, U.S.G.P.O., 1910. 362p.

|  |  |
|---|---|
| VOR | 14<br>Borgese, Elisabeth M. THE DRAMA OF THE OCEAN. New York, H.N. Abrams, 1975. |
| VCS | 16<br>_____ THE OCEAN FRANCHISE. PAPER AT PACEM IN MARIBUS PREPARATORY CONFERENCE ON THE LEGAL FRAMEWORK AND THE CONTINENTAL SHELF, KINGSTON, RHODE ISLAND, January 30-Febraary 1, 1970. University of Rhode Island, 1970. |
| VLOS | 3,7,8,13,15,16<br>_____ THE OCEAN REGIME; A SUGGESTED STATUTE FOR THE PEACEFUL USES OF THE HIGH SEAS AND THE SEA-BED BEYOND THE LIMITS OF NATIONAL JURISDICTION. Center for the Study of Democratic Institutions occasional paper, Vol. 1, no. 5. Santa Barbara, Calif., October, 1968. 39p. |
| VLOS | 1,2,3,5,7,12,13,14,16,18<br>Borgese, Elisabeth M., ed. PACEM IN MARIBUS. New York, Dodd, Mead, and Company, 1972. xxxiv, 382p. |
| VLOS | 14<br>Borgese, Elisabeth M., and David Krieger, eds. THE TIDES OF CHANGE: PEACE, POLLUTION, AND POTENTIAL OF THE OCEANS. New York, Mason/Charter, 1975. xvi, 357p. |
| IIP&H | 13<br>Borland, Stewart, and Martha Oliver. PORT EXPANSION IN THE PUGET SOUND REGION 1970-72. WSG-MP 72-1. Seattle, Division of Marine Resources, University of Washington, 1972. 80p. |
| VB | 12<br>Boroughs, Sir John. THE SOVEREIGNTY OF THE BRITISH SEAS, WRITTEN IN THE YEAR 1633. ed. by Th. Callander Wade. Edinburgh, 1920. 165p. |
| IICZM | 14<br>Bostwick, H. Ketchum, ed. Coastal Zone Workshop, Woods Hole, Mass., 1972. THE WATER'S EDGE: CRITICAL PROBLEMS OF THE COASTAL ZONE. Cambridge, Mass., the M.I.T. Press, 1972. xx, 393p. |
| VB | ART<br>Bouchez, Leo J. THE OUTER BOUNDARY OF THE COASTAL STATES' JURISDICTION OVER THE SEA-BED AND ITS SUBSOIL. Paper at Pacem in Maribus Preparatory Conference on the Legal Framework and the Continental Shelf. Kingston, Rhode Island, January 30-February 1, 1970. University of Rhode Island, 1970. |
| VINTL | 1,5,7,9,11,15<br>_____ THE REGIME OF BAYS IN INTERNATIONAL LAW. Leyden, Sijthoff, 1964. 330p. |
| VLOS | 1,5,7,10,12,14,16<br>Bouchez, Leo J., and L. Kaijen, eds. THE FUTURE OF THE LAW OF THE SEA. Proceedings of the Symposium on the Future of the Sea organized at Den Helder by the Royal Netherlands Naval College and the International Law Institute of Utrecht State University 26 and 27 June 1972. The Hague, Nijhoff, 1973. xi, 164p. |

VC         Boutros-Ghali, B., and Youssef Chlala.  LE CANAL DE SUEZ, 1854-1957;[1]
           CHRONOLOGIE, DOCUMENTS.  Alexandria, Egyptian Society of International Law, 1958.

IIIMM      Bowers, C.A., and R.S. Henderson.  PROJECT DEEP OPS: DEEP OBJECT[***]
           RECOVERY WITH PILOT AND KILLER WHALES.  Report NUC-TP-306.  San Diego, Calif., U.S. Naval Undersea Research and Development Center, November, 1972.  91p.

VOR        Bowett, D.W.  DEEP SEA-BED RESOURCES:  A MAJOR CHALLENGE.  Reprinted[1]
           from The Cambridge Law Journal, Vol. 31, part 1, April 1972.  pp. 50-66.

VLOS       _____  _____  THE LAW OF THE SEA.  England, Manchester University[1,3,5,6,7,8,9,11,12,16]
           Press;  Dobbs Ferry, N.Y., Oceana Publications, Inc., 1967.  117p.

VORM       Bowles, Thomas G.  SEA LAW AND SEA POWER AS THEY WOULD BE AFFECTED[16]
           BY RECENT PROPOSALS.  London, Murray, 1910.  296p.

VENE       Boyd, Dan S.  LEGAL ASPECTS OF STATE-OWNED OIL AND GAS ENERGY RE-[***]
           SOURCES.  Austin, Texas, Governor's Energy Advisory Council, Legal and Regulatory Policy Committee, 1974.  v, 78p.

VOCET      Boykin, Rosemary E.  TEXAS AND THE GULF OF MEXICO; A GENERAL GUIDE[17]
           TO MARINE SCIENCE IN THE TEXAS GULF COAST REGION.  Sea Grant Program.  College Station, Texas A&M University, Center for Marine Resources, 1971.

IIP&H      Bradley, James R.  DEEPWATER TERMINALS - THE CHALLENGE OF THE 70's.[ART]
           In Fifth National Sea Grant Conference, held in Houston, Texas, 1972.  TAMU-SG-73-101.  College Station, Texas A&M University, 1972.

IIP&H      Bragg, Daniel M., and James R. Bradley.  THE ECONOMIC IMPACT OF A[13]
           DEEPWATER TERMINAL IN TEXAS.  TAMU-SG-72-213.  College Station, Texas A&M University, 1972.  vi, 55p.

IIP&H      Bragg, D.M., et al.  A SURVEY OF THE ECONOMIC AND ENVIRONMENTAL AS-[***]
           PECTS OF AN OFFSHORE DEEP-WATER PORT AT GALVESTON, TEXAS:  PART 1: POTENTIAL ECONOMIC EFFECTS.  TAMU-SG-74-213.  College Station, Texas A&M University, 1974.  73p.

IICZM      Brahtz, J.F.P., ed.  COASTAL ZONE MANAGEMENT:  MULTIPLE USE WITH[***]
           CONSERVATION.  New York, John Wiley, 1972.  352p.

VOCET      _____  _____  OCEAN ENGINEERING:  GOALS, ENVIRONMENT, TECHNOLOGY.[18]
           New York, Wiley, 1968.  720p.

|  |  |
|---|---|
| | 13 |
| VOR | Breeding, Clark W., and A. Gordon Burton. INCOME TAXATION OF NATURAL RESOURCES. Englewood Cliffs, N.J., Prentice-Hall, 1971. 1 Vol. |
| | ART |
| VAC | Brennan, D.G. A NOTE ON BRIDGING THE DIFFERING SOVIET AND AMERICAN OBJECTIVES OF SEABED DEMILITARIZATION. Paper at Symposium on the International Regime of the Sea-bed. Rome, 1969. |
| | 17 |
| VOCET | Briggs, Peter. MEN IN THE SEA. New York, Simon and Schuster, 1968. 128p. |
| | 2,5,16 |
| VP | \_\_\_\_\_ \_\_\_\_\_ WATER; THE VITAL ESSENCE. 1st ed. New York, Harper and Row, 1967. ix, 223p. |
| | 1,3,5,7,9,15,16 |
| VLOS | British Institute of International and Comparative Law. DEVELOPMENTS IN THE LAW OF THE SEA, 1958-1964. International Law Series no. 3. Special publication no. 6. London, 1965. 208p. |
| | 1,5,8,15 |
| VINTL | Brittin, Burdick H., and Liselotte B. Watson. INTERNATIONAL LAW FOR SEAGOING OFFICERS. 3d ed. Annapolis, Md., Naval Institute Press, 1972. xx, 536p. |
| | 13 |
| IIP&H | Brockel, Harry C. THE MODERN CHALLENGE TO PORT MANAGEMENT. The University of Wisconsin Sea Grant Program WIS-SG-321. Reprint. Milwaukee, Wis., 1971. |
| | 16 |
| VINTL | Brouwer, Luitzen E. THE NORTH SEA AND THE LAW OF THE CONTINENTAL SHELF. World Land Use Survey occasional paper no. 5. Cornwall, England, Geographic Publications, 1964. 42p. |
| | ART |
| VOR | Brown, E.D. THE PRESENT REGIME OF THE EXPLORATION AND EXPLOITATION OF SEA-BED RESOURCES IN INTERNATIONAL LAW AND IN NATIONAL LEGISLATION. Paper at Symposium on the International Regime of the Sea-bed. Rome, 1969. |
| | 1,7,13,15 |
| VAC | \_\_\_\_\_ \_\_\_\_\_ ARMS CONTROL IN HYDROSPACE: LEGAL ASPECTS. Ocean series 301. Washington, D.C., Woodrow Wilson International Center for Scholars, June 1971. 131p. |
| | 7,18 |
| VLOS | \_\_\_\_\_ \_\_\_\_\_ THE LEGAL REGIME OF HYDROSPACE. Published under the auspices of the London Institute of World Affairs. London, Stevens, 1971. xx, 236p. |
| | 16 |
| IVLOS | \_\_\_\_\_ \_\_\_\_\_ REPORT ON THE LEGAL REGIME OF DEEP-SEA MINING. London, International Law Association, British Branch, Committee on Deep-Sea Mining, 1968. 67p. |

                                                      3,5,6,10,12,13,14,16
VINTL    Brown, Edward D.  THE LEGAL REGIME OF HYDROSPACE.  London, Stevens
         and Sons, 1971.  xx, 236, viiip.


                                                                    12
IVMMR    Brown, Keith C.  BIDDING FOR OFFSHORE OIL; TOWARD AN OPTIMAL STRATE-
         GY.  Dallas, Southern Methodist University Press, 1969.  76p.


                                                                   ***
IICZM    Brown, L.F., Jr., et al.  EVALUATION OF SANITARY LANDFILL SITES,
         TEXAS COASTAL ZONE - GEOLOGIC AND ENGINEERING CRITERIA.  Austin,
         University of Texas, Bureau of Economic Geology, 1972.  18p.


                                                                   ART
IVMMR    Browning, D.  THE LEGAL ENVIRONMENT FOR DEEP OCEAN MINERAL DEVELOP-
         MENT.  Paper at Symposium on Private Investors Abroad.  Dallas, Tex-
         as, 1969.  pp. 9-54.


                                                               5,14a,16
IIIF     Browning, Robert J.  FISHERIES OF THE NORTH PACIFIC:  HISTORY,
         SPECIES, GEAR AND PROCESS.  Anchorage, Alaska Northwest Publishing
         Company, 1974.  vi, 408p.


                                                                   ***
VENE     Brubaker, Sterling.  IN COMMAND OF TOMORROW:  RESOURCE AND ENVIRON-
         MENTAL STRATEGIES FOR AMERICANS.  Published for Resources for the
         Future.  Baltimore, Johns Hopkins University Press, 1975.  xii, 177p.


                                                                   ***
VMT      Bruel, E.  INTERNATIONAL STRAITS.  Vols. 1 and 2.  Copenhagen, Nyt
         nordisk Forlag, 1947.  London, Sweet and Maxwell, 1947.  278, and
         426p.


                                                                    13
IICZM    Brush, Birchard M., and Douglas L. Inman.  COASTAL PROCESSES AND
         LONG RANGE PLANNING.  Preprint from Marine Technology Society Eighth
         Annual Conference preprints.  La Jolla, Calif., Scripps Institution
         of Oceanography, University of California, n.d.  pp. 215-226.


                                                                   ***
IIP&H    Bruun, R.  PORT ENGINEERING.  Houston, Tex., Gulf Publishing Company,
         1973.  443p.


                                                                   ART
IICZM    Buchanan, G. Sidney.  TEXAS NAVIGATION DISTRICTS AND REGIONAL PLAN-
         NING IN THE GULF COAST AREA.  In Houston Law Review, Vol. 10, no. 3,
         March 1973.  pp. 533-597.


                                                                5,13,14
IIILOS   Buck, Eugene.  ALASKA AND THE LAW OF THE SEA:  NATIONAL PATTERNS
         AND TRENDS OF FISHERY DEVELOPMENT IN THE NORTH PACIFIC.  Alaska
         Sea Grant Program.  Anchorage, Arctic Environmental Information and
         Data Center, 1973.  65p.


                                                                   ***
VP       Buggele, Alvin E.  BETTER VACUUM BY REMOVAL OF DIFFUSION-PUMP-OIL
         CONTAMINANTS.  U.S. National Aeronautics and Space Administration,
         February, 1975.  69p.

|  |  |
|---|---|
| | 13 |
| IVP | Buhler, Donald R., ed. MERCURY IN THE WESTERN ENVIRONMENT. Proceedings of a Workshop, Portland, Oregon, February 25-26, 1973. Sponsored by Environmental Health Sciences Center, Oregon State University. Corvallis, Oregon, Continuing Education Publications, 1973. x, 360p. |

14a

IIIP    Bullard, Oral. CRISIS ON THE COLUMBIA. Portland, Or., Touchstone Press, 1968. 151p.

14a

VOCET   Bullen, Frank Thomas. OUR HERITAGE THE SEA. New York, Dutton, 1907. 338p.

\*\*\*

IIIF    Bundesforschungsanstalt für Fischerei, Hamburg. LA PÊCHE MARITIME DANS LES PAYS D'AFRIQUE OCCIDENTALE ASSOCIÉS À LA CEE; ÉTUDE. (Brussels) Commission, Communauté Economique Européenne, 1966. 139p. (European Economic Community. Etudes. Série développement de l'Outre-Mer.)

\*\*\*

VP      Burgess, D., et al. HAZARDS OF SPILLAGE OF LNG (LIQUIFIED NATURAL GAS) INTO WATER. Prepared for Department of Transportation, U.S. Coast Guard, Hazardous Materials Division, Final report; supporting investigation MIPR 2-70099-9-12395. Washington, 1972. 88p.

\*\*\*

VSUB    Burgess, R.F. SHIPS BENEATH THE SEA: A HISTORY OF SUBS AND SUBMERSIBLES. New York, McGraw-Hill Book Company, 1975. 263p.

14

VENV    Burhenne, W.E., and Robert Muecke, comp. INTERNATIONAL ENVIRONMENTAL LAW: MULTILATERAL TREATIES. Beitrage zur Umweltgestaltung; Heft B7. Berlin, E. Schmidt, 1974-    1 Vol. Loose-leaf.

ART

VLOS    Burke, William T. COMMENTS ON CURRENT INTERNATIONAL ISSUES RELATING TO THE LAW OF THE SEA. In Natural Resources Lawyer, July 1971. pp. 660-667.

4,7,11,13,14,15

VLOS    _____ CONTEMPORARY LAW OF THE SEA: TRANSPORTATION, COMMUNICATION AND FLIGHT. Law of the Sea Institute occasional paper no. 28. Kingston, University of Rhode Island, 1975.

7,11,13

VLOS    _____ FOURTH PREPARATORY MEETING, U.N. SEABED COMMITTEE: THE SUBJECT OF MARINE SCIENCE RESEARCH: A REPORT. August 24, 1972. Washington, D.C., National Academy of Sciences, National Research Council, Ocean Affairs Board, 1972. 9p.

1,5,8,11,13,16

VLOS    _____ INTERNATIONAL LEGAL PROBLEMS OF SCIENTIFIC RESEARCH IN THE OCEANS. Prepared for The National Council on Marine Resources and Engineering Development, August 1967. Reproduced by the Clearinghouse for Federal Scientific and Technical Information, Springfield, Va., 1967. 143p.

|         | 1,2,4,5,7,8,14,15,16,18 |
|---------|---|

VLOS　　Burke, William T.　LAW, SCIENCE AND THE OCEAN.　Law of the Sea Institute occasional paper no. 3.　Kingston, University of Rhode Island, 1969.　34p.

VOR　　_____　MARINE RESOURCES AND INTERNATIONAL LAW.　Law of the Sea Institute.　Kingston, University of Rhode Island, 1970.　36p.
[16]

VLOS　　_____　MARINE SCIENCE RESEARCH AND INTERNATIONAL LAW.　Law of the Sea Institute occasional paper no. 8.　Kingston, University of Rhode Island, 1970.　36p.
[1,4,5,7,8,11,13,14,15,16]

VLOS　　_____　OCEAN SCIENCES, TECHNOLOGY, AND THE FUTURE INTERNATIONAL LAW OF THE SEA.　Mershon Center for Education in National Security, pamphlet series no. 2.　Columbus, Ohio State University Press, 1966.　91p.
[1,3,5,6,7,8,11,12,13,14,15,16,18]

VINTL　　_____　A REPORT ON INTERNATIONAL LEGAL PROBLEMS OF SCIENTIFIC RESEARCH IN THE OCEANS.　Prepared for the National Council on Marine Resources and Engineering Development.　Reproduced by the Clearinghouse for Federal Scientific and Technical Information, Springfield, Va., 1967.　143p.
[1,7,16]

VLOS　　_____　SCIENTIFIC RESEARCH ARTICLES IN THE LAW OF THE SEA INFORMAL SINGLE NEGOTIATING TEXT.　Law of the Sea Institute occasional paper no. 25.　Kingston, University of Rhode Island, 1975.
[4,7,11,14]

IIILOS　　_____　SOME THOUGHTS ON FISHERIES AND A NEW CONFERENCE ON THE LAW OF THE SEA.　Law of the Sea Institute occasional paper no. 9.　Kingston, University of Rhode Island, March 1971.　17p.
[1,3,4,5,8,13,14,15,18]

IIILOS　　_____　SOME THOUGHTS ON FISHERIES AND A NEW CONFERENCE ON THE LAW OF THE SEA.　In World Fisheries Policy: Multidisciplinary Views.　Seattle, University of Washington Press, 1972.　pp. 52-73.
[ART]

VLOS　　_____　TOWARDS A BETTER USE OF THE OCEAN.　COMTEMPORARY LEGAL PROBLEMS IN OCEAN DEVELOPMENT.　Comments and recommendations by an international symposium, SIPRI.　Stockholm, Almqvist and Wiksell; N.Y., Humanities Press, 1969.　231p.
[1,3,5,6,9,12,14,15,16]

VLOS　　Burke, William T., comp.　MEMORANDUM TO IMSAP, WITH ENCLOSURES: 1. Copy of a "Statement by IMSAP on U.S. Programs of Technical Assistance," and letter to Dick Vetter.　2. Copy of U.S. position papers on freedom of scientific research for the IOC 7th session ... in Paris.　3. Copy of a paper delivered at Sea Grant Conference, Madison, Wisconsin, October 13, 1971: Fisheries issues in law of the sea negotiations.　Correspondence.　n.p., 1971.
[7,11,13]

                                                                14
VLOS      Burke, William T., et al. NATIONAL AND INTERNATIONAL LAW ENFORCE-
          MENT IN THE OCEAN. Seattle, University of Washington, Institute for
          Marine Studies, 1975. 244p.

                                                    2,12,13,14a,15,16
VOR       Burnell, Elaine R., and Piers von Simson, ed. PACEM IN MARIBUS CON-
          VOCATION, 3d, 1970. PREPARATORY CONFERENCE, SANTA BARBARA, CALIF.
          1970. OCEAN ENTERPRISES; A SUMMARY OF THE PROSPECTS, AND HAZARDS,
          OF MAN'S IMPENDING COMMERCIAL EXPLOITATION OF THE UNDERSEAS. A
          SPECIAL REPORT... Santa Barbara, Center for the Study of Democratic
          Institutions, 1970. xii, 116p.

                                                                14
IVMMR     Burnett, William C. PHOSPHORITE DEPOSITS FROM THE SEA FLOOR OFF
          PERU AND CHILE: RADIOCHEMICAL AND GEOCHEMICAL INVESTIGATIONS CON-
          CERNING THEIR ORIGIN. NSF Grant GX28674. HIG-74-3. Honolulu,
          University of Hawaii, Institute of Geohpysics, 1974. viii, 164p.

                                                                14
IVMMR     Burrell, Robert M., and Alvin J. Cottrell. POLITICS, OIL AND THE
          WESTERN MEDITERRANEAN. The Washington Papers. Vol. I, 7. Beverly
          Hills, Calif., Sage Publications, 1973. ii, 80p.

                                                                ***
VSG       Burroughs, Linda, et al, eds. PROCEEDINGS OF THE FOURTH NATIONAL SEA
          GRANT CONFERENCE HELD IN MADISON, WISCONSIN, OCTOBER 12-13, 1971.
          Sea Grant Publication no. WIS-SG-72-112. Madison, University of
          Wisconsin, 1972?

                                                                ***
VINTL     Bustamante y Rivero, J.L. PRÓLOGO DE LA HISTORIA MARITIMA DEL PERÚ.
          Lima, 1974. 51p.

                                                                1,5
VB        Bustamante y Sirvén, Antonio Sánchez de. EL MAR TERRITORIAL.
          Habana, 1930.

                                                                ***
VP        Butler, Michael J.A., and Fikret Berkes. BIOLOGICAL ASPECTS OF OIL
          POLLUTION IN THE MARINE ENVIRONMENT: A REVIEW. Manuscript Report
          no. 22. Montreal, McGill University, Marine Sciences Centre, 1972.
          121p.

                                                        1,5,7,16,18
VINTL     Butler, William E. THE LAW OF SOVIET TERRITORIAL WATERS; A CASE
          STUDY OF MARITIME LEGISLATION AND PRACTICE. N.Y., Praeger, 1967.
          192p.

                                              3,5,6,7,9,11,13,14,15,16,18
VLOS      _____ SOVIET UNION AND THE LAW OF THE SEA. Baltimore, Johns
          Hopkins Press, 1971. ix, 245p.

                                                                1
VINTL     Butler, William E., ed. SOVIET MARITIME LAW. In Soviet Statutes
          and Decisions, Vol. VI, 1969-70.

                                                        4,7,11,14
VLOS      Buzan, Barry G., and Barbara Johnson. CANADA AT THE THIRD LAW OF
          THE SEA CONFERENCE: POLICY, ROLE AND PROSPECTS. Law of the Sea

Institute occasional paper no. 29. Kingston, University of Rhode Island, 1975.

IICONS    Byrne, John V., and William B. North. LANDSLIDES OF OREGON: NORTH COAST. Sea Grant 5. Corvallis, Oregon State University Extension Service Marine Advisory Program, 1973. 14p.
        13

VLOS    Cabanas, G. Martinez. LESSONS OF U.N. INSTITUTIONAL EXPERIENCE FOR THE INSTITUTIONAL FRAMEWORK OF AN OCEAN REGIME. Paper at Pacem in Maribus Preparatory Conference on the Legal Framework and the Continental Shelf, Kingston, Rhode Island, January 30-February 1, 1970.
        16

VMT    Çaçi, Q. LE RÉGIME JURIDIQUE DES DETROITS ET DES CANAUX INTERNATIONAUX ET LE IMPORTANCE POUR LA NAVIGATION PAR MER DES BATEAUX DE COMMERCE. In Drejtësia Popullore, Vol. 25, no. 2, 1972. pp. 3-13.
        ART

VB    _____ LE RÉGIME JURIDIQUE INTERNATIONAL DES EAUX TERRITORIALES. In Drejtësia Popullore, Vol. 25, no. 6, 1972. pp. 41-59.
        ART

VP    Caflisch, L.C. INTERNATIONAL LAW AND OCEAN POLLUTION. In Revue Belge de Droit International, Vol. 8, 1972. pp. 7-33.
        ART

VORM    Caflisch, Lucius C., ed. ANNALS OF INTERNATIONAL STUDIES, VOL. 4: HYDROSPACE IN INTERNATIONAL RELATIONS. International Publications Service, 1974.
        14

VORM    _____ LES ESPACE MARITIME DANS LES RELATIONS INTERNATIONALES - HYDROSPACE IN INTERNATIONAL RELATIONS. Genève, Association des Anciens Etudiants de l'Institut Universitaire de Hautes Etudes Internationales, 1973. 372p.
        16

IIIF    Calder, Dale R., Peter J. Eldridge and Edwin B. Joseph, eds. THE SHRIMP FISHERY OF THE SOUTHEASTERN UNITED STATES: A MANAGEMENT PLANNING PROFILE. South Carolina Marine Resources Center technical report no. 5. Charleston, 1974. vi, 229p.
        13

VENV    Caldwell, Lynton K. MAN AND HIS ENVIRONMENT: POLICY AND ADMINISTRATION. New York, Harper and Row, 1975. 171p.
        14

IIIP    California. AN ENVIRONMENTAL TRAGEDY; REPORT ON CALIFORNIA SALMON AND STEELHEAD TROUT. Citizens Advisory Committee on Salmon and Steelhead Trout. Sacramento, 1971. 40p.
        ***

VENV    California. Advisory Commission on Marine and Coastal Resources. FIRST ANNUAL REPORT. Sacramento, Calif., 1969. 1st-      1969-
        1,13,14,15,17

VOR     California. Advisory Commission on Ocean Resources. COMPILATION OF RECOMMENDATIONS OF THE GOVERNOR'S ADVISORY COMMISSION ON OCEAN RESOURCES, JANUARY 1965-JANUARY 1967. Sacramento, 1966. 481p.    15

***

IICONS     California. Coastal Zone Conservation Commission. CALIFORNIA COASTAL PLAN. Sacramento, 1975. 443p.

***

VE     _____ _____ ENERGY FINDINGS ADOPTED JANUARY 21, 1975. San Francisco, 1975. vii, 231p.

IIP     California. Department of Health. HAZARDOUS WASTE MANAGEMENT. LAW, REGULATIONS AND GUIDELINES FOR THE HANDLING OF HAZARDOUS WASTE. Sacramento, 1975. 76p.    14

***

IVOL     California. Department of Water Resources. Division of Oil and Gas. BELMONT OFFSHORE OIL FIELD. Sacramento, 1975. 33p.

IIT&L     California. Laws, statutes, etc. INITIATIVE MEASURE TO BE SUBMITTED DIRECTLY TO THE ELECTORS: COASTAL ZONE CONSERVATION ACT; INITIATIVE CREATES STATE COASTAL ZONE CONSERVATION COMMISSION AND SIX REGIONAL COMMISSIONS. Sacramento, 1973. 3p.    13

IVT&L     _____ _____ LEASES AND PROSPECTING PERMITS FOR MINERALS OTHER THAN OIL AND GAS. California Administrative Code. Title 2. Division 3. State property operations. Article 4. Sacramento, n.d.    13

***

IICONS     California. Legislature. Assembly. Committee on Natural Resources, Planning and Public Works. HEARING ON SOUTH SHORELINE OF SAN FRANCISCO BAY. Sacramento, July 9-10, 1964. 182p.

***

IISL     _____ _____ HEARING ON TIDE AND SUBMERGED LANDS. Sacramento, September 17-18, 1964. 268p.

IICR     _____ _____ Subcommittee on Marine Resources. TRANSCRIPT OF PROCEEDINGS. HEARING OF SUBCOMMITTEE ON MARINE RESOURCES ON THE PUBLIC INTEREST IN THE SHORELINE AND COORDINATED MARINE RESOURCE DEVELOPMENT. December 13, 1968, San Diego, California. Sacramento, 1969. 154 l.    2

***

VP     _____ _____ Committee on Public Health. Subcommittee on Environmental Pollutants. HEARING ON ENVIRONMENTAL POLLUTANTS. Sacramento, December 2, 1963. 124p.

***

IIP     _____ _____ Committee on Water. Subcommittee on Water Pollution. HEARINGS ON POLLUTION OF SAN FRANCISCO BAY. Sacramento, December 9-10, 1963. 185p.

IIICONS   California. Legislature. Assembly. Committee on Ways and Means. HEARING ON RESERVATION OF WATER FOR PRESERVATION OF FISHLIFE. Sacramento, January 30-31, 1964. 164p.

IVDRIL   _____ Select Committee on Coastal Zone Resources. OFFSHORE OIL DRILLING: HEARING, APRIL 9, 1974, SANTA MONICA, CALIFORNIA. Transcript and appendices. Sacramento? 1974. 214, 96p.   14

VENE   California. Legislature. Joint Committee on Public Domain. Subcommittee on Geothermal Resources. GEOTHERMAL RESOURCES IN CALIFORNIA, A REPORT. Sacramento, 1973.

VENE   _____ _____ GEOTHERMAL RESOURCES IN CALIFORNIA: MUCH HEAT AND SOME LIGHT, A REPORT. Sacramento, 1974.

IISL   _____ Joint Committee on the Tidelands. HEARING ON JOINT TIDELANDS. Sacramento, March 16, 1964. 48p.

VENE   California. Legislature. Senate. Committee on Governmental Organization. SOLAR ENERGY; ISSUES AND PROBLEMS; A STAFF REPORT. Sacramento, 1974. ii, 44p.

IVMMR   _____ Committee on Natural Resources. HEARING ON AGREEMENTS FOR OIL EXTRACTION; BOUNDARY DETERMINATIONS; LONG BEACH TIDE AND SUBMERGED LANDS. Sacramento, January 6-7, February 27-28, 1964. 4 Vols.

IIIF   California. Marine Research Committee. CALIFORNIA COOPERATIVE OCEANIC FISHERIES INVESTIGATION. DATA REPORT. Sacramento, 1975.

VP   California. Office of Emergency Services. Radiological Section. NUCLEAR POWER PLANT EMERGENCY RESPONSE PLAN. Sacramento, California Department of Health, 1975.   14

IICONS   California. San Francisco Bay Conservation and Development Commission. FINAL EVALUATION REPORT: GUIDELINES BAY PLAN REVISION; BCDC STAFF REPORT, BAY PLAN EVALUATION PROJECT. Sacramento, Office of Planning and Research, 1974. 24p.

VENE   California. State Board of Equalization. CALIFORNIA ENERGY RESOURCES SURCHARGE 1974. Pamphlet no. 10. Sacramento, 1974. 24p.

IVMMR   California. State Lands Commission. State Lands Division. OIL AND GAS RESOURCES ON CALIFORNIA OFFSHORE LANDS. Long Beach, California, 1976.

IVMMR    California. State Lands Commission. OIL AND GAS RESOURCES ON CALIFORNIA OFFSHORE LANDS; A REPORT TO THE LEGISLATURE AT THE REQUEST OF THE JOINT LEGISLATIVE BUDGET COMMITTEE. Sacramento, 1975. 44p.

VSG    California. State University. ANNUAL REPORT. THE HUMBOLDT STATE UNIVERSITY SEA GRANT PROGRAM. HSU-SG-5. California, 1972-

IIWQ    California. University. SALINE WATER CONVERSION RESEARCH PROGRESS REPORT. Los Angeles, 1974/1975. iii, 102p.

14

VSG    ____ ____ SEA GRANT COLLEGE PROGRAM. La Jolla, Calif., 1974-

VSG    ____ ____ Institute of Marine Resources. SEA GRANT COLLEGE PROPOSAL. 1974/75. UCSG-4. San Diego, 1975. 3 Vols.

VOR    ____ ____ INSTITUTE OF MARINE RESOURCES REFERENCE SERIES, REPORT. 1972-1974. Berkeley, Calif., n.d. 50p.

VOCET    California. University. Scripps Institution of Oceanography. NAGA REPORT; SCIENTIFIC RESULTS OF MARINE INVESTIGATIONS OF THE SOUTH CHINA SEA AND THE GULF OF THAILAND, 1951-1961. San Diego, n.d.

13,15

VOR    CALIFORNIA AND USE OF THE OCEAN: A PLANNING STUDY OF RESOURCES, PREPARED FOR THE CALIFORNIA STATE OFFICE OF PLANNING. La Jolla, University of California, Institute of Marine Resources, 1965.

IICR    CALIFORNIA COMPREHENSIVE OCEAN AREA PLAN AND SUPPLEMENT. Sacramento, State of California, Resources Agency, Department of Navigation and Ocean Development, 1972? 188p.

13

IICR    California Marine Advisory Program. MARINE RESOURCES PROBLEMS: THE CALIFORNIA CITIZEN'S VIEWPOINT. CMAP 3. Los Angeles, Sea Grant Advisory Services, University of Southern California, 1974. ii, 13p.

IVMMR    CALIFORNIA OIL AND GAS FIELDS. SOUTH, CENTRAL COASTAL AND OFFSHORE CALIFORNIA. Sacramento, Division of Oil and Gas, 1974. Looseleaf. Vol. 2.

15

IIIF    Cameron, Francis X. CONSTITUTIONAL IMPEDIMENTS TO LIMITED ENTRY FISHERIES LEGISLATION: STATES FROM MAINE TO VIRGINIA. Kingston, University of Rhode Island, 1973.

13

IIIF    Campbell, Blake A. LIMITED ENTRY IN THE SALMON FISHERY: THE BRITISH COLUMBIA EXPERIENCE. Report no. PASGAP 6. Vancouver, University of British Columbia, Centre for Continuing Education, 1972. 14p.

VP        Campbell, F.J. STANDARDIZED HARDWARE FOR OIL SPILL CONTAINMENT BOOMS. Port Hueneme, Calif., U.S. Naval Construction Battalion Center, Civil Engineering Laboratory, 1974. 63p.

IICONS    Campbell, J.F. EROSION AND ACCRETION OF SELECTED HAWAIIAN BEACHES, 1962-1972. Sea Grant Report no. TR-72-02. Honolulu, University of Hawaii, 1972. 34p.

IVMMR     Canada. Department of Energy, Mines and Resources. Resource Administration Division. OFFSHORE EXPLORATION: INFORMATION AND PROCEDURES. Ottawa, 1971. 21p.

VCONS     _____ _____ Department of the Environment. Fisheries and Marine Service. International Fisheries Branch. THE MARINE ENVIRONMENT AND RENEWABLE RESOURCES. Law of the sea discussion paper. Ottawa, 1973. 10p.

VOCET     Canada. Science Council. CANADA, SCIENCE AND THE OCEANS; A MAJOR PROGRAM IN MARINE SCIENCE AND TECHNOLOGY FOR CANADA. Ottawa, 1970. 37p.

VT&L      Canadian Council of Resource Ministers. A DIGEST OF ENVIRONMENTAL POLLUTION LEGISLATION IN CANADA. Montreal, Canada, Secretariat of the CCRM, 1970. 800p. 2 Vols.

VENV      CANADIAN ENVIRONMENTAL LAW NEWS. A joint publication of the Canadian Environmental Law Association and the Canadian Environmental Law Research Foundation. Toronto, Ontario. 1972-

VP        Cannon, James. A CLEAR VIEW: GUIDE TO INDUSTRIAL POLLUTION CONTROL. New York, Inform, Inc., 1975. 235p.

VLOS      Căpătînă, O. CONSIDÉRATIONS CONCERNANT LA RESPONSABILITÉ POUR LES DOMMAGES RÉSULTANT DE L'EXPLORATION ET DE LA MISE EN VALEUR DES MERS ET DE OCEANS, AU-DELÀ DES LIMITES DE LA JURIDICTION NATIONALE. In Revue Roumdine d'Etudes Internationales, Vol. 13, 1971. pp. 113-130.

VLOS      CARACAS '74 (LOS-3): U.N. SOURCE DOCUMENTS ON THE THIRD U.N. LAW OF THE SEA CONFERENCE. Compiled by the editors of Ocean Science News. Holmes Beach, Florida, Wm. W. Gaunt and Sons, Inc., 1974. 2 Vols.

VCONS     Caribbean Study Project. CARIBBEAN STUDY PROJECT WORKING PAPERS AND SELECTION FROM DIALOGUE AT PREPARATORY CONFERENCE, JAMAICA, OCTOBER 1972. Msida, Malta University Press, 1974. x, 225p.

                                                                    5
VOR      Carlisle, Norman. RICHES OF THE SEA; THE NEW SCIENCE OF OCEANOLOGY.
         New York, Sterling Publishing Company, 1968. 128p.

                                                                   ***
IIREC    Carls, E. Glenn. RECREATION. Albany, State University of New York,
         New York Sea Grant Institute, 1975.

                                                                   ***
VSG      Carlson, Douglas M. MANAGEMENT OF THE BIOLOGICAL RESOURCES OF THE
         LAKE ONTARIO BASIN. Albany, New York State Sea Grant Program, 1973.
         264p.

                                                                   ***
IVOCET   Carmichael, A.D. OCEAN ENGINEERING POWER SYSTEMS. Cambridge, Md.,
         Cornell Maritime Press, 1974. 203p.

                                                                     1
IIICONS  Carmona, Ramon. VIGENCIA DE LA CONVENCION SOBRE PESCA Y CONSERVACION
         DE LOS RECURSOS VIVOS DE LA MAR: SUS REPERCUSIONES NACIONALES E IN-
         TERNACIONALES. In Boletín de la Academia de Ciencias Políticas y
         Sociales, no. 34. Caracas, Empresa el Cojo, 1967. 99p.

                                                                    17
VOCET    Carpenter, Malcolm S. EXPLORING SPACE AND SEA. Smithsonian publica-
         tion 4726. Washington, Smithsonian Institution Press, 1967. 28p.

                                                                   ART
IIP&H    Carroll, J.L., et al. PLANNING FOR COASTAL PORTS ON A SYSTEMS BASIS:
         PRELIMINARY METHODOLOGICAL DESIGN. In Report IWR-72-7. University
         Park, Pennsylvania State University, Institute for Research on Land
         and Water Resources, 1972. 245p.

                                                                    14a
IIIF     Carrothers, William A. THE BRITISH COLUMBIA FISHERIES. Toronto,
         Canada, The University of Toronto Press, 1941. xv, 136p.

                                                                   ART
IIIF     Carroz, J.E. LA COMMISSION INTERNATIONAL DES PÊCHES POUR L'ATLAN-
         TIQUE SUD-EST. In Canadian Yearbook of International Law, Vol. 9,
         1971. pp. 3-29.

                                                                   ART
IIICONS  _____ LE ROLE DE LA F.A.O. DANS LA CONSERVATION DES RES-
         SOURCES BIOLOGIQUES DE LA MER. In Société Française pour le Droit
         International. Actualités de droit de la mer: Actes. Paris, 1973.
         pp. 247-268.

                                                                    16
VLOS     _____ REGIONAL FISHERY BODIES AND THE APPORTIONMENT OF THE
         YIELD FROM THE LIVING RESOURCES OF THE SEA. Santa Barbara, Calif.,
         Center for the Study of Democratic Institutions, 1970. 30p.

                                                                    17
VOCET    Carson, Rachel L. THE SEA AROUND US. New York, Oxford University
         Press, 1951. vii, 230p.

                                                                  5,14a
VOCET    _____ THE SEA AROUND US. Rev. ed. New York, Oxford Univer-
         sity Press, 1967. 237p.

|  |  |
|---|---|
| VOCET | ***<br>Carson, Rachel. THE SEA: THE SEA AROUND US. UNDER THE SEA-WIND. THE EDGE OF THE SEA. London, MacGibbon and Kee, 1964. 611p. illus. |
| IICR | 14<br>Carter, Luther J. THE FLORIDA EXPERIENCE: LAND AND WATER POLICY IN A GROWTH STATE. Baltimore, published for Resources for the Future by the Johns Hopkins University Press, 1975. xvi, 354p. |
| VLOS | ***<br>Carvalho, P.P.de. PROPOSIÇOES EM TORNO DO MAR E O DIREITO PENAL. In Arquivos do Ministério da Justiça, Vol. 29, no. 122, 1972. pp. 142-149. |
| IICR | ***<br>Casciano, Frederick M., and Robert Q. Palmer. POTENTIAL OF OFFSHORE SAND AS AN EXPLOITABLE RESOURCE IN HAWAII. Honolulu, University of Hawaii, 1969. 32p. |
| VOCET | 2,5,12,16<br>Casey, S. Russel., Jr. PRECEPT FOR BENTHIC EXPLORATION AND EXPLOITATION. Dallas, UCC Press, 1968. xiv, 89p. |
| VLOS | ART<br>Castagne, A. L'ARCHÉOLOGIE SOUS-MARINE ET LE DROIT: DE LA RÉGLEMENTATION INTERNE AU PROBLÈME DE LA RÉGLEMENTATION INTERNATIONALE. In Société française pour le droit de la mer: Actes. Paris, 1973. pp. 164-183. |
| VLOS | ART<br>Castañeda, J. ... OR DEL COMITÉ PREPARATORIO DE LA TERCERA CONFERENCIA DE LAS NACIONES UNIDAS SOBRE EL DERECHO DEL MAR. In México y el regimen del mar, 1974. pp. 136-165. |
| VLOS | ART<br>_____ LAS POSICIONES DE LOS ESTADOS LATINOAAMERICANOS EN RELACIÓN CON EL DERECHO DEL MAR. In Jurídica. Anuario de la Escuela de Derecho de la Universidad Iberoamericana, 1975. Vol. 5, pp. 209-215. |
| IIIF | ***<br>Castro, Fidel. CUBA WILL NOT RENOUNCE HER RIGHT TO FISH IN INTERNATIONAL WATERS. Speech by Major Fidel Castro Ruz. Havana? Political Editions, 1971. n.p. 32p. |
| VINTL | ART<br>Castroviejo Bolíbar, J.M. LOS FONDOS MARINOS: PRINCIPIOS JURÍDICOS In Revista Española de Derecho Internacional. Vol. 23, 1970. pp. 667-710. |
| VLOS | ART<br>Castro y Castro, F. CONVENIOS BILATERALES DE PESCA: PRÁCTICA Y LEGISLACIÓN MEXICANA. In México y el regimen del mar, 1974. n.p. pp. 106-135. |
| IICZM | 14<br>Cathers, Lincoln D., et al. COASTAL ZONE MANAGEMENT: MULTIPLE USE WITH CONSERVATION. Edited by J. F. Peel Brahtz. New York, Wiley-Interscience, 1972. xii, 352p. |

VMT Cathers, Lincoln D. MARINE TRANSPORT SYSTEMS; STATE OF TECHNOLOGY. ART
In J. F. Peel Brahtz, ed. Coastal Zone Management: multiple use with conservation. New York, John Wiley, 1972. pp. 296-345.

IIIF Cato, James C. ENABLING LEGISLATION: POSSIBILITIES FOR THE COMMERCIAL FISHING INDUSTRY. Staff Paper 8. Gainesville, University of Florida, 1975. 18p. 14

IIIF _____ RECENT TAX DEVELOPMENTS IN COMMERCIAL FISHING. SUSF-SG-74-005. Gainesville, University of Florida, 1974. ***

IIIF Cato, James C., and C. David Veal. RECENT TAX DEVELOPMENTS IN COMMERCIAL FISHING. Rev. Florida Sea Grant publication S USF-SG-75-004. Gainesville, University of Florida, Cooperative Extension Service, 1975. 9p. ***

VP Catoe, Clarence E. THE APPLICABILITY OF REMOTE SENSING TECHNIQUES FOR OIL SLICK DETECTION. In Offshore Technology Conference, 4th, Houston, Tex., 1972. Preprints. Dallas, Tex., 1972. Vol. 1, pp. 887-902. ART

VMLAD Cauchy, Eugene F. LE DROIT MARITIME INTERNATIONAL CONSIDEREE DANS SES ..., ORIGINES ET DANS SES RAPPORTS AVEC LES PROGRES DE LA CIVILISATION. Paris, Guillaumin, 1862. 2 Vols. 3

VP CENTER FOR SHORT-LIVED PHENOMENA. ANNUAL REPORT. New York, UNIPUB, 1968- ***

VOCET Centre d'Etudes et de Recherches de Biologie et d'Oceanographic Medicale. RAPPORT D'ACTIVITE. Nice. Annual, 4 Vols. 17

VOCET Centre national pour l'exploitation des oceans. RAPPORT ANNUEL. Paris. n.d. 17

VLOS Červenka, Zdenek. THE RIGHT OF ACCESS TO THE SEA OF AFRICAN LAND-LOCKED COUNTRIES. In Verfassung und Recht in Uebersee. Vol. 6, 1973. pp. 299-310. ART

VINTL Červenka, Zdenek., ed. LAND-LOCKED COUNTRIES OF AFRICA. Uppsala, Scandinavian Institute of African Studies, 1973. 369p. ***

VLOS Çetingil, E. ÇATMA VE DIĞER DENIZ SEYRÜSEFERI OLAYARINDAN DOĞAN CEZA DAVALARINDA YETKIYE DAIR 1952 BRUEKSEL SOELEŞMESI. In Istanbul Barosu Dergisi.. Vol. 46, 1972. pp. 1091-1101. ART

IICZM Chabreck, Robert H., ed. PROCEEDINGS OF THE COASTAL MARSH AND ESTUARY MANAGEMENT SYMPOSIUM HELD AT LOUISIANA STATE UNIVERSITY, BATON 13

ROUGE, LOUISIANA, JULY 17-18, 1972. Baton Rouge Louisiana State University, Division of Continuing Education, 1973. 316p.

\*\*\*

IICZM   CHALLENGES IN THE ALASKAN COASTAL ZONE. Sea Grant Publication no. 72-1. Anchorage, University of Alaska, 1972. 35p.

\*\*\*

IIIP   Chan, Gordon.L. A STUDY OF THE EFFECTS OF THE SAN FRANSISCO OIL SPILL ON MARINE ORGANISMS. Report no. NOAA-72090817. Washington, U.S. Department of Commerce, National Oceanic and Atmospheric Administration. Part 1- 1972-

ART

VOR   Chapman, Wilbert M. FOOD FROM THE SEA AND PUBLIC POLICY. In English, Thomas Saunders, ed. Ocean resources and public policy. Seattle, Washington University Press, 1973. pp. 64-75

16

VB   _____ JUDICIAL ZONES IN THE OCEAN: THEIR EXTENT AND ATTRIBUTES. Paper for the Fourth Meeting of the Californian Governor's Advisory Commission on Ocean Resources. San Diego, California, June, 1966.

16

VLOS   _____ THE LAW OF THE SEA AND PUBLIC POLICY. University of California Engineering and Physical Science Extension Series, July, 1968. pp. 112-156.

6,8,16

IVMMR   _____ LEGAL PROBLEMS IN HARVESTING MINERALS OF THE DEEP SEABED. Van Camp Foundation, 1963. 17p.

15

IIIOR   _____ SOME PROBLEMS AND PROSPECTS FOR THE HARVEST OF LIVING MARINE RESOURCES TO THE YEAR 2000. San Diego, Calif., Ralston Purina Co., April 1970.

13,16

IIIB   _____ THE THEORY AND PRACTICE OF THE TWELVE MILE FISHERY LIMIT. n.p., Van Camp Foundation, 1963. 29p.

16

IIB   Charteris, A.H. TERRITORIAL JURISDICTION IN WIDE BAYS. Report of the 23rd Conference of the International Law Association, 1906. London, 1907. pp. 103-132.

13

VOCET   Chase, Joseph. OCEANOGRAPHIC OBSERVATIONS ALONG THE EAST COAST OF THE UNITED STATES, JANUARY-DECEMBER 1970. Oceanographic report no. 53. CG 373-53. Washington, D.C., United States Coast Guard Oceanographic Unit, 1972. v, 145p.

13

VOCET   CHEMICAL OCEANOGRAPHIC RESEARCH: PRESENT STATUS AND FUTURE DIRECTION. Deliberations of a workshop held at Naval Postgraduate School, Monterey, California, December 11-15, 1972. Washington, U.S.G.P.O., 1973. viii, 80p.

|  |  | ART |
|---|---|---|
| VLOS | Cheng, T. THE LAW OF THE SEA. In S.Leng, et al. Law in Chinese foreign policy. Dobbs Ferry, New York, Ocean Publications, Inc., 1972. pp. 79-114. | |

***

IIIF    Chestnut, A.F. SYNOPSIS OF MARINE FISHERIES OF NORTH CAROLINA. Part 1. Statistical Information, 1880-1973. Raleigh, University of North Carolina, 1975. 425p.

***

IIIF    Chestnut, A.F., and H.S. Davis. SYNOPSIS OF MARINE FISHERIES. UNC-SG-75-12. Raleigh, North Carolina State University, 1975.

16

VINTL   Chilean Minister of Foreign Relations. THE GOVERNMENT OF CHILE AND THE REPORT OF THE UNITED NATIONS INTERNATIONAL LAW COMMISSION ON REGIME OF THE HIGH SEAS, REGIME OF TERRITORIAL WATERS AND RELATED PROBLEMS. Santiago, Universo, 1957. 40p.

***

IIIT&L  CHILE-USSR: AGREEMENT ON COLLABORATION IN THE DEVELOPMENT OF FISHERIES. Washington, U.S. Department of Commerce, National Marine Fisheries Service, Division of Foreign Fisheries, 1971? 4p.

13

IIIF    Chitwood, Philip E. JAPANESE, SOVIET, AND SOUTH KOREAN FISHERIES OFF ALASKA, DEVELOPMENT AND HISTORY THROUGH 1966. U.S. Fish and Wildlife Service Circular 310. Washington, D.C., January, 1969. iii, 34p.

13

IIIFV&G Chleborowicz, Arthur G. EVALUATION OF TWIN TRAWL SHRIMP FISHING GEAR. University of North Carolina Sea Grant Publication UNC-SG-74-10. Raleigh, 1974. 45p.

***

IVDRIL  Christensen, P. NORWEGIAN OPERATION OF OFFSHORE DRILLING RIGS. Paper presented at Nor-Shipping '73. Fourth International Shipping Exhibition and Technical Symposium, May 10-11, 1973, at Oslo, Norway. Mimeo. 8p.

16

IIIOR   Christol, C. THE LEGAL FRAMEWORK FOR THE DEVELOPMENT OF OCEAN RESOURCES. California Cooperative Oceanic Fisheries Investigations Reports. Sacramento, January, 1969. Vol. 13. pp. 122-126.

16

IIIF    Christy, Francis T., Jr. ALTERNATIVE ARRANGEMENTS FOR MARINE FISHERIES; AN OVERVIEW. Washington, Resources for the Future, 1973. ix, 91p.

ART

IVMMR   _____ ECONOMIC PROBLEMS AND PROSPECTS FOR EXPLOITATION OF THE RESOURCES THE SEABED AND ITS SUBSOIL. In Symposium on the Exploration and Exploitation of the Seabed and its Subsoil. New York, U.S. and World Publications, Inc., Manhattan Publishing Company, 1971?

4,11,13,14,15

IIIF    _____ FISHERMAN QUOTAS: A TENTATIVE SUGGESTION FOR DOMESTIC MANAGEMENT. Law of the Sea Institute occasional paper no. 19.

Kingston, University of Rhode Island, 1973.  7p.

IVMMR     Christy, Francis T., Jr.  MARIGENOUS MINERALS:  WEALTH, REGIMES AND FACTORS OF DECISION.  Reprinted from Symposium on the International Regime of the Sea-bed Proceedings.  Reprint no. 87.  Washington, D.C. Resources for the Future, 1970.  pp. 113-153. [13]

IVMMR     _____  MINERAL RESOURCES OF THE SEA-BED OTHER THAN PETROLEUM AND NATURAL GAS, MARIGENOUS MINERALS:  WEALTH, REGIMES, AND FACTORS OF DECISION.  Paper at Symposium on the International Regime of the Sea-bed.  Rome, 1969. [16]

IIIF     _____  A PROGRAM OF STUDIES ON ALTERNATIVE ARRANGEMENTS FOR MARINE FISHERIES.  Washington, D.C., Resources for the Future, 1971. 6p. [5]

IIIF     Christy, Francis T., Jr., and Anthony Scott.  THE COMMON WEALTH IN OCEAN FISHERIES;  SOME PROBLEMS OF GROWTH AND ECONOMIC ALLOCATION. Published for Resources for the Future, Inc., by the Johns Hopkins Press, Baltimore, 1965.  281p. [1,5,7,15,16]

IIIF     Christy, Francis T. Jr., and A. Scott.  THE COMMON WEALTH IN OCEAN FISHERIES;  SOME PROBLEMS OF GROWTH AND ECONOMIC ALLOCATION.  2d ed. Baltimore, Md., Johns Hopkins Press for Resources for the Future, 1972.  xxxi, 281p. [12]

VLOS     Christy, Francis T., Jr., et al., eds.  THE LAW OF THE SEA:  CARACAS AND BEYOND.  Proceedings of the Ninth Annual Conference of the Law of the Sea Institute.  Kingston, University of Rhode Island, 1975. 422p. [4,7,11]

VLOS     Churchill, Robin, et al., eds.  NEW DIRECTIONS IN THE LAW OF THE SEA. The British Institute of International and Comparative Law, London; Dobbs Ferry, N.Y., Oceana Publications, Inc., 1973-  4 Vols. [13]

IICZM     CITIZEN PARTICIPATION - CZM UPDATE.  In Hawaii Sea Grant Newsletter. Vol. 6, no. 1, January, 1976.  p.4. [ART]

VOR     Citizens for the Northeast Pacific.  MARINE RESOURCE DEVELOPMENT.  Report no. PASGAP 4.  Seattle, Washington State University, Division of Marine Resources, 1972.  24p. [***]

VSUB     CIVIL MANNED UNDERSEA ACTIVITY:  AN ASSESSMENT.  NOAA-73112803. Rockville, Md., U.S. Department of Commerce, National Oceanic and Atmospheric Administration, 1973.  97p. [***]

VOCET     Claiborne, Robert.  ON EVERY SIDE THE SEA:  MAN'S INVOLVEMENT WITH THE OCEANS.  New York, American Heritage Press, 1971.  175p. [17]

| | | |
|---|---|---|
| IIP&H | Clapp, Edwin J. THE PORT OF BOSTON, A STUDY AND A SOLUTION OF THE TRAFFIC AND OPERATING PROBLEMS OF BOSTON, AND ITS PLACE IN THE COMPETITION OF THE NORTH ATLANTIC SEAPORTS. New Haven, Yale University Press, 1916. | 15 |
| IVMMR | Clark, Allen L. SOME PROBABLE IMPACTS OF DEEP OCEAN MINERAL RESOURCE DEVELOPMENT. In Marine Technology Society. Ninth Annual Conference, Washington, D.C., September 10-12, 1973. Washington, D.C., 1973. pp. 253-258. | ART |
| VMT | Clark, Bennett. THE ST. LAWRENCE SEAWAY. An address delivered before the Annual Convention of the Mississippi Valley Association. St. Louis, November 28, 1933. | 1 |
| IIIFP | Clark, Ernest, and Ray Clough. THE SALMON CANNING INDUSTRY. In Food Manufacture, Vol. III, no. 2, June, 1928. pp. 7-11. | ART |
| IICONS | Clark, John. COASTAL ECOSYSTEMS. Washington, D.C., Conservation Foundation, 1974. 178p. | 13 |
| IIIF | Clark, J.M. TOWARD A CONCEPT OF WORKABLE COMPETITION. In American Economic Review, Vol. xxx, June, 1940. pp. 241-256. | ART |
| IIICONS | Clarke, Robert. CONSERVATION OF SEA MAMMALS AND FISH. Wormley, England, National Institute of Oceanography, 1971. | *** |
| IICZM | Clawson, Marion. SOCIAL NEEDS AND THE URBAN-MARINE ENVIRONMENT. In J.F. Peel Brahtz, ed., Coastal Zone Management; Multiple Use with Conservation. New York, John Wiley, 1972. pp. 80-104. | ART |
| VOR | Clawson, Marion, and Hans H. Landsberg, eds. CONSTRUCTION OF NUCLEAR DESALTING PLANTS IN THE MIDDLE EAST. In Desalting Seawater - Achievements and Prospects. New York, Gordon and Breach, Science Publishers, Inc., 1972. | ART |
| IICR | Clawson, Marion, et al. DESALTED SEA WATER FOR AGRICULTURE: IS IT ECONOMICAL? Reprinted from Science, June 6, 1969. Washington, D.C., Resources for the Future, 1969. pp. 1141-1148. | 13 |
| VP | CLEAN SEAS GUIDE FOR OIL TANKERS; THE OPERATION OF LOAD ON TOP. London, International Chamber of Shipping and Oil Companies International Marine Forum, 1973. 21p. | *** |
| VP | Clemons, C.A. A STUDY OF HAZARDOUS WASTE MATERIALS, HAZARDOUS EFFECTS AND DISPOSAL METHODS. Washington, National Technical Information Service. 1972- 3 Vols. | *** |

|        |        |
|--------|--------|
| VAC    | Clift, A. Denis. DEFENSE INTERESTS AND THE NATIONAL OCEANOGRAPHIC PROGRAM. Prepared for the Commission on Marine Science, Engineering, and Resources. Washington, D.C., 1969? 32p. [5] |
| IVMMR  | Clifton, H. Edward. GOLD DISTRIBUTION IN SURFACE SEDIMENTS ON THE CONTINENTAL SHELF OFF SOUTHERN OREGON: A PRELIMINARY REPORT. U.S. Department of the Interior. Geological Survey Circular 587. Washington, U.S. Geological Survey, 1968. III, 6p. [13] |
| VMT    | Clingan, Thomas A., Jr., and Lewis M. Alexander, eds. HAZARDS OF MARITIME TRANSIT. Law of the Sea Institute Workshop held in Nassau, The Bahamas, May 1973. xxv, 138p. [1,3,4,7,11,13,14,16,18] |
| IIIOR  | Clingan, Thomas A., Jr. IMSAP RESPONSE TO THE NACOA REPORT. Draft. Mimeo. Coral Gables, Fla., University of Miami, 1973. 10p. [13] |
| IIIF   | _____ _____ NATIONAL AND INTERNATIONAL FISHERIES MANAGEMENT POLICY. A report of the University of Miami Sea Grant Decision Seminar, November, 1971. Special Bulletin No. 5, NOAA Sea Grant No. 2-35147. Coral Gables, Fla., 1972. iii, 35p. [13] |
| VOSTR  | Clinton, James R. SOIL MECHANICS WITH THE ORB-RUM SEA FLOOR WORK SYSTEM. La Jolla, University of California, Scripps Institution of Oceanography, 1972. 16p. *** |
| VP     | Clopton, J.C., ed. ENVIRONMENTAL RADIOACTIVITY SYMPOSIUM. Baltimore, Md., Johns Hopkins University Press, 1970. 272p. *** |
| IIIAFF | CLOSED-CYCLE MARICULTURE IN MARYLAND, VIRGINIA AND DELAWARE: AN EXAMINATION OF THE ADAPTABILITY OF EXISTING FISHERY LAWS TO NEW TECHNOLOGY. By Joseph Backruth and Diana Wheeler. DEL-SG-2-76. Newark, University of Delaware, Sea Grant Information, College of Marine Studies, 1976. 22p. *** |
| IIP    | COASTAL ESTUARINE POLLUTION. La Jolla, Calif., Ocean Engineering Information Service, n.d. 90p. |
| IIOCET | Coastal Plains Center for Marine Development Services. ABSTRACTS OF MARINE ACTIVITIES (1973) OF THE COASTAL PLAINS REGION (SOUTHEASTERN UNITED STATES). Wilmington, N.C. 74p. [17] |
| IIOCET | _____ _____ PROCEEDINGS OF SEMINAR ON PLANNING AND ENGINEERING IN THE COASTAL ZONE, JUNE 8-9, 1972, CHARLESTON, SOUTH CAROLINA. Seminar series no. 2. Wilmington, N.C., 1972. v, 141p. [13,15] |
| IIOCET | _____ _____ PROCEEDINGS OF A SEMINAR ON PLANNING AND ENGINEERING IN THE COASTAL ZONE. JUNE 8-9, 1972. Seminar series no. 2. Wilmington, N.C., 1972. 141p. *** |

IIREC     Coastal Plains Center for Marine Development Services. PROCEEDINGS OF A SPORT FISHING SEMINAR, JEKYLL ISLAND, GEORGIA, NOVEMBER 18-19, 1971. Seminar series no. 1. Wilmington, N.C., 1972. v, 41p.

IIOCET     _____ _____ REPORT OF THE GOVERNORS' CONFERENCE ON MARINE RESOURCES. Wilmington, N.C., 1973.

VB     COASTAL WATERS AND TERRITORIAL SOVEREIGNTY. Supplemental to Extracts used by Great Britain during the oral argument in the North Atlantic Coast Fisheries Arbitration, 1910.

IIT&L     COASTAL ZONE MANAGEMENT ACT OF 1972: PUBLIC LAW 92-583. College Station, Texas A&M University, 1973.

IICZM     Coastal Zone Management Conference, 2d, Charleston, S.C., 1974. COASTAL ZONE MANAGEMENT: THE COASTAL IMPERATIVE, DEVELOPING A NATIONAL PERSPECTIVE FOR COASTAL DECISION MAKING. Proceedings of the Second Annual Coastal Zone Management Conference, held in Charleston, South Carolina on March 13 and 14, 1974. Prepared at the request of Warren G. Magnuson, chairman, for the use of the Committee on Commerce, pursuant to S.Res.222, National Oceans, i.e. Ocean Policy Study. Washington, U.S.G.P.O., 1974. x, 196p.

IICZM     COASTAL ZONE MANAGEMENT - FROM PLANNING TO PRACTICE. Proceedings of the Third Annual Conference, held in Asilomar, California, May 27-30, 1975. Washington, U.S. Department of Commerce, National Oceanic and Atmospheric Administration, Office of Coastal Zone Management, 1976?

IICZM     COASTAL ZONE MANAGEMENT: THE PROCESS OF PROGRAM DEVELOPMENT. Sandwich, Mass., The Coastal Zone Management Institute, 1974. 326p.

IICZM     COASTAL ZONE MANAGEMENT UPDATE. In Hawaii Sea Grant Newsletter, Vol. 5, no. 12, December, 1975. p. 3.

IVENV     Cobb, David A. THE NEW ENGLAND OFFSHORE MINING ENVIRONMENTAL STUDY. In Offshore Technology Conference, 5th, Houston, Tex., 1973. Preprints. Dallas, Tex., 1973. Vol. 2, pp. 139-143.

IIIF     Cobb, John N. PACIFIC SALMON FISHERIES. Bureau of Fisheries Document no. 902. Washington, U.S. Department of Commerce, 1921.

IVP     Cochran, R.A., et al. OIL RECOVERY SYSTEM UTILIZING POLYURETHANE FOAM, FEASIBILITY STUDY. Washington, Environmental Protection Agency, 1973. xiv, 199p.

VLOS     Cochrane, L. IN SEARCH OF AN INTERNATIONAL SEABED REGIME. The United States draft seabed convention: background, interests represented, and prospects for agreement. In S.W. Wurfel, Current Aspects of Sea Law, Sea Grant Publication UNC-SG-74-03. Chapel Hill, University of North Carolina School of Law, 1974. pp. 1-10.

***

IICZM  Cody, Gene, and Luther W. Hyde. AGENCY IDENTIFICATION AND COORDINATION, ALABAMA COASTAL AREA MANAGEMENT PROGRAM; A PRELIMINARY REPORT. Montgomery, Office of State Planning, 1975. vii, 173p.

15

VOR  Coene, G.T. PROFILE OF MARINE RESOURCES. In Conference on Law, Organization and Security in the Use of the Ocean, 1st, Columbus, Ohio, 1967: Papers and discussions of the Conference. Columbus, Ohio, Mershon Center for Education in National Security, 1967. 55p.

***

VP  Coggle, J.E. WYKEHAM SCIENCE SERIES VOL. 14: BIOLOGICAL EFFECTS OF RADIATION. New York, Springer-Verlag, 1971.

3,16

VMLAD  Cohen, Edward E. ANCIENT ATHENIAN MARITIME COURTS. Princeton, N.J., Princeton University Press, 1973. xii, 233p.

***

IICZM  Cohen, Harry. FLOOD PLAIN AND COASTAL AREA LAND USE CONTROLS. Montgomery, Ala., Office of Development, 1974. 64p.

***

VP  Colas, René. LA POLLUTION DES EAUX. 2 éd. mise a jour. Paris, Presses Universitaires de France, 1968. 126p.

***

IICZM  Cole, B.J., ed. PLANNING FOR SHORELINE AND WATER USES. Kingston, University of Rhode Island, Marine Advisory Service, 1974. 23p.

***

IIIP  Cole, H.A. DISCUSSION ON BIOLOGICAL EFFECTS OF POLLUTION IN THE SEA. London, The Royal Society, 1971.

***

VB  Colegio de abogados de la libertad. EL FORO LIBERTEÑO Y LA DETEUSA DE LAS 200 MILLAS DE MAR TERRITORIAL. Trujillo, 1972. 68p.

13

VB  Coleman, Patrick J. THE WESTERN PACIFIC - ISLAND ARCS - MARGINAL SEAS - GEOCHEMISTRY. New York, Crane, Russak and Company, Inc., 1973. xviii, 675p.

ART

VLOS  Colina, R. de la. EVOLUCIÓN DEL DERECHO DEL MAR EN AMÉRICA: CONTRIBUCIÓN LATINOAMERICANA. In México y el Regimen del Mar, 1974. pp. 37-80.

ART

VOR  Colliard, C.A. LA QUESTION INTERNATIONALE DES RESSOURCES DE LA MER. In Société Française pour le Droit International. Actualités du droit de la mer: Actes. Paris, 1973. pp. 199-229.

1,7

VOR  Colliard, C.A., et al. LE FOND DES MERS; ASPECTS JURIDIQUES, BIOLOGIQUES ET GÉOLOGIQUES. Paris, Librairie Armand Colin, 1971. 208p.

VOR      Collier, J.A. THE REGIME OF THE SEAS; EXPLOITATION AND CONSERVATION. <u>In</u> Report on Conference on Law and Science, London 1964. London, David Davies Memorial Institute of International Studies, 1964. pp. 54-60. [ART]

\*\*\*

IIOSTR      Collier, Jeanne M., et al. HAWAII'S FLOATING CITY DEVELOPMENT PROGRAM. Transportation aspects of offshore complexes. Technical report no. 9. UNIHI-SEAGRANT-CR-76-01. Honolulu, University of Hawaii, 1975. 119p.

\*\*\*

VP      Collins, G.C. RADIOACTIVE WASTES: THEIR TREATMENT AND DISPOSAL. New York, John Wiley, 1961. 239p.

\*\*\*

VOR      Colloque International sur 'Exploitation des Océans, Bordeaux, 1971. COMMUNICATIONS ET RAPPORTS DU COLLOQUE, BORDEAUX, MARS 1971. Paris, Secrétariat du Colloque, 1971?

VP      Colloquium on Pollution of the Sea by Oil Spills, Brussels, 1970. POLLUTION DES EAUX CÔTIÈRES; POLLUTION DE LA MER PAR REJETS D'HYDROCARBURES, RAPPORT. Comité sur les Défis de la Société Moderne. Publication no. 1. Brussels, 1971? [17]

IICZM      Collver, Andrew. PUBLIC IMAGES AND COASTAL ZONE MANAGEMENT: Final report for 1972-73 for Project no. R/S-5. Part one: Policy implications. Sponsored by the National Oceanic and Atmospheric Administration under Sea Grant Program, no. 04-3-158-39 to the New York State Sea Grant Program. NYS Sea Grant Program Report NYSSGP-RS-74-001. Stony Brook, N.Y., State University of New York, 1974. 24p. [13]

VINTL      Colombos, C. John. THE INTERNATIONAL LAW OF THE SEA. London, New York, Longmans, Green, 1954. [7,12]

VINTL      _____ _____ THE INTERNATIONAL LAW OF THE SEA. 4th rev. ed. London, Longmans, 1959. 811p. [8]

VINTL      _____ _____ INTERNATIONAL LAW OF THE SEA. 5th ed. London, Longmans, 1962. [1,3,7,14,16]

VINTL      _____ _____ INTERNATIONAL LAW OF THE SEA. 6th rev. ed. London, Longmans, 1967. xvii, 886p. [1,3,5,6,7,9,10,11,12,15]

\*\*\*

VOSTR      Colunga, Laura, and Richard Stone, eds. PROCEEDINGS: ARTIFICIAL REEF CONFERENCE HELD MARCH 20-22, 1974, HOUSTON, TEXAS, 1974. TAMU-SG-74-103. College Station, Texas A&M University, 1974.

\*\*\*

IIIFV&G      Comitini, S. AN APPROACH TO EVALUATING ALTERNATIVE FISHING TECHNIQUES IN THE HAWAIIAN SKIPJACK TUNA FISHERY. UNIHI-SEAGRANT-JC-73-11. Honolulu, University of Hawaii, 1972. 6p.

|       | ART |
|---|---|
| IIIF | Comitini, S. CONSIDERATIONS OF THE ECONOMIC BENEFITS AND COSTS OF JOINT VENTURES VERSUS INDIGENOUS COMMERCIAL FISHERIES DEVELOPMENT. UNIHI-SEAGRANT-JC-74-20. In Report on Expert Committee on Tropical Skipjack, South Pacific Commission, Papeete, Tahiti, February 25 - March 1, 1974. pp. 21-24. |

|       | 5 |
|---|---|
| VOCET | Commission on Marine Science, Engineering and Resources. INDUSTRY AND TECHNOLOGY. KEYS TO OCEANIC DEVELOPMENT. House Document no. 291-42. Washington, U.S.G.P.O., 1969. 3 Parts. |

|       | 5 |
|---|---|
| VOCET | Commission on Marine Sciences, Engineering and Resources. OUR NATION AND THE SEA: A PLAN FOR NATIONAL ACTION. Report. Washington, U.S.G.P.O., 1969. xi, 305p. |

|       | 15 |
|---|---|
| VORM | Commission to Study the Organization of Peace. REPORT. 1st- November 1940- New York, N.Y., 1940- |

|       | 1 |
|---|---|
| VLOS | \_\_\_\_\_ \_\_\_\_\_ THE UNITED NATIONS AND THE BED OF THE SEA. Nineteenth report. New York, March 1969. 30p. |

|       | 1,13,16 |
|---|---|
| VLOS | \_\_\_\_\_ \_\_\_\_\_ THE UNITED NATIONS AND THE BED OF THE SEA. Nineteenth and twenty-first reports of the Commission to Study the Organization of Peace. New York, 1969-70. 2 Vols. in 1. 30, 45p. |

|       | 7,13,16 |
|---|---|
| VLOS | \_\_\_\_\_ \_\_\_\_\_ THE UNITED NATIONS AND THE OCEANS; CURRENT ISSUES IN THE LAW OF THE SEA. Report no. 23. New York, 1973. 46p. |

|       | 16 |
|---|---|
| IVMMR | Committee on Deep Sea Mineral Resources. American Branch of the International Law Association. INTERIM REPORT (W. Burke rapporteur). New York, 1968. |

|       | 14 |
|---|---|
| IVMMR | Committee on Petroleum Resources under the Ocean Floor. PETROLEUM RESOURCES UNDER THE OCEAN FLOOR. Washington, D.C., National Petroleum Council, 1969. |

|       | 5,16 |
|---|---|
| VORM | Committee to Study the Organization of Peace. NEW DIMENSIONS FOR THE UNITED NATIONS - THE PROBLEMS OF THE NEXT DECADE. N.Y., Dobbs Ferry, Oceana Publications, Inc., 1966. 63p. |

|       | 17 |
|---|---|
| VORM | Commoner, Barry. THE CLOSING CIRCLE; NATURE, MAN, AND TECHNOLOGY. New York, Knopf, 1971. 326, xp. |

|       | 16 |
|---|---|
| VCS | Commonwealth National Library. SELECT READING LIST ON MARGINAL WATERS AND THE CONTINENTAL SHELF. Canberra, Australia, 1955. 3p. |

|       | 1 |
|---|---|
| VC | Compagnie Universelle du Canal Maritime de Suez. THE SUEZ CANAL: NOTES AND STATISTICS. London, 1952. |

\*\*\*

IICZM    COMPARATIVE ASPECTS OF COASTAL ZONE MANAGEMENT: BACKGROUND INFORMATION ON THE LAW OF TEXAS AND OTHER STATES IN VIEW OF THE COASTAL ZONE MANAGEMENT ACT OF 1972. Houston, Texas Law Institute of Coastal and Marine Resources, 1973. 38p.

\*\*\*

IVOI    A COMPREHENSIVE STUDY OF THE OFFHSORE CONTRACT DRILLING INDUSTRY. New York, Walker (G.H.) and Company, 1969. 31p.

7

VP    CONFERENCE MONDIALE INTERCOMMUNALE POUR LA PROTECTION DE LA MER MÉDITERRANÉE CONTRE LA POLLUTION, BEIRUT, 1973. CHARTE DE BEYROUTH: PRINCIPES FONDAMENTAUX; ACTES DE LA CONFERENCE, TENUE À BEYROUTH, 4-6 JUIN 1973. Sponsored jointly by: Fédération Mondiale des Villes Junelées-Cités Unies, Organisation des Villes Arabes and la Ville de Beyrouth. Beyrouth, Conseil Municipal, 1973. 229p.

14

IICZM    Conference on Coastal Management, Beaufort, N.C. PROCEEDINGS OF A CONFERENCE ON COASTAL MANAGEMENT, MAY 16-17, 1974. Center for Marine and Coastal Studies report no. 74-6. Sea Grant UNC-SG-74-16. Raleigh, n.p., 1974. 181p.

\*\*\*

VLOS    CONFERENCE ON CONFLICT AND ORDER IN OCEAN RELATIONS, AIRLIE, VIRGINIA, 1974. Perspectives on ocean policy. Washington, U.S.G.P.O., 1975. 435p.

5,15

VP    CONFERENCE ON INTERNATIONAL AND INTERSTATE REGULATION OF WATER POLLUTION, COLUMBIA UNIVERSITY SCHOOL OF LAW, MARCH 12-13, 1970. New York, Columbia Journal of International Law, 1970. ix, 321p.

\*\*\*

VENV    CONFERENCE ON INTERNATIONAL IMPLICATIONS OF ENVIRONMENTAL PROBLEMS, ISTANBUL, 1971. ENVIRONMENTAL PROBLEMS AND THEIR INTERNATIONAL IMPLICATIONS; PAPERS PRESENTED AT THE CONFERENCE, HELD AT THE MERCHANT MARINE ACADEMY, ISTANBUL, TURKEY, JULY 21-28, 1971. Boulder, Colorado Associated University Press, 1973. 188p.

2,4,6,8,15,16,17

VOR    CONFERENCE ON LAW, ORGANIZATION AND SECURITY IN THE USE OF THE OCEAN. PAPERS, 1st-   1967-   Columbus, Ohio, Mershon Center for Education in National Security, 1967-

\*\*\*

VP    Conference on Law, Science and Politics: Water Pollution and its Effects Considered as a World Problem, Aberystwyth, Wales, 1970. WATER POLLUTION AS A WORLD PROBLEM: THE LEGAL, SCIENTIFIC AND POLITICAL ASPECTS; REPORT OF A CONFERENCE HELD AT THE UNIVERSITY COLLEGE OF WALES, ABERYSTWYTH, 11-12 JULY, 1970. London, Europa Publications for the David Davies Memorial Institute of International Studies, 1971. 240p.

\*\*\*

VLOS    Conference on Local Impacts of the Law of the Sea, Seattle, Wash., 1972. LOCAL IMPACTS OF THE LAW OF THE SEA; PROCEEDINGS OF A CONFERENCE HELD IN SEATTLE, OCTOBER 10-12, 1972. Seattle, University of Washington, Division of Marine Resources, 1973. 141p.

|       |                                                                                                                                                                                                                                                                                                                                                                 |
|-------|-----------------------------------------------------------------------------------------------------------------------------------------------------------------------------------------------------------------------------------------------------------------------------------------------------------------------------------------------------------------|
| VOD   | 13<br>Conference on Marine Pollution, Oslo, 1971. CONVENTION ON THE CONTROL OF MARINE POLLUTION BY DUMPING FROM SHIPS AND AIRCRAFT; REPORT. Oslo, 1971. n.p. n.d. 13, 5p.                                                                                                                                                                                        |
| IICZM | 15,16<br>CONFERENCE ON ORGANIZING AND MANAGING THE COASTAL ZONE, U.S. NAVAL ACADEMY, 1973. PROCEEDINGS. Washington, Council of State Governments, Office of State-Federal Relations, 1973?                                                                                                                                                                      |
| VP    | ***<br>CONFERENCE ON THE ESTABLISHMENT OF AN INTERNATIONAL COMPENSATION FUND FOR OIL POLLUTION DAMAGE, BRUSSELS, 1971. Final act of the Conference with attachments including the text of the adopted Convention. Acte final de la Conference avec documents joints comprenant le texte de la convention adoptee. London, Inter-Governmental Maritime Consultative Organization, 1972. 84p. |
| IIIF  | 16<br>CONFERENCE ON THE FUTURE OF THE U.S. FISHING INDUSTRY, SEATTLE, 1968. PAPERS AND PROCEEDINGS. Seattle, University of Washington, 1968.                                                                                                                                                                                                                    |
| VLOS  | 9<br>CONFERENCE ON THE LAW OF THE SEA, GENEVA, 1958. THE LAW OF THE SEA; THE FINAL ACT AND ANNEXES OF THE UNITED NATIONS CONFERENCE ON THE LAW OF THE SEA, GENEVA, 1958, TOGETHER WITH A SYNOPTICAL TABLE OF CLAIMS TO JURISDICTION OVER THE TERRITORIAL SEA, THE CONTIGUOUS ZONE AND THE CONTINENTAL SHELF. London, Society of Comparative Legislation and International Law, 1958. 42p. Special supplement of The International and Comparative Law Quarterly, 1958. |
| IIP   | 13<br>CONFERENCE ON THE MATTER OF POLUTION OF INTERSTATE WATERS, PUGET SOUND, STRAIT OF JUAN DE FUCA AND THEIR TRIBUTARIES AND ESTUARIES - STATE OF WASHINGTON. 1st, OLYMPIA, 1962. POLLUTION OF INTERSTATE WATERS; TRANSCRIPT OF CONFERENCE. Washington, U.S.G.P.O., 1973. 3 Vols.                                                                              |
| IIP   | 13<br>CONFERENCE ON THE MATTER OF POLLUTION OF THE NAVIGABLE WATERS OF GALVESTON BAY AND ITS TRIBUTARIES, HOUSTON, TEXAS, 1972. FOLLOWUP MEETING. Transcript of proceedings. Washington, U.S.G.P.O., 1973. 215p.                                                                                                                                                |
| VP    | 13<br>CONFERENCE ON THE MATTER OF POLLUTION OF THE NAVIGABLE WATERS OF PEARL HARBOR AND ITS TRIBUTARIES IN THE STATE OF HAWAII, HELD IN HONOLULU SEPTEMBER 21-23, 1971. Honolulu, 1971.                                                                                                                                                                          |
| VP    | 13,14a<br>CONFERENCE ON THE MATTER OF POLLUTION OF THE NAVIGABLE WATERS OF PUGET SOUND, THE STRAIT OF JUAN DE FUCA AND THEIR TRIBUTARIES AND ESTUARIES. 2d. Seattle, Washington, 1967. Transcript of proceedings. Washington, U.S. Department of the Interior, Federal Water Pollution Control Administration, 1968. 3 Vols.                                    |
| VORM  | 13<br>CONFERENCE ON THE OCEANS AND NATIONAL ECONOMIC DEVELOPMENT, SEATTLE, 1973. PROGRAM. Seattle, 1973. 18p.                                                                                                                                                                                                                                                    |

|        |                                                                                                                                                                                                                          |
|--------|--------------------------------------------------------------------------------------------------------------------------------------------------------------------------------------------------------------------------|
| VORM   | 13,15<br>CONFERENCE ON THE UNITED NATIONS OF THE NEXT DECADE, 7th, SOUTH EGREMONT, MASS., 1972. OCEAN MANAGMMENT AND WORLD ORDER. Muscatine, Iowa, Stanley Foundation, 1972. 32p.                                        |
| VP     | 2<br>Congressional Quarterly Service. MAN'S CONTROL OF THE ENVIRONMENT: TO DETERMINE HIS SURVIVAL OT TO LAY WASTE HIS PLANET. Washington, D.C., 1970. 91p.                                                               |
| VOCET  | 13<br>CONTINENTAL SHELF LIMIT AND FREEDOM OF SCIENTIFIC RESEARCH IN THE REGION BEYOND. A statement of the Ocean Affairs Board and the International Marine Science Affairs Policy Committee. Washington, National Academy of Science, 1971. 2p. |
| VP     | ***<br>CONTROL OF HAZARDOUS MATERIAL SPILLS. PROCEEDINGS OF THE 1972 NATIONAL CONFERENCE ON CONTROL OF HAZARDOUS MATERIAL SPILLS. Washington, D.C., Graphics Management Corporation, 1972. 212p.                         |
| VP     | 13<br>CONTROL OF HAZARDOUS MATERIAL SPILLS. Proceedings of the 1974 National Conference on Control of Hazardous Material Spills, August 25-28, 1974, San Francisco, California. N.Y., American Institute of Chemical Engineers, 1974. ix, 377p. |
| IIIT&L | 7<br>CONVENTION ON FISHING AND CONSERVATION OF THE LIVING RESOURCES OF THE HIGH SEAS. U.N. Treaty Series, Vol. 450.                                                                                                      |
| VT&L   | 7<br>CONVENTION ON THE CONTINENTAL SHELF. U.N. Treaty Series, Vol. 499.                                                                                                                                                  |
| VT&L   | 7<br>CONVENTION ON THE TERRITORIAL SEA AND CONTIGUOUS ZONE. U.N. Treaty Series, Vol. 516.                                                                                                                                |
| VT&L   | 16<br>CONVENTION ON THE TERRITORIAL SEA AND THE CONTIGUOUS ZONE BETWEEN THE UNITED STATES OF AMERICA AND OTHER GOVERNMENTS DONE AT GENEVA, APRIL 29, 1958. Washington, U.S.G.P.O., 1964. 70p.                            |
| IIE    | ***<br>Cook, C.E., et al. THE DELINEATION OF AND FACTORS AFFECTING MISSISSIPPI COASTAL ESTUARIES AND TIDAL MARSHES. MSGP-71-002. University, University of Mississippi, 1971. 70p.                                       |
| VENV   | 15<br>Cooley, Richard A., and Geoffrey Wandesforde-Smith, eds. CONGRESS AND THE ENVRIONMENT. Seattle, University of Washington, n.d.                                                                                     |
| IICR   | ***<br>Copeland, B.J., et al. COASTAL RESOURCES AND SHORT TERM RESEARCH NEEDS: A VIEW OF PRIORITIES. UNC-SG-75-18. Raleigh, University of North Carolina, 1975.                                                          |
| IICR   | ***<br>_____ NORTH CAROLINA COASTAL RESOURCES AND SHORT TERM RESEARCH NEEDS: A VIEW OF PRIORITIES. UNC-SG-75-14. Raleigh, North                                                                                     |

Carolina State University, 1975.

VOR  Costlow, J.D., ed. FERTILITY OF THE SEA; PROCEEDINGS OF THE SYMPOSIUM ON FERTILITY OF THE SEA, SAO PAULO, 1969. New York, Gordon and Breach Science Publishers, 1971. 2 Vols.

VORM  Cottrell, Alvin J., and R.M. Burrell, eds. THE INDIAN OCEAN: ITS POLITICAL, ECONOMIC, AND MILITARY IMPORTANCE. New York, Praeger, 1972.

IIIF  Coull, James R. THE FISHERIES OF EUROPE: AN ECONOMIC GEOGRAPHY. London, G. Bell and Sons, 1972. xii, 240p.

VOR  Coulomb, Jean. L'EXPANSION DES FONDS OCÉANIQUES ET LA DÉRIVE DES CONTINENTS. Paris, Presses Universitaires de France, 1969. 224p.

VOCET  _____ SEA FLOOR SPREADING AND CONTINENTAL DRIFT. Dordrecht, Holland, D. Reidel Publishing Company, 1972. 191p.

VP  Coulter, C.G., et al. THERMAL DISCHARGE FROM POWER STATIONS. Thermo-Fluids Conference. Sydney, Australia, Institution of Engineers, 1972? pp. 37-45.

VOCET  Council of Europe, Consultative Assembly. SYMPOSIUM ON THE EXPLORATION OF THE SEA-BED AND ITS SUBSOIL. STRASBOURG, 1970. n.p.

VOCET  _____ SYMPOSIUM ON THE EXPLORATION AND EXPLOITATION OF THE SEA-BED AND ITS SUBSOIL. Papers. 1971. n.p.

VMT  Couper, A.D. THE GEOGRAPHY OF SEA TRANSPORT. London, Hutchinson, 1972.

VMLAD  Courcy, Alfred de. QUESTIONS DE DROIT MARITIME. 1-4 ser. Paris, A. Cotillon..., 1877-88. 4 Vols.

IICONS  Courtenay, W.R., Jr., et al. ECOLOGICAL MONITORING OF BEACH EROSION CONTROL PROJECTS, BROWARD COUNTY, FLORIDA, AND ADJACENT AREAS. Technical memorandum 41. n.p., U.S. Coastal Engineering Research Center, February, 1974. 90p.

IIIF  Couty, Ph. LE COMMERCE DU POISSON DANS LE NORD-CAMEROUN. Paris, France, Office de la Recherche Scientifique et Technique Outre-Mer, 1964. 225p.

VP  Cowen, Edward. OIL AND WATER; THE TORREY CANYON DISASTER. Philadelphia, Lippincott, 1968. xiv, 241p.

| | | ART |
|---|---|---|
IIIP    Crapp, G.B. THE EFFECTS OF OIL POLLUTION AND EMULSIFIER CLEANSING ON LITTORAL ANIMALS AND PLANTS. In Field Studies Council, Oil Pollution Research Unit, Orielton Field Centre, Annual Report. Pembroke, Wales, 1971. pp. 7-13.

***

VOCET   Craven, J. OCEAN ENGINEERING SYSTEMS. Cambridge, Mass., M.I.T. Press, 1971. 520p.

ART

VORM    Craven, J.P. SEA POWER AND THE SEA-BED. In U.S. Naval Institute Proceedings, Vol. 92, 1966. pp. 36-51.

16

VOCET   _____ _____ TECHNOLOGY AND THE LAW OF THE SEA. Paper at the Conference on Law, Organization and Security in the Use of the Ocean. Columbus, Ohio, 1967.

ART

VOR     _____ INDUSTRY/GOVERNMENT RELATIONS IN OFFSHORE RESOURCE DEVELOPMENT. In Offshore Technology Conference, 5th, Houston, Tex., 1973: Preprints. Dallas, Tex., 1973. Vol. 2, pp. 939-968.

***

IIOSTR  Craven, John P., et al. HAWAII'S FLOATING CITY DEVELOPMENT PROGRAM. Annual Report. Waimanalo, University of Hawaii and Oceanic Institute, 1972-    1st-

ART

VOR     Creamer, Robert A. TITLE TO THE DEEP SEABED: PROSPECTS FOR THE FUTURE. In Harvard International Law Journal, Vol. 9, 1968. pp. 205-231.

12,16

VINTL   Crecraft, Earl W. FREEDOM OF THE SEAS. Freeport, N.Y., Books for Libraries Press, 1969. xx, 304p.

3

VMLAD   Cresp, Pierre-Philippe. COURS DE DROIT MARITIME. Paris, Durand et Pedone-Lauriel, 1876-82. 4 Vols.

***

VOR     Critchlow, K. INTO THE HIDDEN ENVIRONMENT: THE OCEANS. New York, Viking Press, 1973. 125p.

17

VOCET   A CRITICAL LOOK AT MARINE TECHNOLOGY; MARINE TECHNOLOGY SOCIETY 4th ANNUAL CONFERENCE AND EXHIBIT, 8-10 JULY, 1968. Washington, D.C., 1968. xiii, 731p.

13,16

VOCET   A CRITICAL REVIEW OF THE MARINE SCIENCE COMMISSION. Proceedings of a Seminar held by the Marine Technology Society Law Committee in conjunction with the George Washington University. January 31, 1969. Washington, George Washington University, 1969. 94p.

1,5,12

VB      Crocker, Henry G., comp. THE EXTENT OF THE MARGINAL SEA. A collection of official documents and views of representative publicists.

Washington, U.S.G.P.O., 1919. 703p.

IICZM     Crooks, Geoffrey. THE WASHINGTON SHORELINE MANAGEMENT ACT OF 1971. Seattle, University of Washington, 1973. 48, 64p.    13

IVM     Cruickshank, Michael J., and Ian J. Collins. DESIGN OF A FACILITY FOR MARINE MINING SYSTEMS RESEARCH. Offshore Technology Conference Paper No. 1034. Preprint. Dallas, Tex., 1969.    13

IVENV     Cruickshank, Michael J., et al. ENVIRONMENT AND TECHNOLOGY IN MARINE MINING. Reprinted from The Journal of Environmental Sciences, April, 1969. pp. 3-11.    13

IIIF     Crutchfield, James A. THE PACIFIC SALMON FISHERIES. Baltimore, Johns Hopkins Press, 1969. xii, 220p.    12

IIIF     Crutchfield, James A., ed. THE FISHERIES; PROBLEMS IN RESOURCE MANAGEMENT. Seattle, University of Washington Press, 1965.    5,12,15

IIIF     Crutchfield, James A., and Giulio Pontecorvo. THE PACIFIC SALMON FISHERIES: A STUDY OF IRRATIONAL CONSERVATION. Baltimore, Johns Hopkins Press, 1969. xii, 220p.    5,12,14,15,16

IIIF     Crutchfield, J.A., and Rowena Lawson. WEST AFRICAN MARINE FISHERIES: ALTERNATIVES FOR MANAGEMENT. Program of International Studies Fishery Arrangements Paper Series, no. 3. Washington, D.C., Resources for the Future, Inc.; Baltimore, Md., Johns Hopkins University Press, 1974. 74p.    1,13,16

VLOS     Cukwurah, A.O. THE THIRD UNITED NATIONS CONFERENCE ON THE LAW OF THE SEA. In Barrister, Vol. 6, 1975. pp. 70-89.    ART

IIIF     Cunningham, B.T. FISHERIES DIVISION PUBLICATIONS 1971. Fisheries Technical Report No. 82. Wellington, New Zealand Marine Department, Fisheries Division, 1972. 11p.    ***

IVOL     Curlin, James W. OUTER CONTINENTAL SHELF OIL AND GAS LEASING OFF SOUTHERN CALIFORNIA: ANALYSIS OF ISSUES. Prepared at the request of Hon. Warren G. Magnuson, Chairman, for the use of the Senate Committee on Commerce, pursuant to S.Res.222. National Ocean Policy Study. 93d Congr., 2d sess., committee print. Washington, U.S. G.P.O., 1974. 100p.    ***

IIP     Cuperus, K.W. WATER RESOURCES LAW: MARINE POLLUTION OF CONTINENTAL ORIGIN. In International Law Association Conference Report, 1972. n.p. pp. 97-106.    ART

                                                                    ART
VOR        Currie, R.I. CONSERVATION AND EXPLOITATION OF THE SEA. In Report
           of Conference on Law and Science, London, 1964. London, David
           Davies Memorial Institute of International Studies, 1964. pp. 49-53.

                                                                    14a
IIIB       Cushing, Caleb. THE TREATY OF WASHINGTON: ITS NEGOTIATION, EXECU-
           TION, AND THE DISCUSSIONS RELATING THERETO. New York, Harper and
           brothers, 1873. viii, 280p.

                                                                    3
VMLAD      Cussy, Ferdinand de Cornot. PHASES ET CAUSES CELEBRES DU DROIT MARI-
           TIME DES NATIONS. Leipzig, F.A. Brockhaus, 1856. 2 Vols.

                                                                    18
IVCS       Dahle, E., Jr. THE CONTINENTAL SHELF LANDS OF THE UNITED STATES:
           MINERAL RESOURCES AND THE LAWS AFFECTING THEIR DEVELOPMENT, EXPLOI-
           TATION, AND INVESTMENT POTENTIAL. UNC-SG-73-11. Chapel Hill, Uni-
           versity of North Carolina, School of Public Health, 1973. 78p.

                                                                    2
VP         Dales, J.H. POLLUTION, PROPERTY AND PRICES. Toronto, University
           of Toronto Press, 1968. vii, 111p.

                                                                    13
VOR        D'Amato, Anthony. WHO PROTECTS THE OCEANS? Chapter one, first
           draft. A project of the American Society's Panel on International
           Law and the Global Environment. Mimeo. n.p., 1971. 34p.

                                                                    1,12,14
VENV       D'Amato, Anthony, and John L. Hargrove. ENVIRONMENT AND THE LAW OF
           THE SEA. Studies in transnational legal policy no. 5. A report for
           American Society of International Law, Working Group on Ocean En-
           vironment. Washington, D.C., May 1974. vi, 60p.

                                                                    ART
VENV       D'Amato, Anthony, and Lawrence Hargrove. A REPORT OF THE WORKING
           GROUP ON OCEAN ENVIRONMENT OF THE AMERICAN SOCIETY OF INTERNATIONAL
           LAW. In Environment and the Law of the Sea, Washington, D.C., May
           1974.

                                                                    13
IIIFV&G    Dang, Bhupinder S., and F.A. Andrews. THE USE OF ACOUSTICS IN FISH
           CATCHING AND FISH STUDY. Washington, D.C., Catholic University of
           America, 1971. iv, 98p.

                                                                    15
VOR        Daniel, Hawthorne, and Francis Minor. THE INEXHAUSTIBLE SEA. New
           York, Dodd, Mead, 1954.

                                                                    ART
VLOS       Danzig, Aaron L. THE IMPACT AND IMPLICATIONS OF GENEVA WORLD CON-
           FERENCE RESOLUTION NO. 15. In Fourth Conference on World Peace
           Through Law, 1969. Proceedings. Genève, 1971. pp. 462-473(1971).

                                                                    13
VP         _____ MARINE POLLUTION - A FRAMEWORK FOR INTERNATIONAL CON-
           TROL. Washington, D.C., Woodrow Wilson International Center for
           Scholars, 1972. iii, 65p.

|       |                                                                                                                                                                                                                                                                                             |
|-------|---------------------------------------------------------------------------------------------------------------------------------------------------------------------------------------------------------------------------------------------------------------------------------------------|
| VOCET | 17<br>Darby, Ray, and Patricia Darby. CONQUERING THE DEEP SEA FRONTIER. New York, McKay, 1971. xiv, 204p.                                                                                                                                                                                   |
| IIP   | 14<br>Davidson, Burton. PROCESS CONTROL MODEL FOR OXYGEN REGENERATION OF POLLUTED RIVERS, PHASES IV AND V AND SPATIALLY AND TEMPORALLY DISTRIBUTED DISCHARGE OF EFFLUENTS IN ESTUARIES: A COMPOSITE. TECHNICAL, RESEARCH PROJECT COMPLETION REPORT. New Brunswick, N.J., Water Resources Research Institute, Rutgers University, 1974. 12p. |
| IIP   | 14<br>Davidson, Burton, and J.V. Hunter. PROCESS CONTROL MODEL FOR OXYGEN REGENERATION OF POLLUTED STREAMS: RESEARCH PROJECT TECHNICAL COMPLETION REPORT. New Brunswick, N.J., Water Resources Research Institute, Rutgers University, 1970. 8p.                                            |
| VP    | 14<br>Davies, J. Clarence, III, and Barbara S. Davies. THE POLITICS OF POLLUTION. 2d ed. Indianapolis, Pegasus, 1975. 254p.                                                                                                                                                                 |
| IVMMR | ***<br>Davis, Fenelon F., et al. NON LIVING RESOURCES. PART 1 - PHYSICAL ENVIRONMENT AND RESOURCES: PHYSIOGRAPHY, GEOLOGY, AND MINERAL RESOURCES OF THE COASTAL ZONE ON LAND. California Comprehensive Ocean Area Plan. Appendix V Vol. 1. Report. Sacramento, Department of Navigation and Ocean Development, 1971. 165p. |
| VENE  | ***<br>Davis, David H. ENERGY POLITICS. New York, St. Martin's Press, 1974. 211p.                                                                                                                                                                                                           |
| IIIB  | 1,5,15,16<br>Davis, Morris. ICELAND EXTENDS ITS FISHERIES LIMITS; A POLITICAL ANALYSIS. Copenhagen, Scandinavian University Books, 1963. 136p.                                                                                                                                              |
| IIIAFF| ***<br>Dawes, Clinton J. ON THE MARICULTURE OF THE FLORIDA SEAWEED, EUCHEUMA ISOFORME. Gainesville, University of Florida, Cooperative Extension Service, 1974. 10p.                                                                                                                        |
| IIP&H | ***<br>Dawson, Amos C., III. DEEPWATER PORT DEVELOPMENT IN NORTH CAROLINA: THE LEGAL CONTEXT. UNC-SG-75-08. Raleigh, University of North Carolina, 1969. 156p.                                                                                                                              |
| IIP&H | ***<br>_____ DEEPWATER PORT DEVELOPMENT IN NORTH CAROLINA: THE LEGAL CONTEXT. UNC-SG-75-08. Chapel Hill, University of North Carolina School of Law, 1974. 41p.                                                                                                                        |
| IIP&H | 14<br>_____ DEEPWATER PORT DEVELOPMENT IN NORTH CAROLINA: THE LEGAL CONTEXT. UNC-SG-75-08. Raleigh, North Carolina State University, March, 1975. 37p.                                                                                                                                 |
| VOCET | 14a<br>Deacon, Margaret. SCIENTISTS AND THE SEA, 1650-1900: A STUDY OF MARINE SCIENCE. London, New York, Academic Press, 1971. xvi, 445p.                                                                                                                                                   |

| | | ART |
|---|---|---|
| VCS | Dean, Arthur H. GENEVA CONVENTION ON THE CONTINENTAL SHELF. In Tulane Law Review, Vol. XLI, no. 2, February 1967. pp. 419-432. | |

***

IVMMR  Deans, Ralph C. OFFSHORE OIL SEARCH. Editorial research reports, Vol. 2, no. 3. Washington, Editorial Research Reports, 1973.

***

VOCET  Deas, Walter, and Clarrie Lawler. BENEATH AUSTRALIAN SEAS. Sydney, Australia, A.H. and A.W. Reed, 1970. 112p.

                                     13,17

VOCET  THE DECADE AHEAD, 1970-1980. Washington, D.C., Marine Technology Society, 1969. xii, 626p.

***

IIP&H  DEEPWATER OIL TERMINALS: POSITION PAPER. Washington, D.C., NAE, Marine Board, 1974. 8p.

***

VOCET  Defant, Albert. PHYSICAL OCEANOGRAPHY. Oxford, Pergamon Press, 1961. 2 Vols.

                                     15

IIP&H  de Frondeville, Bertrand L., et al. FOREIGN DEEP-WATER PORTS: LESSONS FOR AMERICA; CRITICAL ISSUES IN URBAN MANAGEMENT. Washington, D.C., Gryphon House, 1973.

                                     14a,15

IVMMR  Degens, Egon T., and David A. Ross, eds. HOT BRINES AND RECENT HEAVY METAL DEPOSITS IN THE RED SEA; A GEOCHEMICAL AND GEOPHYSICAL ACCOUNT. New York, Springer-Verlag, 1969. xii, 600p.

                                     2,16

VP  Degler, Stanley E., and Sandra C. Bloom. FEDERAL POLLUTION CONTROL PROGRAMS: WATER, AIR, AND SOLID WASTES. Washington, BNA Books, 1969. iii, 111p.

                                     1

VLOS  de Hartingh, Franco. LES CONCEPTIONS SOVIÉTIQUES DU DROIT DE LA MER. Vol. VIII. Paris, Librarie générale de droit et de jurisprudence. R. Richon et R. Durand-Auzias, 1960. 198p.

                                     ART

IICR  de la Cruz, A.A. THE ROLE OF TIDAL MARSHES IN THE PRODUCTIVITY OF COASTAL WATERS. In Association of Southeastern Biologists Bulletin, Vol. 20, no. 4., 1973. pp. 147-156.

***

IVMMR  Delach, M., and B. Horn. FERROMANGANESE DEPOSITS ON THE OCEAN FLOOR. Washington, D.C., National Science Foundation, Office for the International Decade of Ocean Exploration, 1972? 283p.

                                     13

IIREC  Delaune, Kathryn M., ed. PROCEEDINGS OF THE RECREATIONAL BOATING SEMINAR HELD IN GALVESTON, TEXAS ON DECEMBER 17, 1971. Texas A&M University Sea Grant Program, TAMU-SG-72-103. College Station, Texas Engineering Experiment Station, College of Engineering, 1972. 80p.

                                                                    13,16
IICZM   Delaware. Governor's Task Force on Marine and Coastal Affairs.
        THE COASTAL ZONE OF DELAWARE; A PLAN FOR ACTION IN DELAWARE.
        The final report of the Governor's Task Force on Marine and Coastal
        Affairs, April 1970-October 1971. Newark, College of Marine Studies,
        University of Delaware, 1972.

                                                                    11
IIT&L   Delaware. Laws and statutes, etc. COASTAL ZONE ACT. Chapter 70,
        Title 7, Sections 7001-    Mimeo. n.d.

                                                                    ***
VSG     Delaware. University. DELAWARE SEA GRANT PROGRAM; A REPORT ON THE
        UNIVERSITY OF DELAWARE SEA GRANT PROGRAM. 1973/1974. Wilmington,
        1975? 20p.

                                                                    ***
VOCET   _____ RESEARCH VESSELS AND FACILITIES AVAILABLE FOR CHARTER
        FROM THE COLLEGE OF MARINE STUDIES. Lewes, University of Delaware,
        1975. 19p.

                                                                    ***
VCS     _____ A STUDY OF THE SOCIO-ECONOMIC FACTORS RELATING TO THE
        OUTER CONTINENTAL SHELF OF THE MID-ATLANTIC COAST. Wilmington,
        1975? 3 Vols.

                                                                    13
IVMMR   Delaware. Water and Air Resources Commission. PROPOSED MINERAL EX-
        PLORATION REGULATIONS. Fourth draft. n.p. July, 1969. 32p.

                                                                    12
VINTL   Dembski, V. EUROPE AND THE NEW SEA LAW; A MANUAL OF INTERNATIONAL
        POLITICS AND MARITIME LAW. London, Simpkin, 1912. xix, 204p.

                                                                    14
IIOSTR  Denis, Manley St. HAWAII'S FLOATING CITY DEVELOPMENT PROGRAM. THE
        WINDS, CURRENTS AND WAVES AT THE SITE OF THE FLOATING CITY OFF
        WAIKIKI. Technical Report no. 1. UNIHI-SEAGRANT-CR-75-01. Rock-
        ville, Md., U.S. Department of Commerce, 1974. v, 93p.

                                                                    ***
IIIB    DENMARK - FEDERAL REPUBLIC OF GERMAN NETHERLANDS: AGREEMENTS DELIM-
        ITING THE CONTINENTAL SHELF IN THE NORTE (sic) SEA. Washington,
        U.S. Department of Commerce, National Marine Fisheries Service,
        Division of Foreign Fisheries, 1971. 3p.

                                                                    ART
IISL    Denzler, H.E. TIDELANDS OPERATIONS UNDER COAST GUARD REGULATIONS.
        In Slovenko, Ralph, ed., Oil and Gas Operations. Baton Rouge,
        Claitor's, 1963. pp. 268-275.

                                                                    1,5,16
VLOS    De Pauw, Frans. GROTIUS AND THE LAW OF THE SEA. Translated by
        P.J. Arthern. Brussels, Editions de l'Institut de Sociologie, 1965.
        77p.

                                                                    ***
IIP     Der, J.J., and E. Ghormley. OIL CONTAMINATED BEACH CLEANUP. Tech-
        nical Note N-1337. Port Hueneme, Calif., U.S. Naval Construction
        Battalion Center, 1974. 45p.

| | | |
|---|---|---|
| VP | Deran, Elizabeth Y. POLLUTION CONTROL: PERSPECTIVES ON THE GOVERNMENT ROLE. New York, Tax Foundation, 1971. 46p. | 2 |

VP    Deran, Elizabeth Y. POLLUTION CONTROL: PERSPECTIVES ON THE GOVERNMENT ROLE. New York, Tax Foundation, 1971. 46p. [2]

VINTL    De Rocher, Frederic G. FREEDOM OF PASSAGE THROUGH INTERNATIONAL STRAITS: COMMUNITY INTEREST AMID PRESENT CONTROVERSY. Sea Grant technical bulletin no. 23. NOAA Sea Grant no. 2-35147. Coral Gables, Fla., University of Miami Sea Grant Program, 1972. v, 129p. [13]

IIIF    Derouin, D. RÉFLEXIONS SUR QUELQUES ASPECTS ET PROBLÈMES DES PÊCHES NORVÉGIENNES. In Rev Marché Commun, no. 150, January, 1972. pp. 81-88. [ART]

VINTL    de Schutter, Bartholome. THE UNITED NATIONS FLAG, A FULL-FLEDGED SEAFLAG? Reprint from Studies en Voordrachten, 1963-I, University of Brussels. 195p. [1]

VMLAD    Desjardins, Arthur. TRAITE DE DROIT COMMERCIAL MARITIME. Paris, Pedone-Lauriel, 1878-90. 9 Vols. [3]

VP    Despax, Michel. LA POLLUTION DES EAUX ET SES PROBLÈMES JURIDIQUES. Paris, Librairies Techniques, 1968. 219p. [1]

VMLAD    Desty, Robert. THE REVISED STATUTES OF THE UNITED STATES, RELATING TO COMMERCE, NAVIGATION AND SHIPPING, WITH REFERENCES TO THE DECISIONS OF THE FEDERAL COURTS CONSTRUING THEM, TOGETHER WITH THE REGULATIONS PROMULGATED BY THE SECRETARY OF THE TREASURY IN ACCORDANCE THEREWITH, AND A FULL COLLECTION OF FORMS. San Francisco, S. Whitney, and Company, 1880. xxiv, 449p. [6]

IICZM    Devanney, J.W., III. ECONOMIC FACTORS IN THE DEVELOPMENT OF A COASTAL ZONE. Sea Grant Project Office. Cambridge, Massachusetts Institute of Technology, 1970. [17]

VINTL    _____ MARINE DECISIONS UNDER UNCERTAINTY. Cambridge, Md., Cornell Maritime Press, Inc., 1971. [11]

IVMMR    _____ THE OCS PETROLEUM PIE. MITSG 75-10. Cambridge, Massachusetts Institute of Technology, 1975. 130p. [***]

VP    Devos, Anthony, et al., eds. THE POLLUTION READER; BASED ON THE NATIONAL CONFERENCE ON "POLLUTION AND OUR ENVIRONMENT." Montreal, Harvest House, 1968. 264p. [2]

VINTL    de Vries Reilingh, O.G. WARSHIPS IN TERRITORIAL WATERS, THEIR RIGHT OF INNOCENT PASSAGE. In Netherlands Yearbook of International Law, pp. 29-67. 1971. [ART]

14
VP         DeWitt, Floyd A., Jr., and Penelope Mervin.  OIL SPILL AND OIL POL-
           LUTION REPORTS NOVEMBER 1974-FEBRUARY 1975.  EPA-670/2-75-044.  Cin-
           cinnati, Ohio, U.S. Environmental Protection Agency, National En-
           vironmental Research Center, Office of Research and Development,
           May, 1975.  ix, 259p.

                                                                       ***
VENV       Dickert, Thomas G., and Katherine R. Domeny, eds.  ENVIRONMENTAL IM-
           PACT ASSESSMENT:  GUIDELINES AND COMMENTARY.  Berkeley, University
           Of California, 1974.  xi, 238p.

                                                                       ART
IIIENV     Dickie, L.M.  THE INTERACTION BETWEEN FISHERY MANAGEMENT AND ENVIRON-
           MENTAL PROTECTION.  In Ocean Science Review, 1971-72.  Dartmouth,
           Nova Scotia, Bedford Institute of Oceanography, 1973.  pp. 15-33.

                                                                       ART
IVMMR      Diebold, P.  THE RICHNESS OF THE SEA:  MINERALS.  In Symposium on the
           Future of the Sea, Den Helder, 1972.  Proceedings.  The Hague, 1973.
           pp. 51-76.

                                                                       ***
VP         DISPOSAL OF RADIOACTIVE WASTES.  Proceedings of the Scientific Con-
           ference on the Disposal of Radioactive Wastes sponsored by IAEA and
           UNESCO, with the co-operation of FAO, held at the Oceanographic
           Museum of the Principality of Monaco, 16-21 November, 1959.  Proceed-
           ings Series; STI/PUB/18.  n.p.  1960.  2 Vols.

                                                                       17
IIREC      Ditton, Robert B.  THE SOCIAL AND ECONOMIC SIGNIFICANCE OF RECRE-
           ATION ACTIVITIES IN THE MARINE ENVIRONMENT.  Sea Grant Program
           WIS-SG-72-211.  Madison, University of Wisconsin, 1972.  11p.

                                                                       16
VCS        Djordjevic, J.  THE SOCIAL PROPERTY OF MANKIND.  Paper at Pacem in
           Maribus Preparatory Conference on the Legal Framework and the Con-
           tinental Shelf, Kingston, Rhode Island, January 30-February 1, 1970.

                                                                       ***
VOCET      Dobrovol'skii, A.D., S.D. Lappo, and V.L. Tsurikov, eds.  MIROVOI
           OKEAN.  Geograficheskoe Obshchestvo SSSR.  Moskovskii Filial.  Vop-
           rosy geografii, 84.  Moskva, Mysl', 1970.  271p.

                                                                       ***
IIIP       Dodson, Harold L., et al.  FISH KILLS CAUSED BY POLLUTION IN 1971.
           Technical Studies Report no. TS-00-72-10.  Washington, U.S. Environ-
           mental Protection Agency, Office of Water Programs, 1972.  37p.

                                                                       16
IIIINTL    Dodyk, P.  THE INTERNATIONAL LAW OF OCEAN FISHERIES:  PROSPECTS AND
           ALTERNATIVES.  Springfield, Virginia, Government Clearinghouse, 1968.

                                                                       16
IVOL       Dolan, Charles W., Thomas E. Savage, and Robert C. Clark, eds.  EN-
           VIRONMENTAL STATEMENT ON THE PROPOSED LEASING OF PUGET SOUND SHORE-
           LANDS AND BEDS OF NAVIGABLE WATERS FOR OIL AND GAS EXPLORATION, PRE-
           PARED FOR PRESENTATION TO STATE OF WASHINGTON BOARD OF NATURAL RE-
           SOURCES, SUBMITTED BY A JOINT COMMITTEE OF THE MOUNTAINEERS AND
           OTHERS.  n.p., 1970.

|||F Doliber, E.L. LOBSTERING INSHORE AND OFFSHORE. Camden, Maine, International Marine Publishing Company, 1973. 112p.

ART
IIIMM DOLPHIN TRAINING, U.S.S.R. ARTICLES. In Nedleya, no. 37, September 9-15, 1974; Pravda, November 10, 1974. Arlington, Va., Joint Publications Research Service, May 16, 1975. 10p.

ART
IVOSTR Dominguez, Richard F. PREDICTING BEHAVIOR OF SUSPENDED PIPELINES IN THE SEA. In Offshore Technology Conference, 4th, Houston, Texas, 1972. Preprints. Dallas, Tex., 1972. Vol. 1, pp. 619-628.

***
VOD Donohue, G.L., and J.W. Hoyt. HARBOR POLLUTION FROM LARGE SHIPS. San Diego, Calif., U.S. Naval Undersea Research and Development Center, 1973. 23p.

14
IICZM Doolittle, Fred C. LAND USE PLANNING AND REGULATION ON THE CALIFORNIA COAST: THE STATE ROLE. Davis, University of California, Institute of Governmental Affairs, 1972. iii, 85p.

***
IVENE Dorfman, M.G., and D.K. Agagu. GEOTHERMAL RESOURCES FRIO FORMATION, SOUTH TEXAS. Austin, University of Texas, 1975. 36p.

***
VENE Dorfman, Myron, and Ralph O. Kehle. POTENTIAL GEOTHERMAL RESOURCES OF TEXAS. Austin, University of Texas, 1974. 33p.

***
IIIF Dormont, Marcel. PÊCHE MARITIME AU CONGO; POSSIBILITÉS DE DÉVELOPPEMENT. Kinshasa. Université Lovanium. Institut de Recherches Economiques et Sociales. Recherches africaines, 10. Paris, Mouton, 1970. 282p.

ART
VP Dorrler, J.S. SORBENT SYSTEM DEVELOPMENT FOR OIL SPILL CLEANUP. In Proceedings of Joint Conference on Prevention and Control of Oil Spills, Washington, D.C., March 13-15, 1973. pp. 309-314.

ART
VP _____ USE OF SORBENTS FOR OIL SPILL CLEANUP. In Offshore Technology Conference, 4th, Houston, Texas, 1972. Preprints. Dallas, Tex., 1972. Vol. 1, pp. 403-416.

14
IICZM Dorsch, Donald L. LAND USE SURVEY AND ANALYSIS AND LAND DEVELOPMENT PLAN FOR HOLDEN BEACH, NORTH CAROLINA. Raleigh, N.C., Department of Natural and Economic Resources, Division of Community Assistance, 1974. 31p.

ART
IILOS Dorshaw, S.A. THE INTERNATIONAL LEGAL IMPLICATIONS OF OFF-SHORE TERMINAL FACILITIES. In Texas International Law Journal, Vol. 9,

1974.  pp. 205-223.

                                                                                     16

VINTL      Doss, Las Mohun.  THE LAW OF RIPARIAN RIGHTS, ALLUVION, AND FISHERY. Calcutta, Spink, 1891.  439p.

                                                                                     ***

VP         Dotson, G.K., et al.  LAND SPREADING, A CONSERVING AND NON-POLLUTING METHOD OF DISPOSING OF OILY WASTES.  Proceedings of the Fifth International Water Pollution Research Conference, San Francisco, July-August, 1970.  Elmsford, N.Y., Pergamon Press, 1971.

                                                                                     ART

IIIAFF     Doty, Maxwell S., and Vicente B. Alvarez.  SEAWEED FARMS:  A NEW APPROACH FOR U.S. INDUSTRY.  In Marine Technology Society.  Ninth Annual Conference, Washington, D.C., September 10-12, 1973.  Washington, D.C., 1973.  pp. 701-708.

                                                                       2,12,13,17,18

VOR        Doumani, George A.  EXPLOITING THE RESOURCES OF THE SEABED.  Prepared for the Subcommittee on National Security Policy and Scientific Developments of the Committee on Foreign Affairs, U.S. House of Representatives.  Washington, U.S.G.P.O., 1971.  vii, 152p.

                                                                          12,15,16

VOR        _____  _____  OCEAN WEALTH:  POLICY AND POTENTIAL.  New York, Spartan Books:  distributed by Hayden Book Company, Rochelle Park, N.J., 1973.  285p.

                                                                                13

VOD        Draft Convention for the Prevention of Pollution of the Sea by Dumping.  DRAFT ARTICLES OF THE CONVENTION.  March 13, 1972.  University of Oregon School of Law.  Mimeo.  Student paper.  March, 1972.  2 Parts.

                                                                                ***

VENV       Draper, Laurence.  ENVIRONMENTAL CONDITIONS.  Collected Reprints. Wormley, England, National Institute of Oceanography, 1971.  12p.

                                                                                ***

IIDR        Dredging: environmental effects.  PROCEEDINGS OF CONFERENCE HELD AT THE UNIVERSITY OF DELAWARE, APRIL 12-13, 1976.  Lewes, Del., University of Delaware, Cannon Marine Studies Laboratory.  n.y.p.

                                                                           13,15

VOCET     Dubach, Harold W., and Robert W. Taber.  QUESTIONS ABOUT THE OCEANS. Washington, U.S. Naval Oceanographic Office, U.S.G.P.O., 1968. xiii, 121p.

                                                                                 13

VP         Duce, Robert A., ed.  POLLUTANT TRANSFER TO THE MARINE ENVIRONMENT: DELIBERATIONS AND RECOMMENDATIONS OF THE NSF/FDOE POLLUTANT TRANSFER WORKSHOP HELD IN PORT ARANSAS, TEXAS, JANUARY 11-12, 1974. Kingston, Rhode Island, 1974.  vii, 55p.

|     | | 13 |
|---|---|---|

VP	Ducsik, Dennis W., ed. POWER, POLLUTION AND PUBLIC POLICY: ISSUES IN ELECTRIC POWER PRODUCTION, SHORELINE RECREATION, AIR AND WATER POLLUTION FACING NEW ENGLAND AND THE NATION. Massachusetts Institute of Technology Sea Grant Program, Project GH-88. M.I.T. Report No. 24. Cambridge, M.I.T. Press, 1971. xiii, 322p.

          12,16

IICZM	Ducsik, Dennis W. SHORELINE FOR THE PUBLIC; A HANDBOOK OF SOCIAL, ECONOMIC, AND LEGAL CONSIDERATIONS REGARDING PUBLIC RECREATIONAL USE OF THE NATION'S COASTAL SHORELINE. Cambridge, Mass., M.I.T. Press, 1974. xiii, 257p.

          ***

VOS	_____ TEACHING COASTAL ZONE MANAGEMENT: AN INTRODUCTORY COURSE SYLLABUS. MITSG 75-1. Cambridge, Mass., M.I.T., 1974. 148p.

          2

VP	Dudley, George A. COOPERATION BETWEEN STATE AND LOCAL GOVERNMENTS AND INDUSTRY TO SOLVE POLLUTION PROBLEMS. Albany, New York State Environment Facilities Corporation, 1970. 15p.

          3

VMLAD	Dufour, Edmond. DROIT MARITIME; COMMENTAIRE DES TITRES I ET II, LIVRE II, DU CODE DE COMMERCE. Paris, A. Durand, 1859. 2 Vols.

          ***

VOCET	Dugdale, R.C. PROGRESS REPORT - OCEANOGRAPHIC RESEARCH PROGRAM. R65-1. Fairbanks, University of Alaska, Institute of Marine Science, 1975. 12p.

          13

IIIF	Dunham, Fred. A STUDY OF COMMERCIALLY IMPORTANT ESTUARINE-DEPENDENT INDUSTRIAL FISHES. Technical Bulletin no. 4. New Orleans, Louisiana Wild Life and Fisheries Commission, 1972. 63p.

          1,5,7,13,14

VLOS	Dupuy, René-Jean. THE LAW OF THE SEA; CURRENT PROBLEMS. Dobbs Ferry, N.Y., Oceana Publications, Inc.; Leyden, Sijthoff, 1974. xiii, 210p.

          16

IIIP	_____ THE PRESENT AND THE POSSIBLE FUTURE REGIMES FOR THE SEA-BED, THE LIVING RESOURCES OF THE SEA-BED AND THEIR PROTECTION AGAINST POLLUTION CAUSED BY EXPLOITATION OF THE SEA-BED RESOURCES. Paper at Pacem in Maribus Preparatory Conference on the Legal Framework and the Continental Shelf. Kingston, Rhode Island, January 30-February 1, 1970.

          ART

VLOS	Dupuy, R.J., et al. LES APPROPRIATIONS NATIONALES DES ESPACES MARI-IMTES. In Société Française pour le Droit International. Actualités du droit de la mer: Actes. Paris, 1973. pp. 109-157.

          5,16

VINTL	Durante, F. THE PRESENT REGIME OF THE EXPLORATION AND EXPLOITATION OF THE SEA-BED RESOURCES IN INTERNATIONAL LAW AND NATIONAL LEGISLATION. Paper at Symposium on the International Regime of the Sea-bed. Rome, 1969.

|  |  |
|---|---|
| | 5,12 |
| VINTL | Durante, Francesco. LA PIATTAFORMA LITORALE NEL DIRITTO INTERNAZIONALE. Milano, A. Giuffre, 1955. vii, 318p. |
| | *** |
| VREFS | Durrenberger, R.W. DICTIONARY OF ENVIRONMENTAL SCIENCES. Palo Alto, Calif., National Press Books, 1973. 285p. |
| | 17 |
| IVP | Dye, Lee. BLOWOUT AT PLATFORM A; THE CRISIS THAT AWAKENED A NATION. 1st ed. Garden City, N.Y., Doubleday, 1971. viii, 231p. |
| | *** |
| IIIAFF | Dyer, Ira, et al. PROBLEMS AND POTENTIALS OF RECYCLING WASTES FOR AQUACULTURE. MITAF 74-27. Cambridge, Massachusetts Institute of Technology, Marine Resources Information Center, 1974. 170p. |
| | 13 |
| IVOL | Dyer, Morris K., et al. APPLICABILITY OF NASA CONTRACT QUALITY MANAGEMENT AND FAILURE MODE EFFECT ANALYSIS PROCEDURES TO THE USGS OUTER CONTINENTAL SHELF OIL AND GAS LEASE MANAGEMENT PROGRAM. A report to the U.S. Geological Survey. Mimeo. Final Report. Washington, D.C., 1971. 14, 36p. |
| | *** |
| VOCET | Dyrssen, D., and D. Jagner, eds. THE CHANGING CHEMISTRY OF THE OCEANS. Nobel Sympos um 20. New York, Wiley-Interscience, 1972. 365p. |
| | 5,13,17 |
| VP | Easton, Robert O. BLACK TIDE: THE SANTA BARBARA OIL SPILL AND ITS CONSEQUENCES. New York, Delacorte Press, 1972. xvi, 336p. |
| | *** |
| VORM | Eatwell, J.L., et al. PACEM IN MARIBUS III. STUDY PROJECT 3: THE ECONOMIC IMPLICATIONS OF AN OCEAN DEVELOPMENT TAX. Cambridge, Cambridge University. n.d. 133p. |
| | ART |
| IIICONS | Echeverría, F. PRESERVACIÓN DEL MEDIO MARINO. In México y el Regimen del Mar. Tlatelolco, 1974. pp. 225-265. |
| | 2 |
| VP | ECO-CATASTROPHE. By the editors of Ramparts. New York, Harper and Row, 1970. xiii, 158p. |
| | *** |
| VP | THE ECOLOGICAL EFFECTS OF OIL POLLUTION ON LITTORAL COMMUNITIES, INTERNATIONAL CONFERENCE BY THE INSTITUTE OF PETROLEUM AT ZOOLOGICAL SOCIETY OF LONDON, NOVEMBER, 1970. Barking, Essex, England, Applied Science Publishers, 1971. 256p. |
| | 7 |
| VOR | ECONOMIC CONSIDERATIONS CONDUCIVE TO PROMOTING THE DEVELOPMENT OF THE RESOURCES OF THE SEA-BED AND OCEAN FLOOR BEYOND THE LIMITS OF NATIONAL JURISDICTION IN THE INTEREST OF MANKIND. Preliminary note by the Secretariat. Mimeo. A/AC.138/6. 26 February, 1969. 6p. |

|       |                                                                                                                                                                                                                                                                                                    |
|-------|------------------------------------------------------------------------------------------------------------------------------------------------------------------------------------------------------------------------------------------------------------------------------------------------------|
| IICZM | 13<br>ECONOMIC DEVELOPMENT STUDY OF THE TEXAS COASTAL ZONE. Prepared for Coastal Resources Management Program, Interagency Council on Natural Resources and the Environment, State of Texas. TAMU-SG-72-212. College Station, Texas, College of Engineering, Texas A&M University, n.d. x, 130p. |
| IIP&H | 14<br>THE ECONOMIC IMPACT OF A LOUISIANA OFFSHORE OIL PORT. Final Report. Project no. AS-629. Prepared for Louisiana Superport Task Force LOOP Inc., by H.J. Kaiser Company, Gulf South Research Institute. New Orleans, Louisiana State Science Foundation, 1975. vii, 74p. |
| IIIB  | ***<br>ECONOMIC IMPACTS OF EXTENDED FISHERIES JURISDICTION. Proceedings of Conference held at the Clayton Conference Center, University of Delaware, April 29-30, 1976. Sponsored by Delaware Sea Grant Program and National Marine Fisheries Service. Newark, University of Delaware, College of Marine Studies. n.y.p. |
| VOR   | 7<br>ECONOMIC IMPLICATIONS OF EXPLOITATION OF MINERAL RESOURCES OF THE SEA-BED WITH REFERENCE TO WORLD TRADE AND PRICE. Note by the Secretariat. Mimeo. A/AC.135/14. 11 June, 1968. 6p. |
| VENV  | ART<br>Edelstein, L.M., and M.S. Wei. POLLUTION OF THE MARINE ENVIRONMENT AND THE AFFECTS THEREFROM: THE CASE FOR STRICTER ENFORCEMENT. In Oceans Ontario. Technical Symposium held April 23, 1972. Toronto, Canada, James Allister MacInnis Foundation? 1972. |
| VINTL | 1<br>Eek, Hilding. THE HYDROLOGICAL CYCLE AND THE LAW OF NATIONS. Reprinted from Scandinavian Studies in Law, 1965. Göteborg, Almqvist and Wiksell, 1965. 40p. |
| IVM   | ART<br>Eek, W.H. van. TECHNOLOGY AND PROSPECTS FOR THE USE OF AREAS AND MINERAL RESOURCES OF THE SEA-BED AND ITS SUBSOIL. In Symposium on the Exploration and Exploitation of the Sea-Bed and its Subsoil. New York, U.S. and World Publications, Inc., Manhattan Publishing Company, 1971? |
| VP    | ***<br>Ehmer, J. DER GRUNDSATZ DER FREIHEIT DER MEERE UND DAS VERBOT DER MEERESVERSCHMUTZUNG. Berlin, Duncker und Humblot, 1974. 207p. |
| IISL  | 13<br>Edwards, Cecil L. HISTORICAL BACKGROUND OF LAND BOARD LEASE-GRANT ON SUBMERGED AND SUBMERSIBLE LANDS; MEMO TO ATTORNEY-GENERAL. Salem, Or., Advisory Committee to the State Land Board, 1972. 8p. |
| VP    | 13<br>EFFECTS OF OIL SPILLS IN THE MARINE ENVIRONMENT; A SEMINAR - workshop sponsored by the Ocean Affairs Board of the National Academy of Sciences and to be held in early May, 1973, at the Woods Hole Oceanographic Institution, Woods Hole, Mass., 1973. 2p. |

|  |  |
|---|---|
| VENV | Eisenbud, M. ENVIRONMENTAL RADIOACTIVITY. New York, McGraw-Hill, 1963. *** |
| IICZM | 5,12,13,16<br>Eisenbud, Robert. AN EXAMINATION OF THE LAW RELATING TO THE WATER RIGHTS OF THE EVERGLADES NATIONAL PARK: A CASE STUDY IN LEGAL PROBLEMS OF THE COASTAL ZONE. Sea Grant Technical Bulletin no. 21. Coral Gables, Fla., University of Miami Sea Grant Program, 1971. xxxiii, 360p. |
| VORM | *** <br>Eisenstat, Gerlad M. PROFESSIONAL LIABILITY OF SCUBA INSTRUCTORS. Grand Terrace (Colton), Calif. National Association of Underwater Instructors, 1972. |
| IIIF | 14a<br>Elder, John R. THE ROYAL FISHERY COMPANIES OF THE SEVENTEENTH CENTURY. Glasgow, James Maclehose, 1912. vi, 136p. |
| IIIF | *** <br>Eldridge, Peter J., and Steven A. Goldstein, eds. THE SHRIMP FISHERY OF THE SOUTH ATLANTIC UNITED STATES: A REGIONAL MANAGEMENT PLAN. Charleston, S.C., Marine Resources Center, 1975. vi, 66p. |
| IIIFV&G | *** <br>ELECTRONIC FISH SCANNING NET FISHING - FLORIDA - A CASE STUDY. SUSF-SG-76-002. Gainesville, University of Florida, 1976. 9p. |
| VMLAD | *** <br>Eller, Ernest M. THE SOVIET SEA CHALLENGER. New York, Henry Regnery Company, Cowless Book Company, Inc., 1971. 341p. |
| VP | 11<br>Ellington, Juanita, and Gerald Davey. Texas. OUTLINE OF LEGISLATION CONCERNING THE PREVENTION AND CLEANUP OF OIL AND HAZARDOUS SUBSTANCES DISCHARGED INTO WATERS. Houston, Texas Law Institute of Coastal and Marine Resources, University of Houston, 1974. |
| IIIF | 14a<br>Elliott, Charles B. THE UNITED STATES AND THE NORTHEASTERN FISHERIES; A HISTORY OF THE FISHERIES QUESTION. Minneapolis, University of Minnesota, 1887. 151p. |
| IIENV | *** <br>Ellis, Exa, et al., eds. PROCEEDINGS OF THE FIFTH NATIONAL SEA GRANT CONFERENCE HELD IN HOUSTON, TEXAS, 1972. Publication no. TAMU-SG-73-101. College Station, Texas A&M University, 1973. |
| IVMMR | 16<br>Ely, Northcutt. THE LAW GOVERNING THE DEVELOPMENT OF UNDERSEA MINERAL RESOURCES. Paper at Offshore Technology Conference, Dallas, Texas, 1969. 23p. |
| IVMMR | 16<br>_____ THE LAWS GOVERNING EXPLOITATION OF THE MINERALS BENEATH THE SEA. Paper at New York Section of The American Institute of Mining, Metallurgical and Petroleum Engineers, New York, 1966. |

| | | 16 |
|---|---|---|
| IVMMR | Ely, Northcutt. LEGAL PROBLEMS IN UNDERSEA MINERAL DEVELOPMENT. Paper at Meeting of the American Institute of Mining, Metallurgical and Petroleum Engineers, February 19, 1969. | |

| | | 13 |
|---|---|---|
| IVT&L | _____ _____ SUMMARY OF MINING AND PETROLEUM LAWS OF THE WORLD. U.S. Bureau of Mines Information circular 8610. Washington, U.S. Bureau of Mines, 1974. 5 Parts. | |

ART
VB    Ely, Northcutt, and J.M. Marcoux. NATIONAL SEABED JURISDICTION IN THE MARGINAL SEA: THE SOUTH CHINA SEA. In G.T. Yates, III, and J.H. Young, Limits to National Jurisdiction over the Sea. Charlottesville, 1974. pp. 103-151.

***
IIIB    THE EMERGING RIGHT OF PHYSICAL ENFORCEMENT OF FISHERIES MEASURES BEYOND TERRITORIAL LIMITS. WIS-SG-74-222. Madison, University of Wisconsin, 1974.

ART
IVLOS    Emery, K. GEOLOGICAL ASPECTS OF SEA-FLOOR SOVEREIGNTY. In The Law of the Sea: Offshore Boundaries and Zones. Proceedings of the First Annual Conference of the Law of the Sea Institute, Columbus, Ohio State University, 1967. pp. 139-159.

14a
IVMMR    Emery, Kenneth O. THE SEA OFF SOUTHERN CALIFORNIA; A MODERN HABITAT OF PETROLEUM. New York, Wiley, 1960. 366p.

ART
VOCET    _____ _____ AN OCEANOGRAPHER'S VIEW OF THE LAW OF THE SEA. In J. Sztucki, ed., Symposium on the International Regime of the Sea-Bed, Rome, 1969. Proceedings. Rome, Accademia Nazionale dei Lincei, 1970. pp. 47-63.

13
VREFS    Emery, Kenneth O., and Evelyn Sinha. OCEANOGRAPHIC BOOKS OF THE WORLD 1957-1966. Washington, Marine Technology Society, 1967. 57p.

14
VENV    ENERGY AND ENVIRONMENT: METHODS TO ANALYZE THE LONG-TERM RELATIONSHIP. Energie et environment; methodes d'analyse des relations à longe terme. Paris, Organization for Economic Co-operation and Development, 1974. 391p.

***
VP    ENGINEERING ASPECTS OF THERMAL POLLUTION. Proceedings of the National Symposium on Thermal Pollution. Nashville, Tenn., Vanderbilt University Press, 1969. 351p.

1,3,6,9,12,13,14,14a,16
VOR    English, T. Saunders, ed. OCEAN RESOURCES AND PUBLIC POLICY. Seattle, University of Washington Press, 1973. viii, 184p.

2
VENV    ENVIRONMENT REGULATION HANDBOOK. Project director: Steven S. Ross. New York, Environment Information Center, 1973. looseleaf. 1973-

|          | ***                                                                                                                                                                                                  |
|----------|---|

VP      ENVIRONMENTAL ASPECTS OF NUCLEAR POWER STATIONS. Proceedings of a Symposium. New York, UNIPUB 1971. 970p.

2,13
VENV    ENVIRONMENTAL LAW REPORTER. Washington, D.C., Environmental Law Institute, 1970-   looseleaf.

***
IIENV   ENVIRONMENTAL STUDY OF A NUCLEAR POWER PLANT AT CHARLESTOWN, RHODE ISLAND. Marine Technical report no. 33. Narragansett, University of Rhode Island, Marine Advisory Service, 1974. 250p.

***
VP      ENVIRONMENTAL SURVEILLANCE AROUND NUCLEAR STATIONS. Vienna, Austria, International Atomic Energy Agency; New York, UNIPUB, 1974. 909p. 2 Vols.

1,12,16
VENV    Ereli, Eliezer. THE ENVIRONMENTAL REGULATION OF THE SEA AND ITS RESOURCES: CASES AND MATERIALS. 1st draft. 2d printing. Houston, University, College of Law, 1972. xiii, 611p.

5,11,14
IVOSTR  _____ THE LEGAL FRAMEWORK AFFECTING OFFSHORE OIL TERMINALS. Prepared for the Texas Offshore Terminal Commission. Houston, Texas Law Institute of Coastal and Marine Resources, 1973. v, 54p.

6,14
VLOS    _____ THE LEGAL REGIME OF THE SEA AND ITS RESOURCES, CASES AND MATERIALS. 1st draft. Houston, Bates College of Law, University of Houston, 1971. 610p.

***
IICONS  EROSION AND ACCRETION OF SELECTED HAWAIIAN BEACHES, 1962-1972. UNIHI-SEAGRANT-TR-72-02. Honolulu, University of Hawaii, Sea Grant College, 1972. 30p.

***
IIE     ESTUARIES CONFERENCE PROCEEDINGS: TECHNICAL CONFERENCE ON ESTUARIES OF THE PACIFIC NORTHWEST. Corvallis, Oregon State University, Sea Grant Communications. 1st-  1971-

***
VCONS   EUROPEAN CONSERVATION CONFERENCE, STRASBOURG, 1970. THE MANAGEMENT OF THE ENVIRONMENT IN TOMORROW'S EUROPE; PROCEEDINGS OF THE CONFERENCE HELD IN STRASBOURG, 9-12 February, 1970. Compiled by the European Information Centre for Nature Conservation. Strasbourg, Council of Europe, 1971. 255p.

***
IVP     EUROPEAN MODEL CODE OF SAFE PRACTICE FOR THE PREVENTION OF GROUND AND SURFACE WATER POLLUTION BY OIL FROM STORAGE TANKS AND DURING THE TRANSPORT OF OIL. London, Applied Science Publishers, Ltd., 1974. 23p.

1
VINTL   Eustache, François. LE PLATEAU CONTINENTAL DES ÉTATS RIVERAINS DE LA MER DU NORD ET LE DROIT INTERNATIONAL. Lyon, Faculté de droit et des sciences economiques, Université de Lyon, 1967. 182p.

                                                                7,16
VAC     Evensen, J. PRESENT MILITARY USES OF THE SEA-BED -- FORESEEABLE
        DEVELOPMENTS. Paper at Symposium on the International Regime of
        the Seabed, Rome, 1969.

                                                                16
VB      _____  SOME PROBLEMS RELATIVE TO THE DELIMITATION OF COASTAL
        WATERS: AN INVESTIGATION OF TERMINOLOGY AND CLASSIFICATION. Un-
        published paper submitted for Professor L. Sohn's Seminar in Inter-
        national Law problems, Harvard University, 1953. 111p.

                                                                17
VOR     EXPLOITING THE OCEAN; TRANSACTIONS OF THE 2d ANNUAL MTS CONFERENCE
        AND EXHIBIT, JUNE 27-29, 1966. Washington, D.C., Marine Technology
        Society, 1966. x, 570p.

                                                                ***
IIP     FACILITIES IN PORTS FOR THE RECEPTION OF OIL RESIDUES. RESULTS OF
        AN INQUIRY MADE IN 1963. London, Inter-Governmental Maritime Con-
        sultative Organization, n.d. 59p.

                                                                ***
IIP     FACILITIES IN PORTS FOR THE RECEPTION OF OIL RESIDUES. London,
        Inter-Governmental Maritime Consultative Organization, 1973. 145p.

                                                                11
VINTL   Falk, Richard A., and Cyril E. Black, eds. FUTURE OF INTERNATIONAL
        LEGAL ORDER. STRUCTURE OF INTERNATIONAL ENVIRONMENT. N.J., Prince-
        ton University Press, 1969-

                                                                ***
VP      FALLOUT FROM NUCLEAR WEAPONS TESTS CONDUCTED BY FRANCE IN THE SOUTH
        PACIFIC DURING JUNE AND JULY 1972, AND COMPARISONS WITH PREVIOUS
        TEST SERIES. New Zealand, Department of Health, National Radiation
        Laboratory, 1972. 24p.

                                                                2
VENV    Fallows, James M. THE WATER LORDS; RALPH NADER'S STUDY GROUP RE-
        PORT ON INDUSTRY AND ENVIRONMENTAL CRISIS IN SAVANNAH, GEORGIA.
        New York, Grossman Publishers, 1971. xxi, 294p.

                                                                ART
IIDR    Faris, W.M. LIABILITY ARISING FROM DREDGING OPERATIONS. In Ocean
        Mining Symposium. San Pedro, Calif., World Dredging Conference
        Association, 1973. pp. 151-165.

                                                                13
VP      Farrell, Richard J. LET THE POLLUTER BEWARE. In Case and Comment,
        Vol. 75, no. 5, September-October, 1970. pp. 3-5.

                                                                ***
VENV    Farvar, M. Taghi, and John P. Milton, eds. THE CARELESS TECHNOLOGY:
        ECOLOGY AND INTERNATIONAL DEVELOPMENT. Garden City, N.Y., Double-
        day and Company, Inc., Natural History Press, 1972. 1086p.

                                                                1,5,7
VB      Fattal, Antoine. LES CONFERENCES DES NATIONS UNIES ET LA CONVENTION
        DE GENEVE DU 29 AVRIL 1958 SUR LA MER TERRITORIALE ET LA ZONE CON-
        TIGUE. Beyrouth, Librairie du Liban, 1968. 319p.

|       |                                                                                                                                                                                                                           |
|-------|---------------------------------------------------------------------------------------------------------------------------------------------------------------------------------------------------------------------------|
|       | 13                                                                                                                                                                                                                        |
| IIIP  | Fay, Rimmon C., et al. SOUTHERN CALIFORNIA'S DETERIORATING MARINE ENVIRONMENT; AN EVALUATION OF THE HEALTH OF THE BENTHIC MARINE BIOTA OF VENTURA, LOS ANGELES AND ORANGE COUNTIES. Claremont, Calif., Center for California Public Affairs, 1973. 76p. |
|       | 13                                                                                                                                                                                                                        |
| IIIF  | Feddern, Henry A. FIELD GUIDE TO THE ANGELFISHES (POMACANTHIDAE) IN THE WESTERN ATLANTIC. NOAA Technical Report NMFS CIRC-369. Seattle, Wash., 1972. 10p.                                                                  |
|       | ***                                                                                                                                                                                                                       |
| VENV  | FEDERAL PLAN FOR MARINE ENVIRONMENTAL PREDICTION. FISCAL YEAR 1973. Report. NOAA-72072419. Washington, U.S. Department of Commerce, National Oceanic and Atmospheric Administration, March, 1972. 88p.                    |
|       | ***                                                                                                                                                                                                                       |
| VP    | FEDERAL WATER POLLUTION CONTROL ACT OF 1972: PUBLIC LAW 92-500. TAMU-SG-73-602. College Station, Texas A&M University, 1973.                                                                                              |
|       | 13                                                                                                                                                                                                                        |
| IIIP  | Federal Water Quality Administration. 1969 FISH KILLS CAUSED BY POLLUTION. Washington, U.S.G.P.O., 1970. 20p.                                                                                                             |
|       | 2                                                                                                                                                                                                                         |
| VP    | Federation of Tax Administrators. STATE PREFERENTIAL TAX TREATMENT FOR POLLUTION CONTROL FACILITIES. Research report no. 61. Chicago, 1971. 58p.                                                                          |
|       | ART                                                                                                                                                                                                                       |
| IIIF  | Felando, August. FISHERIES USES OF THE SEA; INDUSTRY INTERESTS. In Conference on Local Impacts of the Law of the Sea; proceedings of a conference held in Seattle, October 10-12, 1972. Seattle, University of Washington, Division of Marine Resources, 1973. pp. 44-67. |
|       | 5,14a                                                                                                                                                                                                                     |
| IIIF  | Fenn, Percy T., Jr. THE ORIGIN OF THE RIGHT OF FISHERY IN TERRI- TORIAL WATERS. Harvard University Press, 1926. xiv, 2, 3, 245p.                                                                                          |
|       | 13                                                                                                                                                                                                                        |
| VOCET | Ferrero, Eduardo. THE LATIN AMERICAN MEETING ON ASPECTS OF THE LAW OF THE SEA AND OCEANOGRAPHIC RESEARCH. n.p., 1972. 24p.                                                                                                |
|       | ***                                                                                                                                                                                                                       |
| IVMMR | FERROMANGANESE DEPOSITS OF THE OCEAN FLOOR. Honolulu, University of Hawaii, 1974. 249p.                                                                                                                                   |
|       | 14                                                                                                                                                                                                                        |
| IVMMR | FERROMANGANESE DEPOSITS OF THE OCEAN FLOOR. Cruise Report Mn-74-01 R/V Moana Wave. HIG-74-9. Honolulu, University of Hawaii, Insti- tute of Geophysics, 1974. vi, 194p.                                                   |
|       | 14                                                                                                                                                                                                                        |
| IVMMR | FERROMANGANESE DEPOSITS OF THE OCEAN FLOOR. Cruise Report Mn-74-02 R/V Moana Wave. HIG-75-17. Honolulu, University of Hawaii, Insti- tute of Geophysics, 1975. v, 121p.                                                   |

5,12
VINTL    Ferron, Olivier de. LE DROIT INTERNATIONAL DE LA MER. Tome I, II. Paris, Librairie E. Droz, 1958. 2 Vols.

IIP      Field, R., et al. WATER POLLUTION AND ASSOCIATED EFFECTS FROM STREET SALTING. Washington, U.S.G.P.O., May, 1973. 48p.

VP       Field Studies Council, Oil Pollution Research Unit, Orielton Field Centre. ANNUAL REPORT. Pembroke, Wales, 1971. 46p.

VOR      Fifer, Sheila Kean. THE INTERNATIONAL POLITICS OF OCEAN EXPLOITATION. Dissertation. Virginia. University. Woodrow Wilson Department of Government and Foreign Affairs, Ann Arbor, Mich., University Microfilms, 1973. 212p.

IIIF     Figueiredo, Rómolo de. ANÁLISE DO SECTOR DE PESCA NO ULTRAMAR. SUBSIDIOS PARA O SEU ESTUDO. Lisboa, Agência-Geral do Ultramar, 1966. 296p.

VP       Finger, Stanley M., and T.S. Yu. TECHNOLOGIES FOR SHIPBOARD OIL POLLUTION ABATEMENT EFFECTS OF OPERATIONAL PARAMETERS ON COALESCENCE. Report no. NSRDC-28-155. Annapolis, Md., U.S. Naval Ship Research and Development Center, 1972. 22p.

ART
VCS      Finlay, L.W. REALISM VS. IDEALISM AS THE KEY TO THE DETERMINATION OF THE LIMITS OF NATIONAL JURISDICTION OVER THE CONTINENTAL SHELF. In G.T. Yates, III, and J.H. Young, Limits to National Jurisdiction over the Sea. Charlottesville, 1974. pp. 75-99.

IIIAFF   Finn, Earl L., Jr. PROGRESS REPORT: FISH FARM INVESTIGATIONS, CAPITOL LAKE FALL CHINOOK REARING PROGRAM. Olympia, Washington, Department of Fisheries, December, 1973. 33p.

VP       First, Melvin W., ed. MUNICIPAL WASTE DISPOSAL BY SHIPBORNE INCINERATION AND SEA DISPOSAL OF RESIDUES. Report. Boston, Mass., Harvard University, School of Public Health, 1972. 592p.

ART
IIICONS  FISH CONSERVATION, CULTIVATION AND MANAGEMENT. Conference papers. In Oceanology International 72 Conference, Brighton, England, 1972. London, 1972. pp. 77-99.

IIIAFF   FISH FARMING IN EUROPE: PROSPECTS FOR GROWTH AND THE PROBLEMS. n.p., 1974? 118p.

IIIP     FISH KILLS CAUSED BY POLLUTION IN 1970. Eleventh Annual Report. Washington, D.C., U.S. Environmental Protection Agency, Office of Water Programs, Division of Applied Technology, Technical Data and Information Branch, 1972. 23p.

                                                                                     \*\*\*

VP        Fisher, Hugo B. A LAGRANGIAN METHOD FOR PREDICTING POLLUTANT DISPERSION IN BOLINAS LAGOON, MARIN COUNTY, CALIFORNIA. Professional Paper no. 582-B. Washington. D.C., U.S. Geological Survey, 1972. 36p.

                                                                                     \*\*\*

IIIF      FISHERIES MANAGEMENT DIVISION PUBLICATIONS 1972. Technical Report 121. Wellington, New Zealand, Ministry of Agriculture and Fisheries, Fisheries Management Division, 1973. 9p.

                                                                                     13

IIIF      FISHERIES OF JAPAN. Tokyo, Japan Fisheries Association, 1973. 57p.

                                                                                     13

IIIFV&G   FISHING VESSEL AND GEAR DEVELOPMENTS. Reprinted from Commercial Fisheries Review, Vol. 25, no. 1, January, 1961. pp. 15-16.

                                                                                       2

VENV     Flack, J. Ernest, and Margaret C. Shipley, eds. Western Resources Conference, 9th, University of Colorado, 1967. MAN AND THE QUALITY OF HIS ENVIRONMENT. Boulder, University of Colorado Press, 1968. x, 251p.

                                                                                       3

VMLAD    Flanders, Henry. A TREATISE ON MARITIME LAW. Boston, Little, Brown and Company, 1852. xvi, 444p.

                                                                                       6

VMLAD    _____ A TREATISE ON THE LAW OF SHIPPING. Philadelphia, T.&.J.W. Johnson, 1853. 33, 580p.

                                                                                     13

IVM      Flipse, John E., and Richard J. Greenwald. THE MARINE OPERATOR'S ROLE IN THE RATIONAL FORMULATION OF PRINCIPLES OF LAW GOVERNING MINING ACTIVITIES IN "SHARED" OCEAN SPACE. Reprint. Marine Technology Society, 6th Annual Preprints. Washington, Marine Technology Society. 1970.

                                                                                     14

VSG      Florida. State University System of Florida Sea Grant Program 1974. ANNUAL REPORT 1974 - THE YEAR IN REVIEW. Gainesville, University of Florida, 1974. 28p.

                                                                                      1

VCS      Flouret, Teresa H.I. LA DOCTRINA DE LA PLATAFORMA SUBMARINA. Madrid, 1952.

                                                                                   \*\*\*

IIIREC   Floyd, Charles F., and C.F. Sirmans. THE ECONOMIC IMPACT OF RECREATIONAL LAND-USE IN AN ISLAND ENVIRONMENT: A CASE STUDY OF JEKYLL ISLAND, GEORGIA. Athens, University of Georgia, 1975. 184p.

                                                                                     13

IIIP     Food and Agriculture Organization of the United Nations. FAO TECHNICHAL CONFERENCE ON MARINE POLLUTION AND ITS EFFECTS ON LIVING RESOURCES AND FISHING. ROME, ITALY, DECEMBER 9-18, 1970. 35p.

IIIB	Food and Agriculture Organization of the United Nations. LIMITS AND STATUS OF THE TERRITORIAL SEA, EXCLUSIVE FISHING ZONES, FISHERY CONSERVATION ZONES AND THE CONTINENTAL SHELF (WITH PARTICULAR REFERENCE TO FISHERIES). FAO Fisheries Technical Paper no. 79. Rome, FAO, Legislation Branch, 1968. 30p.  
                          1

IIIB	_____ LIMITS AND STATUS OF THE TERRITORIAL SEA, EXCLUSIVE FISHING ZONES, FISHERY CONSERVATION ZONES AND THE CONTINENTAL SHELF (WITH PARTICULAR REFERENCE TO FISHERIES). FAO Legislative series 3. New York, FAO, 1969. 53p.  
   14

IIIP	_____ POLLUTION; AN INTERNATIONAL PROBLEM FOR FISHERIES. World food problems, no. 14. Rome, FAO, 1971. 85p.  
   1,5

IIIF	_____ REHABILITATION AND DEVELOPMENT OF AGRICULTURE, FORESTRY, AND FISHERIES IN SOUTH KOREA; report prepared for the United Nations Korean Reconstruction Agency by a mission selected by the Food and Agriculture Organization of the United Nations. New York, Columbia University Press, 1954. xviii, 428p.  
   14a

VOD	_____ SCIENTIFIC CRITERIA FOR THE SELECTION OF SITES FOR DUMPING OF WASTES INTO THE SEA. Rome, 1975. New York, UNIPUB.  
   ***

IIIP	_____ WATER POLLUTION AND ITS EFFECTS ON LIVING AQUATIC RESOURCES AND FISHING. Rome? FAO, 1971? 170p.  
   1

IIIFV&G	_____ World Fishing Gear Congress, 2d, London, 1963. MODERN FISHING GEAR OF THE WORLD 2: PAPERS AND DISCUSSIONS. London, Fishing News (Books), 1964. xvi, 603p.  
   13

IIB	Ford, John I. ECOLOGICAL BASELINE STUDY OF THE INTERTIDAL ZONE, KAPOHO, HAWAII:: A PRELIMINARY REPORT. Working Paper no. 1. Honolulu, University of Hawaii, 1973. 44p.  
   ***

IIIF	Forman, Shepard. THE RAFT FISHERMEN; TRADITION AND CHANGE IN THE BRAZILIAN PEASANT ECONOMY. Bloomington, Indiana University Press for International Affairs Center, 1970. xv, 158p.  
   14a

IICZM	Forste, Robert H., ed. PROCEEDINGS. THE NEW ENGLAND COASTAL ZONE MANAGEMENT CONFERENCE. APRIL 28-29, 1970. Durham, New England Center for Continuing Education, 1970. ii, 159p.  
   13,16

IIIOCET	Foster, J.J. A TOWED SUBMERSIBLE FOR FISHERIES RESEARCH - WITH SPECIAL REFERENCE TO FISH CAPTURE STUDIES. In Scottish Mini-Symposium 1972, held in Glasgow, Scotland, October 14, 1972. Underwater Association of Malta 1966 Ltd. Glasgow, University of Strathclyde, Department of Civil Engineering, 1972?  
   ART

VENV     Fowler, John M. ENERGY AND THE ENVIRONMENT. New York, McGraw-Hill, 1975. 496p.     14

***

VOR     France. Conseil Economique et Social. LA PROTECTION ET L'EXPLOITATION DES OCÉANS ET DES FONDS SOUS-MARINS; AVIS ADOPTÉ PAR LE CONSEIL ET RAPPORT PRÉSENTÉ, AU NOM DU CONSEIL par J. Martray. Avis et rapports, no. 15, 19 Avril 1974. Paris, 1974. 40p.

***

VP     France. Direction de la Documentation. LA LUTTE INTERNATIONALE CONTRE LA POLLUTION DES EAUX MARINES par M. Hippolyte-Manigat. Notes et études documentaires, 3903-3904. Paris, 1972. 75p.

***

VOCET     France. Délégation Générale à la Recherche Scientifique et Technique. LA RECHERCHE OCÉANOGRAPHIQUE FRANÇAISE, 1964. Répertoire national des laboratoires. Paris, 1965. 216p.

***

VP     _____ LES POLLUTIONS ET NUISANCES D'ORIGINE INDUSTRIELLE ET URBAINE. Documents de travail établis par J.A. Ternisien. Le progres scientifique. Numero special. Paris, 1966-1967. 2 Vols.

***

IIIOR     France. Institut National de la Statistique et des Etudes Economiques. SERVICE DE COOPÉRATION. LE POISSON DE FLEUVE DANS L'OUEST AFRICAIN; ÉTUDE D'ÉCONOMIE ALIMENTAIRE par P. Cantrell et C. Laurent. Paris, 1961. 69p. maps.

VT&L     France. Laws, statutes, etc. CODE PERMANENT: ENVIRONMENT ET NUISANCES. Rédacteur en chef: Pierre Gousset. Paris, Editions législatives et administratives, 1973-     looseleaf.     2

ART

VORM     Franck, Thomas M. TO DEFINE AND PUNISH PIRACIES - THE LESSON OF THE SANTA MARIA: A COMMENT. Reprinted from New York University Law Review, Vol. 36, no. 4, April 1961.

VP     Frank, Richard A., and Eldon V.C. Greenberg. INTERNATIONAL CONVENTION FOR THE PREVENTION OF POLLUTION FROM SHIPS, 1973: COMMENTS ON THE DRAFT TEXT. Washington, D.C., Center for Law and Social Policy, 1973. 36p.     16

***

IIP&H     Frankel, E. STUDIES ON THE FUTURE OF ATLANTIC PORTS. Report MITSG 72-18. Cambridge, Massachusetts Institute of Technology, Sea Grant Project Office, 1973. 346p.

***

VMT     Frankel, E.G., and H.S. Marcus. OCEAN TRANSPORTATION. Cambridge, Mass., M.I.T. Press, 1973. 833p.

IICZM     Frankel, Moses M. LAW OF SEASHORE, WATERS, AND WATER COURSES: MAINE AND MASSACHUSETTS. Forge Village, Mass., Murray Printing Company, 1969. xxi, 196p.     18

                                                              3,8,9,16
VLOS     Franklin, Carl M. THE LAW OF THE SEA; SOME RECENT DEVELOPMENTS.
         With particular reference to the United Nations Conference of 1958.
         International law studies, 1959-1960; Vol. LIII. Washington, U.S.
         G.P.O., 1961. 312p.


                                                                      9
VLOS     _____  _____ LAW OF THE SEA. Texts of conventions and resolutions,
         1958. U.S. Naval War College. International Law Studies. 1959-
         1960. Vol. 52.


                                                                  14,16
VOCET    Frankowska, Maria, ed. SCIENTIFIC AND TECHNOLOGICAL REVOLUTION AND
         THE LAW OF THE SEA. Wrocław, Zakład Narodowy im. Ossolińskich,
         1974. 153p.


                                                                     13
VLOS     Franssen, Herman. THE ATTITUDES OF THE DEVELOPING COUNTRIES TOWARDS
         THE LAW OF THE SEA. n.p., 1972. 74, iiip.


                                                                    ***
VLOS     Franssen, Herman T., et al. THIRD U.N. LAW OF THE SEA CONFERENCE.
         Prepared for use of the Senate Committee on Commerce and National
         Ocean Study Policy, pursuant to S.Res.222. 94th Congr., 1st sess.,
         committee print. Washington, U.S.G.P.O., 1975. viii, 66p.


                                                                     12
VORM     Frascona, Joseph L. VISIT, SEARCH, AND SEIZURE ON THE HIGH SEAS.
         Privately published, 1938. xiv, 161p.


                                                                    14a
IIIF     Fraser, Thomas M. FISHERMEN OF SOUTH THAILAND; THE MALAY VILLAGERS.
         New York, Holt, Rinehart and Winston, 1966. 110p.


                                                                    ART
VB       Freeman, Robert O. POSSIBLE SOLUTIONS TO THE 200-MILE TERRITORIAL
         LIMIT. In International Lawyer, April, 1973. pp. 387-395.


                                                                      1
VORM     Freeman, William. THE ABSTENTION DOCTRINE. University of North
         Carolina Sea Grant Publication UNC-SG-74-07. Chapel Hill, June
         1974. ii, 34p.


                                                                     17
VORM     French, Herbert E. OF RIVERS AND THE SEA. New York, Putnam, 1970.
         318p.


                                                                    ***
VOR      Frey, H.R., ed. RESOURCES OF THE WORLD'S OCEANS. New York, New
         York Institute of Ocean Resources, 1972. 281p.


                                                                    14a
IIIOR    Frey, H.W., ed. CALIFORNIA'S LIVING MARINE RESOURCES AND THEIR
         UTILIZATION; ed. by H.W. Frey... Sacramento, California Department
         of Fish and Game, 1971. 148p.


                                                                     16
VCS      Friedheim, R. THE CONTINENTAL SHELF ISSUE AT THE UNITED NATIONS: A
         QUANTITATIVE CONTENT ANALYSIS. Arlington, Virginia, Center for Na-
         val Analyses, 1970. Professional Paper no. 7. 251p.

|       | ART |
|-------|-----|
| VOR | Friedheim, R.L. INTERNATIONAL ORGANIZATIONS AND THE USES OF THE OCEAN. In R.S. Jordan, Multinational cooperation. New York, 1972. n.p. pp. 223-281. |

VLOS    Friedheim, Robert L. A LAW OF THE SEA CONFERENCE - WHO NEEDS IT? Professional paper no. 97. Arlington, Va., Center for Naval Analyses, 1972. 30p.
    14

VOR    _____ _____ UNDERSTANDING THE DEBATE ON OCEAN RESOURCES. Monograph series in world affairs, Vol. 6, no. 3, 1968-69. Denver, University of Denver.
    1,2,5,7,8,12,13,16,18

VLOS    Friedheim, Robert L., and Judith T. Kildow. REPORT OF THE OCEAN POLICY RESEARCH WORKSHOP. Law of the Sea Institute occasional paper no. 26. Kingston, University of Rhode Island, 1975. 49p.
    4,7,11,14

VOR    Friedmann, W. JOINT EXPLORATION OF OCEAN BED RESOURCES -- SOME ORGANIZATIONAL ASPECTS. Paper at Pacem in Maribus Preparatory Conference on the Legal Framework and the Continental Shelf, Kingston, Rhode Island, January 30-February 1, 1970.
    16

VOR    Friedmann, Wolfgang. THE FUTURE OF THE OCEANS. New York, George Braziller, 1971. 132p.
    1,2,5,7,9,12,13,14a,16,17,18

IIIF    Friends, Society of. American Friends Service Committee. AN UNCOMMON CONTROVERSY; AN INQUIRY INTO THE TREATY-PROTECTED FISHING RIGHTS OF THE MUCKLESHOOT, PUYALLUP, AND NISQUALLY TRIBES OF THE PUGET SOUND. Prepared for the American Friends Service Committee. Published by the National Congress of American Indians, 1967. 200p.
    14a

VOCET    Friis, Herman R., and Shelby G. Bale, Jr., eds. CONFERENCE ON UNITED STATES POLAR EXPLORATION, WASHINGTON, UNITED STATES POLAR EXPLORATION. National Archives Conference, Vol. 1. Athens, Ohio University Press, 1970. xvii, 199p.
    17

VLOS    FROM THE LAW OF THE SEA TOWARDS AN OCEAN SPACE REGIME. PRACTICAL AND LEGAL IMPLICATIONS OF THE MARINE REVOLUTION. Hamburg, Forschungsstelle für Völkerrecht und ausländisches öffentliches Recht der Universität Hamburg, 1972. 174p.
    ***

VAC    Frosch, R.A. MILITARY USES OF THE OCEAN. Paper at Second Conference on Law Organization and Security in the Use of the Oceans. Columbus, Ohio, October 5-7, 1967. pp. 154-174.
    16

VOR    Frosch, Robert A., et al. THIRD ANNUAL SEA GRANT LECTURE AND SYMPOSIUM. THE OCEANS: PLANETARY ENGINEERING AND INTERNATIONAL MANAGEMENT. MITSG 75-3. Cambridge, Massachusetts Institute of Technology, 1974. 50p.
    ***

|        |        |
|--------|--------|
| VLOS   | 14<br>Frucht, Jamie. LAW OF THE SEA - FLOATING MONOPOLY GAME, PHASE II. Texas Coastal and Marine Council, January, 1975. Houston, University of Houston, Texas Law Institute of Coastal and Marine Resources, Bates College of Law, 1975. 20p. |
| VOCET  | ART<br>Fuglister, F.C. THE THERMAL STRUCTURE IN THE DEEP SEA. In von Arx, William S., ed: Proceedings of the Symposium on Aspects of Deep-Sea Research, Washington, D.C., 1956. Washington, Committee on Undersea Warfare, National Academy of Sciences-National Research Council, 1957. pp. 10-18. |
| VORM   | 17<br>Fuller, Richard B. OPERATING MANUAL FOR SPACESHIP EARTH. Carbondale, Southern Illinois University Press, 1969. 143p. |
| VCONS  | 17<br>Fuller, W.A., and P.G. Kevan, eds. Conference on Productivity and Conservation in Northern Circumpolar Lands, Edmonton, Canada, 1969. PROCEEDINGS. IUCN publications, new ser., no. 16. Morges, Switzerland, International Union for Conservation of Nature and Natural Resources, 1970. 344p. |
| IIIF   | 13<br>Fulton, Leonard A. SPAWNING AREAS AND ABUNDANCE OF STEELHEAD TROUT AND COHO, SOCKEYE, AND CHUM SALMON IN THE COLUMBIA RIVER BASIN - PAST AND PRESENT. Special Scientific Report - Fisheries No. 618. Washington, U.S. Department of Commerce, National Oceanic and Atmospheric Administration, 1970. iii, 37p. |
| VINTL  | 5,7,9,12,16,17<br>Fulton, T.W. THE SOVEREIGNTY OF THE SEA. AN HISTORICAL ACCOUNT OF THE CLAIMS OF ENGLAND TO THE DOMINION OF THE BRITISH SEAS, AND OF THE EVOLUTION OF THE TERRITORIAL WATERS: WITH SPECIAL REFERENCE TO THE RIGHTS OF FISHING AND THE NAVAL SALUTE. London, William Blackwood, 1911. xxvi, 799p. |
| VINTL  | 5,17<br>Fulton, Thomas Wemyss. THE SOVEREIGNTY OF THE SEA; AN HISTORICAL ACCOUNT OF THE CLAIMS OF ENGLAND TO THE DOMINION OF THE BRITISH SEAS, AND OF THE EVOLUTION OF THE TERRITORIAL WATERS; WITH SPECIAL REFERENCE TO THE RIGHTS OF FISHING AND THE NAVAL SALUTE. Millwood, N.Y., Kraus Reprint Company, 1973. |
| IICZM  | 13<br>THE FUTURE MANAGEMENT OF THE OREGON COAST. Proceedings of a Symposium held at the Law Center, University of Oregon, October 27, 1972, sponsored by the Ocean Resources Law Program, a part of the Sea Grant Program in Oregon. Eugene, University of Oregon Law School, 1972. 167p. |
| VOI    | ***<br>THE FUTURE OF OREGON MARITIME INDUSTRIES. Proceedings of a Conference held in Portland, Oregon, May 23-24, 1973. Corvallis, Oregon State University Extension Service, 1973. |
| VENE   | ***<br>Fryer, J.J. ENERGY FOR AUSTRALIA'S FUTURE AND ITS IMPLICATIONS FOR MARINE WORKS. Thermo-Fluids Conference. Sydney, Australia Insti- |

tution of Engineers, 1972? pp. 20-27.

IIIF
                                                          14a
Gabriel, Ralph H. TOILERS OF LAND AND SEA. New Haven, Yale University Press, 1926. 340p.

                                                      \*\*\*

IIP&H Gagliano, Sherwood H., and John W. Day, Jr. Louisiana Superport Studies. Report no. 1. ENVIRONMENTAL ASPECTS OF A SUPERPORT OFF THE LOUISIANA COAST. Preliminary. Publication no. LSU-SG-72-03. Baton Rouge, Louisiana State University, Center for Wetland Resources, 1972. 37p.

                            1,2,4,5,7,8,11,13,14,15,18
VOCET Galey, Margaret E. THE INTERGOVERNMENTAL OCEANOGRAPHIC COMMISSION: ITS CAPACITY TO IMPLEMENT AN INTERNATIONAL DECADE OF OCEAN EXPLORATION. Law of the Sea Institute occasional paper no. 20. Kingston, University of Rhode Island, 1973. 28, 10p.

                                   14a
IIIF Gallagher, Hubert R., and John Van Oosten. INTERNATIONAL BOARD OF INQUIRY FOR THE GREAT LAKES FISHERIES. REPORT AND SUPPLEMENT. Washington, U.S.G.P.O., 1943. iii, 213p.

                          1,2,4,5,6,7,11,13,14,15,16
VLOS Gamble, John K., and Giulio Pontecorvo, eds. LAW OF THE SEA: THE EMERGING REGIME OF THE OCEANS. Proceedings of the Eighth Annual Conference of the Law of the Sea Institute, June 18-21, 1973, Kingston, University of Rhode Island. Cambridge, Mass., Ballinger Publishing Company, 1973. xiv, 393p.

                                          \*\*\*
IICZM Gamman, John K., et al. FEDERAL INVOLVEMENT IN THE CALIFORNIA COASTAL ZONE: A TOPICAL INDEX TO AGENCY RESPONSIBILITY. IMR technical report IMR TR-42. USDC2-35208. Berkeley, University of California, Institute of Marine Resources, 1974. 171p.

                                          \*\*\*
IICZM _____ STATE INVOLVEMENT IN THE CALIFORNIA COASTAL ZONE: A TOPICAL INDEX TO AGENCY RESPONSIBILITY. Sea grant publication no. 42. San Diego, University of California, Institute of Marine Resources, 1975. iv, 143p.

                                          \*\*\*
IIIF Ganoza Bustamante, Jorge. LA VERDAD SOBRE LA CRISIS PESQUERA. Lima, Editora Italperú, 1967. 124p.

                              1,2,3,5,7,11,12,15,16
VLOS García Amador y Rodríguez, F.V. THE EXPLOITATION AND CONSERVATION OF THE RESOURCES OF THE SEA; A STUDY OF CONTEMPORARY INTERNATIONAL LAW. 2d ed., 2d, enlarged, printing. Leyden, Sijthoff, 1963. 240p.
        _____ _____ ADDENDUM, 1963.

                            1,3,4,5,7,8,10,13,14,15,18
VLOS _____ _____ LATINEAMERICA AND THE LAW OF THE SEA. Law of the Sea occasional paper no. 14. Kingston, University of Rhode Island, 1972. i, 52p.

|  | | 5,12 |
|---|---|---|

VOR    García Amador y Rodríguez, F.V. LA UTILIZACION Y CONSERVACION DE LAS RIQUEZAS DEL MAR, ESTUDIO DE DERECHO INTERNACIONAL CONTEMPORANEO... Habana, 1956.

        ART

VLOS    García Robles, A. DESARROLLO Y CODIFICACIÓN DE LAS NORMAS BÁSICAS DEL DERECHO DEL MAR HASTA 1960. In México y el regimen del mar. Tlatelolco, 1974. pp. 15-36.

        1,5

VB    _____ LA CONFERENCIA DE GINEBRA Y LA ANCHURA DEL MAR TERRITORIAL. México, 1959.

        13

IICZM    Gardner, Barbara S., ed. THE CROWDED COAST; THE DEVELOPMENT AND MANAGEMENT OF THE COASTAL ZONE OF CALIFORNIA. Los Angeles, University of Southern California, Center for Marine Affairs, 1971. iii, 147p.

        ART

IVENV    Garland, Charles and Royal Hagerty. ENVIRONMENTAL PLANNING CONSIDERATIONS FOR DEEP OCEAN MINING. In Marine Technology Society. Eighth Annual Conference, Washington, D.C., September 11-13, 1972. Washington, D.C., 1972. pp. 381-394.

        6

VMT    Garoche, Pierre. ...STOWAGE, HANDLING AND TRANSPORT OF SHIP CARGOES. New York, Cornell Maritime Press, 1941. viii, 137p.

        5,12

IICZM    Garretson, Albert. THE LAND-SEA INTERFACE OF COASTAL ZONE OF U.S.; LEGAL PROBLEMS ARISING OUT OF MULTIPLE USE AND CONFLICTS OF PRIVATE AND PUBLIC RIGHTS AND INTERESTS. Springfield, Va., Clearinghouse for Federal Scientific and Technical Information, 1968. 152p.

        ***

VP    Garrett, William D., and William R. Barger. CONTROL AND CONFINEMENT OF OIL POLLUTION ON WATER WITH MONOMOLECULAR SURFACE FILMS. Memorandum report no. 2451. Washington, D.C., 1972. 61p.

        ***

IIIF    Garron, R. LE MARCHÉ COMMUN DE LA PÊCHE MARITIME. Collection de droit maritime et des transports, 8. Paris, Libraries Techniques, 1971. 165p.

        ***

VSG    Garten, David, comp. SEA GRANT ANNUAL REPORT; A REPORT ON THE VIRGINIA INSTITUTE OF MARINE SCIENCE SEA GRANT PROGRAM. Gloucester Point, Va., Institute of Marine Science, 1973. 32p.

        2

VENE    Garvey, Gerald. ENERGY, ECOLOGY, ECONOMY. New York, Norton, 1972. 235p.

        16

IVMMR    Gaskell, Thomas F. OIL AND NATURAL GAS. EXPLORATION, EVALUATION AND EXPLOITATION OF DEEP WATER PETROLEUM. Paper at Symposium on the International Regime of the Sea-bed, Rome, 1969.

IVMMR      Gaskell, Thomas F. OFFSHORE OIL AND SEA FLOOR RESEARCH. In Off-  ART
shore Technology Conference, 6th, Houston, Texas, 1974: Preprints.
Dallas, Tex., 1974. Vol. 2, pp1 551-560.

IVMMR      _____ OIL AND NATURAL GAS; EVALUATION, EXPLORATION AND EX-  ART
PLOITATION OF DEEP WATER PETROLEUM. In Sztucki, J., ed., Symposium
on the International Regime of the Sea-bed, Rome, 1969. Proceedings,
June 30-July 5, 1969. Rome, Accademia Nazionale dei Lincei, 1970.
pp. 75-94.

VOR        _____ USING THE OCEANS. London, Queen Anne Press, 1970.  17
142p.

IIIAFF     Gates, John M. AQUACULTURE IN LESS DEVELOPED NATIONS: SOME ECONO-  ART
MIC CONSIDERATIONS. In Marine Technology Society. Seventh Annual
Conference, Washington, D.C., August 16-18, 1971. Washington, D.C.,
1971. pp. 579-583.

IIIAFF     _____ AQUACULTURE IN NEW ENGLAND. Marine technical report  ***
no. 18. Kingston, University of Rhode Island, 1974. 81p.

IIIF       Gates, John M., and Virgil J. Norton. THE BENEFITS OF FISHERIES  13
REGULATION: A CASE STUDY OF THE NEW ENGLAND YELLOWTAIL FLOUNDER
FISHERY. Sea Grant Resource Economics. Marine Technical Report no.
21. Kingston, University of Rhode Island, 1974. 35p.

IIIAFF     Gaucher, Thomas A., ed. AQUACULTURE: A NEW ENGLAND PERSPECTIVE.  13,15
BASED ON A CONFERENCE CONDUCTED BY THE RESEARCH INSTITUTE OF THE
GULF OF MAINE. New England Marine Resources Information Program.
Sea Grant Program. Durham, New England Marine Resources Information
Program, 1971. vi, 119p.

IIP        General Dynamics Corporation. Electric Boat Division. POTENTIAL  13
ENVIRONMENTAL EFFECTS OF AN OFFSHORE SUBMERGED NUCLEAR POWER PLANT.
Prepared for the Water Quality Research Office, Environmental Pro-
tection Agency. Water pollution control research series. Groton,
Conn., 1971. 2 Vols.

IIIF       George, Carl J. THE ROLE OF THE ASWAN HIGH DAM IN CHANGING THE  ART
FISHERIES OF THE SOUTHEASTERN MEDITERRANEAN. In The Careless Tech-
nology: Ecology and International Development. Conference on the
Ecological Aspects of International Development, held in Warrenton,
Va., December 8-11, 1968. Garden City, N.Y., Doubleday and Company,
Inc., 1972. pp. 152-178.

IVP        George Washington University. Program of policy studies in science  1
and technology. LEGAL, ECONOMIC, AND TECHNICAL ASPECTS OF LIABILITY
AND FINANCIAL RESPONSIBILITY AS RELATED TO OIL POLLUTION. A study
performed for the United States Coast Guard. Washington, D.C., December 1970. National Technical Information Service, PB 198 776.

13
IIT&L    Georgia. Laws, statutes, etc. MARSHLAND PROTECTION ACT OF 1970. Mimeo. Brunswick, Ga., 1970. 13p.

***
VP    Gerhard, Glen C. A STUDY OF THE COST EFFECTIVENESS OF REMOTE SENSING SYSTEMS FOR OCEAN SLICK DETECTION AND CLASSIFICATION. Report no. UNHSG-101. Durham, University of New Hampshire, 1972. 27p.

***
IIP    Gerhardt, R.R., et al. PUBLIC OPINION ON INSECT PEST MANAGEMENT IN COASTAL NORTH CAROLINA. UNC-SG-73-03. Raleigh, North Carolina State University, 1973.

1,4,5,7,11,13,14,15,16,18
VLOS    Gerstle, Margaret L. THE POLITICS OF U.N. VOTING: A VIEW OF THE SEA-BED FROM THE GLASS PALACE. Law of the Sea Institute occasional paper no. 7. Kingston, University of Rhode Island, 1970. 12p.

13
IIIF    Gersuny, Carl, and John J. Poggie, Jr. A FISHERMEN'S CO-OPERATIVE: OPEN SYSTEM THEORY APPLIED. Marine reprint no. 25. Sea Grant 04-3-158-3. Kingston, University of Rhode Island, 1974.

13
IIIF    _____ THE UNCERTAIN FUTURE OF FISHING FAMILIES. Reprinted from The Family Coordinator, April 1973. pp. 241-244.

***
IIIB    Gersuny, Carl, et al. SOME EFFECTS OF TECHNOLOGICAL CHANGE ON NEW ENGLAND FISHERMEN. Narragansett, University of Rhode Island, URI Marine Advisory Service, 1975. 40p.

ART
VENE    Geyer, R.A. ENERGY FROM THE OCEANS. In T.S. English, Ocean Resources and Public Policy. Seattle, University of Washington, 1973. pp. 94-104.

5,7
VLOS    Gidel, Gilbert. LE DROIT INTERNATIONAL PUBLIC DE LA MER. les Establissements Mellottee, 1932. 3 Vols.

1,5
VCS    _____ LE PLATEAU CONTINENTAL. The Hague, 1952.

5
VB    Gihl, Torsten. THE BASELINE OF THE TERRITORIAL SEA. Stockholm, Almqvist and Wiksell, 1967.

5,15,16
IIIF    Gilbert, D., ed. THE FUTURE OF THE FISHING INDUSTRY OF THE UNITED STATES. Seattle, University of Washington Press, 1968.

ART
IIP    Gilbert, Jerome, and Ronald B. Robie. CONTROL OF ESTUARINE POLLUTION. In Natural Resources Journal, Vol. 11, 1971. pp. 256-273.

                                                            13,15
VP        Gilmore, George A., et al. SYSTEMS STUDY OF OIL SPILL CLEANUP PRO-
          CEDURES. Final Report to Committee for Air and Water Conservation,
          American Petroleum Institute. La Jolla, Dillingham Corporation,
          1970. 2 Vols.

                                                               13
IIIF      Ginter, J.J.C. MARINE FISHERIES CONSERVATION IN NEW YORK STATE:
          POLICY AND PRACTICE OF MARINE FISHERIES MANAGEMENT. NYSSGP-SS-74-
          012. Albany, New York State Sea Grant Program, 1974. 72p.

                                                               16
VAC       Girard, C. MILITARY USES OF THE CONTINENTAL SHELF AND THE SEABED
          BEYOND. SIPRI, TOWARDS A BETTER USE OF THE OCEANS: A STUDY AND
          PROGNOSIS. Stockholm, Almqvist and Wiksell, 1969. pp. 259-269.

                                                               16
VP        Gissberg, John G. CIVIL LIABILITY FOR OIL POLLUTION FROM TANKERS
          AND OTHER OCEAN-GOING VESSELS. Ann Arbor, University Microfilms,
          1971. xi, 276p.

                                                              1,8
VINTL     Glass, Henry. MARINE INTERNATIONAL LAW. Proceedings of the United
          States Naval Institute, Vol. XI, no. 3, 1885. Whole No. 34. Anna-
          polis, Md., 1885. xviii, 271p.

                                                          5,7,11,15
VINTL     Glassner, Martin I. ACCESS TO THE SEA FOR DEVELOPING LAND-LOCKED
          STATES. The Hague, Nijhoff, 1970.

                                                               13
IICZM     Glynn County, Ga. Beach and Dune Study Commission. GLYNN COUNTY
          BEACH AND DUNE STUDY. Brunswick, Ga., 1973. 28p.

                                                              ***
VOCET     Goldberg, E.D., ed. NORTH SEA SCIENCE. NATO North Sea Science
          Conference. Cambridge, Mass., M.I.T. Press, 1973. 384p.

                                                              ***
VLOS      Goldenberg, Samuel, ed. LOCAL IMPACTS OF THE LAW OF THE SEA. Sea
          Grant Publication. Seattle, University of Washington Press, 1973.
          111p.

                                                              ART
VB        Goldie, Louis F.E. DELIMITING CONTINENTAL SHELF BOUNDARIES. In
          G.T. Yates, III, and J.H. Young, Limits to National Jurisdiction
          over the Sea. Charlottesville, 1974. pp. 3-74.

                                                               16
IIIB      _____ STATE FISHERY LAWS AND THE THREE-MILE LIMIT. Unpub-
          lished paper submitted to Professor J. Stone's seminar on Inter-
          national Law problems, Harvard University, 1957. 76p.

                                                                2
VP        Goldman, Marshall I., ed. CONTROLLING POLLUTION; THE ECONOMICS OF
          A CLEANER AMERICA. Englewood Cliffs, N.J., Prentice-Hall, 1967.
          xiii, 175p.

                                                                 2
VP         Goldstein, Jerome. HOW TO MANAGE YOUR COMPANY ECOLOGICALLY. Emmaus,
           Pa., Rodale Press; distribued by McKay, New York, 1971. 119p.

                                                                 13
IISL       Goldstein, John H. WETLANDS/FARMLANDS. Adapted from his Competition
           for Wetlands in the Midwest: an Economic Analysis. In Resources,
           no. 38, September 1971. Washington, Resources for the Future, 1971.
           pp. 4-5.

                                                                 16
VCONS      Gomasevich, J. INTERNATIONAL AGREEMENTS ON CONSERVATION OF MARINE
           RESOURCES. Palo Alto, Stanford University Press, 1943. 297p.

                                                           1,5,12,13,16
IVMMR      Goodier, J. Leslie. U.S. FEDERAL AND SEACOASTAL STATE OFFSHORE
           MINING LAWS. Washington, Nautilus Press, 1972. xiv, 221p.

                                                                 ***
VP         Goodier, J. Leslie, et al. THE PREVENTION OF SPILLS OF OIL AND
           CHEMICALS INTO BALTIMORE HARBOR AND ENVIRONS. Report no. C-72919.
           Cambridge, Mass., Little (Arthur D.) Inc., 1971. 285p.

                                                                 2
VENV       Goodman, Gordon T., R.W. Edwards, and J.M. Lambert, eds. ECOLOGY
           AND THE INDUSTRIAL SOCIETY; a symposium of the British Ecological
           Society, Swansea, 13-16 April 1964. New York, Wiley, 1970, Black-
           well Scientific Publications, 1965. viii, 395p.

                                                                 ***
VOR        Goodman, Joel M. DECISIONS FOR DELAWARE: SEA GRANT LOOKS AT OCA
           DEVELOPMENT. DEL-SG-1-75. Newark, University of Delaware, College
           of Marine Studies, 1975. 43p.

                                                                 ***
IICZM      _____ THE DELAWARE COASTAL EXPERIENCE. DEL-SG-18-75. New-
           ark, University of Delaware, College of Marine Studies, 1975. 21p.

                                                                 17
IIE        Goodwin, C.R., et al. TIDAL STUDY OF THREE OREGON ESTUARIES. Ore-
           gon State University, Engineering Experiment Station Bulletin no. 5.
           Corvallis, 1970.

                                                                 14
VSG        Goodwin, Robert F. WASHINGTON SEA GRANT: THE FIRST FIVE YEARS: AN
           EVALUATION OF SELECTED PROJECTS. WSG-PM 74-1. Seattle, University
           of Washington, Division of Marine Resources, 1974. vii, 91p.

                                                                 ART
IICZM      Gopalakrishnan, Chennat and Justin Rutka. SOME INSTITUTIONAL CON-
           STRAINTS TO COASTAL ZONE MANAGEMENT: A CASE STUDY: HAWAII. In
           The American Journal of Economics and Sociology, Vol. 33, no. 2,
           1974. pp. 225-232.

                                                                 ***
IICZM      Gopalakrishnan, F. SPHERES OF INFLUENCE IN HAWAII'S COASTAL ZONE:
           VOLUME 1. FEDERAL AGENCY INVOLVEMENT. UNIHI-SG-AR-72-03. Hono-
           lulu, University of Hawaii, 1973. 92p.

VCS      Góralczyk, Wojciech. SZELF KONTYNENTALNY; STUDIUM PRAWNOMIEDZYNA-RODOWE. (Wyd. 1.) Warszawa, 1957.
     1

VOCET    Gordon, Bernard L., ed. MAN AND THE SEA; CLASSIC ACCOUNTS OF MARINE EXPLORATIONS. 1st ed. Garden City, N.Y., Natural History Press, 1970. xxiv, 498p.
     17

VP      Government Affairs Seminar, 5th. Washington, D.C., 1971. TRANSCRIPT OF A SEMINAR ON ADMINISTRATIVE AND LEGISLATIVE CHALLENGES IN WATER POLLUTION CONTROL. Washington, D.C., Water Pollution Control Federation, 1971. 54p.
     2

VP      Graebel, William P., and Vernon A. Phelps. FAST CURRENT OIL CONTROL STUDY; INTERIM REPORT. U.S. Department of Transportation, Coast Guard. Springfield, Va., National Technical Information Service, 1974. 195p.
     ***

VP      Graham, Gerald F. THE CANADIAN ARCTIC WATERS POLLUTION PREVENTION ACT OF 1970 AND THE CONCEPT OF SELF-PROTECTION. Thesis (M.A.) Carleton University, 1974. Microfiche of typescript, no. 19481. Ottawa: National Library of Canada, 1974. 220p.
     14

IICZM    Grant, Malcolm J. APPROACHES TO STATE COASTAL MANAGEMENT. Coastal Resources Center Sea Grant. University of Rhode Island marine bulletin series no. 13. Narragansett, R.I., Marine Advisory Service, 1973. 7p.
     13

IICZM    _____ MARINE TRADES AND THE COASTAL CRISIS. PERSPECTIVES ON COASTAL MANAGEMENT. Marine Bulletin no. 18. Kingston, University of Rhode Island, 1974. 8p.
     ***

IICZM    _____ PERSPECTIVES ON COASTAL MANAGEMENT: MARINE TRADES AND THE COASTAL CRISIS. Marine bulletin 8. Kingston, University of Rhode Island, Coastal Resources Center, n.d. 8p.
     ***

IIIF     GRANT-IN-AID FOR FISHERIES PROGRAM ACTIVITIES 1974. Washington, U.S. National Oceanic and Atmospheric Administration, 1974. 98p.

IIIENV   Gray, David D. SELECTION OF MATERIALS PREPARED FOR THE MERCHANT MARINE AND FISHERIES COMMITTEE ON GROWTH AND THE ENVIRONMENT. 93d Congr., 2d sess., committee print. Washington, U.S.G.P.O. xii, 148p.
     14

IIENE    Gray, T.J., and O.K. Gashus, eds. TIDAL POWER. New York, Plenum Press, 1972.
     14

IIP      Great Britain. COASTAL POLLUTION. Observations on the report of the Select Committee on Science and Technology. Cmnd. 3880. London, HMSO, January 1969. 24p. [1]

VENE      _____ _____ Conservative Party. Research Department. ENERGY. Notes on current politics, no. 2. London, Conservative Central Office, n.d. [***]

VP      Great Britain. Department of Local Government and Regional Planning. THE PROTECTION OF THE ENVIRONMENT: THE FIGHT AGAINST POLLUTION: presented to Parliament by the Secretary of State for Local Government and Regional Planning, the Secretary of State for Scotland, and the Secretary of State for Wales. London, H.M.S.O., 1970. 29p. [2]

VT&L      Great Britain. Foreign Office. AGREEMENT BETWEEN THE UNITED KINGDOM OF GREAT BRITAIN AND NORTHERN IRELAND AND THE FEDERAL REPUBLIC OF GERMANY RELATING TO THE DELIMITATION OF THE CONTINENTAL SHELF UNDER THE NORTH SEA BETWEEN THE TWO COUNTRIES. Cmnd. 5192. Treaty series no. 7, 1973. London, H.M.S.O., 1973. 5p. [***]

VT&L      _____ _____ AGREEMENT BETWEEN THE GOVERNMENT OF THE UNITED KINGDOM OF GREAT BRITAIN AND NORTHERN IRELAND, AND THE KINGDOM OF DENMARK RELATING TO THE DELIMITATION OF THE CONTINENTAL SHELF BETWEEN THE TWO COUNTRIES. London, n.d. [3]

VP      Great Britain. Royal Commission on Environmental Pollution. FIRST REPORT PRESENTED TO PARLIAMENT BY COMMAND OF HER MAJESTY. Chairman: Sir Eric Ashby. London, H.M.S.O., 1971. vii, 51p. [2]

VENE      Greely, Richard S. ENERGY USE AND CLIMATE: POSSIBLE EFFECTS OF USING SOLAR ENERGY INSTEAD OF "STORED" ENERGY. NSF-RA-N-75-052. Washington, D.C., U.S.G.P.O., 1975. [14]

VB      Green, Leslie C. CANADA'S JURISDICTION OVER THE ARCTIC AND THE LITTORAL SEA. In G.T. Yates, III, and J.H. Young, Limits to National Jurisdiction over the Sea. Charlottesville, Press of the University of Virginia, 1974. pp. 207-229. [ART]

VCS      _____ _____ THE CONTINENTAL SHELF. London, University College, 1951. 80p. [1,16]

VP      Greenberg, Michael, et al. SOLID WASTE PLANNING IN METROPOLITAN AREAS. New Brunswick, N.J., Rutgers University, Center for Urban Policy Research, 1975. 256p. [***]

VCONS      Gregory, David D. THE EASEMENT AS A CONSERVATION TECHNIQUE. With the collaboration of A. Diot (French appendix), and H.H. Dietrich (German appendix). IUCN environmental law paper no. 1. Morges, Switzerland, 1972. 47p. [13]

                                                                13
VENV     Gregory, David D.  STANDING TO SUE IN ENVIRONMENTAL LITIGATION IN
         THE UNITED STATES OF AMERICA.  IUCN environmental law paper no. 2.
         Morges, Switzerland, International Union for Conservation of Nature
         and Natural Resources, 1972.  33p.

                                                                14,14a
IIIF     Gregory, Homer E., and Kathleen Barnes.  NORTH PACIFIC FISHERIES,
         WITH SPECIAL REFERENCE TO ALASKA SALMON.  San Francisco, New York,
         American Council, Institute of Pacific Relations, 1939.  xviii, 322p.

                                                                13,16
VB       Griffin, William L.  DELIMITATION OF OCEAN SPACE BOUNDARIES BETWEEN
         ADJACENT COASTAL STATES OF THE UNITED STATES.  Presented before
         Third Annual Law of the Sea Institute, University of Rhode Island,
         Kingston, R.I., June 24-27, 1968.  13p.

                                                                ***
IVMMR    Grigalunas, T.A.  OFFSHORE PETROLEUM AND NEW ENGLAND:  A STUDY OF
         THE REGIONAL ECONOMIC CONSEQUENCES OF POTENTIAL OFFSHORE OIL AND
         GAS DEVELOPMENT.  Marine technology reports 30 and 39.  Kingston,
         University of Rhode Island, 1975.

                                                                ***
IIIOR    Grigg, Richard W.  STATUS OF THE PRECIOUS CORAL INDUSTRY IN JAPAN,
         TAIWAN, AND OKINAWA:  1970.  UNIHI-SEAGRANT-AR-71-02.  Honolulu,
         University of Hawaii, 1971.  14p.

                                                                ***
IIIOR    Grigg, Richard W., and Lucius G. Eldredge.  THE COMMERCIAL POTENTIAL
         OF PRECIOUS CORALS IN MICRONESIA.  PART 1.  THE MARIANA ISLANDS.
         UGSG-75-01.  Honolulu, University of Hawaii Sea Grant, 1975.  16p.

                                                                ART
VP       Grimes, C.  A SURVEY OF MARINE ACCIDENTS WITH PARTICULAR REFERENCE
         TO TANKERS.  In Journal of Navigation, Vol. 25, 1972.  pp. 496-510.

                                                                13
IIIAFF   Grizzell, Roy A.  CATFISH FARMING:  A NEW FARM CROP.  U.S. Depart-
         ment of Agriculture.  Farmers' Bulletin No. 2244.  Washington, U.S.
         G.P.O., 1969.  22p.

                                                                ***
VP       Gromiec, M.J., and E.F. Gloyna.  RADIOACTIVITY TRANSPORT IN WATER -
         FINAL REPORT.  Technical Report to the Atomic Energy Commission.
         Texas, University at Austin, Environmental Health Engineering Re-
         search Laboratory, 1973.  78p.

                                                                14,17
VOCET    Gross, Meredith G.  OCEANOGRAPHY:  A VIEW OF THE EARTH.  Englewood
         Cliffs, N.J., Prentice-Hall, 1972.  ix, 581p.

                                                                ***
VP       _____  WASTE DISPOSAL.  Albany, State University of New York,
         New York Sea Grant Institute, 1975.

                                                                5,11,14,16
VINTL    Grotius, Hugo.  THE FREEDOM OF THE SEAS;  OR, THE RIGHT WHICH BE-
         LONGS TO THE DUTCH TO TAKE PART IN THE EAST INDIAN TRADE.  New York,
         Arno Press, 1972, 1916.

|  |  | ART |
|---|---|---|
| VP | Gruenfeld, M. IDENTIFICATION OF OIL POLLUTANTS. In Proceedings of Joint Conference on Prevention and Control of Oil Spills, Washington, D.C., March 13-15, 1973. pp. 179-193. | |

ART
IVMMR    Guilcher, Andre. LOCATION AND EVALUATION OF THE MINERAL RESOURCES OF THE SEA-BED AND ITS SUBSOIL. In Symposium on the Exploration and Exploitation of the Sea-Bed and its Subsoil. New York, U.S. and World Publications, Inc., Manhattan Publishing Company, 1971?

ART
IVMMR    Guillen, Oscar. VARIACIÓN DE FOSFATOS EN LA REGIÓN MARITIMA DEL CALLAO COMO MEDIDA DE LA PRODUCCIÓN PRIMARIA. In Seminario Latinoamericano sobre el Océano Pacifico Oriental. 1st, Lima, 1964. Memoria del Primer Seminario; estado del conocimiento del Océano Pacifico Oriental. Lima, Universidad Nacional Mayor de San Marcos, 1966. pp. 73-76.

5
IIIF     Gulf and Caribbean Fisheries Institute. PROCEEDINGS OF THE 25th ANNUAL SESSION, MIAMI, FLORIDA, NOVEMBER, 1972. Edited by James B. Higman. Coral Gables, Fla., Rosenstiel School of Marine and Atmospheric Science, 1973. viii, 184p.

***
IICZM    GULF STATES CONFERENCE ON COASTAL ZONE MANAGEMENT. Proceedings, Biloxi, Mississippi: 1974. MASGP-74-043. Ocean Springs, Mississippi-Alabama Sea Grant Consortium, 1974.

5,7
IIIF     Gulland, John A. THE MANAGEMENT OF MARINE FISHERIES. Seattle, University of Washington Press, 1974. viii, 190p.

13,14a
IIIF     _____ POPULATION DYNAMICS OF WORLD FISHERIES. University of Washington Sea Grant Publication WSG72-1. Seattle, University of Washington, 1972. xiii, 336p.

13,16
IIIF     Gulland, John A., comp. THE FISH RESOURCES OF THE OCEAN. West Byfleet, Surrey, England, Fishing News (Books), 1971. xi, 255p.

1,2,8,12,14a,16,17,18
VOR      Gullion, Edmund A., ed. USES OF THE SEAS. American Assembly. Englewood Cliffs, N.J., Prentice-Hall, 1968. xv, 202p.

***
VP       Gumtz, Garth D., et al. CHARACTERIZATION OF VESSEL WASTES IN DULUTH-SUPERIOR HARBOR. National Environmental Research Center, Office of Research and Development, Cincinnati, Ohio, 1974. vii, 52p.

12
VINTL    Gutierrez Olivos, S. MAR TERRITORIAL Y DERECHO MODERNO. Santiago, Editorial Juridica de Chile. 132p.

ART
IICZM    Haas, Bay. COASTAL ZONE MANAGEMENT: THE LOCAL PERSPECTIVE. In Proceedings of the Coastal Leaders Conference on Coastal Zone Management. MASGP-75-012. Mobile, Mississippi-Alabama Sea Grant Consor-

tium, April 30, 1975. pp. 26-29.

VINTL     Hague. International Court of Justice. NORTH SEA CONTINENTAL SHELF CASES; FEDERAL REPUBLIC OF GERMANY/DENMARK; FEDERAL REPUBLIC OF GERMANY/NETHERLANDS. Leyden, A.W. Sijthoff, 1969. 2 Vols.     5,11,15

VINTL     _____ NUCLEAR TESTS CASE: JURISDICTION OF THE COURT AND ADMISSIBILITY, AUSTRALIA v. FRANCE; VERBATIM RECORD OF ORAL PROCEEDINGS. Canberra, Australian Government Publishing Service, 1974.     ***

IIIINTL     Hague. Permanent Court of Arbitration. North Atlantic Coast Fisheries. PROCEEDINGS IN THE NORTH ATLANTIC COAST FISHERIES ARBITRATION BEFORE THE PERMANENT COURT OF ARBITRATION AT THE HAGUE. Under the provisions of the general treaty of arbitration of April 4, 1908, and the special agreement of January 27, 1909, between the United States of America and Great Britain. U.S. 61st Congr., 3d sess., Senate document 870. Washington, U.S.G.P.O., 1912, 1913.     14a

IIIFV&G     Haines, R.G. ECHO FISHING. London, Leonard-Hill, 1969. xiii, 116p.     13

IIIF     Hale, Williams E., and Dag F. Wittusen. WORLD FISHERIES: A "TRAGEDY OF THE COMMONS"? Woodrow Wilson Association Monograph Series in Public Affairs, no. 4. N.J., Princeton University Press, 1971. 63p.     1,5,6,12,16

IIIF     Hall, D.N.F. A NOTE ON THE ZANZIBAR ROCK-LOBSTER FISHERY. In East African Marine Fisheries Resources Organisation, Annual Report. n.p., 1960.     ART

VMLAD     Hall, Robert G. HALL'S ESSAY ON THE RIGHTS OF THE CROWN AND THE PRIVILEGES OF THE SUBJECT IN THE SEA SHORES OF THE REALM. London, Stevens and Haynes, 2d ed., 1875. 220p.     16

VLOS     Hallman, Robert M. TOWARDS AN ENVIRONMENTALLY SOUND LAW OF THE SEA. Washington, D.C., the International Institute for Environment and Development, 1974. vii, 83p.     5,7,13,14

IICZM     Halperin, David J. COASTAL ZONE MANAGEMENT: INTERGOVERNMENTAL RELATIONS AND LEGAL LIMITATIONS. In Proceedings of the Symposium on Social and Economic Aspects of Water Resources Development, held in Ithaca, New York, June 21-23, 1971. Urbana, Ill., American Water Resources Association, 1972. pp. 201-208.     ART

VCONS     Halstead, Bruce W., comp. A GOLDEN GUIDE TO ENVIRONMENTAL ORGANIZATIONS. New York, Golden Press, 1972. 63p.     17

VODAS     Hamilton, R.C., and E.G. Ward. OCEAN DATA GATHERING PROGRAM - QUALITY AND REDUCTION OF DATA. In Offshore Technology Conference, 6th, Houston, Texas, 1974: Preprints. Vol. 2, pp. 749-770.     ART

ART
IIP&H      Hammon, Alfred. REPORT OF STUDY ON SHIPS CHANNELS AND HARBORS. In Proceedings of the National Security Industrial Association, Ocean Science and Technology Advisory Committee Annual Meeting, and National Oceanography Association/National Security Industrial Association Symposium, held in Washington, D.C., June 2-3, 1971. Washington, D.C., 1971.

***
IIP&H      Hammon, Alfred, and L.M. Krieger. PORT FACILITIES AND COMMERCE. Albany, State University of New York, New York Sea Grant Institute, 1975.

ART
IIIAFF     Hampson, Alfred A. SETTING UP A MARICULTURE BUSINESS: LEGAL CONSIDERATIONS. In Northwest Mariculture Laws - papers and presentations from a symposium held at the Law Center, University of Oregon, Eugene, June 7, 1974. Corvallis, Oregon State University, Sea Grant Communications, 1975.

ART
IIENV      Hann, Roy W., Jr., and Wesley P. James. ENVIRONMENTAL ASPECTS OF A TEXAS SUPERPORT. In Proceedings of the Fifth National Sea Grant Conference held in Houston, Texas, 1972. Sea Grant Publication no. TAMU-SG-73-101. College Station, Texas A&M University, 1973.

13
IIIAFF     Hanson, Joe E., ed. OPEN SEA MARICULTURE: PERSPECTIVES, PROBLEMS, AND PROSPECTS. Stroudsburg, Pa., Dowden, Hutchinson and Ross, Inc., 1974. xi, 410p.

ART
IVMMR      Hardoin, J.L. CALIFORNIA'S OFFSHORE PETROLEUM POTENTIAL. In Society of Petroleum Engineers of AIME: 44th Annual California Regional Meeting. n.p., 1974. 8p.

13
IICZM      Hargis, William J. THE ROLES AND ORGANIZATION OF SCIENCE AND ENGINEERING IN COASTAL ZONE PLANNING AND MANAGEMENT. Testimony before the Subcommittee on Oceanography of the House Merchant Marine and Fisheries Committee, 22 June 1971. Mimeo. Washington, D.C. n.p., 1971.

13,14
VENV       Hargrove, John L. LAW, INSTITUTIONS AND THE GLOBAL ENVIRONMENT. N.Y., Dobbs Ferry, Oceana Publications, Inc., 1972. 394p.

14
VLOS       Hargrove, John L., ed. WHO PROTECTS THE OCEAN? ENVIRONMENT AND THE DEVELOPMENT OF THE LAW OF THE SEA. St. Paul, West Publishing Company, 1975. 250p.

13
IIIFV&G    Harrington, David L., et al. SHRIMP FISHING WITH TWIN TRAWLS. Marine Extension Bulletin no. 1. Savannah, Georgia, Georgia Sea Grant Program and the Marine Extension Center of the University of Georgia. November, 1972.

|        |                                                                                                                                                                                                                 |
|--------|-----------------------------------------------------------------------------------------------------------------------------------------------------------------------------------------------------------------|
| IIIAFF | ***<br>Harris, A.H., et al. MARICULTURE IN ESTUARINE OIL-PIPELINE CANALS IN LOUISIANA. Paper presented at World Mariculture Society, Fourth Annual Meeting and Workshop, January 24-26, 1973, in Monterey, Mexico. n.p. n.d. 9p. |
| VP     | ***<br>Hartung, R., and R.D. Dinman, eds. ENVIRONMENTAL MERCURY CONTAMINATION. Ann Arbor, Mich., Science Publishers, 1972.                                                                                      |
| VINTL  | ***<br>Haucke, M. PIRATENSENDER AUF SEE. Muenchen, Beck, 1969. 212p.                                                                                                                                            |
| VMT    | 3<br>Haumont, Amand. LES TRANSPORTS MARITIMES; ELEMENTS DE DROIT MARITIME APPLIQUE. Paris, Berger-Levrault, etc., 1893. xii, 372p.                                                                              |
| IICZM  | 14<br>Hawaii. Department of Transportation. HAWAII SHORE WATERS REGULATIONS. Honolulu, Harbors Division, 1969? iv, 32p.                                                                                         |
| IIOSTR | ***<br>Hawaii. University. HAWAII'S FLOATING CITY DEVELOPMENT PROGRAM: TRANSPORTATION ASPECTS OF OFFSHORE. UNIHI-SG-76-4. Honolulu, 1976.                                                                        |
| IISL   | ***<br>Hawley, A.J. THE PRESENT AND FUTURE STATUS OF EASTERN NORTH CAROLINA WETLANDS. Raleigh, North Carolina State University, Water Resources Research Institute, 1974. 176p.                                 |
| IIIFP  | ***<br>Hayden, Mildred. HISTORY OF THE SALMON INDUSTRY IN OREGON (Master of Arts Thesis). Eugene, University of Oregon, 1930.                                                                                   |
| IVMMR  | ART<br>Head, Ivan L. THE CANADIAN OFFSHORE MINERALS REFERENCE. In University of Toronto Law Journal, Vol. XVIII, no. 3, 1968, pp. 131-157.                                                                      |
| IVB    | 16<br>Hedberg, Hollis. JURISDICTION OVER OFFSHORE MINERAL RESOURCES. Paper at A.A.P.C. Annual Meeting. Dallas, Texas, April 15, 1969.                                                                           |
| VB     | 1,4,5,7,8,10,11,13,14,16,18<br>_____ NATIONAL-INTERNATIONAL JURISDICTIONAL BOUNDARY ON THE OCEAN FLOOR. Law of the Sea Institute occasional paper no. 16. Kingston, University of Rhode Island, 1972. 19p. |
| IVP    | ART<br>Hedgpeth, Joel. OIL AND HARD MINERALS; POLLUTION PROBLEMS. In Conference on Local Impacts of the Law of the Sea, Seattle, Washington, 1972. Proceedings of a Conference held in Seattle, October 10-12, 1972. Seattle, University of Washington, Division of Marine Resources, 1973. pp. 112-119. |
| VP     | ART<br>_____ _____ RADIOACTIVE CONTAMINATION IN THE ANTARCTIC. In Proceedings of the Colloquium on Conservation Problems in Antarctica, held in Blacksburg, Va., September 10-12, 1971. Lawrence, Kansas, Allen Press, Inc., 1972. pp. 97-109. |

***
IISL    Helfgott, T., et al., eds. WETLANDS CONFERENCE. 1st. Proceedings. Storrs, University of Connecticutt, 1973. 211p.

***
IIDR    Helfrich, Philip. AN ASSESSMENT OF THE EXPECTED IMPACT OF A DREDGING PROJECT PROPOSED FOR PALA LAGOON, AMERICAN SAMOA. UNIHI-SEA-GRANT-TR-76-02. Honolulu, University of Hawaii, 1975. 76p.

***
VP      Henaine Hernandez, Reyna. LA CONTAMINACIÓN DEL MEDIO MARINO. México, Mexico City, Universidad Nacional, Facultad de Ciencias Politicas y Sociales, Centro de Relaciones Internacionales, 1972. 231p.

ART
IVLOS   Henkin, Louis. THE CHANGING LAW OF THE SEA-MINING. In Inter-University Program of Research on Ferromanganese Deposits of the Ocean Floor. Phase 1 report, 1973. pp. 337-351.

1,3,7,12,14,16,18
IVLOS   _____ LAW FOR THE SEA'S MINERAL RESOURCES. ISHA monograph no. 1. New York, Institute for the Study of Science in Human Affairs, Columbia University, 1968. 75p.

2,5,15,18
VOR     Henry, Harriet P., and David J. Halperin. MAINE LAW AFFECTING MARINE RESOURCES. Partial report under a study carried out under the joint sponsorship of the School of Law and the University of Maine and the National Science Foundation. Portland, University of Maine School of Law, 1969-70. 4 Vols. in 2. xiii, 903p.

***
VP      Hepple, P., ed. POLLUTION PREVENTION. Proceedings of 1968 Meeting of the Institute of Petroleum, Harrison and Sons, London, 1971. 223p.

16
VP      _____ SCIENTIFIC ASPECTS OF POLLUTION OF THE SEA BY OIL; PROCEEDINGS OF A SYMPOSIUM HELD ON OCTOBER 1968. Essex, England, Applied Science Publishers; London, Institute of Petroleum, 1968. 68p.

***
VP      _____ WATER POLLUTION BY OIL. PROCEEDINGS OF A SEMINAR, INVERNESSSHIRE, SCOTLAND, MAY 1970. New York, Elsevier, 1971. 393p.

ART
IVDRIL  Herbaux, R. FIRST COMPLETION OF ABANDONED WELL IS UNDERTAKEN OFFSHORE LABRADOR BY GROUP. In Offshore, Vol. 33, 1973. pp. 66-66.

***
VP      Herber, R. INTERNATIONALES UEBEREINKOMMEN UEBER DIE HAFTUNG FUER SCHAEDEN DURCH OELVERSCHMUTZUNG AUF SEE. Schriften des Deutshcen Vereins fuer Internationales Seerecht. Reihe B, Heft 10. Hamburg, 1972. 54p.

***
IIDR    Herbich, John B. COASTAL AND DEEP OCEAN DREDGING. Houston, Texas, Gulf Publishing Company, 1975. 633p.

IIDR      Herbich, John B. CONTINENTAL SHELF AND DEEP OCEAN DREDGING. Event Number 182, American Society for Engineering Education Annual Meeting, June 23-26, 1969. Photocopy. University Park, Pennsylvania State University, 1969.   13

IIDR      _____ PROCEEDINGS OF THE SEVENTH DREDGING SEMINAR. TAMU-SG-76-105. College Station, Texas A&M University, 1975. 249p.   ***

VOR       Herfindahl, Orris C. NATURAL RESOURCES INFORMATION FOR ECONOMIC DEVELOPMENT. Baltimore, Johns Hopkins Press, 1969. xv, 212p.   17

VENV      Herfindahl, Orris C., and Allen V. Kneese. QUALITY OF THE ENVIRONMENT: AN ECONOMIC APPROACH TO SOME PROBLMES IN USING LAND, WATER, AND AIR. Washington, Resources for the Future, Inc., 1965. viii, 96p.   13

VB        Herrera, Caceres, H.R. ESTATUTO JURIDICO DE LA BAHIA DE FONSECA Y REGIMEN DE SUS ZONAS ADYACENTES. Tegucigalpa, Dept. de Publicaciones de la Universidad de Honduras, 1974. 288p.   7

VINTL     _____ HONDURAS Y LA PROBLEMÁTICA DEL DERECHO INTERNACIONAL PUBLICO DEL MAR. Tegucigalpa, Editorial Universitaria UNAH, 1975. 264p.   7

VOCET     Herring, Peter J., and Malcolm R. Clarke, eds. DEEP OCEANS. New York, Praeger Publishers, 1971. 320p.   16,17

IIIF      Herrington, William C. OPERATION OF THE JAPANESE FISHERY MANAGEMENT SYSTEM. Law of the Sea Institute occasional paper no. 11. Kingston, University of Rhode Island, 1971. 21p.   1,4,5,7,8,11,13,14,15,18

IIOSTR    Herrmann, H.G. FOUNDATIONS FOR SMALL SEAFLOOR INSTALLATIONS. Port Hueneme, Calif., U.S. Naval Civil Engineering Laboratory, 1972. 39p.   ***

IICZM     Hershman, Marc J. COASTAL ZONE MANAGEMENT AFTER THE GREENING OF AMERICA; MEMORANDUM. Mimeo. Baton Rouge, La., Coastal Resources Law, Louisiana State University, n.d. 4p.   13

IICZM     _____ COMPARISON AND ANALYSIS OF TWO COASTAL ZONE MANAGEMENT BILLS: LENNON'S H.R.2492 AND LENNON'S H.R.2493; MEMORANDUM. Baton Rouge, La., Louisiana State University, May 28, 1971. 17p.   13

IIP&H     Hershman, Marc J., and H. Gary Knight. LEGAL ASPECTS OF A SUPERPORT OFF LOUISIANA'S COAST. Louisiana Superport studies. Report no. 1. Preliminary. In Louisiana, State University and Agricultural and Mechanical College. Center for Wetland Resources. Publication no. LSU-SG-72-03. Baton Rouge, 1972. 136p.   ART

|      |                                                                                                                                                                                                                                                                                                      |
|------|------------------------------------------------------------------------------------------------------------------------------------------------------------------------------------------------------------------------------------------------------------------------------------------------------|
| VCS  | Heselton, L.R., Jr. THE CONTINENTAL SHELF. Center for Naval Analyses research contribution no. 106 (Contract N00014-68-A-0091). Arlington, Va., Center for Naval Analyses, 1968. [17] |
| IIDR | Hess, Harold D. MARINE SAND AND GRAVEL MINING INDUSTRY OF THE UNITED KINGDOM. NOAA Technical Report ERL 213-MMTC 1. Boulder, Colorado. September 1971. ix, 176p. [13] |
| IVENV | _____ A PROPOSED NATIONAL OFFSHORE MINING ENVIRONMENTAL STUDY IN MASSACHUSETTS WATERS. Mimeo. Paper presented at Coastal Zone Workshop Lecture Series, May 25, 1972. Mass., Woods Hole Oceanographic Institution, 1972. [13] |
| IIIF | Hester, Frank J. MAN IN THE SEA AND FISHERIES OF THE FUTURE. In Marine Technology Society. Second Annual Conference, Washington, D.C., June 27-29, 1966. Washington, D.C., 1966. pp. 524-529. [ART] |
| VP | Heyerdahl, Thor. MAN AGAINST NATURE. Strasbourg, 1972. 9p. [17] |
| VENE | Hezlet, A. ELECTRONICS AND SEA POWER. New York, Stein and Day, 1975. [***] |
| IIIAFF | Hickling, C.F. FISH CULTURE. London, Faber and Faber, 1962. [***] |
| VINTL | Higgins, Alexander P., and C. John Colombos. THE INTERNATIONAL LAW OF THE SEA. London, New York, etc., Longmans, Green and Company, 1943. 2, 647p. [5,6,7] |
| IIIF | Higman, James B., ed. GULF AND CARIBBEAN FISHERIES INSTITUTE. PROCEEDINGS OF THE 26th ANNUAL SESSION, NEW ORLEANS, LOUISIANA, OCTOBER, 1973. Coral Gables, Fla., Rosenstiel School of Marine Atmospheric Science, 1974. 180p. [13] |
| IIIF | _____ GULF AND CARIBBEAN FISHERIES INSTITUTE. PROCEEDINGS OF THE 24th ANNUAL SESSION, MIAMI, FLORIDA, NOVEMBER, 1971. Coral Gables, Fla., Rosenstiel School of Marine and Atmospheric Science, 1972. vii, 147p. [5,13] |
| IIIF | _____ GULF AND CARIBBEAN FISHERIES INSTITUTE. PROCEEDINGS OF THE 25th ANNUAL SESSION, MIAMI, FLORIDA, NOVEMBER, 1972. Coral Gables, Fla., Rosenstiel School of Marine and Atmospheric Science, 1973. viii, 184p. [13] |
| VLOS | Hilbert, Lothar W. LE RÔLE RESPECTIF DES CONSIDÉRATIONS STRATÉGIQUES, DES INTERÊTS ÉCONOMIQUES, DES IDEOLOGIES POLITIQUES, DES FACTEURS HISTORIQUES ET GÉOGRAPHIQUES, DANS LA FORMATION DES RÈGLES DU DROIT INTERNATIONAL DE LA MER. La Haye, Rapport établi au Centre de Recherches de l'Académie de Droit International de La Haye, 1959. [1] |

|||
|---|---|
| VOCET | ***<br>Hill, M.N., ed. THE SEA; IDEAS AND OBSERVATIONS ON PROGRESS IN THE STUDY OF THE SEAS. New York, Interscience Publishers, 1962. 3 Vols. |
| IIIF | 13<br>Hinshaw, Russell N. POLLUTION AS A RESULT OF FISH CULTURAL ACTIVITIES. Prepared for the U.S. Environmental Protection Agency. Reproduced by National Technical Information Service, U.S. Department of Commerce, Springfield, Va., February 1973. vi, 209p. |
| VAC | 16<br>Hirdman, Sven. PROSPECTS FOR ARMS CONTROL IN THE OCEAN. SIPRI research report no. 7. Stockholm, Almqvist and Wiksell; New York, Humanities Press, 1972. 25p. |
| IVENV | ART<br>Hirsch, A. NOAA'S ROLE AND RESPONSIBILITIES WITH RESPECT TO OUTER CONTINENTAL SHELF DEVELOPMENT IN THE EASTERN GULF OF MEXICO. In Proceedings of Marine Environmental Implications of Offshore Drilling in the Eastern Gulf of Mexico. Edited by R.E. Smith. St. Petersburg, State University System of Florida, Institute of Oceanography, 1974. pp. 39-41. |
| VENV | 14,17<br>Hite, James C., and Eugene A. Laurent. ENVIRONMENTAL PLANNING: AN ECONOMIC ANALYSIS; APPLICATIONS FOR THE COASTAL ZONE. New York, Praeger Publishers, 1972. xiv, 155p. |
| IICR | 13,16,17<br>Hite, James C., and James M. Stepp, eds. COASTAL RESOURCE MANAGEMENT. New York, Praeger Publishers, 1971. xxii, 169p. |
| VLOS | 1,5,7,10,11,12,14,15,16<br>Hjertonsson, Karin. THE NEW LAW OF THE SEA; INFLUENCE OF THE LATIN AMERICAN STATES ON RECENT DEVELOPMENTS OF THE LAW OF THE SEA. A study of the law on coastal jurisdiction as it has emerged in Latin America and its impact on present and future law. Leyden, Sijthoff; Stockholm, P.A. Norstedt and Söners, 1973. 187p. |
| VB | 1,4,5,7,13,15,18<br>Hodgson, Robert D., and Lewis M. Alexander. TOWARDS AN OBJECTIVE ANALYSIS OF SPECIAL CIRCUMSTANCES: BAYS, RIVERS, COASTAL AND OCEANIC ARCHIPELAGOS AND ATOLLS. Law of the Sea Institute occasional paper no. 13. Kingston, University of Rhode Island, April, 1972. 54p. |
| VB | ART<br>Hodgson, Robert D., and T.V. McIntyre. NATIONAL SEABED BOUNDARY OPTIONS. In G.T. Yates, III, and J.H. Young, Limits to National Jurisdiction over the Sea. Charlottesville, 1974. pp. 152-173. |
| VINTL | ***<br>Hoepker, W. WELTMACHT ZUR SEE: DIE SOWJETUNION AUF ALLEN MEEREN. Stuttgart, Seewald, 1971. 211p. |
| IIIAFF | ***<br>Hofstede, A.E., et al. FISHCULTURE IN INDONESIA. Indo-Pacific Fisheries Council special publication no. 2. n.p., 1953. |

|  |  | ART |
|---|---|---|
| IIIP | Holden, A.V., and G. Topping. OCCURRENCE OF SPECIFIC POLLUTANTS IN FISH IN THE FORTH AND TAY ESTUARIES. In Proceedings of a Symposium held in Edinburgh, Scotland, October 29, 1971. n.p., 1972. |  |
| VOR | Hollick, Ann L., and Robert E. Osgood. NEW ERA OF OCEAN POLITICS. Baltimore, Johns Hopkins University Press, 1974. xi, 131p. | 5,14,16,18 |
| VORM | Hollick, Ann L. UNITED STATES OCEAN POLICY: 1948-1971. Thesis. Baltimore, Johns Hopkins University, 1971. iv, 319p. | 18 |
| VENV | Holliman, Jonathon. CONSUMER'S GUIDE TO THE PROTECTION OF THE ENVIRONMENT. 2d rev. ed. London, Pan Books (for) Friends of the Earth. n.d. | 14 |
| VP | Holmes, Beatrice H., and William D. Anderson. LAWS AND INSTITUTIONAL MECHANISMS CONTROLLING THE RELEASE OF PESTICIDES INTO THE ENVIRONMENT. Washington, Environmental Protection Agency, Office of Water Programs, Water Quality and Non-Point Source Control Division, Non-Point Source Control Branch, 1972. iii, 140p. | 13 |
| IIIFV&G | Holmsen, Andreas A. RHODE ISLAND'S FLOATING FISH TRAP FISHERY. Agricultural Experiment Station Marine Advisory Service, Resource Economics. University of Rhode Island Marine bulletin series no. 14. Narragansett, Marine Advisory Service, University of Rhode Island, 1973. 7p. | 13 |
| IIIF | _____ SOME NORTHEASTERN STATE REGULATIONS FOR NON-RESIDENT FISHERMEN. Marine memorandum no. 38. Narragansett, University of Rhode Island, Marine Advisory Service, 1975. 11p. | *** |
| IIIOR | Holt, D.J. THE LIVING RESOURCES OF THE SEA-BED. Paper at Symposium on the International Regime of the Sea-bed. Rome, 1969. | 16 |
| VOCET | Hood, D.W. MARINE RESEARCH DEVELOPMENT IN ALASKA. Fairbanks, University of Alaska, Institute of Marine Science, 1975. 6p. | *** |
| VP | Hood, Donald W., ed. IMPINGEMENT OF MAN ON THE OCEANS. New York, Wiley-Interscience, 1971. x, 738p. | 5,14,14a,15,16,17 |
| VCONS | Hooft, H. Ph. Visser't. LES NATIONS UNIES ET LA CONSERVATION DES RESSOURCES DE LA MER. Netherlands, 1958. | 7 |
| IVMMR | Horn, D.R., et al, eds. FERROMANGANESE DEPOSITS ON THE OCEAN FLOOR. Washington, D.C., National Science Foundation, Office for the International Decade of Ocean Exploration, 1972? 283p. | *** |

|  |  |
|---|---|
| | 5,13,14a,17 |
| VOCET | Horsfield, Brenda, and Peter B. Stone.  THE GREAT OCEAN BUSINESS.  New York, Coward, McCann and Geoghegan Inc., 1972.  x, 360p. |

| | ART |
|---|---|
| IICR | Hortig, Francis J.  CONSERVATION OF MINERAL RESOURCES OF THE COASTAL ZONE.  In J.F. Peel Brahtz, ed., Coastal Zone Management; Multiple Use with Conservation.  New York, John Wiley, 1972.  pp. 149-189. |

| | 9 |
|---|---|
| VORM | Houck, Louis.  A TREATISE ON THE LAW OF NAVIGABLE RIVERS.  Boston, Little, Brown, and Company, 1868.  xix, 235p. |

| | 14a,17 |
|---|---|
| VP | Hoult, David P., ed.  OIL ON THE SEA; PROCEEDINGS OF A SYMPOSIUM ON THE SCIENTIFIC AND ENGINEERING ASPECTS OF OIL POLLUTION OF THE SEA, HELD IN CAMBRIDGE, MASSACHUSETTS, 1969.  New York, Plenum Press, 1969.  vii, 114p. |

| | 14 |
|---|---|
| IICZM | HOW DOES SHORELINE MANAGEMENT AFFECT ME?  SHORELINE MANAGEMENT ACT OF 1971: A DISCUSSION OF THE IMPACT OF THIS ACT ON PROPERTY OWNERS IN THE STATE OF WASHINGTON.  Association of Washington Cities, Washington State Association of Counties, Olympia, Washington, Department of Ecology, 1972.  6p. |

| | ART |
|---|---|
| IIIP | Howe, C., and S. Ottway.  SOME EFFECTS OF CRUDE OIL, OIL FRACTIONS AND PRODUCTS ON THE PRAWN LEANDER SQUILLA.  In Field Studies Council, Oil Pollution Research Unit, Orielton Field Centre, Annual Report.  Pembroke, Wales, 1971.  pp. 22-28. |

| | *** |
|---|---|
| VB | Huang, K.  CHUNG HUA MIN KUO TI LING HAI CHI CH'I HSIANG KUAN CHIH TU.  Territorial Waters of the Republic of China and the Related Regulations.  (Jên jên wên k'u, tê'247.)  Tapei, T'ai-wan shang wu yin shu kuan, 1973.  13p. |

| | 14 |
|---|---|
| VENE | Hubbert, M.C.  ENERGY RESOURCES, RESOURCES AND MAN.  The Committee on Resources and Man, National Academy of Sciences.  San Francisco, W.H. Freeman and Company, 1969. |

| | *** |
|---|---|
| IVMMR | Huggard, J.P.  THE DEEP OCEAN AND ITS NON-LIVING RESOURCES:  A NEW LEGAL REALM.  In S.W. Wurfel, Emerging Ocean Oil and Mining Law.  Sea Grant Publication UNC-SG-74-02.  Chapel Hill, University of North Carolina School of Law, 1974.  pp. 40-50. |

| | ART |
|---|---|
| IIIF | Hughes, Steven E., and Charles D. Gill.  SAURY IS PROMISING 'NEW' FISH ON WEST COAST.  JAPAN, SOVIETS FISHING LARGE STOCK OFF U.S.  Reprinted from National Fisherman, April, 1970. |

| | 13 |
|---|---|
| VP | Hull, E.W. Seabrook.  THE EARTH COMMONS: LIMITS AND RIGHTS OF ACCESS.  The Nautilus Papers no. 3.  Washington, Nautilus Press.  November 8, 1972. |

|  |  |
|---|---|
| | 4,5,7,11,13,14,15,18 |
| VENV | Hull, E.W. Seabrook, and Albert W. Koers. INTRODUCTION TO A CONVENTION ON THE INTERNATIONAL ENVIRONMENT PROTECTION AGENCY. Law of the Sea Institute occasional paper no 12. Kingston, University of Rhode Island, September 1971. 21p. |
| | *** |
| VOD | Hunter, Lawson A.W. THE QUESTION OF AN OCEAN DUMPING CONVENTION: CONCLUSIONS OF THE WORKING GROUP ON AN OCEAN DUMPING CONVENTION AND BACKGROUND PAPER. Studies in Transnational Legal Policy no. 2. Washington, American Society of International Law, n.d. |
| | 14 |
| IICZM | Hurd, Bronwyn, ed. THE MASSACHUSETTS COASTLINE: CHOICE OR CONSEQUENCE. Boston, Executive Office of Environmental Affairs, Office of Coastal Zone Management, 1975. |
| | *** |
| VP | Hutton, John. IMPACTS OF OFFSHORE OIL ON NORTH EAST SCOTLAND. A lecture presented by the MIT Sea Grant Program, 28 April 1975. Cambridge, Massachusetts Institute of Technology, 1975. 29p. |
| | ART |
| IICZM | Hyde, L. Willis. COASTAL ZONE MANAGEMENT: THE STATE PERSPECTIVE. In Proceedings of the Coastal Leaders Conference on Coastal Zone Management. MASGP-75-012. Mobile, Mississippi-Alabama Sea Grant Consortium, April 30, 1975. pp. 16-25. |
| | 8,16 |
| VINTL | Hydeman, Lee M., and William H. Berman. INTERNATIONAL CONTROL OF NUCLEAR MARITIME ACTIVITIES. Ann Arbor, Atomic Energy Research Project, The University of Michigan Law School, 1960. 384p. |
| | 5,7 |
| VB | Iceland. THE EVOLVING LIMIT OF COASTAL JURISDICTION. Published by the Government of Iceland, Reykjavik, June 1974. |
| | 8,10,12,13,14,16 |
| VOCET | Idyll, C.P. EXPLORING THE OCEAN WORLD; A HISTORY OF OCEANOGRAPHY. New York, Crowell, 1969. viii, 280p. |
| | 14 |
| IIIAFF | \_\_\_\_\_ \_\_\_\_\_ FARMING THE SEA: A SPECIAL SECTION ON AQUACULTURE. Reprinted from NOAA, Vol. 1, no. 4, 1971. U.S. Department of Commerce, National Oceanic and Atmospheric Administration. Washington, U.S. G.P.O., 1971. 23p. |
| | 14a |
| IIIF | \_\_\_\_\_ \_\_\_\_\_ THE SEA AGAINST HUNGER. New York, Crowell, 1970. xii, 221p. |
| | 14a |
| IVMMR | Igelsrud, Iver, et al. THE DISTRIBUTION OF PHOSPHATES IN THE SEA WATER OF THE NORTHEAST PACIFIC. Seattle, University of Washington Press, 1936. 34p. |
| | *** |
| VLOS | Illanes Fernández, J. EL DERECHO DEL MAR Y SUS PROBLEMAS ACTUALES. Buenos Aires, Editorial Universitaria de Buenos Aires, 1974. 199p. |

VP        Illinois. Legislative Investigating Commission. CHEMICAL LEAK AT THE BULK TERMINALS TANK FARM. A report to the Illinois General Assembly. Chicago, June, 1975. x, 192p.

VINTL     Imbart de Latour, J.J.B. LA MER TERRITORIALE AU POINT DE VUE THEORIQUE ET PRATIQUE. Paris, G. Pedone-Lauriel, 1889. 380p.

***

IIP       IN THE MATTER OF POLLUTION OF THE NAVIGABLE WATERS OF DADE COUNTY, FLORIDA, AND TRIBUTARIES, EMBAYMENTS AND COASTAL WATERS. Proceedings of Conference held in Miami, Florida, July 2-3, 1971. Third session. Washington, D.C., Environmental Protection Agency, 1971. 481p.

VOCET     India. National Institute of Oceanography. COLLECTED REPRINTS, VOL. 2; 1968-1970. Panaji, India, Council of Industrial and Scientific Research, 1972?

***

IIIF      Indo-Pacific Fisheries Council. Secretariat. PROCEEDINGS: SECTION I: COASTAL AQUACULTURE AND ENVIRONMENT. Bangkok, Thailand, FAO Regional Office for Asia and the Far East, 1974. 99p.

***

IIIF      Indo- Pacific Fisheries Council. SECTION III: SYMPOSIUM ON COASTAL AND HIGH SEAS PELAGIC RESOURCES. PROCEEDINGS. 15th SESSION. Bangkok, 1974. n.p. 511p.

***

VOI       Industry and the ocean. Conference papers. OCEANOLOGY INTERNATIONAL 72 CONFERENCE, BRIGHTON, ENGLAND, 1972. London, 1972.

***

IVM       INFORMATION AND PROCEDURES FOR OFFSHORE OPERATORS. Canada, Resource Management and Conservation Branch, Offshore Exploration, 5 February, 1973. n.p. 67p.

***

IVDRIL    INITIAL REPORTS OF THE DEEP SEA DRILLING PROJECT. Washington, U.S. G.P.O., 1970-    Vol. 1-

VOI       INSTITUTE FOR POLITICS AND PLANNING. MULTINATIONAL INVESTMENT IN OCEAN ACTIVITIES. Springfield, Va., U.S. Government Clearinghouse, 1969. 92p.

***

VENV      INSTITUTE OF ENVIRONMENTAL SCIENCES: 21st ANNUAL TECHNICAL MEETING: VOL. I: ENERGY AND THE ENVIRONMENT. Mr. Prospect, Ill., Institute of Environmental Sciences, 1975. 260p.

***

VP        INSTITUTE OF PETROLEUM, LONDON, SCIENTIFIC ASPECTS OF POLLUTION OF THE SEA BY OIL. New York, Elsevier, 1968. 80p.

| | | 15 |
|---|---|---|
| VENV | Institute of Public Administration. THE MARINE ENVIRONMENT: A STATE AND LOCAL PERSPECTIVE; REPORT SUBMITTED TO THE COMMISSION ON MARINE SCIENCE, ENGINEERING AND RESOURCES. New York, June, 1968. | |

15
IVMMR   Institute on Economics of the Petroleum Industry, Dallas, 1963. ECONOMICS OF THE PETROLEUM INDUSTRY: NEW IDEAS, NEW METHODS, NEW DEVELOPMENTS; PAPERS. Houston, Gulf Publishing Company, n.d.

16
VCONS   INTER-AMERICAN SPECIALIZED CONFERENCE ON CONSERVATION OF NATURAL RESOURCES: THE CONTINENTAL SHELF AND MARINE WATERS. Washington, D.C., Pan American Union, 1956. pp. 1-42.

***
VOD   INTERGOVERNMENTAL CONFERENCE ON THE CONVENTION ON THE DUMPING OF WASTE AT SEA, LONDON, 1972. Documents of the final drafting conference for the Convention on the Prevention of Marine Pollution by Dumping of Wastes and other Matter. London, 1972. n.p.

***
VP   Intergovernmental Maritime Consultative Organization. CHARTS OF PROHIBITED ZONES; INTERNATIONAL CONVENTION FOR THE PREVENTION OF POLLUTION OF THE SEA BY OIL. London, 1975.

13
VOD   Intergovernmental Meeting on Ocean Dumping, Reykjavik, 1972. REPORT OF THE INTERGOVERNMENTAL MEETING ON OCEAN DUMPING ADOPTED AT REYKJAVIK, ICELAND, ON 15 APRIL 1972. IMOD/4. Reykjavik, 1972. 1 Vol.

1,2
VODAS   Intergovernmental Oceanographic Commission. LEGAL PROBLEMS ASSOCIATED WITH OCEAN DATA ACQUISITION SYSTEMS (ODAS). A STUDY OF EXISTING NATIONAL AND INTERNATIONAL LEGISLATION, PREPARED JOINTLY BY THE SECRETARIATS OF UNESCO AND IMCO, 1962-68. Revised under the authority of and with the assistance of the IOC Group of Experts on the Legal Status of Ocean Data Acquisition Systems. Paris, UNESCO, 1969. 40p.

17
VOCET   _____ PROJET D'UN CADRE SCIENTIFIQUE GÊNÊRAL POUR L'ÉTUDE DE L'OCÉAN MONDIAL. UNESCO document IOC/89/K. Paris, Commission Océanographique Intergouvernementale, UNESCO, 1964. 85p.

***
IIP&H   INTERNATIONAL ASSOCIATION OF PORTS AND HARBORS: 9th BIENNIAL CONFERENCE: CONFERENCE PAPERS. n.p., 1975? 75p.

***
VP   International Atomic Energy Agency. DISPOSAL OF RADIOACTIVE WASTES INTO RIVERS, LAKES AND ESTUARIES. New York, UNIPUB, 1971. 77p.

***
VP   _____ DISPOSAL OF RADIOACTIVE WASTES INTO SEAS, OCEANS, AND SURFACE WATERS. Vienna, 1966. 898p.

|||
|---|---|
| | ***|
| VMT | International Atomic Energy Agency. Editorial Staff. MARITIME CARRIAGE OF NUCLEAR MATERIALS. Vienna, I.A.E.A., 1973. 418p. |
| | 16 |
| VB | International Bar Association. Committee on Coastal Waters and Appurtenant Subsoil. THE CHARACTER AND SCOPE OF RIGHTS ASSERTED OR EXERCISED BY STATES IN THE WESTERN HEMISPHERE OVER COASTAL WATERS AND APPURTENANT SOIL. The Hague, Nijhoff, 1950. 17p. |
| | *** |
| IIIMM | INTERNATIONAL COMMISSION ON WHALING: TWENTY-SECOND REPORT. London, 1972. 148p. |
| | *** |
| IIIMM | INTERNATIONAL COMMISSION ON WHALING: TWENTY-THIRD REPORT. London, International Commission on Whaling, 1973. 263p. |
| | 7,14 |
| VT&L | International Conference on Marine Pollution, London, 1973. FINAL ACT OF THE CONFERENCE WITH ATTACHMENTS, INCLUDING: INTERNATIONAL CONVENTION FOR THE PREVENTION OF POLLUTION FROM SHIPS, 1973 AND PROTOCOL RELATING TO INTERVENTION ON THE HIGH SEAS IN CASES OF MARINE POLLUTION BY SUBSTANCES OTHER THAN OIL. London, Inter-Governmental Maritime Consultative Organization, 1973. 171p. |
| | 12,16 |
| VP | INTERNATIONAL CONFERENCE ON OIL POLLUTION OF THE SEA, 3d, ROME, 1968. REPORT OF RROCEEDINGS, OCTOBER 7-9, 1968. Winchester, Warren and Son, 1969? 414p. |
| | *** |
| VOCET | INTERNATIONAL CONGRESS MARINE TECHNOLOGY: CONGRESS REPORT, HAMBURG, 1974. Hamburg, Hamburg Messe und Kongress, Gmb H., 1974? 403p. |
| | *** |
| VP | INTERNATIONAL CONVENTION ON PREVENTION OF POLLUTION OF THE SEA BY OIL, 1962- London, Inter-governmental Maritime Consultative Organization, 1962- |
| | *** |
| VP | INTERNATIONAL CONVENTION ON THE PREVENTION OF POLLUTION OF THE SEA BY OIL, 1954, AS AMENDED IN 1962, WITH SUPPLEMENTS INCLUDING AMENDMENTS ADOPTED IN 1969 AND 1971. (Resolutions 175, 232, 246.) London, Inter-governmental Consultative Organization, 1972? |
| | *** |
| VOCET | INTERNATIONAL COUNCIL FOR THE EXPLORATION OF THE SEA. CONTRIBUTIONS TO SPECIAL IGY MEETING 1959. Rapports et procèsverbaux des réunions, 149. Copenhague, Andr. Fred. Høst, 1961. 218p. |
| | *** |
| VOCET | INTERNATIONAL COUNCIL FOR THE EXPLORATION OF THE SEA. 61st- STATUTORY MEETING. Charlottenlund, Denmark, January, 1974- |
| | 13 |
| VOCET | International Decade of Ocean Exploration. PROGRESS REPORT: January 1970/July 1972-July 1972/April 1973. Washington, National Oceanic and Atmospheric Administration, 1973- |

|       |                                                                                                                                                                                                                              |
|-------|------------------------------------------------------------------------------------------------------------------------------------------------------------------------------------------------------------------------------|
| VMMR  | INTERNATIONAL GEOLOGICAL CONGRESS. Twenty-fourth session. Section 8: Marine Geology and Geophysics, held in Montreal, Canada, 1972. Ottawa, Canada, 1972? 249p.                                                              |
| VOCET | INTERNATIONAL INDIAN OCEAN EXPLORATION, 1965-1972. Collected reprints (1-8) and atlas. Paris, UNESCO, 1972?                                                                                                                  |
| VOR   | [8] International Institute for Peace and Conflict Research. TOWARDS A BETTER USE OF THE OCEANS; A STUDY AND PROGNOSIS. Stockholm International Peace Research Institute. Stockholm, 1968. 322p.                             |
| VP    | International Joint Commission. U.S. and Canada. SPECIAL REPORT ON POTENTIAL OIL POLLUTION, EUTROPHICATION AND POLLUTION FROM WATERCRAFT. Washington, D.C., 1970. 36p.                                                       |
| VP    | INTERNATIONAL LEGAL CONFERENCE ON MARINE POLLUTION DAMAGE 1969- Official Records. London, Intergovernmental Consultative Organization, 1969-                                                                                 |
| VP    | INTERNATIONAL LEGAL CONFERENCE ON MARINE POLLUTION DAMAGE, BRUSSELS, 1969. OFFICIAL RECORDS. London, Inter-governmental Maritime Consultative Organization, 1973. 918p.                                                       |
| VMT   | INTERNATIONAL LEGAL CONFERENCE ON MARITIME CARRIAGE OF NUCLEAR SUBSTANCES. London, Inter-governmental Maritime Consultative Organization, 1971.                                                                              |
| VOI   | International Management and Engineering Group of Britain, Ltd. STUDY OF POTENTIAL BENEFITS TO BRITISH INDUSTRY FROM OFFSHORE OIL AND GAS DEVELOPMENTS. London, H.M.S.O., 1972. 136p.                                        |
| VOCET | [17] International Marine Information Symposium, Washington, D.C., 1968. PAPERS PRESENTED. Washington, D.C., Marine Technology Society, 1969. viii, 20.a, 200p.                                                              |
| VOCET | [5,13] INTERNATIONAL MARINE SCIENCE AFFAIRS. A REPORT BY THE INTERNATIONAL MARINE SCIENCE AFFAIRS PANEL OF THE COMMITTEE ON OCEANOGRAPHY. Washington, National Academy of Sciences, 1972. xi, 92p.                           |
| VLOS  | [16] INTERNATIONAL OCEAN AFFAIRS - A SPECIAL REPORT ON THE IMPLEMENTATION OF THE UNITED NATIONS RESOLUTION ON THE RESOURCES OF THE SEA. FAO Fisheries Reports No. 41, Rome, Supp. 3, 1967. 37p.                              |
| VOR   | [16] INTERNATIONAL OCEAN INSTITUTE. REPORT OF THE DIRECTOR 1972/73- Msida, Royal University of Malta, 1974-                                                                                                                  |

                                                                    17
VOCET     International Oceanographic Congress, 2d, Moscow, 1966. MORNING
          REVIEW LECTURES. UNESCO document SC/NS.67/D.59/AF. Paris, UNESCO,
          1969. 256p.

                                                                    16
IVMMR     International Offshore Exploration Conference, 1st, Athens, 1968.
          OECON: MIDDLE EAST, PROCEEDINGS. Long Beach, Calif., Offshore
          Exploration Conference, 1968. 480p.

                                                                   ART
IIP       INTERNATIONAL REGULATION OF POLLUTION FROM LAND-BASED SOURCES. In
          Marine Affairs Journal, Report no. 3. Narragansett, University of
          Rhode Island, 1975.

                                                                   ***
IVMMR     INTERNATIONAL SYMPOSIUM ON OFFSHORE PETROLEUM AND CANADA'S CONTINEN-
          TAL MARGINS, held in Calgary, Canada, September 23-October 2, 1973.
          Proceedings. Calgary, Alberta Society of Petroleum Geologists,
          1974?

                                                                   ***
IVMMR     INTERREGIONAL SEMINAR ON THE DEVELOPMENT OF THE MINERAL RESOURCES OF
          THE CONTINENTAL SHELF, PORT-OF-SPAIN, 1971. United Nations techni-
          cal papers ST/TAO/SER.C/138. New York, United Nations, 1972. 172p.

                                                                   ***
VOR       Irby, Bobby N., and Della McCaughan. GUIDE TO THE MARINE RESOURCES
          OF MISSISSIPPI. MASGAP-75-015. Ocean Springs, Mississippi/Alabama
          Sea Grant Consortium, 1975. 351p.

                                                                    13
VENE      Irwin, John N. THE INTERNATIONAL IMPLICATIONS OF THE ENERGY SITUA-
          TION. Reprinted from Department of State Bulletin, May 1, 1972.

                                                                   ART
IVMMR     Isaacs, Charles R. DREDGING FOR BULK SAMPLES OF MANGANESE NODULES.
          In Offshore Technology Conference, 5th, Houston, Texas, 1973: Pre-
          prints. Dallas, Tex., 1973. Vol. 2. pp. 359-368.

                                                                   ***
VP        Isakson, J.S., et al. COMPARISON OF ECOLOGICAL IMPACTS OF POSTU-
          LATED OIL SPILLS AT SELECTED ALASKAN LOCATIONS. Prepared by Mathe-
          matical Sciences Northwest, Inc., Bellevue, Wash. Washington, D.C.,
          U.S. Department of Transportation, Coast Guard, 1975. xi, 852p.

                                                                    14
IIIF      Isely, Mary B., et al. UNCOMMON CONTROVERSY; FISHING RIGHTS OF THE
          MUCKLESHOOT, PUYALLUP, AND NISQUALLY INDIANS. A report prepared for
          the American Friends Service Committee. Seattle, University of
          Washington Press, 1975. xxxv, 232p.

                                                                     1
VLOS      Instituto Affari Internazionali (IAI) Rome, Italy. SYMPOSIUM ON
          THE INTERNATIONAL REGIME OF THE SEA-BED. June 30 - July 5, 1969.

                                                                   13,15
IIIAFF    Iversen, F.S. FARMING THE EDGE OF THE SEA. London, Fishing News
          (Books) Ltd., 1968. 301p.

| | | |
|---|---|---|
| VP | Ives, Joseph S., ed. POLLUTION CONTROL AND THE MARINE INDUSTRY; PROCEEDINGS OF THE CONFERENCE SPONSORED BY THE INTERNATIONAL ASSOCIATION FOR POLLUTION CONTROL, HELD AT NEW ORLEANS, LA., APRIL 1-3, 1971. Bethesda, Md., 1971. 250p. | *** |
| VORM | Izrael', Yu A. PEACEFUL NUCLEAR EXPLOSIONS AND ENVIRONMENT, U.S.S.R. Arlington, Va., Joint Publications Research Service, 1974. 143p. | *** |
| VCONS | Jackson, Barbara W., and René Dubos. ONLY ONE EARTH; THE CARE AND MAINTENANCE OF A SMALL PLANET. 1st ed. New York, Norton, 1972. xxv, 225p. | 17 |
| IIIF | Jackson, Gerry A. A SPORT FISHING SURVEY OF BILOXI BAY AND THE ADJACENT MISSISSIPPI SOUND. Master's thesis, Mississippi State University, 1972. MSGP-72-013. Ocean Springs, Mississippi-Alabama Sea Grant Consortium, 1972. | *** |
| VCS | Jackson, Henry M. SELECTED MATERIALS ON THE OUTER CONTINENTAL SHELF. Memorandum by Senator Henry M. Jackson of Washington, Chairman of the Committee on Interior and Insular Affairs, United States Senate. 91st Congr., 1st sess., committee print. Washington, U.S.G.P.O., 1969. vii, 47p. | 13,16 |
| VENV | Jackson, W. MAN AND THE ENVIRONMENT. 2d ed. Dubuque, Iowa, William C. Brown Company Publishers, 1973. 338p. | *** |
| IICZM | Jackson, William L. THE EVOLVING ROLE OF THE FEDERAL GOVERNMENT IN THE MANAGEMENT OF LAKE MICHIGAN. Sea Grant Technical report no. 24. MICHU-SG-72-209. Ann Arbor, University of Michigan Sea Grant Program, 1972. xiii, 129p. | 13 |
| VLOS | Jacobsen, Friedrich J. LAW OF THE SEA. Baltimore, Coale, 1818. 636p. | 16 |
| VLOS | Jacobson, Jon L. BRIDGING THE GAP TO INTERNATIONAL FISHERIES AGREEMENT: A GUIDE FOR UNILATERAL ACTION. Reprinted from The San Diego Law Review, Vol. 9, no. 3., 1972. pp. 455-490. | 13 |
| VB | ———— OCEAN ZONES AND BOUNDARIES - INTERNATIONAL LAW AND OCEANS. Oregon State University Sea Grant Extension Marine Advisory Program, Man and his Ocean Publication No. 10. Corvallis, Oregon State University, n.d. 8p. | 13 |
| VMLAD | Jados, Stanley S. CONSULATE OF THE SEA, AND RELATED DOCUMENTS. University, Ala., University of Alabama Press, 1975. xiii, 326p. | 14,16 |
| IIIF | Jaeger, Sig, and Lois Hansen. A LIMITED ENTRY COLLAGE: SOME PUBLISHED ASPECTS, 1974/1975. Seattle, Washington Sea Grant Program, | *** |

Division of Marine Resources, 1975.

IIIF  Jaeger, Sigfryed. AN OVERVIEW OF COMMERCIAL FISHING VESSEL SAFETY IN THE NORTHWEST AND ALTERNATIVES FOR LOSS PREVENTION. A joint publication, Marine Advisory Services, Washington Sea Grant Program, Alaska Sea Grant Program. Division of Marine Resources, Seattle, University of Washington, April 1974. 32p.
[14]

VENV  Jamaica Bay Environmental Study Group. JAMAICA BAY AND KENNEDY AIRPORT: A MULTIDISCIPLINARY ENVIRONMENTAL STUDY; A REPORT. Washington, National Academy of Sciences, 1971.
[15]

IIP&H  James, W.P., et al. ENVIRONMENTAL ASPECTS OF A SUPERTANKER PORT ON THE TEXAS GULF COAST. TAMU-SG-73-201. College Station, Texas A&M University, 1972. 460p.
[***]

VLOS  Janis, Mark W. THE DEVELOPMENT OF EUROPEAN REGIONAL LAW OF THE SEA. A paper prepared for the Conference on Developments in the law of the sea, sponsored by the American Society of International Law and the Northwestern School of Law of Lewis and Clark College, Portland, Oregon, May 12, 1973. 25p.
[1]

VLOS  Janis, Mark W., and Donald C.F. Daniel. THE U.S.S.R.: OCEAN USE AND OCEAN LAW. Law of the Sea Institute occasional paper no. 21. Kingston, University of Rhode Island, May 1974. 22p.
[1,4,7,8,10,11,13,14,15,18]

VP  Janssen, H.M.J. DE VERVUILING VAN DE ZEE EN HET VOLKENRECHT. Zwolle, Tjeenk Willink, 1973. 64p.
[***]

VOI  Jantscher, Gerald R. BREAD UPON THE WATERS, FEDERAL AIDS TO THE MARITIME INDUSTRIES. Washington, D.C., n.p., 1975. 164p.
[14]

VENV  Japan. Environmental Agency of the Japanese Government. ENVIRONMENTAL LAWS AND REGULATIONS IN JAPAN. Tokyo, 1974. 317p.
[***]

VINTL  The Japan Federation of Bar Associations. WE APPEAL AGAIN TO THE LAWYERS OF THE WORLD: ILLEGALITY OF "RHEE LINE" AND UNLAWFUL ARREST OF JAPANESE FISHERMEN. Tokyo? 1960.
[1,16]

IIIF  Japan Fisheries Association. STATEMENT BEFORE THE SUB-COMMITTEE ON MERCHANT MARINE AND FISHERIES OF THE COMMERCE COMMITTEE OF THE UNITED STATES SENATE, MAY 1965.
[1]

VP  Jardas, I., and I. Munjko. PRELIMINARY OBSERVATIONS OF OIL AND PHENOL DISTRIBUTION IN THE CENTRAL ADRIATIC. Split, Yugoslavia, Institut za Oceanogrifiju i Ribarstvo, 1972. 7p.
[***]

                                                                    2
VENV     Jeans, James W., ed. UTILIZING SCIENTIFIC TESTIMONY - ENVIRONMENTAL
         HEALTH. Contributors: Horace Campbell, and others. Cincinnati,
         W.H. Anderson, 1970. 85p.

                                                                  ***
VP       Jenkins, S.H., ed. ADVANCES IN WATER POLLUTION RESEARCH. Sixth
         Conference of the International Association on Water Pollution Re-
         search. Oxford, Pergamon Press, 1973. 898p.

                                                                  ***
IIIOSTR  Jensen, Albert C. ARTIFICIAL FISHING REEFS. Atlas Monograph 18.
         Albany, State University of New York, New York Sea Grant Institute,
         1975. 28p.

                                                                  ***
IIIF     Jensen, John W. PROGRESS REPORT ON FISHERIES DEVELOPMENT IN NORTH-
         EAST BRAZIL. Alabama, Auburn University, International Center for
         Aquaculture, 1976. 7p.

                                                                  ***
IIIF     Jensen, William S. THE SALMON PROCESSING INDUSTRY. PART ONE: THE
         INSTITUTIONAL FRAMEWORK AND ITS EVOLUTION. Sea Grant publication
         no. ORESU-T-76-003. Corvallis, Oregon State University, Sea Grant
         College Program, 1976. 37p.

                                                                   13
IVMMR    Jenkins, Richard L., and Alvin H. Lense. MARINE HEAVY METALS PRO-
         JECT OFFSHORE NOME, ALASKA JULY - AUGUST 1967. Bureau of Mines Tech-
         nical Progress Report - 4 Heavy Metals Program. Washington, U.S.
         Department of the Interior, 1968. 11p.

                                                                  ART
VP       Jernelov, A. ENVIRONMENTAL DYNAMICS OF MERCURY. In Environmental
         Mercury Contamination, ed. by R. Hartung and R.D. Dinman. Ann Arbor,
         Mich., Science Publishers, 1972. pp. 167-178.

                                                        1,3,5,7,8,12,16
VINTL    Jessup, Philip C. THE LAW OF TERRITORIAL WATERS AND MARITIME JURIS-
         DICTION. New York, G.A. Jennings Company, Inc., 1927. 548p.

                                                                  ***
VLOS     Johnson, B. LAW OF THE SEA. New York, Dobbs Ferry, Oceana Publica-
         tions, Inc., 1974.

                                                                    1
VINTL    Johnson, Bo. SUVERÄNITET I HAVET OCH LUFTRUMMET. FOLKRÄTTSLIGA
         STUDIER KRING SUVERÄNITETSANSPRAK I ÖPPNA HAVET SAMT DEN NATIONELLA
         JURISDIKTIONENS GRÄNSER I HAVET OCH LUFTRUMMET. (Souveraineté sur
         la mer et dans les Airs. Étude sur les droits de souveraineté en
         haute mer et les limites de la juridiction nationale sur la mer et
         dans l'espace aérien.) Stockholm, P.A. Norstedt and Söners Förlag,
         1972. 413p.

                                                                   16
VENV     Johnson, Brian. THIRD WORLD AND ENVIRONMENTAL INTERESTS IN THE LAW
         OF THE SEA. New York, International Institute for Environment and
         Development, 1974? 37p.

                                                              1
VMT        Johnson, D.H.N.  SOME LEGAL PROBLEMS OF INTERNATIONAL WATERWAYS,
           WITH PARTICULAR REFERENCE TO THE STRAITS OF TIRAN AND THE SUEZ CANAL.
           Reprinted from The Modern Law Review, March 1968, pp. 153-164.

                                                             17
VENV       Johnson, Huey D., ed.  National Conference on UNESCO, 13th, San Fran-
           cisco, 1969.  NO DEPOSIT - NO RETURN.  MAN AND HIS ENVIRONMENT:  A
           VIEW TOWARD SURVIVAL.  Reading, Mass., Addison-Wesley Publishing
           Company, 1970.  xvi, 351p.

                                          1,2,3,5,7,9,12,13,14
IIIINTL    Johnston, Douglas M.  THE INTERNATIONAL LAW OF FISHERIES:  A FRAME-
           WORK FOR POLICY-ORIENTED INQUIRIES.  New Haven, Yale University
           Press, 1965.  xi, 554p.

                                       1,4,5,7,8,10,11,13,14,15
VEZ        Johnston, Douglas M., and Edgar Gold.  THE ECONOMIC ZONE IN THE LAW
           OF THE SEA:  SURVEY, ANALYSIS AND APPRAISAL OF CURRENT TRENDS.  Law
           of the Sea Institute occasional paper no. 17.  Kingston, University
           of Rhode Island, 1973.  iii, 53p.

                                                       14,15,16
VP         JOINT CONFERENCE ON PREVENTION AND CONTROL OF OIL SPILLS, WASHINGTON,
           D.C., 1971.  PROCEEDINGS, Washington, D.C., American Petroleum
           Institute, 1971?  vii, 544p.

                                                            ***
VP         JOINT CONFERENCE ON PREVENTION AND CONTROL OF OIL SPILLS, WASHINGTON,
           D.C., 1973.  PROCEEDINGS.  Washington, D.C., 1973.  834p.

                                                            ***
VOI        THE JOINT PROBLEMS OF THE OIL AND WATER INDUSTRIES.  PROCEEDINGS OF
           A SYMPOSIUM OF THE OIL AND WATER INDUSTRIES WORKING GROUP.  Barking,
           Essex, England, Applied Science Publishers, 1967.  159p.

                                         2,3,5,6,7,12,13,14,16
VLOS       Jones, Erin B.  LAW OF THE SEA; OCEANIC RESOURCES.  Dallas, South-
           ern Methodist University Press, 1972.  xiv, 162p.

                                                             13
IIIOCET    Jones, F.R. Harden, ed.  SEA FISHERIES RESEARCH.  London, Paul Elek
           (Scientific Books) Ltd., 1974.  xvii, 510p.

                                                             13
IICZM      Jones, Lamar B., and G. Randolph Rice.  AN ECONOMIC BASE STUDY OF
           COASTAL LOUISIANA.  Condusted under the auspices of Louisiana State
           University's Sea Grant Program... LSU-SG-72-02.  Baton Rouge, Cen-
           ter for Wetland Resources, Louisiana State University, 1972.  xiii,
           172p.

                                                             14
VINTL      Jones, Nancy K.  FLAGS OF CONVENIENCE IN THE PACIFIC:  PROSPECTS
           FOR PROLIFERATION, IMPACT, AND REGULATION.  Working paper no. 7.
           Honolulu, University of Hawaii, Sea Grant College, 1975.  28p.

                                                             15
VINTL      Jones, Stephen B.  BOUNDARY-MAKING, A HANDBOOK FOR STATESMEN, TREATY
           EDITORS AND BOUNDARY COMMISSIONERS.  Washington, Carnegie Endowment
           for International Peace, Division of International Law, 1945.

                                                                13
VINTL     Jonsson, Hannes. ICELAND AND THE LAW OF THE SEA. Reykjavik, Ice-
          land, Government of Iceland, 1972. 48p.

                                                               ART
VP        Jordan, Leo, and Louis K. Bragaw. COAST GUARD OIL POLLUTION CONTROL
          SYSTEMS. In Offshore Technology Conference, 6th, Houston, Texas,
          1974: Preprints. Dallas, Tex., 1974. Vol. 1, pp. 550-558.

                                                                14
VLOS      Josephson, Karla. ALASKA AND THE LAW OF THE SEA: USE OF THE SEA BY
          ALASKA NATIVES - A HISTORICAL PERSPECTIVE. Anchorage, Arctic Envir-
          onmental Information and Data Center, 1974. 94p.

                                                                13
IICZM     Journal of the State Bar of California. SYMPOSIUM ISSUE: CALIFOR-
          NIA'S COASTLINE. Vol. 47, 1972. pp. 395-544.

                                                                14
IVLOS     Joyner, Christopher C. INTERNATIONAL LAW OF THE SEA AND THE FUTURE
          OF DEEP SEABED MINING. Charlottesville, Va., John Bassett Moore
          Society, 1975. 8.50.

                                                              14,16
VB        Juda, Lawrence. OCEAN SPACE RIGHTS: DEVELOPING U.S. POLICY. New
          York, Praeger, 1975. xiii, 300p.

                                                               ***
VOCET     Jue, Martin F., et al. AN AUTOMATIC TERRAIN-FOLLOWING CONTROL SYS-
          TEM FOR A DEEP-TOWED SUBMERSIBLE. Paper presented at the Sixth
          Annual Offshore Technology Conference, Houston, Texas, 7 May, 1974.
          MASGP-74-045. Ocean Springs, Mississippi-Alabama Sea Grant Consor-
          tium, 1974.

                                                                16
VMLAD     Justice, Alexander. A GENERAL TREATISE OF THE DOMINION OF THE SEA.
          London, 1710. 107p.

                                                               ***
IIIFP     Kahn, Lesie N., and Sun-de Tong. SQUID PROTEIN CONCENTRATES.
          MITSG 75-16. Cambridge, Massachusetts Institute of Technology,
          1975. 13p.

                                                                13
IIIF      Kalikstein, Paul H. THE MARKETABILITY OF SQUID. MITSG 74-24. Cam-
          bridge, Massachusetts Institute of Technology, May 20, 1974. iv,
          108p.

                                                               2,13
VOR       Kallen, Horace M. TOWARD A PHILOSOPHY OF THE SEAS. Charlottesville,
          University Press of Virginia, 1973. ix, 44p.

                                                                 3
VMLAD     Kaltenborn und Stachau, Carl. GRUNDSÄTZE DES PRAKTISCHEN EUROPAI-
          SCHEN SEERECHTS, BESONDERS IM PRIVATVERKEHRE, MIT RUCKSICHT AUF ALLE
          WICHTIGEREN PARTIKULARRECHTE, NAMENTLICH DER NORDDEUTSCHEN SEESTAAT-
          EN, BESONDERS PREUSSENS UND DER HANSESTÄDTE, SOWIE HOLLANDS FRANK-
          REICHS, SPANIENS, ENGLANDS, NORDAMERIKAS, DÄNEMARKS, SCHWEDENS, RUSS-
          LANDS, VNSW. Berlin, C. Heymann, 1851. 2 Vols.

|         |                                                                                                                                                                                                                                                                                                       |
|---------|-------------------------------------------------------------------------------------------------------------------------------------------------------------------------------------------------------------------------------------------------------------------------------------------------------|
|         | ***                                                                                                                                                                                                                                                                                                   |
| VENE    | Kalter, Robert J., et al. ATLANTIC OUTER CONTINENTAL ENERGY RESOURCES: AN ECONOMIC ANALYSIS. Ithaca, N.Y., Cornell University, Sea Grant Services, 1974. 88p.                                                                                                                                         |
|         | ***                                                                                                                                                                                                                                                                                                   |
| IVMMR   | Kalter, Robert J., and Wallace E. Tyner. ATLANTIC OUTER CONTINENTAL SHELF ENERGY RESOURCES: ECONOMIC IMPLICATIONS FOR LONG ISLAND. Cornell Agricultural Economics Staff Paper no. 75-1. Albany, State University of New York, Sea Grant Institute, 1975. 76p.                                         |
|         | ***                                                                                                                                                                                                                                                                                                   |
| IVOL    | Kalter, Robert J., et al. THE ECONOMICS OF ACCELERATED OUTER CONTINENTAL SHELF LEASING. Cornell Agricultural Economics Staff Paper no. 74-18. Albany, State University of New York, Sea Grant Institute, 1974. 18p.                                                                                   |
|         | ART                                                                                                                                                                                                                                                                                                   |
| IIIF    | Kambona, J.J. SHORE AND REEF FISHERIES. In International Conference on Marine Resources Development in Eastern Africa, held at The University of Dar es Salaam, Tanzania, April 4-9, 1974, in cooperation with the International Center for Marine Resource Development of the University of Rhode Island. Kingston, University of Rhode Island, 1974. pp. 15-28. |
|         | 1,5,6,12,16,18                                                                                                                                                                                                                                                                                        |
| IIIAFF  | Kane, Thomas E. AQUACULTURE AND THE LAW. Sea Grant technical bulletin no. 2. Miami, Fla., University of Miami, 1970. iv, 98p.                                                                                                                                                                         |
|         | ART                                                                                                                                                                                                                                                                                                   |
| IICZM   | _____ LEGAL ASPECTS AND PROBLEMS OF THE NORTH CAROLINA COAST. In Planning and Engineering in the Coastal Zone. Proceedings of Seminar held in Charleston, S.C., June 8-9, 1972. Seminar series no. 2. Wilmington, N.C., 1972. pp. 91-94.                                                           |
|         | ART                                                                                                                                                                                                                                                                                                   |
| IIISF   | Kasahara, Hiroshi. FOOD PRODUCTION FROM THE OCEAN. In Conference on Law, Organization and Security in the Use of the Ocean, 1st, Columbus, Ohio, 1967: Papers and discussions of the Conference. Columbus, Ohio, Mershon Center for Education in National Security, 1967. 43p.                       |
|         | 14a                                                                                                                                                                                                                                                                                                   |
| IIIF    | Kasahara, Hiroshi, and William T. Burke. INTERNATIONAL FISHERY MANAGEMENT IN THE NORTH PACIFIC: PRESENT AND FUTURE. Seattle? University of Washington? 1972. 248p.                                                                                                                                    |
|         | 13                                                                                                                                                                                                                                                                                                    |
| IIIOR   | Kasahara, Hiroshi. PROBLEMS OF ALLOCATION AS APPLIED TO THE EXPLOITATION OF THE LIVING RESOURCES OF THE SEA. Law of the Sea Institute, Kingston, University of Rhode Island, 1972. 11p.                                                                                                               |
|         | 5,16                                                                                                                                                                                                                                                                                                  |
| IIIF    | Kasahara, Hiroshi, and William T. Burke. NORTH PACIFIC FISHERIES MANAGEMENT. Washington, D.C., Resources for the Future, 1973. xiv, 91p.                                                                                                                                                              |

                                                                13,16
VENE    Kash, Don E., et al.  ENERGY UNDER THE OCEANS:  A TECHNOLOGY ASSESS-
        MENT OF OUTER CONTINENTAL SHELF OIL AND GAS OPERATIONS.  Norman, Uni-
        versity of Oklahoma Press, 1973.  xxii, 378p.

                                                1,3,4,5,11,13,14,15
IIIF    Kask, J.L.  TUNA - A WORLD RESOURCE.  Law of the Sea Institute oc-
        casional paper no. 2.  Kingston, University of Rhode Island, May,
        1969.  32, ixp.

                                                                    ART
IICZM   Kassas, M.  IMPACT OF RIVER CONTROL SCHEMES ON THE SHORELINE OF THE
        NILE DELTA.  In The Careless Technology.  Garden City, New York,
        Doubleday and Company, Inc., Natural History Press, 1972.

                                                                 16,18
VLOS    Katin, Ernest.  THE LEGAL STATUS OF THE CONTINENTAL SHELF AS DETER-
        MINED BY THE CONVENTIONS ADOPTED AT THE 1958 UNITED NATIONS CONFER-
        ENCE ON THE LAW OF THE SEA; AN ANALYTICAL STUDY OF AN INSTANCE OF
        INTERNATIONAL LAW MAKING.  Ann Arbor, University Microfilms, 1967.
        272p.

                                                                    16
VC      Keasbey, Lindley M.  THE NATIONAL CANAL POLICY.  Washington, U.S.
        G.P.O., 1903.  In Annual Report of the American Historical Associ-
        ation for 1902, Vol. I, pp. 276-288.

                                                                  5,15
VB      Kehden, Max I.  DIE INANSPRUCHNAHME VON MEERESZONEN UND MEERESBODEN-
        ZONEN DURCH KÜSTENSTAATEN.  Hamburg, Alfred Metzner Verlag, 1971.

                                                                    13
IVMMR   Keiffer, Elisabeth, ed.  MINERAL RESOURCES OF THE WORLD OCEAN.  Pro-
        ceedings of a Symposium held at the Naval War College, Newport,
        Rhode Island, July 11-12, 1968.  Occasional publication no. 4.  King-
        ston, University of Rhode Island, 1968.  108p.

                                                                    14
IIREC   Kelly, Ernest S.  CANADIAN BOATING LAW.  Self-Counsel series.  Van-
        couver:  International Self-Counsel Press, 1974.  104p.

                                                                    16
IISL    Kerrins, Joseph A.  COAST GUARD REGULATIONS IN THE TIDELANDS.  In
        Slovenko, Ralph, ed., Oil and Gas Operations.  Baton Rouge, Clai-
        tor's, 1963.  pp. 256-267.

                                                      2,5,12,15,16,17
IICZM   Ketchum, Bostwick H., ed.  THE WATER'S EDGE:  CRITICAL PROBLEMS OF
        THE COASTAL ZONE.  The Institute of Ecology Coastal Zone Workshop,
        Woods Hole, Mass., 22 May-3 June, 1972.  Cambridge, Massachusetts
        Institute of Technology Press, 1972.  ix, 393p.

                                                                     1
VMT     Khatib, M. Fathalla El, and Omar Z. Ghobashy.  THE SUEZ CANAL:
        SAFE AND FREE PASSAGE.  Arab Information Center, Information paper
        no. 9.  New York, November, 1960.

                                                                     1
VMT     Khoshkish, Anoushiravan.  THE RIGHT OF INNOCENT PASSAGE:  A STUDY
        IN INTERNATIONAL MARITIME LAW.  Thesis, University of Geneva.

Geneva, Éditions Générales, 1954. 168p.

***

VINTL    Kiel, Universität. Institut für Internationales Recht. DIE NUTZUNG DES MEERESGRUNDES AUSSERHALB DES FESTLANDSOCKELS (TIEFSEE); VORTRÄGE UND DISKUSSIONEN EINES SYMPOSIUMS, VERANSTALTET VOM INSTITUT FÜR INTERNATIONALES RECHT AN DER UNIVERSITÄT KIEL 25.-28. MÄRZ 1969. Hamburg, Hansischer Gildenverlag, 1970.

ART
VOR    Kilian, W. EXPLOITATION OF THE RESOURCES OF THE SUBSOIL OF THE SEA: THE CASE FOR AN INTERIM ARRANGEMENT. In Conference on World Peace through Law. Fourth World Conference, Bangkok, 1969. Proceedings. Genève, 1971. pp. 486-501.

***

VOCET    Killen, Harold B., and Richard D. Benton. A TIME-SHARED TELEMETRY SYSTEM FOR A TOWED UNMANNED OBSERVATION PLATFORM. Paper presented at the Fourth Annual Offshore Technology Conference, Houston, Texas, 2 May 1972. MSGP-72-016. Ocean Springs, Mississippi-Alabama Sea Grant Consortium, 1974.

***

IVMMR    Kilpatrick, Joseph E. THE ROLE OF NORTH CAROLINA IN REGULATING OFFSHORE PETROLEUM DEVELOPMENT. UNC-SG-75-09. Raleigh, North Carolina State University, April, 1975. 29p.

14
VLOS    Kimball, Lee. THE LAW OF THE SEA CONFERENCE: A MAJOR TEST OF INTERNATIONAL COOPERATION. Communique Series; no. 27. Washington, D.C., Overseas Development Council, 1976.

***

IVOCET    King, Cuchlaine A.M. INTRODUCTION TO MARINE GEOLOGY AND GEOMORPHOLOGY. London, Edward Arnold Ltd.; New York, Crane, Russak and Company, 1975. 314p.

5
VOCET    _____ AN INTRODUCTION TO OCEANOGRAPHY. McGraw-Hill Book Company, Inc., 1969.

***

VOCET    _____ OCEANOGRAPHY FOR GEOGRAPHERS. London, Edward Arnold, 1962. 337p.

13
VOCET    King, Lauriston R. OCEANOGRAPHERS, POLITICAL INTELLIGENCE, AND FREEDOM OF OCEAN RESEARCH. Woods Hole, Mass., Woods Hole Oceanographic Institution, 1972. 28p.

***

VENV    Kinne, O. MARINE ECOLOGY. New York, Wiley-Interscience, 1971. 681p.

***

VENV    Kinne, O., ed. MARINE ECOLOGY. New York, Wiley-Interscience, 1972. 1774p.

                ***

VP        Kinney, P.J., and D.R. Button. A QUANTITATIVE ASSESSMENT OF OIL POLLUTION PROBLEMS IN ALASKA'S COOK INLET. Fairbanks, University of Alaska, Institute of Marine Science, 1975. 116p.

                6,14,16

VINTL    Kish, John. THE LAW OF INTERNATIONAL SPACES. Leyden, Sijthoff, 1973. xi, 236p.

                13,14

VENV     Kisicki, Donald R. ENVIRONMENTAL MANAGEMENT OF THE GREAT LAKES INTERNATIONAL BOUNDARY AREAS; A CASE STUDY OF THE NIAGARA URBAN REGION. Great Lakes Management Problems series. Albany, New York State Sea Grant Program, 1973. xiv, 301p.

                17

VENV     Klausner, Samuel Z., ed. SOCIETY AND ITS PHYSICAL ENVIRONMENT. The Annals of the American Academy of Political and Social Science, Vol. 389. Philadelphia, American Academy of Political and Social Science, 1970. vii, 187p.

                ***

VENE     Klineburg, Otto, ed. SOCIAL IMPLICATIONS OF THE PEACEFUL USES OF NUCLEAR ENERGY. New York, UNIPUB, 1964. 169p.

                13

VLOS     Knauss, John A. DEVELOPMENT OF THE FREEDOM OF SCIENTIFIC RESEARCH ISSUE OF THE THIRD LAW OF THE SEA CONFERENCE. Mimeo. Kingston, R.I., 1973. 34, 15p.

                1,2,3,4,7,8,11,13,14,15

VLOS     _____ FACTORS INFLUENCING A U.S. POSITION IN A FUTURE LAW OF THE SEA CONFERENCE. Law of the Sea Institute occasional paper no. 10. Kingston, University of Rhode Island. April, 1971. 30p.

                13

VP        _____ OCEAN POLLUTION - STATUS AND PROGNOSTICATION. Presented at the Eighth Annual Law of the Sea Conference, Kingston, Rhode Island. June 21, 1973. 20p.

                13

VLOS     _____ THE STATUS OF SCIENTIFIC RESEARCH AT THE SECOND PREPARATORY CONFERENCE FOR LOS-73. Remarks made as a panel member on Geneva Report, a seminar sponsored by the Marine Technology Society, October 18, 1971, Washington, D.C.; Geneva, 1971. 7p.

                ART

VOCET    _____ UNSOLVED PROBLEMS IN MARINE SCIENCE - 1977. *In* Conference on Law, Organization and Security in the Use of the Ocean, 1st, Columbus, Ohio, Mershon Center for Education in National Security, 1967. Vol. 2. 14p.

                ***

VP        Knebel, H.J. MOVEMENT AND EFFECTS OF SPILLED OIL OVER THE OUTER CONTINENTAL SHELF - INADEQUACY OF EXISTENT DATA FOR THE BALTIMORE CANYON TROUGH AREA. Circular 702. n.p., U.S. Geological Survey, 1974. 20p.

                                                                    15
VENV        Kneese, Allen V., and Blair T. Bower, eds. ENVIRONMENTAL QUALITY
            ANALYSIS; THEORY AND METHOD IN THE SOCIAL SCIENCES. PAPERS FROM
            A RESOURCES FOR THE FUTURE CONFERENCE. Baltimore, Md., n.d.

                                                                     2
VENV        Kneese, Allen V., et al. ECONOMICS AND THE ENVIRONMENT; A MATERI-
            ALS BALANCE APPROACH. Washington, Resources for the Future; dis-
            tributed by the Johns Hopkins Press, Baltimore, 1970. x, 120p.

                                                                    13
VLOS        Knight, H. Gary. ALTERNATIVES TO A LAW OF THE SEA TREATY. Paper
            prepared for the Conference on the Law of the Sea sponsored by the
            American Enterprise Institute for Public Policy Research and the
            U.S. Treasury Department, February 14, 1975. n.p. 24p.

                                                                    13
IVMMR       _____ THE DEEP SEABED HARD MINERAL RESOURCES ACT - A NEGA-
            TIVE VIEW. Reprinted from the San Diego Law Review, Vol. 10, no.
            3, May 1973. pp. 446-466.

                                                                    13
VLOS        _____ THE DRAFT UNITED NATIONS CONVENTION ON THE INTERNATION-
            AL SEABED AREA: BACKGROUND, DESCRIPTION AND SOME PRELIMINARY
            THOUGHTS. Reprinted from The San Diego Law Review, Vol. 8, May,
            1971. pp. 459-550.

                                                                     1
VLOS        _____ IMPACTS OF SOME LAW OF THE SEA PROPOSALS ON GULF AND
            CARIBBEAN OCEAN RESOURCE DEVELOPMENT. In Pacem in Maribus IV,
            Caribbean Study Project Working Papers. International Ocean Insti-
            tute, University of Malta, 1973. pp. 366-413.

                                                                   1,13
IIINTL      _____ INTERNATIONAL LEGAL ASPECTS OF DEEP DRAFT HARBOR
            FACILITIES. Reprinted from Journal of Maritime Law and Commerce,
            Vol. 4, no. 3, April 1973. pp. 367-395.

                                                                     1
VLOS        _____ ISSUES BEFORE THE THIRD UNITED NATIONS CONFERENCE ON
            THE LAW OF THE SEA. Reprinted from Louisiana Law Review, Vol. 34,
            no. 2, Winter 1974, pp. 155-196.

                                                                 14,15,18
VLOS        _____ LAW OF THE SEA: CASES, DOCUMENTS, AND READINGS. Wash-
            ington, D.C., Nautilus Press, Inc., 1975. 871p.

                                                                    13
VLOS        _____ LEGAL ASPECTS OF THE SEA. A paper prepared for the
            Conference on Seapower and Contemporary History, organized by the
            Woodrow Wilson International Center for Scholars, Washington, D.C.,
            February 20, 1973. 16p.

                                                                    13
VLOS        _____ THE 1971 UNITED STATES PROPOSALS ON THE BREADTH OF
            THE TERRITORIAL SEA AND PASSAGE THROUGH INTERNATIONAL STRAITS.
            n.p., 1972. 45, 19p.

                                                                    16
IICZM     Knight, H. Gary. ORGANIZATION TO DEAL WITH COASTAL ZONE PROBLEMS:
          THE LOCAL PERSPECTIVE. Paper at First Annual Institute of Ocean
          Law, University of Miami, Florida, December 10, 1969.

                                                                    16
IICZM     _____ THE ROLE OF THE CONTINENTAL SHELF IN SYSTEMS OF COAST-
          AL MANAGEMENT. Paper at the Conference on Management Systems for
          the Resources of the Coastal Zone. Charleston, South Carolina, June
          8, 1970.

                                                                   1,16
VORM      _____ SPECIAL DOMESTIC INTERESTS AND UNITED STATES OCEANS
          POLICY. In Wirsing, ed., International Relations and the Future of
          Ocean Space. University of South Carolina Press, 1974. pp. 10-43.

                                                                    13
IVMMR     _____ STATEMENT ON H.R. 13904 (THE "DEEP SEABED HARD MINERAL
          RESOURCES ACT"), BEFORE THE SUBCOMMITTEE ON OCEANOGRAPHY OF THE COM-
          MITTEE ON MERCHANT MARINE AND FISHERIES, U.S. HOUSE OF REPRESENTA-
          TIVES. MAY 12, 1972. Photocopy. New Orleans, Louisiana State Uni-
          versity, 1972. 11p.

                                                                    13
VLOS      _____ STATEMENT ON UNITED STATES OCEAN POLICY AND THE IN-
          TERNATIONAL LAW OF THE SEA NEGOTIATIONS, BEFORE THE SUBCOMMITTEE
          ON INTERNATIONAL ORGANIZATIONS AND MOVEMENTS OF THE COMMITTEE ON
          FOREIGN AFFAIRS, UNITED STATES HOUSE OF REPRESENTATIVES, TUESDAY,
          APRIL 11, 1972. Washington, D.C., 1972. 16p.

                                                                    14
VLOS      _____ THE THIRD UNITED NATIONS LAW OF THE SEA CONFERENCE,
          CARACAS. East Coast South America series; Vol. 18, no. 1. Han-
          over, N.H., American Universities Field Staff, 1974. 15p.

                                                                    13
VLOS      _____ U.S. OCEANS POLICY: PERSPECTIVE 1973. Reprinted from
          the Proceedings of the 20th Annual Institute on Mineral Law, March
          16-17, 1973. n.p.

                                                                     1
VLOS      _____ UNITED STATES OCEAN POLICY: PERSPECTIVE 1974. Re-
          printed from Notre Dame Lawyer, Vol. 49, no. 2, December 1973.
          pp. 241-275.

                                                                  14,16
IIIF      Knight, H. Gary, ed. THE FUTURE OF INTERNATIONAL FISHERIES MANAGE-
          MENT. St. Paul, Minn., West Publishing Company, 1975. xiii, 253p.

                                                                 1,15,16
VLOS      _____ THE LAW OF THE SEA: DOCUMENTS AND NOTES. Materials
          prepared exclusively for use by students at Louisiana State Univer-
          sity. Mimeo. 1969. 514p.
          _____ SUPPLEMENTAL MATERIALS. 1972. 266p.

                                                                   ***
IIIF      Knight, H. Gary, and James P. Lambert. LEGAL ASPECTS OF LIMITED
          ENTRY FOR COMMERCIAL MARINE FISHERIES. Baton Rouge, Louisiana
          State University, Center for Wetland Resources, 1975. 127p.

IIIF        Knight, H. Gary, and T. Victor Jackson. LEGAL IMPEDIMENTS TO THE
USE OF INTERSTATE AGREEMENTS IN COORDINATED FISHERIES MANAGEMENT
PROGRAMS: STATES IN THE N.M.F.S. SOUTHEAST REGION. Baton Rouge,
L          Louisiana State University, Office of Sea Grant Development, Sea
Grant Legal Program, 1973. 120p.

                                                                                  1,3,5,11,12,13
IIIINTL    Kobayashi, Teruo. THE ANGLO-NORWEGIAN FISHERIES CASE OF 1951 AND
THE CHANGING LAW OF THE TERRITORIAL SEA. University of Florida monographs; social sciences, no. 26. Gainesville, University of Florida Press, 1965.

                                                                                                          ART
IVMMR      Koegler, F.C. SURFACE CONCENTRATIONS OF DEEP-SEA MANGANESE NODULES.
In Twenty-fourth session of the International Geological Congress,
held in Montreal, Canada, 1972. Ottawa, 1972?

                                        1,4,5,7,8,11,13,14,15,16
IIIINTL    Koers, Albert W. THE ENFORCEMENT OF FISHERIES AGREEMENTS ON THE
HIGH SEAS: A COMPARATIVE ANALYSIS OF INTERNATIONAL STATE PRACTICE.
Law of the Sea Institute occasional paper no. 6. Kingston, University of Rhode Island, 1970. 54p.

                                                   1,3,5,7,12,13,15,16
IIIINTL            INTERNATIONAL REGULATION OF MARINE FISHERIES; A
STUDY OF REGIONAL FISHERIES ORGANIZATIONS. West Byfleet, Surrey,
England, Fishing News (Books), 1973. 368p.

                                                                                     16
VCS         Koh, Kwang Lim. THE CONTINENTAL SHELF - AN ANALYTICAL STUDY OF THE
DRAFT ARTICLES ON THE CONTINENTAL SHELF ADOPTED BY THE INTERNATIONAL
LAW COMMISSION. Cambridge, Harvard University Press, 1954. 508p.

                                                                                    16
VCS             THE CONTINENTAL SHELF, A STUDY OF THE DRAFT ARTICLES
ON THE CONTINENTAL SHELF AND RELATED SUBJECTS PREPARED BY THE INTERNATIONAL LAW COMMISSION. Unpublished paper submitted for Professor Louis B. Sohn's seminar on International Law Problems, Harvard University, 1953. 62p.

                                                                                    16
IIIINTL           INTERNATIONAL REGULATION OF FISHERIES WITH SPECIAL
REFERENCE TO THOSE IN THE NORTH PACIFIC OCEAN. Ph.D. Dissertation.
New Brunswick, N.J., Photoduplication Department, Rutgers University Library, 1967. iii, vi, 331p. Microfilm.

                                                                                     16
VINTL       Kolodkin, A., and K. Zhudro. POSSIBLE FUTURE REGIME OF THE SEA-BED.
SOME LEGAL ASPECTS OF THE USING OF THE SEA-BED. Paper presented at
Symposium on the International Regime of the Sea-bed, Rome, 1969.

                                                                               ***
VLOS        Kolodkin, A.L., und S.V. Molodcov. SEEFRIEDENSRECHT DAS VOELKERRECHTLICHE REGIME DER TERRITORIALGEWAESSER, DER ANSCHLUSSZONE UND
DES HOHEN MEERES. Werkhefte der Forschungsstelle fuer Voelkerrecht
und auslaendisches oetfentliches Recht der Universitaet Hamburg,
21. Hamburg, Metzner, 1973. 169p.

|||| | | |
|---|---|---|

VOR　　Kolodkin, Anatolii L.　THE WORLD OCEAN, 1974.　Translation of Russian-language book by A.L. Kolodkin: MIROVOY OKEAN. Izdatel'stvo Mezhdunarodnyye Otnosheniya, Moscow, 1973. 232p.　　　　　　　　7

IIIP　　Kolpad, R.L.　BIOLOGICAL AND OCEANOGRAPHIC SURVEY OF THE SANTA BARBARA CHANNEL OIL SPILL 1969-70.　Allan Hancock Foundation, Los Angeles, University of Southern California, 1971.　477p.　　　***

IICONS　Komar, Paul D., and C. Cary Rea.　THE CAUSES OF EROSION TO SILETZ SPIT, OREGON.　ORESU-T-75-001.　Corvallis, Oregon State University Sea Grant College Program, 1975.　20p.　　　***

VOCET　　Konecci, Eugene B., and Seymour Schwartz, eds.　MARINE SCIENCES AND BUSINESS POTENTIALS; PROCEEDINGS OF SYMPOSIUM, CORPUS CHRISTI, TEXAS, SEPTEMBER 26-27, 1968.　Transference of technology series no. 3.　Austin, Bureau of Business Research, University of Texas, 1969. xvii, 376p.　　　　17

IIOSTR　Koningsberger, Rosine M., and Stephen B. Ribakoff.　HAWAII'S FLOATING CITY DEVELOPMENT PROGRAM: CONSTRUCTION SITE SELECTION. UNIHI-SEAGRANT-CR-74-04.　Honolulu, University of Hawaii, 1974.　51p.　　　***

IICZM　　Koppelman, Lee E.　A METHODOLOGY TO ACHIEVE THE INTEGRATION OF COASTAL ZONE SCIENCE AND REGIONAL PLANNING.　N.Y., Praeger Publishers, 1974. 118p.　　　14

IIOSTR　Korolev, A.B., et al.　PRESSURIZED UNDERWATER HOUSES AND SHELTERS. In Nekotoryye Rezultaty i Perspektivy Primeneñiya Podvodnykh Domov v Morskikh Issledovaniyakh, Moscow, June 18, 1973.　pp. 134-142.　　　ART

IIIP　　Korringa, P.　MARINE POLLUTION AND ITS BIOLOGICAL CONSEQUENCES. In Costlow, J.D., ed., Fertility of the Sea; Proceedings of the Symposium on Fertility of the Sea, São Paulo, 1969.　N.Y., Gordon and Breach Science Publishers, 1971.　Vol. 1, pp. 215-229.　　　ART

VP　　_____　THE OCEAN AS FINAL RECIPIENT OF THE END PRODUCTS OF THE CONTINENT'S METABOLISM.　In Sioli, H., ed., Oekologie und Lebenschutz in Internationaler Sicht.　Freiburg, Switzerland, Verlag Rombach, 1973. pp. 91-104.　　　ART

IIIINTL　Kouloris, Michel A.　LES NOUVELLES TENDANCES DEPUIS 1962 DANS LE RÉGIME INTERNATIONAL DES PÊCHES MARITIMES.　Athens, 1972.　219p.　　　1,5,7

IIIFV&G　Kowalski, T., and J. Giannotti.　CALCULATION OF TRAWLING GEAR DRAG. Marine technical report no. 16.　Kingston, University of Rhode Island, Marine Advisory Service, 1974.　44p.　　　13,14,15

IIOSTR　Kowalski, T., ed.　1974 FLOATING BREAKWATERS.　Conference papers.　　　13

Floating Breakwaters Conference held in Newport, Rhode Island, April 23-25, 1974, and co-sponsored by the University of Rhode Island, and the University of Washington. Kingston, University of Rhode Island, 1974. 304p.

***

IIIP     Kreag, R., and Frederic J. Smith. SEAFOOD SOLID WASTE IN OREGON: DISPOSAL OR RECOVERY? Special Report 395. Corvallis, Oregon State University, Cooperative Extension Service, Marine Advisory Program, 1973. 22p.

ART

VP     Kremling, K. THE BALTIC SEA AS AN EXAMPLE OF POLLUTION OF INTERNATIONAL WATERS. In Conference on International Implications of Environmental Problems, Istanbul, 1971. Environmental problems and their international implications; papers presented at the conference held at the Merchant Marine Academy, Istanbul, Turkey, July 21-28, 1971. Boulder, Colorado Associated University Press, 1973. pp. 135-152.

ART

VP     _____ METHODS AND PROBLEMS OF in situ RECORDING OF CHEMICAL PROPERTIES IN THE MARINE ENVIRONMENT WITH SPECIAL REGARD TO POLLUTION CONTROL. In Conference on International Implications of Environmental Problems, Istanbul, 1971. Environmental problems and their international implications; papers presented at the conference held at the Merchant Marine Academy, Istanbul, Turkey, July 21-28, 1971. Boulder, Colorado Associated University Press. pp. 153-164.

***

IIIF     Krenkel, P.A., and F.L. Parker. BIOLOGICAL ASPECTS OF THERMAL POLLUTION. Nashville, Tenn., Vanderbilt University Press, 1969. 351p.

***

VP     Krenkel, P.A. and F.L. Parker, eds. ENGINEERING ASPECTS OF THERMAL POLLUTION. Nashville, Tenn., Vanderbilt University Press, 1968. 351p.

15

VP     _____ NATIONAL SYMPOSIUM ON THERMAL POLLUTION, PORTLAND, OREGON, 1968. BIOLOGICAL ASPECTS OF THERMAL POLLUTION: PROCEEDINGS. n.p., 1968.

***

IVOSTR     Kretschmer, T.R., et al. SEAFLOOR CONSTRUCTION EXPERIMENT, SEACON I - AN INTEGRATED EVALUATION OF SEAFLOOR CONSTRUCTION EQUIPMENT AND TECHNIQUES. Technical report R817. Port Heuneme, Calif., U.S. Naval Construction Battalion Center, Civil Engineering Laboratory, 1975. 172p.

***

IIIF     Kreuzer, Rudolf, ed. FISH INSPECTION AND QUALITY CONTROL. FAO CONFERENCE. London, Fishing News (Books) Ltd.; New York, UNIPUB, Inc., 1971. 229p.

|||15
IIIF    Kreuzer, Rudolf, ed. Food and Agricultural Organization of the United Nations. SYMPOSIUM ON THE SIGNIFICANCE OF FUNDAMENTAL RESEARCH IN THE UTILIZATION OF FISH, HUSUM, GERMANY, 1964. THE TECHNOLOGY OF FISH UTILIZATION; CONTRIBUTIONS FROM RESEARCH. London, Fishing News (Books), 1965. xxii, 280p.

|||14
VCONS   Krieger, David. THE OCEANS: A COMMON HERITAGE. Oakville, Ontario, Canadian Peace Research Institute, 1974. 63p.

|||13
VINTL   Krieger, David, ed. PACEM IN MARIBUS-IV. MALTA, JUNE 23-26, 1973. Proceedings. Msida, The Royal University of Malta Press, 1974. xxi, 382p.

|||ART
IVMMR   Krishnaswamy, S. MANGANESE NODULES AND BUDGET OF TRACE SOLUBLES IN OCEANS. In Proceedings of the Changing Chemistry of the Oceans. Nobel Symposium, 20th, held in Aspenaesgaarden, Lerum, Sweden, August 16-20, 1971. pp. 307-320.

|||ART
IIFV&G  Kristinsson, G.E. COMBINATION FISHING VESSELS. In Modern Fishing Gear of the World: 3. London, Fishing News (Books) Ltd.; New York, UNIPUB, Inc., 1971. pp. 306-312.

|||***
IIIFV&G Kristjonsson, Hilmar, ed. MODERN FISHING GEAR OF THE WORLD: 3. Congress on Fishing Gear organized by Food and Agricultural Organization of the United Nations. London, Fishing News (Books) Ltd.; New York, UNIPUB, Inc., 1972.

|||16
IICR    Krueger, R. THE DEVELOPMENT OF THE PACIFIC COAST - THE TIDELANDS AND BEYOND. Paper and Address delivered at the Southwest Regional Conference of the American Institute of Real Estate Appraisers, 1968.

|||ART
VINTL   _____ THE STATE OF INTERNATIONAL LAW AS APPLIED TO OCEAN MINING AND AN EXAMINATION OF THE OFFSHORE MINING LAWS OF SELECTED NATIONS. In Offshore Technology Conference. n.p., 1969. pp. 333-374.

|||16
IVMMR   _____ UNDERWATER EXPLOITATION OF MINERAL RESOURCES, U.S.S.R. Springfield, Va., Government Clearinghouse, 1969.

|||13
VOR     Krueger, Robert B. RESOURCE MANAGEMENT OF THE WORLD'S OCEANS AND COASTAL ZONES. Stanford University School of Earth Sciences, Hoots Lecture Series, November 29, 1971. Photocopy. Stanford, Stanford University, 1971. 49p.

|||1,7,13,15
VAC     Kruger-Sprengel, Friedheim. THE ROLE OF NATO IN THE USE OF THE SEA AND THE SEABED. Edited by Gerard J. Mangone. Ocean series 304. Washington, D.C., Woodrow Wilson International Center for Scholars, 1972. 45p.

|||
|---|---|
| VAC | Kuehne, W. DAS VOELKERRECHT UND DIE MILITAERISCHE NUTZUNG DES MEERESBODENS. Leyden, Sijthoff, 1975. 182p. *** |
| IVOCET | Kuenen, Philip H. MARINE GEOLOGY. New York, Wiley, 1957. 15 |
| IIIFV&G | Kulagin, V.D. THEORY AND LAYOUT OF SEAGOING COMMERCIAL FISHING VESSELS, U.S.S.R. Arlington, Va., Joint Publications Research Service, May 20, 1975. 51p. *** |
| IVOSTR | Kuliyev, I.P., and Yu P. Vladimirov. PROSPECTS FOR UTILIZATION OF UNDERWATER HOUSES AND CHAMBERS IN DEVELOPMENT OF MARINE OIL DEPOSITS. In Nekotoryye Rezultaty i Perspektivy Primeneniya Podvodnykh Domov v Morskilch Issledovaniyakh. Moscow, June 18, 1973. pp. 83-86. ART |
| IVMMR | Kulm, LaVerne D., et al. A PRELIMINARY INVESTIGATION OF THE HEAVY MINERAL SUITES OF THE COASTAL RIVERS AND BEACHES OF OREGON AND NORTHERN CALIFORNIA. Reprinted from The Ore Bin, Vol. 30, no. 9. September, 1968. pp. 168-184. 13 |
| VINTL | Kuribayashi, T. THE RÉGIME OF PASSAGE THROUGH INTERNATIONAL STRAITS. In Hogaku Kenkyu, 1975. no. 4, pp. 35-69; no. 5, pp. 15-39. ART |
| VLOS | LA ACTUAL REVISION DEL DERECHO DEL MAR. UNA PERSPECTIVA ESPAÑOLA. Madrid, Instituto de Estudios Politicos Centro de Documentacion, 1974. 2 Vols. *** |
| VLOS | Laard, Evan. THE CONTROL OF THE SEABED. London, Heinemans, 1974. 5 |
| VINTL | Ladner, Leon J., et al. INTERNATIONAL LAW; RIVERS AND MARGINAL SEAS. Vancouver, University of British Columbia, 1956. ii, 45p. 1,13,16 |
| IIIF | Laevastu, Taivo, and Ilmo Hela. FISHERIES OCEANOGRAPHY; NEW OCEAN ENVIRONMENTAL SERVICES. London, Fishing News (Books), 1970. xv, 238p. 13 |
| IIIOCET | LaFond, E.C. and K.G. LaFond. OCEANOGRAPHY AND ITS RELATION TO MARINE ORGANIC PRODUCTION. In Costlow, J.D., Fertility of the Sea; Proceedings of the Symposium on Fertility of the Sea, São Paulo, 1969. N.Y., Gordon and Breach Science Publishers, 1971. Vol. 1, pp. 241-265. ART |
| VB | LaForest, G.V. BOUNDARY WATERS PROBLEMS IN THE EAST. Conference on Canada-United States Treaty Relations, Duke University Commonwealth-Studies Center, June 1961. 1 |

ART
VP        Lafornara, J.P., and I. Wilder. SOLUTION OF THE HAZARDOUS MATERIAL SPILL PROBLEM IN THE LITTLE MENOMONEE RIVER. In Proceedings, 1974 National Conference on Control of Hazardous Material Spills, San Francisco, Calif., August 25-28, 1974. pp. 202-207.

13
IVMMR     Lahman, H.S., and J.B. Lassiter, III. THE EVOLUTION AND UTILIZATION OF MARINE MINERAL RESOURCES. Report no. MITSG 72-9. Cambridge, Massachusetts Institute of Technology, 1972.

ART
IVOSTR    Lamb, M.J. UNDERWATER PIPELINES. In Marine Technology Society. Second Annual Conference, Washington, D.C., June 27-29, 1966. Washington, D.C., 1966. pp. 293-308.

***
IIIF      Lampe, Harlan C., and Robert D. Niehaus. DEMAND AND SUPPLY POTENTIALS FOR SOUTH VIETNAM'S FISHERY INDUSTRY. Washington, U.S. Department of Agriculture. Economic Research Service, July, 1974. x, 54p.

13
IIIF      Lampe, Harlan C., et al. PROSPECTS FOR FISHERIES DEVELOPMENT ASSISTANCE. International Center for Marine Resource Development, University of Rhode Island. Marine Technical report series no. 19. Kingston, R.I., 1974. vi, 41p.

ART
VP        Landau, Norman J. WATER POLLUTION CASES. In Legal Control of the Environment, Seminar, August-September, 1972. New York, Practising Law Institute, 1972.

5,17
VINTL     Lang, Jack. LE PLATEAU CONTINENTAL DE LA MER DU NORD; ARRÊT DE LA COUR INTERNATIONAL DE JUSTICE, 20 FÉVRIER 1969. Avant propos de Charles Chaumont. Bibliothèque de droit international, t. lviii. Paris, Librairie Générale de Droit et de Jurisprudence, 1970. vii-xiv, 163, 5p.

***
IVMMR     Langley, Van E. MIDDLE EAST OFFSHORE MINERAL LAW. New York, 1970- looseleaf.

13
IIIAFF    Lannan, James E. NETARTS BAY CHUM SALMON HATCHERY; AN EXPERIMENT IN OCEAN RANCHING. ORESU-H-75-001. Corvallis, Oregon State University Sea Grant Program, 1975. 28p.

5,9
VB        Lapradelle, Paul de. LA FRONTIÈRE; ÉTUDE DE DROIT INTERNATIONAL. Paris, Les Editions Internationales, 1928. 368p.

ART
IVM       Laque, Frank L. DEEP-OCEAN MINING: PROSPECTS AND ANTICIPATED SHORT-TERM BENEFITS. In Elisabeth M. Borgese, ed., Pacem in Maribus. New York, Dodd, Mead, 1972. pp. 131-145.

VP      La Rocque, Gene R. SECURITY THROUGH MUTUAL VULNERABILITY. Occasional paper no. 2. Muscatine, Iowa, Stanley Foundation, 1973. 12p.
13

VMT     Lassiter, J.B., and J.W. Devanney. THE ECONOMICS OF ARCTIC OIL TRANSPORTATION. Reprinted from Schiff und Hafen, November, 1970. MIT Sea Grant Program. Report no. MITSG 71-4. Cambridge, Massachusetts Institute of Technology, 1971. pp. J15-J21.
13

***

VP      Laster, R. A COMPILATION OF ISRAELI LAWS FOR THE PREVENTION OF POLLUTION OF THE SEA. Mimeo. Jerusalem, State of Israel Environmental Protection Service, 1974. 42p.

***

IISL    Latimer, Edward B. TIDELANDS LAW OF SOUTH CAROLINA. In Planning and Engineering in the Coastal Zone. Proceedings of seminar held in Charleston, S.C., June 8-9, 1972. Seminar series no. 2. Wilmington, N.C., 1972. pp. 95-97.

***

IIWQ    Lau, L.S. THE QUALITY OF COASTAL WATERS: FIRST ANNUAL PROGRESS REPORT. Technical Report no. 60. UNIHI-SEAGRANT-72-01. Honolulu, University of Hawaii, Water Resources Research Center. 1-    1972-

IIE     Lauff, George H. Conference on Estuaries, Jekyll Island, 1964. ESTUARIES; PAPERS. Washington, American Association for the Advancement of Science, 1967. xv, 757p.
14a

IIIF    Laurs, R.M., and R.J. Lynn. THE ASSOCIATION OF OCEANIC BOUNDARY FEATURES AND ALBACORE TUNA IN THE NORTHEAST PACIFIC. In STD Conference and Workshop Proceedings. San Diego, Calif., Plessy Environmental Systems, 1975.
ART

VINTL   Lauterpacht, E., ed. THE SUEZ CANAL SETTLEMENT: A SELECTION OF DOCUMENTS RELATING TO THE SETTLEMENT OF THE SUEZ CANAL DISPUTE, THE CLEARANCE OF THE SUEZ CANAL AND THE SETTLEMENT OF THE DISPUTES BETWEEN THE UNITED KINGDOM, FRANCE AND THE UNITED ARAB REPUBLIC, NOVEMBER 1956 - MARCH 1959. London, Stevens; New York, Praeger, 1960.
1

***

IVLOS   Law of the Sea. PARTICULAR ASPECTS AFFECTING THE PETROLEUM INDUSTRY. Washington, D.C., National Petroleum Council, 1973. 84p.

VLOS    THE LAW OF THE SEA: A TEST OF INTERNATIONAL COOPERATION. Address by Secretary Kissinger before the Foreign Policy Association, the U.S. Council of the International Chamber of Commerce, and the U.N. Association of the U.S.A., at New York, on April 8, 1976. In U.S. Department of State Bulletin, Vol. LXXIV, no. 1922, April 26, 1976. pp. 533-542.
ART

|       |       |
|---|---|
| VLOS | 4,7,11,14<br>LAW OF THE SEA BRIEFING: REFLECTIONS ON THE CARACAS SESSION OF THE UNITED NATIONS LAW OF THE SEA CONFERENCE, verbatim transcript of briefing co-sponsored by Law of the Sea Institute and the Marine Technology Society, September 1974. Law of the Sea Institute occasional paper no. 24. Kingston, University of Rhode Island, 1975. |
| VLOS | 16<br>LAW OF THE SEA - IMPLICATIONS FOR COASTAL STATES, A SYMPOSIUM HELD IN HOUSTON, FEBRUARY 1, 1974 BY THE TEXAS COASTAL AND MARINE COUNCIL, IN CO-OPERATION WITH THE TEXAS JUDICIAL INSTITUTE. Houston, Texas Law Institute of Coastal and Marine Resources, 1974. ii, 122p. |
| VSG | 8,16<br>Law of the Sea Institute. ANNUAL REPORT. 1971-   Kingston, University of Rhode Island. |
| VREFS | 1,4,5,7,11,13,14,15,16<br>Law of the Sea Institute. INDEX TO PROCEEDINGS II-VII (1974) CONTAINING THE RESULTS OF THE INSTITUTE'S 1966-1972 ANNUAL CONFERENCES. Special publication no. 2. Kingston, University of Rhode Island, August, 1974. 22p. |
| VLOS | 14<br>_____ LAW OF THE SEA: CARACAS AND BEYOND. PROCEEDINGS OF THE NINTH ANNUAL LAW OF THE SEA INSTITUTE. Cambridge, Mass., Ballinger Publishing Company, 1975. 368p. |
| VLOS | ***<br>_____ LAW OF THE SEA: CONFERENCE OUTCOMES AND PROBLEMS OF IMPLEMENTATION. Proceedings of the Tenth Annual Conference. Kingston, University of Rhode Island, June 22-25, 1976. n.y.p. |
| VLOS | 5,14,16,18<br>_____ OCCASIONAL PAPERS. 1-   Kingston, University of Rhode Island, 1969- |
| VLOS | 1,5,11,13,14,15,16<br>_____ PROCEEDINGS. Kingston, University of Rhode Island, 1966-   1st- |
| VLOS | 3,14,15,16<br>LAW OF THE SEA REPORTS: A YEAR OF CRISIS, FEBRUARY 19, 1971; GENEVA REPORT, OCTOBER 18, 1971. Washington, Marine Technology Society, 1972. ix, 204p. |
| VENV | ***<br>Lawrence, John, ed. LAWS, INSTITUTIONS, AND THE GLOBAL ENVIRONMENT. Conference on Legal and Institutional Responses to Problems of the Global Environment held in Harriman, New York, September, 1971. Jointly sponsored by American Society of International Law and Carnegie. |
| VMT | 16<br>Lawrence, Samuel A. INTERNATIONAL SEA TRANSPORT; THE YEARS AHEAD. Lexington, Mass., Lexington Books, 1972. xvi, 316p. |
| IIWQ | 13<br>LAWS FOR A BETTER ENVIRONMENT. Seminar conducted by Water Resources Research Institute. Fall Quarter 1971. Corvallis, Oregon State |

University, 1972. 97p.

***

IIIF     LAWS OF VIRGINIA RELATING TO FISHERIES OF TIDAL WATERS. Charlottesville, Va., Michie Company, 1974. 170p.

***

IICZM     LAWS PERTAINING TO PROPERTY. MASGP-74-034. Ocean Springs, Mississippi-Alabama Sea Grant Consortium, 1973. 208p.

***

IIENV     LAWS RELATING TO ENVIRONMENTAL CONTROL. Parts 1 and 2. MASGP-74-029 and MASGP-74-030. Ocean Springs, Mississippi-Alabama Sea Grant Consortium, 1973. 287p.

***

IICZM     LAWS RELATING TO GENERAL ADMINISTRATION AND MANAGEMENT. MASGP-74-033. Ocean Springs, Mississippi-Alabama Sea Grant Consortium, 1973. 181p.

***

IIICR     LAWS RELATING TO LIVING RESOURCES. MASGP-74-032. Ocean Springs, Mississippi-Alabama Sea Grant Consortium, 1973. 114p.

***

VMT     LAWS RELATING TO NAVIGATION. MASGP-74-036. Ocean Springs, Mississippi-Alabama Sea Grant Consortium, 1973. 93p.

***

IIREC     LAWS RELATING TO RECREATIONAL ACTIVITIES. MASGP-74-031. Ocean Springs, Mississippi-Alabama Sea Grant Consortium, 1973. 82p.

14a
VCS     Lawson, Andrew C. THE CONTINENTAL SHELF OFF THE COAST OF CALIFORNIA. Bulletin of the National Research Council, no. 44, Vol. 8, pt. 2, April, 1924. Washington, D.C., National Research Council of the National Academy of Sciences, 1924. 23p.

6,7,10,13,14,15,16
VLOS     Lay, S. Houston, Robin Churchill, and Myron Nordquist, comp. NEW DIRECTIONS IN THE LAW OF THE SEA. Dobbs Ferry, N.Y., Oceana Publications, Inc., 1973-     4 Vols.

13
IVLOS     Laylin, John G. INTERIM PRACTICES AND POLICY FOR THE GOVERNING OF SEABED MINING BEYOND THE LIMITS OF NATIONAL JURISDICTION. Tuesday session, June 27, 1972, Law of the Sea Institute, Seventh Annual Conference. Mimeo. n.p., 1972. 5p.

***

VLOS     Lazarev, M.I., ed. SOVREMENNOE MEZHDUNARODNOE MORSKOE PRAVO: REZHIM VOD I DNA MIROVOGO OKEANA. Moscow, izd-vo Nauka, 1974. 307p.

2
VOR     Lazzaro, Fortunato. IL REGIME GIURIDICO DEI MEZZI DE RICEREA E SFRUTTAMENTO CHE OPERANO IN MARE. Piacenza, La tribuna, 1967? 137p.

VSG  Leahy, T.M., and William Seaman, eds. ANNUAL REPORT. THE SEA GRANT PROGRAM FOR JANUARY 1 - DECEMBER 31, 1973. Gainesville, University of Florida, 1974.

VOD  Lear, D.W. EFFECTS OF OCEAN DISPOSAL ACTIVITIES ON MID-CONTINENTAL SHELF ENVIRONMENT OFF DELAWARE AND MARYLAND. EPA 903/9-75-015. Philadelphia, U.S. Environmental Protection Agency, 1975. 213p.

VOD  _____ ENVIRONMENTAL SURVEY OF TWO INTERIM DUMPSITES: MIDDLE ATLANTIC BIGHT: SUPPLEMENTAL REPORT. EPA-903/9-74-0106. Philadelphia, U.S. Environmental Protection Agency, 1974. 107p.

IIIINTL  Lecvona, Daniel C. THE ECUADOR FISHERIES DISPUTE. In Journal of Maritime Law and Commerce, Vol. 2, no. 1, October 1972. pp. 91-114.

VORM  Ledbetter, B.G. STEPS TOWARD A STATE OIL TRANSPORTATION POLICY. Remarks before the U.S. Coast Guard Maritime Conference, 6 May, 1975. In Pacific Northwest Sea, Vol. 8, no. 1, 1975. pp. 8-12.

IICZM  Leed, Roger, ed. SHORELINES MANAGEMENT - THE WASHINGTON EXPERIENCE. Proceedings of a Symposium held in Seattle Center in 1972. Seattle, University of Washington Press, 1973. 184p.

VP  Le Faucheux, O. POLLUTION ET PROTECTION DES MERS ET DES PLAGES. In Bibliotheque de l'Environment, J.A. Ternisien, comp. Paris, Guy Te Prat, 1971. Vol. 2, pp. 81-122.

VOR  LE FOND DES MERS; ASPECTS JURIDIQUES, BIOLOGIQUES, ET GÉOLOGIQUES, by C.A. Colliard. Paris, Armand Colin, 1971. 205p.

VP  THE LEGAL AND ECONOMIC ASPECTS OF POLLUTION. A discussion by University of Chicago faculty members: George Anastaplo and others. Chicago, University of Chicago, Center for Policy Study, 1970. viii, 37p.

IICZM  LEGAL AND ECONOMIC STRATEGIES FOR SHORELINES MANAGEMENT. Proceedings of Workshop at University of Washington, September 26, 1975. Seattle, University of Washington, Division of Marine Resources, 1976. 36p.

VLOS  LEGAL ASPECTS OF THE QUESTION OF THE RESERVATION EXCLUSIVELY FOR PEACEFUL PURPOSES OF THE SEA-BED AND THE OCEAN FLOOR, AND THE SUBSOIL THEREOF, UNDERLYING THE HIGH SEAS BEYOND THE LIMITS OF PRESENT NATIONAL JURISDICTION, AND THE USE OF THEIR RESOURCES IN THE INTERESTS OF MANKIND. Study prepared by the Secretariat. Mimeo. A/AC.135/19. 21 June, 1968. 92p.

VORM  LEGAL ASPECTS OF UNDERWATER INSTRUCTION. Papers. Grand Terrace (Colton), Calif., National Association of Underwater Instructors,

        1972. 44p.

                                                                                            ***

IVOSTR    LEGAL CONSIDERATIONS FOR THE CONSTRUCTION AND OPERATION OF A DEEP-WATER OIL TERMINAL IN THE DELAWARE BAY. Newark, University of Delaware, 1975. 27p.

                                                                                             ***

VENV     LEGAL CONTROL OF THE ENVIRONMENT. Seminar, August-September, 1972. New York, Practising Law Institute, 1972. 314p.

                                                                                             14

VODAS    LEGAL PROBLEMS ASSOCIATED WITH OCEAN DATA ACQUISITION SYSTEMS (ODAS). A study of existing national and international legislation, prepared jointly by the Secretariats of UNESCO and IMCO. 1962-68. Rev. under the authority of and with the assistance of the IOC group of experts on the legal status of ocean data acquisitions stations. IOC technical series no. 5. UNESCO, 1969. 40p.

                                                                                         ***

IISL     LEGAL SYMPOSIUM ON WETLANDS. AN EXECUTIVE SUMMARY. Gloucester Point, Virginia Institute of Marine Science, 1974. 8p.

                                                                             5,12,13,16

VB       Legg, Billy J. SEABED REGIMES AND THE LIMITS OF NATIONAL JURISDICTION. University of Miami Sea Grant Program, NOAA Sea Grant no. 2-35147, special bulletin no. 19, January, 1972. Coral Gables, Fla., 1972. 125p.

                                                                                            13

IICZM    A LEGISLATOR'S GUIDE TO LAND MANAGEMENT. Lexington, Ky., The Council of State Governments, 1974. viii, 63p.

                                                                                          ART

IIIAFF    Le Mare, D.W. APPLICATION OF THE PRINCIPLES OF FISH CULTURE TO ESTUARINE CONDITIONS IN SINGAPORE. In Proceedings of the Indo-Pacific Fisheries Council, 2d session, 2-3. n.p., 1950. pp. 180-183.

                                                                                         ***

IIENV    LeMay, Joseph, and Eugene Harrison, eds. ENVIRONMENTAL LAND USE PROBLEMS. A STUDY OF NORTHERN NEW JERSEY. New York, Marcel Dekker, Inc., 1974. xvi, 275p.

                                                                       1,3,5,9,12

IIIF     Leonard, Leonard L. INTERNATIONAL REGULATION OF FISHERIES. Washington, Carnegie Endowment for International Peace, Division of International Law, 1944. 201p.

                                                                            13

IIIP     Lepple, Frederick K. MERCURY IN THE ENVIRONMENT; A GLOBAL REVIEW INCLUDING RECENT STUDIES IN THE DELAWARE BAY REGION. DEL-SG-8-73. Newark, College of Marine Studies, University of Delaware, 1973. 75p.

                                                                                         ***

VOR      Levine, Sumner S., ed. SELECTED PAPERS ON DESALINATION AND OCEAN TECHNOLOGY. New York, Daven Publications, 1968. 437p.

| | | |
|---|---|---|
| IVMMR | L'EXPLOITATION DES RESSOURCES MINÉRALES. In Le Fond des Mers; Aspects Juridiques, Biologiques et Géologiques, by C.A. Colliard. Paris, Armand Colin, 1971. pp. 65-95. | ART |
| VP | Lewin, Stuart F., Alan H. Gordon, and Channing J. Hartelius. LAW AND THE MUNICIPAL ECOLOGY: AIR, WATER, NOISE, OVER-POPULATION. NIMLO research report no. 156. Washington, D.C., National Institute of Municipal Law Officers, 1970. xvi, 243p. | 2 |
| IVOL | Lewis, Austin W. THE STATE-FEDERAL INTERIM AGREEMENT CONCERNING OFFSHORE LEASING AND OPERATIONS. In Slovenko, Ralph, ed., Oil and Gas Operations. Baton Rouge, Claitor's, 1963. pp. 93-100. | ART |
| VMLAD | Lewis, William, ed. DAS DEUTSCHE SEERECHT. EIN KOMMENTAR ZUM V. BUCH DES ALLGEMEINEN DEUTSCHEN HANDELSGESETZBUCHS. Leipzig, Duncker und Humblot, 1877-78. 2 Vols. | 3 |
| IICZM | Liang, Tung, et al. A DYNAMIC WATER AND RELATED LAND RESOURCE PLANNING MODEL: ITS APPLICATION TO AN HAWAIIAN SMALL WATER SYSTEM. Honolulu, University of Hawaii, Water Resources Research Center, 1974. vi, 55p. | *** |
| VLOS | Liang, Y. CODIFICATION OF THE LAW OF THE SEA UNDER THE AUSPICES OF THE UNITED NATIONS. 1964 Annals of the Chinese Society of International Law 3-23. | 16 |
| IIIF | Liao, David S., and Joe B. Stevens. OREGON'S COMMERCIAL FISHERMEN: CHARACTERISTICS, PROFITS AND INCOMES IN 1972. ORESU-T-1-75-001. Corvallis, Oregon State University, 1975. 20p. | 14 |
| VP | Librizzi, W. REVIEW AND COMMENT ON WASTE TREATMENT TECHNIQUES FOR COMMERCIAL VESSELS. In T.F.P. Sullivan, ed., Pollution Control in the Marine Industries. International Association for Pollution Control, 1972. pp. 163-180. | ART |
| IIWQ | Lieber, Harvey. FEDERALISM AND CLEAN WATERS: THE 1972 WATER POLLUTION CONTROL ACT. Lexington, Mass., Lexington Books, 1975. xiv, 288p. | *** |
| VP | Liebermann, M. OIL POLLUTION SOURCE IDENTIFICATION. Environmental Protection Technology Series EPA-R2-73-102. Edison, N.J., U.S. Environmental Protection Agency, Office of Research and Monitoring, 1973. 173p. | *** |
| IIENV | Lilja, Jack. ENVIRONMENTAL HEALTH GUIDELINES FOR MARINA DEVELOPMENT AND OPERATION. Olympia, Washington Department of Social and Health Services, Office of Environmental Health Programs, 1974. | 14 |

                                                            1
VOR      Lillich, Richard B.  WHOSE IS THE BED OF THE SEA? Reprinted from
         New York State Bar Journal, Vol. 40, no. 8, December 1968, pp. 601-
         604.

                                                            5,12,13,16
VINTL    Limitone, Anthony, Jr.  THE REGISTRATION OF SHIPS BY INTERNATIONAL
         AND INTERGOVERNMENTAL ORGANIZATIONS.  University of Miami Sea Grant
         Program, NOAA Sea Grant no. 2-35147, special bulletin no. 2, Novem-
         ber, 1971.  Fla., University of Miami, 1971.  iii, 28p.

                                                            ***
IIOSTR   Lin, A.C.M.  A FEASIBILITY STUDY OF A STABLE MOBILE OCEAN PLATFORM
         AS A NAVAL BASE.  Report NSRDC-3743.  Bethesda, Md., U.S. Naval
         Ship Research and Development Center, 1973.  84p.

                                                            ART
IIIAFF   Lin, S.Y.  FISH CULTURE PROJECT IN HAITI.  In Proceedings of the
         Fourth Annual Session of the Gulf and Caribbean Fisheries Institute,
         1951.  Miami, University of Miami, 1952.  pp. 110-118.

                                                            ***
IIP      Lindsay, Cedric E.  THE BIO-ASSAY APPROACH TO ESTUARINE POLLUTION
         PROBLEMS.  Olympia, Washington, Department of Fisheries, 1958.

                                                            ***
IIENV    Lipp, R.L.  THE ENVIRONMENT OF OFFSHORE AND ESTUARINE ALABAMA.
         Geological Survey for the State Oil and Gas Board.  University,
         Alabama, 1974.  135p.

                                                            ART
VP       List, E.J.  THERMAL DISCHARGE CONSIDERATIONS IN POWER PLANT SITING.
         In Thermo-Fluids Conference.  Sydney, Australia, Institution of En-
         gineers, 1972?  pp. 1-6.

                                                            ***
VORM     LITTORAL COMMUNITIES.  PROCEEDINGS OF A SYMPOSIUM, PEMBROKE, WALES.
         FIELD STUDIES COUNCIL.  Pembroke, Wales, 1968.

                                                            13
IIIP     Livingstone, Robert J.  A SYSTEM FOR THE DETERMINATION OF CHRONIC
         EFFECTS OF POLLUTANTS ON THE PSYCHOLOGY AND BEHAVIOR OF MARINE OR-
         GANISMS.  Florida Sea Grant publication 04-3-158-43.  Gainesville,
         Fla., 1974.  15p.

                                                            5,13,14,16
VLOS     LOCAL IMPACTS OF THE LAW OF THE SEA; PROCEEDINGS OF A CONFERENCE
         HELD IN SEATTLE, OCTOBER 10-12, 1972.  WSG-AS 73-8.  Seattle, Di-
         vision of Marine Resources, University of Washington, 1973.  x,
         141p.

                                                            ***
IIIF     Loesch, H.C.  SOME ALTERNATIVES FOR A NEW SHRIMP LAW AFFECTING
         SHRIMPING IN LOUISIANA INTERNAL WATERS.  Speech.  Annual Louisiana
         Shrimp Association Meeting, January, 1973.  Mimeo.  n.p.  n.d.  14p.

                                                            17
VOR      Loftas, Tony.  THE LAST RESOURCE.  London, Hamilton, 1969.  256p.

|||
|---|---|
|VOR|***<br>Loftas, Tony. THE LAST RESOURCE; MAN'S EXPLOITATION OF THE OCEANS. New, rev. ed. Chicago, Ill., Henry Regnery, 1970. 276p.|
|VOR|14<br>_____ _____ THE LAST RESOURCE: MAN'S EXPLOITATION OF THE OCEANS. Rev. ed. Harmondsworth, Penguin, 1972. 317p.|
|VOR|7<br>_____ _____ WEALTH FROM THE OCEANS. London, Phoenix House, 1967. 69p.|
|VLOS|5,14,15<br>Logan, R.M. CANADA, THE UNITED STATES, AND THE THIRD LAW OF THE SEA CONFERENCE. Montreal, Canadian-American Committee, 1974. viii, 117p.|
|VLOS|1,5,10,12,13,14,15,16,18<br>Logue, John J., ed. THE FATE OF THE OCEANS. World Order Research Institute. Pennsylvania, Villanova University Press, 1972. xxix, 237p.|
|IIIOI|ART<br>Lokken, Harold. FISHERIES USES OF THE SEA; INDUSTRY INTERESTS. In Conference on Local Impacts of the Law of the Sea, Seattle, Washington, October 10-12, 1972. Seattle, University of Washington, Division of Marine Resources, 1973. pp. 38-43.|
|IIOCET|15<br>LONG ISLAND SOUND CONFERENCE, SIXTH, MONTAUK, NEW YORK, 1973. CURRENT RESEARCH IN AN URBAN SEA: LONG ISLAND SOUND; ABSTRACTS. Montauk, New York Ocean Science Laboratory, 1974?|
|IICZM|***<br>Longest, J.W. INVESTIGATION OF THE PUBLIC AND PRIVATE INTERESTS IN THE DEVELOPMENT OF THE CHESAPEAKE BAY AREA. College Park, University of Maryland, 1973. 41p.|
|IIIF|ART<br>Lonsdale, Adrian L. 'NO CONTEST' ON THE FISHING GROUNDS. In U.S. Naval Institute Proceedings, July, 1968. pp. 62-70.|
|VCS|7,12<br>Lopez Villamil, Humberto. LA PLATAFORMA CONTINENTAL Y LOS PROBLEMAS JURIDICOS DEL MAR. Madrid, J. Bravo, 1958.|
|VINTL|***<br>Loriot, F. LA THEORIE DES EAUX HISTORIQUES ET LE REGIME JURIDIQUE DU GOLFE SAINT-LAURENT EN DROIT INTERNE ET INTERNATIONAL. Quebec, 1972. n.p. 705p.|
|IIIP|17<br>Los Angeles, University of Southern California. Allen Hancock Foundation. BIOLOGICAL AND OCEANOGRAPHICAL SURVEY OF THE SANTA BARBARA CHANNEL OIL SPILL. 1969-1970. Its Sea Grant publication no. 2. 1971. 2 Vols.|
|VP|14<br>Loth, David, and Morris L. Ernst. THE TAMING OF TECHNOLOGY. New York, Simon and Schuster, Inc., 1972. 236p.|

16
IISL    Louisiana. Attorney General's Office. A PRIMER ON THE TIDELANDS CONTROVERSY AND LOUISIANA'S EXPERIENCE IN THE DISPUTE. Baton Rouge, 1963. 40p.

***
VOS     Louisiana. State University. Center for Wetland Resources. MARINE RESEARCH INTEREST IN LOUISIANA UNIVERSITIES. LSU-SG-75-02. Baton Rouge, 1975-    1st-    iv, 35p.

13
IISL    _____ _____ WETLANDS: RESOURCE OF THE FUTURE. Baton Rouge, 1971. 1 Vol.

16
IIIT&L  Louisiana. Wildlife and Fisheries Commission. COMPILATION OF LOUISIANA LAWS PERTAINING TO WILD LIFE AND FISHERIES. Baton Rouge, 1958. 212p.

***
IIP&H   LOUISIANA COASTAL LAW. Louisiana Coastal Law Report no. 19. Baton Rouge, Louisiana State University, Louisiana Sea Grant Legal Program, 1975. 4p.

***
IICZM   LOUISIANA GOVERNMENT AND THE COASTAL ZONE - 1972. Report. Baton Rouge, Louisiana Advisory Commission on Coastal Marine Resources, 1972. 194p.

***
IVMMR   Louisiana Offshore Oil Scouts Association. STATUS OF THE LOUISIANA OFFSHORE OIL INDUSTRY AS OF JANUARY 1, 1973; STATISTICAL REVIEW OF EVENTS BETWEEN JULY 1, 1972 AND JANUARY 1, 1973. n.p. 1973.

1,5,13
IIP&H   Louisiana Superport Studies. FIVE SEPARATE SUPERPORT-RELATED STUDIES, Baton Rouge, Louisiana State University, 1972-

1,5,13
IIP&H   _____ _____ PRELIMINARY RECOMMENDATIONS AND DATA ANALYSIS. Report 1. LSU-SG-72-03. Baton Rouge, Louisiana State University, 1972. 419p.

1,5,13
IIP&H   _____ _____ RECOMMENDATIONS FOR THE ENVIRONMENTAL PROTECTION PLAN. Report 3. Baton Rouge, Louisiana State University, 1973. 530p.

1,5,13
IIP&H   _____ _____ TECHNICAL APPENDICES TO RECOMMENDATIONS FOR THE ENVIRONMENTAL PROTECTION PLAN. LSU-SG-74-04. Baton Rouge, Louisiana State University, 1974. 227p.

14a
IIIF    Lounsbury, Ralph G. THE BRITISH FISHERY AT NEWFOUNDLAND, 1634-1763. New Haven, Yale University Press; London, H. Milford, Oxford University Press, 1934. viii, 398p.

|||
|---|---|
|IIP|14<br>Low, Seth T. AN INVESTIGATION OF THE FEDERAL, STATE, AND LOCAL OIL SPILL CONTINGENCY PLANS FOR THE LONG ISLAND SOUND AREA. Albany, Office of Science Adviser to the New York State Assembly, 1973. 180p.|
|VLOS|5,14,18<br>Luard, David E.T. THE CONTROL OF THE SEA-BED; A NEW INTERNATIONAL ISSUE. New York, Taplinger, 1974. x, 309p.|
|VINTL|2<br>Luard, Evan, ed. THE INTERNATIONAL REGULATION OF FRONTIER DISPUTES. New York, Praeger, 1970. 247p.|
|IIIAFF|***<br>Lubet, P.E. RAPPORT AU GOUVERNEMENT DE LA YOUGOSLAVIE SUR L'OSTREI-CULTURE ET LA MYTILICULTURE (2e Miss.). FAO/ETAP 1425. 1961.|
|IIIF|1,3,4,5,7,8,11,13,14,15,18<br>Lucas, C.E. INTERNATIONAL FISHERY BODIES OF THE NORTH ATLANTIC. Law of the Sea Institute occasional paper no. 5. Kingston, University of Rhode Island, 1970. 32p.|
|VP|ART<br>Ludnholm, Bengt. THE OCEANS - THEIR PRODUCTION AND POLLUTION; THE BALTIC AS A CASE STUDY. In Elisabeth M. Borgese, ed., Pacem in Maribus. New York, Dodd, Mead, 1972. pp. 25-31.|
|IICZM|13<br>Ludwigson, John O. MANAGING THE ENVIRONMENT IN THE COASTAL ZONE. Reprinted from Environmental Reporter, monograph no. 3, Vol. 1, no. 1.|
|VP|13<br>Lukens, H.R. INSTRUCTION MANUAL FOR OIL SLICK IDENTIFICATION BY TRACE ELEMENT PATTERNS MEASURED WITH NEUTRON ACTIVATION ANALYSIS. GULF-RT-A-10973. San Diego, California, Gulf Radiation Technology. n.d.|
|VINTL|3,5,12,16<br>Lumb, R.D. THE LAW OF THE SEA AND AUSTRALIAN OFF-SHORE AREAS. St. Lucia, Brisbane, University of Queensland Press, 1966. 86p.|
|VP|2<br>Lund, Herbert F., ed. INDUSTRIAL POLLUTION CONTROL HANDBOOK. New York, McGraw-Hill, 1971.|
|IIP|14<br>Luoma, Samuel N. MERCURY CYCLING IN A SMALL HAWAIIAN ESTUARY. Technical Memorandum Report no. 42. Working paper no. 5. Honolulu, University of Hawaii, Water Resources Center, 1974. vi, 38p.|
|VORM|13,14<br>Luttwak, Edward. THE POLITICAL USES OF SEA POWER. Studies in international affairs, no. 23. Baltimore, Johns Hopkins University Press, 1974. vii, 79p.|
|IICZM|***<br>Lutz, Robert, et al. THE DEVELOPMENT CRITERIA OF THE PRELIMINARY COASTAL PLAN. USC-SG-ASI-75. Los Angeles, University of Southern|

California, Marine Advisory Services, Sea Grant Program, 1976. 35p.

13
IIIFV&G   Lyles, Charles H. STATISTICS OF THE VESSELS DOCUMENTED - FISHING CRAFT 1957-66. Fishery leaflet 610. Washington, U.S.G.P.O., December, 1967. 62p.

13
IICONS   Lynch, M.P., B.L. Laird, et al, eds. MARINE AND ESTUARINE SANCTUARIES. PROCEEDINGS OF THE NATIONAL WORKSHOP ON SANCTUARIES, 28-30 NOVEMBER, 1973. WASHINGTON, D.C. Gloucester Point, Virginia Institute of Marine Science, February 1974. vii, 213p.

14
IIE   Lynam, Leslie. ESTUARIES...A RESOURCE WORTH SAVING. Olympia, Washington State Department of Game, 1972. 21p.

14a
IIIFP   Lynn, Kenneth M. A STUDY ESTIMATING THE MAXIMUM MARKET POTENTIAL OF A PROCESSED FISH PRODUCT. A thesis submitted in partial fulfillment of the requirements for the degree of Master of Business Administration. Tacoma, Washington, University of Puget Sound, 1971. 68p.

***
IIIF   Lyone, Cicely. SALMON: OUR HERITAGE; THE STORY OF A PROVINCE AND AN INDUSTRY. Vancouver, B.C., Mitchell Press, 1969.

***
VENV   McCaffrey, Stephen C. PRIVATE REMEDIES FOR TRANSFRONTIER ENVIRONMENTAL DISTURBANCES. Morges, Switzerland, International Union for Conservation of Nature and Natural Resources, 1975. 157p.

***
IIIF   McCain, John C., and James M. Peck, Jr. THE EFFECTS OF A HAWAIIAN POWER PLANT ON THE DISTRIBUTION AND ABUNDANCE OF REEF FISHES. UNIHI-SEA-GRANT-AR-73-03. Honolulu, University of Hawaii, 1973. 16p.

***
IIOR   McCauley, James E. OREGON'S NEARSHORE OCEAN. Corvallis, Oregon State University, Cooperative Extension Service, Marine Advisory Program, 1973. 8p.

ART
IICZM   MacCutcheon, Edward M. TRAFFIC AND TRANSPORT NEEDS AT THE LAND-SEA INTERFACE. In J.F. Peel Brahtz, Coastal Zone Management; Multiple Use with Conservation. New York, John Wiley, 1972. pp. 105-148.

ART
IIIF   McDonagh, M. IRISH COASTAL FISHERIES; THE EEC AND FISHERIES POLICY. In Technology Ireland, Vol. 6, 1975. pp. 13-15.

ART
VORM   MacDonald, Gordon J.F. AN AMERICAN STRATEGY FOR THE OCEANS. In Edmund A. Gullion, ed., Uses of the Sea. Englewood Cliffs, N.J., Prentice-Hall, 1968. pp. 163-194.

***
VENV   MacDonald, James B., and John E. Conway. ENVIRONMENTAL LITIGATION. Madison, University of Wisconsin, Department of Law, 1972. 450p.

                                                                  1,7
VINTL     McDougal, Myres S., and William T. Burke. CRISIS IN THE LAW OF THE
          SEA: COMMUNITY PERSPECTIVES VERSUS NATIONAL EGOISM. Reprinted from
          Yale Law Journal, Vol. 67, no. 4, February 1958.

                                     1,3,5,6,7,8,9,12,14,15,16
VINTL     _____ THE PUBLIC ORDER OF THE OCEANS; A CONTEMPORARY INTER-
          NATIONAL LAW OF THE SEA. New Haven, Yale University Press, 1962.
          xxv, 1226p.

                                                                   ***
VOR       McEachern, John, and E.L. Towle. RESOURCE MANAGEMENT PROGRAMS FOR
          OCEANIC ISLANDS. PAPER PRESENTED AT THE 37th NORTH AMERICAN WILD-
          LIFE AND NATURAL RESOURCES CONFERENCE, MEXICO CITY, MARCH 12-15,
          1972. St. Thomas, Virgin Islands, Caribbean Research Institute,
          1972. 21p.

                                                                   ART
IVENV     McErlean, A. ENVIRONMENTAL PROTECTION AGENCY'S ROLE, INTERESTS AND
          RESPONSIBILITIES WITH RESPECT TO THE OUTER CONTINENTAL SHELF DEVEL-
          OPMENT. In Proceedings of Marine Environmental Implications of Off-
          shore Drilling in the Eastern Gulf of Mexico. St. Petersburgh,
          State University System of Florida, Institute of Oceanography, 1974.
          pp. 33-35.

                                                                     2
VENV      McEvoy, James. THE AMERICAN PUBLIC'S CONCERN WITH THE ENVIRONMENT:
          A STUDY OF PUBLIC OPINION. Davis, Institute of Governmental Af-
          fairs, University of California, 1971. 29p.

                                                                    17
VOS       McFadden, James T., and John M. Armstrong. A MULTIDISCIPLINARY UNI-
          VERSITY PROGRAM IN MARINE SCIENCES AND ENGINEERING FOR THE GREAT
          LAKES. n.p., 1970.

                                                                   ***
VOD       McFarlane, C.F. OCEAN WASTE DISPOSAL PRACTICES IN METROPOLITAN
          AREAS OF CALIFORNIA. Anaheim, Interstate Electronics Corporation,
          Oceanics Division, 1974. 95p.

                                                                    14a
IIIF      McFarland, Raymond. A HISTORY OF THE NEW ENGLAND FISHERIES, WITH
          MAPS. Philadelphia, University of Pennsylvania; New York, D.
          Appleton and Company, agents, 1911. 457p.

                                                                 1,5,9,16
VLOS      McFee, William. THE LAW OF THE SEA. Philadelphia, Lippincott,
          1950. 318p.

                                                                    17
VOCET     McGill University, Montreal. Marine Science Center. ANNUAL REPORT.
          n.d.

                                                                   ***
IIENV     McGreevy, Randall. SEATTLE SHORELINE ENVIRONMENT. Seattle, Uni-
          versity of Washington, 1973. 41p.

                                                                   ***
IIENV     McGreevy, R. SEATTLE SHORELINE ENVIRONMENT. NOAA 74092307. Rock-
          ville, Md., U.S. National Oceanic and Atmospheric Administration,

1975. 46p.

***

IIIF    McHugh, J.L. BIOLOGICAL CONSEQUENCES OF ALTERNATIVE REGIMES. NYSSGP-SS-75-003. Stony Brook, State University of New York, 1974. 21p.

***

IIIF    McHugh, J.L., and Jay J.C. Ginter. FISHERIES. Albany, State University of New York, New York Sea Grant Institute, 1975.

***

VP    MacKay, D., and W. Harrison, eds. OIL AND THE CANADIAN ENVIRONMENT. Canada, University of Canada, Institute of Environmental Sciences and Engineering, 1973? 149p.

***

IVMMR    MacKay, D.I., and G.A. MacKay. POLITICAL ECONOMY OF NORTH SEA OIL. London, Martin Robertson, 1975. 193p.

16

IIIINTL    MacKay, Robert A. PRELIMINARY REPORT ON THE INTERNATIONAL CONTROL OF FISHERIES ON THE HIGH SEAS. Honolulu, Institute of Pacific Relations, 1929. 5, 42p.

***

IIIAFF    McKee, A. FARMING THE SEA. London, Souvenir Press, 1967.

13,15

IIIAFF    _____ FARMING THE SEA. New York, Thomas Y. Crowell Company, 1971. 198p.

***

VSG    McKee, J. Chester. SEA GRANT: CATALYST FOR UNIVERSITY CONSORTIA IN MISSISSIPPI. Paper presented at the Seventh Annual meeting of the Sea Grant Association, Seattle, Washington, 30 October 1974. MASGP-74-040. Ocean Springs, Mississippi-Alabama Sea Grant Consortium, 1974.

13

IVMMR    McKelvey, V.E. MINERALS IN THE SEA - A COMPREHENSIVE REPORT ON THE MINERAL POTENTIAL OF THE SUBMERGED PARTS OF THE UNITED STATES. Reprint. Ocean Industry. Houston, Gulf Publishing Company, September, 1968. 6p.

5,13,16

IVMMR    McKelvey, V.E., et al. SUBSEA MINERAL RESOURCES AND PROBLEMS RELATED TO THEIR DEVELOPMENT. U.S. Department of the Interior, Geological Survey circular 619. Washington, 1969. V, 26p.

***

VP    McKenna, Q.H., et al. ELECTROCHEMICAL FLOTATION CONCEPT FOR REMOVING OIL FROM WATER. Final Report. USCG-734305.2/4. Washington, U.S. Coast Guard, January, 1973. 131p.

13

IIIF    McKenzie, Daniel H., and Ole A. Mathisen. A SYSTEMS ANALYSIS OF THE BRISTOL BAY SOCKEYE SALMON FISHERY. Fisheries Research Institute Circular no. 71-11. Washington Sea Grant no. 71-5. Seattle, Division of Marine Resources, University of Washington, 1971. 31p.

VENV    McKenzie, Garry D., and Russell O. Utgard. MAN AND HIS PHYSICAL ENVIRONMENT: READINGS IN ENVIRONMENTAL GEOLOGY. 2d ed. Minneapolis, Burgess Publishing Company, 1975. 388p.  
         14

VT&L    McKernan, Donald L. SCIENTIFIC RESEARCH. Statement by the Honorable Donald L. McKernan, alternate United States Representative to the Committee on the Peaceful Uses of the Seabed and the Ocean Floor Beyond the Limits of National Jurisdiction Subcommittee III, August 11, 1972. Geneva, U.S. Information Service, 1972. 4p.  
         13

VP    McLaughlin, John J.A., and James E. Alexander. THE OCEAN AS A SOLUTION TO POLLUTION. In Marine Technology Society. Ninth Annual Conference, Washington, D.C., September 10-12, 1973. Washington, D.C., 1973. pp. 551-562.  
         ART

VP    McLeod, W.R., and D.L. McLeod. MEASURES TO COMBAT OFFSHORE ARCTIC OIL SPILLS. In Offshore Technology Conference, 4th, Houston, Texas, 1972: Preprints. Dallas, Tex., 1972. Vol. 1, pp. 141-162.  
         ART

IIICONS    McLin, Jon. RESOURCES AND AUTHORITY IN THE NORTH-EAST ATLANTIC; FISHERIES CONSERVATION. American Universities Field Staff. Reports. West Europe series, Vol. 8, no. 6. Hanover, N.H., 1973. 13p.  
         ***

VP    McLoughlin, James. THE LAW RELATING TO POLLUTION; AN INTRODUCTION. Manchester, Manchester University Press, 1972. xiii, 133p.  
         2

IICONS    McMillan, George. REPORT TO THE WINSTON CHURCHILL MEMORIAL TRUST ON A TOUR OF PACIFIC RIM COUNTRIES TO STUDY MARITIME AND MARINE PARKS AND GENERAL COASTLINE PROTECTION. Wellington, N.Z., Department of Lands and Survey, 1975. 30p.  
         ***

IVMMR    McNichols, Walter J. LEGAL PROBLEMS REGARDING THE EXTRACTION OF MINERALS (INCLUDING OIL AND GAS) FROM THE CONTINENTAL SHELF. Sea Grant Technical Bulletin no. 14 Miami, Fla., University of Miami, 1971. v, 120p.  
         3,5,12,16,18

VINTL    Macpherson, David. ANNALS OF COMMERCE, MANUFACTURES, FISHERIES, AND NAVIGATION, WITH BRIEF NOTICES OF THE ARTS AND SCIENCES CONNECTED WITH THEM. New York, Johnson Reprint, 1972; London, Nichols and Son, 1805. 4 Vols.  
         14a

IIIP    Mackin, J.G. A REVIEW OF SIGNIFICANT PAPERS ON EFFECTS OF OIL SPILLS AND OIL BRINE DISCHARGES ON MARINE BIOTIC COMMUNITIES. College Station, Texas A&M Research Foundation, 1973.  
         13

VENV    Maddox, John R. THE DOOMSDAY SYNDROME. New York, McGraw-Hill, 1972. vii, 293p.  
         17

|||||||||||||||||||||||||||||||||||||||||||||||||||||||||||||||||||||||||||||||||||||||||||||||||||||||

IIIF Magoon, Charles D. SHRIMP FISHING IN WASHINGTON.[14] Information Booklet no. 3. Olympia, Department of Fisheries, n.d. 21p.

VP Mahoney, James R. EVALUATION OF AN OCEAN BASED SOLID WASTE DISPOSAL SYSTEM: AIR POLLUTION CONTROL ASPECTS. Boston, Mass., Harvard University, School of Public Health, 1972. 78p. [***]

IICZM Maine. STATE OF MAINE GUIDELINES FOR MUNICIPAL SHORELAND ZONING ORDINANCES, ADOPTED BY THE BOARD OF ENVIRONMENTAL PROTECTION AND THE LAND USE REGULATION COMMISSION. Augusta, 1973. 16p. [14]

IIIT&L Maine. Commissioner of Sea and Shore Fisheries. MAINE SEA AND SHORE FISHERIES LAWS AND REGULATIONS. Augusta, 1961. 225p. [3]

IIIFV&G Maine. Department of Marine Resources. NAVIGATIONAL CHARTS, DIAGRAMS, AND INFORMATION TO AID IN THE PREVENTION OF DESTRUCTION OF FISHING GEAR SET OUT BY STATE OF MAINE FISHING VESSELS. Augusta, 1975. 16p. [***]

IVT&L Maine. Laws, statutes, etc. THE MAINE MINING LAW FOR STATE-OWNED LANDS - TITLE 10, CHAPTER 401. Revised Statutes, 1964, as amended by Public Laws of 1965, 1967 and 1969. Augusta, Maine Mining Bureau, 1969. 35p. [13]

IICONS Maine. State Planning Office. MAINE COASTAL RESOURCES RENEWAL. Augusta, 1971. 178p. [2]

VOR Maine. University. School of Law. MAINE LAW AFFECTING MARINE RESOURCES. Portland, University of Maine, 1970. 903p. 4 Vols. [5,16]

IIIOR Mais, K.F., comp. CALIFORNIA DEPARTMENT OF FISH AND GAME FISHERIES RESOURCES SEA SURVEY CRUISES. 1974. Sacramento, California Marine Research Committee, 1975. ix, 86p. [***]

VENV Maldonado, Tomás. DESIGN, NATURE, AND REVOLUTION; TOWARD A CRITICAL ECOLOGY. Translated from the Italian by Mario Domandi. 1st U.S. ed. New York, Harper and Row, 1972. xi, 139p. [17]

VOR Mallan, Lloyd. SECRETS OF THE SEA. New York, Arco, 1965. 112p. [13]

IIILOS Mallon, Lawrence G. A MULTI-DISCIPLINARY ANALYSIS OF THE VARIOUS PROPOSALS PRESENTED FOR THE 1974 LAW OF THE SEA CONFERENCE ON EXCLUSIVE FISHERIES ZONES. Sea Grant technical bulletin no. 28. Coral Gables, University of Miami, 1974. 81p. [13,14,16]

IICZM MANAGING OUR COASTAL ZONE. Proceedings. New York State Sea Grant Program. n.p., 1973. 74p. [***]

|         | 6,11,16 |
|---|---|

VMLAD     Manca, Plinio. INTERNATIONAL MARITIME LAW. Antwerpen, European Transport Law, 1970. 3 Vols.

                                                                             16

VMT     Mance, Sir Harry O. INTERNATIONAL RIVER AND CANAL TRANSPORT. London, Oxford University Press, 1945. 115p.

                                                                             14

IIENE     Mandell, David A. THERMAL POWER PLANT WASTE HEAT UTILIZATION. Department of Lighting, City of Seattle. Bulletin 334. Pullman, Washington State University, 1974. 36p.

                                                                             15

IVMMR     MANGANESE NODULE DEPOSITS IN THE PACIFIC. SYMPOSIUM/WORKSHOP PROCEEDINGS OCTOBER 16-17, 1972. Honolulu, University of Hawaii, 1973. 220p.

                                                                             13

VOS     Mangone, Gerard J. OCEAN STUDIES PROGRAM AT THE WOODROW WILSON INTERNATIONAL CENTER FOR SCHOLARS. Washington, Woodrow Wilson International Center for Scholars, 1971. 16p.

                                                                     5,12,13,15,18

VLOS     _____ THE UNITED NATIONS, INTERNATIONAL LAW, AND THE BED OF THE SEAS. Ocean series 303. Washington, Woodrow Wilson International Center for Scholars, 1972. 44p.

                                                                            ***

VCS     Mangone, Gerard J., and J. Homer. DECISIONS FOR DELAWARE: SEA GRANT LOOKS AT LEGAL ASPECTS OF OCS DEVELOPMENT. DEL-SG-1-75(2). Newark, University of Delaware, 24p.

                                                                            ***

VORM     Mangone, Gerard J., and John L. Pedrick. CONTEMPORARY RESEARCH IN MARINE AFFAIRS. Sea Grant Report DEL-SG-10-74. Newark, University of Delaware, 1974. 54p.

                                                                             13

VOS     Mangone, Gerard J., and John L. Pedrick. MARINE AFFAIRS AND HIGHER EDUCATION. DRL-SG-17-73. Newark, Delaware, College of Marine Studies, University of Delaware. September 1973. 223p.

                                                                            ***

IICZM     Mangum, Fred, Jr. THE NORTH CAROLINA COASTAL ZONE; ECONOMIC PROBLEMS AND COURSES OF ACTION. Raleigh, North Carolina State University, Agricultural Extension Service, 1975.

                                                                             1

VLOS     Manley, Robert H. THE GENEVA CONFERENCES ON THE LAW OF THE SEA AS A STEP IN THE INTERNATIONAL LAW-MAKING PROCESS. Reprinted from The Albany Law Review, Vol. 25, no. 1, January 1961. 21p.

                                                                            ***

VOCET     MANNED UNDERSEA SCIENCE AND TECHNOLOGY: FISCAL YEAR 1974 REPORT. Rockville, Md., U.S. National Oceanic and Atmospheric Administration, 1975. 55p.

| | | 16 |
|---|---|---|
VOR  Manner, E. COMMENTS ON PROFESSOR WILLIAM T. BURKE'S REPORT. SIPRI, TOWARDS A BETTER USE OF THE OCEANS: A STUDY AND PROGNOSIS. Stockholm, Almqvist and Wiksell, 1969. pp. 271-277.

\*\*\*

IIIF  Manor, Thomas A., ed. MARINE FISHERIES REVIEW. Washington, U.S. Department of Commerce, NOAA, 1974-

\*\*\*

VP  MANUAL ON OIL POLLUTION: PRACTICAL INFORMATION ON MEANS OF DEALING WITH OIL SPILLAGES. London, Inter-governmental Maritime Consultative Organization, 1972. 82p.

14

IICZM  Maraist, Frank L. LAWS PERTAINING TO PROPERTY. STATE LAWS THAT AFFECT MISSISSIPPI'S MARINE AND COASTAL ZONE. Mississippi/Alabama Sea Grant Consortium, MASGP-74-034. Ocean Springs, 1974. 202p.

\*\*\*

IICZM  _____ LAWS RELATING TO GENERAL ADMINISTRATION AND MANAGEMENT. Mississippi/Alabama Sea Grant Consortium, MASGAP-74-033. Ocean Springs, University of Mississippi Law Center, 1974. 10 Vols.

\*\*\*

IIIF  Marasco, Richard J. AN ANALYSIS OF FUTURE DEMANDS, SUPPLIES, PRICES AND NEEDS FOR FISHERY RESOURCES OF THE CHESAPEAKE BAY. College Park, Md., Agriculture Experiment Station, 1975. vii, 65p.

\*\*\*

IICZM  Marcus, Norman, and M.W. Groves, eds. THE NEW ZONING: LEGAL, ADMINISTRATIVE AND ECONOMIC CONCEPTS AND TECHNIQUES. New York, Praeger, 1974.

15

VLOS  Mariani, Georgette C. LE DROIT DE LA MER E LA VEILLE DE LA 3 CONFERENCE DES NATIONS-UNIES. Nice, Institut de La Paix et du Developpement, 1974. 49p.

\*\*\*

VENV  MARINE ECOLOGY, ENVIRONMENTAL FACTORS. New York, John Wiley, 1970. 681p.

\*\*\*

VOS  MARINE EDUCATION FOR HAWAII: A PROSPECTUS - A REPORT FOR THE HAWAII MARINE EDUCATION COUNCIL. Honolulu, University of Hawaii, Sea Grant College Program, 1975. 33p.

15

VORM  MARINE GEODESY SYMPOSIUM. PROCEEDINGS. 1st-    1966-    Washington, U.S. Environmental Science Services Administration, U.S.G.P.O., 1966-

\*\*\*

VOI  MARINE INDUSTRIES: PROBLEMS AND OPPORTUNITIES. Washington, D.C. Marine Technology Society, 1973. 719p.

14

IIIP  MARINE POLLUTION AND SEA LIFE: SURVEY OF PROBLEMS AND TREATMENTS. Surrey, England, Fishing News (Books) Ltd., 1972. 624p.

|  |  |
|---|---|
| VCONS | ***<br>MARINE PROTECTION, RESEARCH, AND SANCTUARIES ACT OF 1972: PUBLIC LAW 92-532. TAMU-SG-73-602. College Station, Texas A&M University, 1973. |
| VOS | ***<br>MARINE RESEARCH INTEREST IN LOUISIANA UNIVERSITIES 1975. LSU-SG-75-02. Baton Rouge, Louisiana State University, 1975. 35p. |
| VOR | ***<br>MARINE RESOURCES PROBLEMS: THE CALIFORNIA CITIZENS' VIEWPOINT. Los Angeles, University of Southern California, 1974. 18p. |
| VOR | ART<br>MARINE RESOURCES SPECIAL EDITION. In Los Angeles Daily Journal, Report section, September 24, 1968, pp. 19-25. |
| IIOSTR | ***<br>MARINE STRUCTURES AND SYSTEMS. A FIVE-DAY SHORT COURSE. Lecture Notes. Held in Los Angeles, Calif., July 24-28, 1972. Los Angeles, University of California, 1972? 333p. |
| VOCET | 5,13,17,18<br>Marine Technology Society. ANNUAL CONFERENCE AND EXPOSITION PREPRINTS. 6- 1970- |
| VOCET | 5<br>_____ _____ "THE DECADE AHEAD, 1970-1980." Washington, 1969. xii, 626p. |
| VOR | 5,13,18<br>_____ _____ EXPLOITING THE OCEAN. Transactions of the 2d Annual MTS Conference and Exhibit, June 27-29, 1966. Washington, Marine Technology Society, 1966. x, 520p. |
| IIP&H | 15<br>_____ _____ HANDBOOK FOR OFFSHORE PORT PLANNING; the edited text of a Marine Technology Society, Texas A&M University and University of Delaware short course held at Washington, D.C., September 10 to 14, 1973. Washington, Marine Technology Society, 1973. |
| VLOS | 1,5,8,12,13,18<br>_____ _____ LAW OF THE SEA REPORTS: A YEAR OF CRISIS, FEBRUARY 19, 1971; GENEVA REPORT, OCTOBER 18, 1971. Washington, Marine Technology Society, 1972. ix, 204p. |
| VOCET | 1<br>_____ _____ PREPRINTS, EIGHTH ANNUAL CONFERENCE AND EXPOSITION. Washington, D.C., September 11-13, 1972. xviii, 782p. |
| IICZM | 13,16<br>_____ _____ TOOLS FOR COASTAL ZONE MANAGEMENT CONFERENCE, WASHINGTON, D.C., 1972. PROCEEDINGS. Washington, D.C., Marine Technology Society, 1972. xvi, 213p. |
| VOCET | 16<br>_____ _____ TRANSACTIONS OF THE ANNUAL MTS CONFERENCE AND EXHIBIT. Washington, 1965- |

|  |  |
|---|---|
| VOCET | 5,15,17<br>Marine Technology Society. Law Committee. A CRITICAL REVIEW OF THE MARINE SCIENCE COMMISSION REPORT. PROCEEDINGS OF A SEMINAR HELD BY THE ... COMMITTEE IN CONJUNCTION WITH THE GEORGE WASHINGTON UNIVERSITY. Washington, D.C., n.d. 94p. |

***

VMT    MARITIME CARRIAGE OF NUCLEAR MATERIALS. Proceedings series. Vienna, Austria, International Atomic Energy Agency; New York, UNIPUB, 1973. 402p.

***

VMT    MARITIME TRANSPORT: 1974. OECD, Marine Transport Committee. Paris, Organization for Economic Cooperation and Development, 1975. 149p.

ART
VP    Marland, Richard. THE GOVERNOR'S TASK FORCE ON PEARL HARBOR. In Conference in the Matter of Pollution of the Navigable Waters of Pearl Harbor and its Tributaries in the State of Hawaii, Honolulu, September 21-23, 1971. n.p. n.d. 62p.

17
VOCET    Marr, John C., ed. SYMPOSIUM ON THE COOPERATIVE STUDY OF THE KUROSHIO AND ADJACENT REGIONS (CSK) HONOLULU, 29 APRIL - 2 May, 1968. REPORT AND ABSTRACTS OF PAPERS. FAO fisheries report no. 63. FAO, 1968. 57p.

***

IICZM    Marr, Paul D., and Eugene K. Schuler, Jr. GOVERNMENTAL JURISDICTIONS OF THE NEW YORK STATE COASTAL ZONE. Albany, State University of New York, Sea Grant Institute, 1975. 176p.

5,16
VMLAD    Marsden, Reginald, ed. DOCUMENTS RELATING TO LAW AND CUSTOM OF THE SEA. London, Navy Records Society, 1915. 2 Vols.

3,6
VMLAD    Marsden, Reginald G. A TREATISE ON THE LAW OF COLLISIONS AT SEA. 7th ed., by Marcus W. Slade. London, Stevens and Sons, Limited; New York, Baker, Voorhis and Company, 1919. lxxx, 610p.

3,6,11
VMLAD    _____ THE LAW OF COLLISIONS AT SEA. 11th ed. by Kenneth C. McGuffie. London, Stevens and Sons, Ltd., 1961. lxxxvi, 975p.
_____ _____ SUPPLEMENT, 1970. Vol. 4

17
VOR    Marsh, George P. MAN AND NATURE. Edited by David Lowenthal. Cambridge, Belknap Press of Harvard University Press, 1965. xxix, 472p.

5,16
IVMMR    Marshall, Hubert R., and Betty Zisk. THE FEDERAL-STATE STRUGGLE FOR OFFSHORE OIL. Indianapolis, Bobbs-Merrill, 1966. 53p.

13
VOS    Marshall, Nelson. PLANNING WORKSHOPS ON THE DEVELOPMENT OF UNIVERSITY MARINE PROGRAMS. Kingston, International Center for Marine Resource Development, University of Rhode Island. 13 June, 1973. 6p.

| | | ART |
|---|---|---|
| VP | Marstrand, P.K. POLLUTION OF THE SEAS. In A.D. McKnight, et al, Environmental Pollution Control. London, 1974. pp. 150-173. | |

14
IIENE    Martin, Bob. A REPORT ON ENERGY AND SOLID WASTE FOR TASK FORCE IV ENERGY POLICY COUNCIL. Olympia, Washington, Department of Ecology, 1974. 9, 5p.

2,3,5,12,13,16,18
VLOS    Martin, Cabot. FORMULATING AN OCEANIC JURISPRUDENCE. University of Miami Sea Grant Program, no. 2-35147. Special bulletin no. 1. November, 1971. Coral Gables, Fla., University of Miami, 1971. iii, 25p.

***
VOCET    Martin, D.F. MARINE CHEMISTRY. New York, Marcel Dekker, 1969-

***
VP    Martin, Seelye, and W.J. Campbell. OIL SPILLS IN THE ARCTIC OCEAN: EXTENT OF SPREADING AND POSSIBILITY OF LARGE-SCALE THERMAL EFFECTS. Seattle, University of Washington, Department of Atmospheric Sciences, 1974. 6p.

***
VB    Marvin, U.B. CONTINENTAL DRIFT: THE EVOLUTION OF A CONCEPT. Washington, D.C., Smithsonian Institution Press; distr. New York, George Braziller, 1973. 239p.

5,12,14a,15
VCONS    Marx, Wesley. THE FRAIL OCEAN. New York, Coward-McCann, 1967.

5,17
VP    _____ OILSPILL. The Sierra Club battlebook series, 5. San Francisco, Sierra Club, 1971. 139p.

***
VCONS    _____ THE PROTECTED OCEAN; HOW TO KEEP THE SEAS ALIVE. New York, McCann and Geoghen, Inc., 1972. 95p.

13
IIIFP    Maryland. Bureau of Commercial Fisheries. MARINE PROTEIN CONCENTRATE - A SUMMARY REPORT ON THE DEVELOPMENT OF A PROPOSED COMMERCIAL MANUFACTURING PROCESS AND ON THE PROPERTIES OF A TEST SAMPLE. Fishery Leaflet 584. By Bureau of Commercial Fisheries Technological Laboratory, College Park, Maryland. U.S. Department of the Interior. U.S. Fish and Wildlife Service. Bureau of Commercial Fisheries, n.d.

***
IIP&H    Mascenik, John. DEEPWATER OFFSHORE PETROLEUM TERMINALS. Meeting Preprint. Ann Arbor, Mich., American Society of Civil Engineers, 1972? 29p.

***
IIOL    Massachusetts. Office of Coastal Zone Management. COMMENTS ON LEASING ON THE OUTER CONTINENTAL SHELF - NORTH ATLANTIC. Boston, 1975. 15p.

|  |  |
|---|---|
| | \*\*\* |

IVMMR    Massachusetts. Special Legislative Commission on Marine Boundaries and Resources. REPORT ON THE MATTER OF OFFSHORE OIL DEVELOPMENT ON GEORGES BANK. Boston, 1964-    1-

                                                                    13,15
VOD    Massachusetts Institute of Technology. ECONOMIC ASPECTS OF SOLID WASTE DISPOSAL AT SEA; A REPORT PREPARED FOR THE NATIONAL COUNCIL ON MARINE RESOURCES AND ENGINEERING DEVELOPMENT. Economic aspects of ocean activities, PB 195 225. Cambridge, Mass., M.I.T., 1970. 3 Vols.

                                                                    13,15
IIIFP    _____ THE ECONOMICS OF FISH PROTEIN CONCENTRATE; A REPORT PREPARED FOR THE NATIONAL COUNCIL ON MARINE RESOURCES AND ENGINEERING DEVELOPMENT. PB 195 226. Cambridge, Mass., M.I.T., 1970. 195p.

                                                                    13
IICZM    _____ ECONOMIC FACTORS IN THE DEVELOPMENT OF A COASTAL ZONE. A report prepared for the National Council on Marine Resources and Engineering Development. Economic aspects of ocean activities, Vol. 2. PB 195 224. Cambridge, Mass., 1970.

                                                                    17
VSG    _____ A PROPOSAL FOR 1972/73- INSTITUTIONAL SEA GRANT PROGRAM. Cambridge, Mass., 1972-    2 Vols.

                                                                    13
VOCET    _____ THIRD ANNUAL SEA GRANT LECTURE ON TECHNOLOGY, OCTOBER 3, 1971. Report no. MITSG 75-3. Index no. 75-603-Wpe. Cambridge, M.I.T., 1972?

                                                                    16
IVMMR    _____ Offshore Oil Task Group. THE GEORGES BANK PETROLEUM STUDY: IMPACT ON NEW ENGLAND REAL INCOME OF HYPOTHETICAL REGIONAL PETROLEUM DEVELOPMENT. Report no. MITSG 73-5. Cambridge, Mass., M.I.T., Sea Grant Project Office, 1973. III Vols.

                                                                    14
VCONS    Massachusetts Institute of Technology. Sea Grant Program. USING THE SEAS TO SERVE PEOPLE: a report. Cambridge, Mass., 1974. 16p.

                                                                    1,5,16
VB    Masterson, William E. JURISDICTION IN MARGINAL SEAS. New York, Macmillan, 1929; reprint Kennikat, 1970. 423p.

                                                                    16
VB    _____ NATIONAL JURISDICTION IN THE MARGINAL SEAS OVER FOREIGN SMUGGLING VESSELS. In Grotius, Society, Problems of Peace and War. London, 1928. Vol. 13, pp. 53-74.

                                                                    15
VOCET    Masabuchi, Koichi. MATERIALS FOR OCEAN ENGINEERING. Cambridge, M.I.T. Press, 1970.

                                                                    1,5,12
VB    Mateesco, Nicholas. DEUX FRONTIÈRES INVISIBLES DE LA MER TERRITORIALE À L'AIR "TERRITORIAL". Paris, Pedone, 1965. 294p.

                                                                    1,3
VMLAD      Mateesco, Mircea. LE DROIT MARITIME SOVIÉTIQUE FACE AU DROIT OCCI-
           DENTAL. Paris, Pedone, 1966. 214p.

                                                                    1,5
VINTL      Mateesco, Nicolas. VERS UN NOUVEAU DROIT INTERNATIONAL DE LA MER.
           Paris, 1950.

                                                                    ART
IIIF       Mathisen, Ole A., and Donald E. Bevan. SOME INTERNATIONAL ASPECTS
           OF SOVIET FISHERIES. In Conference on Law, Organization and Secu-
           rity in the Use of the Ocean, 2d, Columbus, Ohio, 1967. Papers pre-
           sented at the Conference. National Council of Applied Economic Re-
           search. Export prospects of fish and fish products. New Delhi,
           1965. 129p. Columbus, Ohio, Mershon Center for Education in Na-
           tional Security, 1967. Vol. 1, pp. 78-136.

                                                                    3
VLOS       Matine-Daftary, Ahmad. COURS ABREGE SUR LA CONTRIBUTION DES CONFER-
           ENCES DE GENEVA AU DEVELOPMENT PROGRESSIF DE DROIT INTERNATIONAL DE
           LA MER. In Hague. Academy of International Law. Recueil des cours,
           1961, Leyden. Vol. 102 (1962), pp. 635-673.

                                                                    5,13
VENV       Maton, Gilbert. A PERSPECTIVE OF REGIONAL AND STATE MARINE ENVIRON-
           MENTAL ACTIVITIES. A QUESTIONNAIRE SURVEY, STATISTICS AND OBSERVA-
           TIONS. Conducted by John I. Thompson and Company. Springfield,
           Va., Commerce Clearing House Federal Scientific and Technical Infor-
           mation Center, 1968.

                                                                    ***
VB         Matte, Nicolas M. DE LA MER TERRITORIALE A L'AIR "TERRITORIAL."
           Editions A. Pedone, 1965.

                                                                    ART
IIIAFF     Matthes, H. COASTAL AND ESTUARINE AQUACULTURE. In International
           Conference on Marine Resources Development in Eastern Africa. Held
           at The University of Dar es Salaam, Tanzania, April 4-9, 1974, in
           cooperation with the International Center for Marine Resource De-
           velopment at the University of Rhode Island. Kingston, University
           of Rhode Island, 1974. pp. 28-37.

                                                                    ***
IIIAFF     Mathews, Stephen B., and Harry G. Senn. CHUM SALMON HATCHERY REAR-
           ING IN JAPAN. Washington Sea Grant publication WSG-TA-75-3.
           Seattle, University of Washington, Division of Marine Resources,
           1975. 24p.

                                                                    ***
IVB        Matthews, J.B. BASELINE DATA SURVEY FOR VALDEZ PIPELINE TERMINAL
           ENVIRONMENTAL DATA STUDY. Fairbanks, University of Alaska, In-
           stitute of Marine Science, 1975. 240p.

                                                                    ART
VP         Matthews, William H. GLOBAL POLLUTION AND INTERNATIONAL COOPERA-
           TION. In Matthews, William H., et al, eds., Man's Impact on the
           Climate, Cambridge, Mass., M.I.T. Press, 1971. pp. 564-579 (1971).

VENV     Matthews, William H., et al, eds. MAN'S IMPACT ON THE CLIMATE. Cambridge, Mass., M.I.T. Press, 1971. 604p.

VENV     _____ _____ MAN'S IMPACT ON TERRESTRIAL AND OCEANIC ECOSYSTEMS. Cambridge, Mass., M.I.T. Press, 1972. 540p.

    ART
IIP     Mattis, W.E., and R.D. Klafler. OPTIMAL WASTE DISCHARGE IN ESTUARIES AND BAYS. In Proceedings of the Fifth World Congress of The International Federation of Automation Control, held in Paris, France, June 12-17, 1972.

IICZM     Mattox, Bruce W. SEA GRANT: A CATALYST FOR COMMUNITY ACTION. Paper presented at the Seventh Annual meeting of the Sea Grant Association, Seattle, Washington, 30 October 1974. MASGP-74-039. Ocean Springs, Mississippi-Alabama Sea Grant Consortium, 1974.

    ART
IICZM     Mattson, H., ed. THE STATE INDUSTRY WORKSHOP ON THE COASTAL ZONE MANAGEMENT ACT OF 1972. In Report MITSG 74-1, August, 1973. Boston, Massachusetts Institute of Technology, Sea Grant Project Office, 1973. 16p.

VLOS     Matysik, Stanislaw. PRAWO MORSKIE. ZARYS SYSTEMU (THE LAW OF THE SEA - OUTLINE OF THE SYSTEM.) Wrocklaw, Warsaw, Crakow, Gdańsk: Zakład Narodowy Imienia Ossolińskich Wydawnictwo, 1971, 1973. 2 Vols.

    ART
IIENV     Maurer, Don, and Hsiang Wang. ENVIRONMENTAL VULNERABILITY OF THE DELAWARE BAY AREA TO DEEPWATER PORTS. In Proceedings of the Fifth National Sea Grant Conference held in Houston, Texas, 1972. Sea Grant Publication no. TAMU-SG-73-101. College Station, Texas A&M University, 1973.

IVENV     _____ ENVIRONMENTAL VULNERABILITY OF THE DELAWARE BAY AREA TO SUPERTANKER ACCOMMODATION. Dover, Del., Council on Environmental Quality, 1973. 4 Vols.

IIIOD     Maurer, Don, et al. EFFECT OF SPOIL DISPOSAL ON BENTHIS COMMUNITIES NEAR THE MOUTH OF DELAWARE BAY. Report DEL-SG-4-74. Newark, University of Delaware, 1974. 229p.

    ART
IICZM     Max, Joe C. NATIONAL SHORELINE STUDY. In Planning and Engineering in the Coastal Zone. Proceedings of seminar held in Charleston, S.C., June 8-9, 1972. Seminar Series no. 2. Wilmington, N.C., 1972. pp. 17-22.

    ART
IIP     Maxwell, J.V. THE NORTH CAROLINA OIL POLLUTION CONTROL LAW; A MODEL FOR STATE EFFORTS TO CURB POLLUTION OF THE SEA. In S.W. Wurfel, Emerging Ocean Oil and Mining Law. Sea Grant Publication UNC-74-02. Chapel Hill, University of North Carolina, 1974. pp. 51-59.

                                                                                                   ***

IIOSTR    Maxwell-Cook, P.V., ed. CONCRETE SEA STRUCTURES. London, Federation Internationale de la Precontrainte, 1973. 259p.

                                                                           ***

IVOSTR    May, A.E., et al. STABLE FLOATING PLATFORM. Technical progress report AOEL-42. La Jolla, California University, Scripps Institution of Oceanography, Advanced Ocean Engineering Laboratory, 1973. 25p.

                                                          ***

IIP&H    Mayer, Harold M. WISCONSIN'S GREAT LAKES PORTS: BACKGROUND AND FUTURE ALTERNATIVES. Prepared for the Department of Transportation, Division and Planning. Milwaukee, University of Wisconsin, Center for Great Lakes Studies, 1975. 66, 6p.

                                                       ART

VENE    Mayne, W. Harry. A STATUS REPORT: MARINE SEISMIC ENERGY SOURCES. In Undersea Technology and Oceanology International Offshore. Vol. 13, no. 8, 1972. pp. 24-27.

                                                       16

IVOI    Mead, John B. INSURANCE COVERAGE OF OFFSHORE DRILLING AND PRODUCTION OPERATIONS. In Slovenko, Ralph, ed., Oil and Gas Operations. Baton Rouge, Claitor's, 1963. pp. 617-627.

                                                       15

VENV    Meadows, Donella H., et al. THE LIMITS TO GROWTH; A REPORT FOR THE CLUB OF ROME'S PROJECT ON THE PREDICAMENT OF MANKIND. New York, Universe Books, 1972.

                                                       17

VENV    Meadows, Dennis L., and Donella H. Meadows, eds. TOWARD GLOBAL EQUILIBRIUM: COLLECTED PAPERS. Cambridge, Mass., Wright-Allen Press, 1973. x, 358p.

                                                        1

IVM    Meeresbergbau und Völkerrecht. DIE VÖLKERRECHTLICHEN PROBLEME DER GEWINNUNG MINERALISCHER ROHSTOFFE DES MEERES AUS DER SICHT DER DEUTSCHEN INDUSTRIE. Wirtschaftsvereinigung Bergbau, Wirtschaftsvereinigung Industrielle Meerestichnik, Bundesverband der Deutschen Industrie, Fruhjahr 1972. 74p.

                                                       ***

IIILOS    Meijers. H. EEG OP ZEE: VRIJE VESTIGING VOOR VISSERS. Studiekring "Prof. Mr. J. Offerhaus", reeks Internationaal privaatrecht, 8. Deventer, Kluwer, 1973. 60p.

                                                       ART

VAC    Melkov, G.M. ON THE QUESTION OF FULL DEMILITARISATION OF THE SEA-BED. In 1973 Soviet Yearbook of International Law, n.p. 1975. pp. 216-234.

                                                       16

VB    Menard, H. THE CONFIGURATION OF THE OCEAN FLOOR AND ITS SUBSOIL: GEOPOLITICAL IMPLICATIONS. Paper at Symposium on the International Regime of the Sea-bed. Rome. 1969.

VINTL     Méndez Silva, R. EL MAR PATRIMONIAL EN AMERICA LATINA. México, Instituto de investigaciones jurídicas, Universite nacional Autónoma de México, 1974. 137p.    ***

VP     Mensah, T.A. THE LAW RELATING TO THE POLLUTION OF THE SEAS. In A.D. McKnight, et al, Environmental Pollution Control. London, 1974. pp. 174-208.    ART

VLOS     Mensbrugghe, Y. van der. RÉFLEXIONS SUR LA DEFINITION DU NAIVRE DANS LE DROIT DE LA MER. In Sociéte française pour le droit international. Actualites du droit de la mer: Actes. Paris, 1973. pp. 62-75.    ART

VLOS     Menzel, E. FUTURE POSSIBILITIES WITH RESPECT TO MACHINERY FOR INTERNATIONAL COOPERATION FOR THE PROMOTION OF THE FREEDOM OF RESEARCH. Paper at Symposium on the International Regime of the Sea-bed. Rome. 1969.    16

VENV     Menzies, R.J., et al. ABYSSAL ENVIRONMENT AND ECOLOGY OF THE WORLD OCEANS. New York, John Wiley and Sons, Wiley-Interscience, 1973. 505p.    ***

IIP     Mercedes, Ruth. COSTS AND BENEFITS OF THE ABATEMENT OF POLLUTION OF BISCAYNE BAY, MIAMI, FLORIDA. Technical bulletin no.4. Coral Gables, University of Miami Sea Grant Program, 1972. 101p.    ***

VP     Mercer, B.W., et al. TREATMENT OF HAZARDOUS MATERIAL SPILLS WITH FLOATING MASS TRANSFER MEDIA. Report NCSL-198-73. Richland, Wash., Battelle Memorial Institute, December, 1973. 24p.    ***

IVENV     MERCURY AND THE ENVIRONMENT: STUDIES OF MERCURY USE, EMISSION, BIOLOGICAL IMPACT AND CONTROL: APPENDICES. Paris, Organisation for Economic Co-operation and Development, 1974. 40p.    ***

IIP     MERCURY POLLUTION INVESTIGATION IN GEORGIA: 1970-1971. Report. Atlanta, Georgia Water Quality Control Board, 1971. 123p.

VENE     Meredith, Dennis L. NUCLEAR POWER PLANT SITING: A HANDBOOK FOR THE LAYMAN. Rev. Marine Advisory Service Sea Grant. Marine Bulletin No. 6. Kingston, University of Rhode Island, January 1973. 32p.    13

IVMMR     Mero, John L. THE MINERAL RESOURCES OF THE SEA. Amsterdam; New York, Elsevier Pub. Co., 1965. XIII, 312p.    5,9,12,13,14,14a,15,16,17

IVMMR     _____ _____ REVIEW OF MINERAL VALUES ON AND UNDER THE OCEAN FLOOR. In Marine Technology Society. 2nd Annual Conference, Washington, D.C., June 27-29, 1966. Washington, D.C., 1966. pp. 61-78.    ART

                                                                    13
IIIF     Merrell, Theodore R., Jr. ALASKA'S FISHERY RESOURCES - THE CHUM
         SALMON. Fishery Leaflet 632. Washington, U.S. Department of the
         Interior, Fish and Wildlife Service, Bureau of Commercial Fisheries,
         1970. iii, 7p.

                                                                    13
IICZM    Merryman, John H. SOME PROBLEMS OF GREEK SHORELAND DEVELOPMENT.
         Lecture series 17. Athens, Greece, Center of Planning and Economic
         Research, 1965. 78p.

                                                                    13
IICZM    Merselis, William B., ed. PROCEEDINGS: COASTAL ZONE MANAGEMENT
         AND THE WESTERN STATES FUTURE. Marine Technology Society, Los
         Angeles Region Section Conference, December 3-4, 1973, Newport
         Beach, California. Washington, D.C., Marine Technology Society,
         1974. vi, 269p.

                                                                    ***
IIWQ     Merselis, William B., et al. A NATIONAL OVERVIEW OF EXISTING COAST-
         AL WATER QUALITY MONITORING. Report no. 445-A. Anaheim, Cal.,
         Interstate Electronics Corporation, Oceanic Division, 1972. 538p.

                                                                    14
VENV     Meshenberg, Michael J., ed. ENVIRONMENTAL PLANNING: A GUIDE TO
         INFORMATION SOURCES. Detroit, Gale Research Co., 1975.

                                                                    1,18
VOR      Messick, T. Paul, Jr. MARITIME RESOURCE CONFLICTS - PERSPECTIVES
         FOR RESOLUTION. University of North Carolina, Sea Grant Publication
         UNC-SG-74-06. Chapel Hill, May, 1974. iii, 98p.

                                                                    11
IVORM    Meurs, A.P. van. PETROLEUM ECONOMICS AND OFFSHORE MINING LEGISLA-
         TION. Amsterdam, Elsevier, 1971.

                                                                    16
IIB      Meyer, Christopher V. THE EXTENT OF JURISDICTION IN COASTAL WATERS.
         Leyden, Sijthoff, 1937. 533p.

                                                                    ART
IIIFV&G  Meyer, J. FISHING BOATS AND EQUIPMENT. In International Confer-
         ence on Marine Resources Development in Eastern Africa. Held at the
         University of Dar es Salaam, Tanzania, April 4-9, 1974, in cooper-
         ation with the International Center for Marine Resource Development
         at the University of Rhode Island. Kingston, University of Rhode
         Island, 1974. pp. 43-54.

                                                                    1,5,11,16
VINTL    Meyers, H. THE NATIONALITY OF SHIPS. The Hague, Nijhoff, 1967.
         xiii, 395p.

                                                                    13
IIIAFF   Miami. University. AQUACULTURE: THE NEW SHRIMP CROP. University
         of Miami Sea Grant Institutional Program. Information Leaflet No.1.
         Coral Gables, University of Miami, 1970. 5p.

                                                                    16
VAC      Michael, D. AVOIDING THE MILITARIZATION OF THE SEAS. Seventeenth
         Report of the Commission to Study the Organization of Peace. New

York, n.p., 1966. pp. 167-170.

IIIFV&G  13
Micuta, Jurate E. UNITED STATES TARIFFS ON SELECTED ITEMS OF COMMERCIAL FISHING GEAR. Fishery Leaflet 625. Washington, U.S.G.P.O., 1969. 11p.

IIENV  14
Miernyk, William L. ENVIRONMENTAL MANAGEMENT AND REGIONAL ECONOMIC DEVELOPMENT. Morgantown, West Virginia University, Regional Research Institute, 1971.

VENV  ART
MIGHTY RIVER, NUCLEAR RIVER. THE FATE OF HANFORD RADIONUCLIDES IN THE COLUMBIA RIVER AND NORTHEAST PACIFIC OCEAN. In Pacific Northwest Sea, Vol. 6, no. 3, 1973. pp. 4-11.

IVMMR  13
Mikhailov, Stefan. MARINE ORES IN THE USSR. Moscow, Novosti Press Agency, 1971. 6p.

VP  13
Mikolaj, Paul G., et al. INVESTIGATION OF THE NATURE, EXTENT AND FATE OF NATURAL OIL SEEPAGE OFF SOUTHERN CALIFORNIA. Preprint. In Offshore Technology Conference, Dallas, Texas, 1972. pp. I-366-I-376.

IIIF  1,5,13
Miles, Edward. ORGANIZATIONAL ARRANGEMENTS TO FACILITATE GLOBAL MANAGEMENT OF FISHERIES. Program of international studies of fishery arrangements, no. 4. Washington, D.C., Resources for the Future, Inc., June, 1974. xii, 23p.

IICZM  14
Milhous, Robert T., and Greg Sorlie. BACKGROUND INFORMATION FOR WATER RESOURCES MANAGEMENT PLANNING IN THE COASTAL BASINS OF WASHINGTON. WRIS technical bulletin no. 6. Olympia, Washington Department of Ecology, Water Resources Information System, April, 1975. 345p.

VINTL  1
Milić, Milenko. OSNOVE PRAVNOG PORETKA NA OTVORENOM MORU. (BASIC PRINCIPLES OF THE REGIME OF HIGH SEAS.) Reprinted from Ponorskog zbornika, knj. 3/1965. pp. 583-639. English summary, pp. 633-639.

VINTL  1
_____ PRAVNA PROBLEMATIKA NOVIH PROSTORA PODMORJA. (LEGAL PROBLEMS OF THE OCEAN FLOOR AREAS.) Reprinted from Pomorskog zbornika, knj. 6, 1968, pp. 289-315. English summary, pp. 314-315.

IICZM  14
Miller, Barbara J., and Robert F. Goodwin. LEGAL AND ECONOMIC STRATEGIES FOR SHORELINES MANAGEMENT. Washington Sea Grant Communications Program. WSG-WO 75-3. Seattle, University of Washington, Division of Marine Resources, 1976. 54p.

16
IICZM    Miller, Douglas K.  THE CALIFORNIA COASTAL ZONE CONSERVATION ACT: CASES AND CONTROVERSIES, 1973-74.  Stanford, Calif., Stanford Environmental Law Society, 1974.  98p.

1,3,5,10,12,13
VINTL    Miller, H. Crane.  INTERNATIONAL LAW AND MARINE ARCHAEOLOGY.  Belmont, Mass., Academy of Applied Science, 1973.  xii, 47p.

ART
VMT      Miller, Richard A.  INDONESIA'S ARCHIPELAGO DOCTRINE AND JAPAN'S JUGULAR.  In Proceedings of the U.S. Naval Institute, Annapolis, Md., Vol. 98, no. 10, October, 1972.  pp. 26-33.

***
IIIFP    Miller, T.M., et al.  PROCEEDINGS OF THE WORKSHOP ON SEAFOOD PROCESSING AND MARKETING IN THE COASTAL PLAINS AREA.  UNC-SG-75-24. Raleigh, North Carolina State University, UNC Sea Grant Program, 1975.  155p.

13
IIIAFF   Milne, P.H.  FISH AND SHELLFISH FARMING IN COASTAL WATERS.  London, Fishing News (Books), 1972.  208p.

13
IIB      Miloy, Leatha F., ed.  LAW AND THE COASTAL MARGIN - SELECTED PAPERS FROM THE LAW AND THE COASTAL MARGIN WORKSHOP SPONSORED BY GULF UNIVERSITIES RESEARCH CORPORATION.  Texas A&M University, National Science Foundation Sea Grant Program.  TAMU-SG-70-108.  College Station, Texas A&M University, 1970.  iii, 83p.

13
VP       Milwaukee. Sewerage Commission.  EVALUATION OF CONDITIONING AND DEWATERING SEWAGE SLUDGE BY FREEZING.  Prepared for the Environmental Protection Agency.  Water Pollution Center Research Series.  Raleigh, N.C., Environmental Protection Agency, 1971.  vi, 67p.

7,14
IVMMR    MINERAL RESOURCES OF THE SEA.  United Nations Report E/4973, 26 April, 1971.

16
VLOS     Miron, G.  PROBLEMS OF AN OPERATING COMPANY IN DEALING WITH AN INTERNATIONAL AUTHORITY.  Paper at the Institute of Ocean Law Conference on Coastal Zone and Ocean Law: Problems of the User.  Miami, Fla., December 10-12, 1969.  n.p.

13
VOR      Missick, T. Paul, Jr.  MARITIME RESOURCE CONFLICTS - PERSPECTIVES FOR RESOLUTION.  Sea Grant Publication UNC-SG-74-06.  Raleigh, North Carolina State University, 1974.  98p.

***
VSG      MISSISSIPPI-ALABAMA SEA GRANT CONSORTIUM.  ANNUAL REPORT.  Ocean Springs, 1973-

***
IICZM    Mississippi-Alabama Sea Grant Consortium.  PROCEEDINGS OF THE ALABAMA COASTAL LEADERS CONFERENCE ON COASTAL ZONE MANAGEMENT, APRIL 30, 1975, MOBILE, ALABAMA.  MASGP-75-012.  Montgomery, Development

Office and Alabama Coastal Area Board, 1975. i, 71p.

***
IICZM MISSISSIPPI GOVERNOR'S CONFERENCE ON COASTAL ZONE MANAGEMENT. Proceedings, Biloxi, Mississippi, 1974. MASGP-74-027. Ocean Springs, Mississippi-Alabama Sea Grant Consortium, 1974.

***
VSG MISSISSIPPI SEA GRANT PROGRAM. PROGRESS REPORT. Ocean Springs, 1971-

1
VMT Mississippi Valley Association. WHY EVERY STATE IN THE MISSISSIPPI VALLEY SHOULD OPPOSE THE RATIFICATION OF THE ST. LAWRENCE WATERWAY TREATY IN ITS PRESENT FORM. January, 1934. 8p.

ART
VLOS Mitchell, J.C. THE REGULATION OF OFFSHORE LEGAL SURVEYS. In Canadian Hydrographic Conference: Fourteenth Annual. n.p., Canada Department of the Environment, Canadian Hydrographic Service, Ocean and Aquatic Affairs, 1975? pp. 139-145.

14
IICONS Mitchell, James K. COMMUNITY RESPONSE TO COASTAL EROSION: INDIVIDUAL AND COLLECTIVE ADJUSTMENTS TO HAZARD ON THE ATLANTIC SHORE. Chicago, University of Chicago, Department of Geography, 1974. xii, 209p.

***
IICR Moberly, Ralph, et al. OFFSHORE AND OTHER SAND RESOURCES FOR OAHU, HAWAII. UNIHI-SEAGRANT-TR-75-03. Honolulu, University of Hawaii, 1975. 36p.

14
IIMMR Moen, Wayne S. MINERAL RIGHTS AND LAND OWNERSHIP IN WASHINGTON. Washington Department of Conservation, Division of Mines and Geology, Information circular no. 36. Olympia, Wash., 1962. iv, 24p.

14
IICZM Mogulof, Melvin B. SAVING THE COAST: CALIFORNIA'S EXPERIMENT IN INTERGOVERNMENTAL LAND-USE CONTROL. Lexington, Mass., Lexington Books, 1975. xiii, 136p.

ART
IIIOR Moiseev, P.A. VLIIANIE CHELOVEKA NA BIOLOGICHESKUIU PRODUKTIVNOST' OKEANA. In Izvestiia Akademii Nauk SSSR Seriia geograficheskaia, Vol. 6, 1971. pp. 15-18.

1,15
VINTL Monteil Arguello, Alejandro. ARTICULOS SOBRE DERECHO DEL MAR. Managua, Nicaragua, Publicaciones del Ministerio de Relaciones Exteriores, Abril, 1971. 135p.

ART
IVDRIL Montgomery, N.E. DRILLING IN THE SEA FROM FLOATING PLATFORMS. In Marine Technology Society. Second Annual Conference, Washington, D.C., June 27-29, 1966. Washington, D.C., 1966. pp. 230-250.

5,14
VP Moorcraft, Colin. MUST THE SEAS DIE? Boston, Gambit, 1973. x, 194p.

IIIF    Moore, Denton R. RATIONAL OCEAN FISHERY MANAGEMENT AND THE UNITED NATIONS. Mimeo. Seattle, University of Washington School of Law, May 19, 1966. 48p.

ART
IVMMR   Moore, J. Robert. EXPLOITATION OF OCEAN MINERALS RESOURCE - PERSPECTIVES AND PREDICTIONS. In Proceedings of the Second International Congress on the History of Oceanography held in Edinburgh, Scotland, September 12-20, 1972.

14a,15
VOCET   Moore, James R., comp. OCEANOGRAPHY; READINGS FROM SCIENTIFIC AMERICAN. San Francisco, W.H. Freeman, 1971. 417p.

***
IIIF    Moore, Remedios W., ed. PROGRESS IN FISHERY AND FOOD SCIENCE. Fiftieth Anniversary Celebration Symposium, Seattle, Washington. Proceedings. Seattle, University of Washington Press, 1972. 1975p.

ART
IIENV   Moore, Stephen F. SOME ASPECTS OF DEEPWATER TERMINAL SITE SELECTION IN NORTHERN NEW ENGLAND COASTAL AREAS. In Proceedings of the Fifth National Sea Grant Conference held in Houston, Texas, 1972. Publication no. TAMU-SG-73-101. College Station, Texas A&M University, 1973.

16
IIB     Moore, Stuart A. A HISTORY OF THE FORESHORE AND THE LAW RELATING THERETO. London, Stevens and Haynes, 1888. 984p.

16
IIIF    Moore, Stuart A., and H.S. Moore. THE HISTORY AND LAW OF FISHERIES. London, Stevens and Haynes, 1903. 446p.

***
VP      Moore, S.F., et al. A PRELIMINARY ASSESSMENT OF THE ENVIRONMENTAL VULNERABILITY OF MACHIAS BAY, MAINE TO OIL SUPERTANKERS. MITSG 73-6. Cambridge, Massachusetts Institute of Technology, 1973. 169p.

ART
VLOS    Morales, Paul I. EL RÉGIMEN DE LA ALTA MAR. In F. Orrego Vicuña, Tendencias del derecho del mar contemporaneo. Buenos Aires, 1974. n.p. pp. 115-143.

***
IICONS  Moreland, R., et al. RESOURCE ANALYSIS OF OREGON'S COASTAL UPLANDS. Florence, Coastal Conservation and Development Commission, 1975. 204p.

***
IVMMR   Morgan, Charles L., and J.R. Moore. ROLE OF THE NUCLEUS IN FORMATION OF FERROMANGANESE NODULES: PROCESSING GUIDELINES FOR THE MARINE MINER. WIS-SG-75-356. Madison, University of Wisconsin, 1975. 8p.

13
IICZM   Morgan, Robert. ON THE LEGAL ASPECTS OF NORTH CAROLINA COASTAL PROBLEMS. 49 North Carolina Law Review. Special Issue. 1971. pp. 857-1003.

IVMMR     Morgenstein, M., and J. Andrews. MANGANESE RESOURCES IN THE HAWAIIAN REGION. In Marine Technological Society Journal, Vol. 5, no. 6, 1971. pp. 27-30.     ART

IVMMR     Morgenstein, Maury, ed. PAPERS ON THE ORIGIN AND DISTRIBUTION OF MANGANESE NODULES IN THE PACIFIC AND PROSPECTS FOR EXPLORATION. An International Symposium organized by the Valdivia Manganese Exploration Group and the Hawaii Institute of Geophysics, Honolulu, Hawaii, July 23-25, 1973. Honolulu, University of Hawaii, 1973. 173p.     13,14

VP     Morin, J.Y. LA POLLUTION DES MERS AU REGARD DU DROIT INTERNATIONAL. In Hague. Academy of International Law. La protection de l'environnement et le droit international. Leyden, 1975. pp. 239-352.     ART

IICZM     Morrell, Dorothy C. THE SEACOAST MANAGEMENT ACT: A LEGISLATIVE HISTORY. Bellevue, Wash., 1970. 8p.     13

IIIF     Morris, R.E. PRIORITIES IN DEVELOPMENT OF THE SHELF FISHERIES. In International Conference on Marine Resources Development in Eastern Africa. Held at The University of Dar es Salaam, Tanzania, April 4-9, 1974, in cooperation with the International Center for Marine Resource Development at the University of Rhode Island. Kingston, University of Rhode Island, 1974. pp. 37-42.     ART

IICZM     Morry, Susan P. 1970 SEACOAST MANAGEMENT BILL: BACKGROUND AND ANALYSIS. Washington Sea Grant publication WSG-MP 71-1. Seattle, University of Washington, Division of Marine Resources, 1971. 27p.     17

VB     Morton, Robert A., and Mary J. Pieper. SHORELINE CHANGES ON BRAZOS ISLAND AND SOUTH PADRE ISLAND; AN ANALYSIS OF HISTORICAL CHANGES OF THE TEXAS GULF SHORELINE. Austin, University of Texas, 1975. 30p.     ***

VP     Mostert, Neal. SUPERSHIP. New York, Knopf, 1974.     15

IVOL     Mountaineers. ENVIRONMENTAL STATEMENT ON THE PROPOSED LEASING OF PUGET SOUND SHORELANDS AND BEDS OF NAVIGABLE WATERS FOR OIL AND GAS EXPLORATION. Seattle, Washington, 1970. n.p. 75p.     16

VCS     Mouton, Martinus W. THE CONTINENTAL SHELF. The Hague, M. Nijhoff, 1952. xi, 367p.     3,5,9,12,16

VCS     _____ THE CONTINENTAL SHELF. The Hague, Nijhoff, 1969. xi, 367p. reprint.     11

IIIAFF     Mshigeni, K.E. SEAWOOD RESOURCES IN TANZANIA. Mimeo. Dar es Salaam, University College, Botany Department, 1970.     ***

| | | 14 |
|---|---|---|
VOR        Msangi, A.S., and J.J. Griffin, eds. INTERNATIONAL CONFERENCE ON MARINE RESOURCES DEVELOPMENT IN EASTERN AFRICA. Held at The University of Dar es Salaam, Tanzania, April 4-9, 1974, in cooperation with The International Center for Marine Resource Development of the University of Rhode Island. Kingston, University of Rhode Island, 1974. 130p.

16

IVM        Muench, F. LEX LATA OF DEEP SEA MINING. Paper at Pacem in Maribus Preparatory Conference on the Legal Framework and the Continental Shelf. Kingston, Rhode Island, January 30-February 1, 1970.

***

IIP&H      MULTI-PURPOSE, OFFSHORE INDUSTRIAL/PORT ISLANDS. Summary of conceptual studies and research needs. Newark, University of Delaware, 1976. 23p.

***

IIIF       Mundt, J. Carl. LIMITED ENTRY INTO THE COMMERCIAL FISHERIES: PROCEEDINGS OF THE CONFERENCE. Conference held at the University of Washington Lake Wilderness Continuing Education Center on September 12 and 13, 1974. Institute for Marine Studies publication series 75-1. Seattle, University of Washington, 1975. ix, 143p.

15

IIP        Municipality of Metropolitan Seattle. DISPOSAL OF DIGESTED SLUDGE TO PUGET SOUND; THE ENGINEERING AND WATER QUALITY ASPECTS. Seattle, Washington, n.d.

17

VP         Murdoch, William W., ed. ENVIRONMENT; RESOURCES, POLLUTION AND SOCIETY. Stamford, Conn., Sinauer Associates, 1971. vii, 440p.

17

VP         Murray, S.P., W.G. Smith, and C.J. Sanu. OCEANOGRAPHIC OBSERVATIONS AND THEORETICAL ANALYSIS OF OIL SLICKS DURING THE CHEVRON SPILL, MARCH 1970. Coastal Studies Institute, technical report no 87. Baton Rouge, Louisiana State University, 1970.

***

IIP&H      Murray, Thomas J. OREGON COASTAL PORT DEVELOPMENT PLAN. Portland, Or., Thomas J. Murray and Associates, 1975. 100p.

ART

IVLOS      Muscarella, Giuseppe. INTERNATIONAL REGIME OF THE SEA-BED; OIL AND NATURAL GAS EXPLORATION AND EXPLOITATION OF DEEP WATER PETROLEUM. In J. Sztucki, ed., Symposium on the International Regime of the Sea-Bed, Rome, 1969. Proceedings, June 30-July 5, 1969. Rome, Accademia Nazionale dei Lincei, 1970. pp. 95-111.

18

IICZM      Mutscher, Gus F. POLITICAL CONSIDERATION IN THE MANAGEMENT OF THE COASTAL ZONE. Sea Grant Program. College Station, Texas A&M University, n.d.

ART

VENE       Nachtsheim, John J., and Wallace T. Sansone. AN INTERIM STATUS REPORT ON THE ENERGY CRISIS AND ITS EFFECT ON WORLD SHIPPING. In Marine Technology, Vol. 11, 1974. pp. 134-135.

|  |  |
|--|--|
| | ART |
| VP | Nadeau, R.J., and R.T. Dewling. HAZARDOUS MATERIAL SPILLS vs. OIL SPILLS COMMON BIOLOGICAL DENOMINATOR. In Proceedings of the 1972 National Conference on Control of Hazardous Material Spills, University of Houston, March 21-23, 1972. Houston, Texas, 1972? pp. 211-216. |

2,13

VOCET Naftalin, Micah H., and John P. Earner. FEDERAL AUTHORITY FOR MARINE SCIENCE ACTIVITIES; A STUDY OF THE LEGAL AUTHORITIES UNDER WHICH THE U.S. GOVERNMENT IS CONDUCTING AND SUPPORTING MARINE SCIENCE ACTIVITIES. Washington, U.S.G.P.O., 1969. ix, 149p.

***

IIIAFF Nair, K.K. REPORT TO THE GOVERNMENT OF NIGERIA ON EXPERIMENTS IN BRACKISHWATER FISH CULTURE IN THE NIGER DELTA, 1965-1968. FAO/UNDP(TA)2759. n.p., 1969.

***

VOCET Nairn, A.E.M., and F.G. Stehli, eds. THE OCEAN BASINS AND MARGINS: VOL. 2: THE NORTH ATLANTIC. New York, Plenum Publishing Corporation, Plenum Press, 1974. 617p.

13

IIIF Nakamura, Hiroshi. TUNA DISTRIBUTION AND MIGRATION. London, Fishing News (Books) Ltd., 1969. 76p.

13

IIREC Napoli, James J., ed. BOATING IN NEW ENGLAND; A REPORT ON THE 1971 MARINE RECREATION CONFERENCE. Narragansett, R.I., New England Marine Resources Information Program, 1972. 23p.

13,14

VP Nash, A.E. Keir, Dean E. Mann, and Phil G. Olsen. OIL POLLUTION AND THE PUBLIC INTEREST: A STUDY OF THE SANTA BARBARA OIL SPILL. Berkeley, University of California, Institute of Governmental Studies, 1972. xiii, 157p.

***

IICZM Nash, Robert A. CALIFORNIA COMPREHENSIVE OCEAN AREA PLAN. APPENDIX I: PERMANENT COASTAL ZONE DATA INVENTORY AND INFORMATION SYSTEM. Report. Sacramento, Department of Navigation and Ocean Development, Resources Agency, 1970. 137p.

14

VOR Nathan (Robert R.) Associates, Washington, D.C. THE ECONOMIC VALUE OF OCEAN RESOURCES TO THE UNITED STATES; prepared at the request of Warren G. Magnuson, chairman, for the use of the Committee on Commerce, pursuant to S.Res.222, National Ocean Policy Study. 93d Congr., 2d sess., committee print. Washington, U.S.G.P.O., 1974. xi, 109p.

13

IVDRIL National Academy of Engineering. OFFSHORE DRILLING PROCEDURES REVIEWED BY MARINE BOARD OUTER CONTINENTAL SHELF RESOURCE DEVELOPMENT SAFETY: A REVIEW OF TECHNOLOGY AND REGULATION FOR THE SYSTEMATIC MINIMIZATION OF ENVIRONMENTAL INTRUSION FROM PETROLEUM PRODUCTS. Washington, D.C., 1973. 4p.

IVOCET  National Academy of Engineering. Marine Board. TOWARD FULFILLMENT OF A NATIONAL OCEAN COMMITMENT. Washington, D.C., 1972. xiii, 255p.   1,5,13,17

IIODAS  National Academy of Engineering. Panel on Buoy Technology Assessment. DIRECTIONS FOR DATA BUOY TECHNOLOGY, 1978-1983. Washington, National Academy of Engineering, 1974. vii, 101p.   14a

VP  _____ _____ Panel on Operational Safety in Offshore Resource Development. OUTER CONTINENTAL SHELF RESOURCE DEVELOPMENT SAFETY: A REVIEW OF TECHNOLOGY AND REGULATION FOR THE SYSTEMATIC MINIMIZATION OF ENVIRONMENTAL INTRUSION FROM PETROLEUM PRODUCTS. Washington, NTIS, 1972. 197p.   ***

VINTL  National Academy of Sciences. COPIES OF OFFICIAL COMMUNICATIONS TO THE STATE DEPARTMENT CONCERNING FREEDOM OF SCIENTIFIC RESEARCH AND THE CONTINENTAL SHELF. Washington, D.C., 1971. 14p.   13

IIWQ  _____ _____ DESALINATION RESEARCH AND THE WATER PROBLEM. Report of the Desalination Research Conference convened by the National Association of Sciences-National Research Council at Woods Hole, Mass. Publication 941. Washington, D.C., 1962. 85p.   13

VENV  _____ _____ MARINE ENVIRONMENTAL QUALITY; SUGGESTED RESEARCH PROGRAMS FOR UNDERSTANDING MAN'S EFFECT ON THE OCEANS. The report of a special study held under the auspices of the Ocean Science Committee of the NAS-NRC Ocean Affairs Board, August 9-13, 1971. Washington, D.C., NAS, 1971. x, 107p.   1

VOCET  _____ _____ NATIONAL RESEARCH COUNCIL GOALS, NEW EMPHASIS, LABORATORY RELATIONSHIPS, EDUCATIONAL AND TRAINING NEEDS AND SCIENTIFIC AWARENESS IN MARINE SCIENCE. Washington, D.C., n.d.   5

VOCET  _____ _____ OCEANOGRAPHY - ACHIEVEMENTS AND OPPORTUNITIES. Washington, D.C., National Academy of Sciences-National Research Council, 1967.   ***

IIIF  _____ _____ A PRELIMINARY REPORT ON INTERNATIONAL FISHERIES MANAGEMENT RESEARCH. REPORT OF THE WORKING GROUP ON INTERNATIONAL FISHERIES MANAGEMENT OF THE COMMITTEE ON INTERNATIONAL MARINE SCIENCE AFFAIRS POLICY OF THE OCEAN AFFAIRS BOARD. Washington, National Academy of Science, 1971. 57p.   13

VOCET  _____ _____ A REPORT BY THE INTERNATIONAL MARINE SCIENCE AFFAIRS PANEL OF THE COMMITTEE ON OCEANOGRAPHY. Washington, D.C., 1972. xi, 92p.   1

VMT  _____ _____ Committee on Hazardous Materials. CONFERENCE PROCEEDINGS ON BULK TRANSPORTATION OF HAZARDOUS MATERIALS BY WATER IN THE   15

FUTURE; A LONG-RANGE FORECAST. Washington, D.C., National Research Council, 1974. iv, 274p.

15
VOCET   National Academy of Sciences. Committee on Oceanography. OCEANOGRAPHY 1960-1970; INTRODUCTION AND SUMMARY OF RECOMMENDATIONS. Washington, D.C., National Research Council, n.d.

13
VINTL   _____ Ocean Affairs Board. FREEDOM FOR SCIENCE IN THE OCEANS (A PROPOSED U.S. POSITION). Prepared under the auspices of the NAS Ocean Affairs Board. Revised May 1972. Washington, 1972. 4p.

16
IIIF    _____ Ocean Affairs Board. Committee on International Marine Science Affairs Policy. A PRELIMINARY REPORT ON INTERNATIONAL FISHERIES MANAGEMENT RESEARCH; REPORT OF THE WORKING GROUP ON INTERNATIONAL FISHERIES MANAGEMENT OF THE COMMITTEE ON INTERNATIONAL MARINE SCIENCE AFFAIRS POLICY (IMSAP) OF THE OCEAN AFFAIRS BOARD. Washington? 1971. 57p.

15
IICZM   _____ Steering Committee on Coastal Wastes Management. WASTES MANAGEMENT CONCEPTS FOR THE COASTAL ZONE; REQUIREMENTS FOR RESEARCH AND INVESTIGATION. Washington, D.C., National Academy of Sciences, 1970. 126p.

13
VOCET   National Academy of Sciences-National Research Council. Ocean Science Committee. FORMATS FOR MARINE GEOPHYSICAL DATA EXCHANGE. A report of an Ad Hoc working group of the Ocean Science Committee. Washington, D.C., June 1972. iv, 19p.

14
IVOCET  National Advisory Committee on Oceans and Atmosphere. ENGINEERING IN THE OCEAN. A report for the Secretary of Commerce. Washington, U.S.G.P.O., November 15, 1974. iii, 54p.

13,14
VOCET   _____ A REPORT TO: THE PRESIDENT AND THE CONGRESS. Washington, U.S.G.P.O. 1-    1972-

13,17
VOR     National Association of Manufacturers of the United States of America. Science and Technology Division. NEW WEALTH FROM THE SEAS. New York, 1966. 80p.

13
IIIF    National Commission on Productivity. PRODUCTIVITY IN THE FISHING INDUSTRIES. Washington, U.S.G.P.O., 1973. 18p.

15
VSG     NATIONAL CONFERENCE ON THE CONCEPT OF A SEA-GRANT UNIVERSITY. Newport, R.I., 1965.

5
VOR     National Council on Marine Resources and Engineering Development. THE ECONOMIC POTENTIAL OF THE MINERAL AND BOTANICAL RESOURCES OF THE U.S. CONTINENTAL SHELF AND SLOPE. Washington, U.S.G.P.O., n.d.

                                                                    14a
VOCET      National Council on Marine Resources and Engineering Development.
           INTERNATIONAL DECADE OF OCEAN EXPLORATION: A REPORT. Washington,
           U.S.G.P.O., 1968. iii, 7p.

                                                                  13,15,17
VOCET      _____ _____ MARINE SCIENCE ACTIVITIES OF CANADA AND THE NATIONS
           OF EUROPE. Washington, U.S.G.P.O., 1968. iv, 159p.

                                                                13,14a,15,17
VOCET      _____ _____ MARINE SCIENCE ACTIVITIES OF THE NATIONS OF AFRICA.
           Washington, U.S.G.P.O., 1968. iv, 76p.

                                                                      1,13
VOCET      _____ _____ MARINE SCIENCE ACTIVITIES OF THE NATIONS OF AFRICA,
           CANADA AND THE NATIONS OF EUROPE; EAST ASIA; LATIN AMERICA; NEAR
           EAST, AND SOUTH ASIA. Washington, D.C., April, 1968. 5 Vols.

                                                                     15,17
VOCET      _____ _____ MARINE SCIENCE ACTIVITIES OF THE NATIONS OF EAST ASIA.
           Washington, U.S.G.P.O., 1968. iv, 80p.

                                                                     15,17
VOCET      _____ _____ MARINE SCIENCE ACTIVITIES OF THE NATIONS OF LATIN
           AMERICA. Washington, U.S.G.P.O., 1968. iv, 76p.

                                                                  13,15,17
VOCET      _____ _____ MARINE SCIENCE ACTIVITIES OF THE NATIONS OF THE NEAR
           EAST AND SOUTH ASIA. Washington, U.S.G.P.O., 1968. iv, 55p.

                                                                        14
VT&L       NATIONAL LEGISLATION AND TREATIES RELATING TO THE LAW OF THE SEA.
           United Nations Legislative Series. N.Y., United Nations, 1974.

                                                                       ***
VOCET      National Oceanic and Atmospheric Administration. ASSESSING TECH-
           NOLOGY FOR MARINE RESOURCE DEVELOPMENT. Proceedings of a conference-
           workshop held by the Marine Technology Society at Arlington, Va., on
           May 15-17, 1972. Washington, U.S. Department of Commerce, 1972.
           94p.

                                                                       ***
VOD        _____ _____ ASSESSMENT OF OFFSHORE DUMPING IN NEW YORK BIGHT ...
           edited by Robert L. Charnell. Washington, U.S. Department of Com-
           merce, 1975. vii, 83p.

                                                                       ***
VOCET      _____ _____ MANNED UNDERSEA SCIENCE AND TECHNOLOGY. Washington,
           D.C., U.S. Department of Commerce, 1975. iv, 51p.

                                                                       ***
VOD        _____ _____ OCEAN DUMPING IN NEW YORK BIGHT. Washington, D.C.,
           1975. vi, 78p.

                                                                       ***
VOD        _____ _____ REPORT TO CONGRESS ON OCEAN DUMPING RESEARCH, JANUARY
           TO DECEMBER, 1974. Washington, D.C., 1975. viii, 48p.

VENV     National Oceanic and Atmospheric Administration. REPORT TO CONGRESS ON OCEAN POLLUTION, OVERFISHING, AND OFFSHORE DEVELOPMENT, JULY 1973-JUNE 1974. Washington, U.S. Department of Commerce, 1975. vi, 77p. ***

IICZM     \_\_\_\_\_ \_\_\_\_\_ STATE COASTAL ZONE MANAGEMENT ACTIVITIES 1974. Washington, U.S. Department of Commerce, 1974. 124p. ***

IVMMR     National Petroleum Council. PETROLEUM RESOURCES UNDER THE OCEAN FLOOR. Washington, D.C., 1969. 107p.    1,5,7,12,13,15,16

VP     \_\_\_\_\_ \_\_\_\_\_ Committee on Environmental Conservation - the Oil and Gas Industries. ENVIRONMENTAL CONSERVATION, THE OIL AND GAS INDUSTRIES; A REPORT OF THE NATIONAL PETROLEUM COUNCIL'S COMMITTEE ON ENVIRONMENTAL CONSERVATION - THE OIL AND GAS INDUSTRIES, with the assistance of the Coordinating Subcommittee. Washington? 1971-    2

IVMMR     \_\_\_\_\_ \_\_\_\_\_ Committee on Petroleum Resources. PETROLEUM RESOURCES UNDER THE OCEAN FLOOR. An interim report by the Committee. Washington, July 9, 1968. 12p.    1

IVMMR     \_\_\_\_\_ \_\_\_\_\_ OCEAN PETROLEUM RESOURCES: AN INTERIM REPORT. Washington, 1974. 39p. ***

IVMMR     National Petroleum Council. Committee on Petroleum Resources Under the Ocean Floor. LAW OF THE SEA: PARTICULAR ASPECTS AFFECTING THE PETROLEUM INDUSTRY, MAY 1973. Washington, D.C., 1973. 90p.    16

IVMMR     \_\_\_\_\_ \_\_\_\_\_ OCEAN PETROLEUM RESOURCES: REPORT OF THE NATIONAL PETROLEUM COUNCIL. Washington, the Council, 1975. 98p.    16

IVOCET     NATIONAL POLICY ON SEABED ENGINEERING. Proceedings, British National Committee on Ocean Engineering, Society for Underwater Technology, n.p., summer, 1974. ***

IVM     National Research Council. Assembly of Engineering, Marine Board. Panel on Operational Safety in Marine Mining. MINING IN THE OUTER CONTINENTAL SHELF AND IN THE DEEP OCEAN. Washington, D.C., National Academy of Sciences, 1975. 140p. ***

IIIP     National Research Council. Committee on Effects of Atomic Radiation on Oceanography and Fisheries. THE EFFECTS OF ATOMIC RADIATION ON OCEANOGRAPHY AND FISHERIES, REPORT. Washington, National Academy of Sciences-National Research Council, 1957. ix, 137p.    14a

VOCET     \_\_\_\_\_ \_\_\_\_\_ Committee on Oceanography. ECONOMIC BENEFITS FROM OCEANOGRAPHIC RESEARCH, A SPECIAL REPORT. Washington, National Academy of Sciences-National Research Council, 1966.    15

|       |                                                                                                                                                                                                                  |
|-------|------------------------------------------------------------------------------------------------------------------------------------------------------------------------------------------------------------------|
| VOCET | 15<br>National Research Council. Committee on Oceanography. OCEANOGRAPHY INFORMATION SOURCES; A STAFF REPORT. Washington, National Academy of Sciences-National Research Council, 1966.                          |
| VOCET | ***<br>_____ AN OCEANIC QUEST; A REPORT ON THE INTERNATIONAL DECADE OF OCEAN EXPLORATION, PREPARED UNDER THE AUSPICES OF THE COMMITTEE ON OCEANOGRAPHY, NATIONAL RESEARCH COUNCIL AND COMMITTEE ON OCEAN ENGINEERING, NATIONAL ACADEMY OF ENGINEERING. Washington, D.C., 1969. 115p. |
| VOCET | 5<br>_____ OCEANOGRAPHY INFORMATION SOURCES, 70; A STAFF REPORT OF THE COMMITTEE. Compiled by R.C. Vetter. Washington, D.C., National Academy of Sciences, 1970. 51p.                                       |
| VOCET | 17<br>_____ OCEANOGRAPHY 1951: A REPORT ON THE PRESENT STATUS OF THE SEA. National Research Council publication 208. Washington, National Academy of Sciences, n.d. 36p.                                   |
| VOCET | 14a,17<br>_____ OCEANOGRAPHY, 1960 TO 1970. Washington, National Academy of Sciences-National Research Council, 1959-   12 Vols.                                                                            |
| VOCET | 15,17<br>_____ OCEANOGRAPHY 1966: ACHIEVEMENTS AND OPPORTUNITIES: A REPORT. Washington, National Academy of Sciences-National Research Council, 1967. 183p.                                                 |
| VOCET | 14a<br>National Research Council. Committee on Undersea Warfare. PROCEEDINGS OF THE SYMPOSIUM ON ASPECTS OF DEEP-SEA RESEARCH, National Academy of Sciences-National Research Council, Washington, D.C., February 29-March 1, 1956. William S. von Arx, ed. Prepared for the Office of Naval Research. Washington, 1957. ix, 181p. |
| VOCET | 15<br>National Research Council. International Marine Science Affairs Panel. INTERNATIONAL MARINE SCIENCE AFFAIRS: A REPORT. Washington, National Academy of Sciences-National Research Council, 1971. 126, 5, 4p. |
| VOCET | 14a,16,17<br>_____ _____ INTERNATIONAL MARINE SCIENCE AFFAIRS; A REPORT. Washington, National Academy of Sciences, 1972. xi, 92p.                                                                      |
| VOCET | 13<br>National Research Council. International Marine Science Affairs Policy Committee. INTERNATIONAL MARINE SCIENCE AFFAIRS; A REPORT. Washington, National Academy of Sciences-National Research Council. 1971. |
| VOCET | 13<br>National Research Council. Marine Chemistry Panel. MARINE CHEMISTRY; A REPORT. Washington, National Academy of Sciences, 1971. ix, 61p.                                                                    |

                                                                        18
VMLAD      National Research Council. Maritime Transportation Research Board.
           FOREIGN MARITIME POLICIES: STUDY DEFINITION; A REPORT. Washington,
           D.C., National Academy of Sciences, 1971. vii, 17p.

                                                                      14a,17
VP         National Research Council. Panel on Monitoring Persistent Pesticides
           in the Marine Environment. CHLORINATED HYDROCARBONS IN THE MARINE
           ENVIRONMENT, A REPORT. Washington, National Academy of Sciences,
           1971. vii, 42p.

                                                                      14a,17
VP         National Research Council. PANEL ON RADIOACTIVITY IN THE MARINE EN-
           VIRONMENT. A SUMMARY. Washington, National Academy of Sciences,
           1971. ix, 272p.

                                                                         14a
VP         National Research Council. Study Panel on Assessing Potential Ocean
           Pollutants. ASSESSING POTENTIAL OCEAN POLLUTANTS; a report of the
           Study Panel on Assessing Potential Ocean Pollutants to the Ocean
           Affairs Board. Commission on Natural Resources, National Research
           Council. Washington, National Academy of Sciences, 1975. xx, 438p.

                                                                      5,7,13
VOCET      National Science Foundation. INTERNATIONAL DECADE OF OCEAN EXPLORA-
           TION. NSF 71-34. October, 1971. Washington, National Science
           Foundation, 1971. 64p.

                                                                1,2,3,4,16
VSG        NATIONAL SEA GRANT CONFERENCE. PROCEEDINGS. 1st-    1965-

                                                                          14
VSG        National Sea Grant Conference. PROCEEDINGS - NATIONAL SEA GRANT
           CONFERENCE. 4th-    1972-    Madison, University of Wisconsin.

                                                                          13
IVM        National Security Industrial Association. REPORT OF THE COASTAL
           STATES CONFERENCE ON THE MULTIPLE USE APPROACH TO OCEAN MINING LAW.
           Portland, Or., December 11-13, 1968.

                                                                         ART
VOR        NATURAL RESOURCES. In Policy Positions, October, 1975. Washington,
           National Conference of State Legislatures, 1975. pp. 41-51.

                                                                         ***
VENV       NATURAL RESOURCES AND RECREATION AGENCIES PROGRAMS, NEEDS, GOALS.
           Annual report. Olympia, Washington Natural Resources and Recreation
           Agencies, 1973. 61p.

                                                                          17
VOCET      Nautilus Research. SEAWORK CAPABILITIES REPORTS. E.W. Seabrook
           Hull, director. ZULU 1968, Analysis Division, Vol. 1, sec. 2.
           Washington, D.C., Nautilus Press, 1968.

                                                                          17
VOCET      _____   SEAWORK CAPABILITIES REPORTS. John O. Ludwigson,
           checklist editor; E.W. Seabrook Hull, director. ZULU 1968, Check-
           list Division, Vol. 1, sec. 2. Washington, D.C., 1968. vi, 173p.

17
VOCET    Nautilus Research. THE ZULU SERIES OF SEA WORK CAPABILITIES REPORTS THRU DECEMBER 31, 1967. Checklist, edited by John Ludwigson. ZULU 1968. Checklist Division, Vol. ICL, Vol. 1, no. 1. Washington, D.C., Nautilus Press, 1968. 2 p.l., 111p.

***

IIIF    Needler, A.W.H. PROCEEDINGS, CONFERENCE ON THE CANADIAN SHRIMP FISHERY. Canadian Fish Report no. 17, n.p., May, 1971. 501p.

15
IVMMR    Nef, Urs Ch. DAS RECHT ZUM ABBAU MINERALISCHER ROHSTOFFE VOM MEERESGRUND UNTER BESONDERER BERUCKSICHTIGUNG DER STELLUNG DER SCHWEIZ. Zurich, Schulthess, 1974.

15
IVMMR    _____ _____ TEMPORARE ARBEIT. Bern, Verlag Stampfli, 1971.

***

IVT&L    Neff, John Lewis, and Robert L. Magnuson. MINING LAWS OF THE STATE OF WASHINGTON. Olympia, Washington, Department of Natural Resources, 1974. xi, 109p.

ART
VLOS    Neild, R. ALTERNATIVE FORMS OF INTERNATIONAL REGIME FOR THE OCEANS. In SIPRI, Towards a Better Use of the Oceans: A Study and Prognosis. Stockholm, Almqvist and Wiksell, 1969. pp. 279-292.

***

IIE    Nelson, B.W., ed. ENVIRONMENTAL FRAMEWORK OF COASTAL PLAIN ESTUARIES. Geological Society of America Memoir 133. Bouder, Colo., Geological Society of America, 1973. 604p.

***

IICZM    Nelson, J.G., et al. CANADIAN PUBLIC LAND USE IN PERSPECTIVE. Ottawa, Social Science Research Council, 1975. 579p.

13,15
VMT    Nelson, Stewart B. OCEANOGRAPHIC SHIPS FORE AND AFT. Office of the Oceanographer of the Navy. Washington, U.S.G.P.O., 1971. xvii, 240p.

ART
IVMMR    Nelson, T.W., and C.A. Burk. PETROLEUM RESOURCES OF THE CONTINENTAL MARGINS OF THE UNITED STATES. In Marine Technology Society. Second Annual Conference, Washington, D.C., June 27-29, 1966. Washington, D.C., 1966. pp. 116-133.

***

VP    Nelson-Smith, A. OIL POLLUTION AND MARINE ECOLOGY. New York, Plenum Publishing Corporation, Plenum Press, 1973. 266p.

16
IVMMR    Netherlands Branch of International Law Association. THE EXPLORATION AND EXPLOITATION OF MINERALS ON THE OCEAN BED AND ITS SUBSOIL. In Report, Fifty-Second Conference of the International Law Association. L. Bouchez, rapporteur, 1966. pp. 793-798.

|     |     |
| --- | --- |
| IICZM | New England Coastal Zone Management Conference, Durham, New Hampshire, 1970. PROCEEDINGS. Sponsored by The New England Council, Inc., n.d.    15 |
| IIENV | New England River Basins Commission. LAWS AND PROCEDURES OF POWER PLANT SITING IN NEW ENGLAND. Boston, n.p., 1970.    15 |
| IICZM | _____ _____ LONG ISLAND SOUND REGIONAL STUDY. New Haven, Conn., 1973.    15 |
| IICZM | _____ _____ STATE COASTAL MANAGEMENT LEGISLATION. A STAFF REPORT. Boston, New England River Basins Commission, 1970.    13 |
| VOR | New Hampshire. University. THE SCIENCE AND TECHNOLOGY OF UTILIZING THE BOTTOM RESOURCES OF THE CONTINENTAL SHELF: A SECOND YEAR PROGRESS REPORT TO THE NATIONAL SEA GRANT PROGRAM OF THE NATIONAL OCEANIC AND ATMOSPHERIC ADMINISTRATION, U.S. DEPARTMENT OF COMMERCE. Second annual report covering Grant no. DC 1-36114, June, 1971 to June 1972. A cooperative university-industry research project. Cooperating institutions: University of New Hampshire, Submarine Signal Division, Raytheon Company. Durham, N.H., 1972. v, 187p.    13 |
| VOCET | _____ _____ Engineering Design and Analysis Laboratory. UNIVERSITY SEALAB; DESIGN AND ANALYSIS OF A SATURATION DIVING FACILITY FOR THE NATIONAL OCEANOGRAPHIC COMMUNITY. Durham, N.H., 1967. xii, 266, 13p.    15 |
| VP | New Jersey. PLAIN FACTS ABOUT NEW JERSEY'S ENVIRONMENT - DETERGENTS. New Jersey, Department of Environmental Protection, 1975.    *** |
| IICZM | _____ _____ Department of Environmental Protection. AN INVENTORY OF THE NEW JERSEY COASTAL AREA; A REPORT. Trenton, N.J., 1975.    *** |
| VP | New Jersey. Legislature. General Assembly. Committee on Agriculture, Conservation and Natural Resources. PUBLIC HEARING ON ASSEMBLY BILL NO. 827 (OCEAN SANCTUARY) held: May 23, 1972. Trenton, 1972. ii, 99p.    2 |
| VOCET | THE NEW THRUST SEAWARD; TRANSACTIONS OF THE THIRD ANNUAL MTS CONFERENCE AND EXHIBIT, 5-7 JUNE, 1967, SAN DIEGO, CALIFORNIA. Washington, Marine Technology Society, 1967. xiii, 717p.    17 |
| VP | New York. Bureau of Radiological Pollution. EXPLANATION OF REGULATIONS FOR THE PREVENTION AND CONTROL OF ENVIRONMENTAL POLLUTION BY RADIOACTIVE MATERIALS. Report no. BRCP-1. Albany, 1973. iii, 13p.    *** |

VCONS    New York. Legislature. Joint Interim Committee. REPORT ON REVISION OF THE CONSERVATION LAW. Albany, 1956. 106p.  
                                                            16

IVM    New York (State). Office of General Services. REMOVING MATERIAL FROM UNDERWATER LANDS. Albany, N.Y., n.d. 5p.    13

IISL    _____  _____ UNDERWATER LAND EASEMENTS. Albany, N.Y., n.d. 5p.    13

VSG    NEW YORK STATE SEA GRANT PROGRAM. Annual Report. A report on the New York State Sea Grant Program from October 1972 to November 1973. State University of New York and Cornell University, 1973. 52p.    13

IICZM    New York State Sea Grant Program. MANAGING OUR COASTAL ZONE; PROCEEDINGS OF A CONFERENCE ON COASTAL ZONE MANAGEMENT. Albany, N.Y., 1973.    15

IIIP    Newcastle-upon-Tyne. University. Advisory Committee on Oil Pollution of the Sea. RESEARCH UNIT ON THE REHABILITATION OF OILED SEABIRDS. ANNUAL REPORT. University of Newcastle-upon-Tyne, 1974. 28p.    ***

VLOS    Newman, Barry. MARITIME MUDDLE: TIDE OF PESSIMISM IS HIGH AS TALKS ON LAW OF SEA NEAR OPENING; FORMIDABLE AGENDA AWAITS U.N. MEETING IN CARACAS: FISHING, MINING, POLLUTION; A PLETHORA OF POSITIONS. In The Wall Street Journal, Tuesday, June 18, 1974.    ART

VP    Newsom, G., and J.G. Sherratt. WATER POLLUTION. Altricham, England, John Sherratt and Son, 1972. 330p.    ***

VENV    Nicholls, Yvonne I., comp. SOURCE BOOK, EMERGENCE OF PROPOSALS FOR RECOMPENSING DEVELOPING COUNTRIES FOR MAINTAINING ENVIRONMENTAL QUALITY. Morges, Switzerland: International Union for Conservation of Nature and Natural Resources, 1973. 142p.    14

IICZM    Nierenberg, William A. NATIONAL GOALS, STATE'S INTERESTS, AND JURISDICTIONAL FACTORS. In J.F. Peel Brahtz, ed., Coastal Zone Management; Multiple Use with Conservation. N.Y., John Wiley, 1972. pp. 21-34.    ART

VOR    Nightingale, Charles. EXPLOITING THE OCEANS. London, Methuen, 1968. 93p.    5

IVM    Nightingale, W.G., ed. WALTER R. SKINNER'S OIL AND GAS INTERNATIONAL YEAR BOOK, 1973. London, Financial Times, Ltd., 1973. 822p.    ***

IVMMR    Noble, I. SOME INVESTMENT IMPLICATIONS OF NORTH SEA OIL AND GAS - A SCOTTISH VIEW. Paper presented at the North Sea Conference.    ***

Mimeo. n.p., 1972. 10p.

              ***

VOCET    Niiler, Pearn P., and Christopher N.K. Mooers, eds. PROGRAMS IN SHELF DYNAMICS, REPORT ON CONFERENCE ON PHYSICAL OCEANOGRAPHY OF CONTINENTAL SHELVES, ANNAPOLIS, MD., APRIL 3-6, 1974, HELD UNDER AUSPICES OF INTERNATIONAL DECADE OF OCEAN EXPLORATION. Washington, D.C., National Science Foundation, 1974. iv, 20p.

              ART

IVMMR    Niino, Hiroshi. ON THE MINERAL RESOURCES OF THE SEA FLOOR AROUND THE JAPANESE ISLANDS AND THE PROBLEMS OF BANKS AND ROCKS SITUATED OUTSIDE THE CONTINENTAL SHELF. In J. Sztucki, ed., Symposium on the International Regime of the Sea-Bed, Rome, 1969. Proceedings, June 30-July 5, 1969. Rome, Accademia Nazionale dei Lincei, 1970. pp. 65-73.

              ***

VOR    1973-1973 SALINE WATER SUMMARY REPORT. Washington, U.S. Office of Saline Water, 1972-1973. 75p.

              ***

IIIF    THE 1968 STATUS REPORT OF THE COLUMBIA RIVER COMMERCIAL FISHERIES. Fish Commission of Oregon/Washington Department of Fisheries. Salem, Or.? 1969. 89p.

              ART

IIOSTR    Niven, R.G. ARTIFICIAL ISLAND CONSTRUCTION IN THE BEAUFORT SEA. In Oceans Ontario, Technical Symposium held April 22, 1972. Toronto, Canada, James McAllister MacInnis Foundation, 1972? 106p.

              13

IIP&H    Nixon, Scott W., et al. ECOLOGY OF SMALL BOAT MARINAS. Graduate School of Oceanography. Sea Grant Marine technical report series no. 5. Kingston, University of Rhode Island, 1973. 20p.

              13

VOR    NO MAN'S SEA. Resources for the Future, Inc., no. 26. September, 1967. Photocopy. Washington, Resources for the Future, Inc., 1967.

              ART

IVMMR    Noakes, John E., et al. LOCATING OFFSHORE MINERAL DEPOSITS BY NATURAL RADIOACTIVE MEASUREMENTS. In Marine Technology Society Journal, Vol. 8, no. 5, 1974. pp. 36-39.

              ***

IIOSTR    _____ _____ RADIOACTIVE MONITORING OF OFFSHORE NUCLEAR POWER STATIONS. Offshore Technology Conference Paper no. OTC 1988. n.p. 6p.

              5,16

VLOS    Noland, F.L. A CASE FOR AN INTERNATIONAL REGIME FOR THE SEABEDS. M.A. Thesis, American University. Ann Arbor, University Microfilms, 1972. 121p.

              ***

IVMMR    NON-LIVING RESOURCES. PART 2 - OIL AND GAS RESOURCES IN THE ONSHORE COASTAL ZONE. California Comprehensive Ocean Area Plan. Appendix V, Vol. 11. Report. Sacramento, Department of Navigation and Ocean Development, 1971. 78p.

***
IVMMR   NON-LIVING RESOURCES. PART 3 - MINERAL DEVELOPMENT ON STATE TIDE LAND AND SUBMERGED LANDS. Sacramento, Department of Navigation and Ocean Development, 1971. 131p.

***
VOI     NOR-SHIPPING '73. Fourth International Shipping Exhibition and Technical Symposium, at Oslo, Norway. Mimeo. n.p. 1973?

***
IIENV   Nordstrom, K.R., et al. AN ENVIRONMENTAL ASSESSMENT OF MAINTENANCE DREDGING OF THE NEW JERSEY INTRACOASTAL WATERWAY. Technical Report 74-1. New Brunswick, N.J., Rutgers University, Marine Sciences Center, 1974.

***
IICZM   North Carolina. Coastal Resources Commission. HANDBOOK ON PUBLIC PARTICIPATION IN THE DEVELOPMENT OF LAND USE PLANS IN THE COASTAL AREAS OF NORTH CAROLINA. Raleigh, 1975. 9p.

***
VP      North Carolina. Department of Natural and Economic Resources. Division of Environmental Management. REGULATION ADOPTING EFFLUENT LIMITATIONS AND GUIDELINES FOR WASTEWATER DISCHARGE TO THE SURFACE WATERS OF NORTH CAROLINA. Raleigh, 1975. 143p.

***
IICZM   North Carolina. University. PROCEEDINGS OF A CONFERENCE ON COASTAL MANAGEMENT, MAY 16-17, 1974, BEAUFORT, NORTH CAROLINA, SPONSORED BY CENTER FOR MARINE AND COASTAL STUDIES. Sea Grant Program. Raleigh, Coastal Plains Center for Marine Development Services, North Carolina State University, 1974. 181p.

1,13,18
VLOS    _____ School of Law. ATTITUDES REGARDING A LAW OF THE SEA CONVENTION TO ESTABLISH AN INTERNATIONAL SEABED REGIME. Sea Grant Publication. Chapel Hill, April, 1972. 143p.

***
IVOI    NORTH EAST SCOTLAND AND THE OFFSHORE OIL INDUSTRY. Aberdeen, North East Scotland Development Authority, 1975. 40p.

14
IICZM   Northam, R.M., et al. OREGON COASTAL ZONE LAND: USE, OWNERSHIP AND VALUE CHANGE. ORESU-T-75-006. Corvallis, Oregon State University Sea Grant College Program, 1975. 56p.

***
IIIF    NORTH-EAST ATLANTIC FISHERIES COMMISSION. Report of the mid-term meeting, November 1974, and the special meeting, Bergen, January, 1975. London, n.p., 1975. 89p.

14
VENV    NORTHEAST PACIFIC ENVIRONMENTAL SCENARIO. Prepared by The Naval Weather Service Environmental Detachment. Ashville, N.C., Naval Weather Service Command, June, 1974.
        _____ _____ SUPPLEMENT. October, 1974.

                                                              ***
VT&L    NORWAY/UNITED KINGDOM: CONTINENTAL SHELF. U.K. Treaty Series 101.
        London, H.M.S.O., 1973.

                                                              13
IIIAFF  NORTHWEST MARICULTURE LAWS - PAPERS AND PRESENTATIONS FROM A SYM-
        POSIUM HELD AT THE LAW CENTER, UNIVERSITY OF OREGON, EUGENE, JUNE
        7, 1974. ORESU-W-74-005. Corvallis, Oregon State University, Sea
        Grant Communications, 1975. 32p.

                                                              14
IIIAFF  Nosho, Terry Y., et al, eds. OCEAN RANCHING IN WASHINGTON: A WORK-
        SHOP SUMMARY. WSG-WO 75-1. Seattle, University of Washington,
        1974. vi, 24p.

                                                              ***
IIIAFF  Nosho, Terry Y., et al. WORKSHOP ON SALMONID AQUACULTURE - A SUM-
        MARY REPORT. PASGAP Publication WSG-WO 74-1. Seattle, University
        of Washington, Sea Grant Communications, 1974. 29p.

                                                              15
VCS     Nossaman, Waters, Scott, Krueger, and Riordan. STUDY OF THE OUTER
        CONTINENTAL SHELF LANDS OF THE UNITED STATES. Los Angeles, Calif.,
        1968. 2 Vols.

                                                              ART
IIIAFF  Novotny, Anthony J. LEGAL ASPECTS OF MARINE FARMING OPERATIONS - A
        GAME OF TOURNAMENT CHESS. In Northwest Mariculture Laws - papers
        and presentations from a symposium held at The Law Center, University
        of Oregon, Eugene, June 7, 1974. Corvallis, Oregon State University,
        Sea Grant Communications, 1975.

                                                              ***
VENE    NUCLEAR POWER PLANT SITING: A HANDBOOK FOR THE LAYMAN. Kingston,
        University of Rhode Island, Marine Advisory Service, 1975.

                                                              ***
IICZM   Nunez, Richard I., and Peter Bluhm. THREE LEGAL ASPECTS OF COASTAL
        ZONE MANAGEMENT IN NEW YORK STATE. Albany, State University of New
        York, Sea Grant Institute, 1975. 84p.

                                                              7
VINTL   Nweiheid, Kaldone G. LA VIGENCIA DEL MAR. UNA INVESTIGACIÓN ACERCA
        DE LA SOBERANÍA MARÍTIMA Y LA PLATAFORMA CONTINENTAL DE VENEZUELA
        DENTRO DEL MARCO INTERNACIONAL DEL DERECHO DEL MAR. n.p. 1973-
        2 Vols.

                                                              ***
VENV    Nybakken, J.W., ed. READINGS IN MARINE ECOLOGY. New York, Harper
        and Row, 1971. 544p.

                                                              ***
IIIAFF  Nyegaard, Curtis W. COHO SALMON FARMING IN PUGET SOUND. Rev. Pull-
        man, Washington State University, Cooperative Extension Service,
        1975. 14p.

                                                              1,13,16
VINTL   Obieta, Joseph A. THE INTERNATIONAL STATUS OF THE SUEZ CANAL.
        2d ed. The Hague, Nijhoff, 1970. ix, 164p.

|       |                                                                                                                                                                                                  |
|-------|--------------------------------------------------------------------------------------------------------------------------------------------------------------------------------------------------|
|       | 1,5,7,13,14a,16                                                                                                                                                                                  |
| VOR   | THE OCEAN. San Francisco, W.H. Freeman, 1969. viii, 140p.                                                                                                                                        |
|       | ***                                                                                                                                                                                              |
| VOR   | OCEAN LAND GRAB. WHO OWNS WHAT RESOURCES IN THE OCEAN? VIDEOTAPE. WSG-AV 75-2. Seattle, University of Washington, Sea Grant Communications, 1975. Videotape cassette.                            |
|       | ***                                                                                                                                                                                              |
| IVM   | OCEAN MINING SYMPOSIUM: OSM II. San Pedro, Calif., World Dredging Conference Association, 1973. 168p.                                                                                            |
|       | ***                                                                                                                                                                                              |
| VOCET | OCEAN '74. IEEE INTERNATIONAL CONFERENCE ON ENGINEERING IN THE OCEAN ENVIRONMENT. New York, Institute of Electrical and Electronic Engineers, 1974? 2 Vols.                                      |
|       | ***                                                                                                                                                                                              |
| IVMMR | OCEAN PETROLEUM RESOURCES: AN INTERIM REPORT OF THE NATIONAL PETROLEUM COUNCIL. Washington, National Petroleum Council, Committee on Ocean Petroleum Resources, 1974. 42p.                       |
|       | 1,5,14,17                                                                                                                                                                                        |
| VOR   | OCEAN RESOURCES. Stanford Journal of International Studies, Vol. 4. California, Stanford University School of Law, 1969. vii, 142p.                                                              |
|       | ***                                                                                                                                                                                              |
| VOR   | OCEAN RESOURCES MANAGEMENT; LEGAL AND POLICY ASPECTS. Proceedings of Workshop, July 11-16, 1976. Cambridge, Massachusetts Institute of Technology, Office of Summer Session, 1976.               |
|       | ART                                                                                                                                                                                              |
| VOR   | OCEAN SCIENCE AND MARINE RESOURCES. By Paul M. Fye et al. In Edmund A. Gullion, ed., Uses of the sea. Englewood Cliffs, N.J., Prentice Hall, 1968. pp. 17-68.                                    |
|       | 5,14                                                                                                                                                                                             |
| VLOS  | OCEAN SCIENCE NEWS. THE STORY OF THIS SUMMER'S TEN-WEEK U.N. SESSION ON THE LAW OF THE SEA. Washington, D.C., Nautilus Press, 1974. 2 Vols.                                                      |
|       | ***                                                                                                                                                                                              |
| IICR  | OCEAN UTILIZATION AND COASTAL ZONE DEVELOPMENT. Report no. MITSG-73-3. Cambridge, Massachusetts Institute of Technology, Sea Grant Project Office. n.d. 29p.                                     |
|       | ***                                                                                                                                                                                              |
| VOD   | OCEAN WASTE DISPOSAL IN SELECTED GEOGRAPHIC AREAS. Anaheim, Cal., Interstate Electronics Corporation, Oceanics Division, 1973. 394p.                                                             |
|       | 1,5,13,14a,15,17                                                                                                                                                                                 |
| VOCET | AN OCEANIC QUEST - THE INTERNATIONAL DECADE OF OCEAN EXPLORATION. Washington, National Academy of Sciences, 1969. vii, 115p.                                                                     |
|       | 13                                                                                                                                                                                               |
| VENE  | Oceanographic Institute of Washington. OFFSHORE PETROLEUM TRANSFER SYSTEMS FOR WASHINGTON STATE; A FEASIBILITY STUDY. Seattle, Oceanographic commission of Washington. December 16, 1974. xx, 62p. |

                                                                14
IIP&H    Oceanographic Institute of Washington.  OFFSHORE PETROLEUM TRANSFER
         SYSTEMS FOR WASHINGTON STATE:  A FEASIBILITY STUDY;  prepared by the
         Oceanographic Institute of Washington for the Oceanographic Commis-
         sion of Washington;  submitted by the Oceanographic Commission of
         Washington to the 44th Legislature of the State of Washington, 16
         December 1974.  Seattle, 1975?  523p.

                                                                ***
IIE      Oceanographic Institute of Washington.  A PROPOSAL FOR A MAINTENANCE
         PROGRAM OF THE COMPENDIUM OF "CURRENT ENVIRONMENTAL STUDIES OF PUGET
         SOUND AND NORTHWEST ESTUARINE WATERS."  Seattle, Washington, 1975.
         40p.

                                                                14,14a
VOR      OCEANOGRAPHIC RESOURCES OF THE PACIFIC NORTHWEST.  Seattle, Univer-
         sity of Washington Press, 1967.  263p.

                                                                14a
VCS      OCEANOGRAPHIC SURVEY OF THE CONTINENTAL SHELF AREA OF SOUTHERN CAL-
         IFORNIA.  Submitted to the California State Water Pollution Control
         Board.  Los Angeles, Allen Hancock Foundation, University of Southern
         California, 1959.  169p.

                                                                ***
VOCET    OCEANOGRAPHY AND THE PUGET SOUND MODEL.  WSG-AV 74-1.  Seattle Uni-
         versity of Washington, Sea Grant Communications, 1974.  FILM.

                                                                13
VOCET    OCEANOGRAPHY; READINGS FROM SCIENTIFIC AMERICAN.  With introduc-
         tions by J. Robert Moore.  San Francisco, W.H. Freeman, 1971.  417p.

                                                                13,17
VOR      Oceanography Study Committee.  OCEANOGRAPHIC RESOURCES OF THE PAC-
         IFIC NORTHWEST.  INVENTORY OF CAPABILITIES FOR OCEANOGRAPHIC AND
         MARINE ACTIVITIES.  Seattle, University of Washington Press, 1967.

                                                                ***
VOCET    OCEANOLOGY INTERNATIONAL 72 CONFERENCE, BRIGHTON, ENGLAND, 1972.
         Conference papers; Oceanology International 72, 19-24 Mar., 1972.
         London, 1972.  507p.

                                                                ***
VOR      THE OCEANS;  COMING INDUSTRIAL FRONTIER.  Interview with aquanaut
         Scott Carpenter.  In U.S. News and World Report.  Volume 68, March
         30, 1970.  pp. 38-40.

                                                                ART
VINTL    O'Connell, D.P.  THE EQUIVALENCE OF THE NAUTICAL LEAGUE AND THE
         CANNON-SHOT IN THE LAW OF NATIONS.  In D. Blumenwitz, und A. Randel-
         shofer.  Festschrift fuer Friedrich Berber zum 75. Geburtstag.
         Muenchen, 1973.  pp. 367-375.

                                                                14
VOR      _____  _____  LEGAL PROBLEMS OF THE EXPLOITATION OF THE OCEAN FLOOR.
         Reprinted from Impact of Science on Society, vol. 21, no.3.  July/
         Sept. 1971.  UNESCO, 1971.  pp. 255-264.

14
VLOS     O'Connor, Dennis M., ed. OCEAN LAW - AN ANONYMOUS DRAFT TREATY ON THE LAW OF THE SEA. Sea Grant 04-5-158-14. Technical Bulletin no. 29. Coral Gables, Fla., University of Miami, 1975. xi, 126p.

ART
VOR      Oda, Shigeru. COMMENTS ON PROFESSOR WILLIAM T. BURKE'S REPORT. In SIPRI, TOWARDS A BETTER USE OF THE OCEANS: A STUDY AND PROGNOSIS. Stockholm, Almqvist and Wiksell, 1969. pp. 293-308.

1,2,3,5,7,9,12,15,16
VOR      _____ INTERNATIONAL CONTROL OF SEA RESOURCES. Leyden, A.W. Sijthoff, 1963. 215p.

1,5,7,9,12,14,15,16,18
VINTL    _____ THE INTERNATIONAL LAW OF THE OCEAN DEVELOPMENT. BASIC DOCUMENTS. Leyden, Sijthoff, 1972- xiv, 519p. 2 Vols.

16
VLOS     _____ POSSIBLE FUTURE REGIMES OF THE SEA-BED RESOURCES. Paper at Symposium on the International Regime of the Sea-bed. Rome. 1969.

14
IICZM    Odell, Rice. THE SAVING OF SAN FRANSISCO BAY; A REPORT ON CITIZEN ACTION AND REGIONAL PLANNING. Washington, Conservation Foundation, 1972. xii, 115p.

***
IIIF     Oetting, Russel. THE SOVIET UNION'S FAR-FLUNG NETS. In U.S. Naval Institute Proceedings, November, 1970. pp. 48-57

ART
IVMMR    Officer, Charles B. MINERAL DEVELOPMENT IN THE DEEP OFFSHORE; RESOURCES AND TECHNOLOGY. In Virginia Cameron, ed. Private investors abroad; problems and solutions in international business in 1969. New York, Matthew Bender, 1969. pp. 1-7.

***
IICR     OFFSHORE AND OTHER SAND RESOURCES FOR OAHU, HAWAII. Sea Grant. Honolulu, University of Hawaii, 1974.

***
IVMMR    Offshore Oil Task Group. THE GEORGES BANK PETROLEUM STUDY. MITSG-73-5. Cambridge, Massachusetts Institute of Technology, 1973. 3 Vols.

***
IVOI     OFFSHORE REPORT: SUMMARY OF INDUSTRY OIL AND GAS ACTIVITIES OFFSHORE. Offshore Report 8/74. Canada, Resource Management and Conservation Branch, May 31, 1974. n.p. 16p.

***
IVOI     OFFSHORE REPORT: A SUMMARY OF INDUSTRY OIL AND GAS ACTIVITIES OFFSHORE. Offshore Report 9/74. Canada, Resource Management Branch, 1974. n.p. 57p.

***
IICZM    Ohio. Legislative Service Commission. A STATE ROLE IN LAND USE MANAGEMENT. By John F. Gallagher, John P. Bay, project officer.

Columbus, Ohio Legislative Service Commission, 1974. vi, 68p.

\*\*\*

VP      OIL AND THE ENVIRONMENT: THE PROSPECT. Houston, Texas, Shell Oil Co., Public Affairs, May, 1973. 32p.

13,15,16

IIP     OIL ON PUGET SOUND. AN INTERDISCIPLINARY STUDY IN SYSTEMS ENGINEERING. SUPERVISED BY JURIS VAGNERS. Sea Grant Publication. Coordinated by Paul Mar. Seattle, distributed by University of Washington Press, 1972. xvii, 629p.

\*\*\*

VP      OIL ON WASHINGTON WATERS. VIDEOTAPE OF A PROGRAM AIRED ON KCTS-TV, PBS. WSG-AV 75-1. Seattle, University of Washington, Sea Grant Communications, 1975. Videotape cassette.

\*\*\*

IIIP    OIL POLLUTION AND THE SIGNIFICANT BIOLOGICAL RESOURCES OF PUGET SOUND: COMPOSITE FACT SHEETS, HABITATS. Olympia, Washington, Department of Ecology, 1975. 129p.

\*\*\*

VP      OIL POLLUTION AND THE SIGNIFICANT BIOLOGICAL RESOURCES OF PUGET SOUND. Baseline Study Program, North Puget Sound. Prepared for Washington (State) Department of Ecology. Portland, Beak Consultants, Inc., 1975. 2 Vols.

9

IIIF    Oke, George C. OKE'S FISHERY LAWS, CONTAINING THE SALMON AND FRESH-WATER FISHERIES ACT, 1923, WITH NOTES THEREON; AND CHAPTERS ON THE COMMON LAW RELATING TO FISHERIES, THE LAW AS TO SEA FISHERIES, AND THE PREVENTION OF POLLUTION; TOGETHER WITH FORMS FOR USE IN LEGAL PROCEEDINGS AND A LIST OF FISHERY DISTRICTS, BY HUBERT HULL. 4th ed. London, Butterworth Co., 1924. 232p.

5,15

IVMMR   Oklahoma. University. Science and Public Policy Program. Technology Assessment Group. ENERGY UNDER THE OCEANS; A SUMMARY REPORT OF A TECHNOLOGY ASSESSMENT OF OCS OIL AND GAS OPERATIONS. Norman, University of Oklahoma Press, 1973. xxii, 378p.

12,14,16

VB      Olenicoff, S.M. TERRITORIAL WATERS IN THE ARCTIC: THE SOVIET POSITION. A report prepared for Advanced Research Projects Agency. Santa Monica, Calif., Rand, 1972. ix, 52p.

13

IIIFV&G Oliver, R.C., Comp. TRAWLERMEN'S HANDBOOK. Rev. Ed. London, Fishing News (Books) Ltd., 1968. 234p.

\*\*\*

IIIF    Olsen, Stephen B., and D.K. Stevenson. COMMERCIAL MARINE FISH AND FISHERIES OF RHODE ISLAND. Marine Technical Report no. 34. Kingston, University of Rhode Island, 1975. 117p.

14

IISL    Olson, Arden, and David Jamison. MARINE LAND MANAGEMENT IN WASHINGTON. Olympia, Washington Department of Natural Resources, Division of Surveys and Marine Land Management, 1973. 22p.

IICONS  Olson, Stephen B., and John A. Jagschitz. ANCHORING THE SAND BY A NETWORK OF LITTLE CABLES, THE BEACHGRASS HOLDS THE DUNES. The Coastal Resources Center. Plant and Soil Science. NOAA Sea Grant. Marine Publication Number 19. Kingston, University of Rhode Island, n.d. [13]

VENV  Olson, Theodore A., and Frederick J. Burgess, eds. PROCEEDINGS, CONFERENCE ON THE STATUS OF KNOWLEDGE, CRITICAL RESEARCH NEEDS, AND POTENTIAL RESEARCH FACILITIES RELATING TO ECOLOGY AND POLLUTION PROBLEMS IN THE MARINE ENVIRONMENT, GALVESTON, 1966. New York, Interscience Publishers, 1967. [5,14]

VP  O'Malley, C., ed. Conference on International and Interstate Regulation of Water Pollution, New York, 1970. INTERNATIONAL AND INTERSTATE REGULATION OF WATER POLLUTION; PROCEEDINGS OF THE CONFERENCE ... HELD AT COLUMBIA UNIVERSITY SCHOOL OF LAW, March 12-13, 1970. Proceedings editor Cormac K.H. O'Malley. New York, Columbia Journal of Transnational Law, 1970. ix, 321p. [16]

IIIF  Oregon. Legislative Assembly. Interim Fisheries Committee. ECONOMIC VALUES OF ANADROMOUS FISHES IN OREGON RIVERS. Salem, Or., 1952. 28p. [16]

IIIF  _____ REPORT OF THE INTERIM FISHERIES COMMITTEE TO THE FORTY-SECOND LEGISLATIVE ASSEMBLY. Salem, Or., 1943. 15p. [16]

IIIF  _____ REPORT OF THE INTERIM FISHERIES COMMITTEE TO THE FORTY-FOURTH LEGISLATIVE ASSEMBLY. Salem, Or., 1947. 8p. [16]

IIWQ  Oregon. State University. MULTI-DISCIPLINARY STUDY OF WATER QUALITY RELATION TO SHIPS: A CASE STUDY OF YAQUINA BAY, OREGON. Oregon State University Sea Grant Program, Special Report 348. Corvallis, Oregon State University, 1972. vii, 135p. [13]

VOR  _____ PROCEEDINGS OF THE THIRD SEA GRANT CONFERENCE. March, 1970. Corvallis, Oregon State University, Sea Grant Administration, 1970. v, 97p. [13]

VSG  _____ SEA GRANT, A REPORT ON THE OREGON STATE UNIVERSITY SEA GRANT PROGRAM FOR 1973-1974. Corvallis, Or., 1975. 30p. [14]

IIE  _____ TECHNICAL CONFERENCE ON ESTUARIES OF THE PACIFIC NORTHWEST. Circular 44. Corvallis, Engineering Experiment Station, 1972. 108p. [***]

VOR  _____ Marine Science Center. THE USES OF THE SEA. American Assembly. Newport, Oregon, May 8-11, 1969. Corvallis, Oregon State University, 1969. [13]

VOI  Oregon. State University. Sea Grant College Program. THE FUTURE[13] OF OREGON MARITIME INDUSTRIES; A CONFERENCE SPONSORED BY OREGON STATE UNIVERSITY EXTENSION SERVICE MARINE ADVISORY PROGRAM, PORTLAND, OREGON, MAY 23-24, 1973. Proceedings. Corvallis, 1973. 47p.

VSG  _____ _____ SEA GRANT; a report on the Oregon State University[13] Sea Grant Program for 1971-72- Corvallis, Or., 1972.

IICR  Oregon, University, Bureau of Governmental Research. CENTRAL ORE-[13] GON COAST. Eugene, 1969. IX Vols.

IICZM  _____ _____ PRELIMINARY LAND USE PLAN FOR THE YAQUINA BAY AREA.[13] Eugene, 1969. 97p.

IIE  Oregon. University. Oregon Institute of Marine Biology. COOS BAY[13] STUDY: AN INTERDISCIPLINARY STUDY OF MAN AND THE ESTUARY. Eugene, 1971. 205p.

IICONS  Oregon Coastal Conservation and Development Commission. BEACHES ***
AND DUNES OF THE OREGON COAST. Florence, 1975.

IICZM  _____ _____ COMPREHENSIVE PLANNING RECOMMENDATIONS FROM DAVID BRAD-[13] WELL AND ASSOCIATES AND THE OFFICE OF RICHARD REYNOLDS, ECOLOGICAL RESEARCH, PLANNING AND DESIGN. San Francisco, 1972. 1 Vol.

IIE  _____ _____ ESTUARINE RESOURCES OF THE OREGON COAST; A NATURAL ***
RESOURCE INVENTORY REPORT. Prepared by Wilsey and Ham, Inc. Florence, 1974. 233p.

IIE  _____ _____ ESTUARY PLANNING GUIDELINES. Florence, Or., Oregon[13] Coastal Conservation and Development Commission, January 31, 1973. 37p.

IIWQ  _____ _____ FRESHWATER RESOURCES. OREGON COASTAL ZONE; A NATURAL ***
RESOURCE. Inventory report prepared by State Water Resources Board. Florence, 1975. 76p.

IICR  _____ _____ HISTORICAL AND ARCHAEOLOGICAL RESOURCES OF THE OREGON ***
COASTAL ZONE; A RESOURCE INVENTORY. Florence, 1974. 41p.

IICONS  _____ _____ HISTORICAL AND ARCHAEOLOGICAL SITE INVENTORY. Flor-[13] ence, Or., 1973. 72p.

IICONS  _____ _____ INTERIM REPORT. Florence, 1973. 22p. ***

| | | 13 |
|---|---|---|
IICR    Oregon Coastal Conservation and Development Commission. OREGON COAST NATURAL RESOURCES MANAGEMENT: CONCEPTS WORKBOOK. Florence, Or., Oregon Coastal Conservation and Development Commission, March 1973. iii, 37p.

IICZM    \_\_\_\_ \_\_\_\_ OVERALL PROGRAM DESIGN. Preliminary report for review only. Florence, Or., 1973. 68p.    13

IICONS    \_\_\_\_ \_\_\_\_ PRELIMINARY POLICY PROPOSALS. Florence, Or., June 26, 1974.    13

IICZM    \_\_\_\_ \_\_\_\_ A STATUS REPORT TO THE LEGISLATURE. December 1972. Florence, Or., 1973.    13

IICONS    \_\_\_\_ \_\_\_\_ SUMMARY FINAL REPORT 1975. Florence, 1975. iv, 37p.    ***

IICONS    \_\_\_\_ \_\_\_\_ WORKSHOP. Florence, Or., 1973.    13

IICZM    \_\_\_\_ \_\_\_\_ Special Economic Study Team. ECONOMIC ANALYSIS AND PROFILE OF THE OREGON COASTAL ZONE. Florence, Or., 1974.    ***

IICZM    Oregon Coastal Planning Group. A STUDY DESIGN. Prepared for the Oregon Coastal Conservation and Development Commission. Draft. San Francisco, n.p., February, 1972. 59p.    13

IICZM    \_\_\_\_ \_\_\_\_ STUDY DESIGN. Prepared for the Oregon Coastal Conservation and Development Commission. San Francisco, n.p., March 1972. 79p.    13

VOCET    OREGON'S NEARSHORE OCEAN. By James E. McCauley. OSU-SG-16. Corvallis, Oregon State University, Sea Grant Marine Advisory Program, Corvallis, 1973. 8p.    ***

IIIOSTR    Oren, O.H. ARTIFICIAL REEFS: A SHORT REVIEW AND APPEAL. FAO Fish Circ. FRS/C305. n.p., 1968.    ***

IIIF    Organisation for Economic Co-operation and Development. Committee for Fisheries. SUBSIDIES AND OTHER FINANCIAL SUPPORT TO THE FISHING INDUSTRIES OF OECD MEMBER COUNTRIES; ADOPTED BY THE COMMITTEE FOR FISHERIES AND APPROVED BY THE COUNCIL AT ITS MEETING ON THE 21st JULY 1964. Paris, 1965. 252p.    ***

IIIF    \_\_\_\_ \_\_\_\_ SUBSIDIES AND OTHER FINANCIAL SUPPORT TO THE FISHING INDUSTRIES OF OECD MEMBER COUNTRIES; ADOPTED BY THE COMMITTEE FOR FISHERIES ON THE 12-13 MAY 1970 AND APPROVED BY THE COUNCIL AT ITS MEETING ON THE 29 SEPTEMBER 1970. Paris, 1971. 149p.    ***

IIIF    Organisation for Economic Co-operation and Development. FISHERY
        POLICIES AND ECONOMIES, 1957-1966. Paris, 1970. 514p.

                                                                    14a
IIIF    _____ _____ INTERNATIONAL SYMPOSIUM ON FISHERIES ECONOMICS, PARIS,
        1971. ECONOMIC ASPECTS OF FISH PRODUCTION. Distributed by OECD
        Publications Center, Washington, D.C., 1972. iii, 480p.

                                                                    ***
VMT     _____ _____ Marine Transport Committee. MARINE TRANSPORT 1972.
        Paris, 1973. 138p.

                                                                    ***
VMT     _____ _____ MARITIME TRANSPORT: 1974. Paris, 1975. 149p.

                                                                    14
IVMMR   Organisation for Economic Co-operation and Development. Special
        Committee for Oil. THE EXPLORATION FOR AND EXPLOITATION OF CRUDE
        OIL AND NATURAL GAS IN THE OECD EUROPEAN AREA INCLUDING THE CONTI-
        NENTAL SHELF; MINING AND FISCAL LEGISLATION. Paris, 1973. 71p.

                                                                    ***
IIIOI   Organisation for Economic Co-operation and Development. PACKAGES
        AND PACKAGING MATERIAL FOR FISH. Paris, 1970. 95p.

                                                                5,7,14a,15
IIIF    _____ _____ REVIEW OF FISHERIES IN OECD MEMBER COUNTRIES 1967-
        Paris, 1968-

                                                                    ***
IIIORM  Organization for European Economic Co-operation. POLITIQUES DE
        PÊCHE EN EUROPE OCCIDENTALE ET EN AMERIQUE DU NORD. Paris, 1960.
        332p.

                                                                    13
VCS     Orlin, Hyman. POSITIONING ON THE CONTINENTAL SHELF. Presented at
        the Law of the Sea Institute, Third Annual Conference, University
        of Rhode Island, Kingston, Rhode Island, June 24-27, 1968. Kingston,
        1969. 14p.

                                                                    ***
VLOS    Orrego Vicuña, Fransisco. CHILE Y EL DERECHO DEL MAR. Santiago de
        Chile, Andres Bello, 1972. 399p.

                                                                    ***
VLOS    _____ _____ LATIN AMERICAN POLICIES ON THE LAW OF THE SEA: THE
        PROSPECTS OF A WORLD COMPROMISE AGREEMENT. Santiago, University of
        Chile, 1974. v, 23p.

                                                                    ***
VLOS    _____ _____ TENDENCIAS DEL DERECHO DEL MAR CONTEMPORANEO. Buenos
        Aires, El Ateneo, 1974. 236p.

                                                                    ***
IIIF    Orth, F.L., et al. THE ALASKA CLAM FISHERY: A SURVEY AND ANALYSIS
        OF ECONOMIC POTENTIAL. Fairbanks, University of Alaska, Institute
        of Marine Science, 1975.

|        |                                                                                                                                                                                              |
|--------|----------------------------------------------------------------------------------------------------------------------------------------------------------------------------------------------|
| VCONS  | Osborn, Fairfield. OUR PLUNDERED PLANET. Boston, Little, Brown, 1948. xiv, 217p.                                                                                               17            |
| VENV   | Otto, L. ENVIRONMENTAL FACTORS IN OPERATIONS TO COMBAT OIL SPILLS. Reports on Marine Science Affairs 9. New York, UNIPUB, 1973. 28p.                                        *** |
| VP     | Ottway, S.M. THE THUNTANK 6 SPILL. In Field Studies Council, Oil Pollution Research Unit, Orielton Field Centre, Annual Report. Pembroke, Wales, 1971. pp. 29-38.          ART |
| VB     | Oudendijk, Johanna K. STATUS AND EXTENT OF ADJACENT WATERS; A HISTORICAL ORIENTATION. Leyden, Sijthoff, 1970. 160p.                                                1,5,7,12,16 |
| IIIOR  | OUR FUTURE FROM THE SEA - A SYMPOSIUM ON THE ECONOMIC POTENTIAL OF NORTH COAST MARINE RESOURCES, JUNE 19, 1971, EUREKA, CALIFORNIA. Humboldt State College Sea Grant - 2. Arcata, Humboldt State College, 1971. 72p.  13 |
| VP     | Oviatt, Candace, and Melvin W. First. OCEANOGRAPHIC STUDIES. Boston, Harvard University, School of Public Health, 1972.                                                   *** |
| VENV   | Owen, D.F. WHAT IS ECOLOGY? Oxford University Press, 1974.                                                                                                                  7 |
| IIIF   | Owers, James. COSTS AND EARNINGS OF ALASKAN FISHING VESSELS - AN ECONOMIC SURVEY. Alaska Commercial Fisheries Entry Commission, n.p., 1974. 40p.                           13 |
| VLOS   | Oxman, Bernard H. OCEAN POLLUTION: WHAT CAN THE LAW OF THE SEA CONFERENCE DO? Kingston, University of Rhode Island, Law of the Sea Institute, June 21, 1973. 4p.           13 |
| VCS    | _____ THE PREPARATION OF ARTICLE 1 OF THE CONVENTION ON THE CONTINENTAL SHELF. Washington, D.C., U.S. Department of Commerce, National Bureau of Standards, 1968. 202p.  1,7,16 |
| VLOS   | PACEM IN MARIBUS CONFERENCE. Dodd, Mead and Company, 1971.                                                                                                                  *** |
| VLOS   | PACEM IN MARIBUS CONFERENCE. PROCEEDINGS. 1st-    1970. Malta, Royal University of Malta Press, 1971.                                                                    7,15 |
| VLOS   | Pacem in Maribus-II, Malta, 1971. DRAFT PROCEEDINGS. n.p. 549p.                                                                                                         15,17 |
| VLOS   | PACEM IN MARIBUS-IV. Proceedings of the Fourth Pacem in Maribus Convocation. Held in Malta, 23-26 June, 1973. n.p.                                                        5,7 |

                                                                    16
VLOS      PACEM IN MARIBUS CONVOCATION, MALTA, 1970. AGENDA, LIST OF PARTICI-
          PANTS, TENTATIVE TABLE OF CONTENTS FOR PUBLISHED PROCEEDINGS, SELEC-
          TED PAPERS AND COMMITTEE REPORTS. Malta? 1970.

                                                                    ***
IICR      Pacific Northwest River Basins Commission. ECOLOGY AND THE ECONOMY.
          Vancouver, Wash., 1975.

                                                                    ***
IIICONS   _____ _____ FISH AND WILDLIFE. Vancouver, Washington, 1975.

                                                                    ***
IVMMR     _____ _____ LAND AND MINERAL RESOURCES. Vancouver, Wash., 1969-

                                                                    ***
VSG       _____ _____ A PROPOSAL TO THE NATIONAL SCIENCE FOUNDATION FOR CON-
          TINUED SEA GRANT INSTITUTIONAL SUPPORT TO BE ADMINISTERED BY THE DI-
          VISION OF MARINE SCIENCES, UNIVERSITY OF WASHINGTON, 1969. Vancou-
          ver, Wash. 245p.

                                                                    ***
VENV      _____ _____ SOURCES OF INFORMATION ON NUCLEAR POWER AND THE EN-
          VIRONMENT. Vancouver, Wash., 1973. 23p.

                                                                    ***
IIWQ      _____ _____ WATER QUALITY AND POLLUTION CONTROL. Pacific region
          comprehensive framework study, appendix 7. Vancouver, Wash., 1971.
          531p.

                                                                    14
VENE      _____ _____ Power Planning Committee. PANEL DISCUSSION ON THER-
          MAL POWER PLANT SITING IN THE PACIFIC NORTHWEST. Vancouver, Wash.,
          1973. 42p.

                                                                    ***
VENE      _____ _____ SOURCES OF INFORMATION ON NUCLEAR POWER AND THE EN-
          VIRONMENT. Vancouver, Wash., 1975. 30p.

                                                                    ***
IICZM     Pacific Northwest River Basins Commission. Surveys and Marine Land
          Management Division. WASHINGTON MARINE ATLAS. Vancouver, Wash.,
          1972.

                                                                    14a
IIIF      Pacific Science Congress. Ninth, Bangkok, Thailand, 1957. FISH-
          ERIES. BANGKOK, SECRETARIAT, NINTH PACIFIC SCIENCE CONGRESS, 1961.
          Proceedings. 91p. Vol. 10.

                                                                    18
VLOS      Padelford, Norman J. ALTERNATIVES FOR POLICY RELATING TO THE SEAS
          (ADDRESS GIVEN TO THE DEPARTMENT OF NAVAL ARCHITECTURE AND MARINE
          ENGINEERING, M.I.T.). April 22, 1969. Cambridge, Massachusetts
          Institute of Technology, 1969.

                                                                    18
VMT       _____ _____ OCEAN COMMERCE AND THE PANAMA CANAL. MITSG 73-13.
          Washington, D.C., Jefferson Law Book Company, 1973.

VMT  Padelford, Norman J. THE PANAMA CANAL IN PEACE AND WAR. New York,[1] The MacMillan Company, 1942. xii, 327p.

VLOS  ———— ———— PROSPECTS FOR A NEW REGIME OF THE SEAS: INTERNATIONAL POLITICAL CONSIDERATIONS. Presented at the Seventh Annual Conference of the Marine Technology Society, Washington, D.C., August 16, 1971. Rev. September 21, 1971. Report no. MITSG 72-5. Cambridge, M.I.T. Press, 1971. 13p. [13]

VLOS  ———— ———— PUBLIC POLICY FOR THE SEAS. Rev. ed. Cambridge, M.I.T. Press, 1970. viii, 338p. [2,3,5,6,8,12,13,14,15,16,18]

VORM  Padelford, Norman J., and Jerry E. Cook, comps. NEW DIMENSIONS OF U.S. MARINE POLICY. MITSG 71-5. Cambridge, Massachusetts Institute of Technology, 1971. xi, 250p. [1,11,12,13,14,15,16,18]

VMT  Padelford, Norman J., and S.R. Gibbs. MARITIME COMMERCE AND THE FUTURE OF THE PANAMA CANAL. MITSG 74-28. Cambridge, Massachusetts Institute of Technology, 1975. 206p. ***

VMT  Page, R.C., and A. Ward Gardner. PETROLEUM TANKSHIP SAFETY. London, Maritime Press Limited, 1971. 231p. ***

VLOS  Pak, C. -s. HAEYANGPŎP T'USU YŎN'GU. Haksul ch'ongsŭ, 2. Seoul, Tan'guk taehakkyo ch'ulp'anbu, 1973. 423p. ***

IIIAFF  Pakrasi, B.B., et al. CULTURE OF BRACHISHWATER FISHES IN IMPOUND-MENTS IN WEST BENGAL, INDIA. Indo-Pacific Fisheries Council occasional paper 66/5. n.p., 1964.

VLOS  Pan American Union. Department of International Law. BACKGROUND MATERIAL ON THE ACTIVITIES IN THE ORGANIZATION OF AMERICAN STATES RELATING TO THE LAW OF THE SEA. Washington, The Union, 1957. 47p. [8,11,16]

VCS  ———— ———— BACKGROUND MATERIAL ON THE JURIDICAL ASPECTS OF THE CONTINENTAL SHELF AND MARINE WATERS. Washington, D.C., 1956. 34p. [16]

VB  Paolillo, F.H. EL MAR TERRITORIAL Y LA ZONA CONTIGUA. In Orrego Vicuña, F., Tendencias del Derecho del Mar Contemporaneo. Buenos Aires, 1974. n.p. pp. 1-38. [ART]

IIIB  Papandreou, Alexandre. LA SITUATION JURIDIQUE DES PÊCHERIES SÉDENTAIRES EN HAUTE-MER. Thesis, University of Geneva, Faculty of Law. Athens, 1958. [1]

VOD  Parasas-Carayannis, G. OCEAN DUMPING IN THE NEW YORK BIGHT: AN ASSESSMENT OF ENVIRONMENTAL STUDIES. Technical Memorandum 39. ***

Ft. Belvoir, Va., U.S. Coastal Engineering Research Center, May 1973. 168p.

VORM     Pardo, Arvid. THE COMMON HERITAGE: SELECTED PAPERS ON OCEANS AND WORLD ORDER, 1967-74. I.O.I. occasional paper no. 3. Msida, Malta University Press, 1975. xxiii, 549p. [16]

VLOS     _____ THE FUTURE OF THE SEA. In Symposium on the Future of the Sea, Den Helder, 1972. Proceedings. The Hague, 1973. pp. 1-20. [ART]

VLOS     _____ A NEW ORDER IN OCEAN SPACE. In Symposium on the Exploration and Exploitation of the Sea-Bed and its Subsoil, held in Strasbourg, France, December 3-5, 1970. New York, U.S. and World Publications, Inc., Manhattan Publishing Company, 1971. [ART]

VLOS     _____ PERSPECTIVES ON THE LAW OF THE SEA NEGOTIATIONS. USC-SG-LS-1-75. Los Angeles, University of Southern California, 1975. 8p. [***]

VLOS     _____ POLITICAL REQUIREMENTS OF AN EFFECTIVE INTERNATIONAL REGIME FOR THE SEA-BED. Paper at Pacem in Maribus Preparatory Conference on the Legal Framework and the Continental Shelf. Kingston, Rhode Island, January 30-February 1, 1970. [16]

VLOS     _____ POSSIBLE FUTURE REGIMES OF THE SEA-BED RESOURCES. Paper at Symposium on the International Regime of the Sea-bed. Rome, 1969. [16]

VOR     _____ WHO WILL CONTROL THE SEABED? In Foreign Affairs, Vol. 47, no. 1, 1968. pp. 123-137. [ART]

IICS     Park, Choon-ho. CONTINENTAL SHELF ISSUES IN THE YELLOW SEA AND THE EAST CHINA SEA. Law of the Sea Institute occasional paper no. 15. Kingston, University of Rhode Island, September, 1972. 64p. [1,3,4,5,7,11,13,14,15,18]

IIIB     _____ FISHERIES ISSUES IN THE YELLOW SEA AND THE EAST CHINA SEA. Law of the Sea Institute occasional paper no. 18. Kingston, University of Rhode Island, September, 1973. 32p. [1,3,4,5,7,11,13,14,15,18]

VCONS     Parker, Bruce C., ed. PROCEEDINGS OF THE COLLOQUIUM ON CONSERVATION PROBLEMS IN ANTARCTICA, held in Blackburg, Va., September 10-12, 1971. Lawrence, Kansas, Allen Press, Inc., 1972. 363p. [***]

VP     Parker, Frank L. NATIONAL SYMPOSIUM ON THERMAL POLLUTION, VANDERBILT UNIVERSITY, 1968. ENGINEERING ASPECTS OF THERMAL POLLUTION; PROCEEDINGS. n.p. [15]

                                                                    13,14
IIILOS    Parker, Walter B.  ALASKA AND THE LAW OF THE SEA:  INTERNATIONAL
          FISHERIES REGIMES OF THE NORTH PACIFIC.  Anchorage, Arctic Environ-
          mental Information and Data Center, University of Alaska, 1974.  65p.

                                                                    16
VORM      PARLIAMENTARY DEBATES, QUESTIONS - SEA-BED NATURE RESOLUTION, MO-
          TION - MARINE SCIENCE AND TECHNOLOGY.  United Kingdom, Parliamentary
          Debates, House of Lords, 5th Series, 303(86) 1969.

                                                                    ***
IICZM     Parnell, James F., and Robert F. Soots, eds.  PROCEEDINGS OF A CON-
          FERENCE ON MANAGEMENT OF DREDGE ISLANDS IN NORTH CAROLINIAN ESTU-
          ARIES.  Sea Grant Program.  Chapel Hill, University of North Caroli-
          na, 1975.  142p.

                                                                    ***
IICZM     Paterson, K.W., et al.  THE HUMAN DIMENSION OF COASTAL ZONE DEVELOP-
          MENT.  Bulletin 679.  Baton Rouge, Louisiana State University, 1974.
          61p.

                                                                    15
VOCET     Pauli, D.C., and G.P. Clappet, eds.  U.S. Office of Naval Research.
          PROJECT SEALAB REPORT; AN EXPERIMENTAL 45-DAY UNDERSEA SATURATION
          DIVE AT 205 FEET, by Sealab II project group.  Washington, D.C.,
          n.d.

                                                                    16
VCS       Pavicevic, V.  THE UNITED NATIONS SEA-BED COMMITTEE:  PERSPECTIVES
          AND CHALLENGES.  Paper at Pacem in Maribus Preparatory Conference
          on the Legal Framework and the Continental Shelf.  Kingston, Rhode
          Island, January 30-February 1, 1970.

                                                                    ART
VB        Pearcy, G.E.  MEASUREMENT OF THE U.S. TERRITORIAL SEA.  Reprinted
          from U.S. Department of State Bulletin, 1959.

                                                                    14
VENV      Pearson, Charles S.  INTERNATIONAL MARINE ENVIRONMENT POLICY, THE
          ECONOMIC DIMENSION.  Baltimore, Johns Hopkins, 1975.  xiv, 127p.

                                                                    ART
VOD       Pearson, Erman A.  MARINE WASTE DISPOSAL SYSTEMS; ALTERNATIVES AND
          CONSEQUENCES.  In J.F. Peel Brahtz, ed., Coastal Zone Management;
          Multiple Use with Conservation.  New York, John Wiley, 1972.
          pp. 286-295.

                                                                    14
IVM       Pearson, John S.  OCEAN FLOOR MINING.  Park Ridge, N.J., Noyes Data
          Corp., 1975.  ix, 201p.

                                                                    ART
IVM       Pehrson, Gordon O.  MINING INDUSTRY'S ROLE IN DEVELOPMENT OF UNDER-
          SEA MINING.  In Marine Technology Society.  Second Annual Conference,
          Washington, D.C., June 27-29, 1966.  Washington, D.C., 1966.  pp. 182-
          196.

                                                                    15,16,17
VOCET     Pell, Claiborne, and Harold L. Goodwin.  CHALLENGE OF THE SEVEN SEAS.
          New York, Morrow, 1966.  xi, 306p.

| | | |
|---|---|---|
| VOR | Pell, Claiborne, and Jacob Javits. THE UNITED NATIONS: THE WORLD AS A DEVELOPING COUNTRY. Report to the Committee on Foreign Relations, United States Senate. 92d Congr., 1st sess., committee print. Washington, U.S.G.P.O., 1971. v, 114p. | 2,13 |
| VLOS | Pell, Claiborne, et al. THE THIRD U.N. LAW OF THE SEA CONFERENCE: REPORT TO THE SENATE by the advisers to the U.S. Delegation. Caracas, June-August, 1974. 94th Congr., 1st sess. Washington, U.S.G.P.O., 1975. v, 85p. | 14 |
| VOCET | Pennington, Howard. THE NEW OCEAN EXPLORERS; INTO THE SEA IN THE SPACE AGE. Boston, Little, Brown, 1972. 282p. | 5,17 |

***

| | | |
|---|---|---|
| IICZM | Penumalli, B.R., et al. ESTABLISHMENT OF OPERATIONAL GUIDELINE FOR TEXAS COASTAL ZONE MANAGEMENT; SPECIAL REPORT I: WATER QUALITY MODELLING AND MANAGEMENT STUDIES FOR CORPUS CHRISTI BAY: A LARGE SYSTEMS APPROACH. Austin, University of Texas, Center for Research and Water Resources, 1974? xii, 223p. | |

***

| | | |
|---|---|---|
| VOCET | Penzias, Walter, and Maxwell W. Goodman. MAN BENEATH THE SEA; A REVIEW OF UNDERWATER ENGINEERING. New York, John Wiley and Sons, Inc., Wiley-Interscience, 1973. 848p. | |
| IIE | Percy, Katherine L., et al. DESCRIPTIONS AND INFORMATION SOURCES FOR OREGON ESTUARIES. Oregon Sea Grant College Program. Corvallis, Oregon State University, 1974. 294p. | 14 |
| VINTL | Perels, Ferdinand. DAS INTERNATIONALE ÖFFENTLICHE SEERECHT DER GEGENWART. Berlin, E.S. Mittler und Sohn, 1882. xxii, 425, 1p. | 3 |

***

| | | |
|---|---|---|
| IIIOCET | Perkins, E.J. THE BIOLOGY OF ESTUARIES AND COASTAL WATERS. London, Academic Press, 1974. 678p. | |
| VP | Perry, John. OUR POLLUTED WORLD; CAN MAN SURVIVE? Rev. ed. New York, Watts, 1972. xvii, 237p. | 13,17 |

***

| | | |
|---|---|---|
| VOR | Perry, R. THE UNKNOWN OCEAN. New York, Taplinger Publishing, 1972. 288p. | |
| VORM | Peru. Instituto del Mar. Memoria anual, 1969- Callao. | 17 |
| VINTL | Peru. Ministerio de Relaciones Exteriores. EXPOSICIONES OFICIALES PERUANAS SOBRE EL NUEVO DERECHO DEL MAR. Lima, 1972. 235p. | 7 |

***

| | |
|---|---|
| IIIF | PERU-U.S.S.R.: AGREEMENT ON CO-OPERATION FOR THE DEVELOPMENT OF THE FISHING INDUSTRY. Washington, U.S. Department of Commerce, National Marine Fisheries Service, Division of Foreign Fisheries, 1971? 5p. |

|||||
|---|---|
| | ***|
| IVMMR | PETROLEUM IN THE MARINE ENVIRONMENT. Washington, D.C., National Academy of Sciences, 1975. 117p. |
| | 15 |
| VOR | Pettersson, Hans. THE OCEAN FLOOR. New York, Hafner, 1969- |
| | *** |
| VSG | Peyton, Patricia, and Sharon Schreiber, eds. PROCEEDINGS OF THE SEVENTH NATIONAL SEA GRANT ASSOCIATION CONFERENCE. Seattle, University of Washington, Division of Marine Resources, October 29-31, 1974. 250p. |
| | 13 |
| VOR | Peyton, Patricia, ed. MARINE RESOURCE DEVELOPMENT; A BLUEPRINT BY CITIES FOR THE NORTHEAST PACIFIC. PASGAP 4. Seattle, published for the Pacific Sea Grant Advisory Program by Washington Sea Grant Advisory Services, University of Washington, Division of Marine Resources, 1972. 31p. |
| | 1,3,5,14;15,16 |
| VLOS | Pharand, Donat. THE LAW OF THE SEA OF THE ARCTIC WITH SPECIAL REFERENCE TO CANADA. Ottawa, University of Ottawa Press, 1973. xxii, 367p. |
| | 14 |
| IICZM | Phillabaum, Stephen D. A GEOMORPHIC INVENTORY OF WHATCOM COUNTY MARINE SHORELINE WITH CONSIDERATIONS FOR ITS MANAGEMENT. Photocopy. Bellingham, Wash., Western Washington State College, Department of Geography, 1973. 176p. |
| | 7 |
| VLOS | THE PHILIPPINES: THE LAW OF THE SEA: ITS VARIOUS ASPECTS AND THE PHILIPPINE VIEWPOINT. In Philippines Yearbook of International Law. Volume III, 1974. |
| | *** |
| VP | Phillips, John H., et al. ANALYSIS OF DYNAMICS OF DDT IN MARINE SEDIMENTS. Corvallis, Or., National Environmental Research Center, Office of Research Center, May, 1975. vii, 98p. |
| | 14a |
| IIIF | Pierce, Wesley G. GOIN' FISHIN'; THE STORY OF THE DEEP-SEA FISHERMEN OF NEW ENGLAND. Salem, Mass., Marine Research Society, 1934. xiii, 323p. |
| | *** |
| VP | Piersall, Charles H., Jr., and Robert E. Borgstrom. COST ANALYSIS OF OPTIMAL METHODS OF SHIPBOARD DOMESTIC WASTE DISPOSAL. Professional paper no. 91. Arlington, Va., Center for Naval Analyses, 1972. 31p. |
| | *** |
| IIIAFF | Pillay, T.V.R. PROCEEDINGS OF THE FAO WORLD SYMPOSIUM ON WARM WATER POND FISH CULTURE. FAO Fisheries Report no. 44, Vol. 4. n.p. 1967. |
| | 13 |
| IIIAFF | Pillay, T.V.R., ed. COASTAL AQUACULTURE IN THE INDO-PACIFIC REGION. Papers presented at the Indo-Pacific Fisheries Council Symposium on Coastal Aquaculture, Bangkok, Thailand, 18-21 November, 1970. West |

Byfleet, Surrey, England, Fishing News (Books) Ltd., 1972. xiii, 497p.

***

IIIOCET    Pimlott, Douglas H., et al. SCIENTIFIC ACTIVITIES IN FISHERIES AND WILDLIFE RESOURCES; BACKGROUND STUDY FOR THE SCIENCE COUNCIL OF CANADA. Science Council of Canada. Special study, 15. Ottawa, 1971. 191p.

1,5,16

VINTL    Piper, Don C. THE INTERNATIONAL LAW OF THE GREAT LAKES; A STUDY OF CANADIAN-UNITED STATES COOPERATION. Duke University, Commonwealth-Studies Center. Durham, N.C., Duke University Press, 1967. 165p.

***

IVOSTR    PIPELINES IN THE OCEAN. New York, American Society of Civil Engineers, Pipeline Division, Task Committee on Pipelines in the Ocean, n.d. 106p.

15

VOR    Piquemal, A. LE FOND DES MERS: PATRIMOINE COMMUN DE L'HUMANITÉ. Nice, Institut de la Paix et du Développement, Université de Nice, 1973. 278p.

16

VOR    Pirie, R. Gordon, ed. OCEANOGRAPHY; CONTEMPORARY READINGS IN OCEAN SCIENCES. New York, Oxford University Press, 1973. 530p.

13

IIP&H    Pitkin, M. MARAD PORT STUDY. Speech, June 3, 1971, before OSTA panel meeting and NOA/NSIA Symposium, State Department. Washington, D.C., 1971. 10p.

***

VOCET    PLANNING AND ENGINEERING IN THE MARINE ENVIRONMENT. Los Angeles, University of California, Continuing Education in Engineering and Science, 1973. 308p.

16

VP    Plano, Jack C. INTERNATIONAL APPROACHES TO THE PROBLEMS OF MARINE POLLUTION. ISIO monographs, 1st series, no. 7. Brighton, England, Institute for the Study of International Organisation, University of Sussex, 1972. 38p.

7,14

VLOS    Platzroeder, Renate, comp. THIRD UNITED NATIONS CONFERENCE ON THE LAW OF THE SEA: DOCUMENTS OF THE CARACAS SESSION 1974. Werkhefte des Instituts für Internationale Angelegenheiten der Universität Hamburg; Heft 26. Publ. by D. Verein f. Internat. Seerecht, Dt. Landesgruppe d. Comité Maritime Internat. and Inst. f. Internat. Angelegenheiten d. Univ. Hamburg. Hamburg: Deutscher Verein f. Internat. Seerecht; Hamburg: Institut für Internat. Angelegenheiten d. Univ. Hamburg; Frankfurt (am Main): Metzner in. Komm., 1975. xvii, 371p.

***

VLOS    _____ THIRD UNITED NATIONS CONFERENCE ON THE LAW OF THE SEA-DOCUMENTS OF THE GENEVE SESSION, 1975. Frankfurt, Germany, Metzner; South Hackensack, N.J., Fred B. Rothman, 1976. xiv, 322p.

VLOS      Platzroeder, Renate, and Wolfgang Graf Vitzthum. ZUR NEUORDNUNG DES MEERES VÖLKERRECHTS AUF DER DRITTEN SEERECHTSKONFERENZ DER VEREINTEN NATIONEN. Mai, 1974.

IVOSTR    Pliskin, Lucien. DEEP AND VERY DEEP OIL-STORAGE TANKS. In Offshore Technology Conference, 6th, Houston, Texas, 1974. Preprints. Dallas, Tex., 1974. Vol. 1. pp. 113-118.

IIIP      Plymouth Laboratory. TORREY CANYON POLLUTION AND MARINE LIFE. Biological Association, United Kingdom Cambridge University Press, 1969.

IIIF      Poggie, John J., Jr., and Carl Gersuny. FISHERMEN OF GALILEE: THE HUMAN ECOLOGY OF A NEW ENGLAND COASTAL COMMUNITY. Sociology and Anthropology - Sea Grant Marine Bulletin Series no. 17. Kingston, University of Rhode Island. 116p.

IIIOR     Poh, Kok-kian. ECONOMICS AND MARKET POTENTIAL OF THE PRECIOUS CORAL INDUSTRY IN HAWAII. UNIHI-SEAGRANT-AR-71-03. Honolulu, University of Hawaii, 1972. 22p.

VLOS      POLICY ISSUES IN OCEAN LAW. St. Paul, West Publishing Company, 1975. ix, 189p.

VORM      Pollack, H. UNITED STATES FOREIGN POLICY AND THE MARINE SCIENCES. Paper at Second Conference on Law, Organization and Security in the Use of the Oceans. Columbus, Ohio. October 5-7, 1967.

VP        Pollak, E.G. DEVELOPMENT OF A PROTOTYPE OFFSHORE OIL CONTAINMENT SYSTEM. In Offshore Technology Conference, 4th, Houston, Texas, 1972: Preprints. Dallas, Tex., 1972. Vol. 1. pp. 913-924.

VP        Pollock, Walter E., and Wyatt M. Rogers, Jr. TRANSPORTATION OF RADIOACTIVE MATERIALS IN THE WESTERN STATES. Prepared by the Western Interstate Nuclear Board Committee on Transportation of Radioactive Materials. Lakewood, Colo, 1974. 134p.

VP        POLLUTION ABSTRACTS. La Jolla, Calif., Oceanic Library and Information Center, n.d.

VP        POLLUTION CONTROL IN MARINE INDUSTRIES. International Association for Pollution Control, Washington, D.C., 1972. 350p.

VP        POLLUTION EVENTS REPORT. New York, UNIPUB, 1975-

VP        POLLUTION OF THE SEA BY OIL. RESULTS OF AN INQUIRY MADE IN 1963. New York, UNIPUB, 1964. 104p.

***
VAC      Polmar, N. SOVIET NAVAL POWER: CHALLENGE FOR THE 1970s. Rev. ed. National Strategy Information Center, Inc., Strategy Paper no. 13. New York, Crane, Russak and Company, 1974. 132p.

ART
VP       Polvani, Carlo. RADIOACTIVE SOLID WASTE DISPOSAL INTO THE OCEANS: IMPLICATIONS AND PERSPECTIVES. In J. Sztucki, ed., Symposium on the International Regime of the Sea-Bed, June 30-July 5, 1969. Rome, 1969. Proceedings. Rome, Accademia Nazionale dei Lincei, 1970. pp. 195-214.

2
VCONS    Ponce Miranda, Neftalí. DOMINIO MARÍTIMO. Quito, 1971. 169p.

***
VP       Pontavice, Emmanuel du. LA POLLUTION DES MERS PAR LES HYDROCARBURES À PROPOS DE L'AFFAIRE DU "TORREY CANYON". Paris, Librairie Générale de Droit et de Jurisprudence, 1968. 142p.

3,4,5,7,11,12,14,16
IIIB     Pontecorvo, Giulio, ed. FISHERIES CONFLICTS IN THE NORTH ATLANTIC: PROBLEMS OF JURISDICTION AND ENFORCEMENT. Cambridge, Mass., Ballinger Publishing Company, 1974. xix, 203p.

1
IIIMT    Porter, Paul A. THE GULF OF AQABA: AN INTERNATIONAL WATERWAY. Its significance to international trade. Washington, D.C., Public Affairs Press, 1957.

***
IIP&H    PORTS AND WATERWAYS SAFETY ACT OF 1972: PUBLIC LAW 92-340. TAMU-SG-73-602. College Station, Texas A&M University, 1973.

5,12,13,16
VP       Post, Thomas R. PRIVATE COMPENSATION FOR INJURIES SUSTAINED BY DISCHARGE OF OIL FROM VESSELS ON THE NAVIGABLE WATERS OF THE UNITED STATES. University of Miami Sea Grant Program technical bulletin no. 22. Coral Gables, Fla., 1972. vi, 72p.

ART
IVM      POTENTIAL ENVIRONMENTAL IMPACT OF MANGANESE-NODULE MINING THE DEEP SEA. By T.C. Malone, et al. In Offshore Technology Conference, 5th, Houston, Texas, 1973. Preprints. Dallas, Tex., 1973. Vol. 2, pp. 129-138.

13
VP       Potter, Jeffrey, DISASTER BY OIL. OIL SPILLS: WHY THEY HAPPEN, WHAT THEY DO, HOW WE CAN END THEM. New York, The MacMillan Company, 1973. xii, 307p.

5,16
VINTL    Potter, Pitman B. THE FREEDOM OF THE SEAS IN HISTORY, LAW, AND POLITICS. New York, Longmans, 1924. 299p.

5,13
VINTL    Poulantzas, Nicholas M. THE RIGHT OF HOT PURSUIT IN INTERNATIONAL LAW. Leyden, A.W. Sijthoff, 1969. xv, 451p.

IICZM     Power, Garrett. THE FEDERAL ROLE IN COASTAL DEVELOPMENT. In Environmental Law Institute. St. Paul, Minnesota, 1974. pp. 792-843. ART

\*\*\*

VORM     Practising Law Institute. OCEAN LAW AND COASTAL LAW - A COURSE HANDBOOK. Elize Anne Gettzer, chairman. New York, 1976.

\*\*\*

VP     Pratt, S.D., et al. BIOLOGICAL EFFECTS OF OCEAN DISPOSAL OF SOLID WASTE. Marine technical report series no. 9. Marine Experiment Station, Graduate School of Oceanography. Kingston, University of Rhode Island, 1973. v, 53p. 13

\*\*\*

IICZM     THE PRESENT AND FUTURE OF COASTS. Proceedings, First Annual Conference of The Coastal Society held in Arlington, Virginia, November 26-27, 1975. Bethesda, Md., The Coastal Society, 1976?

\*\*\*

IIIF     Prins, Adriaan H. SAILING FROM LAMU; A STUDY OF MARITIME CULTURE IN ISLAMIC EAST AFRICA. Assen, Van Gorcum, 1965. xii, 320p.

\*\*\*

IIE     PROCEEDINGS. SECOND ANNUAL TECHNICAL CONFERENCE ON ESTUARIES OF THE PACIFIC NORTHWEST. March 16th and 17th, 1972. Corvallis, Oregon State University, 1972. 111p. 13

\*\*\*

VP     PROCEEDINGS: INDUSTRY - GOVERNMENT SEMINAR - OIL SPILL TREATING AGENTS. New York, American Petroleum Institute, n.d.

\*\*\*

IICZM     PROCEEDINGS OF A CONFERENCE ON COASTAL MANAGEMENT, MAY 16-17, 1974, BEAUFORT, NORTH CAROLINA. Sponsored by Center for Marine and Coastal Studies, UNC Sea Grant Program, Coastal Plains Center for Marine Development Services. UNC-SC-74-16. Raleigh, Center for Marine and Coastal Studies, North Carolina State University, 1974. 181p.

\*\*\*

IIP     PROCEEDINGS OF A MEETING ON FRESHWATER AND ESTUARINE STUDIES OF THE EFFECTS OF INDUSTRY, HELD IN LONDON ON JUNE 3-4, 1971. Royal Society of London, Series B: Biological Sciences 180(1061):(March 21, 1972).

\*\*\*

IICZM     PROCEEDINGS OF ALABAMA COASTAL LEADERS CONFERENCE ON COASTAL ZONE MANAGEMENT. Sponsored for the Alabama Coastal Area Board by The Mississippi-Alabama Sea Grant Consortium. MASGP-75-012. Mobile, April 30, 1975. i, 71p. 14

\*\*\*

VP     PROCEEDINGS OF SYMPOSIA ORGANIZED BY THE INSTITUTE OF WATER POLLUTION CONTROL. Maidstone, Kent, England, Institute of Water Pollution Control.

\*\*\*

VENV     PROCEEDINGS OF THE ANNUAL NEW JERSEY ENVIRONMENTAL CONGRESS. New Jersey, Association of New Jersey Environmental Commissions, 1974-

VP    PROCEEDINGS OF THE CONFERENCE FOR THE PREVENTION AND CONTROL OF OIL SPILLS. Washington, D.C., American Petroleum Institute, Publications Management Corporation, 1971. 552p.

VP    PROCEEDINGS OF THE CONFERENCE IN THE MATTER OF POLLUTION OF THE NAVIGABLE WATERS OF PEARL HARBOR AND ITS TRIBUTARIES IN THE STATE OF HAWAII. Held in Honolulu, Hawaii, September 21-23, 1971. 62p.

IIIENV    PROCEEDINGS OF THE CONFERENCE ON MARINE BIOLOGY IN ENVIRONMENTAL PROTECTION HELD AT SAN CLEMENTE ISLAND, CALIFORNIA, ON 13-15, NOVEMBER, 1973. San Diego, Calif., Naval Underwater Center, 1974. 186p.

VP    PROCEEDINGS OF THE EIGHTH INDUSTRIAL WATER AND WASTEWATER CONFERENCE. Austin Tex., Texas Water Pollution Control Association, 1968. 146p.

VP    PROCEEDINGS OF THE EIGHTEENTH SOUTHERN WATER RESOURCES AND POLLUTION CONTROL CONFERENCE. Chapel Hill, N.C., Industrial Extension Service, North Carolina State University, 1969. 192p.

VOI    PROCEEDINGS OF THE FUTURE OF OREGON MARITIME INDUSTRIES. A conference sponsored by Oregon State University Extension Service Sea Grant Marine Advisory Program held in Portland, Oregon, May 22-23, 1974. Corvallis, Oregon State University, 1974. 62p.

VP    PROCEEDINGS OF THE INTERNATIONAL SYMPOSIUM OF THE COMMISSION OF THE EUROPEAN COMMUNITIES HELD IN ROME, ITALY, SEPTEMBER 7-10, 1971. n.p., 1972. 2 Vols.

VP    PROCEEDINGS OF THE 1971 JOINT CONFERENCE FOR THE PREVENTION AND CONTROL OF OIL SPILLS. Washington, D.C., Publications Management Corporation, 1971. 544p.

IIIOR    PROCEEDINGS OF THE SYMPOSIUM ON THE OCEANOGRAPHY AND FISHERIES RESOURCES OF THE TROPICAL ATLANTIC, ABIDJAN, IVORY COAST, 20-28 OCTOBER, 1966. New York, UNIPUB, 1969. 430p.

IIIF    Prochaska, Frederick J. FLORIDA COMMERCIAL MARINE FISHERIES: GROWTH, RELATIVE IMPORTANCE, AND INPUT TRENDS. Report no. 11. Gainesville, University of Florida, 1976. 50p.

IIIF    Prochaska, Frederick J., and James R. Baarda. FLORIDA'S FISHERIES MANAGEMENT PROGRAMS: THEIR DEVELOPMENT, ADMINISTRATION, AND CURRENT STATUS. Gainesville, Agricultural Experiment Stations, 1975. iii, 64p.

IIIF    _____ _____ REGULATORY MANAGEMENT PROGRAMS FOR FLORIDA MARINE FISHERMAN. SUSF-SG-74-003. Gainesville, University of Florida, 1974.

|||||||||||||||||||||||||||||||||||||||||||||||||||||||||||||||||

\*\*\*
IIIFV&G  Prochaska, Frederick J., and James C. Cato. NORTHWEST FLORIDA GULF COAST RED SNAPPER-GROUPER PARTY BOAT OPERATIONS - AN ECONOMIC ANALYSIS, 1974. SUSF-SG-75-007. Gainesville, University of Florida, 1975. 12p.

17
VOCET  PROGRESS INTO THE SEA SYMPOSIUM, WASHINGTON, D.C., 1969. TRANSACTIONS. Washington, D.C., Marine Technology Society, 1970. ix, 297p.

5,13,14
VOCET  A PROPOSAL FOR A WASHINGTON STATE COMMISSION ON OCEANOGRAPHY. Seattle, Battelle-Northwest, 1966. 62p.

13
VP  PROPOSED LEGISLATION FOR THE PREVENTION AND COMBATTING OF OIL POLLUTION AT SEA. Reprinted from South African Shipping News and Fishing Industry Review, 1971. pp. 31-35.

13
VMT  Pruett, J.M. AIR CUSHION VEHICLES IN THE GULF OFFSHORE OIL INDUSTRY: A FEASIBILITY STUDY. Sea Grant publication LSU-SG-73-04. Baton Rouge, Louisiana State University and Agricultural and Mechanical College, Center for Wetland Resources, 1974? 68p.

ART
IIIF  Pruter, A.T. FISHERIES USES OF THE SEA; PUBLIC POLICY ISSUES. In Conference on Local Impacts of the Law of the Sea, Seattle, Wash., 1972. Local impacts of the law of the sea; proceedings of a conference held in Seattle, October 10-12, 1972. Seattle, Wash., University of Washington, Division of Marine Resources, 1973. pp. 17-22.

ART
IICZM  PUBLIC ACCESS TO BEACHES IN THE UNITED STATES. In Marine Affairs Journal, Report no. 3. Narragansett, University of Rhode Island, 1975.

14
IICZM  Purpura, James A., and William M. Sensabaugh. COASTAL CONSTRUCTION SETBACK LINE. SUSF-SG-74-002. Gainesville, Fla., Marine Advisory Program, 1974. 18p.

13
VENE  Quarles, John R., Jr. THE ECONOMY, ENERGY AND THE ENVIRONMENT - LAST CHANCE FOR THE ESTABLISHMENT. Remarks by John R. Quarles, Jr., to the corporations Banking and Business Law Section of the Philadelphia Bar Association. December 2, 1974. Washington, U.S. Environmental Protection Agency, Office of Public Affairs, 1974. 14p.

13
VP  _____ WATER POLLUTION AND THE RULE OF LAW; AN ADDRESS PRESENTED AT THE AMERICAN BAR ASSOCIATION NATIONAL INSTITUTE. October 26, 1972. New York City, 1972. 8p.

16
IIILOS  Quast, Werner C. WASHINGTON'S FISHERMEN AND THE LAW OF THE SEA; A LINK BETWEEN LOCAL POLITICS AND INTERNATIONAL LAW. Unpublished Ph.D. Thesis. Seattle, University of Washington Library, 1966.

|  |  |
|---|---|
| | 9,13,14,16 |
| VOD | THE QUESTION OF AN OCEAN DUMPING CONVENTION. Studies in transnational legal policy, no. 2. Washington, American Society of International Law, 1972. vi, 53p. |

| | 1,5 |
|---|---|
| VINTL | Rabbath, Edmond. MER ROUGE ET GOLFE D'AQABA DANS L'ÉVOLUTION DU DROIT INTERNATIONAL. Egyptian Society of International Law brochure no. 16. Alexandria, 1962. 52p. |

| | 2,14 |
|---|---|
| VP | Rabin, Edward H., and Mortimer D. Schwartz, eds. THE POLLUTION CRISIS: OFFICIAL DOCUMENTS. Dobbs Ferry, N.Y., Oceana Publications, Inc., 1972-1975. 2 Vols. |

| | *** |
|---|---|
| VP | RADIOACTIVE CONTAMINATION OF THE MARINE ENVIRONMENT. Symposium on the interaction of radioactive contaminants with the constituents of the marine environment. International Atomic Energy Agency Proceedings Series. Vienna. New York, UNIPUB, 1973. 726p. |

| | 5,12 |
|---|---|
| VB | Raestad, Arnold. LA MER TERRITORIALE, ETUDES HISTORIQUES ET JURIDIQUES. Paris, 1913. n.p. |

| | 3 |
|---|---|
| VMLAD | Raikes, Francis W., Tr. THE MARITIME CODES OF ITALY. London, E. Wilson, 1900. xii, 2, 264p. |

| | 3 |
|---|---|
| VMLAD | Raikes, Francis W., ed. THE MARITIME CODES OF SPAIN AND PORTUGAL. London, E. Wilson, 1896. 212p. |

| | *** |
|---|---|
| IIOSTR | Raissi, H. WAVE RESPONSE OF BOTTOMLESS HARBORS AND OFFSHORE OIL STORAGE TANKS. Berkeley, University of California, College of Engineering, 1973. 164p. |

| | 3 |
|---|---|
| VMLAD | Ramadan, Ibrahim Hafez. THE LIBYAN MARITIME CODE. Tripoli, Translation Office, 1967? iii, 117p. |

| | *** |
|---|---|
| VP | Ramseier, R.O., et al. OIL SPILL AT DECEPTION BAY, HUDSON STRAIT. Scientific Series no. 29. Ottawa, Canada Department of the Environment, Inland Waters Branch, Glaciology Subdivision, 1973. 61p. |

| | *** |
|---|---|
| VENE | Ramsey, William and Phillip R. Reed. LAND USE AND NUCLEAR POWER PLANTS, CASE STUDIES OF SITING PROBLEMS. Atomic Energy Commission. Washington, U.S.G.P.O., 1974. 58p. |

| | ART |
|---|---|
| IICZM | Randall, Charles H., Jr. STATUS OF COASTAL ZONE LEGISLATION. In Planning and Engineering in the Coastal Zone. Proceedings of seminar held in Charleston, S.C., June 8-9, 1972. Seminar Series no. 2. Wilmington, N.C., 1972. pp. 77-82. |

ART
IVMMR    Rankin, J.E. THE LEGAL ATTITUDES OF THE PEOPLE'S REPUBLIC OF CHINA TOWARD OFF-SHORE OIL EXPLORATION AND EXPLOITATION. In S.W. Wurfel, Emerging Ocean Oil and Mining Law. Sea Grant Publication UNC-SG-74-02. Chapel Hill, University of North Carolina, 1974. pp. 21-29.

13
VOR    Rao, Pemmaraju. OFFSHORE NATURAL RESOURCES. AN EVALUATION OF AFRICAN INTERESTS. Reprinted from The Indian Journal of International Law, Vol. 12, no. 3, July 1972. pp. 345-367.

***
IICZM    Rapp, Gerald R., et al. ECONOMIC DEVELOPMENT IN THE TEXAS COASTAL ZONE; A CONCEPTUAL REPORT. Prepared for: Office of the Governor, Division of Planning Coordination; Coastal Resources Management Program and the Interagency Council on Natural Resources and the Environment. College Station, Texas A&M University, Sea Grant Office, 1973.

ART
IIIF    Rass, T.S. GEOGRAPHICAL FISHERIES COMPLEX OF THE NORTH SEA AND CHANGES IN IT. In Okeanologiia, 1973.

2
VENV    Rathlesberger, James, ed. NIXON AND THE ENVIRONMENT; THE POLITICS OF DEVASTATION: THIRTEEN ESSAYS. New York, Taurus Communications, 1972. ix, 279p.

ART
VOD    RATIFICATION OF PROPOSED CONVENTION ON THE PREVENTION OF MARINE POLLUTION BY DUMPING OF WASTES AND OTHER MATTER. In Final Environmental Impact Statement ELR-0177. January, 1973. Washington, U.S. Department of State, 1973. 160p.

ART
IVMMR    Ratiner, Leigh. OIL AND HARD MINERALS; GOVERNMENT PROPOSALS. In Conference on Local Impacts of the Law of the Sea, Seattle, Wash., 1972. Local impacts of the law of the sea; proceedings of a conference held in Seattle, October 10-12, 1972. Seattle, University of Washington, Division of Marine Resources, 1973. pp. 103-111.

ART
IIE    Ravan, Jack E. ESTUARIES - A LIMITED RESOURCE. In Planning and Engineering in the Coastal Zone. Proceedings of Seminar held in Charleston, S.C., June 8-9, 1972. Seminar Series no. 2. Wilmington, N.C., 1972. pp. 63-66.

***
IIIP    Ravanko, O. THE PALVA OIL TANKER DISASTER IN THE FINNISH SW ARCHIPELAGO. V. THE LITTORAL AND AQUATIC FLORA OF THE POLLUTED AREA. Publication 181. Turku, Finland, University of Turku, Department of Turku, n.d. 4p.

15
VCONS    Ray, Carleton. MARINE PARKS FOR TANZANIA. Washington, Conservation Foundation, 1968.

***
IIIMM    Ray, G.C., et al. BESMEX: BERING SEA MARINE MAMMAL EXPERIMENT. NASA-TM-X-62399. Washington, D.C., U.S. National Aeronautics and

Space Administration, 1974. 55p.

VENV     Ray, Hurlon C. REVIEWING ENVIRONMENTAL IMPACT STATEMENTS AT THE REGIONAL LEVEL - APPRAISALS, EVALUATIONS, COMMENTS AFTER 15 MONTHS WITH NEPA. Seattle, U.S. Environmental Protection Agency, Region X, 1972.     13

IIISF     Raymont, J.E.G. ALTERNATIVE SOURCES OF FOOD IN THE SEA. In J.D. Costlow, ed., Fertility of the Sea; Proceedings of the Symposium on Fertility of the Sea, São Paulo, 1969. New York, Gordon and Breach Science Publishers, 1971. Vol. 2, pp. 383-399. Abstract in Portuguese.     ART

VENV     RECENT ENVIRONMENTAL DEVELOPMENTS IN MARINE AND OFFSHORE ACTIVITIES. Proceedings of conference, November, 1971, reprinted from Houston Law Review, Vol. 9, no. 4, 1972.     11

VENV     RECENT FEDERAL LEGISLATION SIGNIFICANT IN ENVIRONMENTAL PLANNING PROGRAMS OF THE STATE OF TEXAS. Sea Grant Publication TAMU-SG-73-602. College Station, Texas A&M University, February, 1973. 21p.     ***

IIIP     RECOMMENDED TREATMENT OF OILED SEABIRDS. Report. England, University of Newcastle-upon-Tyne, Department of Zoology, Research Unit on the Rehabilitation of Oiled Seabirds, Advisory Committee on Oil Pollution of the Sea, 1972. 11p.     ***

VMLAD     Reddie, James. RESEARCHES, HISTORICAL AND CRITICAL, IN MARITIME INTERNATIONAL LAW. Edinburgh, Thomas Clark, 1844-45; Ann Arbor, Mich., University Microfilms, 1973. 2 Vols.     16

IIIF     Redfield, Michael. COSTS AND PROFITABILITY IN THE COMMERCIAL FISHING INDUSTRY: THE INSURANCE DILEMMA. A Washington Sea Grant Publication WSG-MP 71-4. Seattle, University of Washington, 1971. 59p.     13,16

VOR     Reed, Laurence. OCEAN-SPACE - EUROPE'S NEW FRONTIER; TOWARDS A LONG-RANGE, CONCERTED PROGRAMME FOR EXPLOITING THE RESOURCES OF THE SEA. London, Bow Publications, Ltd., 1969. 60p.     16

IIE     REGULATION OF ACTIVITIES AFFECTING BAYS AND ESTUARIES: A PRELIMINARY STUDY. Texas Law Institute of Coastal and Marine Resources, University of Houston, n.d.     11

IICZM     REGULATION OF THE COAST: LAND AND WATER USES. Portland, University of Maine School of Law, 1970. 208p.     ***

VENV     Rehbinder, Eckard. GERMAN LAW ON STANDING TO SUE. IUCN environment law paper, no. 3. Morges, Switzerland, International Union for Conservation of Nature and Natural Resources, 1972. 22p.     13

                                                    5,8,15,16
VINTL    Reiff, Henry.  THE UNITED STATES AND THE TREATY LAW OF THE SEA.
         Minneapolis, University of Minnesota Press, 1959.  451p.

                                                          ***
IIE      Reih, G.K.  ECOLOGY OF INLAND WATERS AND ESTUARIES.  New York, Reinhold, 1961.  392p.

                                                          13
VENV     Reitze, Arnold W., Jr.  ENVIRONMENTAL LAW.  Washington, North American International, 1972.  Vol. 1.

                                                          13,15
VENV     _____ _____  ENVIRONMENTAL PLANNING:  LAW OF LAND AND RESOURCES.
         Washington, North American International, 1974.

                                                          13
IIWQ     _____ _____  THE FEDERAL WATER POLLUTION CONTROL LAW OF 1972 AND
         OTHER MATTERS.  A supplement to Environmental Law, Vol. 1, 2d ed.
         Washington, D.C., North American International, 1973, 64p.

                                                          ***
IIIF     REPORT OF THE DIRECTOR OF MARINE FISHERY RESEARCH FOR THE YEARS
         1969-1971.  Suffolk, Great Britain Ministry of Agriculture, Fisheries and Food, Fisheries Laboratory, February, 1973.  86p.

                                                          ***
VORM     A REPORT TO:  THE PRESIDENT AND THE CONGRESS.  Annual report.  1st-
         Washington, D.C., National Advisory Committee on Oceans and Atmosphere, 1972-

                                                          15
IIIAFF   Research Institute of the Gulf of Maine.  AQUACULTURE:  THE DETERMINANTS TO SUCCESS;  PRE-CONFERENCE LITERATURE.  Portland, Maine,
         TRIGOM, 1970.

                                                          ***
VOR      _____ _____  RENEWABLE MARINE RESOURCES DEVELOPMENT PROJECT.  Castine, Maine, Maritime Academy, 1972?  122p.

                                                          ***
IIIOR    RESEARCH TO MEET U.S. AND WORLD FOOD NEEDS.  Report of a working
         conference sponsored by the Agricultural Research Policy Advisory
         Committee (ARPAC).  Kansas City, Mo., 1975.  2 Vols.

                                                          ***
VOR      Resources for the Future, Washington, D.C.  SELECTING POLICIES FOR
         THE DEVELOPMENT OF MARINE RESOURCES;  WORKING PAPER PREPARED BY
         RESOURCES FOR THE FUTURE AT THE REQUEST OF THE COMMISSION ON MARINE
         SCIENCE, ENGINEERING AND RESOURCES.  Washington, D.C., 1968.  54p.

                                                          ***
VOR      RESOURCES FROM THE SEA AND FEDERAL LIMITATIONS ON STATE CONTROL.
         Portland, University of Maine School of Law, 1970.  274p.

                                                          13
IIIF     Rettig, R. Bruce.  THROUGH A GLASSY SEA DARKLY:  THE ECONOMICS OF
         LIMITING ENTRY TO A COMMERCIAL FISHERY.  Sea Grant no. 04-3-158-4.
         Corvallis, Oregon, Agricultural Experiment Station.  22p.

IIOSTR    Rettinger, M., and Don W. Green. A PROPOSED LITTORAL AIRPORT. In Proceedings of Inter-noise 72. International Conference on Noise Control Engineering, held in Washington, D.C., October 4-6, 1972. New York, Poughkeepsie, Institute of Noise Control Engineering, 1972. pp. 344-349.
ART

***

VP    RÉUNION INTERNATIONALE D'OCÉANOGRAPHIE MÉDICALE. 2nd, NICE, 1964. COLLOQUE INTERNATIONAL SUR "LA POLLUTION DU MILIEU MARIN." Centre d'Etudes et de Recherches de Biologie et d'Océanographie Médicale, Nice. Cahiers, 16-17. Nice, 1964-65. 2 Vols.

***

VLOS    REUNIÓN LATINOAMERICANA SOBRE ASPECTOS DEL DERECHO DEL MAR, LIMA, 1970. Documentos officiales. Lima, 1970. n.p.

***

VOCET    Revelle, R. SCIENTIFIC RESEARCH ON THE SEA-BED - INTERNATIONAL CO-OPERATION IN SCIENTIFIC RESEARCH AND EXPLORATION OF THE SEA-BED. Paper at Symposium on the International Regime of the Sea-bed. Rome, 1969.
16

***

VINTL    Reynaud, André. LA VOLONTÉ LA NATURE ET LE DROIT. LES DIFFÉRENDS DU PLATEAU CONTINENTAL DE LA MER DU NORD DEVANT LA COUR INTERNATIONALE DE JUSTICE. Paris, Librairie Générale de Droit et de Jurisprudence; R. Pichon et R. Durand-Auzias, 1975. 245p.

***

VLOS    Reynolds, Clark G. HISTORY IN THE MAKING: LAW OF THE SEA. Maine Sea Grant Information Leaflet, no. 7. Walpole, University of Maine, 1975.
18

***

VOS    Reynolds, Clark G., and William J. McAndrew, eds. 1973 SEMINAR IN MARITIME AND REGIONAL STUDIES. Proceedings of Conference held at the University of Maine. MSG-B-6-75. Portland, Maine, 1974. 205p.

***

VENE    Rhode Island. University. MARINE BULLETIN. NUCLEAR POWER PLANT SITING: A HANDBOOK FOR THE LAYMAN. 1972. Kingston, University of Rhode Island, Marine Advisory Service, 1972. 31p.

***

IIIOR    _____ NEW ENGLAND MARINE RESOURCES INFORMATION PROGRAM. FLORIDA LEGISLATION. Narragansett, University of Rhode Island, 1969. 11p.
13

IIIOR    _____ International Center for Marine Resources Development. ANNUAL REPORT. Kingston, R.I., 1972-
13

IIIF    _____ SOCIO-ECONOMIC RESEARCH ISSUES IN FISHERIES DEVELOPMENT. A report on a workshop, held jointly by the International Center for Marine Resource Development and the Agriculture Development Council at the University of Rhode Island, October 25-27, 1972. Marine Technical Report Series no. 14. Kingston, University of Rhode Island, 1973. 12p.
13

                                                                    13
IIIF      Rhode Island. University. Law of the Sea Institute. COMMENTS RE-
          CEIVED ABOUT OCCASIONAL PAPER # 19: "FISHERMAN QUOTAS: A TENTATIVE
          SUGGESTION FOR DOMESTIC MANAGEMENT" by Francis T. Christy. Mimeo.
          Kingston, n.d. 4, 2p.

                                                                   ART
VOR       Rich, Alexander, and Vladimir A. Engelgardt. A PROPOSAL FROM A
          U.S. AND A SOVIET SCIENTIST; OCEANIC RESOURCES AND DEVELOPING NA-
          TIONS. In Bulletin of Science Organization, Vol. 24, February,
          1968. pp. 2-3.

                                                                   ***
VENV      Richardson, Dan K. THE COST OF ENVIRONMENTAL PROTECTION: REGULA-
          TING HOUSING DEVELOPMENT IN THE COASTAL ZONE. New Brunswick, N.J.,
          Rutgers University, Center for Urban Policy Research, 1975. 250p.

                                                                    1
VMT       Richel, Alan L. ISRAEL'S NAVIGATIONAL RIGHTS IN THE GULF OF AQABA
          AND STRAITS OF TIRAN. Thesis. Washington, April 29, 1972. 137p.

                                                                    13
IICZM     Richmond, Henry R. THE OREGON COAST AND THE OREGON COASTAL AND DE-
          VELOPMENT COMMISSION: THE FOX GUARDING THE CHICKENS? A balance
          for the public interest: OSPIRG reports. Portland, Or., OSPIRG,
          1973. 96p.

                                                                   14a
IIIF      Ricker, William E. METHODS OF ESTIMATING VITAL STATISTICS OF FISH
          POPULATIONS. Bloomington, Indiana University, 1948. v, 101p.

                                                                    2
VP        Rienow, Robert. MAN AGAINST HIS ENVIRONMENT. New York, Ballantine
          Books, 1970. xii, 307p.

                                                           1,3,5,11,12,14a
IIICONS   Riesenfeld, Stefan A. PROTECTION OF COASTAL FISHERIES UNDER INTER-
          NATIONAL LAW. Washington, Carnegie Endowment for International
          Peace, 1942. xii, 296p.

                                                                   ART
VENE      Rigassi, D.A. EUROPEAN OIL GAS INDUSTRY UNDERGOING DYNAMIC CHANGES.
          In World Oil, Vol. 156, January, 1963. pp. 92-101.

                                                                   ***
IIP       Riley, Charles D. WASTE DISPOSAL AND WATER QUALITY IN THE ESTUARIES
          OF NORTH CAROLINA. Raleigh, North Carolina State University, School
          of Engineering, Department of Civil Engineering, 1972. 97p.

                                                                    14
VOCET     Riley, J.P., and R. Chester. INTRODUCTION TO MARINE CHEMISTRY.
          New York, Academic Press, 1971. 465p.

                                                                   ***
VOCET     Riley, J.P., and G. Skirrow. CHEMICAL OCEANOGRAPHY. New York, Aca-
          demic Press, 1965. 2 Vols.

                                                                   ART
IIB       Riphagen, W. THE JURISDICTION OF THE COASTAL STATE. In Symposium
          on the Future of the Law of the Sea, Den Helder, 1972. Proceedings.

The Hague, 1973. n.p. pp. 154-162.

ART
VMT RISK ANALYSIS OF THE OIL TRANSPORTATION SYSTEM. AN OIW REPORT. In Pacific Northwest Sea, Vol. 5, no. 4, 1972. pp. 3-22.

16
VAC Ritchie-Calder, Peter R. ARMS AND THE OCEAN BED "IN QUIET ENJOYMENT." Paper at Pacem in Maribus Preparatory Conference on the Legal Framework and the Continental Shelf. Kingston, Rhode Island, January 30-February 1, 1970.

15,16
VP _____ _____ THE POLLUTION OF THE MEDITERRANEAN SEA. Berne, Switzerland, Herbert Lang, 1972. 148p.

13
IIE Robas, Ann K. SOUTH FLORIDA'S MANGROVE-BORDERED ESTUARIES - THEIR ROLE IN SPORT AND COMMERCIAL FISH PRODUCTION. University of Miami Sea Grant Institutional Program. Information Bulletin No. 4. Coral Gables, Fla., 1970. 28p.

***
VP Roberts, A.C. SHORE TERMINATION FOR OIL SPILL BOOMS. EPA-R2-73-114. Edison, N.J., U.S. Environmental Protection Agency, Office of Research and Monitoring, 1973. 23p.

13
IIIAFF Roberts, Kenneth J. ECONOMICS OF HATCHERY SALMON DISPOSAL IN OREGON. Oregon State University Sea Grant Marine Advisory Program, Sea Grant no. 17. Corvallis, Or., 1972? 20p.

13
IIE _____ _____ UNDERSTANDING THE USE AND MANAGEMENT OF OREGON ESTUARIES. Oregon State University Sea Grant Marine Advisory Program. Man and his Ocean. Sea Grant publication no. 18. Corvallis, Or., 1972? 10p.

13,14
VENV Roberts, Kenneth J., and J. Bruce Rettig. LINKAGES BETWEEN THE ECONOMY AND THE ENVIRONMENT: AN ANALYSIS OF ECONOMIC GROWTH IN CLATSOP COUNTY, OREGON. Oregon Sea Grant ORESU-T-74-005. Corvallis, Oregon State University, 1975. 27p.

2,3,5,13,14,16
IVOL ROCKY MOUNTAIN MINERAL LAW FOUNDATION. Law of federal oil and gas leases. New York, Mathew Bender. 1964- 2 Vols.

***
VLOS Rodino, W. DIGEST OF THE LAW OF THE SEA. N.Y., Dobbs Ferry, Oceana Publishers, Inc., n.d.

***
IVENV Roels, O.A., et al. ENVIRONMENTAL IMPACT OF DEEP-SEA MINING, PROGRESS REPORT. Washington, U.S. Department of Commerce, NOAA, 1973. iv, 185p.

IIIB      Rojahn, Ondolf. DIE ANSPRÜCHE DER LATEINAMERIKANISCHEN STAATEN ***
          AUF FISCHEREIVORRECHTE JENSEITS DER ZWÖLFMEILENGRENZE. Kiel. Universität, Institut für Internationales Recht. Veröffentlichungen, 69. Hamburg, Hansischer Gildenverlag, 1972. 308p.

VINTL     Rojas Garciduenas, Jose. EL CASO INTERNACIONAL DE LA SALINIDAD DE [3]
          LAS AGUAS ENTREGADAS A MEXICO EN EL RIO COLORADO. Reprinted from Revista de la Facultad de Derecho de Mexico, Vol. XIV, no. 54, April-June 1964.

VOCET     Rona, Peter A. EXPLORATION METHODS FOR THE CONTINENTAL SHELF: GEO- [13]
          LOGY, GEOPHYSICS, GEOCHEMISTRY. NOAA technical report ERL 238-AOML & Boulder, Colo., National Oceanic and Atmospheric Administration, 1972. iii, 47p.

IVMMR     _____ PLATE TECTONICS AND MINERAL RESOURCES. In Scientific  ART
          American, Vol. 229, July, 1973. pp. 86-95.

IIIINTL   Root, Elihu. NORTH ATLANTIC COAST FISHERIES ARBITRATION AT THE [12]
          HAGUE. Cambridge, Harvard University Press; London, H. Milford, 1917.

IVMMR     Rose, Curt D. PETROLEUM IN THE ESTUARY. College Park, University ***
          of Maryland, Natural Resources Institute, 1974. 15p.

VENV      Rose, Jerome G., ed. LEGAL FOUNDATIONS OF ENVIRONMENTAL PLANNING. ***
          New Brunswick, N.J., Rutgers University, Center for Urban Policy Research, 1975. 318p.

VENV      Rosenburg, Donald H., ed. PROCEEDINGS OF THE CONFERENCE WORKSHOP ***
          TO REVIEW THE DRAFT STUDY PLAN FOR ENVIRONMENTAL ASSESSMENT OF THE GULF OF ALASKA, SOUTHEASTERN BERING AND BEAUFORT SEAS. Sea Grant Report 75-4. Anchorage, Alaska, February 18-21, 1975. 184p.

VOCET     Rosenburg, D.H., et al. RESEARCH VESSEL ACTIVITIES 1969-70. Fair- ***
          banks, University of Alaska, Institute of Marine Science, 1975. 35p.

IICZM     Rosentraub, Robert W., et al. COASTAL ZONE DEVELOPMENT AND COASTAL ***
          POLICY IN SOUTHERN CALIFORNIA: A TWO-YEAR ANALYSIS OF THE SOUTH COAST REGIONAL COMMISSION. USC-SG-6-75. Los Angeles, University of Southern California, 1975. 95p.

IVOCET    Ross, E.A. AN INTRODUCTION TO NORTH SEA OFFSHORE EXPLORATION. In  ART
          K.D. Troup, ed., NORSPEC 70, London: the North Sea Spectrum. Proceedings of a conference on the ships, materials, equipment and the problems involved in the exploitation of the North Sea. London, Thomas Reed Publications, 1971. pp. 31-36.

|  |  |
|---|---|
| IIP | 5,13,14,16<br>Ross, William M. OIL POLLUTION AS AN INTERNATIONAL PROBLEM; A STUDY OF PUGET SOUND AND THE STRAIT OF GEORGIA. Seattle, University of Washington Press, 1973. xiii, 279p. |
| IIIF | 1,5,15,16,18<br>Rothschild, Brian J., ed. WORLD FISHERIES POLICY; MULTIDISCIPLINARY VIEWS. Public policy issues in resource management, Vol. 4. Seattle, University of Washington Press, 1972. xix, 272p. |
| IVM | ART<br>Rothstein, Arnold J., and Raymond Kaufman. THE APPROACHING MATURITY OF DEEP OCEAN MINING - THE PACE QUICKENS. In Offshore Technology Conference, 5th, Houston, Texas, 1973: Preprints. Dallas, Tex., 1973. Vol. 2, pp. 323-344. |
| VOR | ***<br>Rouch, Jules Alfred Pierre. LES OCÉANS. Collection Armand Colin. Section de physique, 320. Paris, 1957. 216p. |
| IIIF | 14a<br>Rounsefell, George A., and W. Harry Everhart. FISHERY SCIENCE, ITS METHODS AND APPLICATIONS. New York, Wiley, 1953. 444p. |
| VB | ART<br>Rousseau, C. LA CONDITION JURIDIQUE DES ESPACES MARITIMES ADJACENTS AU TERRITOIRE FRANÇAISE. In J. Tittel, Multitudo Legum ius unum: Mélanges en l'honneur de Wilhelm Wengler zu seinem 65. Geburtstag. Berlin, 1973. Vol. 1, pp. 325-335. |
| IIE | 13<br>Rousseau, Rollie. ESTUARIES - WHERE RIVERS MEET THE SEA. In Oregon State Game Commission Bulletin. Vol. 25, no. 8. Portland, August, 1970. |
| IVLOS | ART<br>Routh, J.A.S. INTERNATIONAL REGULATION OF PETROLEUM EXPLORATION AND EXPLOITATION ON THE HIGH SEAS. In S.W. Wurfel, Emerging Ocean Oil and Mining Law. Sea Grant publication UNC-SG-74-02. Chapel Hill, University of North Carolina School of Law, 1974. pp. 1-11. |
| IIP | ***<br>Royal Commission on Environmental Pollution. POLLUTION IN SOME BRITISH ESTUARIES AND COASTAL WATERS. Third Report. Comnd. 5054. London, Her Majesty's Stationery Office, 1972. 133p. |
| IIIF | 5,13<br>Royce, William F. INTRODUCTION TO THE FISHERY SCIENCES. Academic Press, 1972. |
| IIIFV&G | 13,14a,16<br>Royce, William F., et al. SALMON GEAR LIMITATION IN NORTHERN WASHINGTON WATERS; AN ECONOMIC, BIOLOGICAL, AND LEGAL SURVEY OF THE SALMON RESOURCE OF NORTHERN PUGET SOUND AND STRAIT OF JUAN DE FUCA. Seattle, University of Washington, 1963. vi, 123p. |
| VB | 4,7,11,14<br>Rozakis, Christol L. THE GREEK-TURKISH DISPUTE OVER THE AEGEAN CONTINENTAL SHELF. Law of the Sea Institute occasional paper no. 27. Kingston, University of Rhode Island, 1975. |

IIIFP   Rubenstein, Mark E. THE HISTORY OF CONCENTRATION IN THE CANNED SALMON INDUSTRY OF THE UNITED STATES. (Honors Thesis) Cambridge, Mass., Harvard College, 1966.

ART
VINTL   Rubin, Alfred P. LAND-LOCKED AFRICAN COUNTRIES AND RIGHTS OF ACCESS TO THE SEA. In Červenka Zdenek, Land-locked Countries of Africa. Uppsala, Scandinavian Institute of African Studies, 1973.

VSG     Rucker, James B. SEA GRANT: A CATALYST FOR LEGISLATIVE ACTION. Paper presented at the Seventh Annual meeting of the Sea Grant Association, Seattle, Washington, 30 October, 1974. MASGP-74-041. Ocean Springs, Mississippi-Alabama Sea Grant Consortium, 1974.

ART
VB      Ruda, J.M. EL LÍMITE EXTERIOR DE LA PLATAFORMA CONTINENTAL. In Estudios de derecho internacional publico y privado: homenaje al Profesor Luis Sela Sampil. Oviedo, 1970. pp. 633-656.

ART
VINTL   Rudolf, W. DIE MALAKKA-STRASSE, EIN NEUES VOELKERRECHTS-PROBLEM. In D. Blumenwitz, und A. Randelzhofer. Festschrift fuer Friedrich Berber zum 75. Geburtstag. Muenchen, 1973. pp. 433-448.

VP      Ruel, M., et al. GUIDELINES ON THE USE AND ACCEPTABILITY OF OIL SPILL DISPERSANTS. EPS 1-EE-73-1. Canada, Department of the Environment, Environmental Emergency Branch, 1973. 63p.

ART
IIIINTL Ruester, B. UEBERLEGUNGEN ZUM ISLAENDISCHEN FISCHEREISTREIT. In D. Blumenwitz, und A. Randelshofer. Festschrift fuer Friedrich Berber zum 75. Geburtstag. Muenchen, 1973. pp. 449-466.

7
VINTL   _____ VERTRAEGE UND DEKLARATIONEN UEBER DEN FESTLANDSOCKEL, CONTINENTAL SHELF. Dokumente, 42. Frankfurt am Main, 1975. 181p.

14
VENV    Ruester, Bernd, and Bruno Simma, eds. INTERNATIONAL PROTECTION OF THE ENVIRONMENT: TREATIES AND RELATED DOCUMENTS. N.Y., Dobbs Ferry, Oceana Publishers, Inc., 1975-    10 Vols.

VORM    Ruhe, W.J. TECHNICAL SUPPORTING SERVICES FOR THE NATIONAL OCEAN PROGRAM. Washington, D.C., National Council on Marine Resources and Engineering Development, 1968. 85p.

1,13,16
IIIP    Ruivo, Mario, ed. MARINE POLLUTION AND SEA LIFE. La pollution des mers et les ressources biologiques. La contaminación del mar y los recursos vivos. West Byfleet, Surrey, England, Fishing News (Books), 1972. xxiv, 624p. (In French, English, Spanish.)

16
IIIOCET Rulifson, Robert L. GEOPHYSICAL OFFSHORE OIL EXPLORATION AND ASSOCIATED FISHERY PROBLEMS. Portland, Oregon, Fish Commission, 1963. 46p.

|  |  |
|---|---|
| | 13 |
| VENV | Russell, Clifford S., and Hans H. Landsberg. THE BORDER CROSSING. Adapted from their International Environmental Problems - a Taxonomy. In Resources, no. 38, September, 1971. Washington, D.C., Resources for the Future, 1971. pp. 5-6. |

15
VORM    RUSSIA IN THE CARIBBEAN. Washington, Center for Strategic and International Studies, Georgetown University, 1973. 2 Vols.

\*\*\*
IICZM   Rutka, J., and C. Gopalakrishnan. SPHERES OF INFLUENCE IN HAWAII'S COASTAL ZONE: VOL. 1, FEDERAL AGENCY INVOLVEMENT. UNIHI-SEAGRANT-AR-72-03. Honolulu, University of Hawaii, Sea Grant Colleges 1973. 85p.

\*\*\*
VORM    Rutka, Susan S. MARINE AND COASTAL-RELATED MEASURES: 1973 HAWAII STATE LEGISLATURE. Working Paper no. 3. Honolulu, University of Hawaii, 1973. 22p.

12,16
VINTL   Ryan, James W. FREEDOM OF THE SEAS AND INTERNATIONAL LAW. New York, The Court Press, 1941. 54p.

14a
IIIF    Sabine, L. REPORT ON THE PRINCIPAL FISHERIES OF THE AMERICAN SEAS. Prepared for the Treasury Department. Washington, R. Armstrong, Printer, 1853.

13,15
VENE    Saila, S.B. PRELIMINARY SITE EVALUATION STUDY ROME POINT. NORTH KINGSTOWN, RHODE ISLAND. FINAL REPORT. Kingston, University of Rhode Island, 1969.

1,5,16
IIIF    Saila, Saul B., and Virgil J. Norton. TUNA: STATUS, TRENDS, AND ALTERNATIVE MANAGEMENT ARRANGEMENTS. Program of international studies of fishery arrangements, no. 6. Washington, D.C., Resources for the Future, Inc., June 1974. x, 59p.

\*\*\*
IIOSTR  St. Denis, Manley. HAWAII'S FLOATING CITY DEVELOPMENT PROGRAM. Technical report no. 1. UNIHI-SEAGRANT-CR-75-01. Honolulu, University of Hawaii, 1974. 93p.

3
IIIFV&G SALMON GEAR LIMITATION IN NORTHERN WASHINGTON WATERS; AN ECONOMIC, BIOLOGICAL, AND LEGAL SURVEY OF THE SALMON RESOURCE OF NORTHERN PUGET SOUND AND THE STRAIT OF JUAN DE FUCA. University of Washington Publications in fisheries, n.s., Vol. 2, nos. 1-2. Contribution no. 145, 160, College of Fisheries. Seattle, University of Washington Printing Plant, 1963.

14a
IIIF    Salter, Luther C. ORGANIZING AND INCORPORATING FISHERY COOPERATIVE MARKETING ASSOCIATIONS. Washington, U.S.G.P.O., 1936. 38p.

IIOSTR   Salter, Richard G. A FLOATING POWER PLATFORM CONCEPT FOR THE WEST COAST. Santa Monica, California, Rand Corporation. December, 1972. 11p. [13]

VP   Saltonstall, Richard. YOUR ENVIRONMENT AND WHAT YOU CAN DO ABOUT IT. New York, Walker, 1970. xvii, 299p. [2]

VLOS   Samet, Jan H., and Robert L. Fuerst. THE LATIN AMERICAN APPROACH TO THE LAW OF THE SEA. Sea Grant Publication no. 73-08. Chapel Hill, University of North Carolina, 1973. 167p. [10,18]

***

VP   Sampedro, Ruth M. COSTS AND BENEFITS OF THE ABATEMENT OF POLLUTION OF BISCAYNE BAY, MIAMI, FLORIDA. Sea Grant Technical Bulletin. Coral Gables, Fla., University of Miami, 1972. 102p.

VINTL   Sandiford, Roberto. DIRITTO MARITTIMO. Milano, Giuffre, 1960. 709p. [1]

IIIB   _____ _____ IL PROBLEMA DELLE ZONE DI PESCA. Reprinted from Il Diritto Marittimo, Special number, 1964. 19p. [1]

VINTL   _____ _____ LES CONVENTIONS INTERNATIONALES DANS LE DOMAINE DE LA NAVIGATION FLUVIALE. Reprinted from Revue Internationale du Droit des Gens, Vol. I, Serie II, 1962. [1]

VINTL   _____ _____ PIRATERIA E DIRITTO DI ASILO. Reprinted from Storia e politica, Vol. II, no. 2, April-June 1963. [1]

IVDRIL   SANTA BARBARA OIL SYMPOSIUM - OFFSHORE PETROLEUM PRODUCTION - AN ENVIRONMENTAL INQUIRY. December 16-18, 1970. Santa Barbara, University of California, 1970. viii, 377p. [5,13]

***

IVOI   Sapp, Daniel C., and Karen E. Richter. REMOTE SURVEILLANCE OF OIL- AND GAS-FIELD ACTIVITIES IN ALABAMA. Alabama, Auburn University, 1975. 22p.

VOR   Sater, John E., A.G. Ronhovde, and L.C. Van Allen. ARCTIC ENVIRONMENT AND RESOURCES. Washington, Arctic Institute of North America, 1971. viii, 309p. [17]

***

VENE   Savage, John A. POTENTIAL OF TIDAL AND GULF STREAM POWER RESOURCES. Prepared for the Governor's Energy Advisory Council. Dallas, Southern Methodist University, Institute of Technology, 1975. iv, 48p.

***

IIIMM   Savini, M.J. REPORT ON INTERNATIONAL AND NATIONAL LEGISLATION FOR THE CONSERVATION OF MARINE MAMMALS: PART I. INTERNATIONAL LEGISLATION. FAO Fisheries Circular 326, June, 1974. 83p.

IIREC Scalpone, Frank. RECREATIONAL BOATING; LIKE FUN? In Marine Technology Society. 9th Annual Conference, Washington, D.C., September 10-12, 1973. Washington, D.C., 1973. pp. 233-235.
ART

***

IIIF Scattergood, Leslie W., and Lola T. Dees, eds. REPORT OF THE BUREAU OF COMMERCIAL FISHERIES FOR THE CALENDAR YEAR 1969. Washington, U.S.G.P.O., 1971. 141p.

IIP Schachter, Oscar, and Daniel Server. MARINE POLLUTION PROBLEMS AND REMEDIES. UNITAR research reports, no. 4. New York, United Nations Institute for Training and Research, 1971. 23, ixp.
13,17

IIICONS Schaefer, Milner B. CONSERVATION OF BIOLOGICAL RESOURCES OF THE COASTAL ZONE. In J.F. Peel Brahtz, ed., Coastal zone management; multiple use with conservation. New York, John Wiley, 1972. pp. 35-79.
ART

IIIOR \_\_\_\_ \_\_\_\_ LIVING RESOURCES OF THE SEA-BED. Rome, 1969.
16

VOR _____ THE RESOURCES BASE: PRESENT AND FUTURE. In Borgese, Elisabeth Mann, ed., Pacem in maribus. New York, Dodd, Mead, 1972. pp. 95-119.
ART

VOR _____ SOME COMMENTS ON INTERACTION BETWEEN THE EXPLOITATION OF THE FOOD RESOURCES AND OTHER USES OF THE OCEAN. In Conference on Law, Organization and Security in the Use of the Ocean, 1st, Columbus, Ohio, 1967: Papers and discussions of the Conference. Columbus, Ohio, Mershon Center for Education in National Security, 1967.
ART

IIIOR _____ SOME CONSIDERATIONS OF LIVING RESOURCES ASSOCIATED WITH THE DEEP SEA-BED. In J. Sztucki, ed., Symposium on the International Regime of the Sea-Bed, Rome, June 30-July 5, 1969. Proceedings. Rome, Accademia Nazionale dei Lincei, 1970. pp. 155-184.
ART

***

VOCET Schaefer, W. ECOLOGY AND PALAEOECOLOGY OF MARINE ENVIRONMENTS. G.Y. Craig, ed. Translated by I. Oertel. Chicago, University of Chicago Press, 1972. 624p.

VP Schaeffer, Francis A. POLLUTION AND THE DEATH OF MAN; THE CHRISTIAN VIEW OF ECOLOGY. Wheaton, Ill., Tyndale House Publishers, 1970. 125p.
17

VOCET Schatz, Gerald S., ed. SCIENCE, TECHNOLOGY, AND SOVEREIGNTY IN THE POLAR REGIONS. Lexington, Mass., Lexington Books, 1974. xv, 215p.
16

***

VP Schatzberg, Paul. INVESTIGATION OF SORBENTS FOR REMOVING OIL SPILLS FROM WATERS. Report no. 8-921. Annapolis, Md., U.S. Naval Ship Research and Development Center, 1971. 88p.

VCS       Scheingold, S. LESSONS OF THE EUROPEAN COMMUNITY FOR AN OCEAN REGIME. Paper at Pacem in Maribus Preparatory Conference on the Legal Framework and the Continental Shelf. Kingston, Rhode Island, January 30 - February 1, 1970.

***

VOS       Schenck, Hilbert V., and J.J. McAniff. MARINE RESEARCH INTEREST IN LOUISIANA UNIVERSITIES. LSU-SG-75-02 Baton Rouge, Louisiana State University, 1975. 35p.

14

IIP&H     Schenker, Eric, and Harry C. Brockel, eds. PORT PLANNING AND DEVELOPMENT AS RELATED TO PROBLEMS OF U.S. PORTS AND THE U.S. COASTAL ENVIRONMENT: A COLLECTION OF EDITED PAPERS PRESENTED AT A CONFERENCE SPONSORED BY THE UNIVERSITY OF WISCONSIN - MILWAUKEE, CENTER FOR GREAT LAKES STUDIES, AND THE U.S. DEPARTMENT OF TRANSPORTATION HELD BETWEEN NOVEMBER 27 AND 30, 1973. Cambridge, Md., Cornell Maritime Press, 1974. xxi, 327p.

***

VOR       Scheuer, P.J. CHEMISTRY OF MARINE NATURAL PRODUCTS. New York, Academic Press, 1973. 208p.

13

IIIMM     Schevill, William E., ed. THE WHALE PROBLEM. A STATUS REPORT. Cambridge, Mass. Harvard University Press, 1974. x, 419p.

***

IICR      Schlee, John S. SAND AND GRAVEL. Albany, State University of New York, New York Sea Grant Institute, 1975.

***

IICZM     Schoenbaum, Thomas J. THE MANAGEMENT OF LAND AND WATER USE IN THE COASTAL ZONE: A NEW LAW IS ENACTED IN NORTH CAROLINA. Reprinted from North Carolina Law Review, Vol. 53, no. 2, December 1974. pp. 276-302.

***

IICZM     _____ PUBLIC RIGHTS AND COASTAL ZONE MANAGEMENT. UNC-SG-72-13. Raleigh, North Carolina State University, 1972.

17

VOS       Schoenfeld, Clarence A., ed. OUTLINES OF ENVIRONMENTAL EDUCATION. From the 1969-70 and 1970-71 issues of the Journal of Environmental Education. Madison, Wis., Dembar Educational Research Services, 1971? x, 246p.

***

IVMMR     Schott, W. MINERALISCHE ROHSTOFFE DES MEERESBODENS. In Kiel. Universitat. Institut fur internationales Recht. Die Nutzung des Meeresgrundes ausserhalb des Festlandsockels. Hamburg, Hansischer Gildenverlag, 1970. pp. 40-47.

ART

IIIB      Schram, G.G. THE CASE FOR COASTAL STATE JURISDICTION. In G. Pontecorvo, Fisheries Conflicts in North Atlantic. Cambridge, Mass., 1974. pp. 105-115.

|       | 13 |
|-------|----|
| VENE  | Schurr, Sam H. MIDDLE EASTERN OIL IN THE NEXT DECADE: SOME PROSPECTS AND PROBLEMS. Reprinted from Proceedings of the Council of Economics, American Institute of Mining, Metallurgical, and Petroleum Engineering Reprint no. 89. Washington, D.C., Resources for the Future, 1970. pp. 109-117. |

***

VB    Schwartzrauber, Sayre A. THE THREE-MILE LIMIT OF TERRITORIAL SEAS. Annapolis, Md., Naval Institute Press, 1972. 325p.

***

VINTL    Schwarzkopf, H. STAATLICHE INFORMATIONSPFLICHTEN IM SEERECHT. Schriften zum Voelkerrecht, 43. Berlin, Duncker und Humblot, 1975. 123p.

13

VOR    Science Council of Canada. CANADA, SCIENCE AND THE OCEANS. Report No. 10, 1970. Ottawa, Information Canada, 1970. 37p.

ART

VODAS    Scott, D.P.D. THE LEGAL STATUS OF OCEAN DATA ACQUISITION SYSTEMS (ODAS). In Colloque International sur' Exploitation des Oceans, held in Bordeaux, France, March, 1971. Proceedings. Paris, Centre National pour l'Exploitation des Oceans, 1971.

5,12,13,16

VB    Scott, Marshall S. FLORIDA'S SEAWARD BOUNDARIES; A DILEMMA. University of Miami Sea Grant Technical bulletin no. 20. Coral Gables, Fla. University of Miami, 1971. iii, 114p.

***

IICZM    Scott, Stanley. GOVERNING CALIFORNIA'S COAST. Berkeley, University of California, Institute of Governmental Studies, 1975. 454p.

***

VSG    SEA GRANT. A REPORT ON THE OREGON STATE UNIVERSITY SEA GRANT PROGRAM FOR 1973-74. Corvallis, Oregon State University, 1975.

***

VSG    SEA GRANT. A REPORT ON THE OREGON STATE UNIVERSITY SEA GRANT COLLEGE PROGRAM 1974-1975. Corvallis, Oregon State University, 1976. 93p.

***

VSG    SEA GRANT ASSOCIATION. PROCEEDINGS OF 8TH ANNUAL MEETING HELD IN BILOXI, MISS., OCTOBER 27-30, 1975. Ocean Springs, Miss., Mississippi - Alabama Sea Grant Consortium, 1976?

15

VSG    THE SEA-GRANT COLLEGE PROGRAM AT THE UNIVERSITY OF RHODE ISLAND; A PROPOSAL FOR INSTITUTIONAL SUPPORT UNDER THE NATIONAL SEA-GRANT COLLEGE AND PROGRAM ACT OF 1966. Kingston, University of Rhode Island, 1966? II, 96p.

17

VSG    Sea Grant Conference, 2d, Newport, R.I., 1968. PROCEEDINGS. Kingston, University of Rhode Island. 88p.

VSG  SEA GRANT NEWSLETTER AND INDEX, 1968-72. NOAA-TM-EDS ESIC-10. Rockville, Md., U.S. Department of Commerce, Environmental Science Information Center, May, 1973. 157p.

ART
VSG  THE SEA GRANT PROGRAM: EXPECTATIONS vs. REALITY. In Marine Affairs Journal, Report no. 3. Narragansett, University of Rhode Island, 1975.

IICZM  Sealy, James E., Jr., and W.M. Ahr. QUANTITATIVE ANALYSIS OF SHORE-LINE CHANGE, SARGENT, TEXAS. TAMU-SG-75-209. College Station, Texas A&M University, 1975. 177p.

IIIF  Seaman, William Jr., ed. SHARKS AND MAN: A PERSPECTIVE. Report no. 10. Gainesville, University of Florida, 1976. 37p.

VOR  SECOND CONFERENCE ON WATER DESALINATION. Proceedings. Bhavnagar, Central Salt and Marine Chemicals Research Institute, 1972? 499p.

IIOSTR  Seidl, Ludwig H. HAWAII'S FLOATING CITY DEVELOPMENT PROGRAM: THEORETICAL INVESTIGATION AND OPTIMIZATION OF THE PLATFORM'S SEA-KEEPING CHARACTERISTICS. UNIHI-SEAGRANT-CR-73-01. Honolulu, University of Hawaii, 1973. 100p.

VENE  Seifert, W.W., et al, eds. ENERGY AND DEVELOPMENT: A CASE STUDY. Sea Grant Report MITSG-72-16. Cambridge, Massachusetts Institute of Technology, Sea Grant Project Office, 1973. 300p.

5,14
VLOS  Selden, John. OF THE DOMINION; OR, OWNERSHIP OF THE SEA. Translation of Mare clausum. Reprint of the 1652 ed. New York, Arno, 1972. 500, 37p.

14
IVMMR  SEMINAR ON PETROLEUM LEGISLATION WITH PARTICULAR REFERENCE TO OFF-SHORE OPERATIONS, BANGKOK, THAILAND, 1971. PROCEEDINGS. United Nations. Document E/CN.11/1052. New York? United Nation, 1973. vii, 154p.

VORM  SEMINARIO LATINOAMERICANO SOBRE EL OCÉANO PACÍFICO ORIENTAL. 1st, LIMA, 1964. Memoria del Primer Seminario; estado del conocimiento del Océano Pacífico Oriental. Lima, Universidad Nacional Mayor de San Marcos, 1966. xxxvi, 218p.

16
IIIF  Sengoku, Takashi. SEDENTARY FISHERIES AND THE CONTINENTAL SHELF. Unpublished paper submitted to Professor Sohn's seminar on contemporary problems in International Law, Harvard University, 1954. 38p.

IICZM  Sensabaugh, W.M. THE BEACH - A NATURAL PROTECTION FROM THE SEA. SUSF-SG-75-002. Tallahassee, Florida Department of Natural

Resources, Bureau of Beaches and Shores, 1975. 6p.

ART
VLOS Sepúlveda, C. EL DERECHO INTERNACIONAL MARÍTIMO DESDE LAS CONVENCIONES DE GINEBRA. In Estudios de derecho internacional publico y privado: homenaje al Profesor Luis Sela Sampil. Oviedo, 1970. pp. 577-592.

14a,17
VCONS Shaler, Nathaniel S. MAN AND THE EARTH. New York, Fox, Duffield and Company, 1905. vi, 240p.

1,5,7,8,12,15
VB Shalowitz, Aaron L. SHORE AND SEA BOUNDARIES, WITH SPECIAL REFERENCE TO THE INTERPRETATION AND USE OF COAST AND GEODETIC SURVEY DATA. Washington, U.S.G.P.O., 1962-64. 2 Vols.

***
IIIAFF Shang, Yung Cheng. ECONOMIC FEASIBILITY OF FRESH WATER PRAWN FARMING IN HAWAII. UNIHI-SEAGRANT-AR-74-05. Honolulu, University of Hawaii, 1974. 49p.

14a,15
IIIF Shapiro, Sidney, ed. OUR CHANGING FISHERIES. National Marine Fisheries Service. Washington, U.S.G.P.O., 1971. x, 534p.

***
IISL Shaw, Samuel P., et al. WETLANDS OF THE UNITED STATES. Circular 39. U.S. Department of the Interior, Fish and Wildlife Service. Washington, U.S.G.P.O., 1971.

13
IIIAFF Shaw, William N., ed. PROCEEDINGS OF THE FIRST U.S.-JAPAN MEETING ON AQUACULTURE AT TOKYO, JAPAN, OCTOBER 18-19, 1971, UNDER THE U.S.-JAPAN COOPERATIVE PROGRAM IN NATURAL RESOURCES. NOAA TR NMFS CIRC-388. Seattle, U.S. Department of Commerce, National Oceanic and Atmospheric Administration, February, 1971. iii, 133p.

7,16
VCS Shawcross. THE LAW OF THE CONTINENTAL SHELF. WORLD LAND USE SURVEY. Bude, Cornwall, English Geographic Publications, Ltd., 1964. 42p.

13
VSUB Shenton, Edward H. DIVING FOR SCIENCE; THE STORY OF THE DEEP SUBMERSIBLE. New York, Norton, 1972. 267p.

15
VOCET Shepard, Francis P. THE EARTH BENEATH THE SEA. Rev. ed. Baltimore, Johns Hopkins Press, 1967. xi, 242p.

***
IVMMR _____ SUBMARINE GEOLOGY. 3d ed. New York, Harper and Row, Publishers, Inc., 1973. 524p.

17
VB Shepard, Francis P., and Harold R. Wanless. OUR CHANGING COASTLINES. New York, McGraw-Hill, 1971. 579p.

|       |                                                                                                                                                                                                                                                                                                           |
|-------|-----------------------------------------------------------------------------------------------------------------------------------------------------------------------------------------------------------------------------------------------------------------------------------------------------------|
| VMT   | ***<br>Shepard, Perry J. ANALYSIS OF THE ROLE OF THE GULF INTRACOASTAL WATERWAY IN TEXAS. TAMU-SG-75-202. College Station, Texas A&M University, Department of Marine Resources Information, Center for Marine Resources, 1974. 254p. |
| IIIF  | ***<br>Shindo, S. GENERAL REVIEW OF THE TRAWL FISHERY AND THE DEMERSAL FISH STOCKS OF THE SOUTH CHINA SEA. FAO Fisheries Technical Paper 120. Tokyo, April 1973. 54p. |
| VP    | 5,16<br>Shinn, Robert A. THE INTERNATIONAL POLITICS OF MARINE POLLUTION CONTROL. New York, Praeger, 1974. xvii, 200p. |
| IICZM | ***<br>SHORELINE USE AND PROTECTION. PART 2 - ROAD TRANSPORTATION. California Comprehensive Ocean Area Plan. Sacramento, Department of Navigation and Ocean Development, 1972. 74p. |
| IICZM | 13,14,16<br>SHORELINES MANAGEMENT: THE WASHINGTON EXPERIENCE; PROCEEDINGS OF A SYMPOSIUM, THE SEATTLE CENTER, JUNE 24, 1972. Published under the auspices of the Environmental Quality Committee, Young Lawyers Section, American Bar Association through cooperation of the Washington Sea Grant Program, University of Washington. WSG-AS 73-4. Seattle, University of Washington Press, 1972. vii, 184p. |
| VENE  | ***<br>Shoupp, W.E. WORLD ENERGY AND THE OCEANS. 2d Annual Sea Grant Lecture and Symposium. Report MITSG 74-7. Cambridge, Mass., M.I.T., 1973. 10p. |
| VINTL | 16<br>Shukairy, Ahmad. TERRITORIAL AND HISTORICAL WATERS IN INTERNATIONAL LAW. Palestine monographs no. 24. Beirut, Research Center, Palestine Liberation Organization, 1967. 211p. |
| VENE  | ***<br>Shupe, John W. HAWAII GEOTHERMAL PROJECT. Overview of Phases I and II. Honolulu, University of Hawaii, 1974. 10p. |
| VP    | 5,12,16,17<br>Sibthorp, M.M. OCEANIC POLLUTION; A SURVEY AND SOME SUGGESTIONS FOR CONTROL. London, David Davies Memorial Institute of International Studies, 1969. 53p. |
| IIIP  | ***<br>Siegel, S.M. MERCURY: ASPECTS OF ITS ECOLOGY AND ENVIRONMENTAL TOXICITY. Hawaiian Botanical Science paper no. 33. Honolulu, University of Hawaii, 1973. |
| VINTL | ***<br>Sigurdsson, P. UM TJÓN AF VOELDUM SKIPA. (Úlfljótur, Vol. 26, no. 4. Fylgirit). Reykjavik, Orator, 1973. 245p. |
| IVMMR | ***<br>Silas, C.J. NORTH SEA PETROLEUM, ITS PRESENT DEVELOPMENT AND FUTURE OPPORTUNITIES. Paper presented at Nor-Shipping '73. Fourth International Shipping Exhibition and Technical Symposium, May |

10-11, 1973, at Oslo, Norway. n.p. 1973? 16p.

                                                                                               ART

IIIOR    Silverthorne, Wesley. MARINE ALGAE AS AN ECONOMIC RESOURCE. In Marine Technology Society. Seventh Annual Conference, Washington, D.C., August 16-18, 1971. Washington, D.C., 1971. pp. 523-533.

                                                                                                14

VLOS     Simmonds, K.R. CASES ON LAW OF THE SEA. N.Y., Dobbs Ferry, Oceana Publishers, Inc., 1976. 8 Vols.

                                                                           7,15,16

VOR      Simmonds, K.R., ed. THE RESOURCES OF THE OCEAN BED; REPORT OF A CONFERENCE AT DITCHLEY PARK, 26-29 SEPTEMBER 1969. Ditchley Park, England, Ditchley Foundation, 1974? 53p.

                                                                           ***

IIIOR    Simpson, A.C. FAO INDICATIVE WORLD PLAN FOR AGRICULTURAL DEVELOPMENT. AREA REVIEWS ON LIVING RESOURCES OF THE WORLD'S OCEANS: MOLLUSCAN RESOURCES. FAO Fisheries Circular 109.8. 1968.

                                                                             ART

VSUB     Sinclair, J.E. OPERATING SMALL MANNED SUBMERSIBLE SYSTEMS WITH PARTICULAR REFERENCE TO THE NORTH SEA. In K.D. Troup, ed., NORSPEC 70, London: the North Sea spectrum. Proceedings of a conference on the ships, materials, equipment and the problems involved in the exploitation of the North Sea. London, Thomas Reed Publications, 1971. pp. 183-185.

                                                                            14

VENV     Singer, Fred S. THE CHANGING GLOBAL ENVIRONMENT. Dordrecht; Boston, D. Reidel Publishing Company, 1975. 423p.

                                                                             ART

VORM     Singh, N. PRESIDENTIAL PROCLAMATIONS OF INDIA ON MARITIME MATTERS. In J. Tittel, Multitudo legum ius unum: mélanges en l'honneur de Wilhelm Wengler zur seinem 65 Geburtstag. Berlin, 1973. Vol. 1, pp. 575-590.

                                                                            ***

IVOCET   Sinha, E., OCEANIC PATENTS 1959-1968. Ocean Engineering Information Series. La Jolla, Calif., Ocean Engineering Information Service, 1969. 90p.

                                                                              1

VOR      SINO-AMERICAN COLLOQUIUM ON OCEAN RESOURCES, TAIPEI, REPUBLIC OF CHINA, APRIL 28-MAY 6, 1971. Sponsored by the Sino-American Science Cooperation Committee, a joint activity of the Academia Sinica and the National Academy of Sciences. n.p. 1972?

                                                                            17

VENV     Sioli, Harald. ÖKOLOGIE UND LEBENSSCHUTZ IN INTERNATIONALER SICHT. ECOLOGY AND BIOPROTECTION; INTERNATIONAL CONCLUSIONS. Freiburg, Rombach, 1973. 548p. English and German. Summaries in English, French, German, and Spanish.

                                                                            ***

IIENE    SITING CONSIDERATIONS FOR OFFSHORE NUCLEAR POWER PLANTS: SEMINAR PROCEEDINGS. Park Ridge, Ill., Dames and Moore, 1974. 98p.

|  |  | ART |
|---|---|---|
| IIIF | Skeesick, Delbert G. ANADROMOUS FISHERY MANAGEMENT: PROBLEMS AND INNOVATIONS FOR SOLUTIONS. In Proceedings of the 27th Annual Meeting of the Soil Conservation Society, held in Portland, Oregon, August 6-19, 1972. Ankeny, Iowa, 1972? pp. 204-208. | |

9
VB    Skelton, Ray H. THE LEGAL ELEMENTS OF BOUNDARIES AND ADJACENT PROPERTIES. Indianapolis, The Bobbs-Merrill Company, 1930. 1x, 580p.

5,12,14,14a
VOR    Skinner, Brian J., and Karl K. Turekian. MAN AND THE OCEAN. Englewood Cliffs, N.J., Prentice-Hall, 1973. viii, 149p.

13
VENE    Skladel, George W. THE COASTAL BOUNDARIES OF NAVAL PETROLEUM RESERVE NO. 4. Sea Grant No. 73-12. Anchorage, University of Alaska, May, 1974. 20p.

***
VP    Skocypec, R.J. OIL/WATER TANK CONTENT PROFILES. Report no. EE.30TMR.71. Florham, N.J., Esso Research and Engineering Company, 132p.

1,3,5,7,11,16
VINTL    Slouka, Zdenek J. INTERNATIONAL CUSTOM AND THE CONTINENTAL SHELF; STUDY IN THE DYNAMICS OF CUSTOMARY RULES OF INTERNATIONAL LAW. The Hague, Nijhoff, 1968. xii, 186p.

16
VINTL    _____ _____ INTERNATIONAL CUSTOM AND THE CONTINENTAL SHELF: A STUDY OF SOME ASPECTS OF THE GROWTH OF CUSTOMARY RULES OF INTERNATIONAL LAW. Microfilm. New York, Columbia University, 1966. 317p.

16
IICR    Slovenko, Ralph, ed. MINERAL AND TIDELANDS LAW. Baton Rouge, Claitor's, 1963. 216p.

16
IISL    _____ _____ OIL AND GAS OPERATIONS: LEGAL CONSIDERATIONS IN THE TIDELANDS AND ON LAND. Baton Rouge, Claitor's, 1963. 806p.

13
VMM    Small, George L. THE BLUE WHALE. New York, Columbia University Press, 1971. 248p.

ART
IIP&H    Small, Sam W. WHAT'S NEXT IN SUPERTERMINALS? In Fifth National Sea Grant Conference, held in Houston, Texas, 1972. TAMU-SG-73-101. College Station, Texas A&M University, 1972?

14,16
IIIORM    Smetherman, Bobbie B., and Robert M. Smetherman. TERRITORIAL SEAS AND INTER-AMERICAN RELATIONS; WITH CASE STUDIES OF THE PERUVIAN AND U.S. FISHING INDUSTRIES. New York, Praeger, 1974. vi, 121p.

ART
VCS    Smets, P.F. LA LOI DU 13 JUIN 1969 SUR LE PLATEAU CONTINENTAL DE LA BELGIQUE. In W.J. Ganshof van der Meersch, Miscellanea. Brussels, 1972. n.p. Vol. 1. pp. 269-295.

|||||||||||||||||||||||||||||||||||||||||||||||||||||||||||||||

***
IIIF     Smit, P.J., and J.L. Rushburne, comp. A SURVEY OF THE FISHING IN-
DUSTRY IN SOUTH AFRICA AND SOUTH WEST AFRICA. Johannesburg, Stats-
inform (Pty) Ltd., 1971. 158p.

ART
IIIF     Smith, Courtland L. OBSERVED AND PERCIEVED IMPACTS OF DISTANT WATER
FISHING: OREGON OTTER TRAWL CASE. Reprinted from Maine Fisheries
Review, Vol. 37, no. 4, 1975. pp. 13-15.

***
VOR     Smith, F.G. Walton, and H. Chapin. THE SUN, THE SEA, AND TOMORROW;
POTENTIAL SOURCES OF FOOD, ENERGY AND MINERALS FROM THE SEA. New
York, Scribner, 1954. 210p.

13
IIISF     Smith, Frederick J. ECONOMIC CONDITION OF SELECTED PACIFIC NORTH-
WEST SEAFOODS FIRMS. Studies in marine economics. OSU Sea Grant
Special report 327. Corvallis, Oregon State University, Agricul-
tural Experiment Station, 1971. 14p.

14
IIIOI     _____ THE ECONOMIST AND THE SEAFOOD PRODUCER. ORESU-R-74-
025. Reprinted from the American Journal of Agricultural Economics,
Vol. 56, no. 5, 1974. pp. 1038-1046.

13
IIISF     _____ PRICING AND MARKETING OREGON SEAFOODS. STUDIES IN
MARINE ECONOMICS. Special Report 289. Corvallis, Oregon State Uni-
versity, Agricultural Experiment Station, April, 1970.

13
IIIFV&G     Smith, Frederick J., and Robert L. Greene. FUEL NEEDS FOR OREGON'S
COMMERCIAL FISHERMEN. Department of Agricultural Economics and
Marine Advisory Program Cooperating, Sea Grant Program. Corvallis,
Oregon State University, 1974. 16p.

ART
VP     Smith, G.E. INTERNATIONAL COOPERATION FOR THE CONTROL OF OIL POL-
LUTION. In S.W. Wurfel, Emerging Ocean Oil and Mining Law. Sea
Grant Publication UNC-SG-74-02. Chapel Hill, University of North
Carolina School of Law, 1974. pp. 12-20.

1,5,8,11
VINTL     Smith, Herbert A. THE LAW AND CUSTOM OF THE SEA. 2d ed. New York,
Praeger, 1950. 216p.

16
VINTL     _____ THE LAW AND CUSTOM OF THE SEA. 3d ed. London, Stevens, 1959. 291p.

14a,16
VP     Smith, J.E., ed. Marine Biological Association of the United King-
dom. Laboratory, Plymouth. 'TORREY CANYON' POLLUTION AND MARINE
LIFE: A REPORT BY THE PLYMOUTH LABORATORY OF THE MARINE BIOLOGICAL
ASSOCIATION OF THE UNITED KINGDOM. London, Cambridge University
Press, 1968. xiv, 196p.

***
VENV     Smith, James N. ENVIRONMENTAL QUALITY AND SOCIAL JUSTICE IN URBAN AMERICA. Washington, The Conservation Foundation, 1974. xii, 145p.

ART
IIIAFF     Smith, J. Owens, and David L. Marshall. MARICULTURE: A NEW OCEAN USE. Reprinted from Georgia Journal of International and Comparative Law, Vol. 4, no. 2, 1974. Athens, University of Georgia, 1974. pp. 307-342.

ART
VP     Smith, J. Wardley. POLLUTION OF WATER BY OIL. In Conference on International Implications of Environmental Problems, Istanbul, 1971. Environmental problems and their international implications; papers presented at the conference held at the Merchant Marine Academy, Istanbul, Turkey, July 21-28, 1971. Boulder, Colorado Associated University Press, 1973. pp. 111-125.

ART
IIIAFF     Smith, Leah J., and John E. Huguenin. THE ECONOMICS OF WASTE WATER-AQUACULTURE SYSTEMS. In 1975 IEEE Conference Record on Engineering in the Ocean Environment, Ocean '75, November, 1975. Massachusetts, Woods Hole Oceanographic Institution, 1975. 11p.

***
VP     Smith, M.F., and P. Lane. PLANNING-EQUIPMENT AND TRAINING FOR OIL POLLUTION CONTROL. Rev. ed. Westport, Conn., Slickbar, 1973.

***
IVM     Smith, Peter A. UNDERWATER MINING - INSIGHT INTO CURRENT U.S. THINKING. WIS-SG-72-330. Madison, University of Wisconsin Sea Grant Program, n.d. 6p.

***
IVENV     Smith, Robert E., ed. PROCEEDINGS OF MARINE ENVIRONMENTAL IMPLICATIONS OF OFFSHORE DRILLING IN THE EASTERN GULF OF MEXICO; CONFERENCE WORKSHOPS. St. Petersburg, State University System, Florida Institute of Oceanography, 1974. 445p.

***
IIIF     Smith, R.T. OBSERVATIONS ON THE SHRIMP FISHERY IN PUGET SOUND. Olympia, Washington Department of Fisheries, 1937. 11p.

13
VOCET     Smith, Wayne J. OUTLINE OF A PROPOSED STRATEGY FOR "FREEDOM OF SCIENTIFIC RESEARCH." Woods Hole, Mass., Woods Hole Oceanographic Institution, 1972. 8, 2p.

14
IICZM     Snohomish County Citizens Advisory Committee on Shoreline Management. SNOHOMISH COUNTY SHORELINE MANAGEMENT MASTER PROGRAM. Everett, Wash., 1974. 150p.

5,7,12
VINTL     Sobarzo, Alejandro. REGIMEN JURIDICO DEL ALTA MAR. Editorial Porrua, 1970.

1,5,15
VINTL     Societe Française pour le Droit International. ACTUALITES DU DROIT DE LA MER. Colloque de Montpellier, Mai, 1972. Paris, Pedone,

1973. 296p.

VLOS     8
Society of Comparative Legislation and International Law. THE LAW OF THE SEA, THE FINAL ACT AND ANNEXES OF THE UNITED NATIONS CONFERENCE ON THE LAW OF THE SEA, GENEVA, 1958, TOGETHER WITH A SYNOPTICAL TABLE OF CLAIMS TO JURISDICTION OVER THE TERRITORIAL SEA, THE CONTIGUOUS ZONE AND THE CONTINENTAL SHELF. London, 1958. 42p.

VINTL     1
_____ THE SUEZ CANAL: A SELECTION OF DOCUMENTS RELATING TO THE INTERNATIONAL STATUS OF THE SUEZ CANAL, AND THE POSITION OF THE SUEZ CANAL COMPANY. November 1854-July 1956. London, 1956. 76p.

VLOS     14,16
Society of Conservative Lawyers. WHOSE SEA?: A STUDY OF MARITIME JURISDICTION. London, Conservative Political Centre, 1974. 31p.

VP     ART
Soell, Herman. SUBVENTION ODER SONDERABSCHREIBUNG? SPECIAL DEPRECIATION ALLOWANCES OR SUBSIDIES? AMORTISSEMENTS EXCEPTIONNELS OU SUBVENTIONS? In Beitraege zuer Umweltsgestaltung. West Berlin, Erich Schmidt Verlag, 1975. Vol. A33. 68p.

VOR     16
Sohn, Louis B. POSSIBLE FUTURE REGIMES OF THE SEA-BED RESOURCES. INTERNATIONAL REGULATORY AGENCY. Paper at Symposium on the International Regime of the Sea-bed. Rome, 1969.

VLOS     14
_____ THE UNITED NATIONS AND THE OCEANS: CURRENT ISSUES IN THE LAW OF THE SEA. Commission to study the organization of peace. Twenty-third report. New York, 1973. 46p.

IIIF     13
Sokolski, Adam A., ed. OCEAN FISHERY MANAGEMENT DISCUSSIONS AND RESEARCH. Proceedings of a workshop sponsored by the Division of Economic Research, National Marine Fisheries Service, November 5-6, 1970. NOAA TR NMFS CIRC-371. Seattle, U.S. Department of Commerce, National Oceanic and Atmospheric Administration, 1973. 173p.

VENE     ***
SOLAR SEA POWER. Pittsburgh, Pa., Carnegie-Mellon University, 1974. 139p.

VP     13
Solow, Robert M. THE ECONOMIST'S APPROACH TO POLLUTION AND ITS CONTROL. Reprinted from Science, Vol. 173, 6 August, 1971. pp. 498-503.

IICZM     ART
Sondheimer, Carol. COASTAL ZONE MANAGEMENT: THE FEDERAL PERSPECTIVE. In Proceedings of Alabama Coastal Leaders Conference on Coastal Zone Management. MASGP-75-012. Mobile, Mississippi-Alabama Sea Grant Consortium, April 30, 1975. pp. 8-15.

VOSTR     1,4,5,7,11,13,14,15,16
Soons, Alfred H.A. ARTIFICIAL ISLANDS AND INSTALLATIONS IN INTERNATIONAL LAW. Law of the Sea Institute occasional paper no. 22. Kingston, University of Rhode Island, 1974. 30p.

ART
IVMMR    Sorem, Ronald K., and Allan R. Foster. MARINE MANGANESE NODULES: IMPORTANCE OF STRUCTURAL ANALYSIS. In Twenty-fourth Session of the International Geological Congress, held in Montreal, Canada, 1972. pp. 192-200.

3,5,8,12,16
VLOS     Sorensen, Max  LAW OF THE SEA. New York, Carnegie Endowment for International Peace, 1958. 255p.

\*\*\*
IICZM    Sorlie, George. BACKGROUND INFORMATION FOR WATER RESOURCES MANAGEMENT PLANNING IN THE WESTERN AND SOUTHERN PUGET SOUND BASINS. WRIS technical bulletin no. 18. Olympia, Washington Department of Ecology, 1975. 167p.

17
VOCET    Soule, Gardner. THE GREATEST DEPTHS; PROBING THE SEAS TO 20,000 FEET AND BELOW. Philadelphia, Macrae Smith Co., 1970. 194p.

\*\*\*
IIIF     South Africa. Division of Sea Fisheries. ANNUAL REPORT. 1974-

\*\*\*
IIP&H    _____ THE CAPE ROUTE, THE STRATEGIC COASTLINE AND MODERN HARBOURS OF SOUTH AFRICA. Pretoria, South Africa, Department of Information; New York, Republic of South Africa Government Information Service, 1975.

\*\*\*
IIE      _____ THE ORANGE RIVER PROJECT: TAMING SOUTH AFRICA'S BIGGEST RIVER. Pretoria, South Africa, Department of Information; New York, Republic of South Africa Government Information Service, 1975.

\*\*\*
VOCET    SOUTH AFRICAN NATIONAL OCEANOGRAPHIC SYMPOSIUM: ABSTRACTS. Cape Town, South African Department of Industries, Sea Fisheries Branch, 1973. 112p.

14
VOR      Southern Growth Policies Board. Land and Natural Resources Committee. LAND AND NATURAL RESOURCES IN THE SOUTH. Research Triangle Park, N.C., 1974.

\*\*\*
VOCET    SOVIET OCEANOGRAPHIC STUDIES, USSR. January 16, 1975. Arlington, Va., Joint Publications Research Service, 1975. 11p.

7
VLOS     Spain. Instituto de Estudios Politicos, Centro de Documentación, Madrid, 1974. LA ACTUAL REVISION DEL DERECHO DEL MAR: UNA PERSPECTIVA ESPANOLA. 2 Vols.

5,15,17
VOR      Spangler, Miller B. NEW TECHNOLOGY AND MARINE RESOURCE DEVELOPMENT; A STUDY IN GOVERNMENT-BUSINESS COOPERATION. New York, Praeger, 1970. xxxiii, 607p.

|  | ART |
| --- | --- |
| IIIF | Spangler, Miller B. U.S. PROJECTIONS OF SUPPLY AND DEMAND FOR FISHERY PRODUCTS. In Marine Technology Society. 7th Annual Conference, Washington, D.C., August 16-18, 1971. Washington, D.C., 1971. pp. 555-574. |

|  | *** |
| --- | --- |
| VLOS | SPECIAL REPORT: TRANSLATIONS ON LAW OF THE SEA. Worldwide 14. November 5, 1974. Arlington, Va., Joint Publications Research Service, November 5, 1974. 143p. |

|  | *** |
| --- | --- |
| VLOS | SPECIAL REPORT: TRANSLATIONS ON LAW OF THE SEA, WORLD WIDE. December 30, 1974. Arlington, Va., Joint Publications Research Service, 1974. 1, 72p. |

|  | *** |
| --- | --- |
| VLOS | SPECIAL REPORT: TRANSLATIONS ON LAW OF THE SEA, WORLDWIDE, JUNE 25, 1975. Arlington, Va., Joint Publications Research Service, 1975. 136p. |

|  | 13,16,17 |
| --- | --- |
| VENV | Spencer, Wallace H. ENVIRONMENTAL MANAGEMENT FOR PUGET SOUND: CERTAIN PROBLEMS OF POLITICAL ORGANIZATION AND ALTERNATIVE APPROACHES. Washington Sea Grant Program publication, WSG-MP 71-2. Seattle, University of Washington, 1971. 50p. |

|  | ART |
| --- | --- |
| IIIFV&G | Spinning, J.N. FISHERIES, VESSELS AND GEAR. In Pilot Chart. Washington, U.S. Defence Mapping Agency, Hydrographic Center, 1972. 16p. |

|  | 14 |
| --- | --- |
| VOR | Sporn, P. FRESH WATERS FROM SALINE WATERS. Oxford, Pergamon Press, 1966. |

|  | 13 |
| --- | --- |
| IIIAFF | Spotte, Stephen. FISH AND INVERTEBRATE CULTURE: WATER MANAGEMENT IN CLOSED SYSTEMS. New York, Wiley-Interscience, a Division of John Wiley and Sons, Inc., 1970. xiv, 145p. |

|  | 17 |
| --- | --- |
| IIWQ | Spring, Robert, Ira Spring, and Harvey Manning. THE KEY TO OUR ENVIRONMENT ... COOL, CLEAR WATER. Seattle, Superior Pub. Co., 1970. 174p. |

|  | 15 |
| --- | --- |
| VORM | Sprout, Harold H., and Margaret Sprout. THE RISE OF AMERICAN NAVAL POWER, 1776-1918. Princeton, Princeton University Press, 1967. |

|  | 14 |
| --- | --- |
| VOR | Sreenivasa Rao, Pemmaraju. THE PUBLIC ORDER OF OCEAN RESOURCES: A CRITIQUE OF THE CONTEMPORARY LAW OF THE SEA. Cambridge, Mass., MIT Press, 1975. 313p. |

|  | *** |
| --- | --- |
| IIIOI | Stansby, Maurice E. INDUSTRIAL FISHERY TECHNOLOGY. New York, Rheinhold Publishing Company, 1963. 393p. |

IIIP      Stanton, Philip B. OPERATION RESCUE. Report of the American Petroleum Institute. Washington, D.C., 1972. 32p.

VP        THE STATE OF MARINE POLLUTION IN THE MEDITERRANEAN AND LEGISLATIVE CONTROLS. Studies and Reviews no. 51. Rome, Food and Agriculture Organization of the United Nations, General Fisheries Council for the Mediterranean, 1972. 71p.

VOR       STATE, PUBLIC, AND PRIVATE RIGHTS, PRIVILEGES AND POWERS. Portland, University of Maine School of Law, 1970. 208p.

IVDRIL    Stavland, A. REGULATIONS FOR MOBILE DRILLING PLATFORMS TO BE ISSUED BY THE MARITIME DIRECTORATE IN NORWAY AND OTHER REGULATORY AGENCIES. Paper presented at Nor-Shipping '73. Fourth International Shipping Exhibition and Technical Symposium, May 10-11, 1973, Oslo, Norway, mimeo. n.p. 1973? 6p.

14

VENV      Stein, Robert E., ed. CRITICAL ENVIRONMENTAL ISSUES ON THE LAW OF THE SEA: A REPORT OF THE INTERNATIONAL INSTITUTE FOR ENVIRONMENT AND DEVELOPMENT, by Patricia W. Birnie, et al. Washington, International Institute for Environment and Development, 1975. 57p.

IIIOR     STEINBECK AND THE SEA. Proceedings of a Conference held at the Marine Science Center Auditorium, Newport Oregon, May, 1974. Corvallis, Oregon State University Sea Grant Program, 1974. 48p.

14a

VP        Steinhart, Carol E., and John S. Steinhart. BLOWOUT; A CASE STUDY OF THE SANTA BARBARA OIL SPILL. North Scituate, Mass., Duxbury Press, 1972. xvi, 138p.

ART

IICZM     Steinitz, Carl, and Douglas Way. A MODEL FOR EVALUATING VISUAL CONSEQUENCES OF URBANIZATION ON SHORELINE LANDSCAPES. In A Study of Resource Use in Urbanizing Watersheds. Plan formulation and evaluation studies. Washington, Department of the Army, Corps of Engineers, 1970.

IICONS    Stephen, Michael F., Paul J. Brown, et al. BEACH EROSION INVENTORY OF CHARLESTON COUNTY, SOUTH CAROLINA: A PRELIMINARY REPORT. SG-SC-75-4. Charleston, South Carolina Sea Grant Program, 1975. 79p.

2

VP        Stepp, James M., and H.M. Macaulay. THE POLLUTION PROBLEM. Washington, American Enterprise Institute for Public Policy Research, 1968. iii, 67p.

13

VP        Stevenage, England. Warren Spring Laboratory. OIL POLLUTION OF THE SEA AND SHORE; A STUDY OF REMEDIAL MEASURES. London, H.M.S.O., 1972. v, 32p.

|  |  |
|---|---|
| IVMMR | Stevens, T.H., and R.J. Kalter. ATLANTIC OUTER CONTINENTAL SHELF OIL AND GAS RESOURCES: BACKGROUND AND POLICY ISSUES. Albany, New York State University Sea Grant Program, 1974. 28p. *** |
| VP | Stewart, George. NOT SO RICH AS YOU THINK. New York, New American Library, 1970. 176p. 2 |
| VOR | Stewart, Harris, B., Jr. DEEP CHALLENGE. Princeton, N.J., Van Nostrand, 1966. 15 |
| IIWQ | Stewart, James M., ed. WATER SUPPLY AND WASTEWATER IN COASTAL AREAS. Reprint no. 83. Raleigh, North Carolina State University, UNC Sea Grant Program, 1976? 195p. *** |
| VOCET | Stewart, Robert W., and L.M. Dickie. AD MARE: CANADA LOOKS TO THE SEA; A STUDY ON MARINE SCIENCE AND TECHNOLOGY, BACKGROUND STUDY FOR THE SCIENCE COUNCIL OF CANADA. Science Council of Canada. Special study, 16. Ottawa, 1971. 175p. *** |
| VOCET | _____ _____ ÉTUDE SUR LES SCIENCES ET LA TECHNOLOGIE DE LA MER. Étude speciale no. 16. Ottawa, Information Canada, 1971. 189p. 17 |
| IICONS | Stirewalt, G.L., and Roy L. Ingram. AERIAL PHOTOGRAPHIC STUDY OF SHORELINE EROSION AND DEPOSITION, PAMLICO SOUND, NORTH CAROLINA. Sea Grant Program. Chapel Hill, University of North Carolina, 1974. iv, 66p. *** |
| VAC | Stockholm International Peace Research Institute. PROSPECTS FOR ARMS CONTROL IN THE OCEAN. Report no. 7, October, 1972. Stockholm, 1973? 5 |
| VAC | Stockholm International Peace Research Institute. SIPRI YEARBOOK OF WORLD ARMAMENTS AND DISARMAMENTS 1969/70. Stockholm, Almqvist and Wiksell; New York, Humanities Press, 1970. 5,15 |
| VAC | Stockholm International Peace Research Institute. TOWARDS A BETTER USE OF THE OCEAN: A STUDY AND PROGNOSIS. Stockholm, Almqvist and Wiksell, 1969. 231p. 7,16 |
| VOCET | Stockman, Robert H. THE INTERGOVERNMENTAL OCEANOGRAPHIC COMMISSION, AN UNCERTAIN FUTURE. WSG-74-3. Seattle, Division of Marine Resources, University of Washington, 1974. 119p. 1,9,13,16 |
| IIENV | Stone, James H. PRELIMINARY ASSESSMENTS OF THE ENVIRONMENTAL IMPACT OF A SUPERPORT ON THE SOUTHEASTERN COASTAL AREA OF LOUISIANA. Louisiana superport studies. Report 2. LSU-SG-72-05. Baton Rouge, Center for Wetland Resources, Louisiana State University, 1972. xxii, 345p. 13 |

16
VINTL    Strabolgi, J.M., and George Young. FREEDOM OF THE SEAS. New York, Liveright, 1928. 283p.

ART
IIREC    Strang, William A. RECREATION AND THE LOCAL ECONOMY: IMPLICATIONS FOR ECONOMIC AND RESOURCE PLANNING. In Marine Technology Society. 7th Annual Conference, Washington, D.C., August 16-18, 1971. pp. 509-521.

15
VORM     Strategy for Peace Conference. CONFERENCE TO PLAN A STRATEGY FOR PEACE. Report 1st- 1960- Muscatine, Iowa, Stanley Foundation.

***
IIIP     Straughan, D. BIOLOGICAL OCEANOGRAPHICAL SURVEY OF THE SANTA BARBARA CHANNEL OIL SPILL 1969-1970. Los Angeles, Calif., Allan Hancock Foundation, University of Southern California. 477p.

***
VENE     Strauss, A.M. SOLAR SEA POWER PLANTS (SSPP): A CRITICAL REVIEW AND SURVEY. NASA-TM-X-70783. U.S. National Aeronautics and Space Administration, 1974. 76p.

14a
IIWQ     Strickland, J.D.M., and T.R. Parsons. A PRACTICAL HANDBOOK OF SEAWATER ANALYSIS. Ottawa, Queen's Printer, 1968. 311p.

13
IIP      Strohbehn, Roger W., et al. LAWS AND INSTITUTIONAL MECHANISMS CONTROLLING RELEASE OF PESTICIDES INTO THE ENVIRONMENT. Pesticide study series -11. U.S. Environmental Protection Agency. Washington, U.S.G.P.O., n.d.

1,5,7,8,12,13
VINTL    Strohl, Mitchell P. THE INTERNATIONAL LAW OF BAYS. The Hague, Martinus Nijhoff, 1963. 426p.

***
IIOSTR   STRUCTURES IN THE OCEAN - FIXED AND FLOATING STRUCTURES OF STEEL AND CONCRETE IN HOSTILE SEAS. Berkeley, University of California, Continuing Education in Engineering, September 22, 1973.

***
VORM     STUDIES ON HUMAN PERFORMANCE IN THE SEA. Vol. 1. UNIHI-SEAGRANT-MR-76-01. Honolulu, University of Hawaii, 1975. 350p.

***
VENV     STUDY OF CRITICAL ENVIRONMENTAL PROBLEMS. WILLIAMS COLLEGE, 1970. MAN'S IMPACT ON THE GLOBAL ENVIRONMENT: ASSESSMENT AND RECOMMENDATIONS FOR ACTION; REPORT OF THE STUDY OF CRITICAL ENVIRONMENTAL PROBLEMS, JULY 1970. Cambridge, Mass., M.I.T. Press, 1970. xxii, 319p.

***
VCS      STUDY OF THE OUTER CONTINENTAL SHELF LANDS OF THE UNITED STATES. PUBLIC LAND LAW REVIEW COMMISSION. Los Angeles, Calif., Nossman, Waters, Scott, Kruger and Riordan, 1968. 2 Vols.

IIIF Suarez-Caabro, Jose A., and M.A. Rolon. STATUS OF FISHERIES IN PUERTO RICO, 1973. Cabo Rojo, PR., Department of Agriculture, 1974. 48p.

***

ART
IIIF Suda, A. TUNA FISHERIES AND THEIR RESOURCES IN THE INDIAN OCEAN. In Bernt Zeitzschel, ed. The biology of the Indian Ocean; proceedings of a symposium held at the University of Kiel, Germany from 31 March to 6 April, 1971 organized by the Scientific Committee on Oceanic Research and the Marine Productivity Section of the International Biological Programme, Berlin, Springer-Verlag, 1973. pp. 431-450.

11,18
IICZM Suher, Thomas, and Keith Hennessee. STATE AND FEDERAL JURISDICTIONAL CONFLICTS IN THE REGULATION OF UNITED STATES COASTAL WATERS. University of North Carolina Sea Grant publication UNC-SG-74-05. Chapel Hill, April, 1974. iv, 75p.

ART
IVMMR Sullivan, Robert J. OIL AND POLICE POWER IN ZONING. In Los Angeles Daily Journal, Report Section, February 27, 1968. pp. 7-17.

ART
IVENE Sullivan, Robert L. COMPARISON OF NORTH SEA GAS SALES CONTRACTS WITH U.S. TYPE CONTRACTS. In Society of Petroleum Engineers of AIME: Second Annual European Meeting. SPE 4328. n.p. 1973. 10p.

***
VP Sullivan, T.F.P., ed. POLLUTION CONTROL IN THE MARINE INDUSTRIES. Washington, D.C., International Association for Pollution Control, 1972. 400p.

***
VP _____ _____ POLLUTION CONTROL IN THE MARINE INDUSTRIES, 1973. Washington, D.C., International Association for Pollution Control, 1973. 407p.

***
IVOI A SUMMARY OF INDUSTRY OIL AND GAS ACTIVITIES OFFSHORE. Offshore Report 3/73. Canada, Resource Management and Conservation Branch, June 30, 1973. 27p.

***
IVM A SUMMARY OF INDUSTRY OIL AND GAS ACTIVITIES OFFSHORE. Offshore Report 4/73. Canada, Resource Management and Conservation Branch, August 31, 1973. 34p.

***
VMT SUMMARY REPORT: ANALYSIS OF THE ROLE OF THE INTRACOASTAL WATERWAY IN TEXAS. TAMV-SG-75-203. College Station, Texas A & M University, 1975.

13
IIIFV&G Sundstrom, Gustaf T. COMMERCIAL FISHING VESSELS AND GEAR. U.S. Department of the Interior. Fish and Wildlife Service. Bureau of Commercial Fisheries. Circular 48. Washington, U.S.G.P.O., 1957. 48p.

|  |  |
|---|---|
| | ***|
| VMT | SUPER OCEAN CARRIER CONFERENCE - THE MILLION TON CARRIER. Proceedings. San Pedro, Calif., 1974. n.p. 702p. |

***
VOSTR    A SURVEY OF UNIQUE TECHNICAL FEATURES OF THE FLOATING NUCLEAR POWER PLANT CONCEPT. Washington, U.S. Atomic Energy Commission, Directorate of Licensing, March, 1974. 105p.

3
VINTL    Surville, Fernand. COURS ELEMENTAIRE DE DROIT INTERNATIONAL PRIVE CONFORME AU PROGRAMME DES FACULTES DE DROIT. DROIT CIVIL. - PROCEDURE - DROIT COMMERCIAL. Paris, A. Rousseau, 1895. 636p.

ART
VP    Swan, Peter N. INTERNATIONAL AND NATIONAL APPROACHES TO OIL POLLUTION RESPONSIBILITY: AN EMERGING REGIME FOR A GLOBAL PROBLEM. Reprinted from Oregon Law Review, V. 50, Spring 1971. Eugene, Or., 1971. pp. 504-586.

1,5,7,9,12,14,15,16
VB    Swarztrauber, Sayre, A. THE THREE-MILE LIMIT OF TERRITORIAL SEAS. Annapolis, Naval Institute Press, 1972. xii, 316p.

***
IIOSTR    Swatzburg, I.P. CAPITAL COST ESTIMATE: FLOATING MARINE COMPLEX. Working Paper no. 2. Honolulu, University of Hawaii, 1973. 77p.

***
IICR    Symonds, Philip J. EQUITY AND EFFICIENCY IN STATE COASTAL RESOURCE MANAGEMENT: AN APPLICATION TO URBAN RECREATIONAL BOATING POLICY. USC-SG-2-75. Los Angeles, University of Southern California, 1975. 138p.

***
VP    SYMPOSIA ORGANIZED BY THE INSTITUTE OF WATER POLLUTION CONTROL. Proceedings. The Trent Research Programme, Nottingham, 1971; Water Pollution by Oil, Aviemore, Scotland, 1970; Water Pollution Control in Coastal Areas, Bournemouth, 1970; Farm Wastes, Newcastle-upon-Tyne, 1970; The Sewerage (Scotland) Act 1968, Edinburgh, 1970; Pollution by Synthetic Detergents: Towards a Solution, Torquay, 1967; Conservation and Reclamation of Water, London, 1967; Trade Wastes, Birmingham, 1957; The Evolution and Development of the Activated-Sludge Process, Blackpool, 1954. Maidstone, Kent, England, Institute of Water Pollution Control. n.d.

11
IIINTL    Symposium. LAW OF THE SEA - IMPLICATIONS FOR COASTAL STATES. Houston, Texas Law Institute of Coastal and Marine Resources, University of Houston, 1973.

5,17
VOR    SYMPOSIUM ON INVESTIGATIONS AND RESOURCES OF THE CARIBBEAN SEA AND ADJACENT REGIONS. Willemstad, Curacao, 1968. Reports and abstracts of papers edited by the Marine Biology and Environment Branch of the Food and Agriculture Organization of the United Nations. FAO fisheries report no. 71.1. Rome, FAO, 1969. 165p.

|     | ***                                                                                                                                                                                                                        |
| --- | -------------------------------------------------------------------------------------------------------------------------------------------------------------------------------------------------------------------------- |
| VP  | SYMPOSIUM ON MARINE POLLUTION, LONDON, 1973. PROCEEDINGS. London, Royal Institution of Naval Architects, 1973. 106p.                                                                                                       |

15,17
VMMR   SYMPOSIUM ON MINERAL RESOURCES OF THE WORLD OCEAN, NAVAL WAR COLLEGE, 1968. Proceedings. Occasional publication no. 4. Kingston, University of Rhode Island, 1968. 108p.

***
VP   SYMPOSIUM ON PREVENTION OF MARINE POLLUTION FROM SHIPS, HELD IN ACAPULCO, MEXICO, MARCH 22-31, 1976. Proceedings. London, Intergovernmental Maritime Consultative Organisation, 1976.

15
IIE   A SYMPOSIUM ON THE BIOLOGICAL SIGNIFICANCE OF ESTUARIES, HOUSTON, TEXAS, FEBRUARY 1970. Sponsored by the Sport Fishing Institute in cooperation with the Sportsmen's Clubs of Texas, Inc., and the National Wildlife Federation. Washington, D.C., Sport Fishing Institute, 1971. xi, 111p.

13,15,17
VOR   SYMPOSIUM ON THE EXPLORATION AND EXPLOITATION OF THE SEA-BED AND ITS SUBSOIL, STRASBOURG, DECEMBER 3-5, 1970. PROCEEDINGS. Document number AS/Coll Mer (70) 1. Council of Europe, 1970. Consultative Assembly.

***
VOC   SYMPOSIUM ON THE EXPLORATION AND EXPLOITATION OF THE SEA-BED AND ITS SUBSOIL, HELD IN STRASBOURG, FRANCE, DECEMBER 3-5, 1970. Organized by Council of Europe, Consultative Assembly, Papers. New York, U.S. and World Publications, Inc., Manhattan Publishing Company, 1971. 292p.

7
VP   Symposium on the Scientific and Engineering Aspects of Oil Pollution of the Sea, Cambridge, Mass., 1969. OIL ON THE SEA. Cambridge, M.I.T., 1970.

***
IIIF   SYMPOSIUM - THE FIRST ANNUAL MARINE RECREATIONAL FISHERIES SYMPOSIUM, HELD IN NEW ORLEANS, LA., ON FEBRUARY 27, 1976. Proceedings. Savannah, Ga., National Coalition for Marine Conservation, 1976?

3
VMLAD   Szirmai, Zsolt, and J.D. Korevaar, eds. THE MERCHANT SHIPPING CODE OF THE SOVIET UNION. Leyden, A.W. Sijthoff, 1960. 151p.

5,12,16,17
VLOS   Sztucki, Jerzy, ed. SYMPOSIUM ON THE INTERNATIONAL REGIME OF THE SEA-BED, ROME, 1969, ISTITUTE AFFARI INTERNAZIONALI. PROCEEDINGS. Rome, Academia nazionale dei Lincei, 1970. xvi, 767p.

13
VENV   Tait, R.V. ELEMENTS OF MARINE ECOLOGY: AN INTRODUCTORY COURSE. Revised by R.S. de Santo. London, Butterworth and Co.; New York, Springer Verlag, 1972. 327p.

                                                                                      1
VINTL      Takabayashi, Hideo. HISTORICAL STUDY OF THE REGIME OF THE TERRITO-
           RIAL SEA. Tokyo, Yushindo Co., 1968. 303p. In Japanese.

                                                                                    ***
IIOSTR     Talkington, H.R. THE FLOATING STABLE PLATFORM: TRANSFERRING NAVY
           TECHNOLOGY TO CIVILIAN APPLICATIONS. San Diego, Naval Undersea Re-
           search and Development Center, 1973. 17p.

                                                                                    ***
VORM       Tangsubkul, Phiphat. LA POLITIQUE THAI'LANDAISE DE MISE EN VALEUR
           DU GOLFE DU SIAM. Thèse. Marseille. Aix-Marseille. Université.
           Unites d'Enseignment et Recherche de Droit et Science Politique,
           1972. 247p.

                                                                                    ***
IIIF       Tanzania, Fisheries Division. ANNUAL REPORTS, 1965-1972. Dar es
           Salaam, 1972.

                                                                                     13
IIIP       Tarzwell, Clarence M., et al. BIOLOGICAL PROBLEMS IN WATER POLLU-
           TION. Third seminar 1962. PB 168 784. Cincinnati, Ohio, U.S. De-
           partment of Health, Education and Welfare, 1965. ix, 315p.

                                                                                    ***
VB         Taska, A. DIE GRENZEN DES KUESTENMEERES ESTLANDS. Kiel, Inaug.-
           Diss, 1974. 156p.

                                                                                    ART
IIIP       Taylor, Gordon Rattray. THE THREAT TO LIFE IN THE SEA. In Saturday
           Review, v.53, no. 31, Aug. 1, 1970. New York, 1970. pp. 40-42.

                                                                                     16
VENV       Teclaff, Ludwik A., and Albert E. Utton, eds. INTERNATIONAL ENVIRON-
           MENTAL LAW. New York, Praeger, 1974. viii, 270p.

                                                                                    ***
IICZM      Terpstra, H., et al. SEASHORES AND COASTS: CHALLENGE IN SHORELINE
           DEVELOPMENT AND CONSERVATION. Berkeley, University of California,
           1968.

                                                                                    ***
VENV       Ternisien, J.A., comp. PRECIS GENERAL DES NUISANCES: NUISANCES
           DUES AUX ACTIVITES INDUSTRIELLES. Bibliotheque de l'Environment.
           Vol. 2. Paris, Guy Le Prat, 1971. 355p.

                                                                                    ***
IIIAFF     Terry, Orville W. AQUACULTURE. Albany, State University of New
           York, New York, Sea Grant Institute, 1975.

                                                                                    ***
IIIAFF     _____ THE NEW YORK AQUACULTURE PROGRAM - PAST, PRESENT AND
           FUTURE. Albany, State University of New York, Sea Grant Institute,
           1974. 18p.

                                                                                     15
VSUB       Terry, Richard D. THE CASE FOR THE DEEP SUBMERSIBLE. Anaheim,
           Calif., Autonetics, 1964.

|  |  |
|---|---|
| VOCET | Terry, Richard D. OCEANOGRAPHY; ITS TOOLS, METHODS, RESOURCES, AND APPLICATIONS. Downey, Calif., Autonetics, 1961. xv, 347p. Vol. 1.     15 |
| VOCET | Terry, Richard G., ed. OCEAN ENGINEERING; A PRELIMINARY REPORT SUBMITTED TO THE CHAIRMAN OF THE INTERAGENCY COMMITTEE OF OCEANOGRAPHY BY THE NATIONAL SECURITY INDUSTRIAL ASSOCIATION. Corrected. North Hollywood, Calif., distributed by Western Periodicals Company, Washington, 1966. 4 Vols.     5,15 |
| VINTL | Tesauro, Giuseppe. L'INQUINAMENTO MARINO NEL DIRITTO INTERNAZIONALE. Milano, Dott. A. Giuffre Editore, 1971. 232p.     *** |
| VINTL | Testa, Carlos. LE DROIT PUBLIC INTERNATIONAL MARITIME. PRINCIPES GENERAUX - REGLES PRATIQUES. Paris, G. Pedone-Lauriel, 1886. vi, 2, 347p.     3 |
| IICZM | Texas. Governor's Advisory Committee on Marine Resources. GOALS FOR TEXAS IN THE COASTAL ZONE AND THE SEA. Sea Grant publications 105, 107, 109-110, 112, 114-115. Houston, 1970. 8 Vols.     17 |
| IICZM | Texas. Interagency Natural Resources Council. THE COASTAL RESOURCES MANAGEMENT PROGRAM OF TEXAS; A SUMMARY. A report to the 62d Texas Legislature. Austin, Texas, 1970.     5,13 |
| IICZM | Texas. SUMMARY OF SELECTED LEGISLATION RELATING TO THE COASTAL ZONE. Texas Law Institute of Coastal and Marine Resources, University of Houston, n.d.     11 |
| IICZM | Texas. University. Division of Natural Resources and the Environment. BAY AND ESTUARINE SYSTEM MANAGEMENT IN THE TEXAS COASTAL ZONE: PHASE II; A CONCEPTUAL REPORT. Prepared for: Office of the Governor, Division of Planning Coordination; Coastal Resources Management Program and the Interagency Council on Natural Resources and the Environment. Austin, 1973.     *** |
| IICZM | _____ A CONCEPTUAL REPORT ON THE MANAGEMENT OF BAY AND ESTUARINE SYSTEMS - PHASE I. Austin, Division of Natural Resources and the Environment, 1972.     *** |
| IICZM | Texas. University. Bates College of Law. MARINE RESOURCES: THE LAW AND ADMINISTRATION OF THE COASTAL ZONE. MARINE RESOURCES INSTITUTE, MAY 18-19, 1970. Houston, 1970. 12p.     6 |
| IICZM | Texas. University. Center for Research in Water Resources. ESTABLISHMENT OF OPERATIONAL GUIDELINES FOR TEXAS COASTAL ZONE MANAGEMENT. Austin, 1975. 218p.     *** |

                                                                    13
VOR         Texas A&M University. PROCEEDINGS, FIFTH NATIONAL SEA GRANT CON-
            FERENCE. TAMU-SG-73-101. College Station, Texas, Department of
            Marine Resources Information, Center for Marine Resources, 1973.
            xii, 251p.

                                                                     5
IICZM       _____ Agricultural Extension Service. COASTAL LAND RE-
            SOURCES CONFERENCE, JUNE, 1970.

                                                                   ***
IIIAFF      _____ Department of Wildlife and Fisheries Sciences. PRO-
            CEEDINGS OF THE FISH FARMING CONFERENCE ANNUAL CONVENTION, CATFISH
            FARMERS OF TEXAS. College Station, 1974. 98p.

                                                                    13
IIDR        Texas A&M University. Center for Dredging Studies. PROCEEDINGS OF
            THE 3rd DREDGING SEMINAR, NOVEMBER 20, 1970. Sea Grant publication
            no. TAMU-SG-71-109. Center for Dredging Studies report no. 148.
            College Station, Texas, 1971. 88p.

                                                                    13
IIP&H       Texas A&M University. College of Architecture and Environmental
            Design. Architecture Research Center. PORT AND HARBOR DEVELOPMENT
            SYSTEM. Phase 1 - Design guidelines work report. TAMU-SG-71-216.
            College Station, 1971. 140p.

                                                                   ***
IICZM       Texas A&M University. The Environmental Engineering Division.
            Civil Engineering Department. WASTE MANAGEMENT IN THE TEXAS COAST-
            AL ZONE. A conceptual report. Prepared for the Office of the Gov-
            ernor, Division of Planning Coordination, Coastal Resources Manage-
            ment Program, Interagency Council on Natural Resources and the En-
            vironment of Texas. College Station, March, 1973.

                                                                   8,18
VB          Texas A&M University. Sea Grant Program. LAW AND THE COASTAL MAR-
            GIN; SELECTED PAPERS FROM THE LAW AND THE COASTAL MARGIN WORKSHOP,
            SPONSORED BY GULF UNIVERSITIES RESEARCH CORPORATION. College Sta-
            tion, 1970. 83p.

                                                                   ***
IIDR        _____ PROCEEDINGS OF THE 6th DREDGING SEMINAR. TAMU-SG-74-
            104. College Station, 1974. 99p.

                                                                    16
VOR         _____ A SUMMARY OF RECENT TEXAS ACTS AND RESOLUTIONS RELATED
            TO MARINE RESOURCE DEVELOPMENT. College Station, Texas, 1970. 12p.

                                                                    14
IICZM       TEXAS COASTAL MANAGEMENT PROGRAM. AUTHORITY OF GOVERNMENTAL ENTI-
            TIES IN THE TEXAS COASTAL ZONE. Austin, Texas, General Land Office,
            1975. 94p.

                                                                    14
IICZM       TEXAS COASTAL MANAGEMENT PROGRAM, SECOND YEAR WORK PROGRAM. Austin,
            Tex., General Land Office, Coastal Management Program, 1975. 47p.

| | | 13 |
|---|---|---|
IICZM    TEXAS COASTAL ZONE LEGISLATION. Austin, Texas Council on Marine-related affairs, 1973.

VORM    Texas Council on Marine-related Affairs. A BRIEF RECAPITULATION COVERING SOME OF THE MAJOR COASTAL AND MARINE-RELATED ACTIVITIES OF THE 63d LEGISLATURE OF TEXAS. Austin, 1973. 5p.
[13]

IICZM    Texas Law Institute of Coastal and Marine Resources. THE BEACHES. PUBLIC RIGHTS AND PRIVATE USE. Proceedings of a Conference, January 15, 1972. University of Houston, n.d. iii, 74p.
[11,13]

IICZM    _____ _____ COMPARATIVE ASPECTS OF COASTAL ZONE MANAGEMENT. Background information on the law of Texas and other states in view of the Coastal Zone Management Act of 1972. TAMU-SG-73-607. Houston, Bates College of Law, 1973. 34p.
[13,16]

IICZM    _____ _____ SUMMARY OF SELECTED LEGISLATION RELATING TO THE COASTAL ZONE; a report prepared for the Coastal Resources Management Program, Office of the Governor, by the Texas Law Institute of Coastal and Marine Resources. Houston, Bates College of Law, 1972. 111p.
[2,12,16]

VOR    THE TEXAS LAW INSTITUTE REPORTER. Houston, Texas Law Institute of Coastal and Marine Resources, University of Houston, 1974-
[11]

VORM    Texas Transportation Institute. TRANSPORTATION IN THE TEXAS COASTAL ZONE; A CONCEPTUAL REPORT. Prepared for the Office of the Governor. Austin, 1973.
***

IIIAFF    TEXTBOOK OF FISH CULTURE: BREEDING AND CULTIVATION OF FISH. Translated by Henry Kahn. Surrey, England, West Byfleet, Fishing News (Books) Ltd., 1970. 436p.
[13]

VLOS    Thacher, P.S. THE UNITED NATIONS SEA-BED COMMITTEE DISCUSSIONS: A REVIEW. Paper at Institute of Ocean Law Conference on Coastal Zone and Ocean Law: Problems of the User. Miami, Florida. December 10-12, 1969.
[16]

VORM    Theberge, James D., ed. SOVIET SEAPOWER IN THE CARIBBEAN: POLITICAL AND STRATEGIC IMPLICATIONS. New York, Praeger Publishers, 1972.
[15]

IIOSTR    THEORETICAL INVESTIGATIONS AND OPTIMIZATION OF THE PLATFORM'S SEAKEEPING CHARACTERISTICS. By Ludwig H. Seidl. Honolulu, University of Hawaii, 1973. vii, 100p.
***

VP    THERMAL DISCHARGE: ENGINEERING AND ECOLOGY. Thermo-Fluids Conference. Sydney, Australia, Institution of Engineers, 1972? 134p.
***

                                                              ***
IIIOI    Thomas, F.B., et al. DEVELOPMENT, FUNCTION AND OPERATION OF THE
         COASTAL SEAFOOD LABORATORY. UNC-SG-73-18. Raleigh, North Carolina
         State University, 1973.

                                                              13,18
VORM     Thomas, Fran. LAW IN ACTION: LEGAL FRONTIERS FOR NATURAL RESOURCES
         PLANNING; THE WORK OF PROFESSOR JACOB H. BEUSCHER, INCLUDING A
         BIBLIOGRAPHY OF HIS PUBLISHED WORK. Madison, Land Economics Jour-
         nal, University of Wisconsin-Madison, 1972. xiv, 93p.

                                                              ***
VORM     Thomas, Russel S. 1975 LEGISLATION RELATING TO MARINE RESOURCES OF
         NEW YORK. Albany, State University of New York, Sea Grant Insti-
         tute, 1975. 38p.

                                                              17
VENV     Thomas, William A., ed. INDICATORS OF ENVIRONMENTAL QUALITY. En-
         vironmental science research. New York, Plenum Press, 1972. x,
         275p. Vol. 1.

                                                              1,5
VINTL    Thommen, Thamarappallil K. LEGAL STATUS OF GOVERNMENT MERCHANT
         SHIPS IN INTERNATIONAL LAW. The Hague, Nijhoff, 1962. 177p.

                                                              ***
IIWQ     Thompson, J.A.J., and F.T. McGomas. DISTRIBUTION OF MERCURY IN THE
         SEDIMENTS AND WATERS OF HOWE SOUND, BRITISH COLUMBIA. Technical
         Report no. 396. Canada, Fisheries Research Board, 1973.

                                                              13
IIENV    Thompson, John R. ECOLOGICAL EFFECTS OF OFFSHORE DREDGING AND BEACH
         NOURISHMENT: A REVIEW. Miscellaneous paper no. 1-73. Springfield,
         National Technical Information Service, 1973.

                                                              5,13
IIIF     Thompson, Robert N., ed. PROCEEDINGS, FROM OREGON'S 1971 NATIONAL
         DISCUSSION FORUM. Marine fisheries resources. Corvallis, Or., 1972.
         x, 235p.

                                                              ***
IIP&H    Thor, Gary, and Gary Haagen. AN ENVIRONMENTAL HEALTH SURVEY OF
         MARINAS AND BOATING IN WESTERN WASHINGTON. Olympia, Wash., Office
         of Environmental Programs, Housing and Recreation Section, 1970.

                                                              16
VOR      Thors, Thor. TO WHAT EXTENT IS APPROPRIATION OF THE SEA POSSIBLE
         OR LEGAL? Unpublished paper submitted for Professor Sohn's course,
         Government 270. Cambridge, Harvard University, 1955.

                                                              ART
IIIF     THREE ASPECTS OF INTERACTION CONCERNING THE PACIFIC SKIPJACK TUNA
         FISHERY. In Marine Affairs Journal, Report no. 3. Narragansett,
         University of Rhode Island, 1975.

                                                              ***
IICZM    Tilley, Steve. CITIZEN PARTICIPATION IN NORTH CAROLINA'S COASTAL
         AREA MANAGEMENT PROGRAM. Raleigh, North Carolina State University,
         Center for Marine and Coastal Studies, 1974.

IICZM   Tilley, William S. PLANNING FOR NORTH CAROLINA'S COASTAL INLETS: AN ANALYSIS OF THE PRESENT PROCESS AND RECOMMENDATIONS FOR THE FUTURE. Raleigh, N.C., North Carolina State University, Center for Marine and Coastal Studies, 1973. 58p. [14]

VORM    Tjassens, Johan. ZEE-POLITE FRT VEREENICHDE NEDERLANDEN VERTHOONT IN EEN TAFEL. In's Graven'hage, I. Veely, 1652. 18, 276p. [3]

VP      Tobias, Leo, et al. FEASIBILITY STUDY OF THE SAND METHOD OF COMBATTING A MAJOR OIL SPILL IN THE OCEAN ENVIRONMENT. Final report, Washington, D.C., U.S. Army Corps of Engineers, 1971. 35p. ***

IICZM   Todd, C.F., Jr. THE COASTAL ZONE: PROBLEMS WITH MAN'S USES. Rand Paper Series P-5081. Santa Monica, Calif., Rand Corporation. 1973. 15p. ***

VLOS    Tolentino, Arturo M. Philippine Delegation. THIRD UNITED NATIONS CONFERENCE ON THE LAW OF THE SEA. SECOND COMMITTEE STATEMENT ON ITEM 16: ARCHIPELAGOS. n.p. August 12, 1974. 7p. [13]

IIIF    Tollefson, Roger, et al. A SUMMARY OF FISHERY STATISTICS OF THE PACIFIC COAST. Prepared for Northwest Pulp and Paper Association. n.p. 1959. 182p. [14a]

VCONS   Tomasevich, J. INTERNATIONAL AGREEMENTS ON CONSERVATION OF MARINE RESOURCES, WITH SPECIAL REFERENCE TO THE NORTH PACIFIC. Reprint of 1943 ed. Kraus Reprints, n.d. Millwood, N.Y. [5,14]

IICZM   TOOLS FOR COASTAL ZONE MANAGEMENT, WASHINGTON, D.C., 1972. PROCEEDINGS. Marine Technology Society. 213p. [15,17]

IIWQ    Touhill, C.J. DEMONSTRATION OF A STATE WATER QUALITY MANAGEMENT INFORMATION SYSTEM. Prepared for Washington Environmental Research Center, U.S. Environmental Protection Agency. Harrisburg, Pa., Bureau of Water Quality Management, 1974. vii, 129p. ***

VP      TOVALOP. (Tanker Owners Voluntary Agreement concerning Liability for Oil Pollution) TOVALOP: EXPLANATORY MEMORANDUM - QUESTIONS AND ANSWERS; THE TANKER OWNERS VOLUNTARY AGREEMENT CONCERNING LIABILITY FOR OIL POLLUTION (TOVALOP); THE MEMORANDUM AND ARTICLES OF ASSOCIATION OF THE INTERNATIONAL TANKER OWNERS POLLUTION FEDERATION LTD.; THE INTERNATIONAL TANKER INDEMNITY ASSOCIATION COMPANY ACT, 1968; THE RULES OF THE INTERNATIONAL TANKER INDEMNITY ASSOCIATION LTD.; THE BYE-LAWS OF THE INTERNATIONAL TANKER INDEMNITY ASSOCIATION LTD. London? 1969? International Legal Materials, Vol. 8, 1969. p. 497. [1]

VOR     TOWARD A BETTER USE OF THE OCEANS; A STUDY AND PROGNOSIS. Symposium held in Stockholm, June 10-14, 1968. Stockholm, SIPRI, 1968. 322p. [15,16]

|     |     |
| --- | --- |
| VOR | ***<br>TOWARD A BETTER USE OF THE OCEAN; A STUDY AND PROGNOSIS. Stockholm, Almqvist and Wiksell; New York, Humanities Press, 1969. 231p. |
| VENV | 13<br>Train, Russell E. ECOLOGY AND ECONOMY: TWO HOUSEHOLD WORDS. An address to the New York Chamber of Commerce and Industry, October 3, 1974. Washington, D.C., Environmental Protection Agency. 15p. |
| VLOS | ***<br>TRANSLATIONS ON THE LAW OF THE SEA. Arlington, Va., Joint Publication Research Service, I- |
| VT&L | ***<br>TREATY BETWEEN THE KINGDOM OF THE NETHERLANDS AND THE FEDERAL REPUBLIC OF GERMANY ON THE DELIMITATION OF THE CONTINENTAL SHELF UNDER THE NORTH SEA. Washington, U.S. Department of Commerce, National Marine Fisheries Service, Division of Foreign Fisheries, 1971? |
| IIIF | 13<br>Trefethen, Parker S. FISH PASSAGE RESEARCH - REVIEW OF PROGRESS, 1961-1966. Circular 254. Washington, U.S. Department of the Interior, U.S. Fish and Wildlife Service, Bureau of Commercial Fisheries, 1968. iii, 24p. |
| IIIFP | 14a<br>Tressler, Donald K., et al. MARINE PRODUCTS OF COMMERCE; THEIR ACQUISITION, HANDLING, BIOLOGICAL ASPECTS, AND THE SCIENCE AND TECHNOLOGY OF THEIR PREPARATION AND PRESERVATION. 2d ed., rev. and enl. New York, Book Division, Reinhold, 1951. xiii, 782p. |
| IIP&H | ***<br>Trisko, Ralph L., et al. U.S. DEEPWATER PORT STUDY. Washington, D.C., U.S. Technical Information Service, 1972. V Vols. |
| VOCET | ***<br>Troup, K.D., ed. NORSPEC 70, LONDON: THE NORTH SEA SPECTRUM; PROCEEDINGS OF A CONFERENCE ON THE SHIPS, MATERIALS, EQUIPMENT AND THE PROBLEMS INVOLVED IN THE EXPLOITATION OF THE NORTH SEA. London, Thomas Reed Publications, 1971. 259p. |
| VCS | 1,13<br>Trumbull, James V.A. ATLANTIC CONTINENTAL SHELF AND SLOPE OF THE UNITED STATES - SAND-SIZE FRACTION OF BOTTOM SEDIMENTS, NEW JERSEY TO NOVA SCOTIA. Geological Survey professional paper 529-K. Washington, U.S.G.P.O., 1972. iii, K45p. |
| VENV | 14<br>Trzyna, Thaddeus C., and Arthur W. Jokela. THE CALIFORNIA ENVIRONMENTAL QUALITY ACT: AN INNOVATION IN STATE AND LOCAL DECISION MAKING. Environmental Studies series, no. 5. Claremont, Calif., Center for California Public Affairs, 1974. ix, 135p. |
| VENV | 15<br>Tucker, Edwin W. TEXT, CASES, PROBLEMS ON LEGAL REGULATION OF THE ENVIRONMENT. St. Paul, West Publishing Company, 1972. |

|         |                                                                                                                                                                                                                                    |
|---------|--------------------------------------------------------------------------------------------------------------------------------------------------------------------------------------------------------------------------------------|

                                                                       \*\*\*

IVMMR      Tucker, P.W. THE PROSPECTS FOR NORTH SEA NATURAL GAS. Paper presented at the North Sea Conference. Mimeo. n.p. 1972? 15p.

                                                                       ART

IICONS     TUG ASSISTANCE BILL. MARINE SHORELINE EROSION AND PROTECTION. <u>In</u> Pacific Northwest Sea; Vol. 8, no. 3, 1975. Seattle, Wash., Oceanographic Commission of Washington, 1975. 15p.

                                                                      14,14a

VOCET      Turekian, Karl K. OCEANS. Englewood Cliffs, N.J., Prentice-Hall, 1968. viii, 120p.

                                                                        15

IIENV      Turekian, Karl K., et al. MARINE SEDIMENTS, NEW HAVEN HARBOR, CONNECTICUT: RESULTS OF ANALYSES AND PROPOSALS FOR DREDGE SPOILS DISPOSAL; ADDENDUM 12 OF THE ENVIRONMENTAL REPORT, COKE WORKS SITE, JUNE 1971. Manchester, New Hampshire, Normandeau Associates, January 1972. vii, 134p.

                                                                        15

IIIOR      Tussing, Arlon R., ed. ALASKA FISHERIES POLICY; ECONOMICS, RESOURCES, AND MANAGEMENT. Fairbanks, Institute of Social, Economic and Government Research, 1972. ix, 470p.

                                                                 1,5,13,14

IIIINTL    Tussing, Arlon R., et al. FISHERIES OF THE INDIAN OCEAN; ISSUES OF INTERNATIONAL MANAGEMENT AND LAW OF THE SEA. RFF/PISFA paper 5. Washington, D.C., Resources for the Future, 1974. xiv, 55p.

                                                                      16

IIIINTL    _____ FISHERIES OF THE INDIAN OCEAN: ISSUES OF INTERNATIONAL MANAGEMENT AND LAW OF THE SEA. Washington, Resources for the Future, 1974. xiv, 55p.

                                                                      16

IIIF       Tussing, Arlon R., et al, eds. ALASKA FISHERIES POLICY: ECONOMICS, RESOURCES, AND MANAGEMENT. ISEGR report no. 33. Fairbanks, Institute of Social, Economic and Government Research, University of Alaska, 1972. ix, 470p.

                                                                    \*\*\*

IIIFV&G    Tyler, J., and M. McKenzie. TO CATCH A MILLION FISH: NORTH CAROLINA COMMERCIAL FISHING GEAR AND METHODS. UNC-SG-73-05. Raleigh, University of North Carolina, 1973. 19p.

                                                                    15

VOCET      UNDERSEA TECHNOLOGY; HANDBOOK DIRECTORY, 1968-   Arlington, Va., Compass Publications, 1968-

                                                                    \*\*\*

VOCET      UNDERWATER ARCHEOLOGY, A NASCENT DISCIPLINE. New York, UNIPUB, 1972. 306p.

                                                                      ART

VSUB       UNDERWATER VEHICLE OPERATIONS. CONFERENCE PAPERS. <u>In</u> Oceanology International 72 Conference, Brighton, England, 1972. London, 1972. pp. 225-285.

                                                                  ***
IIIOSTR    Unger, I., and E.C. Bolster. ARTIFICIAL REEFS: A REVIEW. American
           Littoral Society special publication no. 4. Highlands, N.J. 1966.

                                                                    1
VB         Union Research Service. Hong Kong. COMMUNIST CHINA'S TERRITORIAL
           WATERS. In Hong Kong, Union Research Service, Vol. 8, no. 20,
           September 6, 1957.

                                                                   13
VOR        United Kingdom Atomic Energy Authority. DESALINATION AND ITS ROLE
           IN WATER SUPPLY. Prepared for British Information Services. London,
           Headly Brothers Ltd., 1967. 103p.

                                                                  ***
IVMMR      UK OFFSHORE OIL AND GAS YEARBOOK 1974/75. London, Kogan Page Limi-
           ted, 1974. 291p.

                                                                  ***
IVMMR      UK OFFSHORE OIL AND GAS YEARBOOK 1975-1976. 2d ed. New York, In-
           ternational Publications Service, 1975. 320p. 47.50.


------     UNITED NATIONS DOCUMENTS. To find these materials please consult
           United Nations Yearbook; Monthly Chronicle, etc. Only a very few
           selected materials are included here.

                                                                  ***
VOI        United Nations. MODERNIZATION AND MECHANIZATION OF SALT INDUSTRIES
           BASED ON SEAWATER IN DEVELOPING COUNTRIES. Proceedings of Expert
           Group Meeting, Rome, 25-29 September 1968. New York, UNIPUB, 1970.
           161p.

                                                                  ***
VENE       _____ _____ PROCEEDINGS OF THE INTERGOVERNMENTAL MEETING ON THE
           IMPACT OF THE CURRENT ENERGY CRISIS ON THE ECONOMY OF THE ESCAP RE-
           GION. E.75.II.F.7. New York, UNIPUB, 1974, 229p.

                                                               7,12,14
VAC        _____ _____ SEA-BED - A FRONTIER OF DISARMAMENT. New York? 1972.
           20p.

                                                               7,13,14
VLOS       United Nations. General Assembly. Committee on the Peaceful Uses
           of the Sea-bed and the Ocean Floor Beyond the Limits of National
           Jurisdiction. REPORT. UNGA 24th sess. A/7622. New York, United
           Nations, 1969. 161p.
                      _____ _____ ADDENDUM...Supp. no. 22A.

                                                               7,13,14
VLOS       _____ _____ REPORT. A/872. New York, United Nations, 1972.
           vii, 251p.

                                                                    1
VP         United Nations. Office of Public Information. THE HUMAN ENVIRON-
           MENT... MARINE POLLUTION - POTENTIAL CATASTROPHE. New York, Uni-
           ted Nations, April, 1971. 24p.

VLOS  United Nations. Secretary-General. ECONOMIC IMPLICATIONS OF SEA-BED MINERAL DEVELOPMENT IN THE INTERNATIONAL AREA. United Nations document A/Conf.62/25. New York, United Nations, 1974. 92p.

17
VP  UNITED NATIONS CONFERENCE ON THE HUMAN ENVIRONMENT, STOCKHOLM, 1972. IDENTIFICATION AND CONTROL OF POLLUTANTS EMANATING FROM SHIPS, VESSELS AND OTHER EQUIPMENT OPERATING IN THE MARINE ENVIRONMENT. New York, 1971. 7, 1p.

1,5,7,13,14
VLOS  UNITED NATIONS CONFERENCE ON THE LAW OF THE SEA, 3d, NEW YORK AND CARACAS, 1973-1974. THIRD UNITED NATIONS CONFERENCE ON THE LAW OF THE SEA: OFFICIAL RECORDS. New York, United Nations, 1975- 3 Vols.

VOCET  United Nations Educational, Scientific and Cultural Organization. INTERNATIONAL DECADE OF OCEAN EXPLORATION (IDOE) 1971-1980. New York, UNIPUB, 1974. 87p.

IIIOR  _____ PROCEEDINGS OF THE SYMPOSIUM ON THE OCEANOGRAPHY AND FISHERIES OF THE TROPICAL ATLANTIC, ABIDJAN, IVORY COAST, 20-28 OCTOBER, 1966. Results of the ICITA and of the GTS, organized through the joint efforts of UNESCO, FAO, and OAU. Review Papers and Contributions. New York, UNESCO, 1969. 430p.

IIIOR  _____ SYMPOSIUM ON INVESTIGATIONS AND RESOURCES OF THE CARIBBEAN SEA AND ADJACENT REGIONS PREPARATORY TO THE CO-OPERATIVE INVESTIGATIONS OF THE CARIBBEAN AND ADJACENT REGIONS (CICAR), ORGANIZED JOINTLY BY UNESCO AND FAO, WILLEMSTAD, CURAÇAO, NETHERLANDS ANTILLES, 18-26 NOVEMBER, 1968. Papers on Physical and Chemical Oceanography, Marine Biology. New York, UNESCO, 1971. 545p.

1,5,13,14
VODAS  _____ Secretariat. LEGAL PROBLEMS ASSOCIATED WITH OCEAN DATA ACQUISITION SYSTEMS (ODAS). A study of existing national and international legislation, prepared jointly by the Secretariats of UNESCO and IMCO, 1962-68. Revised under the authority of and with the assistance of the IOC Group of Experts on the Legal Status of Ocean Data Acquisition Systems. Intergovernmental Oceanographic Commission technical series. Paris, UNESCO, 1969. 40p.

IIIAFF  United Nations. Food and Agricultural Organization. FAO AQUACULTURE BULLETIN. NEWS DIGEST OF AQUACULTURE RESEARCH AND DEVELOPMENT. Rome, FAO, 1968-

VEZ  _____ LIMITS AND STATUS OF THE TERRITORIAL SEA, EXCLUSIVE FISHING ZONES, FISHERY CONSERVATION ZONES AND THE CONTINENTAL SHELF (WITH PARTICULAR REFERENCE TO FISHERIES). FAO Legislative Series, 8. Rome, FAO, 1969. 32p. and addendum.

IIIF  _____ WORLD FISHERIES ABSTRACTS. Rome, FAO, 1950-

***
VENE     United Nations Institute for Training and Research. ENERGY CRISIS AND THE FUTURE. New York, UNIPUB, 1975. 117p.

13
VAC     United States. Arms Control and Disarmament Agency. INTERNATIONAL NEGOTIATIONS ON THE SEABED ARMS CONTROL TREATY. Publication no. 68. Washington, D.C., May, 1973. 201p.

15
VC     _____ Atlantic-Pacific Interoceanic Canal Study Commission. INTEROCEANIC CANAL STUDIES 1970. Washington, 1970.

15
VC     _____ _____ INTEROCEANIC CANAL STUDIES; STUDY OF ENGINEERING FEASIBILITY; ANNEX 5. Washington, 1970.

***
VENV     United States. Atomic Energy Commission. NUCLEAR POWER FACILITY PERFORMANCE CHARACTERISTICS FOR MAKING ENVIRONMENTAL IMPACT ASSESSMENTS. Washington, 1974. 231p.

------     UNITED STATES. CONGRESS. UNITED STATES. AGENCIES. To find U.S. Congressional and U.S. Agencies materials please consult the U.S. Monthly Catalog; Congressional Information Service; Congressional Quarterly Weekly Reports, etc. Only a very few selected materials are included here.

14a
IIIOI     United States. Bureau of Fisheries. ALASKA FISHERY AND FUR-SEAL INDUSTRIES. 1893-    Washington, U.S.G.P.O., 1893-

14a
IIIF     _____ _____ REPORT OF ALASKA INVESTIGATIONS IN 1914, by E. Lester Jones, deputy commissioner of fisheries. December 31, 1914. Washington, U.S.G.P.O., 1915. 155p.

8
VMLAD     _____ _____ Bureau of Foreign and Domestic Commerce. NAVIGATION LAWS. Comparative study of principal features of the law of the United States, Great Britain, Germany, Norway, France, and Japan. Prepared by Grosvenor M. Jones, commercial agent, in collaboration with the Bureau of Navigation and Steamboat-inspection Service. Washington, U.S.G.P.O., 1916. 190p.

14
IVOL     _____ _____ Bureau of Land Management. FINAL ENVIRONMENTAL STATEMENT: PROPOSED 1975 OUTER CONTINENTAL SHELF OIL AND GAS GENERAL LEASE, OFFSHORE TEXAS: OCS SALE NO. 37, FES 74-63. Washington, D.C., 1974 or 1975. 4 Vols.

12,13,14a,17
IIE     _____ _____ Bureau of Sport Fisheries and Wildlife. NATIONAL ESTUARY STUDY. Washington, U.S.G.P.O., 1970. 7 Vols.

13
IIE     _____ _____ PROCEEDINGS OF NORTHWEST ESTUARINE AND COASTAL ZONE SYMPOSIUM, PORTLAND, OR., OCTOBER 28-30, 1970. Washington, U.S. Department of the Interior. Bureau of Sport Fisheries and Wildlife,

1970. 224p.

                        13
IIT&L United States. Coast Guard. RULES AND REGULATIONS FOR ARTIFICIAL ISLANDS AND FIXED STRUCTURES ON THE OUTER CONTINENTAL SHELF. (Title 33, CFR parts 140-146 inclusive). CG-3. Washington, U.S.G.P.O., 1972. vi, 56p.

                     14a,15,17
VOR United States. Commission on Marine Science, Engineering and Resources. OUR NATION AND THE SEA: A PLAN FOR NATIONAL ACTION; REPORT. Washington, U.S.G.P.O., 1969. xi, 305p.

                     1,2,13
VOCET _____ PANEL REPORTS OF THE COMMISSION ON MARINE SCIENCE, ENGINEERING AND RESOURCES. Washington, 1969. 3 Vols.

                     14
IVCS United States. Congress. Office of Technology Assessment. AN ANALYSIS OF THE DEPARTMENT OF THE INTERIOR'S PROPOSED ACCELERATION OF DEVELOPMENT OF OIL AND GAS ON THE OUTER CONTINENTAL SHELF, MARCH 5, 1975. Washington, U.S.G.P.O., 1975.

                     14
IVCS _____ AN ANALYSIS OF THE FEASIBILITY OF SEPARATING EXPLORATION FROM PRODUCTION OF OIL AND GAS ON THE OUTER CONTINENTAL SHELF. Congress of the United States, Office of Technology Assessment. Washington, U.S.G.P.O., 1975. xi, 290p.

                     ***
IVM _____ COASTAL EFFECTS OF OFFSHORE ENERGY DEVELOPMENT: OIL AND GAS SYSTEMS. Summary of an Interim Report to The Technology Assessment Board. Prepared for the National Ocean Policy Study. 94th Congr., 2d sess. Washington, U.S.G.P.O., March 16, 1976. i, 40p.

                     14
VMT _____ OIL TRANSPORTATION BY TANKERS: AN ANALYSIS OF MARINE POLLUTION AND SAFETY MEASURES. Washington, U.S.G.P.O., 1975. XIX, 288p.

                     ***
IVENV United States. Council on Environmental Quality. OCS OIL AND GAS - AN ENVIRONMENTAL ASSESSMENT; A REPORT TO THE PRESIDENT. Washington, U.S.G.P.O., 1974. 5 Vols.

                     1,13
VOD _____ OCEAN DUMPING; A NATIONAL POLICY. A report to the President prepared by the Council on Environmental Quality, October 1970. Washington, U.S.G.P.O., 1971. 45p.

                     13
VP _____ THE PRESIDENT'S 1971 ENVIRONMENTAL PROGRAM CONTROLLING POLLUTION. REFORM - RENEWAL FOR THE 70's. Washington, U.S.G.P.O., 1971. 11p.

                     ***
IICONS United States. Department of Agriculture Soil Conservation Service. PROGRAM OF ACTION FOR CENTRAL COAST RESOURCE CONSERVATION AND DEVELOPMENT PROJECT. Washington, D.C., 1974. xviii, 113p.

VCS      United States. Department of Commerce. DEVELOPMENT POTENTIAL OF U.S. CONTINENTAL SHELVES. A report by the Batelle Memorial Institute on its study of the Coast and Geodetic Survey's products and services as related to economic activity in the U.S. continental shelf regions. Washington, U.S.G.P.O., 1966.    5,13

***

IIOSTR      _____ _____ THE ECONOMICS OF DEEP-WATER TERMINALS. Washington, Office of Ports and Intermodal Systems, 1972. 67p.

VORM      _____ _____ THE EFFECTS OF POLLUTION ABATEMENT ON INTERNATIONAL TRADE. The first report of the Secretary of Commerce to the President and Congress in compliance with section 6 of the Federal water pollution control act amendments of 1972 (Public law 92-500). Washington, U.S.G.P.O., 1973. Reproduced by National Technical Information Service.    2

VOD      _____ _____ REPORT OF THE CONGRESS ON OCEAN DUMPING AND OTHER MAN-INDUCED CHANGES TO OCEAN ECOSYSTEMS. OCTOBER 1972 THROUGH DECEMBER 1973. Washington, U.S.G.P.O., March, 1974. ix, 96p.    13

***

IIIOI      _____ _____ Bureau of Fisheries. Alaska Fisheries Service. ALASKA FISHERIES AND FUR-SEAL INDUSTRIES. Washington, U.S.G.P.O., 1916- Annual.

IIIINTL      United States. Department of Commerce. Bureau of Fisheries. INTERNATIONAL REGULATIONS OF THE FISHERIES ON THE HIGH SEAS. Washington, U.S.G.P.O., 1910.    16

***

IIIF      _____ _____ Economic Development Administration. STUDY OF FEASIBILITY OF ESTABLISHING DISTANT-WATER FISHING INDUSTRY IN PUERTO RICO. Washington, 1973. i, 76p.

***

VOCET      _____ _____ Environmental Data Service. INTERNATIONAL DECADE OF OCEAN EXPLORATION, PROGRESS REPORT: APRIL 1973-APRIL 1974. Washington, 1974. vii, 51p. Vol. 3.

***

IIP&H      _____ _____ Maritime Administration. FEASIBILITY OF NORTH ATLANTIC DEEP-WATER OIL TERMINAL, EXECUTIVE PAPER - OFFSHORE MARINE TERMINALS. Soros Associates, Inc., 1972. 48p.

***

VINTL      _____ _____ FOREIGN FLAG MERCHANT SHIPS OWNED BY U.S. PARENT COMPANIES AS OF JUNE 30, 1974. Washington, U.S.G.P.O., 1975. 3, 54p.

***

IIP&H      _____ _____ OFFSHORE OIL TERMINAL DESIGN CONSIDERATIONS FOR UNITED STATES WATERS. By Richard W. Black. Paper presented before Chesapeake Section of Society of Naval Architects and Marine Engineers, January 7, 1974. Washington, 1974.

IVP    United States. Department of Commerce. National Bureau of Standards. MARINE POLLUTION MONITORING (PETROLEUM), PROCEEDINGS OF SYMPOSIUM AND WORKSHOP HELD AT NATIONAL BUREAU OF STANDARDS, GAITHERSBURG, MARYLAND, MAY 13-17, 1974. Washington, U.S.G.P.O., December, 1974. xvi, 316p.

IICR    \_\_\_\_\_ \_\_\_\_\_ National Oceanic and Atmospheric Administration. AESTHETIC RESOURCES OF COASTAL ZONE. Prepared by Roy Mann Associates, Inc., Cambridge, Mass. Rockville, Md., Office of Coastal Zone Management, 1975. vi, 199p.

VOR    \_\_\_\_\_ \_\_\_\_\_ ASSESSING TECHNOLOGY FOR MARINE RESOURCE DEVELOPMENT, PROCEEDINGS OF CONFERENCE-WORKSHOP HELD BY MARINE TECHNOLOGY SOCIETY AT ARLINGTON, VA., ON MAY 15-17, 1972. Washington, 1974. 5, 94p.

IIIFP   \_\_\_\_\_ \_\_\_\_\_ FISH MEAL AND OIL. CURRENT FISHERIES STATISTICS, FM. Washington, D.C., 1974-

VOCET   \_\_\_\_\_ \_\_\_\_\_ MANNED UNDERSEA SCIENCE AND TECHNOLOGY. ANNUAL REPORT. Washington, U.S.G.P.O., 1972-    1st-

VP    \_\_\_\_\_ \_\_\_\_\_ MARINE POLLUTION MONITORING: STRATEGIES FOR A NATIONAL PROGRAM; DELIBERATIONS OF A WORKSHOP HELD AT SANTA CATALINA MARINE BIOLOGICAL LABORATORY OF THE UNIVERSITY OF SOUTHERN CALIFORNIA, ALLAN HANCOCK FOUNDATION, OCTOBER 25-28, 1972. Los Angeles, 1972. 203p.

VSG    \_\_\_\_\_ \_\_\_\_\_ NOAA REPORTS ON SEA GRANT. Rockville, Md., 1974? 43p.

VOD    \_\_\_\_\_ \_\_\_\_\_ REPORT TO THE CONGRESS ON OCEAN DUMPING AND OTHER MAN-INDUCED CHANGES TO OCEAN ECOSYSTEMS, OCTOBER 1972 THROUGH DECEMBER 1973. Washington, 1974. 96p.

IIP&H   United States. Department of Defense. Corps of Engineers. OREGON COASTAL HARBORS. Washington, D.C., 1975.

VORM    \_\_\_\_\_ \_\_\_\_\_ Naval Oceanographic Office. OCEAN FRONTIERS, UNITED STATES NAVY AND OCEANOGRAPHY. Washington, D.C., 1974. 15p.

VOCET   \_\_\_\_\_ \_\_\_\_\_ OCEANOGRAPHIC SURVEY REPORT, SEA OF JAPAN. MAY 1974. Washington, D.C., 1974. 182p.

VAC    United States. Department of Defense. Naval Ordnance System Command. FAMILY OF UNDERWATER WEAPONS, 16th TECHNICAL CONFERENCE OF NAVAL MINEFIELD COMMUNITY, JANUARY 29-30, 1973. Silver Spring, Md., Naval Ordnance Laboratory, 1974. 56p.

IIE     United States. Department of Health, Education, and Welfare. Public Health Service. DELAWARE ESTUARY COMPREHENSIVE STUDY, WATER USE ADVISORY COMMITTEE GUIDE. Division of Water Supply and Pollution Control, Region 2, New York, N.Y., 1964. 3, 52p.

IIP     _____ _____ PROGRESS REPORT NO. 7 OF TECHNICAL COORDINATING COMMITTEE CONSIDERING POLLUTION OF WATERS OF PUGET SOUND, STRAIT OF JUAN DE FUCA, AND THEIR TRIBUTARIES AND ESTUARIES. Region G, Portland, Or., 1962.

IICONS  _____ _____ Department of Labor. KAIMU BEACH, HAWAII, PROPOSED SHORE PROTECTION, FINAL ENVIRONMENTAL STATEMENT. Washington, U.S. Department of Labor, 1973. 43, 77p.

IICONS  _____ _____ Pacific Ocean Division, Corps of Engineers. PREVENTION AND MITIGATION OF SHORE DAMAGES, KAHULUI HARBOR, MAUI, FINAL ENVIRONMENTAL STATEMENT. Honolulu, Hawaii, 1973. 59p.

VT&L    _____ _____ Department of State. FISHERIES, CERTAIN FISHERIES PROBLEMS ON HIGH SEAS IN WESTERN AREAS OF MIDDLE ATLANTIC OCEAN, AGREEMENT BETWEEN UNITED STATES AND UNION OF SOVIET SOCIALIST REPUBLICS, SIGNED FEBRUARY 26, 1975; (ENTERED INTO FORCE APRIL 1, 1975) WITH RELATED LETTERS. Washington, U.S.G.P.O., 1975. 2, 39p.

VLOS    _____ _____ LAW OF THE SEA, 3d UNITED NATIONS CONFERENCE, CARACAS. JUNE 20-AUGUST 29, 1974. Reprinted from Department of State Bulletins, April 15, August 5, and September 23, 1974. Washington, D.C., 1974. 48p.

VOD     _____ _____ PROPOSED OCEAN DUMPING CONVENTION. Draft Environmental Impact Statement ELR-5377. Washington, 1972. 94p.

                                                                  1,3,5
VINTL   _____ _____ SOVEREIGNTY OF THE SEA. Geographic bulletin no. 3. Washington, Department of State, April, 1965.

                                                                  13
VLOS    _____ _____ UNITED STATES DRAFT OF U.N. CONVENTION ON INTERNATIONAL SEABED AREA. Draft United Nations Convention of the International Seabed Area Working Paper. August 3, 1970. Photocopy. Washington.

VENE    _____ _____ Department of the Interior. ALASKAN NATURAL GAS TRANSPORTATION SYSTEMS - ECONOMIC AND RISK ANALYSIS - FINAL CONCLUSION AND RESULTS. Springfield, Va., National Technical Information Service, 1976. 605p.

IIICONS _____ _____ FEDERAL AID MANUAL (IN FISH AND WILDLIFE RESTORATION PROGRAM). Rev. 1975. Washington, 308p.

IIP  United States. Department of the Interior. THE NATIONAL ESTUARINE POLLUTION STUDY. Report of the Secretary of the Interior to the U.S. Congress. Washington, U.S.G.P.O., March 25, 1970.

***

VCONS  _____ OUR NATURAL RESOURCES: THE CHOICES AHEAD. Washington, U.S.G.P.O., 1974. 130p.

***

IVOL  _____ OUTER CONTINENTAL SHELF OIL AND GAS DEVELOPMENT - IMPROVEMENTS NEEDED IN DETERMINING WHERE TO LEASE AND AT WHAT DOLLAR VALUE. Washington, U.S.G.P.O., 1975? 51p.

17

VP  _____ A REPORT ON POLLUTION OF THE NATION'S WATERS BY OIL AND OTHER HAZARDOUS SUBSTANCES, BY THE SECRETARY OF THE INTERIOR AND THE SECRETARY OF TRANSPORTATION. Washington, U.S.G.P.O., 1968. ii, 31p.

***

IVENV  _____ THE TRANS-ALASKA PIPELINE AND THE ENVIRONMENT: A BIBLIOGRAPHY. Richard W. Schoept, comp. Washington, U.S.G.P.O., 1974. 22p.

5,13,14

IVOL  _____ Bureau of Land Management. DRAFT ENVIRONMENTAL STATEMENT. PROPOSED 1973 OUTER CONTINENTAL SHELF OIL AND GAS GENERAL LEASE SALE OFFSHORE MISSISSIPPI, ALABAMA AND FLORIDA. OCS SALE NO. 32. Washington, 1973.

***

IVOL  _____ ENVIRONMENTAL IMPACT STATEMENT ON PROPOSED INCREASE IN OIL AND GAS LEASING ON THE OUTER CONTINENTAL SHELF. Draft Environmental Statement. Washington, U.S.G.P.O., 1975. Vol. 1. 792p.

***

IVOL  _____ FINAL ENVIRONMENTAL STATEMENT PROPOSED 1974 OUTER CONTINENTAL SHELF OIL AND GAS GENERAL LEASE SALE, OFFSHORE LOUISIANA. Washington, U.S.G.P.O., 1974. 3 Vols.

13

IVOL  _____ FINAL ENVIRONMENTAL STATEMENT FOR A PROPOSED 1973 OUTER CONTINENTAL SHELF OIL AND GAS GENERAL LEASE SALE OFFSHORE MISSISSIPPI, ALABAMA, AND FLORIDA. OCSS 32 FES 73-60. Washington, 1973.

13

IVOL  _____ FINAL ENVIRONMENTAL STATEMENT. PROPOSED 1974 OUTER CONTINENTAL SHELF OIL AND GAS GENERAL LEASE SALE OFFSHORE TEXAS. OCSS 34 FES 74-14. Washington, 1974. 3 Vols.

***

IVOL  _____ FINAL ENVIRONMENTAL STATEMENT: PROPOSED 1975 OUTER CONTINENTAL SHELF OIL AND GAS GENERAL LEASE, OFFSHORE TEXAS: OCSS 37 FES 74-63. New Orleans, La., 1975. 4 Vols.

IVOL	United States. Department of the Interior. Bureau of Land Management. PROPOSED INCREASE IN ACREAGE TO BE OFFERED FOR OIL AND GAS LEASING ON OUTER CONTINENTAL SHELF. Draft environmental statement. Washington, D.C., 1974-    Vol. 1-

VCS	_____ A STUDY OF THE SOCIO-ECONOMIC FACTORS RELATING TO THE OUTER CONTINENTAL SHELF OF THE MID-ATLANTIC COAST. Washington, 1975. 9 Vols. plus atlas.

IVOL	_____ Geological Survey. LEASING AND MANAGEMENT OF ENERGY RESOURCES ON THE OUTER CONTINENTAL SHELF. USGS INF-74-33. Washington, U.S.G.P.O., 1976. 40p.

IVP	United States. Department of the Interior. Bureau of Mines. IMPLICATIONS OF THE WATER POLLUTION CONTROL ACT OF 1972 FOR THE MINERAL RESOURCE INDUSTRY, A SURVEY. IC8681. Washington, U.S.G.P.O., 1975. 61p.

VENE	_____ Energy Research and Development Administration. PROBLEMS IN IDENTIFYING, DEVELOPING, AND USING GEOTHERMAL RESOURCES. Report to the Congress. Washington, U.S. General Accounting Office, 1975. 71p.

IVOL	United States. Department of the Interior. Federal Energy Administration. OUTLOOK FOR FEDERAL GOALS TO ACCELERATE LEASING OF OIL AND GAS RESOURCES ON THE OUTER CONTINENTAL SHELF. Report to the Congress by the U.S. Comptroller General. Washington, U.S. General Accounting Office, March 19, 1975. 40p.

VP	_____ Federal Water Pollution Control Administration. WASTE FROM WATERCRAFT, REPORT TO CONGRESS ON POLLUTION OF NAVIGABLE WATER OF U.S. Washington, Department of the Interior, Federal Water Pollution Control Administration, 1967. 103p.

IIICONS	_____ Fish and Wildlife Service. CONSERVING OUR FISH AND WILD LIFE HERITAGE. Washington, 1974. 12p.

VP	_____ Geological Survey. MOVEMENT AND EFFECTS OF SPILLED OIL OVER OUTER CONTINENTAL SHELF, INADEQUACY OF EXISTENT DATA FOR BALTIMORE CANYON TROUGH AREA. By H.J. Knebel. Reston, Va., 1974. iii+ 17p.

IVMMR	_____ SUMMARY OF 1972 OIL AND GAS STATISTICS FOR ONSHORE AND OFFSHORE AREAS OF 151 COUNTRIES. By Sherwood E. Frezon. Reston, Va., 1974. iv+ 163p.

VOR	United States. Department of the Interior. Office of Saline Water. SALINE WATER CONVERSION SUMMARY REPORT, 1973-1974. Washington, U.S.G.P.O., 1974. vii, 64p.

VP　　　　United States. Department of Transportation. VLCC 'METULA' OIL
SPILL. By Roy W. Hann, Jr. Prepared by Texas A&M Research Foundation, College Station, Texas. Washington, National Technical Information Service, 1974. iv, 61p.

***

VMT　　　_____ Coast Guard. EVALUATION OF THE HAZARD OF BULK WATER
TRANSPORTATION OF INDUSTRIAL CHEMICALS. National Academy of Sciences. Washington, National Technical Information Service, 1973. 81p.

***

VP　　　　_____ HAZARDOUS POLLUTING SUBSTANCES SYMPOSIUM, ABSTRACT
OF PROCEEDINGS, SEPTEMBER 14-16, 1970, NEW ORLEANS, LA. Washington, D.C., 578p.

***

VP　　　　_____ PETROLEUM OIL DETECTION BUOY SYSTEM. By Herbert R.
Gram. Prepared by Spectogram Corporation, North Haven, Conn. Washington, National Technical Information Service, 1975. iv, 29p.

14

VP　　　　United States. Environmental Protection Agency. BASIC DOCUMENTS
CONCERNING PROGRAMS TO CONTROL ENVIRONMENTAL POLLUTION FROM FEDERAL GOVERNMENT ACTIVITIES. Washington, 1975. vi, 162p.

***

IIWQ　　　_____ ENVIRONMENTAL IMPACT OF LAND USE ON WATER QUALITY,
WORK PLAN, BLACK CREEK STUDY, MAUMEE RIVER BASIN, ALLEN COUNTY, IND.: PLANNING PHASE, WORK PLAN, REDUCTION OF SEDIMENT AND RELATED POLLUTANTS IN MAUMEE RIVER AND LAKE ERIE. Washington, D.C., May, 1973.

***

IIP　　　　_____ FUTURE OF NORTH CAROLINA COASTAL AREA. NATIONAL ESTUARINE POLLUTION STUDY; FEDERAL WATER POLLUTION CONTROL ADMINISTRATION. Washington, D.C., 1969. 12p.

***

IIP　　　　_____ FUTURE OF SOUTH CAROLINA COASTAL REGION. NATIONAL ESTUARIES POLLUTION STUDY; FEDERAL WATER POLLUTION CONTROL ADMINISTRATION. Washington, D.C., 1969. 20p.

***

VP　　　　_____ HAZARDOUS WASTES. SW series, 138. Washington, D.C., 1975.

13

VOD　　　_____ OCEAN DISPOSAL PRACTICES AND EFFECTS. A report to the
Administrator of the Environmental Protection Agency by the President's Water Pollution Control Advisory Board. Washington, U.S. G.P.O., 1972. iii, 30p.

***

VP　　　　_____ OIL POLLUTION RESEARCH NEWSLETTER. Washington, Office of Research and Monitoring, National Environmental Research Center, Cincinnati, Edison Water Quality Research Laboratory, Environmental Protection Agency. 1974-

***
IIWQ  United States. Environmental Protection Agency. WATER QUALITY MANAGEMENT STUDY: BOSTON HARBOR, MASS., PROJECTIONS OF POPULATION AND MUNICIPAL WASTE LOADINGS. Washington, D.C., 1970. iii, 21p.

16
IIIOR  United States. Fish and Wildlife Service. FISHERY RESOURCES OF THE UNITED STATES. Washington, U.S.G.P.O., 1945. 135p.

16
IIICONS  _____  LAWS AND REGULATIONS FOR THE PROTECTION OF THE COMMERCIAL FISHERIES OF ALASKA. Washington, U.S.G.P.O., 1936, rev. ed. 1948. 67p.

***
VORM  United States. General Accounting Office. INFORMATION ON UNITED STATES OCEAN INTERESTS TOGETHER WITH POSITIONS AND RESULTS OF LAW OF THE SEA CONFERENCE AT CARACAS, MULTIAGENCY. Washington, U.S. G.P.O., March 6, 1975. v, 72p.

14
IICONS  _____  NATIONAL EFFORTS TO PRESERVE THE NATION'S BEACHES AND SHORELINES - A CONTINUING PROBLEM. Corps of Engineers (civil functions), Department of the Army: report to the Congress by the Comptroller General of the United States. Washington, U.S. General Accounting Office, 1975. v, 65p.

14
IVMMR  _____  OUTER CONTINENTAL SHELF OIL AND GAS DEVELOPMENT - IMPROVEMENTS NEEDED IN DETERMINING WHERE TO LEASE AND AT WHAT DOLLAR VALUE. Report to the Congress. U.S. Department of the Interior. Washington, D.C., U.S. Comptroller General, June 30, 1975. 51p.

14
IVOL  _____  OUTLOOK FOR FEDERAL GOALS TO ACCELERATE LEASING OF OIL AND GAS RESOURCES ON THE OUTER CONTINENTAL SHELF, DEPARTMENT OF THE INTERIOR. Federal Energy Administration: report to the Congress by the Comptroller General of the United States. Washington, U.S. General Accounting Office, 1975. 40p.

13
IVP  United States. Geological Survey. OUTER CONTINENTAL SHELF LEASE MANAGEMENT STUDY: SAFETY AND POLLUTION CONTROL. Washington, Water Resources Division, Systems Laboratory Group, 1972. 1 Vol.

13,14,16
VT&L  United States. Laws, statutes, etc. A COMPILATION OF FEDERAL LAWS RELATING TO CONSERVATION AND DEVELOPMENT OF OUR NATION'S FISH AND WILDLIFE RESOURCES, ENVIRONMENTAL QUALITY, AND OCEANOGRAPHY. Washington, U.S.G.P.O., 1972. xxv, 618p.

13,14,16
VT&L  _____  A COMPILATION OF FEDERAL LAWS RELATING TO CONSERVATION AND DEVELOPMENT OF OUR NATION'S FISH AND WILDLIFE RESOURCES, ENVIRONMENTAL QUALITY, AND OCEANOGRAPHY. Washington, U.S.G.P.O., 1973. xxvi, 706p.

|  |  | 13 |
|---|---|---|

VT&L     United States. Laws, statutes, etc. COMPILATION OF FEDERAL LAWS RELATING TO FUEL AND ENERGY RESOURCES. Prepared for the use of the Committee on Interior and Insular Affairs of the House of Representatives. 92d Congr., 2d sess., committee print. Washington, U.S. G.P.O., 1972. lviii, 898p.

                                                                                                                 14

VORM     United States. Library of Congress. Congressional Research Service. SOVIET OCEAN ACTIVITIES: A PRELIMINARY SURVEY: PREPARED AT THE REQUEST OF WARREN G. MAGNUSON, CHAIRMAN, COMMITTEE ON COMMERCE, AND ERNEST F. HOLLINGS, CHAIRMAN, NATIONAL OCEAN POLICY STUDY FOR THE USE OF THE COMMITTEE ON COMMERCE AND THE NATIONAL OCEAN STUDY POLICY, PURSUANT TO S.RES.222. Library of Congress, Congressional Research Service. 94th Congr., 1st sess., committee print. Washington, U.S.G.P.O., 1975. viii, 81p.

                                                                                                                  ***

VLOS     _____ THE THIRD U.N. LAW OF THE SEA CONFERENCE; PREPARED AT THE REQUEST OF HON. WARREN G. MAGNUSON, AND HON. ERNEST F. HOLLINGS, FOR THE USE OF THE COMMITTEE ON COMMERCE AND THE NATIONAL OCEAN STUDY POLICY. 94th Congr., 1st sess., committee print. Washington, U.S.G.P.O., 1975. 66p.

                                                                                                                  ***

VENV     United States. Library of Congress. Environmental Policy Division. CONGRESS AND THE NATION'S ENVIRONMENT: ENVIRONMENTAL AND NATURAL RESOURCES AFFAIRS OF THE 93d CONGRESS. PREPARED BY THE ENVIRONMENTAL POLICY DIVISION, CONGRESSIONAL RESEARCH SERVICE, LIBRARY OF CONGRESS, AT THE REQUEST OF HENRY M. JACKSON, CHAIRMAN, COMMITTEE ON INTERIOR AND INSULAR AFFAIRS, UNITED STATES SENATE. 94th Congr., 1st sess., committee print. Washington, U.S.G.P.O., 1975. vii, 940p.

                                                                                                                  ***

VENV     _____ ENVIRONMENTAL PROTECTION AFFAIRS OF THE NINETY-THIRD CONGRESS. A REPORT PREPARED BY THE ENVIRONMENTAL POLICY DIVISION OF THE CONGRESSIONAL RESEARCH SERVICE OF THE LIBRARY OF CONGRESS FOR THE COMMITTEE ON PUBLIC WORKS, U.S. SENATE, AT THE REQUEST OF SENATOR EDMUND S. MUSKIE. 94th Congr., 1st sess., committee print. Washington, U.S.G.P.O., 1975. x, 330p.

                                                                                                                  ***

IIIF     United States. Library of Congress. Legislative Reference Service. THE POSTWAR EXPANSION OF RUSSIA'S FISHING INDUSTRY. PREPARED AT THE REQUEST OF W.G. MAGNUSON, CHAIRMAN, FOR THE USE OF THE COMMITTEE ON COMMERCE, UNITED STATES SENATE, WITH TRANSLATIONS OF FISHERY ARTICLES AND NEWS FROM SOVIET PUBLICATIONS. 88th Congr., 2d sess., committee print. University of Washington, Fisheries Research Institute, 1964. 50p.

                                                                                               1,2

IIIT&L     _____ TREATIES AND OTHER INTERNATIONAL AGREEMENTS CONTAINING PROVISIONS ON COMMERCIAL FISHERIES, MARINE RESOURCES, SPORT FISHERIES, AND WILDLIFE TO WHICH THE UNITED STATES IS PARTY. Prepared at the request of Warren G. Magnuson, Chairman, for the use of the Committee on Commerce, United States Senate. 89th Congr., 1st sess. Washington, U.S.G.P.O., 1965. 410p.

|  |  | 17 |
|---|---|---|
| VOCET | United States. National Council on Marine Resources and Engineering Development. MARINE RESEARCH. Washington, U.S.G.P.O., 1967/68- | |

|  |  | *** |
|---|---|---|
| IIIF | United States. National Marine Fisheries Service. GULF FISHERIES ANNUAL SUMMARY 1972. Washington, U.S.G.P.O., February 5, 1975. | |

|  |  | 8 |
|---|---|---|
| VLOS | United States. President. FOUR CONVENTIONS AND AN OPTIONAL PROTOCOL FORMULATED AT THE UNITED NATIONS CONFERENCE ON THE LAW OF THE SEA, HELD AT GENEVA FEBRUARY 24-APRIL 27, 1958. Message from the President of the United States. 86th Congr., 1st sess. Senate. Executive documents J-N. Washington, U.S.G.P.O., 1958. 66p. | |

|  |  | 1,17 |
|---|---|---|
| VOR | _____ THE REPORT TO THE CONGRESS ON MARINE RESOURCES AND ENGINEERING DEVELOPMENT. 1st- Washington, U.S.G.P.O., 1967- | |

|  |  | *** |
|---|---|---|
| IVMMR | _____ Council on Environmental Quality. OUTER CONTINENTAL SHELF OIL AND GAS, ENVIRONMENTAL ASSESSMENT, REPORT TO PRESIDENT. Washington, U.S.G.P.O., 1974. 4 Vols. | |

|  |  | 13 |
|---|---|---|
| VT&L | United States. President, 1969-1974 (Nixon). CONVENTION ON THE PREVENTION OF MARINE POLLUTION. Message transmitting the Convention on the Prevention of Marine Pollution by Dumping of Wastes and Other Matter, opened for signature at Washington, London, Mexico City, and Moscow on December 29, 1972. Washington, U.S.G.P.O., 1973. viii, 47p. | |

|  |  | 13 |
|---|---|---|
| VT&L | _____ TWO CONVENTIONS AND AMENDMENT RELATING TO POLLUTION OF THE SEA BY OIL. Message ... transmitting two conventions done in Brussels at the International Legal Conference on Marine Pollution Damage, 1969... Washington, U.S.G.P.O., 1970. 50p. | |

|  |  | 15 |
|---|---|---|
| VORM | _____ THE FEDERAL OCEAN PROGRAM. Washington, D.C., U.S. G.P.O., 1972. ix, 121p. | |

|  |  | 2 |
|---|---|---|
| IVP | United States. President's Panel on Oil Spills. OFFSHORE MINERAL RESOURCES: A CHALLENGE AND AN OPPORTUNITY; second report of the President's Panel on Oil Spills. Executive Office of the President, Office of Science and Technology. Washington, U.S.G.P.O., 1969. v, 12p. | |

|  |  | 5,12,13,17 |
|---|---|---|
| VOR | United States. President's Science Advisory Committee. Panel on Oceanography. EFFECTIVE USE OF THE SEA; REPORT. Washington, U.S.G.P.O., 1966. xv, 144p. | |

|  |  | 13 |
|---|---|---|
| VOR | United States. Public Land Law Review Commission. ONE THIRD OF THE NATION'S LAND. A report to the President and to the Congress by the Public Land Law Review Commission. Washington, U.S.G.P.O., 1970. xii, 342p. | |

                                                                    14a
IIIT&L   United States. Tariff Commission. TREATIES AFFECTING THE NORTH-
         EASTERN FISHERIES. Report no. 152. 2d series. Washington, U.S.
         G.P.O., 1944. 167p.

                                                                    ***
IVORM    United States. Technology Assessment Office. ANALYSIS OF FEASIBILI-
         TY OF SEPARATING EXPLORATION FROM PRODUCTION OF OIL AND GAS ON OUTER
         CONTINENTAL SHELF; MAY, 1975. Washington, U.S.G.P.O., 1975. xi,
         290p.

                                                                    14a
IIIF     United States. Treasury Department. Special Agents Division. SEAL
         AND SALMON FISHERIES AND GENERAL RESOURCES OF ALASKA. Washington,
         U.S.G.P.O., 1898. 4 Vols.

                                                                    ***
IIP&H    UNITED STATES DEEPWATER PORT STUDY. Alexandria, Va., U.S. Army
         Engineer Institute for Water Resources, 1972. 4 Vols.

                                                                    ***
VORM     UNITED STATES MARINE SCIENTIFIC RESEARCH ASSISTANCE TO FOREIGN
         STATES. Proceedings. Washington, D.C., National Academy of Sci-
         ences, 1974. 316p.

                                                                    15
VINTL    U.S.S.R. Academy of Sciences. Institute of State and Law. THE
         LEGAL REGIME OF THE WORLD OCEAN. Moscow, Social Sciences Today
         Editorial Office, 1973.

                                                                    ***
VP       Utton, Albert, ed. POLLUTION AND INTERNATIONAL BOUNDARIES - UNITED
         STATES-MEXICAN ENVIRONMENTAL PROBLEMS. Albuquerque, N.M., Univer-
         sity of New Mexico Press, 1973.

                                                                    ***
VSUB     Vadus, Joseph R. INTERNATIONAL REVIEW OF MANNED SUBMERSIBLES AND
         HABITATS, PRESENTED AT ATLANTIC INTERNATIONAL SEARCH AND RESCUE
         SEMINAR, LANTSAR '75, APRIL 22-25, 1975, NEW YORK, N.Y., Washington
         U.S. Department of Commerce, National Oceanic and Atmospheric Ad-
         ministration, 1975. 6, 81p.

                                                                    ***
IIP      Vagners, Juris, and Paul Mar. OIL ON PUGET SOUND - AN INTERDISCI-
         PLINARY STUDY IN SYSTEMS ENGINEERING. Sea Grant Publication.
         Seattle, University of Washington Press, 1972. 647p.

                                                                    5
VOCET    Vahle, Cornelius W. PLANNING AND COORDINATING OCEANOGRAPHIC PRO-
         GRAMS: THE ACTIVITIES OF THE FEDERAL COUNCIL FOR SCIENCE AND TECH-
         NOLOGY, 1959-1966; A REPORT PREPARED FOR THE COMMISSION ON MARINE
         SCIENCE, ENGINEERING AND RESOURCES. Washington, D.C., Operations
         and Policy Research, Inc., 1968. 55p.

                                                                    17
VOCET    Vaissiere, Raymond. L'HOMME ET LE MONDE SOUS-MARIN... Paris, La-
         rousse, 1969. 406p.

VMLAD    Valin, R.J. COMMENTAIRE SUR L'ORDONNANCE DE LA MARINE, DU MOIS³ D'AOUT 1681. Poitiers, F.A. Saurin, 1829. xxiii, 1, 644p.

VMLAD    Valroger, Lucien M. DROIT MARITIME; COMMENTAIRE THEORIQUE ET PRA-³ TIQUE DU LIVRE IL DU CODE DE COMMERCE (LEGISLATIONS COMPAREES). Paris, L. Larose et Forcel, 1883-86. 5 Vols.

IIIF    Van Cleve, Richard, and Ralph W. Johnson. MANAGEMENT OF THE HIGH 5,12,13,16 SEAS FISHERIES OF THE NORTHEASTERN PACIFIC. University of Washington Publications in Fisheries News Series. Vol. II, no. 2. Seattle, 1963. 63p.

VENE    Van Tassel, Alfred J., ed. ENERGY UNDER THE OCEANS: A SUMMARY REPORT OF A TECHNOLOGY ASSESSMENT OF OCS OIL AND GAS OPERATIONS. In The Environmental Price of Energy. Lexington, Mass., D.C. Heath and Company, Lexington Books, 1975. pp. 265-287.    ART

VENE    _____ _____ THE ENVIRONMENTAL PRICE OF ENERGY. Lexington, Mass., 14 Lexington Books, 1975.

VLOS    Vargas Carreño, E. AMERICA LATINA Y LOS PROBLEMAS CONTEMPORANEOS 7 DEL DERECHO DEL MAR. Santiego de Chile, Bello, 1973. 159p.

VOCET   Vargas, Jorge A. LA INVESTIGACIÓN CIENTÍFICA EN AMÉRICA LATINA. 7 UN NUEVO CAPÍTULO DEL DERECHO DEL MAR. Secretaría de Relaciones Exteriores. Cuestiones Internacionales Contemporáneas/3, Tlatelalco, México, D.F. Primera edición, 1975.

VINTL   _____ _____ "LEGISLACIÓN LATINOAMERICANA SOBRE DERECHO DEL MAR" ART EN MEXICO Y EL REGIMEN DEL MAR. In Secretaría de Relaciones Exteriores, Mexico, 1974. pp. 358-397.

VOCET   _____ _____ NORMATIVE ASPECTS OF SCIENTIFIC RESEARCH IN THE OCEANS: 1,4,7,10,11,13,14 THE CASE OF MEXICO. Law of the Sea Institute occasional paper no. 23. Kingston, University of Rhode Island, October, 1974. 23p.

IIIAFF  Veal, C. David, et al. DEVELOPMENTS IN OFF-BOTTOM OYSTER CULTURE ***  IN MISSISSIPPI. Paper presented at the winter meeting of the American Society of Agricultural Engineers, Chicago, Illinois, December, 1972. MSGP-72-011. Jackson, University of Mississippi, Sea Grant Law Center, 1972.

IIIF    Verhoeven, Leon A. A REPORT TO THE SALMON FISHING INDUSTRY OF ALAS- *** KA ON THE RESULTS OF THE 1947 TAGGING EXPERIMENTS. Seattle, University of Washington, Fisheries Research Institute, 1952.

VINTL   Verzijl, Jan H.W. INTERNATIONAL LAW IN HISTORICAL PERSPECTIVE. 1,2,3,4,5,11,13,14,16 Leyden, A.W. Sijthoff, 1968. 5 Vols.

|        |                                                                                                                                                                                                                |
|--------|----------------------------------------------------------------------------------------------------------------------------------------------------------------------------------------------------------------|
| VMT    | 1<br>Villacres Moscoso, Jorge W. THE INTEROCEAN ROUTES THROUGH (sic) THE AMAZONIAN REGION. Guayaquil, Ecuador, The Tropical Geography Center, 1962. |
| VP     | \*\*\*<br>VILLANOVA OCEAN CONFERENCE, 1971. THE FATE OF THE OCEANS. Villanova, Villanova University, 1972. 237p. |
| IIIF   | 13<br>Virginia. Marine Resources Commission. LAWS OF VIRGINIA RELATING TO FISHERIES OF TIDAL WATERS. Reprinted from the Code of Virginia of 1950 and the 1966 Cumulative Supplement. Charlottesville, The Michie Company, 1966. 125p.<br>\_\_\_\_ \_\_\_\_ SUPPLEMENT. 1968. 30p. |
| IISL   | \*\*\*<br>\_\_\_\_ \_\_\_\_ WETLANDS GUIDELINES. Newport News, 1974. 47p. |
| VSG    | \*\*\*<br>Virginia. Institute of Marine Science. SEA GRANT ANNUAL REPORT. Gloucester Point, 1971- |
| VCONS  | 3,9,12<br>Visser't Hooft, Hendrik P. LES NATIONS UNIES ET LA CONVERSATION DES RESSOURCES DE LA MER; ÉTUDE DES RAPPORTS ENTRE LE CODIFICATEUR ET LE MILIEU POLITIQUE. The Hague, M. Nijhoff, 1958. 425p. |
| VINTL  | 5,7<br>Vitzthum, Wolfgang G. DER RECHTSSTATUS DES MEERESBODENS. Berlin, Duncker and Humblot, 1972. |
| VLOS   | ART<br>Voelckel, M. LE STATUT JURIDIQUE DES SYSTÈMES D'ACQUISITION DE DONNÉES OCÉANIQUES. In Sociéte Française pour le Droit International. Actualités du droit de la mer: Actes. Paris, 1973. pp. 76-89. |
| IIISF  | \*\*\*<br>Vogt, Craig. ALASKAN SEAFOOD PROCESSING. Region X; Surveillance and Analysis Division; Working paper no. 83. Washington, D.C., Environmental Protection Agency, 1973. 4, 39p. |
| VCONS  | 17<br>Vogt, William. ROAD TO SURVIVAL. New York, W. Sloane Associates, 1956. xvi, 335p. |
| VMLAD  | 1,5,18<br>Volkov, Aleksei A. MARITIME LAW. Edited by A.K. Zhudro. Translated from Russian by E.D. Gordon, Jerusalem, Israel Program for Scientific Translations. Springfield, Va., U.S. Department of Commerce National Technical Information Service, 1971. vi, 162p. |
| IIIFV&G | 13<br>von Brandt, Andres. FISH CATCHING METHODS OF THE WORLD. Rev. and enl. West Byfleet, Surrey, England, Fishing News (Books) Ltd., 1972. xvi, 240p. |

                                                                    16
IIIF      Vonreis, John. TOWARD RATIONAL POLICY FORMULATION IN NORTH PACIFIC
          FISHERIES. Unpublished paper in University of Washington Law Library, 1969. 58p.

                                                              3,5,12,13,16
IIIB      Vosper, William J. A FISHING ZONE DELIMITATION OF THE ALASKAN COAST
          INTRODUCING FISHERY BASELINES. University of Miami Sea Program.
          Coral Gables, Fla., 1971. ix, 127p.

                                                                     ***
VLOS      Vyotskiĭ, A.F. PRAVOVYE PROBLEMY SVOBODY NAUCHNYKH ISSLEDOVANII V
          MIROVOM OKEANE. Kiev, Naukova dumka, 1974. 157p.

                                                                     ***
IIOD      Wagner, D.D. AN INVESTIGATION OF THE PHYSICAL IMPACT OF SEWAGE OUTFLOW ON A RIVER-ESTUARINE ENVIRONMENT. Annapolis, Md., U.S. Naval
          Academy, Trident Scholar Project Report, 1974. 1973. 72p.

                                                                      13
VP        Waldichuk, Michael. RADIOACTIVITY IN THE MARINE ENVIRONMENT. Prepared by the Panel on Radioactivity in the Marine Environment on
          the Committee on Oceanography of the National Academy of Sciences
          National Research Council. WASH 1185. UC-48. Washington, D.C.,
          U.S. Atomic Energy Commission, Division of Biology and Medicine,
          1971. vi, 28p.

                                                                     14a
IIIOR     Walford, Lionel A. LIVING RESOURCES OF THE SEA. New York, Ronald
          Press Company, 1958. xv, 321p.

                                                                     ***
IICONS    Walker, Havens and Erikson. VISUAL RESOURCES ANALYSIS OF THE OREGON
          COASTAL ZONE; EXPERIENTIAL QUALITIES OF OREGON COASTAL ENVIRONMENTS. Coastal Conservation and Development Commission. Florence,
          1974.

                                                                     ***
VOCET     Walter, Deas, and Clarrie Lawler. BENEATH AUSTRALIAN SEAS. Sydney,
          Australia, A.H. and A.W. Reed, 1970. 112p.

                                                                     ***
VP        Walter, R.A., et al. USCG POLLUTION ABATEMENT PROGRAM: A PRELIMINARY STUDY OF VESSEL AND BOAT EXHAUST EMISSIONS. Technical Report
          no. DOT-TSC-USCG-72-3. Cambridge, Mass., U.S. Department of Transportation, Transportation Systems Center, 1972. 131p.

                                                                     ART
IVM       Walthier, Thomas N. MINING PANEL REPORT. In Proceedings of the
          Ocean Science and Technology Advisory Committee Annual Meeting, and
          National Oceanography Association/National Security Industrial
          Association Symposium held in Washington, D.C., June 2-3, 1971.
          Washington, National Security Industrial Association, 1971.

                                                                     ***
VP        Walton, A. INTERNATIONAL ACTIONS TO PREVENT POLLUTION OF THE SEAS
          BY SHIPS. Report series BI-R-73-7. Canada, Bedford Institute of
          Oceanography, 1973. 13p.

|  |  |
|---|---|
| IVMMR | Wang, Frank F.H. MINERAL RESOURCES OF THE SEA. (ST/ECA/125).[16] New York, UNIPUB, 1970. 49p. |
| IVMMR | Wang, Frank F.H., and Michael J. Cruickshank. TECHNOLOGIC GAPS IN[13] EXPLORATION AND EXPLOITATION OF SUB-SEA MINERAL RESOURCES. Offshore Technology Conference. Paper No. 1031. Preprint. Dallas, n.p., 1969. |
| VODAS | Ward, E.G. OCEAN DATA GATHERING PROGRAM - AN OVERVIEW. In Offshore Technology Conference, 6th, Houston, Texas, 1974: Preprints. [ART] Dallas, Tex., 1974. Vol. 2. pp. 771-780. |
| VENV | Ward, M.A., ed. MAN AND HIS ENVIRONMENT; PROCEEDINGS. Banff Conference on Pollution, 1st, 1968. Sponsored jointly by The University of Calgary and The Engineering Institute of Canada. Oxford, New York, Pergamon Press, 1970- [2] |
| VP | Warren, Charles E. BIOLOGY AND WATER POLLUTION CONTROL. Philadelphia, Saunders, 1971. [15] |
| IICZM | Warren, Robert, et al. DESIGNING COASTAL MANAGEMENT AGENCIES: PROBLEMS IN ALLOCATING COASTAL RESOURCES. Paper. Los Angeles, University of Southern California, Center for Urban Affairs, 1972? 54p. *** |
| VT&L | Washington. Conservation Commission. FEDERAL LAWS AND STATE OF[14] WASHINGTON LAWS CONCERNING RESOURCE CONSERVATION. Rev. ed. Olympia, 1975. 48p. |
| VENE | Washington. Department of Commerce and Economic Development.[14] ENERGY: PRESENT STATUS AND FUTURE OPPORTUNITIES. Olympia, 1975. 8p. |
| IIT&L | _____ _____ Department of Ecology. COMPENDIUM OF STATE LAWS AND REGULATIONS CONCERNING SOLID WASTE MANAGEMENT IN WASHINGTON STATE. Olympia, May 1, 1974. *** |
| IICZM | _____ _____ FINAL GUIDELINES SHORELINE MANAGEMENT ACT OF 1971.[14] Olympia, 1972. viii, 20p. |
| VENE | _____ _____ GEOTHERMAL ENERGY POTENTIAL OF WASHINGTON STATE. Olympia, October, 1972. 23p. *** |
| IICZM | _____ _____ LAKES CONSTITUTING SHORELINES OF THE STATE. Shoreline Management Act of 1971. Olympia, 1973. 27p. *** |

| | | 14,16 |
|---|---|---|
VP     Washington. Department of Ecology. LEWIS COUNTY SOLID WASTE MANAGEMENT PLAN. Olympia, April 30, 1974.

***

IIIP    _____ _____ OIL POLLUTION AND THE SIGNIFICANT BIOLOGICAL RESOURCES OF PUGET SOUND: A REVIEW AND ANALYSIS OF AVAILABLE INFORMATION. Prepared by Beale Consultants, Inc., Portland, Or. Olympia, 1975. 2 Vols.

14,16

VP    _____ _____ OIL POLLUTION PREVENTION AND CONTROL. Olympia, 1973.

***

IIB   _____ _____ A PROGRAM FOR BASELINE STUDIES RELATED TO MARINE WATERS OF THE STATE OF WASHINGTON; FINAL REPORT PREPARED FOR WASHINGTON STATE DEPARTMENT OF ECOLOGY. Olympia, 1974. 125p.

***

VP    _____ _____ A PROPOSED PROGRAM ON PREVENTION AND CONTROL OF OIL POLLUTION IN WASHINGTON STATE. Olympia, Washington, 1975. iii, 36p.

***

IICZM   _____ _____ SHORELINE MANAGEMENT ACT OF 1971: INVENTORY SUPPLEMENT. no. 1-    Olympia, 1972-

***

IICZM   _____ _____ SHORELINE MANAGEMENT ACT: STREAMS AND RIVERS CONSTITUTING SHORELINES OF THE STATE DEPARTMENT OF HIGHWAYS. Olympia, 1972. 133, 40p.

***

IICZM   _____ _____ SHORELINES LAWS AND REGULATIONS: HOW DOES SHORELINE MANAGEMENT AFFECT ME? Olympia, Association of Washington Cities, Washington State Association of Counties and Department of Ecology. 1972. 6p.

14,16

IICZM   _____ _____ STREAMS AND RIVERS CONSTITUTING SHORELINES OF THE STATE, SHORELINE MANAGEMENT ACT OF 1971, ADOPTED BY JUNE, 1972, AMENDED EFFECTIVE AUGUST, 1973. Olympia, 1973. 163p.

14

VP    _____ _____ WATER POLLUTION INCIDENTS REPORTED IN WASHINGTON STATE. Olympia, 1971-

14a

IIIF    Washington. Department of Fisheries. FISHERIES. Olympia, 1963.

16

IIIF    _____ _____ ORDERS OF THE DIRECTORS OF FISHERIES. 1950-    Olympia, 1950-

14,16

IICZM   _____ _____ Department of Natural Resources. Division of Surveys and Marine Land Management. THE LAND USE ALLOCATION PLAN: DEPARTMENT OF NATURAL RESOURCES MANAGED MARINE LANDS. Olympia, 1973. 24p.

IISL     Washington. Department of Natural Resources. Division of Surveys and Marine Land Management. THE LAND USE ALLOCATION PLAN FOR STATE-OWNED AQUATIC LANDS. Preliminary report. Olympia, Division of Surveys and Marine Land Management, Department of Natural Resources, 1972. 13p.

                              14,16

IIENE    Washington. Energy Policy Council. ENERGY IN THE STATE OF WASHINGTON. Prepared by the Task Force on Energy Profile of Washington. Seattle, 1974. 15p.

                              13

IIP      Washington. Enforcement Project. POLLUTIONAL EFFECTS OF PULP AND PAPER MILL WASTES IN PUGET SOUND; A REPORT OF STUDIES. Portland, Or., U.S. Department of the Interior, Federal Water Pollution Control Administration, Northwest Regional Office, 1967. xxii, 472p.

                              14,16

IICZM    Washington. Garfield County. GARFIELD COUNTY SHORELINES MASTER PLAN. Pomeroy, Wash., 1974. 51p.

                              14,16

IIT&L    Washington. Laws, statutes, etc. CHAPTER 173-20; SHORELINE MANAGEMENT ACT LAKES CONSTITUTING SHORELINES OF THE STATE. Olympia, Washington, Department of Ecology, 1972. 26p.

                              14,16

IIT&L    _____ CHAPTER 173-18 WAC: STREAMS AND RIVERS CONSTITUTING SHORELINES OF THE STATE SHORELINE MANAGEMENT ACT OF 1971: ADOPTED JUNE, 1972, AMENDED EFFECTIVE AUGUST 1973. Olympia, Washington, Department of Ecology, 1973. i, 163p.

                              16

IIIF     Washington. Legislature. Interim Committee on Fisheries. REPORT ON THE PROBLEMS AFFECTING THE FOOD FISHERIES OF THE COLUMBIA RIVER SYSTEM AND THE STATE OF WASHINGTON. Olympia, 1946. 50p.

                              16

IIIF     _____ REPORT ON THE PROBLEMS AFFECTING FOOD FISHERIES OF THE STATE OF WASHINGTON. Olympia, 1949. 59p.

                              14,16

IICZM    Washington. Lewis County. Board of Commissioners. COMPREHENSIVE SOLID WASTE MANAGEMENT PLAN. Chehalis, Wash., 1974.

                              14,16

IIREC    Washington. NATURAL RESOURCES AND RECREATION AGENCIES - PROGRAMS, NEEDS, GOALS. 1973 Annual Report. Olympia, Washington State Library, 1973. 68p.

                              14,16

VP       _____ Oceanographic Commission. RISK ANALYSIS OF THE OIL TRANSPORTATION SYSTEM. A report to the 43d Legislature by the Oceanographic Institute of Washington. Olympia, 8 September, 1972. 551p.

VP    Washington. Oceanographic Commission. RISK ANALYSIS OF THE OIL 14,16
TRANSPORTATION SYSTEM; COMMENTS BY THE OCEANOGRAPHIC COMMISSION OF
WASHINGTON ON THE U.S. ARMY CORPS OF ENGINEERS STUDY OF POTENTIAL
DEEP-WATER PORT FACILITIES ON THE WEST COAST. Olympia, 1973.

IIOSTR    _____ _____ SUBMARINE PIPELINE CROSSINGS OF ADMIRALTY INLET, PU- 14
GET SOUND: A STUDY OF TECHNICAL FEASIBILITY. Submitted to the 44th
Legislature of the State of Washington. Olympia, 22 December, 1975.
199p.

\*\*\*

IICZM    Washington. Office of Program Planning and Fiscal Management.
State Planning Division. INTRODUCTION OF THE ENVIRONMENTAL-LAND USE
PLANNING CONCEPT PREPARED BY STATE PLANNING DIVISION, OFFICE OF PRO-
GRAM PLANNING AND FISCAL MANAGEMENT. Photocopy. Olympia?, 1970.
35p.

\*\*\*

IICZM    Washington. State Legislative Council. SUMMARY OF SEACOAST MANAGE-
MENT - INITIATIVE 43. Olympia, Washington, 1970. 8p.

\*\*\*

VENV    Washington. Thermal Power Plant Site Evaluation Council. DRAFT
ENVIRONMENTAL IMPACT STATEMENT ON PUGET SOUND POWER AND LIGHT COM-
PANY'S SKAGNIT. NUCLEAR POWER PROJECT (APPLICATION NO. 74-1.)
Olympia, Washington, 1975. iv, 537p.

\*\*\*

VENV    _____ _____ DRAFT SUPPLEMENT TO ENVIRONMENTAL IMPACT STATEMENT
ON WPPSS NUCLEAR PROJECT NOS. 1 AND 4 (APPLICATION 74-2.) Olympia,
Washington, 1975. iii, 202p.

\*\*\*

IIIAFF    Washington. University. OCEAN RANCHING IN WASHINGTON. A WORKSHOP
SUMMARY. WSG-WO 75-1. Seattle, 1975. 24p.

\*\*\*

VSG    _____ _____ Division of Marine Resources. A PROPOSAL TO THE NA-
TIONAL SCIENCE FOUNDATION FOR CONTINUED SEA GRANT INSTITUTIONAL
SUPPORT TO BE ADMINISTERED BY THE DIVISION OF MARINE RESOURCES.
Seattle, University of Washington, 1969. 245p.

VSG    _____ _____ WASHINGTON SEA GRANT PROGRAM. SECOND YEAR PROPOSAL, 14
1973-74. Seattle, University of Washington, 1973. xxx, 105p.
Vol. 1.

\*\*\*

VSG    _____ _____ WASHINGTON SEA GRANT PROGRAM: PROPOSAL, 1975-1976.
Seattle, University of Washington, 1975. 2 Vols.

IICZM    Washington. Water Resources Center. REGIONAL PROBLEM ANALYSIS IN 14
THE PACIFIC NORTHWEST. By Harvey R. Doerkson and others. Issued
in cooperation with the Idaho Water Resources Research Institute
and the Oregon Water Resources Research Institute. Pullman,
Washington State University, 1975. xii, 122p.

|  | 7,12,13,16 |
|---|---|

VSG	Washington Sea Grant Program. LOCAL IMPACTS OF THE SEA. Seattle, University of Washington Press, 1973.

14

VCONS	Washington State Conservation Commission. FEDERAL LAWS AND STATE OF WASHINGTON LAWS CONCERNING RESOURCE CONSERVATION. Olympia, 1975.

14a

IIP	Washington State Enforcement Project. POLLUTIONAL EFFECTS OF PULP AND PAPER MILL WASTES IN PUGET SOUND; A REPORT ON STUDIES. Portland, Or., U.S. Department of the Interior, Federal Water Pollution Control Administration, Northwest Regional Office, 1967. xxii, 474p.

14

IICZM	Washington State Land Planning Commission. LAND PLANNING FOR OUR FUTURE: FINAL SUMMARY REPORT. Photocopy. Olympia? 1973? 27p.

***

VOD	Wasp, E.J., et al. BULK TRANSPORT OF WASTE SLURRIES TO INLAND AND OCEAN DISPOSAL SITES. Springfield, Va., U.S. Department of Commerce, Clearinghouse for Federal Scientific and Technical Information, 1970.

13

IICZM	WASTES MANAGEMENT CONCEPTS FOR THE COASTAL ZONE - REQUIREMENTS FOR RESEARCH AND INVESTIGATION. Washington, National Academy of Sciences-National Academy of Engineering, 1970. 126p.

***

VP	Water Pollution by Oil. PROCEEDINGS OF SEMINAR OF THE INSTITUTE OF WATER POLLUTION CONTROL AND THE INSTITUTE OF PETROLEUM AT AVIEMORE, SCOTLAND. Barking, Essex, England, Applied Science Publishers, 1971.

***

IIE	WATER QUALITY INVESTIGATION OF ESTUARIES OF GEORGIA; EIGHTEEN MONTH REPORT. Submitted by Brunswick Junior College. Atlanta, Environmental Protection Division, 1975. 73p.

***

IIIF	Watkinson, J.G., and R. Smith, comp. NEW ZEALAND FISHERIES. Wellington, New Zealand Ministry of Agriculture and Fisheries, 1972. 90p.

13

IVM	Wayland, Russell G. A GOVERNMENT VIEW OF INCENTIVES FOR OUTER CONTINENTAL SHELF MINING. Reprint from Marine Technology 1970, Vol. 1. Washington, Marine Technology Society, 1970.

13

IVMMR	Weaver, L.K., et al. OFFSHORE PETROLEUM STUDIES. Composition of the offshore U.S. petroleum industry and estimated cost of producing petroleum in the Gulf of Mexico. Bureau of Mines Information Circular 8557. Washington, U.S.G.P.O., 1972. v, 168p.

13

IVMMR	_____ OFFSHORE PETROLEUM STUDIES. Historical and estimated future hydrocarbon production from U.S. offshore areas and the impact on the onshore segment of the petroleum industry, Bureau of Mines Information Circular 8575. Washington, U.S.G.P.O., 1973. ii, 30p.

VENE     Weaver, L.K., et al. OFFSHORE PETROLEUM STUDIES: COMPOSITION OF THE OFFSHORE U.S. PETROLEUM INDUSTRY AND ESTIMATED COSTS OF PRODUCING PETROLEUM IN THE GULF OF MEXICO. U.S. Bureau of Mines Information Circular 8557. Washington, U.S.G.P.O., 1973. 168p.   ***

VOR     Weber, A. OUR NEWEST FRONTIER: THE SEA-BOTTOM. In Marine Technology Society, Exploiting the Ocean. Washington, D.C., 1966. pp. 405-411.   ART

VP     Wechsler, A.E., et al. REGULATIONS, PRACTICES AND PLANS FOR THE PREVENTION OF SPILLS OF OIL AND HAZARDOUS POLLUTION SUBSTANCES. Oil and hazardous materials program series OHM 72 05 002. Cambridge, Mass., Arthur D. Little, Inc., for Division of Oil and Hazardous Materials, Office of Water Programs, Environmental Protection Agency, 1971. Vol. 1.   13

VSG     Weedman, Parmula K., comp. SEA GRANT PUBLICATIONS INDEX. Narragansett, R.I. National Sea Grant Depository, Pell Marine Science Library, University of Rhode Island. Washington, U.S. Environmental Science Center, 1968/72-   annual.   5,13,14,16,18

VP     Weisberg, Barry. BEYOND REPAIR; THE ECOLOGY OF CAPITALISM. Boston, Beacon Press, 1971. ix, 201p.   17

VB     Weissberg, Guenther. MAPS AS EVIDENCE IN INTERNATIONAL BOUNDARY DISPUTES: A REAPPRAISAL. Reprinted from American Journal of International Law, Vol. 57, no. 4, October, 1963.   9

IIIINTL     _____ _____ RECENT DEVELOPMENTS IN THE LAW OF THE SEA AND THE JAPANESE-KOREAN FISHERY DISPUTE. The Hague, Nijhoff, 1966. 135p.   1,3,5,10,12,13,15,16

VLOS     Weisberg, R.I. DEVELOPMENTS IN THE OCEAN RIGHTS OF LAND-LOCKED NATIONS. Sea Grant Publication UNC-SG-74-03. In S.W. Wurfel, Current Aspects of Sea Law. Chapel Hill, University of North Carolina School of Law, 1974. pp. 18-27.   ART

VMT     Wells, Robert D. PICTORIAL - THE SOVIET SUBMARINE FORCE. In U.S. Naval Institute Proceedings, August, 1971. pp. 63-79.   ART

IIIAFF     Welsh, James P. MARICULTURE OF THE CRAB CANCER MAGISTER (DANA). UTILIZING FISH AND CRUSTACEAN WASTES AS FOOD. Sea Grant Project HSU-SG-4. California, Humbolt State University, April, 1974. iii, 76p.   13

VMLAD     Welwood, William. AN ABRIDGEMENT OF ALL SEA-LAWES; GATHERED FORTH OF ALL WRITINGS AND MONUMENTS, WHICH ARE TO BE FOUND AMONG ANY PEOPLE OR NATION; VPON THE COASTS OF THE GREAT OCEAN AND MEDITERRANEAN SEA: AND SPECIALLY ORDERED AND DISPOSED FOR THE VSE AND BENEFIT OF ALL BENEUOLENT SEA-FARERS, WITHIN HIS MAIESTIES DOMINIONS OF GREAT   5,6,12,13,14,16

BRITANNE, IRELAND, AND THE ADJACENT ISLES THEREOF. London, Printed by H. Lownes for T. Man, 1613. Amsterdam, Theatrum Orbis Terrarum; New York, Da Capo Press, 1972. 77p.

VOCET Wenk, Edward, Jr. NEW MACHINERY FOR POLICY PLANNING IN MARINE SCIENCES. In Thomas S. English, ed., Ocean Resources and Public Policy. Seattle, Washington University Press, 1973. 184p.   ART

VORM \_\_\_\_\_ \_\_\_\_\_ THE POLITICS OF THE OCEAN. Seattle, University of Washington Press, 1972. xviii, 590p.   1,2,5,9,12,13,14,14a,15,16,17

VOCET Went, A.E.J. SEVENTY YEARS AGROWING; A HISTORY OF THE INTERNATIONAL COUNCIL FOR THE EXPLORATION OF THE SEA 1902-1972. Copenhagen, International Council for the Exploration of the Sea, 1972. 254p.   ***

VMLAD Werner, August-Raynald. TRAITÉ DE DROIT MARITIME GÉNÉRAL: ÉLÉMENTS ET SYSTÈMES, DÉFINITION, PROBLÈMES, PRINCIPES. Geneva, Librairie Droz, 1964. 502p.   1

VOCET Wertenbaker, William. THE FLOOR OF THE SEA: MAURICE EWING AND THE SEARCH TO UNDERSTAND THE EARTH. Boston, Little, Brown and Company, 1974. xi, 275p.   13

IISL WETLAND GUIDELINES. Va., Newport News: Marine Resources Commission, 1974. 26p.   ***

IISL WETLANDS MANAGEMENT SEMINAR. In Proceedings, Nassau-Suffolk Regional Planning Board, Regional Marine Resources Council. n.p. 1972? 122p.   ART

VOCET Weyl, Peter K. OCEANOGRAPHY AN INTRODUCTION TO THE MARINE ENVIRONMENT. John Wiley and Sons, Inc., 1970. xvii, 535p.   5,14a

IIMM WHALING - INTERNATIONAL REGULATIONS. In Marine Affairs Journal, Report no. 3. Narragansett, University of Rhode Island, 1975.   ART

VENV Wheeler, David L., comp. THE HUMAN HABITAT; CONTEMPORARY READINGS. New York, Van Nostrand Reinhold Company, 1971. xii, 275p.   17

VENV Whipple, William, Jr. ENVIRONMENTAL QUALITY AND ITS EVALUATION. New Brunswick, N.J., Rutgers University, Water Resources Research Institute, 1974. 37p.   13,14,16,18

VENV Whisenhunt, Donald W. THE ENVIRONMENT AND THE AMERICAN EXPERIENCE; A HISTORIAN LOOKS AT THE ECOLOGICAL CRISIS. Port Washington, New York, Kennikat Press, 1974. 136p.   14

|        |                                                                                                                                                                                                                                                                                                                |
|--------|--------------------------------------------------------------------------------------------------------------------------------------------------------------------------------------------------------------------------------------------------------------------------------------------------------------------|
| IVMMR  | Whitaker, R.D., et al. INSPECTION OF PETROLEUM OPERATIONS ON OUTER CONTINENTAL SHELF. U.S. Department of Interior, Geological Survey, 1975.  ***                                                                                                                                                                   |
| VORM   | White, Irvin L. DECISION MAKING FOR SPACE: LAW AND POLITICS IN AIR, SEA AND OUTER SPACE. West Lafayette, Ind., Purdue University Studies, 1970. 277p.  6,14                                                                                                                                                        |
| IVMMR  | White, Irvin L., et al. NORTH SEA OIL AND GAS; IMPLICATIONS FOR FUTURE UNITED STATES DEVELOPMENT. Science and Public Policy Program. Technology Assessment Group. A study sponsored by the Council on Environmental Quality. Norman, University of Oklahoma Press, 1973. xiii, 176p.  16                          |
| IIIF   | White hurst, Jonathon W. THE MENHADEN FISHING INDUSTRY IN NORTH CAROLINA. Sea Grant publication UNC-SG-72-12. Chapel Hill, University of North Carolina Sea Grant Program, 1973. 51p.  13                                                                                                                          |
| IIIF   | Whiteleather, Richard T., and Herbert H. Brown. AN EXPERIMENTAL FISHERY SURVEY IN TRINIDAD, TOBAGO AND BRITISH GUIANA WITH RECOMMENDED IMPROVEMENTS IN METHODS AND GEAR. Washington, Anglo-American Caribbean Commission, 1945. iv, 130p.  14a                                                                     |
| VOD    | Whitesides, E., Jr. OCEAN DUMPING, BRIEFING DOCUMENT FOR PRESIDENT'S WATER POLLUTION CONTROL ADVISORY BOARD. Washington, U.S. Environmental Protection Agency, 1972. 2, 45p.  13                                                                                                                                   |
| IIIF   | Wick, Carl I. OCEAN HARVEST. THE STORY OF COMMERCIAL FISHING IN PACIFIC COAST WATERS. Seattle, Wash., Superior Publishing Company, 1946. 185p.  14a                                                                                                                                                                |
| IIE    | Wick, William Q. CRISIS - OREGON ESTUARIES - A SUMMARY OF ENVIRONMENTAL FACTORS AFFECTING OREGON ESTUARIES. Oregon State University Sea Grant Program. Corvallis, Oregon State University, n.d. 7p.  13                                                                                                            |
| IIIF   | Wijkstrom, U.N. PROCESSING AND MARKETING MARINE FISH - POSSIBLE GUIDELINES FOR THE 1975-1976 PERIOD. In International Conference on Marine Resource Development in Eastern Africa. Held at the University of Dar es Salaam, Tanzania, April 4-9, 1974, in cooperation with The International Center for Marine Resource Development at the University of Rhode Island. Kingston, University of Rhode Island, 1974. pp. 55-68.  ART |
| VLOS   | Wike, A.R. THE STOCKHOLM CONFERENCE: SOME IMPLICATIONS FOR THE LAW OF THE SEA. In S.W. Wurfel, Current Aspects of Sea Law. Sea Grant Publication UNC-SG-74-03. Chapel Hill, University of North Carolina School of Law, 1974. pp. 11-17.  ART                                                                      |

                                                              ***

IIIF     Williams, Anne D. EFFECTS OF FOREIGN FISHING ON THE COASTAL MARINE FISHERIES OF NEW YORK STATE. Albany, Office of Science Adviser to The New York Assembly, 1975.

                                                              ***

VOD      Williams, Joseph W., Jr. FY 1973 NAVY PROGRAM FOR SHIPBOARD SEWAGE COLLECTION, HOLDING, AND TRANSFER AND OIL POLLUTION CONTROL SYSTEMS. San Diego, Calif., U.S. Navy, Public Affairs Office, 1972? 18p.

                                                              ***

VP       Wilson, C.A. CRUDE OIL SPILLS RESEARCH: AN INVESTIGATION AND EVALUATION OF ANALYTICAL TECHNIQUES. Washington, U.S. Bureau of Mines, 1975. 32p.

                                                              ***

IIOSTR   Wilson, Douglas. HAWAII'S FLOATING CITY DEVELOPMENT PROGRAM: CONCRETE FOR LARGE FLOATING STRUCTURES. UNIHI-SEAGRANT-CR-74-02. Honolulu, University of Hawaii, 1974. 76p.

                                                             7,18

VORM     Wilson, Gary W. THE WORLD OCEAN: INTERNATIONAL PROBLEMS AND AMERICA'S CHOICES. Master's Thesis. Naval Postgraduate School, September 1971.

                                                              ***

IIWQ     Williams, John R., and Gary D. Tasker. WATER RESOURCES OF THE COASTAL DRAINAGE BASINS OF SOUTHEASTERN MASSACHUSETTS, WEIR RIVER, HINGHAM, TO JONES RIVER, KINGSTON. Prepared in cooperation with United States Geological Survey. Hydrologic investigation atlas HA-504. Boston, Water Resources Commission, 1974.

                                                             13

VP       Wimpress, D.S., et al. Garrett Corporation. AiResearch Manufacturing Division of Los Angeles. OIL/WATER SEPARATION SYSTEM WITH SEA SKIMMER. Prepared for the Office of Research and Monitoring, Environmental Protection Agency. Water pollution control research series. Washington, U.S. Environmental Protection Agency, 1970. xi, 187p.

                                                            ART

IIIAFF   Winget, Rodner R., et al. THE FEASIBILITY OF CLOSED SYSTEM MARICULTURE: PRELIMINARY EXPERIMENTS WITH CRAB MOLTING. In Proceedings of the National Shellfisheries Association, Vol. 63, June 1973. pp. 88-92.

                                                              ***

IIIF     Winn, Edward L., III. SOME LEGAL ASPECTS OF THE ATLANTIC LOBSTER INDUSTRY. UNC-SG-75-07. Raleigh, University of North Carolina, 1975. 15p.

                                                 2,5,12,14,16,18

VINTL    Wirsing, Robert G., ed. SYMPOSIUM ON INTERNATIONAL RELATIONS AND THE FUTURE OF OCEAN SPACE, UNIVERSITY OF SOUTH CAROLINA, 1972. INTERNATIONAL RELATIONS AND THE FUTURE OF OCEAN SPACE. Studies in International Affairs, no. 10. Columbia, S.C., published for the Institute of International Studies, University of South Carolina by the University of South Carolina Press, 1974. xi, 146p.

                                                                    17
VSG      Wisconsin. University. Sea Grant Program. PROGRESS REPORT OF SEA
         GRANT ACTIVITIES; A REPORT OF PROJECT ACTIVITIES CONDUCTED UNDER
         SEA GRANT INSTITUTIONAL SUPPORT AT THE UNIVERSITY OF WISCONSIN.
         Madison, 1969.

                                                                    17
VSG      _____ A PROPOSAL TO THE NATIONAL OCEANIC AND ATMOSPHERIC
         ADMINISTRATION, DEPARTMENT OF COMMERCE, FOR CONTINUATION OF SEA GRANT
         INSTITUTIONAL SUPPORT FOR 1971-72, BY THE UNIVERSITY OF WISCONSIN.
         Vol. II. Madison, 1971. 435p.

                                                                    17
VOI      WISCONSIN SEA GRANT CONFERENCE FOR INDUSTRIAL EXECUTIVES, 2d, MADI-
         SON, 1969. PROCEEDINGS. Sea Grant Office public information report
         no. 2. Madison, University of Wisconsin, 1969. v, 85p.

                                                                     3
IIIF     Wisdom, A.S. WATER RIGHTS, INCLUDING FISHING RIGHTS. London, Oyez,
         1969. 138p.

                                                                     6
VOI      Wissmann, Rudolf W. THE MARITIME INDUSTRY; FEDERAL REGULATION IN
         ESTABLISHING LABOR AND SAFETY STANDARDS. New York, Cornell Maritime
         Press, 1942. xiv, 386p.

                                                                     3
VMLAD    Wiswall, F.L. THE DEVELOPMENT OF ADMIRALTY JURISDICTION AND PRAC-
         TICE SINCE 1800; AN ENGLISH STUDY WITH AMERICAN COMPARISONS. Cam-
         bridge, England, Cambridge University Press, 1970. xxvii, 223p.

                                                                    14
IICZM    Wolf, James M. LAND MANAGEMENT IN THE LAKE ONTARIO BASIN. Great
         Lakes Management Problems Series. Albany, New York State Sea Grant
         Program, 1973. vi, 39p.

                                                                    13
IIIFV&G  Wolf, Robert S. RESEARCH VESSELS OF THE NATIONAL MARINE FISHERIES
         SERVICE. NOAA technical report NMFS CIRC-362. Washington, U.S.
         G.P.O., 1971. iii, 46p.

                                                                   ***
VP       Wolfe, L. Stephen, and David P. Hoult. EFFECTS OF OIL UNDER SEA ICE.
         Publication no. 72-10. Cambridge, M.I.T. Press, 1972. 40p.

                                                                   ***
IIIFP    Wolff, R.P. THE POTENTIAL USE OF TRASH FISH CAUGHT BY SHRIMP TRAWL-
         ERS. Mimeo. Miami, University of Miami, Institute of Marine Sci-
         ence, 1965.

                                         1,4,5,7,8,11,13,14,15,16,18
IIIINTL  Wolff, Thomas. PERUVIAN-UNITED STATES RELATIONS OVER MARITIME FISH-
         ING: 1945-1969. Law of the Sea Institute occasional paper no. 4.
         Kingston, University of Rhode Island, 1970. 26p.

                                                                   ***
VENV     Wood, D.W., ed. IMPINGEMENT OF MAN ON THE OCEANS. New York, Wiley-
         Interscience, 1971. 704p.

                                                              ***
IIIMM    Wood, F.G.  MARINE MAMMALS AND MAN:  THE NAVY'S PORPOISES AND SEA
         LIONS.  New York, David McKay Company, 1973.  270p.

                                                              ***
IVMMR    Woodland, A.W., ed.  PETROLEUM AND THE CONTINENTAL SHELF OF NORTH-
         WEST EUROPE: VOL. I:  GEOLOGY.  New York, John Wiley and Sons,
         Halstead Press, 1975.  465p.

                                                               17
VOS      Woodrow Wilson International Center for Scholars.  OCEAN STUDIES PRO-
         GRAM AT THE WOODROW WILSON INTERNATIONAL CENTER FOR SCHOLARS, 1970-
         1971.  Washington, D.C., 1971.  16p.

                                                              14a
VOCET    Woods, J.D., and J.N. Lythgoe, eds.  UNDERWATER SCIENCE; AN INTRO-
         DUCTION TO EXPERIMENTS BY DIVERS.  London, New York, Oxford Univer-
         sity Press, 1971.  xiii, 330p.

                                                               17
VOR      Woods Hole Oceanographic Institution.  ANNUAL REPORT.  Woods Hole,
         Mass., n.d.

                                                              ***
VOD      Woodward, J.B.  SOURCES OF OIL AND WATER IN BILGES OF GREAT LAKE
         SHIPS.  Washington, U.S.G.P.O., July, 1974.  34p.

                                                  1,2,5,7,12,13,16,18
VINTL    Wooster, Warren S., ed.  FREEDOM OF OCEANIC RESEARCH.  A study con-
         ducted by the Center for Marine Affairs of the Scripps Institution
         of Oceanography, University of California.  New York, Crane, Russak
         and Company, 1973.  255p.

                                                                1
VENV     _____  THE OCEAN AND MAN.  Entire issue of Scientific Ameri-
         can, Vol. 221, no. 3, September 1969.  p. 218.

                                                              14a
VOCET    _____  Symposium on Scientific Exploration of the South
         Pacific.  Scripps Institution of Oceanography, 1968.  SCIENTIFIC
         EXPLORATION OF THE SOUTH PACIFIC; PROCEEDINGS OF A SYMPOSIUM HELD
         DURING THE NINTH GENERAL MEETING OF THE SCIENTIFIC COMMITTEE ON
         OCEANIC RESEARCH.  Washington, National Academy of Sciences, 1970.
         vii, 257p.

                                                               13
IIIF     Workshop on Fisheries Cooperatives, Galilee, R.I., 1972.  FISHERIES
         COOPERATIVES:  THEIR FORMATION AND OPERATION.  University of Rhode
         Island Marine Advisory Service Marine memorandum 30.  Narragansett,
         University of Rhode Island Marine Advisory Service, 1972.  16p.

                                                               17
VENV     Workshop on Global Ecological Problems, University of Wisconsin,
         1971.  MAN IN THE LIVING ENVIRONMENT; REPORT.  Madison, University
         of Wisconsin Press, 1972.  xxiii, 288p.

14a
VP        Workshop on Inputs, Fates, and the Effects of Petroleum in the Marine Environment, Airlie House, 1973. PETROLEUM IN THE MARINE ENVIRONMENT. Workshop on Inputs, Fates, and the Effects of Petroleum in the Marine Environment, May 21-25, 1973, Airlie House, Virginia. Held under the auspices of the Ocean Affairs Board. Commission on Natural Resources, National Research Council. Washington, National Academy of Sciences, 1975. xi, 107p.

13
IIIAFF    World Mariculture Society. PROCEEDINGS OF THE FIRST ANNUAL WORKSHOP: WORLD MARICULTURE SOCIETY, HELD AT LOUISIANA STATE UNIVERSITY, BATON ROUGE, LOUISIANA, FEBRUARY 9-10, 1970. Baton Rouge, Louisiana State University, 1971. 1-    1971-

13
VOCET     World Meteorological Organization. GLOBAL OCEAN RESEARCH. Reports on marine science affairs. Report no. 1, prepared by a Joint Work Party of the Scientific Committee on Oceanic Research (ICSU), the Advisory Committee on Marine Resources Research (FAO) and the Advisory Group on Oceanic Research (WMO) Geneva, Secretariat of the World Meteorological Organization, 1970. xxxvii, 47p.

2
VT&L      World Peace Through Law Center. United Nations Committee. TREATY GOVERNING THE EXPLORATION AND USE OF THE OCEAN BED. Geneva, 1968? 27p.

***
IIE       Wright, F.F. A PRIMER TO ESTUARINE OCEANOGRAPHY. Fairbanks, University of Alaska, Institute of Marine Science, 1975. 106p.

16
VP        Wright, Gordon P., and David G. Olson. DESIGNING WATER POLLUTION DETECTION SYSTEMS: ENVIRONMENTAL LAW ENFORCEMENT ON THE U.S. COASTAL WATERS AND THE GREAT LAKES. Cambridge, Mass., Ballinger Publishing Company, 1974. xix, 227p.

ART
IVMMR     Wright, J.E., et al. RECENT GEOLOGICAL EXPLORATION OF THE CONTINENTAL SHELF AROUND THE BRITISH ISLES. In Twenty-fourth session of the International Geological Congress, held in Montreal, Canada, 1972. pp. 201-211.

ART
IISL      Wright, J. Skelly. JURISDICTION IN THE TIDELANDS. In Ralph Slovenko, ed., Oil and Gas Operations. Baton Rouge, Claitor's, 1963. pp. 20-31.

5,12,13,16
VP        Wulf, Norman. CONTIGUOUS ZONES FOR POLLUTION CONTROL: AN APPRAISAL UNDER INTERNATIONAL LAW. University of Miami Sea Grant Program NSF Grant - GH 100. Technical Bulletin No. 3. Fla., University of Miami, March, 1971. vi, 189p.

1,13,18
VLOS      Wurfel, Seymour W. CURRENT ASPECTS OF SEA LAW. Sea Grant publication UNC-SG-74-03. Raleigh, North Carolina State University, 1974. ii, 105p.

IVM  Wurfel, Seymour W. EMERGING OCEAN OIL AND MINING LAW. Sea Grant Publication UNC-SG-74-02. Raleigh, North Carolina State University, 1974. 61p.  
        13,18

***

IIIINTL  \_\_\_\_\_ \_\_\_\_\_ INTERNATIONAL FISHERY LAW. UNC-SG-74-01. Raleigh, North Carolina State University, 1974.

***

VP  \_\_\_\_\_ \_\_\_\_\_ LEGAL MEASURES CONCERNING MARINE POLLUTION. Sea Grant Program. Chapel Hill, University of North Carolina, 1975. 80p.

IIIINTL  \_\_\_\_\_ \_\_\_\_\_ SOME ASPECTS OF INTERNATIONAL FISHERY LAW. University of North Carolina Sea Grant publication UNC-SG-74-01. Chapel Hill, March, 1974. 90p.  
        1,13,18

VLOS  \_\_\_\_\_ \_\_\_\_\_ THE SURGE OF SEA LAW. Sea Grant Publication UNC-SG-73-01. Chapel Hill, University of North Carolina, School of Public Health, 1973. ii, 246p.  
        1,13,14

***

VLOS  Wurfel, Seymour W., ed. ATTITUDES REGARDING A LAW OF THE SEA CONVENTION TO ESTABLISH AN INTERNATIONAL SEABED REGIME. UNC-SG-72-02. Raleigh, North Carolina State University, 1972.

***

VLOS  \_\_\_\_\_ \_\_\_\_\_ SOME CURRENT SEA LAW PROBLEMS. UNC-SG-75-06. Raleigh, University of North Carolina, 1975. 73p.

IIOSTR  Yamashita, Yoshihiko. HAWAII'S FLOATING CITY DEVELOPMENT PROGRAM. Technical Report no. 3. UNIHI-SEAGRANT-CR-74-01. Honolulu, University of Hawaii, 1973. vi, 134p.  
        13

IISL  Yancey, Benjamin W. INSURANCE AGAINST DAMAGE TO PROPERTY IN THE TIDELANDS. In Ralph Slovenko, ed., Oil and Gas Operations. Baton Rouge, Claitor's, 1963. pp. 599-616.  
        ART

***

VENV  Yannacone, V.J., Jr., et al. ENVIRONMENTAL RIGHTS AND REMEDIES. Rochester, N.Y., Lawyers Co-operative Publishing Company, 1972-1973. 2 Vols. with supplements.

VB  Yates, George T., III, and John H. Young, eds. LIMITS TO NATIONAL JURISDICTION OVER THE SEA. Virginia Legal Studies. Charlottesville, Va., University of Virginia Press, 1974. 224p.  
        10,14,16

***

IIP&H  Yep, W. JAPAN: A SURVEY OF PORTS, DEEPWATER TERMINALS, AND VESSELS. Alexandria, Va., U.S. Army Institute for Water Resources, 1973. 274p.

|  |  |
|---|---|
| IIIOI | ART<br>Yonker, Walter. FISHERIES USES OF THE SEA; INDUSTRY INTERESTS. In Conference on Local Impacts of the Law of the Sea, Seattle, Wash., 1972. Local impacts of the law of the sea; proceedings of a conference held in Seattle, October 10-12, 1972. Seattle, University of Washington, Division of Marine Resources, 1973. pp. 68-74. |
| VLOS | 7,14,16<br>Young, Elizabeth, and Brian Johnson. THE LAW OF THE SEA. London, Fabian Society, 1973. 48p. |
| VLOS | ***<br>Young, E., and P. Fricke. SEA USE PLANNING. London, Fabian Society, 1975. 35p. |
| IVMMR | ART<br>Young, R. INTERNATIONAL POLICY CONSIDERATIONS RELATING TO OCEAN MINERAL RESOURCES. In Narragansett Marine Laboratory occasional publication no. 4. Kingston, University of Rhode Island, 1968. pp. 104-107. |
| VP | 2<br>Young, Wayland H. CONTROLLING OUR ENVIRONMENT. Fabian Society research series, 283. London, Fabian Society, 1970. 20p. |
| VOR | 14<br>Youngquist, Walter. INVESTING IN NATURAL RESOURCES: TODAY'S GUIDE TO TOMORROW'S NEEDS. New York, Dow Jones, 1975. 241p. |
| VMT | ART<br>Yturriaga, J.A. de. NAVIGATION THROUGH THE TERRITORIAL SEA INCLUDING STRAITS USED FOR INTERNATIONAL NAVIGATION. In Hazards of Maritime Transit, Third Law of the Sea Workshop, 1973. Cambridge, Mass., Massachusetts Institute of Technology, 1973. pp. 85-89. |
| IIENE | ***<br>Yumori, Isao R. THE FEASIBILITY OF OFFSHORE COAL-FIRED ELECTRICAL POWER GENERATION. UNIHI-SEAGRANT-CR-75-02. Honolulu, University of Hawaii, 1975. 122p. |
| VENE | ***<br>_____ SEAWARD EXTENSION OF URBAN SYSTEMS. THE FEASIBILITY OF OFFSHORE COAL-FIRED ELECTRICAL POWER GENERATION. Technical report no. 7. UNIHI-SEAGRANT-CR-75-02. Honolulu, University of Hawaii, 1975. 121p. |
| VLOS | 6,7,10,12,14,16<br>Zacklin, Ralph, ed. THE CHANGING LAW OF THE SEA; WESTERN HEMISPHERE PERSPECTIVES. Carnegie Endowment for International Peace, Inter-American Study Group of International Law. Leyden, Sijthoff, 1974. iv, 272p. |
| VINTL | 1<br>Zaragoza, Universidad de. Seminario de Estudios Internacionales. ESTUDIOS DE DERECHO INTERNACIONAL MARITIMO. Zaragoza, 1963. |
| IVMMR | 5,16<br>Zaslawski, Emil K. OIL UNDER THE HIGH SEAS. Carbondale, Southern Illinois University Press, 1960. 39p. |

ART
VENE    Zener, C. SOLAR SEA POWER. In Quarterly Progress Report NSF-RA/
        N-73-063. Washington, D.C., U.S. National Science Foundation,
        1973.

***
VENE    Zener, C., et al. SOLAR SEA POWER. Publication NSF/RA/N-74-14.
        Washington, U.S. National Science Foundation, July 31, 1974. 139p.

***
VINTL   Zhudro, A.K. i Dzhavad, ÎÛ. KH. MORSKOE PRAVO. Moskva, Transport,
        1974. 383p.

***
IVMMR   Zhuravlyev, A.V., et al. THE SAKHALIN SHELF: GEOLOGICAL STRUCTURE.
        OIL AND GAS PROSPECTS AND WAYS OF OIL/GAS DEVELOPMENT. Moscow,
        All-Union Scientific Research, Geological and Geophysical Institute,
        1972? 191p.

13
IIE     Zinn, Jeffrey A. ANALYSIS OF SILETZ BAY ESTUARY. Salem, Or., Di-
        vision of State Lands, 1970. 61p.

14
IIREC   Zook, William J. COASTAL RIVERS SPORT FISHING INVESTIGATIONS IN
        1973; SUPPLEMENTAL PROGRESS REPORT, COASTAL SALMON PROGRAM, APRIL,
        1974. Olympia, Washington State Department of Fisheries, Management
        and Research Division. 23p.

13
VP      Zwick, David R., ed. NADER TASK FORCE REPORT ON WATER POLLUTION.
        WATER WASTELAND. Introduction by Ralph Nader. Preliminary Draft.
        Washington, D.C., Center for Study of Responsive Law, 1971. 2 Vols.


REFERENCE MATERIALS
By Category


II - COAST AND COASTAL ZONE MANAGEMENT

***
IIREFS  Brown, L.F., Jr., et al. COASTAL PROCESSES AND HAZARDS. NATURAL
        HAZARDS OF THE TEXAS COASTAL ZONE. Austin, University of Texas,
        1974. 13p.

***
IIREFS  Brinn, David. A SELECT BIBLIOGRAPHY ON POLLUTION OF ESTUARIES AND
        COASTAL WATERS WITH PARTICULAR REGARD TO INDUSTRIAL EFFLUENTS.
        Bibliographic series no. SM/BIB/785. London, British Steel Corpora-
        tion, Strip Mills Division. n.d. 5p.

***
IIREFS  California. Department of Water Resources. SEA-WATER INTRUSION IN
        CALIFORNIA, INVENTORY OF COASTAL GROUND WATER BASINS. Sacramento,
        1975. xii, 394p.

IIREFS    COMPENDIUM OF CURRENT ENVIRONMENTAL STUDIES IN PUGET SOUND AND NORTH-
WEST ESTUARINE WATERS. Seattle, Oceanographic Institute of Washington, 1975. 370p.

***

IIREFS    Coastal Plains Center for Marine Development Services. DEVELOPMENT ACTIVITIES IN THE MARINE ENVIRONMENT OF THE COASTAL PLAINS REGION. DIRECTORY OF FACILITIES. Washington, D.C., 1971. 84p.

***

IIREFS    _____ _____ A DIRECTORY OF BIBLIOGRAPHIES RELEVANT TO THE ENVIRONMENT AND ACTIVITIES OF THE COASTAL PLAINS REGION. Wilmington, N.C., 1972. 43p.

***

IIREFS    _____ _____ MARINE LITERATURE. SERIAL PUBLICATIONS IN LIBRARIES OF THE COASTAL PLAINS REGION. Wilmington, N.C., 1973. 2 Parts.

***

IIREFS    _____ _____ SUMMARY OF MARINE ACTIVITIES OF THE COASTAL PLAINS REGION. Wilmington, N.C., 1974. 39p.

***

IIREFS    CURRENT ENVIRONMENTAL STUDIES IN PUGET SOUND AND NORTHWEST ESTUARINE WATERS - A COMPENDIUM. Seattle, Oceanographic Institute of Washington, 1974. 370p. Looseleaf.

***

IIREFS    Delaware. University. A GUIDE TO DELAWARE'S COASTLINE MARINAS. Newark, Sea Grant Marine Advisory Service, 1975. 12p.

***

IIREFS    Dolan, Robert, and Bruce Hayden. CLASSIFICATION OF COASTAL ENVIRONMENTS, PROCEDURES AND GUIDELINES. Charlottesville, University of Virginia, Department of Environmental Sciences, 1973.

***

IIREFS    Doran, Edwin, Jr., and B.P. Brown, Jr. A RECREATIONAL GUIDE TO THE CENTRAL TEXAS COAST. TAMU-SG-75-606. College Station, Texas A&M University, 1975. 131p.

IIREFS    Ducsik, Dennis W. A HANDBOOK OF SOCIAL, ECONOMIC, AND LEGAL CONSIDERATIONS REGARDING PUBLIC RECREATIONAL USE OF THE NATION'S COASTAL SHORELINE. MITSG NG-43-72. Cambridge, Massachusetts Institute of Technology, 1974. xiii, 257p.

***

IIREFS    Habercom, G.E., Jr. OFFSHORE STRUCTURES - A BIBLIOGRAPHY WITH ABSTRACTS. Springfield, Va., NTIS, 1974.

***

IIREFS    _____ _____ SUPERTANKERS AND SUPERPORTS. A bibliography with abstracts. Springfield, Va., U.S. Technical Information Service, 1974. 76p.

IIREFS    Heikoff, Joseph. SHORELINES AND BEACHES IN COASTAL MANAGEMENT: A BIBLIOGRAPHY. Monticello, Ill., Council of Planning Librarians,

1975. 63p.

IIREFS  Herbich, John B., and R.H. Snider. BIBLIOGRAPHY ON DREDGING. Texas Engineering Experiment Station. NSF Sea Grant Institutional Grant GH-26. Texas A&M University, Center for Dredging Studies, September, 1969. 20p.

***

VREFS  INDEX OF PUBLICATIONS RELATIVE TO THE MISSISSIPPI GULF COAST. MSGP-72-012. Hattiesburg, University of Southern Mississippi, 1972.

***

IIREFS  McGill, John T. SELECTED BIBLIOGRAPHY OF COASTAL GEOMORPHOLOGY OF THE WORLD. Los Angeles, University of California, 1960. 50p.

***

IIREFS  Marr, Paul D., and April Shelford. A BIBLIOGRAPHY OF REGIONAL PLANNING REPORTS. NYSSGP-RS-75-027. Albany, New York Sea Grant Institute, State University of New York, 1975. 69p.

***

IIREFS  OIL POLLUTION AND THE SIGNIFICANT BIOLOGICAL RESOURCES OF PUGET SOUND: ANNOTATED BIBLIOGRAPHY. Olympia, Washington, Department of Ecology, 1975. 199p.

***

IIREFS  Passero, Barbara, and D.A. Horn. DIRECTORY OF M.I.T. RESEARCH PROJECTS RELATED TO MARINE RESOURCES, OCEAN UTILIZATION, AND COASTAL ZONE MANAGEMENT. MITSG 75-14. Cambridge, Massachusetts Institute of Technology, 1975. 51p.

***

IIREFS  Passero, B., and D.A. Horn, comp. DIRECTORY OF M.I.T. RESEARCH PROJECTS RELATED TO MARINE RESOURCES, OCEAN UTILIZATION AND COASTAL ZONE DEVELOPMENT. Report, MITSG 73-7. Cambridge, Massachusetts Institute of Technology. Sea Grant Project Office, 1973. 56p.

***

IIREFS  Reis, Robert I., ed. COASTAL ZONE LEGAL REFERENCES (SELECTED). Albany, State University of New York, Sea Grant Institute, 1975. 169p.

***

IIREFS  Schwartz, F.J., and A.F. Chestnut. HYDROGRAPHIC ATLAS OF NORTH CAROLINA ESTUARINE AND SOUND WATERS. UNC-SG-73-12. Raleigh, North Carolina State University, 1973.

IIREFS  Sinha, Evelyn. COASTAL/ESTUARINE POLLUTION. AN ANNOTATED BIBLIOGRAPHY. Ocean Engineering Information Series Vol. 3. La Jolla, Calif., Ocean Engineering Information Service, 1970. 87p.

***

IIREFS  _____ COASTAL-ESTUARINE AND NEARSHORE PROCESSESS: AN ANNOTATED BIBLIOGRAPHY. La Jolla, Ocean Engineering Information Service, 1974. 230p.

IIREFS      Sorensen, Jens, and M. Demers. COASTAL ZONE BIBLIOGRAPHY: CITA-
            TIONS TO DOCUMENTS ON PLANNING, RESOURCES MANAGEMENT AND IMPACT
            ASSESSMENT. IMR TR-43. La Jolla, Calif., University of California,
            1973. 89p.

IIREFS      Symonds, P.J. STATISTICAL HANDBOOK OF COASTAL ZONE SOCIO-ECONOMIC
            AND HOUSING CHARACTERISTICS: LOS ANGELES COUNTY. USC-SG-6-74. Los
            Angeles, University of Southern California, 1974. 150p.

IIREFS      United States. Department of Defense. Defense Mapping Agency.
            WORLD PORT INDEX. Washington, U.S.G.P.O., 1971. xxix, 333p.


III - MARINE RESOURCES (LIVING)

IIIREFS     Alaska. Office of the Governor. INTERNATIONAL FISHERIES AND EX-
            TERNAL AFFAIRS. LANGUAGE DIRECTORY. Annual. Juneau, May 1975.
            22p.

IIIREFS     AQUACULTURE BIBLIOGRAPHIC FILE - COMPUTERIZED. Washington, U.S.
            Department of Commerce, National Oceanic and Atmospheric Administra-
            tion, OASIS, 1976.

IIIREFS     California. Department of Fish and Game. DIGEST OF COMMERCIAL FISH
            LAWS. A. Petrovich, Jr., comp. Sacramento, 1976. 31p.

IIIREFS     California. Marine Research Committee. CALIFORNIA COOPERATIVE
            OCEANIC FISHERIES INVESTIGATION. ATLAS. Sacramento, 1975.

                                                                              14a
IIIREFS     Carter, Neal M. INDEX AND LIST OF TITLES, FISHERIES RESEARCH
            BOARD OF CANADA AND ASSOCIATED PUBLICATIONS, 1965-1972. Ottawa,
            Fisheries Research Board of Canada, 1973. 588p.

IIIREFS     Coutant, C.C., et al. THERMAL EFFECTS ON AQUATIC ORGANISMS: ANNO-
            TATED BIBLIOGRAPHY OF THE 1973 LITERATURE. Oak Ridge, Tn., AEC,
            Oak Ridge National Laboratories, 1975.

IIREFS      DeLacy, Allan C., et al. A CHECKLIST OF PUGET SOUND FISHES. PASGAP
            WSG 72-3. Seattle, University of Washington, Sea Grant Communica-
            tions, 1972. 43p.

IIIREFS     Engelhardt, Heinz, ed. THE SOUTH AFRICAN FISHING INDUSTRY HANDBOOK
            AND BUYER'S GUIDE 1972/1973. 11th ed. Cape Town, Thompson Publi-
            cations, South Africa (PTY.) Ltd., 1973. 258p.

IIIREFS     _____ THE SOUTH AFRICAN FISHING INDUSTRY HANDBOOK AND BUY
            ER'S GUIDE: 1974/75. 12th ed. Cape Town, South Africa, Thompson

Publications, 1975? 203p.

IIIREFS   Engett, Mary Ellen, and Lee C. Thorson. FISHERY PUBLICATIONS, CALENDAR YEAR 1970: LISTS AND INDEXES. NOAA Technical Report NMFS CIRC-377. Seattle, Wash., 1972. ix, 34p.   13

\*\*\*

IIIREFS   Food and Agricultural Organization of the United Nations. ATLAS OF THE LIVING RESOURCES OF THE SEA. Rome, FAO, 1973.

\*\*\*

IIIREFS   \_\_\_\_\_  \_\_\_\_\_  CURRENT BIBLIOGRAPHY FOR AQUATIC SCIENCES AND FISHERIES. Compiled by Biological Data Section, Fish Stock Evaluation Branch, Fishery Resources and Exploitation Division, FAO. London, Taylor and Francis, Ltd., 1959. Annual. 3 Vols.

\*\*\*

IIIREFS   \_\_\_\_\_  \_\_\_\_\_  FAO CATALOG OF FISHING GEAR DESIGNS. London, Fishing News (Books), 1973. 155p.

IIIREFS   \_\_\_\_\_  \_\_\_\_\_  MANUAL ON FISHERMEN'S COOPERATIVES. FAO fisheries studies, no. 13. Rome, 1971. vii, 124p.   13

\*\*\*

IIIREFS   \_\_\_\_\_  \_\_\_\_\_  Fishery Economics and Institutions Division and the Fishery Industries Division, Department of Fisheries. FISHING PORTS AND MARKETS. London, Fishing News (Books) Ltd., 1970. 396p.

IIIREFS   Food and Agriculture Organization of the United Nations. Documentation Center. FISHERIES: ANNOTATED BIBLIOGRAPHY. Pêches; bibliographie annotée. Pesca; bibliografia anotada. FAO publications and documents (1945-1969). Rome, 1969. 2 Vols.   13

IIIREFS   Forbes, S.T., and O. Nakken, eds. MANUAL OF METHODS FOR FISHERIES RESOURCE SURVEY AND APPRAISAL. Part 2. The use of acoustic instruments for fish detection and abundance estimation. FAO manuals in fisheries science no. 5. Rome, Food and Agriculture Organization of the United Nations, 1972. xiii, 138p.   13

\*\*\*

IIIREFS   Ginter, Jay J.C. A CATALOG OF MARINE FISHERIES LEGISLATION IN NEW YORK STATE. Albany, State University of New York, Sea Grant Institute, 1974. 89p.

\*\*\*

IIIREFS   Gleason, Robert. RESOURCE INVENTORY, ARCTIC REGION, MARINE BIOLOGICAL RESOURCES. Anchorage, Alaska, Joint Federal-State Land Use Planning Commission. Resource Planning Team, 1974. 22p.

IIIREFS   Heald, Eric J. UNIVERSITY OF MIAMI SEA GRANT PROGRAM (ESTUARINE AND COASTAL STUDIES) FISHERY RESOURCES ATLAS I NEW YORK TO FLORIDA. Sea Grant Technical Bulletin no. 3. Coral Gables, University of Miami, 1970. 225p.   13

IIIREFS  Heald, Eric J. UNIVERSITY OF MIAMI SEA GRANT PROGRAM (ESTUARINE AND COASTAL STUDIES) FISHERY RESOURCES ATLAS II, WEST COAST OF FLORIDA TO TEXAS. Technical Bulletin no. 4. Coral Gables, University of Miami, 1970. 174p.
    13

IIIREFS  KEY BOOK TO WORLD MAP OF FISHERIES. Copenhagen, Denmark, Jorgen Frimodt, 1966.
    15

IIIREFS  Manar, Thomas A. FISHERY PUBLICATIONS, CALENDAR YEAR 1971: LISTS AND INDEXES. NOAA Technical report NMFS CIRC-37. Washington, U.S. G.P.O., 1972. 14, 24p.
    13

IIIREFS  National Geographic Society, Washington, D.C. THE BOOK OF FISHES; GAME FISHES, FOOD FISHES, SHELLFISH AND CURIOUS CITIZENS OF AMERICAN OCEAN SHORES, LAKES AND RIVERS; with 134 illustrations, color plates of 92 familiar salt and fresh-water fishes ... color plates from life by Hashime Murayama. Washington, D.C., The National Geographic Society, 1924. 243p.
    14a

IIIREFS  North Pacific Fur Seal Commission. Standing Scientific Committee. GLOSSARY OF TERMS USED IN FUR SEAL RESEARCH AND MANAGEMENT. Fishery leaflet 546. Washington, D.C., Bureau of Commercial Fisheries, 1969. 9p.
    13

IIIREFS  Nowak, W.S.W., comp. THE LOBSTERS (HOMARIDAE) AND THE LOBSTER FISHERIES: AN INTERDISCIPLINARY BIBLIOGRAPHY. St. John's Memorial University of Newfoundland, 1972. 313p.
    16

IIIREFS  Ovens, Carol, ed. EQUIPMENT AND SUPPLIES DIRECTORIES. DIRECTORY OF SERVICES FOR MARINERS, NORTH PACIFIC COAST. Washington Sea Grant Publication. n.p. 1973. 159p.
    ***

IIIREFS  Rickards, W.L. A BIBLIOGRAPHY OF ARTIFICIAL REEFS AND OTHER MAN-MADE FISH ATTRACTANTS. UNC-SG-73-04. Raleigh, North Carolina State University, 1973.
    ***

IIIREFS  Schuster, W.H. AN ANNOTATED BIBLIOGRAPHY ON THE CULTURE OF MILKFISH CHANOS CHANOS FORSKAL. Indo-Pacific Fisheries Council occasional paper 52/3. n.p. 1952.
    ***

IIIREFS  United States Environmental Data Service. BIBLIOGRAPHY ON MARINE BIOLOGY. Rockville, Md., 1972.

IIIREFS  Wooster, Warren S., et al. ATLAS OF THE ARABIAN SEA FOR FISHERY OCEANOGRAPHY. Prepared for the Food and Agricultural Organization of the United Nations. La Jolla, Calif., University, n.d.
    15

## IV - MARINE RESOURCES (NON-LIVING)

IVREFS     Cruickshank, Michael J. MINING AND MINERAL RECOVERY. Reprinted from Undersea Technology Handbook/Directory. Arlington, Compass Publications, Inc., 1969.   ART

***

IVREFS     EUROPEAN OFFSHORE OIL AND GAS YEARBOOK 1975-1976. 1st ed. New York, International Publications Service, 1975. 300p. A new companion volume to the U.K. Offshore oil and gas yearbook.

***

IVREFS     Habercom, G.E., Jr. OFFSHORE DRILLING - A BIBLIOGRAPHY WITH ABSTRACTS. Springfield, Va., NTIS, 1974.

***

IVREFS     Lai, N.W., et al. A BIBLIOGRAPHY OF OFFSHORE PIPELINE LITERATURE. TAMU-SG-74-206. College Station, Texas A&M University, 1973. 127p.

IVREFS     MAP OF LOUISIANA OFFSHORE GULF OF MEXICO SHOWING OIL AND GAS PIPE LINES. In Offshore, Vol. 32, no. 12, 1972. pp. 1   ART

IVREFS     MAP OF WORLD RESERVES OF OFFSHORE OIL AND GAS. In Offshore, Vol. 33, no. 4, 1973.   ART

IVREFS     NORTH SEA RIGS - WHO DOES WHAT. In Offshore Services, Vol. 6, no. 1, 1972. pp. 38-39; Vol. 8, 1975. pp. 34-37.   ART

***

IVREFS     Pulso, Patricia, and Trudy Wood. A GUIDE TO PUBLICATIONS AND SUBSEQUENT INVESTIGATIONS OF DEEP SEA DRILLING PROJECT MATERIALS. Prepared for National Science Foundation, National Ocean Sediment Coring Program, San Diego, University of California, Scripps Institution of Oceanography, January, 1975.
\_\_\_\_\_ \_\_\_\_\_ SUPPLEMENT. January-August, 1975. 31p.

***

IVREFS     Riggs, Stanley R., and M.P. O'Connor. GEOLOGICAL BIBLIOGRAPHY OF NORTH CAROLINA'S COASTAL PLAIN, COASTAL ZONE, AND CONTINENTAL SHELF. UNC-SG-75-13. Raleigh, University of North Carolina, 1975. 141p.

IVREFS     Texas A&M University. Sea Grant College Program. SEA GRANT PUBLICATIONS FOR THE OFFSHORE INDUSTRY. TAMU-SG-75-605. College Station, Department of Marine Resources, 1975. 12p.   14


## V - GENERAL

***

VREFS     Alaska. State Library. A GUIDE TO THE LAW OF THE SEA HOLDINGS IN JUNEAU. Juneau, 1975. iii, 9p.

|       |                                                                                                                                                                                                                              |
|-------|------------------------------------------------------------------------------------------------------------------------------------------------------------------------------------------------------------------------------|
| VREFS | 17<br>American Geographical Society of New York. SERIAL ATLAS OF THE MARINE ENVIRONMENT. Folio 1- New York, 1962- |
| VREFS | 14,16<br>Andrews, Joseph L. BIBLIOGRAPHY ON THE LAW OF USERS OF INTERNATIONAL RIVERS. New York, New York University School of Law, 1960. v, 119p. |
| VREFS | 13<br>Ashby, Charlotte M., comp. MARINE SCIENCE NEWSLETTERS - 1973; AN ANNOTATED BIBLIOGRAPHY. NOAA technical memorandum EDS NODC-3. Washington, D.C., National Oceanographic Data Center, 1973. ii, 26p. |
| VREFS | ***<br>_____ MARINE SCIENCE NEWSLETTERS - 1975. AN ANNOTATED BIBLIOGRAPHY. NOAA technical memorandum EDS NODC-4. Washington, D.C., National Oceanographic Data Center, 1975. 30p. |
| VREFS | 17<br>Auffhammer, Ida W., and William B. Deichmann. ABSTRACTS AND SUMMARIES OF THE LITERATURE ON DRUGS FROM THE SEA, 1967-1970. Sea Grant technical bulletin no. 16. Miami, Fla., University of Miami, 1971. vii, 191p. |
| VREFS | 13<br>Averitt, Paul, and M. Deveraux Carter. SELECTED SOURCES OF INFORMATION ON UNITED STATES AND WORLD ENERGY RESOURCES: AN ANNOTATED BIBLIOGRAPHY. U.S. Department of the Interior. Geological Survey Circular 641. Washington, U.S. Geological Survey, 1970. III, 21p. |
| VREFS | ***<br>Bacescu, Mihai. BIBLIOGRAPHIE ROUMAINE DE LA MER NOIRE. Bucarest, Comisia Nationala a Republicii Populare Romine pentru UNESCO, 1965. 122p. |
| VREFS | 17<br>Baker, R.B., W.R. Deebel, and R.D. Geisenderfer, eds. GLOSSARY OF OCEANOGRAPHIC TERMS. 2d ed. Special publication 35. Washington, U.S. Naval Oceanographic Office, 1966. vi, 204p. |
| VREFS | 3<br>Bermes, Annick, et J.P. Levy. BIBLIOGRAPHIE DU DROIT DE LA MER. Paris, Editions techniques et economiques, 1974. 138p. |
| VREFS | ***<br>A BIBLIOGRAPHY ON OCEAN WASTE DISPOSAL. Anaheim, Calif., Interstate Electronics Corp., Oceanics Department, 1973. 111p. |
| VREFS | 11<br>Brecher, Joseph J., and Manuel E. Nestle. ENVIRONMENTAL LAW HANDBOOK. Berkeley, California Continuing Education of the Bar, 1970. 343p. |
| VREFS | ***<br>Brown, R.J. OCEAN LAW - A BIBLIOGRAPHY WITH ABSTRACTS. Springfield Va., NTIS, 1975. |

VREFS  Burchell, Robert W., and David Listokin. THE ENVIRONMENTAL IMPACT HANDBOOK. New Brunswick, N.J., Rutgers University, Center for Urban Policy Research, 1975. 256p.

3
VREFS  Caeser, Julius. HANDBUCH DER DEUTSCHEN REICHSGESETZGEBUNG BETREFFEND DIE SEEUNFALLE UND DEREN UNTERSUCHUNG UND VERHUTUNG. n.p. n.d.

VREFS  California. University. Institute of Marine Resources. IMR REFERENCE SERIES 74-6. UNIVERSITY OF CALIFORNIA SEA GRANT COLLEGE PROGRAM DIRECTORY, 1973-74. Publication no. 28. Berkeley, Institute of Marine Resources, 1974. iv, 14p.

VREFS  _____ _____ SEA GRANT COLLEGE PROGRAM DIRECTORY 1974-1975. Sea Grant Publication no. 36. La Jolla, University of California Institute of Marine Resources, 1974. iv, 14p.

VREFS  _____ _____ SEA GRANT COLLEGE PROGRAM DIRECTORY 1975-1976. Sea Grant Publication no. 43. La Jolla, University of California Institute of Marine Resources, 1975. iv, 11p.

13,14
VREFS  Christol, Carl Q. OIL POLLUTION OF THE MARINE ENVIRONMENT - A LEGAL BIBLIOGRAPHY. Prepared for the use of the Committee on Public Works, United States Senate. Washington, U.S.G.P.O., 1971. 93p.

ART
VREFS  Compendium of 1974. MARINE ENVIRONMENTAL STUDIES. In Pacific Northwest Sea, Vol. 8, no. 2, 1975. pp. 4-11, 15.

VREFS  Cross, F.L., Jr., ed. MARINE ENVIRONMENTAL ENGINEERING HANDBOOK. Westport, Conn., Technomic Publishing Company, 1974. 186p.

VREFS  Cross, R., et al. OIL SPILLS CONTROL MANUAL FOR FIRE DEPARTMENTS. Technology series EPA-R2-73-117. Edison, N.J., U.S. Environmental Protection Agency, Office of Research and Monitoring, 1973. 96p.

VREFS  Deacon, G.E.R., ed. OCEANS; AN ATLAS-HISTORY OF MAN'S EXPLORATION OF THE DEEP. 2d ed. London, Paul Hamlyn, 1968. 297p.

VREFS  Dean, Flora. A BIBLIOGRAPHY OF NON-TECHNICAL LITERATURE ON ENERGY. Prepared at the request of H.M. Jackson, Chairman, Committee on Interior and Insular Affairs, U.S. Senate, pursuant to S.Res.45, a national fuels and energy policy study. 92d Congr., 1st sess., committee print. Washington, 1971. 99p.

VREFS  DIRECTORY OF INSTITUTIONS ENGAGED IN POLLUTION INVESTIGATIONS: CONTAMINANTS IN AQUATIC ORGANISMS. FAO Fisheries Circular 325. n.p., March, 1974. 49p.

VREFS   DIRECTORY OF INTERNATIONAL ENVIRONMENTAL MONITORING PROGRAMS. New York, UNIPUB, 1974-

VREFS   DIRECTORY OF MARINE-RELATED ACTIVITIES IN THE STATE OF HAWAII: 1973. UNIHI-SEAGRANT-MS-73-01. Honolulu, University of Hawaii, 1974. 52p.

VREFS   DIRECTORY OF MARINE SCIENCE RESEARCH 1974-1975. Los Angeles, University of Southern California, 1974. 57p.

VREFS   DIRECTORY OF NATIONAL AND INTERNATIONAL POLLUTION MONITORING PROGRAMS (UNITED NATIONS ENVIRONMENT PROGRAMME). New York, UNIPUB, 1974. 3 Vols.

VREFS   Durrenberger, Robert W. DICTIONARY OF ENVIRONMENTAL SCIENCES. Palo Alto, Calif., National Press Books, 1973. 285p.

15
VREFS   _____ ENVIRONMENT AND MAN; A BIBLIOGRAPHY. Palo Alto, Calif., National Press Books, 1970.

VREFS   Edmundson, Eldon, Jr., et al. MARINE RADIOECOLOGY, SELECTED BIBLIOGRAPHY OF NON-RUSSIAN LITERATURE; 1974. Washington, Atomic Energy Commission, 1974. i, 53p.

VREFS   ENVIRONMENTAL ATLAS AND MULTI-USE MANAGEMENT PLAN FOR SOUTH-CENTRAL LOUISIANA. Baton Rouge, Louisiana State University, Center for Wetland Resources, 1975? 2 Vols.

VREFS   Environmental Studies Institute. ENVIRONMENTAL PERIODICALS BIBLIOGRAPHY. Santa Barbara, International Academy, 1975?

17
VREFS   Fairbridge, Rhodes W., ed. THE ENCYCLOPEDIA OF OCEANOGRAPHY. Encyclopedia of Earth Sciences series, Vol. 1. New York, Reinhold Publishing Company, 1966. xiii, 1021p.

5,13
VREFS   Firth, Frank E. THE ENCYCLOPEDIA OF MARINE RESOURCES. Van Nostrand Reinhold Company, 1969. xi, 740p.

VREFS   FLORIDA SEA GRANT/PROGRAM DIRECTORY - 1974. SUSF-SG-74-001. Gainesville, University of Florida, 1974.

VREFS   FLORIDA SEA GRANT/PROGRAM DIRECTORY - 1976. SUSF-SG-76-001. Gainesville, University of Florida, 1976.

13,17
VREFS   Food and Agriculture Organization of the United Nations. Department of Fisheries. ATLAS OF THE LIVING RESOURCES OF THE SEAS. Atlas des ressources biologiques des mers. Atlas de los recursos vivos

del mar. 3d ed. Rome, 1972. vii, 19p.

VREFS Food and Agriculture Organization of the United Nations. Fishery Resources Division. INTERNATIONAL DIRECTORY OF MARINE SCIENTISTS. REPERTOIRE INTERNATIONAL DES EXPERTS DES SCIENCES DE LA MER/GUIA INTERNACIONAL DE EXPERTOS EN CIENCIAS DEL MAR. Rome, FAO. 1970. xiv, 193p.
  17

VREFS Forbes, Lynn. OCEANOGRAPHY IN PRINT; A SELECTED LIST OF EDUCATIONAL SOURCES. Falmouth, Mass., Oceanographic Education Center, 1968. 58p.
  ***

VREFS Fricke, Peter H., and Leif Landberg., comp. INDEX OF RECENT MARITIME RESEARCH. Cardiff, Department of Maritime Studies, University of Wales Institute of Sciences and Technology, 1973. ii, 88p.
  18

VREFS Gaffke, Vicki, and Gwil Evans, eds. INVENTORY NON-TECHNICAL MARINE RESOURCES PUBLICATIONS AND AUDIO-VISUAL MATERIALS. Compiled by Oregon State University Sea Grant Marine Advisory Program. PASGAP 5. Corvallis, Or., October, 1972. 75p.
  13

VREFS Gamble, John K., Jr. GLOBAL MARINE ATTRIBUTES. Cambridge, Mass., Ballinger Publishing Company, 1974. xi, 270p.
  1,5,13,16

VREFS _____ INDEX TO MARINE TREATIES. Washington Sea Grant Ocean Law publication 72-2. Seattle, University of Washington, Division of Marine Resources, 1972. 435p.
  5,13,14,16

VREFS Gamble, John K., Jr., et al. LAW OF THE SEA: A BIBLIOGRAPHY OF THE PERIODICAL LITERATURE OF THE 1970's. Law of the Sea Institute special publication no. 4. Kingston, University of Rhode Island, 1975. 80p.
  4,5,7,11,12,14

VREFS Harrison, Elizabeth A. ECOLOGY OF THE MARINE ENVIRONMENT: A BIBLIOGRAPHY WITH ABSTRACTS. Springfield, Va., National Technical Information Service, 1975. 210p.
  ***

VREFS Hartman, Charles W., and Robert F. Carlson. BIBLIOGRAPHY OF ARCTIC WATER RESOURCES. Fairbanks, University of Alaska, Institute of Water Resources, 1970. 538p.
  14

VREFS Hawaii. University. SEA GRANT COLLEGE PROGRAM MARINE ATLAS OF HAWAII, BAYS, AND HARBORS. Cartographer: Lois S. Nishimoto. UNIHI-SEAGRANT-MR-74-01. Honolulu, 1974. 241p.
  ***

VREFS _____ Sea Grant Program. DIRECTORY OF MARINE-RELATED ACTIVITIES IN THE STATE OF HAWAII. UNIHI-SEAGRANT-MS-73-01. Honolulu, 1974. 52p.

                                                                    ***
VREFS    Ho, Paul. PEOPLE'S REPUBLIC OF CHINA AND INTERNATIONAL LAW, SELEC-
         TIVE BIBLIOGRAPHY OF CHINESE SOURCES. U.S. Library of Congress,
         1972. xiii, 45p.

                                                                     13
VREFS    Hoduski, Bernadine E., comp. ENVIRONMENTAL SERVICES BIBLIOGRAPHY.
         Rev. Kansas City, U.S. Environmental Protection Agency, 1973. 26p.

                                           1,4,5,7,8,11,12,13,14,15,16,18
VREFS    Hollick, Ann L., ed. MARINE POLICY, LAW, AND ECONOMICS; ANNOTATED
         BIBLIOGRAPHY: THE 1960's. Kingston, University of Rhode Island,
         Law of the Sea Institute, 1970. ii, 184p.
         _____ _____ SUPPLEMENT. 1973.

                                                                     17
VREFS    Hunt, Lee M., and Donald G. Groves, eds. A GLOSSARY OF OCEAN SCI-
         ENCE AND UNDERSEA TECHNOLOGY TERMS; AN AUTHORITATIVE COMPILATION OF
         OVER 3,500 ENGINEERING AND SCIENTIFIC TERMS USED IN THE FIELD OF
         UNDERWATER SOUND, OCEANOGRAPHY, MARINE SCIENCES, UNDERWATER PHYSIOL-
         OGY AND OCEAN ENGINEERING. Arlington, Va., Compass Publications,
         1965. vii, 173p.

                                                                     13,18
VREFS    Hurd, Bronwyn, and B. Passero, comp. OCEANS OF THE WORLD: THE LAST
         FRONTIER; AN ANNOTATED BIBLIOGRAPHY ON THE LAW OF THE SEA. M.I.T.
         Sea Grant Program. Report no. MITSG 74-17. Cambridge, Massachusetts
         Institute of Technology, 1974. 10p.

                                                                    ***
VREFS    Hurd, Bronwyn, and Julie Frey. PUBLICATIONS 1970-1974. MITSG 75-9.
         Cambridge, Massachusetts Institute of Technology, 1975. 32p.

                                                                    ***
VREFS    Hurme, A.K. A GLOSSARY OF ECOLOGICAL TERMS FOR COASTAL ENGINEERS.
         Miscellaneous paper 2-74. Fort Belvoir, Va., U.S. Coastal Engineer-
         ing Research Center, 1974. 19p.

                                                                     17
VREFS    Huxley, Anthony J., ed. STANDARD ENCYCLOPEDIA OF THE WORLD'S OCEANS
         AND ISLANDS. 1st ed. New York, Putnam, 1962. 383p.

                                                                    ***
VREFS    Inter-Governmental Maritime Consultative Organization. IMCO PUBLI-
         CATIONS. London, 1975.

                                                                     17
VREFS    Johnson, Philip R., and Charles W. Hartman. ENVIRONMENTAL ATLAS
         OF ALASKA. College, Institute of Arctic Environmental Engineering,
         University of Alaska, 1969. iv, 111p.

                                                                     15
VREFS    Kessler, Myer M., and Gene V. Soccolich, eds. ANNUAL DIRECTORY OF
         ENVIRONMENTAL INFORMATION SOURCES; 1971. Boston, National Founda-
         tion for Environmental Control, 1971.

                                            2,4,7,11,12,13,14,15,16
VREFS    Koers, Albert W. THE DEBATE ON THE LEGAL REGIME FOR THE EXPLORATION
         AND EXPLOITATION OF OCEAN RESOURCES: A BIBLIOGRAPHY FOR THE FIRST
         DECADE, 1960-1970. Law of the Sea Institute special publication

no. 1. Kingston, University of Rhode Island, 1970. 44p.

***

VREFS    LEGAL ASPECTS OF WATER POLLUTION IN NEW JERSEY AND PENNSYLVANIA: A BIBLIOGRAPHY. Washington, U.S. Department of the Interior, Water Resources Scientific Information Center, 1972. 225p.

***

VREFS    Lehman, E.J. OCEAN WASTE DISPOSAL. A BIBLIOGRAPHY WITH ABSTRACTS. NTIS-WIN-74-062. Springfield, Va., U.S. National Technical Information Service, 1974. 146p.

4,5,7,11,12,14

VREFS    Llana, Christopher, John Gamble and Charlene Quinn. LAW OF THE SEA: A BIBLIOGRAPHY OF THE PERIODICAL LITERATURE OF THE 1970's. Law of the Sea Institute special publication no. 4. Kingston, University of Rhode Island, 1975. (See also Gamble, et al.)

***

VREFS    Louisiana. State University and Agricultural and Mechanical College. MARINE RESEARCH INTEREST IN LOUISIANA UNIVERSITIES. LSU-SG-75-02. Baton Rouge. 1-    1975-

***

VREFS    MAJOR OIL SPILL DIRECTORY. New York, UNIPUB, 1975. 142p.

***

VREFS    Mississippi-Alabama Sea Grant Consortium. SEA GRANT PUBLICATIONS 1971-1974. MASGAP-75-001. Ocean Springs, 1975. 15p.

14

VREFS    Muecke, Robert. INTERNATIONALES UMWELTRECHT - MULTILATERALE VERTRAEGE. (Parallel text in English/French/German.) Berlin, E. Schmidt, 1974-    3 Vols. Looseleaf.

14

VREFS    National Environmental Research Center, Cincinnati. ENVIRONMENTAL RESEARCH PUBLICATIONS, 1971-1975. Compiled by Technical Information Staff. Cincinnati, U.S. Environmental Protection Agency, Office of Research and Development, National Environmental Research Center. Washington, U.S.G.P.O., 1975. iv, 96p.

13

VREFS    Neal, Victor T., and Sally A. Kulm. READINGS IN MARINE SCIENCE, A PARTIALLY ANNOTATED BIBLIOGRAPHY FOR YOUNG READERS, NON-PROFESSIONALS AND TEACHERS. Corvallis, Oregon State University, Division of Continuing Education, 1968. 27p.

13

VREFS    New Mexico. University. Technology Application Center. HYDROGEN ENERGY; a bibliography with abstracts. Cumulative volume 1953 through 1973. Technical editor: Kenneth E. Cox. TAC-H 74-500. Albuquerque, N.M., 1974. 1 Vol.

15,17

VREFS    North, Jeannette P., comp. ANNOTATED ACRONYMS AND ABBREVIATIONS OF MARINE SCIENCE RELATED INTERNATIONAL ORGANIZATIONS. U.S. National Oceanographic Data Center general series publication G-18. n.p., 1969. xv, 115p.

　　　　　　　　　　　　　　　　　　　　　　　　　　　　　　　13,15
VREFS　　OCEAN AFFAIRS BIBLIOGRAPHY 1971. A selected list emphasizing international law, politics and economics of ocean uses. Ocean Series no. 302. Washington, Woodrow Wilson International Center for Scholars, 1971. v, 201p.

　　　　　　　　　　　　　　　　　　　　　　　　　　　　　　　17
VREFS　　OCEAN AFFAIRS BIBLIOGRAPHY. Washington, D.C., Woodrow Wilson International Center for Scholars, 1972.

　　　　　　　　　　　　　　　　　　　　　　　　　　　　　　　17
VREFS　　OCEAN RESEARCH INDEX; A GUIDE TO OCEAN AND FRESHWATER RESEARCH INCLUDING FISHERIES RESEARCH. Guernsey, British Isles, F. Hodgson, 1970. 507p.

　　　　　　　　　　　　　　　　　　　　　　　　　　　　　　　14a
VREFS　　OCEANIC ABSTRACTS. Louisville, Kentucky.

　　　　　　　　　　　　　　　　　　　　　　　　　　　　　　　ART
VREFS　　O'Connel, D.P. GERMAN LITERATURE ON THE TERRITORIAL SEA, 18th AND 19th CENTURIES. In J. Tittel, Multitudo legum ius unum: mélanges en l'honneur de Wilhelm Wengler zu seinem 65. Geburtstag. Berlin, 1973. Vol. 1, pp. 325-335.

　　　　　　　　　　　　　　　　　　　　　　　　　　　　　　　***
VREFS　　OIL SPILLAGE: A BIBLIOGRAPHY. Bibliography Series WRSIC 73-207. Washington, U.S. Department of the Interior, Water Resources Scientific Information Center, 1973. 390p.

　　　　　　　　　　　　　　　　　　　　　　　　　　　　　　　***
VREFS　　Ovens, Carol B. DIRECTORY OF SERVICES FOR MARINERS. PASGAP Publication no. 1. Seattle, University of Washington, Sea Grant Communications, 1973. 159p.

　　　　　　　　　　　　　　　　　　　　　　　　　　　　　　　18
VREFS　　Padelford, Norman J., and Joel Zimmerman, comp. ANNOTATED LIST OF PERIODICALS DEALING WITH OCEAN ENGINEERING, OCEANOGRAPHY, NAVAL ARCHITECTURE AND PUBLIC POLICY RELATING TO THE SEAS. Cambridge, Massachusetts Institute of Technology, Sea Grant Program Office, 1969.

　　　　　　　　　　　　　　　　　　　　　　　　　　　　　　　18
VREFS　　Padelford, Norman J. SELECTED BIBLIOGRAPHY ON MARINE RESOURCES AND OCEAN ENGINEERING, MARITIME AFFAIRS, LAW OF THE SEA AND PUBLIC POLICY. Sea Grant Program Project GH-1. Cambridge, Massachusetts Institute of Technology, 1968.

　　　　　　　　　　　　　　　　　　　　　　　　　　　　　　　13
VREFS　　Paradiso, John L., and Robert D. Fisher. MAMMALS IMPORTED INTO THE UNITED STATES IN 1970. Special scientific report - Wildlife no. 161. Washington, D.C., U.S.G.P.O., 1972. ii, 62p.

　　　　　　　　　　　　　　　　　　　　　　　　　　　　　　　14,16
VREFS　　Passero, Barbara, and D.A. Horn, comp. DIRECTORY OF M.I.T. RESEARCH PROJECTS RELATED TO MARINE RESOURCES, OCEAN UTILIZATION AND COASTAL ZONE DEVELOPMENT. Cambridge, Massachusetts Institute of Technology, Sea Grant Project Office, 1973. iii, 56p.

                                                                14
VREFS    Passero, Barbara, and D.A. Horn, comp.  DIRECTORY OF M.I.T. RESEARCH
         PROJECTS RELATED TO MARINE RESOURCES, OCEAN UTILIZATION, AND COASTAL
         ZONE MANAGEMENT 1975.  MITSG-75-14.  Cambridge, Massachusetts Insti-
         tute of Technology, Sea Grant Project Office, 1975.  51p.

                                                              ***
VREFS    Passero, Barbara, and M.J. Seale.  COASTAL ZONE MANAGEMENT: FOCUS
         ON NEW ENGLAND; AN ANNOTATED SELECTED BIBLIOGRAPHY.  MITSG 75-21.
         Cambridge, Massachusetts Institute of Technology, 1976.  37p.

                                                              ***
VREFS    Petersen, Nancy P.  CONGRESSIONAL PUBLICATIONS ON OCEANOGRAPHY:  A
         SELECTED BIBLIOGRAPHY, 1959-1972.  Washington, Congressional Re-
         search Service, Library of Congress, 1972-

                                                              ***
VREFS    Radosevich, G.E., et al.  WATER LAW AND ITS RELATIONSHIP TO ENVIRON-
         MENTAL QUALITY:  A BIBLIOGRAPHY OF SOURCE MATERIAL.  Fort Collins,
         Colorado State University, 1973.  131p.

                                                              ***
VREFS    RHODE ISLAND MARINE BIBLIOGRAPHY.  Marine Technical Report no. 3.
         Kingston, University of Rhode Island, 1972.  183p.

                                                              ***
VREFS    Riggs, Stanley R., and M.P. O'Connor.  GEOLOGICAL BIBLIOGRAPHY OF
         NORTH CAROLINA'S COASTAL PLAIN, COASTAL ZONE, AND CONTINENTAL SHELF.
         UNC-SG-75-13.  Chapel Hill, University of North Carolina, 1975.
         141p.

                                                              ***
VREFS    Rosenburg, D.H.  BIBLIOGRAPHY OF THE OCEANOGRAPHY AND BIOLOGY OF THE
         NORTHERN GULF OF ALASKA.  Fairbanks, University of Alaska, Institute
         of Marine Science, 1975.  218p.

                                                                14
VREFS    Schoepf, Richard W., comp.  THE TRANS-ALASKA PIPELINE AND THE ENVI-
         RONMENT:  A BIBLIOGRAPHY.  Washington, U.S. Department of the Inter-
         ior, 1975.  22p.

                                                              ***
VREFS    Schweitzer, J.P., comp.  DIRECTORY OF MARINE SCIENCE EDUCATION 1973.
         Baton Rouge, Louisiana State University, Center for Wetland Re-
         sources, 1973.  47p.

                                                               7,14
VREFS    THE SEA:  ECONOMIC AND TECHNOLOGICAL ASPECTS:  A SELECT BIBLIOGRAPHY.
         LA MER:  ASPECTS ECONOMIQUES ET TECHNIQUES:  BIBLIOGRAPHIE SELEC-
         TIVE.  New York, United Nations, Dag Hammarskjöld Library, 1974.
         vii, 41p.

                                                               7,14
VREFS    THE SEA:  LEGAL AND POLITICAL ASPECTS:  A SELECT BIBLIOGRAPHY.  LA
         MER:  ASPECTS JURIDIQUES ET POLITIQUES:  BIBLIOGRAPHIE SELECTIVE.
         New York, United Nations, Dag Hammarskjöld Library, 1974.  viii,
         46p.

| | | ART |
|---|---|---|
VREFS    SEA GRANT. In Fish Boat, Vol. 19, no. 4, 1974. pp. 26-27.

                                                                       ART

VREFS    SEA GRANT. In Fish Boat, Vol. 20, no. 4, 1975. pp. 22-23.

                                                                        14

VREFS    SEA GRANT PUBLICATIONS INDEX. Parmula K. Weedman, comp. Narragansett, R.I., National Sea Grant Depository, Pell Marine Science Library, University of Rhode Island. Washington, U.S. Environmental Science Information Center, 1968/1972-

                                                                     1,5,16,17

VREFS    SEA-BED 1968. INDEXED AND ANNOTATED BY HARRY N.M. WINTON. New York, Worldmark Press, 1970. 6 Vols.

                                                                    5,14,16,17

VREFS    SEA-BED 1969. INDEXED AND ANNOTATED BY HARRY N.M. WINTON. New York, Worldmark Press, 1971. 8 Vols.

                                                                     17

VREFS    Shih, H.H. A LITERATURE SURVEY OF OCEAN POLLUTION. The Catholic University of America. Report no. 71-6. Washington, The Catholic University of America, Institute of Ocean Science and Engineering, 1971. 110p.

                                                                     ***

VREFS    Shilling, C.W., and M.F. Werts. UNDERWATER MEDICINE AND RELATED SCIENCES: A GUIDE TO THE LITERATURE. An annotated bibliography, key word index, and microthesaurus. New York, Plenum Publishing Corporation, IFI/Plenum Data Corporation, 1973. 702p.

                                                                     ***

VREFS    Sittig, M. OIL SPILL PREVENTION AND REMOVAL HANDBOOK. Pollution Technology Review, no. 11; Energy Technology Review, no. 2, and Ocean Technology Review no. 1. Park Ridge, N.J., Noyes Data Corporation, 1974. 477p.

                                                                     13

VREFS    Smith, F.G. Walton, ed. HANDBOOK OF MARINE SCIENCE. Cleveland, Ohio, CRC Press, Inc., 1974. 2 Vols.

                                                                     ***

VREFS    Smith, M. OIL SPILL REMOVAL. A BIBLIOGRAPHY WITH ABSTRACTS. NTIS-WIN-74-037. Springfield, Va., National Technical Information Service, 1974. 119p.

                                                                     ***

VREFS    Sorensen, Jens, and M. Demers. COASTAL ZONE BIBLIOGRAPHY: CITATIONS TO DOCUMENTS ON PLANNING, RESOURCES MANAGEMENT AND IMPACT ASSESSMENT. IMR TR-43. Sea Grant publication no. 8. La Jolla, Calif., University of California, 1973. 89p.

                                                                     ***

VREFS    STATE GOVERNMENT ORGANIZATION: AGENCIES DEALING WITH MARINE RESOURCES. Portland, University of Maine School of Law, 1969. 156p.

                                                                     ***

VREFS    Studdard, Gloria J., comp. COMMON ENVIRONMENTAL TERMS: A GLOSSARY. Rev. EPA Region IV, Atlanta, Georgia. Washington, U.S. Environmental Protection Agency, 1974. 23p.

4,7,11,14
VREFS     Székely, Alberto. BIBLIOGRAPHY ON LATIN AMERICA AND THE LAW OF THE SEA. Law of the Sea Institute special publication no. 5. Kingston, University of Rhode Island, 1975.

18
VREFS     Texas A&M University. SEA GRANT PUBLICATIONS FOR THE OFFSHORE INDUSTRY. College Station, 1975.

7
VREFS     Third United Nations Conference on the Law of the Sea. Third Session, Geneva, 17 March - 10 May, 1975. LIST OF BOOKS AND MONOGRAPHS ON THE LAW OF THE SEA. AVAILABLE FOR THE DURATION OF THE CONFERENCE. Mimeo. LOSC/LIB/GVA.75/Misc.1 GE.75-63206. New York, United Nations, 21 March, 1975.

5,15
VREFS     Thompson (John I.) and Company. STATE AND LOCAL GOVERNMENT ACTIVITIES AND ROLES IN MARINE SCIENCE, ENGINEERING AND DEVELOPMENT; A BRIEFLY ANNOTATED CATALOG OF PUBLISHED STUDIES AND REPORTS ON SUCH ORGANIZATIONAL ARRANGEMENTS AND ACTIVITIES IN THE COASTAL STATES AND IN THOSE BORDERING ON THE GREAT LAKES. Washington, D.C., John I. Thompson and Company, 1968.

16
VREFS     Tover, Bill, et al. A BIBLIOGRAPHY OF PACEM IN MARIBUS PUBLICATIONS AND DOCUMENTS. I.O.I occasional paper no. 1. Msida, Malta, International Ocean Institute, The Royal University of Malta, 1973. iii, 49p.

7,14
VREFS     United Nations. Dag Hammarskjöld Library. REGIME OF THE SEA AND THE SEA-BED. BIBLIOGRAPHY. New York, United Nations, 1972.

7
VREFS     United Nations. Secretariat. LAW OF THE SEA TERMINOLOGY. Terminology Bulletin no. 297/Rev.1. ST/CS /SER.F/297/Rev.1. New York, United Nations, 1975. 276p.

7
VREFS     United Nations. THIRD UNITED NATIONS CONFERENCE ON THE LAW OF THE SEA. FOURTH SESSION, NEW YORK, 15 MARCH - 7 MAY, 1976. LIST OF BOOKS AND MONOGRAPHS ON THE LAW OF THE SEA THAT ARE AVAILABLE FOR CONSULTATION IN THE SPECIAL LIBRARY ROOM ESTABLISHED FOR THE DURATION OF THE CONFERENCE AND LOCATED IN THE SECRETARIAT BUILDING AT HEADQUARTERS, NEW YORK. New York, United Nations, 1976. 19p.

***
VREFS     _____ THIRD UNITED NATIONS CONFERENCE ON THE LAW OF THE SEA, THIRD SESSION, GENEVA, 17 MARCH - 10 MAY, 1975. ADDITIONAL LIST OF BOOKS AND ARTICLES ON THE LAW OF THE SEA AVAILABLE FOR THE DURATION OF THE CONFERENCE. Mimeo. LOSC/LIB/GVA.75/Misc.1/Add.1 GE.75-64139. New York, United Nations, 4 April, 1975.

***
VREFS     _____ WORLD ENERGY SUPPLIES 1969-1972. E.74.XVII.7. New York, UNIPUB, 1974. 195p.

|||
|---|---|
| VREFS | UNITED NATIONS ENVIRONMENT PROGRAM: DIRECTORY OF NATIONAL AND INTERNATIONAL POLLUTION MONITORING PROGRAMS. Cambridge, Mass., Smithsonian Institution, Center for Short-Lived Phenomena, February, 1974. 1272p. |

18

| | |
|---|---|
| VREFS | UNITED NATIONS SOURCE DOCUMENTS ON SEABED MINING. Compiled by the editors of Ocean Science News. Washington, Nautilus Press, 1974. 391p. |

18

| | |
|---|---|
| VREFS | UNITED NATIONS SOURCE DOCUMENTS ON THE THIRD U.N. LAW OF THE SEA CONFERENCE; CARACAS '74 (LOS-3). Compiled by the editors of Ocean Science News. Washington, Nautilus Press, 1974. 412p. Companion volume to United Nations source documents on seabed mining. |

***

| | |
|---|---|
| VREFS | United States. Atomic Energy Commission. FICHE INDEX FOR NUCLEAR DOCKETS: OFFSHORE POWER SYSTEMS, FLOATING NUCLEAR PLANTS, PLANT DESIGN REPORT. Faye Horne, ed. Washington, D.C., 1974. 75p. |

***

| | |
|---|---|
| VREFS | _____  _____ SOLAR ENERGY, BIBLIOGRAPHY. Washington. iii, 218, 138p. |

***

| | |
|---|---|
| VREFS | United States. Department of Commerce. Environmental Data Service. ENDEX/OASIS, NOAA ENVIRONMENTAL DATA KEY. Washington, U.S.G.P.O., 1974. 6p. |

***

| | |
|---|---|
| VREFS | _____ USER'S GUIDE TO OASIS, OCEANIC AND ATMOSPHERIC SCIENCE INFORMATION SYSTEM. Rockville, Md., May 1974. viii, 55p. |

13,14

| | |
|---|---|
| VREFS | United States. Department of Commerce. National Oceanic and Atmospheric Administration. SEA GRANT PUBLICATIONS INDEX 1968-1972. NOAA-TM-EDS-ESIC-8,9. Rockville, Md., 1972. 190p. 2 Vols. |

13

| | |
|---|---|
| VREFS | _____ National Technical Information Service. THE OCEANS AND NATIONAL ECONOMIC DEVELOPMENT CONFERENCE, JULY 17-19, 1973, SEATTLE, WASHINGTON. Bibliography. Springfield, Va., 1972. ii, 19p. |

***

| | |
|---|---|
| VREFS | United States. Department of Defense. Army. Engineer Corps. WASHINGTON ENVIRONMENTAL ATLAS. Seattle, 1975. |

***

| | |
|---|---|
| VREFS | _____  _____ Department of the Interior. Sport Fisheries and Wildlife Bureau. BIBLIOGRAPHY OF RESEARCH PUBLICATIONS OF GREAT LAKES FISHERY LABORATORY, 1928-72. Paul H. Eschmeyer, editor. Washington, 1974. 14p. |

***

| | |
|---|---|
| VREFS | United States. Department of the Interior. THE TRANS-ALASKA PIPELINE AND THE ENVIRONMENT: A BIBLIOGRAPHY. Richard W. Schoepf, comp. Washington, U.S.G.P.O., 1974. 22p. |

VREFS    United States. Environmental Protection Agency. BASIC DOCUMENTS CONCERNING PROGRAMS TO CONTROL ENVIRONMENTAL POLLUTION FROM FEDERAL GOVERNMENT ACTIVITIES. Washington, 1975. vi, 162p.

***

VREFS    _____ _____ DIRECTORY OF ENVIRONMENTAL ORGANIZATIONS FOR ALASKA, IDAHO, OREGON, WASHINGTON, AND PROVINCE OF BRITISH COLUMBIA. Seattle, Wash., Office of External Affairs, Region 10, 1975. 151p.

***

VREFS    United States. General Accounting Office. FEDERAL AGENCIES ADMINISTERING PROGRAMS RELATED TO MARINE SCIENCE ACTIVITIES AND OCEANIC AFFAIRS, MULTIAGENCY. Washington, U.S.G.P.O., February 25, 1975. 13, 177p.

***

VREFS    United States. Library of Congress. Congressional Research Service. OFFSHORE OIL: SELECTED REFERENCES 1969-1975. Washington, U.S. G.P.O., 1975. 27p.

***

VREFS    United States. Naval Oceanographic Office. OCEANOGRAPHIC ATLAS OF THE NORTH ATLANTIC OCEAN. Washington, 1963-1968. 6 Vols.

***

VREFS    UNITED STATES DIRECTORY OF MARINE SCIENTISTS 1975. Washington, D.C., National Academy of Sciences, 1975. 327p.

ART

VREFS    Vambery, J.T. LAW OF THE SEA: A SELECTIVE BIBLIOGRAPHY OF ARTICLES. DOCUMENTS AND MONOGRAPHS. In Columbia Journal of Transnational Law, Vol. 13, 1974. pp. 173-187.

7

VREFS    Vargas, Jorge A. BIBLIOGRAFIA ESPECIALIZADA SOBRE ASPECTOS NORMATIVOS DE LA INVESTIGACIÓN CIENTÍFICA EN LOS OCEANOS. 1974. n.p.

17

VREFS    Vetter, Richard C., comp. A DIRECTORY OF OCEANOGRAPHERS IN THE UNITED STATES, 1969. Committee on Oceanography, Division of Earth Sciences, National Research Council. Washington, D.C., National Academy of Sciences, 1969. 4, 72p.

7

VREFS    Vitzthum, Wolfgang. PACEM IN MARIBUS - I. Selected Bibliography for the use of Pacem in Maribus. An International Convocation to Explore Peaceful Uses of the Oceans and the Ocean Floor. Held at Valleta on the Island of Malta, 28 June-3 July, 1970. Vol. 6.

***

VREFS    Washington. Surveys and Marine Land Management Division. WASHINGTON MARINE ATLAS. Olympia, 1972.

***

VREFS    Washington. University. BOOKS IN MARINE STUDIES. TOPICS: PUBLIC POLICY AND THE MARINE ENVIRONMENT, MARINE BIOLOGY, FISHERIES, OCEANOGRAPHY. Seattle, Wash., 1975. 12p.

VREFS   Weedman, Parmula K., comp. SEA GRANT NEWSLETTER INDEX. Narragansett, University of Rhode Island, 1968-

VREFS   _____ _____ SEA GRANT PUBLICATIONS INDEX. Narragansett, University of Rhode Island, 1968-

17
VREFS   Wisconsin. University. Sea Grant Program. DIRECTORY OF MARINE AND MARINE-RELATED INFORMATION RESOURCES AT THE UNIVERSITY OF WISCONSIN. Public information report no. 4. Madison, 1970. 2 Vols.

1,5,12,18
VREFS   Woodrow Wilson International Center for Scholars. OCEAN AFFAIRS BIBLIOGRAPHY, 1971. A SELECTED LIST EMPHASIZING INTERNATIONAL LAW, POLITICS AND ECONOMICS OF OCEAN USES. Ocean Series no. 302. Washington, D.C., September, 1971. 201p.

16
VREFS   Zeydel, Walter H. SELECTIVE SUPPLEMENTAL BIBLIOGRAPHY ON TERRITORIAL WATERS AND THE CONTINENTAL SHELF WITH ADDED MATERIALS ON FISHERIES. New York, International Bar Association, 1952. 10p.


ADDITIONS:

14
VLOS    Anand, Ram P. LEGAL REGIME OF THE SEA-BED AND THE DEVELOPING COUNTRIES. Columbia, Mo., South Asia Books, 1975.

14
VREFS   THIRD UNITED NATIONS CONFERENCE ON THE LAW OF THE SEA: RULES OF PROCEDURE. New York, UNIPUB, 1976.

14
VREFS   THE SEA: A SELECT BIBLIOGRAPHY ON THE LEGAL, POLITICAL, ECONOMIC AND TECHNOLOGICAL ASPECTS, 1975-1976. New York, UNIPUB, 1976.

14
VLOS    Hull, E.W. Seabrook. THE INTERNATIONAL LAW OF THE SEA: A CASE FOR A CUSTOMARY APPROACH. Law of the Sea Institute Occasional Paper no. 30. Kingston, University of Rhode Island, April, 1976. 17p.

***
IVENV   Frank, Richard A. DEEPSEA MINING AND THE ENVIRONMENT: A REPORT OF THE WORKING GROUP ON ENVIRONMENTAL REGULATION OF DEEPSEA MINING. American Society of International Law Studies on Transnational Legal Policy no.10. St. Paul, MN., West Publishing Company, 1976. VII, 54p.

***
VLOS    Pardo, Arvid. THE UNITED NATIONS AND THE OCEANS: A FATEFUL CHALLENGE. Third Annual World Order Lecture. Philadelphia, PA., The World Order Research Institute, Villanova University Press, 1970. 15p.

KEYWORD MASTER LIST
FOR EXPLANATION PLEASE SEE PAGE 427

ABANDONED CABLES AND GEAR
ABANDONED PROPERTY SALVAGE
ABSORBANCE
ABRASIVES
ABSTENTION DOCTRINE
ACCIDENTS AT SEA
ACTIVE CONTINENTAL MARGIN
ABYSSAL PLAINS
ABYSSAL ZONES
ACCESS FOR LAND-LOCKED STATES
ACCESS TO HIGH SEAS
ACCIDENTAL OIL POLLUTION
ACCIDENTS PREVENTION
ACCRETION
ADJACENT COASTAL STATES
ADJACENT SEA
ADJACENT SHELF
ADJACENT SHORELANDS
ADMINISTRATION
ADSORPTION
AERIAL PHOTOGRAPHY
AERIAL SURVEY
AEROBIC CORROSION
AGRICULTURAL POLLUTION
AGRICULTURAL WASTES
AIRSPACE
ALBACORE
ALBACORE BOAT AND RIGGING
ALGAE
ALGAE CULTURE
ALTERNATIVE FISHERY ARRANGEMENTS
ALUMINUM
AMPHIBIANS
ANADROMOUS FISH CONSERVATION
ANADROMOUS SPECIES
ANCHOVIES
ANTI-MARITIME POSITION
ANTI-POLLUTION TECHNIQUES
ANTI-SUBMARINE POSITION
ANTI-SUBMARINE WARFARE
AQUABUSINESS
AQUACULTURE
AQUACULTURE ASSOCIATIONS
AQUACULTURE BUSINESS ASSOCIATION
AQUACULTURE FEED
AQUACULTURE HARVESTING
AQUACULTURE HAZARDS
AQUACULTURE INDUSTRY
AQUACULTURE JURISDICTION
AQUACULTURE LAWS AND REGULATIONS
AQUACULTURE - LEGAL CONSIDERATIONS
AQUACULTURE LICENSING
AQUACULTURE POLLUTION
AQUACULTURE POND SITING
AQUACULTURE POND SITING PROBLEMS

AQUACULTURE PONDS
AQUACULTURE PRIORITIES
AQUACULTURE PROBLEMS
AQUACULTURE REGULATION
AQUACULTURE RESEARCH
AQUACULTURE SITE SELECTION
AQUACULTURE SYSTEMS DEVELOPMENT
AQUACULTURE TECHNOLOGY
AQUACULTURE TRANSPORTATION
AQUACULTURE ZONING
AQUACULTURE ZONING REGULATIONS
AQUANAUTS
AQUATIC LIFE
AQUATIC LIFE ENVIRONMENTAL
   REQUIREMENTS
AQUATIC ORGANISMS
AQUATIC SPORTS
AQUICULTURE . . . . . . . . . . . . . . . . .
         see  AQUACULTURE
ARCHAEOLOGY . . . . . . . . . . . . . . .
         see  MARINE ARCHAEOLOGY
ARCHIPELAGIC SEALANES PASSAGE
ARCHIPELAGIC STATES
ARCHIPELAGIC WATERS
ARCHIPELAGO NATIONS. . . . . . . . . . . .
         see  ARCHIPELAGIC STATES
ARCHIPELAGOES
ARCHIPELAGOES - ENCLOSED
ARCHIPELAGOES - SEMI-ENCLOSED
ARCHIPELAGOES - STRAIGHT BASELINES
ARCS OF CIRCLES . . . . . . . . . . . . . . .
         see  TERRITORIAL SEA
              DELIMITATION
ARMS CONTROL
ARMY
ARTIFICIAL DEEP WATER PORTS
ARTIFICIAL HABITATS
ARTIFICIAL ISLANDS
ARTIFICIAL REEFS
ARTIFICIAL SAND
ARTIFICIAL STRUCTURES . . . . . . . . . . .
         see  OFFSHORE STRUCTURES
ATLAS
ATOLLS
ATOMIC . . . . . . . . . . . . . . . . . . .
         see  NUCLEAR
BAITFISH CULTURE
BALLAST
BARGE CARRIERS
BARGES
BARRICADE . . . . . . . . . . . . . . . . . .
         see  FISHING GEAR
BASELINE
BASELINE ACCRETION
BASELINE CASES

BASELINE CHANGES
BASELINE EROSION
BASELINE HISTORY
BASELINE - LOW TIDE ELEVATIONS . . . . . . .
    see  LOW TIDE ELEVATIONS
BASELINE MEASUREMENT
BASELINE STUDIES
BAYS - BASELINE
BEACH BUILDINGS
BEACH EROSION
BEACH FRONT
BEACH FRONT LITTORAL OWNER
BEACH MINERALS
BEACH POLLUTION
BEACH RESTORATION
BEACH SAND LOSS
BENTHIC COMMUNITIES
BENTHIC EXPLOITATION/EXPLORATION
BENTHIC REGION
BENTHOS
BIBLIOGRAPHIES
BILATERAL AGREEMENTS
BILGE
BILLFISHES
BIOACOUSTICS
BIO-ENGINEERING
BI-STATE WATER BODY
BLUEFIN TUNA
BOATING . . . see  RECREATION
BORDERING  COASTAL STATE
BOTTOM DISTURBANCE
BOTTOM DREDGING
BOTTOM SEDIMENTS
BOTTOM TRAWLING METHODS
BOTTOM-DWELLING SHELLFISH
BOUNDARIES
BOUNDARIES - APPORTIONMENT
BOUNDARIES - EQUIDISTANCE
BOUNDARIES - JURISDICTION
BOUNDARY DEFINITION
BOUNDARY DELIMITATION
BOUNDARY DEMARCATION
BREADTH OF TERRITORIAL SEA
BRINE EFFLUENT
BROAD-ZONE JURISDICTION
BULK CARRIERS
BULKHEAD LINES
BULKHEADS
BUOY TECHNOLOGY
BUOYS
BYPRODUCT RECOVERY
CABLES . . . see  SUBMARINE CABLES
CABOTAGE
CANALS
CANNON SHOT RULE
CARGO MOVEMENT
CARGO PLATFORMS
CARGO TANK SIZE
CATADROMOUS SPECIES

CATCH QUOTAS
CATFISH
CATFISH FARMING
CHANNELS
CHEMICAL EXTRACTION - SEA WATER
CHEMICAL RUNOFF
CHEMICAL TANKERS
CHUM SALMON
CIRCUMJACENT STATES
CIRCUMNAVIGATION
CLOSED SEAS
COAL
COAST
COAST CHANGES
COAST GUARD
COAST GUARD SPILL CLASSIFICATION
COASTAL LAND LOSS
COASTAL ACTIVITIES
COASTAL ARCHIPELAGO
COASTAL AREAS
COASTAL AREAS - STRAIGHT BASELINES
COASTAL BASINS
COASTAL BOUNDARIES
COASTAL COMMISSION
COASTAL COMMUNITIES
COASTAL CONSERVATION
COASTAL CONSTRUCTION SETBACK LINE
COASTAL COUNTRY
COASTAL DEVELOPMENT
COASTAL DREDGING . . . see  DREDGING
COASTAL DRILLING . . . see  DRILLING
COASTAL ECOLOGY
COASTAL ENGINEERING
COASTAL ENGINEERING GEOLOGY
COASTAL ENVIRONMENT
COASTAL FISHERMEN
COASTAL FLORA
COASTAL FRONTAGE
COASTAL GOVERNANCE
COASTAL INDENTATION
COASTAL INLET STUDIES
COASTAL ISLAND WATERS
COASTAL ISLANDS
COASTAL LAGOONS
COASTAL LAND
COASTAL LAND USE PLANS
COASTAL NATION
COASTAL-NATION CONTROL
COASTAL NATION JURISDICTION
COASTAL NATIONS
COASTAL NATIONS - LIMITED AUTHORITY
COASTAL PLANNING
COASTAL OIL POLLUTION
COASTAL POLICIES
COASTAL POLLUTION
COASTAL POLLUTION PREVENTION
COASTAL POWER PLANTS
COASTAL PROBLEMS

COASTAL RELATED INDUSTRIES
COASTAL RESOURCES
COASTAL RESOURCES ADMINISTRATION
COASTAL RESOURCES RESEARCH
COASTAL SAND
COASTAL SCENIC RESOURCES
COASTAL SEA-BED ECONOMIC AREA
COASTAL SEWAGE PLANT OPERATORS
COASTAL SHIPPING
COASTAL SPECIES
COASTAL STATE
COASTAL STATE CONSENT
COASTAL STATE CONTROL
COASTAL STATE CONTROL OF DRILLING
COASTAL STATE FISHERIES
COASTAL STATE JURISDICTION
COASTAL STATE LIABILITY
COASTAL STATE SCIENTIFIC RESEARCH
COASTAL STATE SEA-BED JURISDICTION
COASTAL STATES
COASTAL STATES - EXCLUSIVE RIGHTS
COASTAL STUDIES
COASTAL TERRACES
COASTAL WATERS
COASTAL ZONE ACTIVITIES
COASTAL ZONE ADMINISTRATIVE PERMITS
COASTAL ZONE BASELINE
COASTAL ZONE CONFLICTS
COASTAL ZONE CONSERVATION
COASTAL ZONE DESTRUCTION
COASTAL ZONE DEVELOPMENT CHARGES
COASTAL ZONE DEVELOPMENT NEEDS
COASTAL ZONE DREDGING
COASTAL ZONE ECONOMIC ACTIVITIES
COASTAL ZONE ENVIRONMENT
COASTAL ZONE ENVIRONMENTAL MEASURES
COASTAL ZONE EXTENSION
COASTAL ZONE INSTITUTIONAL BARRIERS
COASTAL ZONE INWARD EXTENSION
COASTAL ZONE LAND ACQUISITION
COASTAL ZONE LAND USE PLANNING
COASTAL ZONE LAND USE REGULATIONS
COASTAL ZONE MANAGEMENT
COASTAL ZONE MANAGEMENT DISPUTES
COASTAL ZONE MANAGEMENT POLICIES
COASTAL ZONE MANAGEMENT PROGRAMS
COASTAL ZONE NAVIGABLE WATERS
COASTAL ZONE OIL SPILLS
COASTAL ZONE POLLUTION
COASTAL ZONE POLLUTION DETECTION . . .
    see  POLLUTION DETECTION
COASTAL ZONE POLLUTION EFFECTS
COASTAL ZONE POLLUTION POLICIES
COASTAL ZONE POLLUTION REGULATORY
  AUTHORITIES
COASTAL ZONE POWER PLANTS
COASTAL ZONE REGULATORY AUTHORITY
COASTAL ZONE RESEARCH

COASTAL ZONE RESOURCE MANAGEMENT
COASTAL ZONE SEAWARD EXTENSION
COASTAL ZONE SILTATION
COASTAL ZONE STUDIES
COASTAL ZONE TRAFFIC CONTROL
COASTAL ZONE USES
COASTAL ZONE WASTE CONTROL
COASTAL ZONE WASTE DISPOSAL
COASTAL ZONE WASTES
COASTAL ZONE WATER USE PLANNING
COASTAL ZONE WATERSHED LOGGING
COASTLINE
COASTLINE ACCRETION AND EROSION
COASTLINE BACKSHORE
COASTLINE CONSERVATION
COASTLINE CONSERVATION LEGISLATION
COASTLINE CONTROL
COASTLINE DEBRIS DEPOSIT
COASTLINE DEVELOPMENT
COASTLINE FORESHORE
COASTLINE HORIZONTAL CONTROL
COASTLINE INLET MIGRATION
COASTLINE MARSHES
COASTLINE MEAN TIDE LEVEL
COASTLINE PROTECTION . . . . . . . . . . .
    see  SHORELINE PROTECTION
COASTLINE RETREAT
COASTLINE - SOUNDING LINE CROSSINGS
COBALT
COD WAR
COHO SALMON
COLLISION AVOIDANCE SYSTEMS
COLLISIONS
COMMERCIAL AQUACULTURE SYSTEMS
COMMERCIAL FISHERIES
COMMERCIAL FISHING
COMMERCIAL MARITIME INTERESTS
COMMON HERITAGE OF MANKIND
COMPLETION SYSTEMS
CONCRETE CONSTRUCTION IN SEAWATER
CONCRETE DRUMS
CONCRETE GRAVITY PLATFORMS
CONCRETE PLATFORMS
CONFERENCE
CONFERENCE PROGRAMS
CONSERVATION
CONSERVATION ZONE
CONSTRUCTION
CONSTRUCTION AND DEMOLITION
CONSTRUCTION WASTE
CONTACT PESTICIDE
CONTAINER PORTS . . . . . . . . . . . . . . .
    see  PORTS AND HARBORS
CONTAMINATED BOTTOM SEDIMENTS
CONTAMINANTS . . . . . . . . . . . . . . .
    see  ENVIRONMENTAL
         CONTAMINENTS
CONTEMPORARY STATE PRACTICE

CONTIGUOUS AIRSPACE
CONTIGUOUS FISHING ZONE
CONTIGUOUS ZONE
CONTIGUOUS ZONES - CUSTOMS
CONTIGUOUS ZONES - DELIMITATION
CONTIGUOUS ZONES - ENVIRONMENTAL
 PROTECTION
CONTIGUOUS ZONES - INTERNATIONAL
 AGREEMENTS
CONTIGUOUS ZONES - NATIONAL SECURITY
CONTIGUOUS ZONES - NEUTRALITY
CONTIGUOUS ZONES - POLLUTION
CONTIGUOUS ZONES - SCIENTIFIC RESEARCH
CONTINENTAL BORDERLAND
CONTINENTAL COASTLINE
CONTINENTAL DRIFT
CONTINENTAL LANDMASS
CONTINENTAL MARGIN BEYOND 200 MILES
CONTINENTAL MARGINS
CONTINENTAL NATIONS
CONTINENTAL PLATFORM
CONTINENTAL RISE
CONTINENTAL RISE GEOLOGY
CONTINENTAL SEA
CONTINENTAL SHELF
CONTINENTAL SHELF ADJACENCY CRITERIA
CONTINENTAL SHELF APPORTIONMENT
CONTINENTAL SHELF ARMS CONTROL . . . . .
   see   ARMS CONTROL
CONTINENTAL SHELF - BASE OF SLOPES
CONTINENTAL SHELF - BASELINES
CONTINENTAL SHELF BED ROCK
CONTINENTAL SHELF - BIOLOGICAL
 ENVIRONMENT
CONTINENTAL SHELF - BOUNDARIES
CONTINENTAL SHELF CANYONS
CONTINENTAL SHELF CLAIMS
CONTINENTAL SHELF CONVENTION
CONTINENTAL SHELF - DEPTH LIMIT
CONTINENTAL SHELF DISPUTES
CONTINENTAL SHELF - ECONOMIC ZONE
CONTINENTAL SHELF EDGE
CONTINENTAL SHELF EXPLOITATION
CONTINENTAL SHELF EXPLORATION RIGHTS
CONTINENTAL SHELF - FISHERIES
CONTINENTAL SHELF - GEODETIC CONTROL
CONTINENTAL SHELF GEOLOGY
CONTINENTAL SHELF GOLD
CONTINENTAL SHELF HARD MINERALS
CONTINENTAL SHELF INSTALLATIONS
CONTINENTAL SHELF - INSULAR TERRACE
CONTINENTAL SHELF -
 INTERNATIONALIZATION
CONTINENTAL SHELF ISLANDS
CONTINENTAL SHELF LEASES . . . . . . . . . .
   see   OFFSHORE LEASES
CONTINENTAL SHELF LIMIT
CONTINENTAL SHELF LINING

CONTINENTAL SHELF - MILITARY
 INSTALLATIONS
CONTINENTAL SHELF - MILITARY USES
CONTINENTAL SHELF - MINERAL DEPOSITS
CONTINENTAL SHELF MINERALS
CONTINENTAL SHELF MINING . . . . . . . . .
   see   MARINE MINING
CONTINENTAL SHELF - NARROW SHELF
CONTINENTAL SHELF - NATURAL RESOURCES
CONTINENTAL SHELF - OIL LAND
CONTINENTAL SHELF - OUTER LIMITS
CONTINENTAL SHELF PETROLEUM
CONTINENTAL SHELF PLACER DEPOSITS
CONTINENTAL SHELF POLLUTION
CONTINENTAL SHELF PRESERVES
CONTINENTAL SHELF REGIME
CONTINENTAL SHELF RESOURCES
CONTINENTAL SHELF RIGHTS
CONTINENTAL SHELF SCIENTIFIC RESEARCH
CONTINENTAL SHELF - SEAWARD EXTENT
CONTINENTAL SHELF SEAWARD LIMITS
CONTINENTAL SHELF - SUBJACENT
CONTINENTAL SHELF - SUPERJACENT
CONTINENTAL SHELF SUBSOIL
CONTINENTAL SHELF SURFACE SEDIMENTS
CONTINENTAL SHELF SURVEY
CONTINENTAL SHELF TREATIES
CONTINENTAL SHELF - TRENCHES
CONTINENTAL SHELF - TROUGHS
CONTINENTAL SHELF WATERS
CONTINENTAL SLOPE
CONTINENTAL SLOPE GEOLOGY
CONTINENTAL TERRACE
CONTINENTAL WATER
CONTINUOUS BUCKET LINE
CONTRACT ZONING
CONVENTION SCHEDULE
CONVENTIONS
CONVERGENT BOUNDARIES
COPPER
CORAL SEAFLOORS
CORE SAMPLE
CRAB
CRAB FISHERY
CRUDE OIL POLLUTION
CUSTOMARY INTERNATIONAL LAW
CUSTOMARY LAW
CUSTOMS ZONE
DDT CONTENT/RESIDUES
DATA BUOY TECHNOLOGY
DEEP DRAFT OFFSHORE PORTS
DEEP OCEAN FAUNA
DEEP OCEAN FLOOR GEOLOGY
DEEP OCEAN FLOOR RESEARCH
DEEP OCEAN STATIONS
DEEP OCEAN SURVEY VEHICLE
DEEP OCEAN TECHNOLOGY . . . . . . . . . . .
   see   OCEAN TECHNOLOGY

DEEP OIL-STORAGE TANKS
DEEP PIPELINES
DEEP SATURATION DIVING TECHNIQUES
DEEP SEA-BED
DEEP SEA-BED EXPLOITATION
DEEP SEA-BED POLLUTION
DEEP SEA-BED SUBSOIL
DEEP SUBMERGENCE OCEAN ENGINEERING
DEEP SUBMERGENCE RESCUE VEHICLE
DEEPSEA DRILLING
DEEPSEA FLOOR
DEEPSEA MINERALS/MINING SITES
DEEPSEA SMELT
DEEPSEA TECHNOLOGY . . . . . . . . . . .
       see   OCEAN TECHNOLOGY
DEEPSEA TRENCH
DEEP-TOWED SUBMERSIBLE
DEEPWATER
DEEPWATER DRILLING
DEEPWATER DRILLING TRACTS
DEEPWATER LEASES
DEEPWATER TERMINALS . . . . . . . . . .
       see   PORTS AND HARBORS
DELIMITATION
DELIMITATION - EXPLOITABILITY CRITERION
DELIMITATION - HORIZONTAL
DELIMITATION - ISOBATH CRITERIA
DELIMITATION OF BOUNDARIES
DELIMITATION OF TERRITORIAL SEA
DELIMITATION - ZIG ZAG
DELTA
DEMERSAL FISHES
DENUCLEARIZATION OF OCEAN SPACE
DESALINATION
DESALINATION - POLLUTION CONTROL
DETERGENT POLLUTION
DEVELOPING COUNTRIES
DEVELOPING NATIONS
DEVELOPING WORLD . . . . . . . . . . .
       see   DEVELOPING COUNTRIES
DIGESTS
DISCARDED AUTOMOBILE BODIES
DISCHARGE
DISPUTE SETTLEMENT
DISPUTE SETTLEMENT PROVISIONS
DISTANT-WATER FISHERIES/NATIONS
DISTANT-WATER FLEETS
DIURNAL INEQUALITY
DIVING EQUIPMENT
DISTRESS CALLS
DIVING SAFETY RESEARCH
DIVURGENT BOUNDARIES
DOMESTIC POLLUTION SOURCES
DOMESTIC SEWAGE
DOMINUS MARIS
DOUBLE BOTTOM TANKERS
DOUBLE HULL TANKERS
DOUBLE SIDE TANKERS . . . . . . . . . .
       see   DOUBLE HULL TANKERS

DRAFT STATUTE
DRAINING
DREDGE SPOILS
DREDGING
DREDGING AND FILLING
DREDGING POLLUTION
DREDGING SPOIL DISPOSAL
DRILLING
DRILLING RIGS
DRY DOCK . . . . . . . . . . . . . . .
       see   PORTS AND HARBORS
DRY CARGO
DUMPED DANGEROUS CHEMICALS
DUMPED EXPLOSIVES
DUMPING
DUMPING - AIR
DUMPING - COASTAL REGULATION
DUMPING - LAND
DUMPING - OCEAN . . . . . . . . . . . .
       see   OCEAN DUMPING
DUMPING - POLLUTION
DUMPING REGULATIONS
DUNGENESS CRAB
EARTH MOVEMENTS
EARTHQUAKE MONITORING
ECHO FISHING
ECOLOGICAL BASELINE STUDIES
ECOLOGY
ECONOMIC RESOURCE ZONE
ECONOMIC ZONE
ECONOMIC ZONE MANAGEMENT
ECONOMIC ZONE RESEARCH
ECONOMICS OF AQUACULTURE
ECOSYSTEMS
EDIBLE FISHERY PRODUCTS. . . . . . . . .
       see   FISH PRODUCTS
EEL
EFFLUENT DISCHARGE
EFFLUENTS
EKISTICS
ELECTRICITY
ELECTRICITY - SEA-BED TRANSPORTATION
ELECTRONIC EAVESDROPPING
EMBAYED ESTUARIES
EMERGENT ISLANDS
EMISSION . . . see   EFFLUENT
ENDLESS BUCKET LINE
ENDANGERED SPECIES
ENERGY
ENERGY CONSERVATION
ENERGY - ENVIRONMENTAL PROTECTION
ENERGY FACILITY SITING
ENERGY NEEDS
ENERGY - OFFSHORE CABLES
ENERGY POLICY
ENERGY RESEARCH
ENERGY RESOURCES RESEARCH
ENERGY SOURCES
ENERGY TECHNOLOGY

ENERGY USE
ENGINEERING RESEARCH
ENTRY IN DISTRESS
ENVELOPE LINE
ENVIRONMENT - CONVENTIONS
ENVIRONMENT DATA SYSTEM
ENVIRONMENT DISRUPTION
ENVIRONMENT MANAGEMENT
ENVIRONMENT REGULATION
ENVIRONMENT RESEARCH
ENVIRONMENTAL CONTAMINANTS
ENVIRONMENTAL ENGINEERING
ENVIRONMENTAL EVALUATION SYSTEM
ENVIRONMENTAL IMPACT ASSESSMENT
ENVIRONMENTAL PROTECTION
ENVIRONMENTAL QUALITY
ENVIRONMENTAL REGULATION
ENVIRONMENTAL RESTRAINTS
ENVIRONMENTAL SCIENCE
EPICONTINENTAL SEA
EQUIDISTANCE BOUNDARY
EQUIDISTANCE LINE
EQUIDISTANCE METHOD
EQUIDISTANCE PRINCIPLE
EQUIDISTANCE RULE
EROSION
EROSION - CAUSE
EROSION - WIND
ESCARPMENT
ESPIONAGE
ESTUARIES
ESTUARIES ADMINISTRATION
ESTUARIES COMMISSIONS
ESTUARIES - GROUNDWATER RIGHTS
ESTUARIES - HUNTING
ESTUARIES - JURISDICTION
ESTUARIES - MANGROVE BORDERED . . . . .
    see   MANGROVE BORDERED
         ESTUARIES
ESTUARIES RESTORATION
ESTUARIES - RIPARIAN RIGHTS
ESTUARIES - WATER QUALITY
ESTUARINE OIL POLLUTION
ESTUARY CONSERVATION
ESTUARY DESTRUCTION
ESTUARY DREDGING
ESTUARY FISHING
ESTUARY - INDUSTRIAL POLLUTION
ESTUARY MANAGEMENT
ESTUARY MOVEMENT
ESTUARY - OIL SPILLS
ESTUARY POLLUTION
ESTUARY RESOURCES
ESTUARY STUDIES
ESTUARY TIDE
ESTUARY TURBIDITY
EUTROPHICATION
EXCLUSIVE ECONOMIC ZONE

EXCLUSIVE FISHERIES ZONES
EXCLUSIVE FISHING RIGHTS
EXCLUSIVE FISHING ZONE
EXCLUSIVE FISHING ZONE CLAIMS
EXCLUSIVE ZONE/SOVEREIGNTY
EXECUTIVE AGREEMENTS
EXPERIMENTAL STUDIES
EXPLOITATION
EXPLOITABILITY CLAUSE
EXPLOITABILITY TEST
EXPLORATION
EXPLORATORY DRILLING
EXTRATERRITORIALITY
FACTORY SHIPS
FACTORY SHIPS - OCEAN DUMPING
FATHOM
FEDERAL AGENCIES
FEDERAL-STATE DISPUTES
FINFISH AQUACULTURE
FISCAL ZONE
FISH - APPORTIONMENT PROBLEM
FISH - BIOMASS BALANCE
FISH - BOTTOM-DWELLING
FISH - BOUNDARIES
FISH CATCH
FISH CITIES
FISH CONSERVATION
FISH - COASTAL STATE PREFERENCE
FISH CONSUMPTION
FISH CONTROL METHODS
FISH CULTURE . . . . . . . . . . . . . .
        see   AQUACULTURE
FISH - DEPLETION
FISH DEVELOPMENT
FISH HABITS
FISH HEALTH MANAGEMENT
FISH INSPECTION
FISH MARKET
FISH MEAL . . . . . . . . . . . . . . . .
        see   FISH PRODUCTS
FISH - MERCURY CONTAMINATION
FISH MUSCLE PROTEIN . . . . . . . . . . .
        see   FISH PROTEIN
FISH - NATURAL MORTALITY
FISH OIL
FISH - POLLUTION DEATHS
FISH PRODUCTS
FISH PROTEIN CONCENTRATE
FISH PROTEIN CONTENT
FISH RESOURCES
FISH RESOURCES - ENHANCEMENT
FISH - RIGHTS OF LANDLOCKED NATIONS
FISH - SPAWNING AREA
FISH SPECIES
FISH STOCKS
FISH TRAPS
FISH YIELD
FISHERIES

FISHERIES - BILATERAL AGREEMENTS
FISHERIES BOUNDARIES
FISHERIES CLAIMS
FISHERIES CLOSING LINE . . . . . . . . . .
      see   ECONOMIC ZONE
FISHERIES - COASTAL JURISDICTION
FISHERIES - COMMERCE CLAUSE
FISHERIES - COMMON HERITAGE OF
  MANKIND
FISHERIES - CONCESSIONS
FISHERIES - CONSERVATION
FISHERIES - DEVELOPMENT
FISHERIES - DISPUTES
FISHERIES - FOREIGN SURVEILLANCE
FISHERIES - HIGH SEAS
FISHERIES - INTERNAL REGULATION
FISHERIES - LIMITED COVERAGE
FISHERIES - LITIGATION
FISHERIES MANAGEMENT
FISHERIES MANAGEMENT OBJECTIVES
FISHERIES - OVEREXPLOITATION . . . . . .
      see   OVERFISHING
FISHERIES - PROBLEMS
FISHERIES PROTECTION
FISHERIES QUOTAS
FISHERIES REGULATION
FISHERIES RESEARCH
FISHERIES - STATE AUTHORITY
FISHERIES STUDIES
FISHERIES - SUBMERGED LAND ACT
FISHERIES - TECHNOLOGY
FISHERIES - TERRITORIAL WATERS
FISHERIES TREATIES
FISHERIES ZONE
FISHERIES ZONE EXTENSION
FISHERIES ZONE JURISDICTION
FISHERMAN QUOTAS
FISHERMEN
FISHERY BYPRODUCTS
FISHERY CONFLICTS
FISHERY CONSERVATION ZONES
FISHERY COOPERATIVES
FISHERY LAWS
FISHERY LAWS - VIOLATION
FISHERY LEGISLATION
FISHERY PRODUCTS - CONSUMPTION
FISHERY PRODUCTS - EDIBLE . . . . . . . .
      see   FISH PRODUCTS
FISHERY PRODUCTS - EXPORT
FISHERY PRODUCTS - IMPORT
FISHERY PRODUCTS - NONEDIBLE
FISHERY PRODUCTS - STATISTICS
FISHERY RESOURCES - EXPLOITATION
FISHERY RESOURCES - GEOGRAPHIC
  DISTRIBUTION
FISHFARMING . . . . . . . . . . . . . . . .
      see   AQUACULTURE
FISHING ALLOCATION

FISHING - ANGLING REGULATIONS
FISHING - CATCH QUOTAS
FISHING - COASTAL STATE'S POSITION
FISHING - CONTIGUOUS ZONES
FISH HATCHERY
FISHING - HISTORICAL RIGHT
FISHING - EXCLUSIVE RIGHTS
FISHING GEAR
FISHING GEAR STOWAGE
FISHING INDUSTRY
FISHING INDUSTRY - CANNING
FISHING INDUSTRY - FACTORY SHIPS
FISHING INDUSTRY - HIGH SEAS
FISHING INDUSTRY - INTERNATIONAL
  WATERS
FISHING INDUSTRY - POLLUTION
FISHING INDUSTRY - PROCESSING . . . . .
      see   FISH PROCESSING
FISHING INDUSTRY - SHRIMP TRAWLERS . .
      see   SHRIMP TRAWLERS
FISHING INDUSTRY - TECHNOLOGY
FISHING INDUSTRY - WHALING . . . . . .
      see   WHALING
FISHING - INTERNATIONAL ACTIVITIES
FISHING MANAGEMENT
FISHING-QUOTA SYSTEM
FISHING - TERRITORIAL WATERS
FISHING REVENUES
FISHING VESSELS - LONG RANGE . . . . .
      see   LONG RANGE FISHING
               VESSELS
FISHING VESSELS AND GEAR
FISHING VESSELS AND GEAR - BOAT AND
  RIGGING
FISHING VESSELS AND GEAR - DAMAGE
FISHING VESSELS AND GEAR LAWS
FISHING VESSELS AND GEAR LICENSES
FISHING VESSELS AND GEAR - LINE TRAWL
FISHING VESSELS AND GEAR SALES
FISHING VESSELS AND GEAR - TROLLING
  BOATS
FISHING VESSELS AND GEAR - UNDERSEA
  SYSTEMS
FISHING WATERS
FISHING ZONES
FIXED BOUNDARIES
FIXED CONTINENTAL SHELF LABORATORY
FIXED STRUCTURE . . . . . . . . . . . . .
      see   OFFSHORE STRUCTURE
FJORDS
FLAG OF REGISTRY
FLAG STATE JURISDICTION
FLAG STATE RIGHTS
FLAG STATES
FLAG TANKERS
FLAGS OF CONVENIENCE
FLAGS OF NECESSITY
FLAGS OF REGISTRY

FLAGS OF SHIPS
FLATFISH
FLOATING AIRPORTS . . . . . . . . . . . .
    see   OFFSHORE STRUCTURES
FLOATING BOOMS
FLOATING CITIES . . . . . . . . . . . . .
    see   OFFSHORE STRUCTURES
FLOATING DRILLING RIGS . . . . . . . .
    see   DRILLING RIGS
           OFFSHORE STRUCTURES
FLOATING FACTORIES
FLOATING FISH TRAPS
FLOATING INVERTIBLE PLATFORMS . . . . .
    see   OFFSHORE STRUCTURES
FLOATING ISLANDS . . . . . . . . . . . .
    see   OFFSHORE STRUCTURES
FLOATING LANDING STAGE
FLOATING PLATFORM COMMUNITIES
FLOATING PLATFORMS . . . . . . . . . . .
    see   OFFSHORE STRUCTURES
FLOATING RIG . . . . . . . . . . . . . . .
    see   OFFSHORE STRUCTURES
FLOATING SALMON TRAP
FLOATING ZONE
FLOODPLAINS
FLOUNDER
FLYWHEELS
FORECAST FISH CONSUMPTION
FOREIGN FISHING
FOREIGN FISHING VESSELS
FOREIGN FLAG VESSELS
FOREIGN TRADE POLICY
FORESHORE
FORESTRY PRODUCTS
FOSSIL FUELS
FREE PORT
FREE TRANSIT
FREE ZONE
FREEDOM OF ACCESS
FREEDOM OF FISHING
FREEDOM OF NAVIGATION
FREEDOM OF PASSAGE
FREEDOM OF THE HIGH SEAS
FREEDOM OF THE SEAS
FREEDOM OF TRANSIT
FRINGING REEFS
FUEL SHIPS
FUGITIVE MINERALS
FUR SEALS
FUSION
GAS
GASES FROM WASTE
GASIFICATION OF COAL
GEODETIC LINES . . . . . . . . . . . . .
    see   BOUNDARIES
GEOGRAPHIC CONTINUITY
GEOGRAPHIC ISOBATH
GEOGRAPHICAL CONFIGURATIONS
GEOGRAPHICALLY FAVORED STATES

GEOGRAPHICALLY DISADVANTAGED STATES
GEOLOGY RESEARCH
GEOTHERMAL DEPOSITS
GEOTHERMAL ENERGY
GLOBAL FISHERY CONTROL
GRAVEL
GULFS
GUYOTS
HADDOCK
HAKE
HAKING
HALIBUT
HARBORS . . . . . . . . . . . . . . . . .
    see   PORTS AND HARBORS
HARBORWORKS
HARBORWORKS BASELINE
HARD MINERAL RESOURCES
HATCHERIES . . . . . . . . . . . . . . .
    see   FISH HATCHERY
HAZARDOUS CARGOES
HAZARDOUS SUBSTANCES
HEADLAND TO HEADLAND BASELINE
HEATED WATER DISCHARGE
HEAVY WASTE DISCHARGE
HELSINKI RULES
HERRING
HIGH SEAS
HIGH SEAS ALLOCATION LINES
HIGH SEAS BEYOND NATIONAL
    JURISDICTION
HIGH SEAS FREEDOM
HIGH SEAS HISTORY
HIGH SEAS OCEAN AREAS
HIGH SEAS OWNERSHIP
HIGH SEAS POSSESSION
HIGH SEAS - REASONABLE USE
HIGH SEAS REGIME
HIGH SEAS REGULATORY AUTHORITY
HIGH SEAS SEIZURES
HIGH TIDE LINE
HIGH WATER MARK
HIGHLY MIGRATORY SYSTEMS
HISTORIC BAYS
HISTORIC WATERS
HISTORIC WATERS DOCTRINE
HOT BRINES
HOT PURSUIT
HOVERCRAFT
HOVERING ACTS
HYDROCARBONS
HYDRONAUTICS
HYDROSPACE - DEMILITERIZATION . . . .
    see   ARMS CONTROL
ICE
ICE AGES
ICE ENGINEERING
ICE-ERODED
ICE ISLANDS

ICE PLATFORM
ICEBERG FARMING
ICEBERGS
ICEBREAKER TANKER
IMMIGRATION
IMMIGRATION CONTROLS
IMMIGRATION PROTECTION
IMMIGRATION RULES
IMMUNITIES
INCOME TAXATION OF NATURAL RESOURCES
INDENTATION
INDUSTRIAL FISHING METHODS
INDUSTRIAL POLLUTANTS
INDUSTRIAL RECOMMENDATIONS
INDUSTRIAL TECHNOLOGY
INDUSTRIAL WASTES
INDUSTRIALIZED COUNTRIES
INDUSTRIES - OCEANWARD MOVEMENT
INLAND ICE FISHING
INLAND WATERS
INLETS
INNOCENT PASSAGE
INNOCENT PASSAGE - STRAITS
INNOCENT TRANSIT . . . . . . . . . . . .
     see  INNOCENT PASSAGE
INSHORE FISHERIES
IN-SOLUTION MINING
INSULAR COAST
INSULAR REGIMES
INSULAR SHELF
INSULAR SLOPE
INSULAR TERRACE
INSULAR WATERS
INTENTIONAL DUMPING
INTENTIONAL OIL SPILLAGE
INTERFERENCE
INTERIOR WATERS . . . . . . . . . . . . .
     see  INLAND WATERS
INTERISLAND WATERS
INTERMEDIATE ZONE
INTERNAL SEA WATERS . . . . . . . . . .
     see  INTERNAL SEAS
INTERNAL SEAS
INTERNAL SEAS - BASELINES
INTERNAL WATERS
INTERNATIONAL ACCESS
INTERNATIONAL AGREEMENTS
INTERNATIONAL AUTHORITY MARINE
  EXPLOITATION
INTERNATIONAL CASE LAW
INTERNATIONAL CODIFICATION
INTERNATIONAL COURT OF JUSTICE
INTERNATIONAL FISHERIES
INTERNATIONAL FISHERIES MANAGEMENT
INTERNATIONAL LAW
INTERNATIONAL LAW - VESSEL SEIZURE
INTERNATIONAL NAVIGATION
INTERNATIONAL NAVIGATIONAL ROUTE

INTERNATIONAL NORMS
INTERNATIONAL ORGANIZATIONS
INTERNATIONAL POLICIES
INTERNATIONAL POLLUTION
INTERNATIONAL POLLUTION REGULATION
INTERNATIONAL REGIME FOR THE SEA-BED
INTERNATIONAL REGIMES
INTERNATIONAL REGISTRY AUTHORITY
INTERNATIONAL RELATIONS
INTERNATIONAL SEA-BED AREA
INTERNATIONAL SEA-BED AUTHORITY
INTERNATIONAL SEA-BED OPERATIONS
INTERNATIONAL SEAS
INTERNATIONAL STANDARDS
INTERNATIONAL STRAITS
INTERNATIONAL TRADE
INTERNATIONAL VESSELS
INTERNATIONAL WATERS
INTERNATIONAL ZONE
INTERNATIONALIZATION OF CONTINENTAL
  SHELF
INTERSECTING ARCS . . . . . . . . . . . .
     see  BOUNDARIES
INTERSTATE AGREEMENTS
INTERSTATE WATERS
INTERTIDAL AQUACULTURE
ISLAND BASELINES
ISLAND BAYS
ISLAND BOUNDARIES
ISLAND CLUSTERS
ISLAND GROUPS
ISLAND SHELF
ISLAND SHORES
ISLAND STATE JURISDICTION
ISLAND STATES
ISLAND-STUDDED COASTS
ISLAND-STUDDED SEA
ISLAND WILDERNESS
ISLANDS
ISLANDS - ARTIFICIAL . . . . . . . . . . .
     see  ARTIFICIAL ISLANDS
ISLANDS - CONTINENTAL SHELF
ISLANDS - DESCRIPTION
ISLANDS - POLITICAL STATUS
ISLANDS - TERRITORIAL SEA
ISOBATH
ISOLATED ISLANDS
JACK-UPS
JETTIES
JELLY FISH
JUS IMPERIUM
JURISDICTION
KELP
KING CRAB
KING SALMON
KNOLLS
KRILL
LAGOON

LAGOON CULTURE
LAGOON POLLUTANTS
LAKES
LAND-BASED POLLUTION
LAND-BASED PRODUCERS
LAND-LOCKED STATE
LAND - SUBMERGED AND SUBMERSIBLE . . .
       see   SUBMERGED LAND
LAND LEASES
LAND OWNERSHIP
LAND USE PLANNING
LAND USE REGULATION
LANDBASED POLLUTION
LANDFILL
LAND-LOCKED COUNTRIES
LANDLOCKED STATES
LAND-SEA RESOURCE INTERPLAY
LAND-SOURCE POLLUTION
LANDSLIDES
LANDSLIDES - PREVENTION
LATERAL BOUNDARIES
LATERAL BOUNDARIES APPORTIONMENT
LATERAL DELIMITATION
LATERAL EQUIDISTANCE BOUNDARIES
LATERAL EQUIDISTANCE LINES
LAW OF THE SEA
LAW OF THE SEA NEGOTIATIONS
LAW OF THE SEA TRIBUNAL
LAWS AND LEGISLATION - FEDERAL
LAWS AND LEGISLATION - GLOBAL
LAWS AND REGULATIONS
LEAD
LEGAL CONTINENTAL SHELF
LEASES - GAS
LEASES - OIL DRILLING
LEASING PRACTICES
LEAST-COST WASTE TREATMENT
LEGAL ACTIONS
LEGAL REGIME FOR DEEP SEA-BED
LEGAL ZONES
LEGISLATION
LIABILITY
LIGHT FISHING
LIGHTERING
LIGHTHOUSES
LIMITED ENFORCEMENT RIGHTS
LINE FISHING
LIQUEFICATION OF COAL
LITIGATION
LITIGATION - FEDERAL
LITIGATION - FOREIGN
LITIGATION - INTERNATIONAL
LITIGATION - STATE
LITTORAL COMMUNITIES
LITTORAL STATES
LITTORAL ZONES
LIVING RESOURCES
LIVING RESOURCES OF HIGH SEAS . . . . .
       see   LIVING RESOURCES

LOBSTER AQUACULTURE
LOBSTER FARMING
LOBSTER WAR
LOBSTERING
LOGGING POLLUTION
LONG-DISTANCE FISHING
LONG-DISTANCE FISHING FLEETS
LONG-LINE CULTURE
LONG RANGE FISHING VESSELS
LONG LINE CRAB POT SYSTEMS
LOW TIDE ELEVATIONS
LOW TIDE LINE
LOW-WATER
LOW-WATER MARK
MACKEREL
MAGNETIC POLES
MAJOR FISH CATCHES
MANAGEMENT OF OCEAN SPACE
MANATEES
MANGANESE MEGANODULES
MANGANESE MINES
MANGANESE MUD
MANGANESE NODULE EXPLORATION
MANGANESE NODULES
MANGANESE TAILINGS
MANGROVE BORDERED ESTUARIES
MANMADE FISH ATTRACTANTS
MANMADE ISLANDS . . . . . . . . . . . .
       see   ARTIFICIAL ISLANDS
MANNED SEAFLOOR COMPLETIONS
MANNED UNDERSEA SCIENCE
MANNED UNDERSEA STATIONS
MANNED UNDERSEA TECHNOLOGY
MAPPING
MARE CLAUSUM . . . . . . . . . . . .
       see   CLOSED SEAS
MARGINAL PLATEAUS
MARICULTURE . . . . . . . . . . . . .
       see   AQUACULTURE
MARINE AGRICULTURE
MARINE ALGAE . . . . . . . . . . . . .
       see   ALGAE
MARINE AQUACULTURE . . . . . . . . . .
       see   AQUACULTURE
MARINE ARCHAEOLOGY
MARINE BIOLOGICAL DAMAGE
MARINE BIOLOGY
MARINE BOUNDARIES . . . . . . . . . . .
       see   BOUNDARIES
MARINE CAVES
MARINE CONSTRUCTION
MARINE DISRUPTION
MARINE ECOLOGY
MARINE ECONOMICS
MARINE ENGINEERING EQUIPMENT
MARINE ENVIRONMENT
MARINE ENVIRONMENTAL POLLUTION
MARINE EXPLOITATION
MARINE FAUNA

MARINE FLORA
MARINE FOOD SUPPLY . . . . . . . . . . . . .
      see SEAFOOD
MARINE GEOLOGY
MARINE GEOTECHNOLOGY
MARINE GEOTECHNIQUES
MARINE LAND MANAGEMENT
MARINE LAW . . . . . . . . . . . . . . . .
      see LAW OF THE SEA
MARINE LIFE
MARINE LIFE CONSERVATION
MARINE LIFE DISRUPTION
MARINE LIFE RESEARCH
MARINE LIFE - TELEMETERING
MARINE LIFE - TIDAL WATERS
MARINE MAMMALS
MARINE MAMMALS - KILLING OF
MARINE MAMMALS - PROTECTION
MARINE MAMMALS - RESEARCH
MARINE MASS TRANSIT SYSTEMS
MARINE MASS TRANSPORTATION
MARINE MINERAL DEPOSITS
MARINE MINERAL EXPLOITATION
MARINE MINERAL EXPLORATION
MARINE MINERAL PRODUCTION
MARINE MINERAL RECOVERY
MARINE MINERAL RESOURCES
MARINE MINERAL RESOURCES - CATEGORIES
MARINE MINERAL RESOURCES - CONTINENTAL
   SHELF
MARINE MINERAL DEPOSITS - DEEP OCEAN
   BASIN
MARINE MINERAL DEPOSITS - DEEP OCEAN BED
MARINE MINERAL RESOURCES - DETECTION
   SYSTEMS
MARINE MINERAL RESOURCES - EVALUATION
MARINE MINERAL RESOURCES - FUGITIVE
   MINERALS
MARINE MINERAL RESOURCES - POTENTIAL
MARINE MINERAL RESOURCES - PRODUCTION
   PROBLEMS
MARINE MINERAL RESOURCES - SEA WATER
MARINE MINERAL RESOURCES - WITHIN
   BEDROCK
MARINE MINERALS - OFFSHORE
MARINE MINERALS - PROSPECTING
MARINE MINING
MARINE MINING LAW
MARINE MINING LICENSES
MARINE MINING MORATORIUM
MARINE MINING OPERATIONS
MARINE MINING POLLUTION
MARINE OIL STORAGE TERMINALS
MARINE POLLUTANTS
MARINE POLLUTION
MARINE POLLUTION CONTROL
MARINE POLLUTION PREVENTION
MARINE POLLUTION RESEARCH
MARINE POWER SYSTEMS

MARINE PRESERVES
MARINE PRODUCTS
MARINE PRODUCTS RESEARCH
MARINE PROTECTION
MARINE RECREATION . . . . . . . . . . . . .
      see RECREATION - MARINE
MARINE RESOURCE ZONES
MARINE RESOURCES
MARINE RESOURCES CONSERVATION
MARINE RESOURCES - DRUGS
MARINE RESOURCES - EXPLOITATION
MARINE RESOURCES - EXPLORATION
MARINE RESOURCES - FOREIGN ACTIVITIES
MARINE RESOURCES - INTERESTS OF
   COASTAL STATES
MARINE RESOURCES - INTERNATIONAL
   ACTIVITIES
MARINE RESOURCES - INTERNATIONAL LAW
MARINE RESOURCES - JURISDICTION
MARINE RESOURCES MANAGEMENT
MARINE RESOURCES - NATIONAL ACTIVITIES
MARINE RESOURCES - SHARING
MARINE SANCTUARIES
MARINE SCIENCE
MARINE SCIENCE - DATA EXCHANGE
MARINE SCIENCE PROGRAMS
MARINE TECHNOLOGY
MARINE TECHNOLOGY TRANSFER
MARINE TRANSPORTATION
MARITIME ADMINISTRATION
MARITIME AFFAIRS
MARITIME BOUNDARIES
MARITIME DOCTRINE
MARITIME HAZARDS
MARITIME INDUSTRY . . . . . . . . . . . . .
      see OCEAN INDUSTRY
MARITIME JURISDICTION
MARITIME SOVEREIGNTY
MARITIME SPACE
MARITIME STATE
MARITIME TRANSIT
MARKER BUOYS
MARSHLANDS
MEAN SEA LEVEL
MECHANICAL SKIMMERS
MEDIAN LINE
MEDIAN-LINE PRINCIPLES
MEDICINES FROM THE SEA
MERCHANT MARINE
MERCURY
MERCURY CONTAMINATION
MERCURY LEVELS
MERCURY POISONING
METAL-RICH DEEP OCEAN MUD
METAL-SEDIMENT INTERACTIONS . . . . . .
      see POLLUTION
METAL TAILINGS
MIGRATORY SPECIES

MILITARY INSTALLATIONS
MILITARY INTERESTS
MILITARY MOBILITY
MILITARY USES OF OCEAN
MILITARY USES OF SEA-BED
MILITARY USES OF STRAITS
MILITARY USES
MILITARY ZONES OF PEACE
MINERAL DEPOSITS
MINERAL LANDS
MINERAL RESOURCES JURISDICTION
MINERAL RESOURCES POLICY
MINERALS
MINES
MINING
MINING CLAIMS
MINING ENGINEERING
MINING - HARD MINERALS
MINING LAWS
MINING OFFSHORE . . . . . . . . . . . . . . .
     see   MARINE MINING
MINING RIGHTS
MINING TECHNOLOGY
MINING VESSELS
MINING ZONES
MISSILE SUBMARINES
MIXED ECONOMIC ZONE
MOBILE PLATFORMS/DRILLING UNITS
MOBILE RIGS
MOLLUSKS
MONITORING
MONITORING DEVICES
MOORING
MOORING BUOYS
MORATORIUM RESOLUTIONS
MORTALITY RATES
MOUNTAINS IN THE SEA
MUD - OCEAN FLOOR . . . . . . . . . . . . . .
     see   SEA-BED MUD
MUDFLATS
MULTILATERAL TREATIES/ACTION
MUNICIPAL SEWAGE
MUSSEL BEDS
MUSSEL CULTURE
MUSSELS
NATIONAL ENERGY POLICY
NATIONAL OCEAN INSTITUTIONS
NATIONAL OCEAN POLICY
NATIONAL SECURITY
NATURAL GAS
NATURAL GAS - OFFSHORE
NATURAL GAS TRANSPORTATION
NATURAL PROLONGATION PRINCIPLE
NATURAL RESOURCES
NATURAL RESOURCES CONSERVATION
NATURAL RESOURCES MANAGEMENT
NAVAL ARCHITECTURE
NAVAL ARMAMENT
NAVAL MOBILITY

NAVIGABLE WATERS
NAVIGABLE WATERS REGULATIONS
NAVIGABLE WATERS RESTRICTIONS
NAVIGATION
NAVIGATION AND COMMUNICATIONS
NAVIGATION CHANNELS
NAVIGATION POLICIES
NEAP TIDE
NEARSHORE
NEARSHORE ACTIVITIES
NEARSHORE ENVIRONMENT
NEARSHORE ZONE
NETS . . . . see   FISHING VESSELS AND GEAR
NICKEL
NODULE MINING/PROCESSING
NOISE POLLUTION
NON-INNOCENT PASSAGE
NON-LIVING RESOURCES . . . . . . . . . . . .
     see   MARINE MINERAL RESOURCES
NON-RENEWABLE RESOURCES
NONSUSPENDABLE INNOCENT PASSAGE
NON-VESSEL MOBILE STRUCTURES
NON-VESSEL STATIONARY STRUCTURES . . .
     see   OFFSHORE STRUCTURES
NUCLEAR AGE
NUCLEAR DAMAGE . . . . . . . . . . . . . . . .
     see   NUCLEAR POLLUTION
NUCLEAR ENERGY
NUCLEAR ENERGY PRODUCTION
NUCLEAR EXPLOSIONS
NUCLEAR FUELS
NUCLEAR MERCHANT SHIPS
NUCLEAR MISSILE SYSTEMS
NUCLEAR POLLUTION
NUCLEAR POWER PLANTS
NUCLEAR POWER PLANTS - FLOATING
NUCLEAR POWER PLANTS - OFFSHORE
NUCLEAR POWER PLANTS - SITE SELECTION
NUCLEAR POWER PLANTS - SUBMERGED
NUCLEAR POWERED SHIPS
NUCLEAR PROPULSION
NUCLEAR RADIATION
NUCLEAR REACTORS
NUCLEAR SEEPAGE
NUCLEAR SHIPS
NUCLEAR TEST FALL-OUT
NUCLEAR TESTING
NUCLEAR WEAPONS
NUISANCE
OCEAN ACTIVITIES
OCEAN AIRPORTS . . . . . . . . . . . . . . . . .
     see   OFFSHORE STRUCTURES
OCEAN BASINS
OCEAN BOTTOM . . . . . . . . . . . . . . . . . .
     see   SEA-BED
OCEAN COMMERCE
OCEAN CONSERVATION
OCEAN CONSERVATORS . . . . . . . . . . . . .
     see   OCEAN CONSERVATION

OCEAN DATA ACQUISITION SYSTEMS
OCEAN DATA SYSTEMS
OCEAN DEFENSE PROBLEMS
OCEAN DEVELOPMENT
OCEAN DEVELOPMENT TAX
OCEAN DRILLING . . . . . . . . . . . . . . . .
       see  MARINE DRILLING
OCEAN DUMPING
OCEAN DUMPING REGULATIONS
OCEAN ECONOMIC POTENTIAL
OCEAN ECONOMICS
OCEAN EDUCATION . . . . . . . . . . . . . .
       see  OCEAN STUDY
OCEAN ENCLOSURE
OCEAN ENERGY GENERATION
OCEAN ENGINEERING
OCEAN EXPLOITATION
OCEAN EXPLORATION
OCEAN EXPLORATION PROGRAM
OCEAN FARMING . . . . . . . . . . . . . . . . .
       see  AQUACULTURE
OCEAN FLOOR
OCEAN FLOOR SUBSOIL
OCEAN FLOOR SYSTEMS . . . . . . . . . . . . .
       see  SUBSEA COMPLETIONS
OCEAN FOOD RESOURCES
OCEAN HARBORS
OCEAN HISTORY
OCEAN INDUSTRY
OCEAN LAW . . . . . . . . . . . . . . . . . . . .
       see  LAW OF THE SEA
OCEAN MINING . . . . . . . . . . . . . . . . .
       see  MARINE MINING
OCEAN MINING LAW . . . . . . . . . . . . .
       see  MARINE MINING LAW
OCEAN OIL LAW
OCEAN ORIENTED ACTIVITIES
OCEAN OUTFALLS
OCEAN PERCH
OCEAN PLATFORM DEVELOPMENT
OCEAN PLATFORMS
OCEAN POLICY
OCEAN POLICY RESEARCH
OCEAN RANCHING . . . . . . . . . . . . . . .
       see  AQUACULTURE
OCEAN REGIME
OCEAN RESOURCES . . . . . . . . . . . . . . .
       see  MARINE RESOURCES
OCEAN SAND
OCEAN SAND RECLAMATION
OCEAN SCIENCE . . . . . . . . . . . . . . . . .
       see  MARINE SCIENCE
OCEAN SCIENCE POLICY
OCEAN SPACE
OCEAN SPACE - BOUNDARIES
OCEAN SPACE - DELIMITATION
OCEAN SPACE JURISDICTIONAL ZONES
OCEAN SPACE - OVERFLIGHT

OCEAN SPACE STRATA
OCEAN SPACE - UNILATERAL CLAIMS
OCEAN STUDY
OCEAN STUDY INSTITUTIONS
OCEAN TECHNOLOGY
OCEAN USES
OCEAN WAVES
OCEAN-BASED ENERGY FACILITIES
OCEAN-RELATED MATTERS
OCEANIC-CONTINENTAL CRUST INTERSECTION
OCEANIC DATA
OCEANIC JURISPRUDENCE
OCEANOGRAPHIC ACTIVITIES
OCEANOGRAPHIC BASIN
OCEANOGRAPHIC RESEARCH
OCEANOGRAPHIC RESEARCH STATIONS
OCEANOGRAPHY
OCEANOLOGY
OCEANS
OCEANS AND ATMOSPHERE
OCEANS - MILITARY ROLE
OCTOPUSES
OFFSHORE ACTIVITIES
OFFSHORE AIRPORTS . . . . . . . . . . . . . .
       see  OFFSHORE STRUCTURES
OFFSHORE BARGE MOORINGS
OFFSHORE BOUNDARIES . . . . . . . . . . . .
       see  BOUNDARIES
OFFSHORE CABLES
OFFSHORE CITIES . . . . . . . . . . . . . . . .
       see  OFFSHORE STRUCTURES
OFFSHORE CONSTRUCTION
OFFSHORE DEEPWATER PORT FACILITY
OFFSHORE DRILLING
OFFSHORE DRILLING PLATFORMS . . . . . . .
       see  OFFSHORE STRUCTURES
OFFSHORE DUMPING
OFFSHORE ENVIRONMENT
OFFSHORE EQUIPMENT
OFFSHORE EXPLORATION . . . . . . . . . . .
       see  OFFSHORE OPERATIONS
OFFSHORE FIXED PLATFORMS . . . . . . . . .
       see  OFFSHORE STRUCTURES
OFFSHORE INSTALLATIONS
OFFSHORE ISLANDS
OFFSHORE LEASING
OFFSHORE LOADING FACILITIES
OFFSHORE MINERAL EXPLOITATION
OFFSHORE NUCLEAR POWER PLANTS
OFFSHORE OIL
OFFSHORE OIL PLATFORMS . . . . . . . . . . .
       see  OFFSHORE STRUCTURES
OFFSHORE OIL SEEPAGE
OFFSHORE OIL STORAGE
OFFSHORE OIL TERMINAL
OFFSHORE OPERATIONS
OFFSHORE PETROLEUM DRILLING
OFFSHORE PIPELINE OPERATIONS

OFFSHORE PIPELINES
OFFSHORE PLATFORM COMPLEXES . . . . . .
       see OFFSHORE STRUCTURES
OFFSHORE PLATFORM DESIGN
OFFSHORE PLATFORMS . . . . . . . . . . . .
       see OFFSHORE STRUCTURES
OFFSHORE POLLUTION
OFFSHORE POLLUTION HAZARDS
OFFSHORE PORTS
OFFSHORE POWER PLANTS . . . . . . . . . .
       see OFFSHORE STRUCTURES
OFFSHORE POWER SYSTEMS
OFFSHORE RECREATION CENTERS
OFFSHORE REFINERIES AND STORAGE
OFFSHORE RIG DESIGN
OFFSHORE RIGHTS
OFFSHORE RIGS
OFFSHORE STORAGE TANKS . . . . . . . . . .
       see OFFSHORE STRUCTURES
OFFSHORE STRUCTURES
OFFSHORE STRUCTURES - SITE SELECTION
OFFSHORE TECHNOLOGY
OFFSHORE TERMINALS
OFFSHORE TEST DRILLING . . . . . . . . . .
       see OFFSHORE DRILLING
OFFSHORE WATERS
OFFSHORE ZONE JURISDICTION
OFFSHORE ZONES
OIL
OIL AND GAS
OIL AND GAS EXPLORATION
OIL AND GAS LEASES
OIL AND GAS SEEPAGE
OIL BASES
OIL CARGO FLAMMABILITY
OIL CONCESSIONS
OIL CONTAMINATED BIRDS
OIL CONTAMINATED WILD LIFE
OIL CONTAMINATION
OIL DERRICKS
OIL DISCHARGE
OIL DISCOVERIES
OIL DISPERSANTS
OIL DRILLING
OIL FIELD BRINES
OIL FIELDS
OIL INDUSTRY
OIL PIPELINES
OIL PLATFORM EQUIPMENT
OIL POLLUTION
OIL POLLUTION - BIOLOGICAL EFFECTS
OIL POLLUTION CLEANUP
OIL POLLUTION CONTAINMENT . . . . . . . .
       see OIL POLLUTION CONTROL
OIL POLLUTION DETECTION
OIL POLLUTION EFFECTS
OIL POLLUTION - FINES
OIL POLLUTION LEGAL ASPECTS

OIL POLLUTION LEGISLATION
OIL POLLUTION - LIABILITIES
OIL POLLUTION MONITORING
OIL POLLUTION PREVENTION
OIL POLLUTION REPORTS
OIL PROCESSING
OIL PRODUCTION
OIL RECOVERY AND HANDLING TECHNIQUES
OIL REFINERIES
OIL RESERVOIRS
OIL RIGS
OIL SANDS
OIL SEARCH . . . . . . . . . . . . . . . . . . .
       see OFFSHORE DRILLING
           OCEAN EXPLORATION
OIL SHALE
OIL SKIMMERS
OIL SLICK
OIL SLOP WATER
OIL SLUDGE
OIL SLUDGE DUMPING
OIL SPILL CLEANUP PROCEDURE
OIL SPILL CLEANUP RESEARCH
OIL SPILL CONTAINMENT
OIL SPILLS
OIL SPILLS - MAIN SOURCES
OIL SPREADING
OIL STORAGE
OIL SUPER TANKERS
OIL TOWNS . . . . . . . . . . . . . . . . . . .
       see OIL BASES
OIL TRANSPORTATION
OIL TRANSPORTATION - ENCASED
    UNDERGROUND CABLES
OIL WASHWATER
OIL WASTES
OIL WELL DRILLING
OIL WELL LOGGING
OIL WELLS
OILBERGS
OILCLEANING MATERIALS
OIL-DRILLING VESSEL
OIL-EATING BACTERIA
OIL WELL SEEPAGE
OPEN SEA AQUACULTURE
OPEN SEAS
OPEN WATER FISHING
OPPOSITE STATES
ORGANIZATIONS
OTTERS
OUTER CONTINENTAL SHELF
OUTER CONTINENTAL SHELF LAND
OUTER CONTINENTAL SHELF LEASES . . . . .
       see OFFSHORE LEASES
OUTER CONTINENTAL SHELF RESOURCE
    ALLOCATION
OUTER CONTINENTAL SHELF RESOURCE
    MANAGEMENT

OUTER LIMIT OF CONTINENTAL SHELF
OUTER SPACE
OVERFISHING
OVERFLIGHT
OYSTER BEDS
OYSTER CULTURE
OYSTER REEFS
OYSTERS
OZONE
PARTICIPATION OF LAND-LOCKED STATES
PATRIMONIAL SEA
PENGUINS
PERMANENT HARBORWORKS
PESTICIDE RUNOFF
PETROLEUM CONSERVATION
PETROLEUM CRACKING
PETROLEUM-DESALTING
PETROLEUM ENGINEERING
PETROLEUM GEOLOGY
PETROLEUM IN SUBMERGED LANDS
PETROLEUM INDUSTRY
PETROLEUM - LAW AND LEGISLATION
PETROLEUM PIPELINES
PETROLEUM REFINERIES
PETROLEUM TECHNOLOGY
PETROLEUM TRANSPORTATION
PIERS
PILCHARD
PIPELINE SAFETY
PIPELINES
PIRACY
PIRATE BROADCASTING
PLANT NUTRIENTS POLLUTION
PLATE MOVEMENT
PLATE TECTONICS
POLAR BEARS
POLITICAL INTELLIGENCE - "OCEAN RESEARCH"
POLITICAL VACUUM OF HIGH SEAS
POLLUTANT DETECTION
POLLUTANT DILUTION
POLLUTANT DISPERSION
POLLUTANT REMOVAL
POLLUTANTS - HARBOR
POLLUTANTS - OFFSHORE
POLLUTED ESTUARY
POLLUTION
POLLUTION - AGRICULTURAL WASTES
POLLUTION ASSESSMENT AND CONTROL
POLLUTION - BALLAST
POLLUTION - CONTIGUOUS ZONE
POLLUTION CONTROL
POLLUTION CONTROL PROGRAMS
POLLUTION DETECTION
POLLUTION - DUMPING
POLLUTION EFFECTS
POLLUTION - ESTUARIES
POLLUTION - EXPLOSIVES
POLLUTION - FALL-OUT
POLLUTION - INTERNATIONAL PROBLEM
POLLUTION HAZARDS
POLLUTION INTERVENTION
POLLUTION - LAND RUN-OFF
POLLUTION - MUNICIPAL DISCHARGE
POLLUTION - NUCLEAR WASTES
POLLUTION - OIL TERMINALS
POLLUTION PREVENTION
POLLUTION PREVENTION PROGRAMS
POLLUTION PREVENTION - STATE OBLIGATION
POLLUTION PROBLEMS
POLLUTION - RADIOACTIVE WASTE
POLLUTION - REGULATION
POLLUTION SOURCES
POLLUTION - SEWAGE
POLLUTION - THERMAL
POLLUTIONAL TRENDS
PORPOISES AND DOLPHINS
PORT DEVELOPMENT
PORT FACILITIES
PORT MANAGEMENT
PORT STATE
PORT-STATE CONTROL
PORT SURVEYS
PORTS AND HARBORS
POWER PLANT LICENSING
POWER PLANT SITING
POWER SOURCES . . . . . . . . . . . . . . . .
    see ENERGY
PREFERENTIAL EXPLOITATION
PREFERENTIAL EXPLORATION
PREFERENTIAL FISHING RIGHTS
PRESERVATION OF MARINE ENVIRONMENT
PRIZE LAWS
PRODUCTION PLATFORMS
PRODUCTION TECHNIQUES/CONTROLS
PROPERTY LEASES
PROTEIN
PUBLIC LAND
PUBLIC WATER
PUBLIC'S RIGHT TO BEACH
PULPMILL EFFLUENT
PURSE-SEIN FISHERY
RADIATION
RADIATION COUNTERMEASURES
RADIATION PROTECTION
RADIATION SOURCES
RADIOACTIVE FALL-OUT
RADIOACTIVE MONITORING
RADIOACTIVE POLLUTION
RADIOACTIVE WASTE
RADIOACTIVE WASTE DISCHARGE
RAW MATERIALS
RAW SEWAGE
REASONABLE USE
REBUS SIC STANTIBUS
RECEIVING WATERS
RECOVERY NETS
RECREATIONAL SUBMERSIBLES

RECREATION
RECREATION - MARINE
RED CLAY DISCARD
RED SALMON
RED SNAPPER
RED TIDE
REDUCING AREA METHOD
REEFS
REEFS - ARTIFICIAL . . . . . . . . . . . . . . .
        see ARTIFICIAL REEFS
REFINERIES
REFRIGERATOR SHIP
REFUSE. . . . . . . . . . . . . . . . . . . . . .
        see SOLID WASTE
REFUSE POLLUTION
REGIME OF STRAITS . . . . . . . . . . . . . .
        see STRAITS
REGIONAL FISHERIES AGENCIES
REGIONAL FISHERY CONTROL
REGIONAL PLANNING . . . . . . . . . . . . .
        see COASTAL ZONE MANAGEMENT
REGULATION OF FREEDOM OF FISHING
RENEWABLE RESOURCES/REPRODUCTIVE CYCLES
RES COMMUNIS
RES NULLIUS
RES PUBLICA
RES UNIVERSITATIS
RESEARCH VESSELS
RESERVOIR
RESOURCE CONSERVATION
RESOURCE EXTRACTION
RESOURCE MANAGEMENT
RESOURCE RECOVERY
RESOURCE ZONE
RESOURCES LEGISLATION
RESTOCKING
RIDGES
RIGHT OF ACCESS
RIGHT OF HOT PURSUIT
RIGHT OF INNOCENT PASSAGE
RIGHT OF PASSAGE . . . . . . . . . . . . . . .
        see FREEDOM OF PASSAGE
RIGHT OF TRANSIT
RIGHT OF COASTAL STATES
RIGS
RIPARIAN PROPERTY
RIPARIAN RIGHTS
RIPARIAN RIGHTS - LEGAL ASPECTS
RIVER BASIN
RIVER CULTURE
RIVER MOUTHS
RIVER POLLUTION
RIVERS
RIVERS - BASELINE
ROADSTEADS
RUBBISH
RULES OF INNOCENT PASSAGE
RUNOFF
SALINE WATER

SALINITY
SALMON
SALMON MIGRATION
SALMON SPAWNING
SALT
SALT MARSHES
SALT WATER ECOSYSTEM
SALT WATER INTRUSION
SALVAGE AND DIVING
SALVAGE RIGHTS
SAND
SAND DRIFT
SAND DUNES
SAND MOVEMENT
SANITARY CONTROLS
SANITARY LANDFILL
SANITARY REGULATIONS
SARDINES
SATURATION DIVING
SAURY FISHERIES
SCALLOPS
SCIENTIFIC RESEARCH
SCIENTIFIC RESEARCH - CONTINENTAL SHELF
SCIENTIFIC RESEARCH - DEEP SEA-BED
SCIENTIFIC RESEARCH - ECONOMIC ZONE
SCIENTIFIC RESEARCH INSTALLATIONS
SCIENTIFIC RESEARCH - MANNED UNDERSEA
    RESEARCH STATIONS
SCIENTIFIC RESEARCH - TERRITORIAL SEA
SCRAP DUMPING
SCUBA DIVING
SEA BASS
SEA BIRDS
SEA BOTTOM
SEA BOTTOM ENTRANCE
SEA BOUNDARY DELIMITATIONS
SEA BOUNDARIES
SEA COWS
SEA DEFENSE ZONES
SEA FRONTAGE
SEA HORSE
SEA LANES
SEA LAW . . . . . . . . . . . . . . . . . . . . .
        see LAW OF THE SEA
SEA OTTERS
SEA STATES . . . . . . . . . . . . . . . . . . .
        see COASTAL STATES
SEA URCHIN FISHERY
SEA WATER
SEA WATER - DRUGS
SEA WATER RECIRCULATING SYSTEMS
SEA-BASED ENVIRONMENT
SEABED . . . . . . . . . . . . . . . . . . . . . .
        see SEA-BED
SEA-BED
SEA-BED - ABYSSAL ZONE
SEA-BED ACTIVITIES
SEA-BED AQUACULTURE

SEA-BED ARMS CONTROL . . . . . . . . . . . .
        see   ARMS CONTROL
SEA-BED ATOLLS
SEA-BED - BEYOND NATIONAL JURISDICTION
SEA-BED COLONIZATION . . . . . . . . . . .
        see   SEA-BED EKISTICS
SEA-BED COMMITTEE
SEA-BED - COMMON HERITAGE OF MAN
SEA-BED - DELIMITATION
SEA-BED - DISARMAMENT OF
SEA-BED EKISTICS
SEA-BED ENGINEERING
SEA-BED - EQUITABLE SHARING OF BENEFITS
SEA-BED - EXPLOITATION
SEA-BED - EXPLORATION
SEA-BED - "FREEZING" OF
SEA-BED - HOT BRINES
SEA-BED IMPLANTATIONS
SEA-BED INSTALLATIONS
SEA-BED - INTERNATIONAL LAW
SEA-BED - INTERNATIONAL REGIME
SEA-BED - LIMITS OF NATIONAL JURISDICTION
SEA-BED - MANNED UNDERSEA RESEARCH
   STATIONS . . . . . . . . . . . . . . . . .
        see   SCIENTIFIC RESEARCH
SEA-BED - MID-OCEANIC RIDGES
SEA-BED MILITARY EMPLACEMENTS
SEA-BED MILITARY INTERESTS
SEA-BED MILITARY USE
SEA-BED MINING . . . . . . . . . . . . . . . .
        see   MARINE MINING
SEA-BED MINING CLAIMS
SEA-BED MUD
SEA-BED - NATIONAL CLAIMS
SEA-BED POLLUTION
SEA-BED QUESTION
SEA-BED - REGULATION OF
SEA-BED RESOURCE EXPLORATION
SEA-BED SAND TRANSPORT
SEA-BED - SOVEREIGNTY
SEA-BED SUBSOIL
SEA-BED - SUPERJACENT STATES
SEA-BED - "SURFACE SYSTEM"
SEA-BED TECHNOLOGY
SEA-BED - TUNNELLING
SEA-BED VEHICLES
SEA-FARMING . . . . . . . . . . . . . . . . .
        see AQUACULTURE
SEAFLOOR . . . . . . . . . . . . . . . . .
        see   SEA-BED
SEAFLOOR CONSTRUCTION
SEAFLOOR SCIENCE . . . . . . . . . . . . . .
        see   MARINE SCIENCE
             OCEANOGRAPHY
SEAFLOOR SPREADING
SEAFOOD
SEAFOOD PROCESSING
SEAGRANT LEGISLATION
SEA-ICE JURISDICTION
SEAKEEPING
SEALAB
SEA LEVEL
SEALING
SEALING ZONE
SEALS
SEAMOUNTS
SEAS
SEASHORE ALTERATIONS
SEASTEADING . . . . . . . . . . . . . . . .
        see   AQUACULTURE
SEAWARD EXTENSION
SEAWEED CULTURE
SEAWEED FARMS
SEAWEED PRODUCTS
SEAWEED RESOURCE MANAGEMENT
SECURITY
SEDENTARY RESOURCES/SPECIES
SEDIMENT PLUMES
SEDIMENT STABILITY
SEDIMENTATION
SEEPAGE
SEGREGATED BALLAST
SEINERS
SEISMIC CABLES
SEISMIC DISTURBANCES
SEISMIC EXPLORATION
SEISMIC MEASUREMENTS
SEISMIC VIBRATIONS
SEMI-CIRCLE CLOSING LINE TEST
SEMI-CIRCULAR RULE
SEMI-ENCLOSED SEAS . . . . . . . . . . . .
        see   ENCLOSED SEAS
SEMI-SUBMERSIBLE DRILLING RIGS
SEMI-SUBMERSIBLE SUPPLY VESSELS
SETBACK - CONSTRUCTION
SEWAGE SLUDGE
SEWAGE SLUDGE DUMPING . . . . . . . . .
        see   OCEAN DUMPING
SEWAGE TREATMENT
SEWERAGE
SHALLOW WATERS
SHARKS
SHELLFISH AQUACULTURE
SHELLFISH CONSERVATION
SHELLFISH CULTURE . . . . . . . . . . . . .
        see   AQUACULTURE
SHELLFISHERY . . . . . . . . . . . . . . . . .
        see   SHELLFISH AQUACULTURE
SHELFLESS STATES
SHELF-LOCKED STATES
SHIP SEIZURES . . . see   VESSEL SEIZURES
SHIPBOARD PROCESSING
SHIP SEWAGE
SHIP-GENERATED POLLUTION . . . . . . . .
        see   VESSEL-SOURCE POLLUTION
SHIPPING INDUSTRY

SHIPPING RULES
SHIPPING SAFETY CONTROL ZONES
SHIPS
SHIPS - NUCLEAR POWERED . . . . . . . . . . .
   see  NUCLEAR POWERED SHIPS
SHIPS - REGISTRATION
SHIPWRECKS
SHIPYARDS
SHORE CLEANUP
SHORE DEVELOPMENT
SHORE DISPLACEMENT
SHORE PROTECTION
SHORE SUPPLY BASES . . . . . . . . . . . . . . .
   see  OIL BASES
SHORELAND BOUNDARIES
SHORELANDS MANAGEMENT UNITS
SHORELANDS REGULATION
SHORELINE CLASSIFICATION
SHORELINE EROSION
SHORELINE - LITTORAL DRIFT
SHORELINE MONITORING . . . . . . . . . . . .
   sa  SHORELINE EROSION
SHORELINE PRESERVATION
SHORT COASTLINE STATES
SHRIMP AGREEMENT
SHRIMP AQUACULTURE
SHRIMP FISHERIES SORTING TRAWLS
SHRIMP FISHERY
SHRIMP TRAWLERS
SILT
SILVICULTURE
SILVICULTURE - POLLUTION
SINKING
SITE EVALUATION
SITING
SKIMMING
SKIPJACKS
SLAVERY
SLOPE-RISE INTERSECTION
SMUGGLING
SMUGGLING - CONTIGUOUS ZONES - CUSTOMS
SOCIALIST LAW OF THE SEA
SOLAR ENERGY
SOLAR POWER
SOLAR RADIATION
SOLAR SEA POWER
SOLES
SOLID WASTE DISPOSAL/POLLUTION
SOLID WASTE - GARBAGE TRASH
SONAR SYSTEMS
SONIC SOUNDING
SONOBUOYS
SORTING TRAWLS
SOVEREIGN IMMUNITY
SOVEREIGN RIGHTS
SOVEREIGNTY AREA
SPACECRAFT
SPAWNING
SPAWNING POPULATIONS

SPECIAL PURPOSE TERRITORY . . . . . . . . . .
   see  EXCLUSIVE ZONE
SPECIALTY CARRIERS
SPECIES
SPECIES - SURVIVAL
SPERM WHALES
SPOIL
SPONGES
SPORT FISHING
SPORTS - MARINE
SPRATS
SQUID FISHERY
STARFISH
STATE - MARINE EXPLOITATION
STATE - MARINE EXPLORATION
STATE FISHERY LAWS
STATISTICS
STEEP SHELF STATES
STORAGE FACILITIES
STORM SURGES
STRAIGHT BASELINES
STRAIGHT BASELINES - ARCHIPELAGOES
STRAIGHT BASELINES - LENGTH
STRAITS
STRAITS - INNOCENT PASSAGE
STRATA
STREAM POLLUTION
STREAMS
STREAMS - CONSERVATION
STUDIES - MARINE ECONOMICS
STUDIES - NATIONAL SHORELINES
SUBJACENT TERRITORIES
SUBLITTORAL AQUACULTURE
SUBLITTORAL CANYONS
SUBLITTORAL ZONES
SUBMARINE ACTIVITY
SUBMARINE BOUNDARIES
SUBMARINE CABLES
SUBMARINE DRILLING
SUBMARINE GEOLOGY
SUBMARINE MISSILE FLEET
SUBMARINE PIPELINES
SUBMARINE PLATEAUS
SUBMARINE TANKER
SUBMARINE TRENCHES
SUBMARINE TROUGHS
SUBMARINE WARFARE
SUBMARINE ZONE
SUBMERGED BODIES
SUBMERGED DOMAIN
SUBMERGED LAND - LEGISLATION
SUBMERGED LANDS
SUBMERGED SHORELINES
SUBMERSIBLES
SUBOCEANIC
SUBSEA ANCHOR DRILLING
SUBSEA BOUNDARIES
SUBSEA COMPLETIONS
SUBSEA MINERAL RESOURCES

SUBSEA PUMPING STATION . . . . . . . . . . .
    see  SUBSEA COMPLETIONS
SUBSEA STORAGE STRUCTURES . . . . . . . .
    see  OFFSHORE STRUCTURES
SUBSEA UNIT INSTALLATION
SUBSEA WELLHEADS
SUCTION LIFT
SUNKEN CITIES
SUNKEN WRECKS/RECOVERY/DISPOSAL
SUPERJACENT WATERS
SUPERPORTS . . . . . . . . . . . . . . . . . . .
    see  DEEP DRAFT OFFSHORE PORTS
SURVEYS
SURVIVAL CAPSULE
SWELLS
SWIMMING - WATER QUALITY FOR
SWORDFISH
SYMMETRICAL SEASCAPE
SYMPOSIUMS
TANK FARM
TANKER BERTHS
TANKER EQUIPMENT
TANKER FLEET
TANKER PORT CAPABILITIES
TANKER TERMINALS
TANKER TRAFFIC
TANKERS
TANKSHIPS
TAX - FOR POLLUTION CONTROL
TECHNOLOGY - MARINE
TECTONIC DAMS
TECTONIC PLATES
TELEMETRY SYSTEM
TERMINALS
TERRACES
TERRITORIAL SEA APPORTIONMENT
TERRITORIAL SEA CLAIM
TERRITORIAL SEA DELIMITATION
TERRITORIAL SEA HISTORY
TERRITORIAL SEA LIMIT
TERRITORIAL SEA RESEARCH
TERRITORIAL SEAS
TERRITORIAL SEAS - ARCHIPELAGOES
TERRITORIAL SEAS - BASELINE DETERMINATION
TERRITORIAL SEAS - BOUNDARIES
TERRITORIAL SEAS - BREADTH
TERRITORIAL SEAS - CANNON SHOT RULE
TERRITORIAL SEAS - CONTIGUOUS ZONES
TERRITORIAL SEAS - ENTRY IN DISTRESS
TERRITORIAL SEAS - FLUCTUATING
  SHORELINES
TERRITORIAL SEAS - GULFS
TERRITORIAL SEAS - HOT PURSUIT
TERRITORIAL SEAS - INNOCENT PASSAGE
TERRITORIAL SEAS - INTERNATIONAL
  REALITIES
TERRITORIAL SEAS - ISLANDS
TERRITORIAL SEAS - LIMITS ON "INNOCENT
  RESEARCH"
TERRITORIAL SEAS - LITTORAL SEA
TERRITORIAL SEAS - MARITIME BOUNDARY
TERRITORIAL SEAS - MARINE MINERAL
  RESOURCES
TERRITORIAL SEAS - MILEAGE LIMITS
TERRITORIAL SEAS - MILITARY ISSUES
TERRITORIAL SEAS - OPPOSITE STATES
TERRITORIAL SEAS - OVERFLIGHT IN
  AIRSPACE OF
TERRITORIAL SEAS - PIRATE RADIO STATIONS
TERRITORIAL SEAS - PROPOSED EXTENSIONS
TERRITORIAL SEAS - REGIME
TERRITORIAL SEAS - ROADSTEADS
TERRITORIAL SEAS - SCIENTIFIC RESEARCH
TERRITORIAL SEAS - STRAITS
TERRITORIAL SEAS - STRATEGIC DETERRENT
TERRITORIAL SEAS - TRACKING STATIONS
TERRITORIAL WATERS
TERRITORIAL WATERS DELIMITATION
TERRITORIAL WATERS - LEGAL STATUS
TERRITORIAL WATERS - MARITIME
  SOVEREIGNTY BELT
TERRITORIAL WATERS - NATIONAL SEA
TERRITORIAL WATERS - SUPERJACENT SEAS
THERMAL BALANCE - GLOBAL
THERMAL DISCHARGES
THERMAL EFFLUENT
THERMAL ENERGY
THERMAL ENERGY PRODUCTION
THERMAL ENERGY PRODUCTION - POLLUTION
THERMAL POLLUTED WATER
THERMAL POLLUTION
THERMONUCLEAR POWER
THERMOPOLLUTION
3 MILE LIMIT
TIDAL BEACH
TIDAL ENERGY
TIDAL ESTUARIES
TIDAL FLATS
TIDAL LIMITS
TIDAL MARSH
TIDAL PLATFORMS
TIDAL POWER
TIDAL POWER PLANTS
TIDAL WATERWAYS
TIDE WATERS
TIDELAND DISPOSAL
TIDELANDS
TIDELANDS DISPUTES
TIDELANDS OWNERSHIP
TIDELANDS - PUBLIC TRUST LIMITATIONS
TIDES
TIDES - BASELINES
TORTS
TOW TUGS
TOWING
TOXIC POLLUTANTS
TRADITIONAL FISHING
TRANSIT PASSAGE

TRANSNATIONAL OCEAN INSTITUTIONS
TRANSPORTATION . . . . . . . . . . . . . . . .
       see  MARINE TRANSPORTATION
            MARITIME TRANSIT
TRANSPORTATION OF NUCLEAR MATERIALS
TRANSPORTATION POLICIES
TRANSPORTATION - RADIOACTIVE MATERIALS
TRANSPORTATION - UNDERWATER
TRAWL NET REELS
TRAWLERS
TREASURE TROVE
TREATIES
TREATIES - ACCESSION
TREATY REVISION
TREATY-MAKING POWER
TRESPASS
TROLLER GEAR
TROLLING BOAT OPERATIONS
TROPICAL MARINE ESTUARY
TROPICAL OCEAN
TROUGHS
TROUT AQUACULTURE
TROUT FARMING
TRUSTEESHIP AREA
TRUSTEESHIP ZONE
TUNA
TUNA TRAPS
TUNA WAR
TURBO DRILL - UNDERWATER . . . . . . . . . .
       see  UNDERWATER TURBO DRILL
TURTLES
12 MILE EXCLUSIVE FISHERIES ZONE
12 MILE TERRITORIAL SEA
TWO-DIMENSIONAL ZONES
200 METER DEPTH
200 MILE ECONOMIC ZONE
200 MILE FISHING JURISDICTION ZONE
200 MILE POLLUTION CONTROL ZONE
U-BOATS
ULTRADEEP WATER DRILLING
UNDERDEVELOPED COUNTRIES . . . . . . . . . .
       see  DEVELOPING COUNTRIES
UNDERGROUND WATER
UNDERSEA BARRIERS
UNDERSEA ENERGY
UNDERSEA OIL STORAGE TANKS
UNDERSEA PIPELINES
UNDERSEA RESEARCH . . . . . . . . . . . . . .
       see  MARINE RESEARCH
UNDERSEA TECHNOLOGY
UNDERSEA VEHICLES
UNDERSEA WARFARE
UNDERWATER ACOUSTICS
UNDERWATER ARCHAEOLOGY . . . . . . . . . .
       see  MARINE ARCHAEOLOGY
UNDERWATER BUOYS
UNDERWATER CONSTRUCTION
UNDERWATER DISTURBANCES
UNDERWATER DRILLING
UNDERWATER EXPLORATION
UNDERWATER EXPLOSIONS
UNDERWATER HABITATS
UNDERWATER HOUSE-LABORATORY
UNDERWATER INSTALLATIONS
UNDERWATER LIVING
UNDERWATER MEDICINE
UNDERWATER OBSERVATION VEHICLES
UNDERWATER PARKS
UNDERWATER POWER SYSTEMS
UNDERWATER RECOVERY VEHICLES
UNDERWATER RESCUE VEHICLES
UNDERWATER RIGS
UNDERWATER SALVAGE
UNDERWATER STRUCTURES
UNDERWATER TECHNOLOGY
UNDERWATER TURBO DRILL
UNENCUMBERED PASSAGE
UNILATERAL ACTS
UNIMPEDED PASSAGE OF STRAITS/TRANSIT
UNSTABLE COASTLINE
UPWELLING
URBAN ESTUARY
VESSEL ACCIDENT CONTROL
VESSEL PASSAGE . . . . . . . . . . . . . . . . .
       see  MARITIME TRANSIT
VESSEL POLLUTION
VESSEL SEIZURES
VESSEL WASTE DISPOSAL . . . . . . . . . . . .
       see  OCEAN DUMPING
VESSEL WASTE POLLUTION
VESSEL-RELEASE REQUIREMENT
VESSEL-SOURCE POLLUTION
VOLCANIC ISLANDS
VOLCANIC PLATE LAYER
VOLCANOES
VOLUME OF OCEAN
WALRUS
WASTE DISCHARGE POLLUTION
WASTE DISPOSAL
WASTE HEAT UTILIZATION
WASTE LUMBER
WASTE MANAGEMENT
WASTE RECYCLING
WASTE REMOVAL
WASTE TREATMENT
WASTE TREATMENT FACILITIES
WASTE-HEAT EFFLUENTS
WATER BOTTOMS
WATER COLUMN
WATER FOWL CLEANUP
WATER FOWL CONSERVATION
WATER LANES
WATER- AIRLIFTS
WATER QUALITY
WATER QUALITY EQUIPMENT
WATER QUALITY MANAGEMENT
WATER QUALITY MANAGEMENT METHODS
WATER QUALITY MANAGEMENT TECHNOLOGY

WATER QUALITY MONITORING STANDARDS
WATER QUALITY MANAGEMENT STANDARDS
WATER QUALITY STANDARDS LEGISLATION
WATER RESOURCES
WATER SPORTS
WATER USE PLANNING
WATERCRAFT
WATERCRAFT WASTES
WATERFRONT
WATERFRONT AREA SAFETY
WATERFRONT HOUSING
WATERFRONT LAND
WATER-POLLUTION-CONTROL SYSTEMS
WEAPON EMPLACEMENT
WEAPONS OF MASS DESTRUCTION
WETLANDS
WETLANDS CONSERVATION
WETLANDS LEGISLATION
WETLANDS PROTECTION
WETLANDS RESOURCES

WHALES
WHALING VESSELS
WHARVES
WHITING
WILDLIFE
WIND POWER
WIRELESS RADIO ZONE
WHISTLING BEACHES
WORLD FISHERIES MANAGEMENT
WORLD ECONOMY
WORLD OCEAN
WORLD TANKER TRADE ROUTES
YELLOWFIN TUNA
YELLOWTAILS
ZONAL APPROACH
ZONES BEYOND NATIONAL JURISDICTION
ZONES OF PEACE AND SECURITY
ZONING
ZOOPLANKTON
ZONING LITIGATION

SELECTED PERIODICAL ARTICLES
by Author and Title

VINTL    ABANDONED PROPERTY AT SEA: WHO OWNS THE SALVAGE "FINDS"? William & Mary Law Review 12:97-110 (1970)

IIP&H    Abbott, E.N.V., et al. A NEW HARBOR FOR THE SHETLANDS. Offshore Services 7(4):30-32 (1974)

IISL    Abbott, L. SOME LEGAL PROBLEMS INVOLVED IN SAVING GEORGIA'S MARSHLANDS. Georgia State Bar Journal 7:27-36 (August, 1970)

IIIAFF    Abbott, Walter. METALLURGICAL MARICULTURE; FICTION OR FORESIGHT? Ocean Industry. 6:43-44 (1971)

VP    Abelson, P.H. MARINE POLLUTION. Science 171:21 (1971)

VC    Abu-El-Hassan, A. SUEZ CANAL DUES: PAST AND FUTURE. Maritime Studies and Management 2:32-37 (1974)

IICZM    ACCESS TO PUBLIC MUNICIPAL BEACHES: THE FORMULATION OF A COMPREHENSIVE LEGAL APPROACH. Suffolk University Law Review. 7:936-972 (1973)

VCONS    Ackerman, Howard A. POPULATION, NATURAL RESOURCES, AND TECHNOLOGY. Ekistics 23:265-268 (1967)

IVM    Acomb, R. INDEMNITY AS APPLIED TO OFFSHORE OIL ACTIVITIES. Louisiana Bar Journal 14:209-220,253-257 (1967)

IVMMR    Acosta-Estevez, R. PETROLEUM DEVELOPMENTS IN MEXICO IN 1970. American Association of Petroleum Geologists Bulletin 55:1676-1685 (1971)

IVMMR    _____ _____ PETROLEUM DEVELOPMENTS IN MEXICO IN 1972. American Association of Petroleum Geologists Bulletin 57:2126-2135 (1973)

VOI    Adams, Bill, and Ted Strachan. NORTH SEA REPORT. Ocean Industry 7:26-32 (1972)

IIIAFF    Adams, James W., Jr. UNEXPLORED FAR-EASTERN AREAS LOOK PROMISING. Ocean Industry 4:53-57 (1969)

VLOS    Adede, A.O. SETTLEMENT OF DISPUTES ARISING UNDER THE LAW OF THE SEA CONVENTION. American Journal of International Law 69:798-818 (1975)

VLOS    _____ _____ THE SYSTEM FOR EXPLOITATION OF THE "COMMON HERITAGE OF MANKIND" AT THE CARACAS CONFERENCE. American Journal of International Law 69:31-49 (1975)

VP    Adeniji, Kola. LEGAL CHALLENGE OF ENVIRONMENTAL POLLUTION TO AFRICA; A CASE STUDY IN THE REGIONAL APPROACH TO ENVIRONMENTAL PROBLEMS. Anglo-American Law Review 4:312-330 (1975)

VLOS    AD HOC COMMITTEE ON PEACEFUL USES OF THE SEA-BED HOLDS FIRST SESSION. U. N. Monthly Chronicle 5(4): 50-51 (1968)

| | |
|---|---|
| VLOS | AD HOC COMMITTEE ON PEACEFUL USES OF THE SEA-BED BEGINS SECOND SESSION. U. N. Monthly Chronicle 5(7):46-49 (1968) |
| VLOS | AD HOC COMMITTEE ON PEACEFUL USES OF THE SEA-BED ADOPTS REPORT TO ASSEMBLY. U. N. Monthly Chronicle 5(8):97-100 (1968) |
| IIP | ADMIRALTY - FLORIDA OIL POLLUTION ACT - STATE OIL POLLUTION REGULATION OF MARITIME ACTIVITIES IS PERMISSIBLE SO LONG AS THERE IS NO FATAL CONFLICT BETWEEN THE STATE LEGISLATION AND FEDERAL MARITIME REGULATORY SCHEMES. Vanderbilt Journal of Transnational Law. 7:183-194 (1973) |
| VP | ADMIRALTY LAW: CALIFORNIA SUES A VESSEL IN REM FOR OIL DISCHARGE DAMAGES TO ITS WATER AND MARINE LIFE. Tulsa Law Journal 6:257-263 (1970) |
| VP | ADMIRALTY REMEDIES FOR VESSEL OIL POLLUTION OF NAVIGABLE WATERS. Texas International Law Journal 7:121-150 (1971) |
| VCS | Adrogué, C.A. EL PROBLEMA DE LA JURISDICCIÓN EN LA PLATAFORMA CONTINENTAL ARGENTINA. Revista del Colegio de Abogados de la Ciudad de Buenos Aires 36(3/4):5-8 (1972) |
| IVDRIL | ADVANCEMENTS IN DRILLING INDUSTRY. World Oil 160:67-71 (1965) |
| VB | AFRICA; MARITIME ZONES. West Africa 911:(July 14, 1972) |
| IIP&H | AFRICA. World Dredging and Marine Construction 10(1):28-29 (1974) |
| IIIOI | Agnello, Richard J. PROPERTY RIGHTS AND EFFICIENCY IN THE OYSTER INDUSTRY. Journal of Law and Economy 18:521-533 (1975) |
| IIIOI | Agnello, Richard J., and L.P. Donnelley. THE INTERACTION OF ECONOMIC, BIOLOGICAL, AND LEGAL FORCES IN THE MIDDLE ATLANTIC OYSTER INDUSTRY. Fisheries Bulletin 73:256-261 (1975) |
| VB | AGREEMENT BETWEEN THE GOVERNMENT OF THE COMMONWEALTH OF AUSTRALIA AND THE GOVERNMENT OF THE REPUBLIC OF INDONESIA ESTABLISHING CERTAIN SEABED BOUNDARIES IN THE AREA OF THE TIMOR AND ARAFURA SEAS, SUPPLEMENTARY TO THE AGREEMENT OF 18 MAY 1971. Indian Journal of International Law 13(1):113-116 (1973) |
| IIIB | AGREEMENT ON FISHERY PROBLEMS IN THE WESTERN AREAS OF THE MIDDLE ATLANTIC OCEAN. International Legal Materials 7:144-148 (1968) |
| VLOS | Aguilar, M. Andrés. PATRIMONIAL SEA OR ECONOMIC ZONE CONCEPT. San Diego Law Review 11:579-602 (1974) |
| VCS | Ahern, W., Jr. BENEATH THE BANK. Oceanus 17:24-27 (1973) |
| VOR | Ahluwalia, S.S. PEACEFUL USES OF THE SEA-BED. India Quarterly (New Delhi) 27:149-152 (1971) |
| IVMMR | Aidlin, Joseph W. REPRESENTING THE GEOTHERMAL RESOURCES CLIENT. Rocky Mountain Mineral Law Institute 19:27-46 (1974) |
| IVOL | Aitkens, A. NEW OUTER CONTINENTAL SHELF OPERATIONS AND LEASING REGULATIONS AND OIL AND GAS LEASE FORM. Natural Resources Lawyer 3(2):298-314 (1970) |

VLOS    Akesson, R. THE LAW OF THE SEA CONFERENCE. Journal of World Trade Law 8:283-297 (1974)

IIIF    THE ALASKAN FISHERIES. Fishboat 20:30-31, 34-38 (1975)

IIIB    ALASKA WINS: PROTEST TO JAPAN. Newsweek 11:12-12 (Apr. 4, 1938)

IIIF    ALASKAN FISHERMEN ORGANIZE FORCES UNDER SINGLE BANNER. National Fisherman 53(2):A2 (1972)

IVMMR   Albers, John P. SEABED MINERAL RESOURCES; A SURVEY. Bulletin of the Atomic Scientists 29:33-38 (1973)

VOR     Albers, John P., and R.F. Meyer. NEW INFORMATION ON WORLDWIDE SEA-BED RESOURCES. Ocean Management 2(1):61-74 (1974)

IIOR    Alexander, Lewis M. AMERICA'S COASTAL AND OFFSHORE WATERS: USE PROBLEMS AND POTENTIALS. In Problems and Trends in American Geography 113-123 (1967)

VOR     _____ _____ INDICES OF NATIONAL INTEREST IN THE OCEANS. Ocean Development and International Law Journal 1:21-49 (1973)

VLOS    _____ _____ LAW OF THE SEA AT THE END OF THE DECADE - A PREDICTION. Marine Technology Society Journal 8(6):60-65 (1974)

VB      _____ _____ NATIONAL JURISDICTION AND THE USE OF THE SEA. Natural Resources Journal 8:373-400 (1969)

VLOS    _____ _____ REGIONALISM AND THE LAW OF THE SEA: THE CASE OF SEMI-ENCLOSED SEAS. Ocean Development and International Law 2:151-186 (1974)

IIOR    _____ _____ RESOURCES OF THE SEA; NATIONAL JURISDICTION AND THE USE OF THE SEA. Natural Resources Journal 8:373-400 (1968)

VLOS    Alexander, Lewis M., and Robert D. Hodgson. THE ROLE OF THE GEOGRAPHICALLY-DISADVANTAGED STATES IN THE LAW OF THE SEA. San Diego Law Review 13(3):558-582 (1976)

VOCET   Alexander, T. OCEAN ENGINEERING TAKES PLUNGE. Fortune 73:145-216 (1966)

IIIF    Alfirević, S., and P. Cetinić. SCIENTIFIC AND ECONOMIC ASPECTS OF YUGOSLAV INTERESTS IN THE FIELD OF FISHERY ON HIGH SEAS. Naša Zakonitost 28:747-758 (1974)

IIIFV&G ALGUNS TIPOS DE EMBARCACOES PESQUEIRAS CONSTRUIDAS E PROJETADAS NA POLONIA (I). Revista Nacional da Pesca 13(109):19-21 (1971)

IIIFV&G ALGUNS TIPOS DE EMBARCACOES PESQUEIRAS CONSTRUIDAS E PROJETADAS NA POLONIA (II). Revista Nacional da Pesca 13(110):19-21 (C1971)

VP      Alhéritière, Dominique. ÉLÉMENTS POUR UNE ÉTUDE COMPARATIVE ELES DIX ORGANISMES PROVINCIAUX AU CANADA CHARGÉS DE MENER LA LUTTE CONTRE LA POLLUTION ELES EAUX. Revue Générale de Droit 3:280-290 (1973)

IIP     Allen, Alan A., and R.S. Schlueter. NATURAL OIL SEEPAGE AT COAL OIL POINT, SANTA BARBARA, CALIFORNIA. Science 170:974-977 (1970)

VCS         Allen, Donald R., and Patrick H. Mitchell. THE LEGAL STATUS OF THE CONTINENTAL SHELF OF THE EAST CHINA SEA. Oregon Law Review 5(4):789-812 (1972)

IIILOS      Allen, Edward W. CONTROL OF FISHERIES BEYOND THREE MILES. Washington Law Review 14:91-98 (1939)

IIICONS     _____ _____ DEVELOPING FISHERY PROTECTION. American Journal of International Law 36:115-116 (1942)

IIIF        _____ _____ FISHERY PROCLAMATION OF 1945. American Journal of International Law 45:177-178 (1951)

VINTL       _____ _____ FREEDOM OF THE SEAS. American Journal of International Law 60:814-816 (1966)

IIIINTL     _____ _____ INTERNATIONAL LAW AND DEEP SEA FISHERIES. Pacific Fisherman 35:35-37 (1937)

IIIINTL     _____ _____ INTERNATIONAL LAW, WAR AND FISH. Tulane Law Review 13:118-121 (1943)

IIIB        _____ _____ LEGAL LIMITS OF COASTAL FISHERY PROTECTION. Washington Law Review 21:1-4 (1946)

IIIF        _____ _____ A NEW CONCEPT FOR FISHERY TREATIES. American Journal of International Law 46:319-324 (1952)

IIIF        _____ _____ SALMON ON THE PEACE TABLE. Rotarian 62:25-27 (Feb., 1943)

IIP&H       Allen, Ronald C. FEDERAL EVALUATION OF RIPARIAN PROPERTY: SECTION 111 OF THE RIVERS AND HARBORS ACT OF 1970. Maine Law Review 24:175-214 (1972)

VP          Alsup, William. ROLE OF THE COMMONWEALTH IN MANAGING SOLID WASTE DISPOSAL. Suffolk University Law Review 8:555-597 (1974)

IIILOS      ALTERNATE PLAN ASKED BY CANADIAN COUNCIL. Fish Boat 19(7):26,39 (1974)

VOR         Alverson, Dayton L. MANAGEMENT OF THE OCEAN'S LIVING RESOURCES: AN ESSAY REVIEW. Ocean Development and International Law 3:99-125 (1975)

IVMMR       Amann, H. ERDOEL- UND ERDGASGEWINNUNG AUS GROESSEREN WASSERTIEFEN: ENTWICKLUNGSTENDENZEN, AUFSCHLUSS- UND PRODUKTIONSTECHNISCHE PROBLEME. Zeit-Schrift fuer Bohr und Foerder Technik 90:14-25 (1974)

IVM         _____ _____ MOEGLICHKEITEN ZUR OPTIMALEN SCHIFFSZEITNUTZUNG BEI DER MARINEN GROSSFLAECHENPROSPEKTION. Meerestechnik 4:109-113 (1973)

IVMMR       _____ _____ PRINCIPLES FOR AN INTERNATIONAL ORGANIZATION TO EXPLORE AND UTILIZE DEEP OCEAN MINERAL RESOURCES. Meerestechnik 4:159-160 (1973)

VOCET       Amari, Shoichi. WHAT'S NEW IN OCEANOGRAPHIC MACHINERY IN JAPAN? Ocean Industry 4:51-52 (1969)

| | |
|---|---|
| VP | AMENDMENTS TO OIL POLLUTION ACT. South African Shipping News and Fishing Industry Review 27(7):27-27 (1972) |
| VP | AMENDMENTS TO OIL POLLUTION ACT. South African Shipping News and Fishing Industry Review 28(7):31,33,35 (1973) |
| VENV | AMERICAN BAR ASSOCIATION NATIONAL INSTITUTE - LAW OF THE ENVIRONMENT. Natural Resources Lawyer 7:189-371 (1974) |
| VOR | American Bar Association National Institute on Marine Resources. PAPERS PRESENTED. JUNE, 1967, LONG BEACH, CAL. Natural Resources Lawyer 1(2)(3): (1968) |
| VOR | AMERICAN BAR ASSOCIATION RESOLUTION RE NATURAL RESOURCES OF THE SEA ADOPTED BY THE HOUSE OF DELEGATES AUGUST 6, 1973 AND REPORT OF THE SECTION OF NATURAL RESOURCES LAW RECOMMENDING ADOPTION OF THAT RESOLUTION. Natural Resources Lawyer 6:589-633 (1973) |
| VOR | American Society of International Law. Regional meeting, 1971, Chapel Hill, North Carolina. LAW OF MARINE RESOURCES. North Carolina Law Review 49, Special Issue (1971) |
| VLOS | Amersinghe, C.F. BASIC PRINCIPLES RELATING TO THE INTERNATIONAL REGIME OF THE OCEANS AT THE CARACAS SESSION OF THE U. N. LAW OF THE SEA CONFERENCE. Journal of Maritime Law and Commerce 6(2):213-248 (1975) |
| VINTL | Amerasinghe, C.F. PROBLEM OF ARCHIPELAGOES IN THE INTERNATIONAL LAW OF THE SEA. International and Comparative Law Quarterly 23:539-575 (1974) |
| VLOS | Amor, Bernardo Sepulveda. DERECHO DEL MAR; APUTES SOBRE EL SISTEMA LEGAL MEXICANO. Foro Internacional 13:232-271 (1972) |
| VMT | Anand, R.P. FREEDOM OF NAVIGATION THROUGH TERRITORIAL WATERS AND INTERNATIONAL STRAITS. Indian Journal of International Law 14:169-189 (1974) |
| VLOS | _____ _____ INTERESTS OF THE DEVELOPING COUNTRIES AND THE DEVELOPING LAW OF THE SEA. Annales d'Etudes Internationales 4:13-29 (1973) |
| VLOS | _____ _____ INTERNATIONAL MACHINERY FOR SEABED: ISSUES AND PROSPECTS. Indian Journal of International Law 13(3):351-366 (1973) |
| VCS | _____ _____ LEGAL CONTINENTAL SHELF AND THAT IT INCLUDES. Institute for Defense Studies Analysis Journal 5:358-416 (1973) |
| VB | _____ _____ LIMITS OF NATIONAL JURISDICTION IN THE SEA-BED. India Quarterly 29:79-103 (1973) |
| VINTL | _____ _____ TYRANNY OF THE FREEDOM-OF-THE-SEAS DOCTRINE. International Studies 12:416-429 (1973) |
| IIIB | Andersen, H.G. THE ICELANDIC FISHERY LIMITS AND THE CONCEPT OF THE EXCLUSIVE ECONOMIC ZONE. Ulfljótur (supplement to no.3): 3-18 (1974) |
| VMMR | Anderson, Alan. CHAOS AT SEA AND THE RAPE OF THE SEABED. Saturday Review/World :14-21 (November 6, 1973) |

IIIF   Anderson, Chandler P. THE FINAL OUTCOME OF THE FISHERIES ARBITRA-
       TION. American Journal of International Law 7:1-16 (1913)

VENV   Anderson, David. LAW AND OUR ENVIRONMENT. GOVERNMENT AND THE EN-
       VIRONMENT: A NEED FOR PUBLIC PARTICIPATION. University of British
       Columbia Law Review 6:111-114 (1971)

VLOS   Anderson, E.V. LAW OF THE SEA BATTLE - AN OVERVIEW. Marine Tech-
       nology Society Journal 8(6):4-14 (1974)

IIILOS Anderson, Lee G. ECONOMIC ASPECTS OF FISHERIES UTILIZATION IN THE
       LAW OF THE SEA NEGOTIATIONS. San Diego Law Review 11:656-678 (1974)

IICZM  Anderson, S.H. COASTAL ZONE PLANNING: THE IMPACT OF REGIONAL
       EFFORTS IN NEW ENGLAND. Marine Affairs Journal 1:78-90 (1973)

VOR    Andraši, J. THE SEABED: HERITAGE OF MANKIND? Anali Pravnog
       Fakulteta u Beogradu 19(1/3):25-37 (1972)

IVMMR  Andrassy, Juraj. THE EXPLOITATION OF DEEP SEA RESOURCES. Jugo-
       slovenska Revija Za Medvnarodno Pravo :98-110 (1968)

VLOS   Andrassy, J. NEŠTO O ČI. 5 KONVENCIJEO EPIKONTINENTALNOM POJASU.
       Zbornik Pravnog Fakulteta u Zagrebu 22:57-63 (1972)

VC     Andrews, Burton. SUEZ CANAL CONTROVERSY. Albany Law Review
       21(1):25p (1957)

IVMMR  Angerstein, J. AMERICAN PETROLEUM GEOLOGIST ON THE HISTORY AND
       FUTURE OF NORTH SEA DEPOSITS. Northern Offshore 2(2):91-   (1973)

IVMMR  _____ _____ AN AMERICAN SURVEYS THE NORTH SEA. Northern Offshore
       2(1):96-   (1973)

IVODAS _____ _____ DATA BUOY PROJECTS OF VAST IMPORTANCE IN OFFSHORE OIL
       FIELD OPERATIONS. Northern Offshore 2:34,37-38 (1973)

IVM    _____ _____ MEETING RISING OFFSHORE COSTS. Northern Offshore
       3(4):107-108,111-112,115 (1974)

IIIAFF AQUACULTURE PROJECTS: REQUIREMENTS FOR APPROVAL OF DISCHARGES.
       Federal Register 39(115):20769-20775 (June 13, 1974)

VLOS   Aramburu Menchaca, A. LA COSTUMBRE Y LA DELIMATICIÓN DE LOS
       ESPACIOS MARÍTIMOS EN EL CONTINENTE AMERICANO. Revista Uruguayo
       de Derecho Internacional 2:105-126 (1973)

VLOS   Arbuet Vignaly, H. LA SOBERANÍA URUGUAYA EN LOS ESPACIOS MARÍTIMOS.
       Revista Uruguaya de Derecho Internacional 2:127-155 (1973)

IVMMR  Archer, A.A. ECONOMICS OF OFF-SHORE EXPLORATION AND PRODUCTION OF
       SOLID MINERALS ON THE CONTINENTAL SHELF. Ocean Management 1:5-40
       (1973)

IIIF   ARGENTINA: FISHERIES. Latin American Newsletters :32 (January 26,
       1973)

VLOS   Armas, Barea C. NUEVAS NORMAS JURÍDICAS PARA LA REGULACION DE
       FONDOS MARINOS Y OCEÁNICOS FUERA DE LOS LIMITES DELLA JURISDICION
       ESTATAL. Revista Uruguaya de Derecho Internacional 2:157-190 (1973)

VAC        ARMS AND THE OCEAN: HIDDEN DEPTHS. Economist 231:35-35 (1969)

IICZM      Armstrong, John M., and Earl H. Bradley, Jr. STATUS OF STATE COASTAL ZONE MANAGEMENT PROGRAMS. Marine Technology Society Journal 6:7-16 (1972)

IVSUB      Armstrong, J.R.C. SUBMERSIBLE PLAYS KEY ROLE IN LAYING TRANSATLANTIC CABLE. Ocean Industry 10(2):121-123 (1975)

VSUB       Arnold, H.A. MANNED SUBMERSIBLES FOR RESEARCH. Science 158:84-91 (1967)

IIIF       Arnold, Victor L., and Daniel W. Bromley. SOCIAL GOALS, PROBLEM PERCEPTION, AND PUBLIC INTERVENTION: THE FISHERY. San Diego Law Review 7:469-487 (1970)

IVOSTR     ARTIFICIAL ISLANDS FOR ARCTIC DRILLING. Petroleum Engineer 45(6):76-76 (1972)

IIIFV&G    ASBEL EQUIPARA LAGOSTA NO MERCADO INTERNACIONAL. Revista Nacional da Pesca 13(109):34-35 (1971)

IIAH       ASIA. World Dredging and Marine Construction 10(1):31-33 (1974)

IVM        Askevold, Gerald. OCEAN MINING IN PERSPECTIVE. Stanford Journal of International Studies 4:115-142 (1970)

IVM        Atkinson, T. UNDERWATER DEVELOPMENT AND OFFSHORE MINING. Offshore Technology 4(4):17-18 (1972)

IVDRIL     ATLANTIC AND ALASKAN OIL DRILLING PROSPECTS. Marine Technology Society Journal 8:8-13 (1974)

IVMMR      ATLANTIC STATES' CLAIM TO OFFSHORE OIL RIGHTS: UNITED STATES V. MAINE. Environmental Affairs 2:827-839 (1973)

IVP        Atlas, R.M., and R. Bartha. FATE AND EFFECTS OF POLLUTING PETROLEUM IN THE MARINE ENVIRONMENT. Residue Reviews; Residues of Pesticides and other Contaminants in the Total Environment 49:49-85 (1973)

IIIB       AT SEA WITH THE 89TH CONGRESS: THE UNITED STATES FISHERIES ZONE. Hastings Law Journal 18:937-957 (1967)

VP         Aubert, M. POLLUTIONS CHIMIQUES ET CHAINES TROPHODYNAMIQUES MARINES. Revue Internationale d'Oceanographie Medicale 28:9-25 (1972)

VP         Aubert, M., et al. EFFETS DES POLLUTIONS CHIMIQUES VIS-A-VIS DE TELEMEDIATEURS INTERVENANT DANS L'ECOLOGIE MICROBIOLOGIQUE ET PLANCTONIQUE EN MILIEU MARIN. Revue Internationale d'Oceanographie Medicale 28:129-166 (1972)

IVMMR      Auburn, F.M. THE DEEP SEABED HARD MINERAL RESOURCES BILL. San Diego Law Review 9:491-513 (1972)

IVM        _____ _____ DEEP SEA MINING. American Bar Association Journal 56:975-976 (1970)

VB         _____ _____ INTERNATIONAL LAW AND SEA-ICE JURISDICTION IN THE ARCTIC OCEAN. International and Comparative Law Quarterly 22:552-557 (1973)

VLOS      Auburn, F. M.  INTERNATIONAL SEABED AREA.  International and Comparative Law Quarterly 20:173-194 (1971)

IVMMR     _____ _____ SOME LEGAL PROBLEMS OF THE COMMERCIAL EXPLOITATION OF MANGANESE NODULES IN THE PACIFIC.  Ocean Development and International Law Journal 1:185p. (1973)

IICZM     Ausness, Richard C.  LAND USE CONTROLS IN COASTAL AREAS.  California Western Law Review 9:391-428 (1973)

IVM       Austin, C.F.  IN THE ROCK; A LOGICAL APPROACH FOR UNDERSEA MINING OF RESOURCES.  Engineering and Mining Journal :82-88 (1967)

IIP&H     AUSTRALIA AND NEW ZEALAND.  World Dredging and Marine Construction 10(1):34-35 (1974)

VCS       AUSTRALIA: CONTINENTAL SHELF.  Guardian :3-3 (May 15, 1973)

IIIMM     AUSTRALIA; FISHERIES.  Australian News :2-2 (August 10, 1972)

IIIB      AUSTRALIA: FISHING LIMITS.  Aftenposten :6-6 (April 21, 1973)

VINTL     AUSTRALIA-INDONESIA: BOUNDARY.  Australian Foreign Affairs Record :107-107 (February, 1973)

VP        AUSTRALIA; POLLUTION.  Australian News :2-2 (August 31, 1972)

IIIB      AUSTRALIA: PROTECTION OF FISHING RIGHTS.  Australian News no.3 (December 14, 1972)

IVOCET    AUTOMATIC RIG FOR OFFSHORE DRILLING.  Ocean Industry 10(2):108-109 (1975)

VENV      Axtmann, R.C.  ENVIRONMENTAL IMPACT OF A GEOTHERMAL POWER PLANT.  Science 187:795-802 (March 7, 1975)

VENV      Azar, Robert F.  IMPACT OF RADIATION ON OUR ENVIRONMENT.  Loyola Law Review 18:695-716 (1971-72)

VLOS      Azcárraga Bustamante, J.L.de.  ALGUNAS CONSIDERACIONES SOBRE PÉRIDAS DE FLETE COMO CONSECUENCIA DE UN SINIESTRO MARÍTIMO.  Revista Espanola de Derecho Internacional 25:69-76 (1972)

IIP       Azcárraga, J.L.de.  CONTAMINACIÓN DE AGUAS Y COSTAS.  Lectures Jurídicas 42:75-114 (1970)

IIDRIL    Baars, C.  DREDGING IN DEEP WATER.  Offshore Services 5(6):51,53 (1972)

VLOS      Babović, B.  ON THE OCCASION OF THE INTERNATIONAL CONFERENCE ON THE LAW OF THE SEA: NEW CODIFICATION OR THE NEW LAW OF THE SEA?  Medunarodni Problemi 26:69-90 (1974)

VENV      Bacon, T.C.  ROLE OF THE UNITED NATIONS ENVIRONMENT PROGRAM (UNEP) IN THE DEVELOPMENT OF INTERNATIONAL ENVIRONMENTAL LAW.  Canadian Yearbook of International Law 12:255-266 (1974)

VLOS      Baikoyse, K.G.  _TO DIKAION TES THALĀSSES: NOMIKA KAI EPISTEMONIKA PROBLEMATA EK TĒS ETHEREYNESŌS TOY BYTHOY TŌN THALASSŌN KAI ŌKEANÓN.  Epitheōrēsis toy Emporikoy Dikaioy 23:449-459 (1972)

IVOSTR    Bainbridge, C.A. ANALYZING FIXED STEEL PLATFORMS IN THE NORTH SEA. Petroleum Engineer 46(5):98,101,105 (1974)

IVMMR     Bakke, Donald R. RUSSIA SAMPLES DEEP OCEAN FOR GAS AND OIL. Offshore 32(10):67-68 (1972)

IVDRIL    _____ _____ SOVIETS ENCOUNTER TROUBLE IN LIFTING OFFSHORE OIL FLOW. Offshore 33(7):198- (1973)

IVM       _____ _____ SOVIETS TO STEP UP OFFSHORE OIL FLOW. Offshore 32(12)40,42,44 (1972)

VP        Baksheyeva, I.P., et al. RADIOACTIVITY OF THE WATER OF THE NORTH-EASTERN PART OF THE ATLANTIC OCEAN. Oceanology 11(6):861-867 (1972)

VLOS      Balboa, Marie M. THE LAW OF THE SEA. Phi Delta Delta 37:18-23 (1959)

IVENV     Baldwin, Malcolm F. PUBLIC POLICY ON OIL - AN ECOLOGICAL PERSPECTIVE. Ecology Law Quarterly 1:245-303 (1971)

IVMT      Balhaser, H. MULTI-VESSEL-TANK (MVT) FUER DEN SCHIFFSTRANSPORT VON VERFLUES-SIGTEN GASEN. Zeitschrift fuer Bohr und Foerder Technik 89:467-469 (1973)

IVMMR     Ball, Norma R. THE EAST COAST OF SCOTLAND AND NORTH SEA OIL. Geography 58:51-55 (1973)

IVOL      Ballem, John B. CONTINUING ADVENTURES OF THE OIL AND GAS LEASE. Canadian Bar Review 50:423- (1972)

IVMMR     Balogh, Lord. THE NORTH SEA OIL BLUNDER. Banker 124:281-288 (1974)

IIIP      BALTIC SEA; FISHERIES AND POLLUTION. Aftenposten 6: (September 4, September 11, September 14, 1973)

VB        Balupuri, S. TERRITORIAL WATERS IN SOVIET LAW AND PRACTICE. Indian Journal of International Law 14:217-229 (1974)

IIILOS    Bandanov, T.B. ADMINISTRATIVE RESPONSIBILITY FOR INFRINGING OBLIGATORY DECISIONS AT MARITIME FISHING PORTS. Translation of Rybnoe Khozyaistvo 7:34-40 (1971)

IVMMR     Banks, L.M. HOW GOOD ARE ARGENTINA'S OFFSHORE OIL PROSPECTS? World Oil 165:116-122 (1967)

VP        Baram, Michael S. LEGAL AND REGULATORY FRAMEWORK FOR THERMAL DISCHARGE FROM NUCLEAR POWER PLANTS. Environmental Affairs 2:505- (1972)

IIIAFF    Bardach, J.E. AQUACULTURE. Science 161:1098-1106 (1968)

IIIB      Bardonnet, D. LA DÉNONCIATION PAR LE GOUVERNEMENT SÉNÉGALAIS DE LA CONVENTION SUR LA MER TERRITORIALE ET LA ZONE CONTIGUE ET DE LA CONVENTION SUR LA PÊCHE ET LA CONSERVATION DES RESSOURCES BIOLIGUQUES DE LA HAUTE MER, EN DATE 29 AVRIL 1958 À GENÈVE. Annuaire Français de Droit International 18:123-180 (1972)

IIILOS    Bardonnet, D., et J. Carroz. LES ETATS DE L'AFRIQUE D'L'OUEST ET LE
          DROIT INTERNATIONAL DES PEÂCHES MARITIMES. Annuaire Française de
          Droit International 19:837-874 (1973)

IIICONS   Barea, C.A., e F.P. de Armas. PESCA Y CONSERVACIÓN DE LOS RECURSOS
          VIVOS EM LAS AGUAS DE ALTA MAR. Arquivos do Ministério da Justiça
          29(122):153-188 (1972)

VOD       Barnes, E.S. SEWAGE POLLUTION FROM TOURIST HOTELS IN JAMAICA.
          Marine Pollution Bulletin 4:102-105 (1973)

IIIB      Barnes, K. JAPANESE FISHERY CONTROL AND BRISTOL BAY. Far Eastern
          Survey 6:102-103 (1937)

IIIF      Barnes, Kathleen and Homer E. Gregory. ALASKA SALMON IN WORLD POL-
          ITICS. Far Eastern Survey 7:47-53 (1938)

VINTL     Barracca, P.S. HISTORY OF MARINE SALVAGE IN THE U.S. Marine Engi-
          neering/Log 79(6):45-47,49 (1974)

IIB       Barrie, G.N. HISTORICAL BAYS. Comparative and International Law
          Journal of Southern Africa 6:39-62 (1973)

IIILOS    _____  _____ INTERNATIONAL ENFORCEMENT OF CONVENTIONS ON FISHERIES.
          Tydskrif vir Hedendaagse Romeins-Hollandse Reg 38:140-152 (1975)

VLOS      Barrie, George N. THE THIRD LAW OF THE SEA CONFERENCE: A FINAL
          SUMMATION. Tydskrif vir Hedendaagse Romeins-Hollandse Reg 37:245-
          255 (1974)

VOI       Barrow, Thomas D. OFFSHORE INDUSTRY IN CRUCIAL PHASE OF DEVELOPMENT.
          Undersea Technology 11:38 (1970)

IVMMR     Barry, C.B. OIL INDUSTRY BACKGROUND CAN PAY OFF IN SULFUR PRODUC-
          TION. Oil and Gas Journal 65:120-124 (1967)

IICS      Barry, F. THE ADMINISTRATION OF THE OUTER CONTINENTAL SHELF LANDS
          ACT. Natural Resources Lawyer 1(3):38-48 (1968)

VLOS      Barrie, G.N. THE THIRD LAW OF THE SEA CONFERENCE: A PREVIEW OF
          SOME OF THE ISSUES. Tydskrif vie Hedendaagse Romeins-Hollandse Reg
          36:23-46 (1973)

VAC       Barry, James A., Jr. THE SEABED ARMS CONTROL ISSUE 1967-1971. A
          SUPERPOWER SYMBIOSIS. U.S. Naval War College 25(2):87-101 (1972)

IIIB      Barston, R.P., and H.W. Hanneson. THE ANGLO-ICELANDIC FISHERIES
          DISPUTE. International Relations 4:559-584, 628 (1974)

IVOL      Bartlett, R.H., and P.F. Rhodes. IMPLIED COVENANTS IN OIL AND GAS
          LEASES IN CANADA. Missouri Law Review 39:363-397 (1975)

IIIB      Barton, G. TERRITORIAL SEA AND FISHING ZONE ACT, 1965 AND CONTINEN-
          TAL SHELF ACT, 1964. New Zealand Universities Law Review 2:81-86
          (1966)

VOD       Bascom, W. THE DISPOSAL OF WASTE IN THE OCEAN. Scientific American
          231:16-25 (1974)

| | |
|---|---|
| IVM | Bascom, W. MINING THE OCEAN DEPTHS. Geoscience News 1:10-11, 26-28 (1967) |
| VOCET | Bascom, Willard. TECHNOLOGY AND THE OCEAN; SUCH ADVANCES AS RESISTANT MATERIALS AND HUGE SHIPS EXPAND THE USES OF THE SEA. Scientific American 221:198-217 (1969) |
| VOR | Basiuk, Victor. MARINE RESOURCES DEVELOPMENT, FOREIGN POLICY, AND THE SPECTRUM OF CHOICE. Orbis 12:39-72 (1968) |
| VC | Bassiouni, M. Cherif. THE NATIONALIZATION OF THE SUEZ CANAL AND THE ILLICIT ACT IN INTERNATIONAL LAW. DePaul Law Review XIV(2):40p (1965) |
| VOR | Basu, M.C. DEVELOPMENT OF OCEAN RESOURCES FOR MAN. Environment this Month. The International Science 1(2):40-46 (1972) |
| IVMMR | Bates, Charles C. JAPAN; AN EMERGING POWER IN OFFSHORE OIL AND GAS EXPLORATION. Ocean Industry 7:37-42 (1972) |
| VLOS | Baty, Thomas. THE FREE SEA - PRODUCE THE EVIDENCE. American Journal of International Law 35:227-242 (1941) |
| IICONS | Baum, Alvin. SAN FRANCISCO BAY CONSERVATION AND DEVELOPMENT COMMISSION. Lincoln Law Review 5:98-118 (1970) |
| IIIF | Bayitch, S.A. INTERNATIONAL FISHERY PROBLEMS IN THE WESTERN HEMISPHERE. University of Miami Law Quarterly 10:499-506 (1956) |
| IICONS | BEACH EROSION: CAN MANKIND HELP NATURE REGAIN DELICATE BALANCE? National Fisherman 52(13):82-83, 90 (1972) |
| IICONS | BEACH RESTORED WITH DREDGED SAND. World Dredging and Marine Construction 8(11):40-40 (1972) |
| VINTL | Beall, Kenneth S., Jr. STATE REGULATION OF SEARCH FOR AND SALVAGE OF SUNKEN TREASURE. Natural Resources Lawyer 4:1-18 (1971) |
| IVM | Beall, J.V. OCEAN MINING FACES PROBLEMS; PUSH IN OCEANOGRAPHY MAY YIELD SOLUTIONS. Mining Engineering 52-57 (1967) |
| VLOS | Beaucourt, C. A PROPOS D'UN BEST-SELLER MAL CONNU ET PEU LU: LES FAUSSES CORROBATIONS DU CONSULAR DE LA MER. Droit Maritime Français 27:131-138 (1975) |
| IIB | Beauchamp, K., et al. JURISDICTIONAL PROBLEMS IN CANADA'S OFFSHORE. Public Land and Resources Law Digest 12:72-89 (1975) reprinted from Alberta Law Review Vol. II, 1973. |
| IVDRIL | BEAUFORT SEA DRILLING MAY BE FEASIBLE. Offshore 35:128- (1975) |
| VAC | Bechhoefer, Bernard G. NUCLEAR TEST BAN TREATY IN RETROSPECT. Case Western Reserve Journal of International Law 5:125-154 (1974) |
| VOCET | Becker, Gordon L. SHORT CRUISE ON THE GOOD SHIPS TOVALOP AND CRISTAL. Journal of Maritime Law and Commerce 5:609-632 (1974) |
| VP | \_\_\_\_\_ \_\_\_\_ VEHICLES FOR REIMBURSEMENT OF OIL POLLUTION DAMAGES. Houston Law Review 9:669-675 (1972) |

| | |
|---|---|
| IIIB | Becker, L. BREADTH OF THE TERRITORIAL SEA AND FISHERIES JURISDICTION. U.S. Department of State Bulletin 40:369-374 (1959) |
| VP | Beckmann, Walter C. APPLIED OCEANOGRAPHY VITAL TO POLLUTION-CONTROL EFFORTS. Undersea Technology 11:26-29 (1970) |
| VLOS | Beesly, J.A. THE LAW OF THE SEA CONFERENCE. International Perspectives :28-35 (July/August 1972) |
| IIB | Beesley, J. Allen. RIGHTS AND RESPONSIBILITIES OF ARCTIC COASTAL STATES: THE CANADIAN VIEW. Journal of Maritime Law and Commerce 3:1-12 (1971) |
| IIE | Begg, R.W.D. NEW ESTUARY LAND RECLAMATION SCHEME COMMENCES AT CARDIFF. Public Cleansing 63(7):309-318 (1973) |
| IIIT&L | BELGIUM-ICELAND: FISHERIES AGREEMENT ON THE EXTENSION OF THE ICELANDIC FISHERY LIMITS TO 200 MILES. (DONE AT REYKJAVIK, NOVEMBER 28, 1975). International Legal Materials Current Documents XV(1):1-4 (January, 1976) |
| IVM | Bell, W.E. THE EQUIPMENT REQUIREMENTS FOR OIL AND GAS IN THE NORTH SEA. Northern Offshore 3(4):116,119-120,123-124,127 (1974) |
| IIE | Bella, D.A. STRATEGIC APPROACH TO ESTUARINE ENVIRONMENTAL MANAGEMENT. American Society of Civil Engineers Journal 101(WW1):73-92 (1975) |
| VLOS | Bellanger, F. L'ÉVOLUTION CONTEMPORAINE DE DROIT DE LA MER. Archiv des Voelkerrechts 16:194-203 (1974) |
| IICZM | Beller, W.S. OCEAN ISLANDS - CONSIDERATIONS FOR THEIR COASTAL ZONE MANAGEMENT. Coastal Zone Management Journal 1:27-45 (1973) |
| VOCET | Bello, Emmanuel G. THE PRESENT STATE OF MARINE SCIENCE AND OCEANOGRAPHY IN THE LESS DEVELOPED COUNTRIES. International Lawyer 8:231-241 (1974) |
| VOR | Belman, M. THE ROLE OF THE STATE DEPARTMENT IN FORMULATING FEDERAL POLICY REGARDING MARINE RESOURCES. Natural Resources Lawyer 1:14-22 (1968) |
| VP | Bendiner, Robert. TAKING OIL OFF THE SHELF. New York Times Magazine :12-14,16,18,20 (June 29, 1975) |
| IICZM | Benner, Richard P. SHORELANDS GOAL: KEY TO STRONG COASTAL PROGRAM. 1,000 Friends of Oregon Newsletter 1(4):3-3 (1976) |
| VCONS | Beradelli, Phillip J. CONGRESS ESTABLISHES MARINE SANCTUARIES. Offshore 32:38-38 (1972) |
| IVOL | Berardelli, Phillip J. INTERIOR RESUMES SCHEDULING OF LEASES AFTER NINE-MONTH DELAY. Offshore 32:34-34 (1972) |
| VOI | BERGEN DISTRICT NOW CLOSER TO OFFSHORE ACTIVITY. Northern Offshore 2:54,57-58 (1973) |
| VP | Bergman, S. NO FAULT LIABILITY FOR OIL POLLUTION DAMAGE. Journal of Maritime Law and Commerce 5:1-50 (1973) |

VP          Berman, Tom, et al. SPECIAL SECTION ON WATER POLLUTION. THE SEA OF GALILEE: POLLUTION PROBLEMS AND PROSPECTS. Environmental Affairs 2:365-    (1972)

VP          Bermingham, P. FEDERAL GOVERNMENT AND AIR AND WATER POLLUTION. Business Lawyer 23:467-492 (1968)

IVENV       Bermingham, Paul E. PETROLEUM INDUSTRY AND ENVIRONMENTAL POLLUTION. Institute on Mineral Law (La SU) 17:3-    (1970)

VOR         Bernfeld, Seymour S. DEVELOPING THE RESOURCES OF THE SEA; SECURITY OF INVESTMENT. The International Lawyer 2:67-76 (1967)

VOR         \_\_\_\_\_ \_\_\_\_\_ DEVELOPING THE RESOURCES OF THE SEA; SECURITY OF INVESTMENT. Natural Resources Lawyer 1:82-90 (1968)

IVM         \_\_\_\_\_ \_\_\_\_\_ THE MINING INDUSTRY AND THE CONTINENTAL SHELF CONVENTION. Institute of Mining and Metallurgy 78:A10-A19 (1969)

IVMMR       \_\_\_\_\_ \_\_\_\_\_ PITFALLS AND PANACEAS FOR THE ACQUISITION OF HARD-ROCK MINERALS BENEATH THE HIGH SEAS. Rocky Mountain Mineral Law Institute 14:613-641 (1968)

IVMMR       Bernhardt, J. Peter A. SPITZBERGEN: JURISDICTIONAL FRICTION OVER UNEXPLOITED OIL RESERVES. California Western International Law Journal 4:61-120 (1973)

IIOSTR      Bernstein, L.B. RUSSIAN TIDAL POWER STATION IS PRECAST OFFSITE, FLOATED INTO PLACE. Civil Engineering 44:46-49 (1974)

IVMMR       Bernstein, Peter J. ATLANTIC OFFSHORE OIL: PREPARING TO TAKE THE PLUNGE. Nation 217:203-207 (September 10, 1973)

IVMMR       Berryhill, H.L., Jr. THE WORLDWIDE SEARCH FOR PETROLEUM OFFSHORE. Scientific and Technical Aerospace Reports 12:2169-2170 (1974)

IIIF        Beurier, J.P. VERS UNE RESTRUCTURATION ADMINISTRATIVE DES PÊCHES MARITIMES FRANÇAISES. Droit Administratif 30:124-129 (1974)

VLOS        Beurier, J.P., et P. Cadenat. LE CONTENU ÉCONOMIQUE DES NORMES JURIDIQUES DANS LE DROIT DE LA MER CONTEMPORAIN. Revue Générale de Droit International Public 78:575-622 (1974)

VLOS        \_\_\_\_\_ \_\_\_\_\_ LES RESULTATS DE LA CONFÉRENCE DE GENÈVE SUR LE DROIT DE LA MER. Revue Générale de Droit International Public 79:750-762 (1975)

VENE        Best, Judith A. RECENT STATE INITIATIVES ON POWER PLANT SITING: A REPORT AND COMMENT. Natural Resources Lawyer 5:668-680 (1972)

VLOS        Bethill, Charles D. PEOPLE'S CHINA AND THE LAW OF THE SEA. The International Lawyer 8:724-751 (1974)

VINTL       THE BETTER PART OF VALOUR - APPLICABILITY OF THE JONES ACT TO THE FLAGS OF CONVENIENCE FLEET. San Diego Law Review 7:674-683 (1970)

VENE        Bevan, George A. ENERGY DEVELOPMENT: A NEED FOR VISION AND STATESMANSHIP. Alberta Law Review 12:1-25 (1974) (Petroleum Law Suppl.)

| | |
|---|---|
| VINTL | Bevans, C. CONTEMPORARY PRACTICE OF THE UNITED STATES RELATING TO INTERNATIONAL LAW. <u>American Journal of International Law</u> 62:150-151, 485-488 (1968) (Navigation) |
| IIP | Bevenue, A., et al. PESTICIDE RESIDUES IN OUR WATERS. <u>Hawaii Farm Science</u> 20(3):1-3 (1971) |
| IIIP | Beyer, Donald L., et al. EFFECTS OF SALMON CANNERY WASTES ON WATER QUALITY AND MARINE ORGANISMS. <u>Journal of Water Pollution Control Federation</u> 47(7):1857-1869 (1975) |
| VP | Bidleman, T.F., and C.E. Olney. DDT IN THE OCEAN: IS THE ATMOSPERE THE SOURCE? <u>Maritimes</u> 18(2):1-3 (1974) |
| VLOS | Biemiller, C. TOMORROW'S SEAS. <u>Vista of U. N. Association</u> 3:43-53 (1967) |
| VINTL | Bierzanek, R. FREEDOM OF THE SEAS IN THE DIPLOMATIC CORRESPONDENCE OF SIGISMUNDUS AUGUSTUS, KING OF POLAND, 16TH CENTURY. <u>Polish Yearbook of International Law</u> 3:131-141 (1970) |
| IVMMR | BIG NEWS FROM MEDITERRANEAN IS THE STRIKE OFF GREECE. <u>Offshore</u> 33(7):136,139 (1973) |
| VMT | BIGGER ROLE FOR SMALL WARSHIPS. <u>Shipbuilding and Marine Engineering International</u> 95(1158):453-456 (1972) |
| VOR | Biggs, Gonzalo. DEEPSEA'S ADVENTURES: GROTIUS REVISITED. <u>International Lawyer</u> 9:271-281 (1975) |
| IIIB | Bilder, Richard B. THE ANGLO-ICELANDIC FISHERIES DESPUTE. <u>Wisconsin Law Review</u> 1973:37-132 (1973) |
| VP | \_\_\_\_\_ \_\_\_\_\_ THE CANADIAN ARCTIC WATERS POLLUTION PREVENTION ACT: NEW STRESSES ON THE LAW OF THE SEA. <u>Michigan Law Review</u> 69(1): (1970) |
| VP | \_\_\_\_\_ \_\_\_\_\_ CONTROLLING GREAT LAKES POLLUTION: A STUDY IN UNITED STATES-CANADIAN ENVIRONMENTAL COOPERATION. <u>Michigan Law Review</u> 70:469-556 (1972) |
| VOR | Bilder, Richard. EMERGING LEGAL PROBLEMS OF THE DEEP SEAS AND POLAR REGIONS. <u>Naval War College Review</u> 20:34-39 (1967) |
| IISL | Binder, Dennis. TAKING VERSUS REASONABLE REGULATION: A REAPPRAISAL IN LIGHT OF REGIONAL PLANNING AND WETLANDS. <u>University of Florida Law Review</u> 25:1- (1972) |
| VB | Birken, Arthur M. GULF OF VENEZUELA: BORDER DISPUTE. <u>Lawyer of the Americas</u> 6:52-68 (1974) |
| VENV | Birnie, P.W. MARINE ENVIRONMENT AND THE LAW OF THE SEA. <u>Marine Pollution Bulletin</u> 6:10-12 (1975) |
| IIILOS | Bishop, W.W., Jr. INTERNATIONAL LAW COMMISSION DRAFT ARTICLES ON FISHERIES. <u>American Journal of International Law</u> 50:627-636 (1956) |
| VENE | Bjorge, K.R. DEVELOPMENT OF GEOTHERMAL RESOURCES AND THE 1970 GEOTHERMAL STEAM ACT - LAW IN SEARCH OF DEFINITION. <u>University of Colorado Law Review</u> 46:1-25 (1974) |

IIP      Black, J. PREVENTION OF SPILLAGE AT MONO-MOORING TERMINALS. Tanker and Bulk Carrier 20:28,30-32 (1973)

VP       Blackman, R.A.A., et al. THE DONA MARIKA OIL SPILL. Marine Pollution Bulletin 4:181-182 (1973)

IVM      Blaiklock, K.V. POSITION FIXING FOR NORTH SEA OIL: II - POSITION FIXING IN THE NORTH SEA. Journal of Navigation 27:212-219 (1974)

VOR      Blanchard, F.A., and R.W. Corell. MAN'S ADAPTATION TO THE SEA; A KEY TO THE OCEAN'S RESOURCES. Stanford Journal of International Studies 4:71-83 (1969)

IVOSTR   Bleakley, W.B. LOCKHEED, SHELL FLANGE UP SUBSEA WELL. Oil and Gas Journal 70(43):64-66 (1972)

IVOSTR   _____ _____ SHELL INSTALLS UNDERWATER WELLHEAD CHAMBER, TESTS CAPSULE. Oil and Gas Journal 70(31):58-60 (1972)

VOI      _____ _____ SUBSEA TECHNIQUES READY FOR NORTH SEA CHALLENGE. Ocean Industry 10(2):81-84,88 (1975)

VENV     Bleicher, Samuel A. OVERVIEW OF INTERNATIONAL ENVIRONMENTAL REGULATION. Ecology Law Quarterly 2:1-90 (1972)

VOI      Blenkarn, K.A. COPING WITH NATURE OFFSHORE - AN SPE-AIME DISTINGUISHED LECTURE. Journal of Petroleum Technology 25:257-266 (1973)

IVMT     Blenkey, N. TANKER PROSPECTS TAKE DOWNTURN. Marine Engineering/Log 79(7):101-103,226 (1974)

VENE     Bloch, Ivan. NUCLEAR POWER PLANT PROLIFERATION. Environmental Law 2:376-410 (1972)

VCS      Blum, Annette. THE CONTINENTAL SHELF CONVENTION AND AFRICAN RATIFICATION. African Law Studies No.6, June, 1972

VP       Blumer, M. OIL POLLUTION OF THE OCEAN. Oceanus 15:2-7 (1969)

VP       Blumer, M., and J. Sass. OIL POLLUTION; PERSISTENCE AND DEGRADATION OF SPILLED FUEL OIL. Science 176:1120-1122 (1972)

VP       Blumer, Max. SCIENTIFIC ASPECTS OF THE OIL SPILL PROBLEM. Environmental Affairs 1:54-73 (1971)

VLOS     Boas, Frank. LANDLOCKED COUNTRIES AND THE LAW OF THE SEA. American Bar Association. Section of International and Comparative Law. Bulletin. pp. 22-27 (December 1959)

IIT&L    BOATS AND ASSOCIATED EQUIPMENT: SAFE LOADING AND POWERING STANDARDS. Federal Register 40(45):10649-10654 (March 6, 1975)

IIP&H    Bockrath, J. ENVIRONMENT, DEVELOPMENT, AND THE NATIONAL INTEREST: PROBLEMS IN DEFINITION AND PREROGATIVES. Natural Resources Lawyer 8(1):29-40 (1975)

IIIAFF   Bockrath, Joseph, and D. Wheeler. CLOSED-CYCLE MARICULTURE IN MARYLAND, VIRGINIA AND DELAWARE: AN EXAMINATION OF THE ADAPTABILITY OF EXISTING FISHERY LAWS TO NEW TECHNOLOGY. DEL-SG-2-76. William and Mary Law Review 17(1):85-107 (1976)

VENV    Boehme, E. DER BEITRAG DER VEREINTEN NATIONEN ZUM MARINEN UMWELT-SCHUTZ. Vereinte Nationen 20:73-77 (1972)

VLOS    Boehringer, K.H. DER NOTWENDIGE ABSCHIED VON DER THEORIE DER FREI-HEIT DER MEERE. Neue Zeitschrift fuer Wehrrecht 14:201-209 (1972)

VLOS    _____ _____ ON SALE: DIE FREIHEIT DER MEERE. Neue Zeitschrift fuer Wehrrecht 15:201-215 (1973)

IIWQ    Boettger, Thomas E. WATER QUALITY MAINTENANCE. Pennsylvania Bar Association Quarterly 44:196-202 (1973)

VT&L    Boggs, S. Whittemore. DELIMITATION OF THE TERRITORIAL SEA: THE METHOD OF DELIMITATION PROPOSED BY THE DELEGATION OF THE UNITED STATES AT THE HAGUE CONFERENCE FOR THE CODIFICATION OF INTERNATIONAL LAW. Journal of International Law: Supplement 24:541-555 (1930)

VB      _____ _____ NATIONAL CLAIMS IN ADJACENT SEAS. The Geographical Review XLI(2):25p (1951)

VENV    Boisserée, Klaus. CHANCES AND PROBLEMS OF INTERNATIONAL AGREEMENTS ON ENVIRONMENTAL POLLUTION. Natural Resources Journal 12:218-241 (1972)

IIIB    Bold, J.I.T. OHIO, INDIANA, ILLINOIS V. KENTUCKY FISHING RIGHTS IN THE OHIO RIVER. Indiana Law Journal 14:431-450 (1939)

VOCET   Booda, Larry L. DEEP OCEAN PHOTOGRAPHY. Undersea Technology 14:20-23 (1973)

IIOSTR  _____ _____ GULF OFFSHORE PORT PROJECT WAITING FOR CONGRESSIONAL ACTION. Sea Technology 15:30-31 (1974)

VOS     _____ _____ MARINE SCIENCES AND ASW RECEIVE BIG BUDGET INCREASES. Undersea Technology 13:30-32 (1972)

VOS     _____ _____ OCEAN PROGRAMS TAKE SHARE OF FEDERAL BUDGET INCREASES. Sea Technology 16(3):20-22,46 (1975)

IIOSTR  _____ _____ OFFSHORE NUCLEAR POWER PLANTS. Sea Technology 15:16-17 (1974)

VOS     _____ _____ PRIORITIES SHIFTED IN FY 1974 FEDERAL MARINE SCIENCE PROGRAMS. Undersea Technology and Oceanology International Offshore Technology 14:31,33-35 (1973)

VOCET   _____ _____ WHAT'S NEW IN UNDERWATER PHOTOGRAPHY? Undersea Technology 13:28-34 (1972)

VOI     THE BOOMING OFFSHORE MARINE INDUSTRY. Ocean Industry 8(6):47, A47-H47 (1973)

IIP&H   Borbe, L. GROSSSCHIFTE UND IHRE AUSWIRKUNG AUF DIE SEEHAFEN. Seewirtschaft 4(6):453-456 (1972)

VLOS    Borgese, Elizabeth M. BOOM, DOOM, AND GLOOM OVER THE OCEANS: THE ECONOMIC ZONE, THE DEVELOPING NATIONS, AND THE CONFERENCE ON THE LAW OF THE SEA. San Diego Law Review 11:541-556 (1974)

VLOS        Borgese, Elisabeth M. FOREWORD: PACEM IN MARIBUS. Oregon Law Review 50:373-377 (1971)

VLOS        _____ _____ THE LAW OF THE SEA. The Center Magazine 7:25-34 (November/December 1974)

VLOS        _____ _____ OCEAN RESOURCES LAW. FOREWORD: PACEM IN MARIBUS. Oregon Law Review 50(Part 2):373-377 (1971)

VLOS        Borgese, E.M. RECOMMENDATIONS BY PACEM IN MARIBUS V TO THE U. N. CONFERENCE ON THE LAW OF THE SEA. Environment Conservation 2:14-16 (1975)

VLOS        Borgese, Elizabeth M. THE REPUBLIC OF THE DEEP SEAS. The Center Magazine 4:18-27 (1968)

VOCET       Borowikow, P.A. VERGLEICHENDE UNTERSUCHUNG VON UNTERWASSER - LABORATORIEN. Meerestechnik 5:25-27 (1974)

IIIP        Borowitzka, M.A. INTERTIDAL ALGAE SPECIES DIVERSITY AND THE EFFECT OF POLLUTION. Australian Journal of Marine and Freshwater Research 23:73-84 (1972)

VLOS        Bos, A. THE THIRD U. N. CONFERENCE ON THE LAW OF THE SEA. Internationale Spectator 28:372-381 (1974)

IVMMR       Bostrom, K., et al. ALUMINUM-POOR FERROMANGANOAN SEDIMENTS ON ACTIVE OCEANIC RIDGES. Journal of Geophysical Research 74:3261-3270 (1969)

VP          Bouchez, L.J. DE VERONTREINIGING VAN DE ZEE EN HET VOLKENRECHT. INTERNATIONAL LAW ASSOCIATION. NETHERLANDS BRANCH. Medelingen 65:7-68 (1972)

VLOS        _____ _____ HERWAARDERING VAN HET RECHT VAN DE ZEE. Nederlands Juristenblad 24:749-759 (1974)

VLOS        _____ _____ THE LEGAL REGIME OF SCIENTIFIC RESEARCH ON THE SEA-BED. Paper at the Symposium on the International Regime of the Sea-bed. Rome. (1969)

IIIFV&G     Boulten, J. ADVANTAGES OF STANDARD DESIGN FOR FISHING VESSELS. Australian Fisheries 33(2):14-16 (1974)

IVMMR       Bouma, Arnold H., and Richard Resak. OIL FOUND ON KNOLLS ON GULF'S CONTINENTAL RISE. Ocean Industry 4:73-77 (1969)

VP          Bourne, C.B. INTERNATIONAL LAW AND POLLUTION OF INTERNATIONAL RIVERS AND LAKES. University of British Columbia Law Review 6:115-136 (1971)

IVMMR       Bouysse, P. LA RECHERCHE MINIÈRE SOUS-MARINE. Annales des Mines 4:41-52 (1970)

IICONS      Bowden, Gerald. LEGAL BATTLES ON THE CALIFORNIA COAST: A REVIEW OF THE RULES. Coastal Zone Management Journal 2(3):273-296 (1976)

VOR         Bowett, D.W. DEEP SEA-BED RESOURCES: A MAJOR CHALLENGE. The Cambridge Law Journal 31(1):50-66 (1972)

| | |
|---|---|
| VLOS | Bowett, D.W. SECOND UNITED NATIONS CONFERENCE ON THE LAW OF THE SEA. International and Comparative Law Quarterly 9:415-435 (1960) |
| IVOSTR | BP'S FORTIES FIELD PLATFORM NEARS COMPLETION. Ocean Industry 10(2):78-80 (1975) |
| IVMMR | Bradley, Keith. OIL AND GAS RESOURCES OF THE WORLD. PART 2. THE NORTH SEA RESOURCES. The International Journal of Environmental Science 1(2):64-69 (1972) |
| VP | Bradley, Paul G. MARINE OIL SPILLS: A PROBLEM IN ENVIRONMENTAL MANAGEMENT. Natural Resources Journal 14:337-359 (1974) |
| IVM | Braadlie, T. DEEP WATER PIPE LINING. Northern Offshore 2(1):18, 21-22 (1973) |
| IIIP | Braham, H.W. LEAD IN THE CALIFORNIA SEA LION (ZALOPHUS CALIFORNIANUS). Environmental Pollution 5:253-258 (1973) |
| VOR | Branco, Raul. RATIONAL DEVELOPMENT OF SEA-BED RESOURCES; ISSUES AND CONFLICTS. Ocean Management 1:41-54 (1973) |
| IVMMR | _____ _____ THE TAX REVENUE POTENTIAL OF MANGANESE NODULES. Ocean Development and International Law Journal 1:201-208 (1973) |
| VOR | Brandel, Roland E. OCEANS: TWO-THIRDS OF THE WORLD UP FOR GRABS. Brief/Case 21:7-9 (1971) |
| VLOS | Brantley, Thomas H. LAW OF THE SEA. Harvard International Law Journal 14:555-565 (1973) |
| IVM | Brasier, G.A., et al. TEST PROVES RELIABILITY OF SUB-SEA WELL WORK-OVER TOOLS. World Oil 165:129-136 (1967) |
| IIIB | BRASIL DEFENDE AS 200 MILHAS NA CONFERENCIA SOBRE DIREITO DO MAR. Revista Nacional da Pesca 13(108):25-28 (1971) |
| IIIB | BRASIL FIRMA ACORDO COM TRINIDAD-TOBAGO. Revista Nacional da Pesca 13(108):10-10 (1971) |
| VP | Brask, G. OIL CATASTROPHES, LIABILITY, INSURANCE. Nordisk Foersaekrings Tidskrift 54:125-136 (1974) |
| IIIF | BRAZIL; FISHERIES. Bolsa Review 67:388-388 (July, 1972) |
| IIIF | BRAZIL - NETHERLANDS: FISHING. Bolsa Review 74: (February, 1973) |
| IIIF | BRAZIL/USA: FISHERIES. O Estado de S. Paulo :1 (February 15, 1973) |
| VB | BREADTH OF THE TERRITORIAL SEA AND CONTIGUOUS ZONES OF STATES REPRESENTED AT THE UNITED NATIONS CONFERENCE ON THE LAW OF THE SEA. Revue de Droit International pour le Moyen-Orient 7:19-32 (1958) |
| VENE | Breazeale, W.V., and M.M. Neel. POWER PLANT OFFERS VERSATILITY. Ocean Industry 8:148-152 (1973) |
| VENV | Briet, Ludwig, A.E. ENVIRONMENTAL PROTECTION IN THE NETHERLANDS. Business Lawyer 27:827-832 (1972) |

| | |
|---|---|
| VOI | BRINGING IT ASHORE. Offshore Services 7(5):55,57 (1974) |
| IISL | Brion, Denis J. VIRGINIA NATURAL RESOURCES LAW AND THE NEW VIRGINIA WETLANDS ACT. Washington and Lee Law Review 30:19-71 (1973) |
| IIP | Brisou, J. LA POLLUTION MICROBIENNE, VIRALE ET PARASITAIRE DES EAUX LITTORALES ET SES CONSEQUENCES POUR LA SANTÉ PUBLIQUE. Bulletin of the World Health Organization 38(1):70-118 (1968) |
| IVOSTR | British Gas Council. GIANT BACTON TERMINAL HANDLING 4 BILLION CFD OF NORTH SEA GAS. Petroleum Engineer 45(6):49-50,54 (1972) |
| IIIF | Broadhead, M. COMMENT L'AMERIQUE INVESTIT DANS L'INDUSTRIE THONIERE. France Peche 166:88-89 (1971/1972) |
| VINTL | Brock, J. LEGALITY OF WARNING AREAS AS USED BY THE UNITED STATES. JAG Journal 21:69-72 (1966-67) |
| IVLOS | _____ _____ MINERAL RESOURCES AND THE FUTURE DEVELOPMENT OF THE INTERNATIONAL LAW OF THE SEA. JAG Journal 22:39-49 (1967) |
| VMT | _____ _____ THREATS TO FREEDOM OF NAVIGATION. JAG Journal 24:75-78 (1969-70) |
| VLOS | Brock, John R. INTRODUCTION TO THE 1971 ISSUE ON LAW OF THE SEA. JAG Journal XXV(3):67-68 (1971) |
| VMT | Brockel, H.C. THE SEAWAY SYSTEM: NEW FORECAST REFLECTS OPTIMISM. World Ports 36(5):10-11,13-14,27 (1974) |
| VENE | Bronstein, Daniel A. STATE REGULATION OF POWERPLANT SITING. Environmental Law 3:273-315 (1973) |
| IVMMR | Brooks, D.L. DEEP SEA MANGANESE NODULES; FROM SCIENTIFIC PHENOMENON TO WORLD RESOURCE. Natural Resources Journal 8:401-423 (1968) |
| IVP | Brooks, David K. LIABILITY OF AN OIL AND GAS LESSEE FOR CAUSING DRAINAGE: A STANDARD FOR TEXAS. Texas Law Review 51:546-577 (1973) |
| IIIP | Brooks, R.R. HEAVY METALS IN SOME NEW ZEALAND COMMERCIAL SEA FISHES. New Zealand Journal of Marine and Freshwater Research 8:155-166 (1974) |
| IVM | Brown, E. DEEP-SEA MINING: THE LEGAL REGIME OF "INNER SPACE". 1968 Yearbook of World Affairs. pp. 165-190 |
| VCS | _____ _____ OUTER LIMIT OF THE CONTINENTAL SHELF. Juridicial Review pp. 111-146 (1968) |
| IIIB | Brown, E.D. ICELAND'S FISHERY LIMITS: THE LEGAL ASPECT. The World Today February 1973 |
| VP | _____ _____ INTERNATIONAL LAW AND MARINE POLLUTION: RADIOACTIVE WASTE AND "OTHER HAZARDOUS SUBSTANCES". Natural Resources Journal 11:221-255 (1971) |
| VP | _____ _____ THE PREVENTION AND CONTROL OF MARINE POLLUTION. Anglo-American Law Review 1:51-78 (1972) |

| | |
|---|---|
| VB | Brown, Philip M. THE MARGINAL SEA. <u>American Journal of International Law</u> 18:89-95 (1923) |
| IVOSTR | Brown, R.J. HOW DEEP SHOULD AN OFFSHORE LINE BE BURIED FOR PROTECTION? <u>Oil and Gas Journal</u> 69-90-92 (1971) |
| VOR | Brown, S. NATIONAL INTERESTS VERSUS INTERNATIONAL NEEDS. <u>Marine Technology Society Journal</u> 8(6):29-39 (1974) |
| VINTL | Brown, S., and L.L. Fabian. TOWARD MUTUAL ACCOUNTABILITY IN THE NONTERRESTRIAL REALMS. <u>International Organization</u> 29:877-892 (1975) |
| IVMMR | Browning, D. EXPLOITATION OF SUBMARINE MINERAL RESOURCES BEYOND THE CONTINENTAL SHELF. <u>Texas International Law Forum</u> 4:1-27 (1968) |
| IIIF | \_\_\_\_\_ \_\_\_\_\_ INTER-AMERICAN FISHERIES RESOURCES: A NEED FOR COOPERATION. <u>Texas International Law Forum</u> 2:1-39 (1966) |
| VLOS | \_\_\_\_\_ \_\_\_\_\_ THE SEA AND OCEAN POLITICS. <u>Ocean Industry</u> 4:53-55 (1969) |
| VOR | \_\_\_\_\_ \_\_\_\_\_ UNITED NATIONS AND MARINE RESOURCES. <u>William and Mary Law Review</u> 10:690-704 (1969) |
| VCS | \_\_\_\_\_ \_\_\_\_\_ WHO HAS WHAT RIGHTS ON THE CONTINENTAL SHELVES. <u>Ocean Industry</u> 3:52-56 (1968) |
| VENV | Brownlie, Ian. A SURVEY OF INTERNATIONAL CUSTOMARY RULES OF ENVIRONMENTAL PROTECTION. <u>Natural Resources Journal</u> 13:177-390 (1973) |
| IIP&H | Bruckshaw, G.V. DEVELOPMENT OF MARINE OIL TERMINAL EQUIPMENT. <u>Tanker and Bulk Carrier</u> 20:23-24 (1973) |
| IVDRIL | Bruechner, K.W. TRENDS IN UNDERWATER DRILLING COMPLETIONS. <u>Ocean Industry</u> 2:27-29 (1967) |
| IVDRIL | Brun, Andre. DRILLING CONTROL, EFFICIENCY AT PEAK ON NEW DRILLSHIP. <u>World Oil</u> 175(7):45-45,48,51-52 (1972) |
| IVMMR | Brundage, H.T. EXPLORATION'S WIDENING TECHNOLOGY. <u>World Oil</u> 160:87-92 (1965) |
| IVMMR | \_\_\_\_\_ \_\_\_\_\_ NORTH AMERICA OFFSHORE; GULF OF MEXICO, WESTERN U.S., EASTERN CANADA DRAW TOP INTEREST. <u>World Oil</u> 164:94-99 (1967) |
| VLOS | Brunet, Edward J. MUSING ON THE BOTTOM: ECONOMIC AND LEGAL IMPLICATIONS OF THE UNITED STATES' PROPOSED DRAFT UNITED NATIONS CONVENTION ON THE INTERNATIONAL SEABED. <u>University of Illinois Law Forum</u> 1974:251-284 (1974) |
| IVOCET | Bruun, A. NEW IDEAS IN DEEP WATER OIL PRODUCTION SYSTEMS; PART I, THE MANUAL APPROACH. <u>World Oil</u> 167:78-81 (1968) |
| IVDRIL | Buchanan, L.G. HALIBUT GROUP'S DRILLING PROGRAM SPEEDS DEVELOPMENT OF THISTLE FIELD. <u>Petroleum Engineering</u> 46(5):40-43,46 (1974) |
| IVOSTR | Buckman, D. SEAL INSTALLS SUBSEA UNIT IN MOBIL'S BERYL FIELD. <u>Ocean Industry</u> 10(7):39-41 (1975) |

| | |
|---|---|
| IIIOR | THE BUDGET. Fish Boat 19(4):36-37,65 (1974) |
| IIOSTR | BUILDING A MULTI-PURPOSE ISLAND IN THE SEA. Ocean Industry 8(4): 187-190,192-194 (1973) |
| VLOS | Burger, W. TREATY PROVISIONS CONCERNING MARINE SCIENCE RESEARCH. Ocean Development and International Law Journal 1:159-184 (1973) |
| IICONS | Burgweger, Francis J. THE CALIFORNIA COASTAL ZONE CONSERVATION ACT OF 1972: A SAMPLING OF DEVELOPER'S PROBLEMS. Environmental Comment :4-7 (April 20, 1975) |
| VENV | Burhenne, Wolfgang E., and Thomas J. Schoenbaum. EUROPEAN COMMUNITY AND MANAGEMENT OF THE ENVIRONMENT: A DILEMMA. Natural Resources Journal 13:494-503 (1973) |
| IVMMR | Burke, Robert G. NORTH SEA TAKES SHAPE AS OIL AND GAS PROVINCE. Offshore 32(11):33-36 (1972) |
| IIIF | Burke, William T. ASPECTS OF INTERNAL DECISION-MAKING PROCESSES IN INTERGOVERNMENTAL FISHERY COMMISSIONS. Washington Law Review 43:115-178 (1967) |
| VOR | _____ _____ CONTEMPORARY LEGAL PROBLEMS IN OCEAN DEVELOPMENT. The International Lawyer 3:536-559 (1969) |
| VLOS | _____ _____ LAW OF THE SEA. Oceanology 57-58 (June, 1966) |
| VLOS | _____ _____ LAW OF THE SEA. Oceanology International 3:38-38 (1968) |
| VLOS | _____ _____ LAW, SCIENCE AND THE OCEAN. Natural Resources Lawyer 3:195-226 (1970) |
| VLOS | _____ _____ A NEGATIVE VIEW OF A PROPOSAL FOR UNITED NATIONS OWNERSHIP OF OCEAN MINERAL RESOURCES. Natural Resources Lawyer 1(2):42-62 (1968) |
| VP | Burrows, Paul, et al. TORREY CANYON: A CASE STUDY IN ACCIDENTAL POLLUTION. Scottish Journal of Political Economy 21:237-258 (1974) |
| IICZM | Burton, Ian, and Robert W. Kates. FLOODPLAIN AND THE SEASHORE: A COMPARATIVE ANALYSIS OF HAZARD-ZONE OCCUPANCE. Geographical Review 44-367-385 (1954) |
| VLOS | Butler, W.E. SEERECHTS- UND MEERESPOLITIK DER SOWJETUNION. Europa Archiv 27:673-682 (1972) |
| IIB | Butler, William E. LEGAL REGIME OF RUSSIAN TERRITORIAL WATERS. American Journal of Internal Law 62:51-77 (1968) |
| VP | _____ _____ POLLUTION CONTROL AND THE SOVIET ARCTIC. International and Comparative Law Quarterly 21(3):557-560 (1972) |
| VCS | _____ _____ SOVIET UNION AND THE CONTINENTAL SHELF. American Journal of International Law 63:103-107 (1969) |
| IIIF | Butlin, J.A. THE ROLE OF ECONOMICS IN FISHERIES MANAGEMENT RESEARCH. Maritime Studies and Management 2:56-65 (1974) |

VLOS    Butte, Woodfin L. LAW OF THE SEA - BREAKERS AHEAD. The International Lawyer 6:237-257 (1972)

VLOS    Buzan, B. LAW OF THE SEA CONFERENCE: THE DANGER OF DELAY. International Perspectives :25-29 (November/December, 1974)

VLOS    _____ _____ SEABED ISSUES AT THE LAW OF THE SEA CONFERENCE: THE CARACAS SESSION. Canadian Yearbook of International Law 12:222-238 (1974)

IIOSTR  Byars, Carlos. BURNED PLATFORM COMES BACK IN GULF COAST. Oil and Gas Journal 70(31):96-98 (1972)

IVOL    _____ _____ DISCOVERIES MULTIPLY ON NEW LEASES OFF LOUISIANA. Oil and Gas Journal 71:29-33 (1973)

IVOL    _____ _____ DISCOVERY RATE LOOKS HIGH ON JUNE LEASES OFF TEXAS. Oil and Gas Journal 72:17-19 (1974)

IVP     _____ _____ INDUSTRY GROUP READY FOR OIL SPILLS. Oil and Gas Journal 70:77-79 (1972)

IVOL    _____ _____ SEARCH PAYS OFF IN TEXAS STATE WATERS. Oil and Gas Journal 70(48):32-34 (1972)

VODAS   _____ _____ SEISMIC WORK IN THE GULF BUILDING TO ALL-TIME HIGH. Oil and Gas Journal 71:53-55 (1973)

IVOL    _____ _____ STAMPEDE FOR GULF BLOCKS SMASHES ALL BONUS RECORDS. Oil and Gas Journal 70(52):37-41 (1972)

IIIFP   Bykov, B.P. INTERNATIONAL CONFERENCE ON THE PROBLEM OF PRODUCING ALBUMIN CONCENTRATES FROM FISH. National Marine Fisheries Service, Division of Foreign Fisheries. Trans. of Rybnoe Khozyaistvo 7:90-92 (1970)

VB      Byrne, J. CANADA AND THE LEGAL STATUS OF OCEAN SPACE IN THE CANADIAN ARCTIC ARCHIPELAGO. Faculty of Law Review 28:1-16 (1970) (University of Toronto)

IIIMM   CACA DA BALEIA NAS COSTAS BRASILEIRAS. Revista Nacional da Pesca 13(110): (1971)

VLOS    Caflish, L. FUTURE OF THE LAW OF THE SEA. Review of the International Commission of Jurists 11:35-47 (1973)

VLOS    _____ _____ LA REVISION DU DROIT INTERNATIONAL DE LA MER. Schweizerisches Jahrbuch fuer Internationales Recht 29:48-91 (1973)

VP      _____ _____ SOME ASPECTS OF OIL POLLUTION FROM MERCHANT SHIPS. Annales d'Etudes Internationales 4:213-236 (1973)

VLOS    Caflish, Lucius. FUTURE OF THE LAW OF THE SEA. The Review of the International Commission of Jurists 11:35-47 (1973)

IVM     Cahill, F.B. THE DEVELOPMENT OF IRISH OFFSHORE OIL AND GAS. Technology Ireland 5(2):11-13 (1973)

VENE    _____ _____ OFFSHORE ENERGY. Technology Ireland 5:23-24 (1974)

VLOS    Calder, N. UNDERSEA COLONIALISM. New Statesman 77:322-323 (March 7, 1969)

VENV    Caldwell, Lynton K. CONCEPTS IN DEVELOPMENT OF INTERNATIONAL ENVIRONMENTAL POLICIES. Natural Resources Journal 13:177-390 (1973)

VENV    \_\_\_\_\_ \_\_\_\_\_ ENERGY CRISIS AND ENVIRONMENTAL LAW: PARADOX OF CONFLICT AND REINFORCEMENT. New York Law Forum 20:751-801 (1975)

IICZM   CALIFORNIA BEACH ACCESS: THE MEXICAN LAW AND THE PUBLIC TRUST. Ecology Law Quarterly 2:571-611 (1972)

VENV    CALIFORNIA ENVIRONMENTAL QUALITY ACT: THE LEGISLATIVE AND JUDICIAL RESPONSE TO THE ENVIRONMENTAL CRISIS. University of West Los Angeles Law Review 5:21-31 (1973)

VCZM    CALIFORNIANS NEED BEACHES - MAYBE YOURS! San Diego Law Review 9:605-626 (1970)

IISL    CALIFORNIA'S TIDELANDS TRUST FOR MODIFIABLE PUBLIC PURPOSES. Loyola of Los Angeles Law Review 6:485-525 (1973)

IISL    CALIFORNIA'S TIDELANDS TRUST: SHORING IT UP. Hastings Law Journal 22:759-781 (1971)

IIIF    Callarias, G. FISH IN THE ICELANDIC SEA? Oxford Lawyer 2:13-20 (1959)

VENV    Cameron, Francis X. NEDA AND THE CZMA: THE ENVIRONMENTAL IMPACT STATEMENT AND SECTION 306 GUIDELINES. William and Mary Law Review 16:773-792 (1975)

VLOS    Caminos, Hugo. LAW OF THE SEA AT THE CARACAS SESSION: A BRIEF EVALUATION. Columbia Journal of Transnational Law 14:80-86 (1975)

IVOSTR  Campbell, P.J.D. PLATFORMS IN THE SOUTHERN NORTH SEA. Journal of Petroleum Technology 25:1046-1048 (1973)

IIIFV&G Campbell, William F., Jr. AUTOMATIC PILOTS FOR THE FISHING FLEET. Fish Boat 17:33,61-63 (1972)

IVP     Campbell, W.J., and S. Martin. OIL AND ICE IN THE ARCTIC OCEAN: POSSIBLE LARGE-SCALE INTERACTIONS. Science 181:56-58 (1973)

IIISF   Campos, Joao C.D. ALGAS: EXPLORACAO DOS CAMPOS NATURAIS. Revista Nacional da Pesca 1972:38-40

VP      CANADA; ARCTIC WATERS POLLUTION. Canadian Weekly Bulletin :2-2 (November 8, 1972)

IIIMM   CANADA - NORWAY SEALING COMMISSION: DAVIS STRAIT. Bulletin of Legal Developments 3:28-28 (February 12, 1975)

VOR     CANADA TO STUDY PROPOSALS THAT WOULD ESTABLISH A NATIONAL OCEANS POLICY TO ENSURE A ROLE FOR DOMESTIC INDUSTRIES. Offshore 33:95-96 (1973)

IIIF    CANADA/USA: FISHERIES. International Perspectives :59-59 (July-August, 1973)

IVMMR    CANADA'S "FRONTIER" SEARCH. Petroleum Press Service 40:246-249
         (1973)

VP       CANADIAN ARCTIC WATERS POLLUTION PREVENTION ACT: AN ANALYSIS.
         Louisiana Law Review 31:632-649 (1971)

IVCS     CANADIAN PROVINCES SEEK DETERMINATION OF OFFSHORE SHELF. Offshore
         32(10):75-75 (1972)

IVM      CANADIAN REPORT CITES ECONOMIC IMPACT OF OFFSHORE OIL AND GAS DEVEL-
         OPMENT. Offshore 32(10):71-72 (1972)

IIIFV&G  CANADIANS USING U.S. SUCTION-LIFT SYSTEM. World Fishing 23:23-23
         (January-February 1974)

VSUB     Candland, Shelby V. MOTORLESS SUB WILL GLIDE ACROSS THE OCEAN.
         Ocean Industry 6:57-59 (1971)

IVOL     Canfield, Monte, Jr. OIL AND GAS LEASING OF THE OUTER CONTINENTAL
         SHELF. GAO Review 10:33-40 (1975)

IIISF    CANNED AND PRESERVED SEAFOOD PROCESSING POINT SOURCE CATEGORY:
         EFFLUENT LIMITATIONS GUIDELINES. Federal Register 39(124):23133-
         23156 (June 26, 1974)

IISL     CAN NEW YORK'S TIDAL WETLANDS BE SAVED? A CONSTITUTIONAL AND COM-
         MON LAWS SOLUTION. Albany Law Review 39:451-493 (1975)

VLOS     CAN THE U.N. PARCEL OUT THE SEA-BED? Business Week 1993:66-68
         (Nov.-Dec. 1967)

IVMMR    Caplan, N. LEGAL ISSUES OF THE OFFSHORE MINERAL RIGHTS DISPUTE IN
         CANADA. McGill Law Journal 14:475-493 (1968)

VLOS     CARACAS, 1974: INTERNATIONAL REGULATION OF OCEAN ECOLOGY. Golden
         Gate Law Review 5:325-365 (1975)

IIOSTR   Cardoso, L.deL. CONSTRUCTING AN ARTIFICIAL ISLAND OFF BRAZIL.
         Ocean Industry 9:29-31 (1974)

VP       Carpenter, E.J., and K.L. Smith, Jr. PLASTICS ON THE SARGASSO SEA
         SURFACE. Science 175:1240-1241 (1972); 177:85-85 (1972)

IVOSTR   Carrive, F., and B. Julien. DESIGNING HIGHLY STABLE FLOATING PLAT-
         FORMS. Ocean Industry 4:48-52 (1969)

IIIINTL  Carroz, J., and A. Roche. INTERNATIONAL POLICING OF HIGH SEA FISH-
         ERIES. Canadian Yearbook of International Law 6:61-90 (1968)

IIIINTL  _____  _____  THE PROPOSED INTERNATIONAL COMMISSION FOR THE CONSER-
         VATION OF ATLANTIC TUNAS. American Journal of International Law
         61:673-702 (1967)

IVOL     Carter, L. CONTINENTAL SHELF: SCRAMBLE FOR FEDERAL OIL-LEASE REV-
         ENUES. Science 160:1431-1433 (1968)

VLOS     _____  _____  DEEP SEABED: WHO SHOULD CONTROL IT? U. N. ASKS.
         Science 159:66-68 (Jan. 1968)

IIILOS      Carter, L.J. LAW OF THE SEA: FISHERIES PLIGHT POSES DILEMMA FOR UNITED STATES. Science 185(4148):336-339 (1974)

VENE        _____ _____ TRIDENT: LAWSUIT CHALLENGES THE NAVY'S BILLION-DOLLAR BABY. Science 185(4155):928-929 (1974)

VP          Cartwright, Robert E. HANDLING OF AIR AND WATER POLLUTION CASES BY THE PLAINTIFF. The Forum 9:639-648 (1974)

VOR         Carver, John A., Jr. TREND TO STATE PROTECTIONISM IN NATURAL RESOURCE MANAGEMENT. Rocky Mountain Mineral Law Institute 18:253-269 (1973)

IIP&H       THE CASE FOR A SUPERPORT. Surveyor 6(4):24-29 (1972)

VINTL       Castaneda, Jorge. THE CONCEPT OF PATRIMONIAL SEA IN INTERNATIONAL LAW. Indian Journal of International Law 12:535-542 (1972)

VENV        Casto, D. USE OF THE CORPS OF ENGINEER PERMIT AUTHORITY AS A TOOL FOR DEFENDING THE ENVIRONMENT. Natural Resources Journal 11:1-47 (1971)

VP          Cernkovich, John C. QUI TAM ACTIONS AGAINST POLLUTERS OF NAVIGABLE WATERS: AN ATTEMPTED AUGMENTATION OF REFUSE ACT ENFORCEMENT. St. Mary's Law Journal 3:278-293 (1971)

VP          CERTIFICATE OF FINANCIAL RESPONSIBILITY (OIL POLLUTION). NOTICE OF CERTIFICATES ISSUED AND NOTICE OF CERTIFICATES REVOKED. Federal Register 38(30):4438-4440 (February 14, 1973)

IIP&H       Chabert, Georges. CONSTRUCTING A NEW SEA-LOADING SYSTEM OFF EGYPT. Ocean Industry 4:28-35 (1969)

IVMMR       Challis, H. NORTH SEA OIL AND GAS - WHAT POTENTIAL FOR UK. Engineering 213:149-151,153,157-159,161 (1973)

IVMMR       THE CHANGING MAP OF A NEW OIL PROVINCE. Ocean Industry 10(2):56-57 (1975)

IIIOR       Chapman, W. GOVERNMENTAL ASPECTS OF HARVESTING THE LIVING RESOURCES OF THE SEA. Natural Resources Lawyer 1(3):119-129 (1968)

IIIF        _____ _____ UNITED STATES POLICY ON HIGH SEAS FISHERIES. U.S. Department of State Bulletin 20:67-71 (1919)

VLOS        _____ _____ WHO OWNS THE SEA? Oceanology International 2:24-27 (May/June 1967)

IIIAFF      Chapman, W.M. AQUABUSINESS; THE HARVEST FROM THE SEA. Columbia Journal of World Business 50:45-52 (1970)

IIIINTL     Chapman, Wilbert M. THE THEORY AND PRACTICE OF INTERNATIONAL FISHERY DEVELOPMENT MANAGEMENT. San Diego Law Review 7:408-454 (1970)

VOR         Chapman, W.T. THE BANK OF THE WORLD'S FERTILITY. Columbia Journal of World Business 2:71-79 (1967)

VLOS        Chappell, D. CONFERENCE ON THE LAW OF THE SEA. Tasmanian University Law Review 1:323-333 (1959)

IIIB       CHARGE JAPS RAID ALASKA SALMON. Business Week pp.17-18 (July 3, 1937)

IIICONS    Charne, J.B. FISH AND GAME - POWER OF THE STATE TO REGULATE TAKING OF. Wisconsin Law Review 181-184 (1949)

VLOS       Charney, Jonathan I. INTERNATIONAL REGIME FOR THE DEEP SEABED: PAST CONFLICTS AND PROPOSALS FOR PROGRESS. Harvard International Law Journal 17:1-50 (1976)

IISL       _____ _____ JUDICIAL DEFERENCE IN THE SUBMERGED LANDS CASES. Vanderbilt Journal of Transnational Law 7:383-455 (1974)

VOCET      Chase, J. NOAA AND OCEANOGRAPHIC RESEARCH; WET NASA IDEA DRIES UP. Science 173:216-217 (1971)

VCS        Chaturvedi, S.C. THE NORTH SEA CONTINENTAL SHELF: CASES ANALYSED. Indian Journal of International Law 13(3):481-493 (1973)

IVM        Chaziteodo, G., and A. Wienen. EXTRACTION AND HAULAGE OF MANGANESE NODULES FROM THE DEEP SEA. Meerestechnik 5(2):37-43 (1974)

IIIF       Cheatley, R.D. FISH MARKETING IN AUSTRALIA: QUEENSLAND. Australian Fisheries 31(5):21-24 (1972)

VLOS       Cheek, Conrad H. LAW OF THE SEA: EFFECTS OF VARYING COASTAL STATE CONTROLS ON MARINE RESEARCH. Ocean Development and International Law Journal 1(2):209-219 (1973)

VLOS       _____ _____ LAW OF THE SEA: EFFECTS ON MARINA RESEARCH. Ocean Development and International Law Journal 1:202-210 (1973)

VOR        Cheever, D. THE ROLE OF INTERNATIONAL ORGANIZATION IN OCEAN DEVELOPMENT. International Organization 22:629-647 (1968)

VLOS       Cheng, T. COMMUNIST CHINA AND THE LAW OF THE SEA. American Journal of International Law 63:47-73 (1969)

IVMMR      Chernow, Ron. THE NEW SHEIKDOM OFF THE JERSEY SHORE. Philadelphia 66:162-164,166-176,178 (June, 1975)

VP         Chester, R., et al. MERCURY IN SOME SURFACE WATERS OF THE WORLD OCEAN. Marine Pollution Bulletin 4(2):28-29 (1973)

IIIP       Chia, Fu-Shiang. KILLING OF MARINE LARVAE BY DIESEL OIL. Marine Pollution Bulletin 4(2):29-30 (1973)

VLOS       Childs, P. THE INTERESTS OF LAND-LOCKED STATES IN LAW OF THE SEAS. San Diego Law Review 9:701-732 (1972)

IVMMR      Chilton, J.R., et al. ARCTIC ISLANDS DEVELOPMENT MAY REQUIRE $8 BILLION. World Oil 174:118-119 (1972)

IVMMR      CHINA MAKES MOVE TO ENTER EXPORTING RANKS FROM OFFSHORE. Offshore 33(7):141-141 (1973)

IVMMR      Chopey, N.P. ATLANTIC OFFSHORE OIL: STILL MIRED IN WASHINGTON. Chemical Engineering 82(16):43-45 (1975)

IIP      Chow, T.J., et al. LEAD POLLUTION: RECORDS IN SOUTHERN CALIFORNIA COASTAL SEDIMENTS. Science 181:551-552 (1973)

IIWQ     Christensen, B.A. RATIONAL PROTECTION OF WATER RESOURCES IN COASTAL ZONES THROUGH PLANNED DEVELOPMENT. Water Resources Bulletin 9:1201-1209 (1973)

VP       Christol, Carl Q. INTERNATIONAL LAW AND OIL POLLUTION OF THE MARINE ENVIRONMENT. Journal of the State Bar of California 46(4):459-465 (1971)

IIIF     Christy, Francis T., Jr. A LOOK AT FISHERIES ISSUES. Marine Technology Society Journal 8(6):56-59 (1974)

VLOS     _____ _____ ALTERNATIVE REGIMES FOR THE MARINE RESOURCES UNDERLYING THE HIGH SEAS. Natural Resources Lawyer 1(2):63-77 (1968)

IIILOS   _____ _____ DISPARATE FISHERIES: PROBLEMS FOR THE LAW OF THE SEA CONFERENCE AND BEYOND. Ocean Development and International Law 1(4):337-353 (1974)

IVMMR    _____ _____ ECONOMIC CRITERIA FOR RULES GOVERNING EXPLOITATION OF DEEP SEA MINERALS. International Lawyer 2:224-242 (1968)

IIILOS   _____ _____ FISHERIES AND THE NEW CONVENTIONS ON THE LAW OF THE SEA. San Diego Law Review 7:455-468 (1970)

VINTL    _____ _____ MARINE RESOURCES AND THE FREEDOM OF THE SEAS. Natural Resources Journal 8(3):424-433 (1968)

VOR      _____ _____ NEW DIMENSIONS FOR TRANSNATIONAL MARINE RESOURCES. American Economic Review 60:109-113 (1970)

IIIF     _____ _____ NORTHWEST ATLANTIC FISHERIES ARRANGEMENTS: A TEST OF THE SPECIES APPROACH. Ocean Development and International Law Journal 1:65-91 (1973)

VOR      _____ _____ PROPERTY RIGHTS IN THE WORLD OCEAN. Natural Resources Journal 15:695-712 (1975)

VOR      _____ _____ REALITIES OF OCEAN RESOURCES. Marine Technology Society Journal 3:33-38 (1969)

IVMMR    _____ _____ SOCIAL SCIENTIST WRITES ON ECONOMIC CRITERIA FOR RULES GOVERNING EXPLOITATION OF DEEP SEA MINERALS. The International Lawyer 2:224-242 (1968)

IVMMR    Christy, Francis T., Jr., and J. Goodier. LEGAL ASPECTS OF THE EXPLOITATION OF OFFSHORE MINERAL DEPOSITS. Mining Engineering 20:149-152 (1968)

VB       CHRONIQUE: EXTENSION A 12 MILES DES EAUX TERRITORIALES FRANCAISES. Centre National pour l'Exploitation des Oceans Bulletin 37:11-12 (1972)

IIIF     Churchill, R.R. THE FISHERIES JURISDICTION CASES: THE CONTRIBUTION OF THE INTERNATIONAL COURT OF JUSTICE TO THE DEBATE ON COASTAL STATES' FISHERIES RIGHTS. International and Comparative Law Quarterly 24:82-105 (1975)

| | |
|---|---|
| VOR | Chwen, W.W. FUNDAMENTAL PROBLEMS FOR THE EXPLOITATION AND THE USE OF DEEP SEABED NATURAL RESOURCES IN THE INTERNATIONAL LAW. Chung Hsing Law Review 9:1-14 (1974) |
| IIOSTR | Ciani, John B., et al. UNDERWATER CONSTRUCTION SURVEY. Journal of the Society of American Military Engineers 64(421):315-318 (1972) |
| VB | Cisneros, M. 200 MILE LIMIT IN THE SOUTH PACIFIC: A NEW POSITION IN INTERNATIONAL LAW WITH A HUMAN AND JURIDICAL CONTENT. American Bar Association Section of International and Comparative Law 56-61 (1964) |
| VP | CIVIL LIABILITY FOR OIL POLLUTION. Houston Law Review 10:394-425 (1973) |
| VP | CIVIL PENALTIES FOR VIOLATION OF OIL POLLUTION PREVENTION REGULATIONS: INTERIM REGULATIONS. Federal Register 39(169):31601-31603 (1974) |
| VB | Clagett, Brice M. SURVEY OF AGREEMENTS PROVIDING FOR THIRD-PARTY RESOLUTION OF INTERNATIONAL WATER DISPUTES. American Journal of International Law 55:645-669 (1961) |
| IIIP | Clark, John R. THERMAL POLLUTION AND MARINE LIFE. Scientific American 220:19-27 (1969) |
| IVOL | Clarkson, Kenneth W. ECONOMIC EFFECTS OF WORK REQUIREMENTS IN LEASES TO DEVELOP SEABED RESOURCES. Virginia Journal of International Law 15:795-814 (1975) |
| VINTL | _____ _____ INTERNATIONAL LAW, U.S. SEABEDS POLICY AND OCEAN RESOURCE DEVELOPMENT. Journal of Law and Economics 17:117-142 (1974) |
| VMT | Clautice, W.G. SUBMARINE TANKER NAVIGATION IN THE ARCTIC. Marine Technology Society Journal 8(8):29-37 (1974) |
| VP | CLEANUP EQUIPMENT FOR SPILLS IS ARRAYED FOR IMMEDIATE USE IN GULF OF MEXICO. Offshore 33:61-62 (1973) |
| IIE | Clineburg, W. and J. Krahmer. LAWS PERTAINING TO ESTUARINE LANDS IN SOUTH CAROLINA. South Carolina Law Review 23:7-24 (1971) |
| VENV | Clingan, Thomas A., Jr. LAW AFFECTING THE QUALITY OF THE MARINE ENVIRONMENT. University of Miami Law Review 26:223-254 (1971) |
| VOR | _____ _____ THE OCEANS. Lawyer of the Americas 4(3):576-584 (1972) |
| VOR | _____ _____ ORGANIZING TO PROBE THE OCEANS: AN EXERCISE IN POLITICAL SCIENCE. Oregon Law Review 50:398-424 (1971) |
| VOCET | _____ _____ SCIENTIFIC INQUIRY IN THE OCEANS: LEGAL REGULATION AND RESPONSIBILITY. Lex et Sciento 6(2):77-91 (1969) |
| IIIF | _____ _____ A SECOND LOOK AT UNITED STATES FISHERIES MANAGEMENT. San Diego Law Review 9:432-453 (1972) |
| VOR | _____ _____ TRIUMPHANTLY ON THE REEFS. Marine Technology Society 3(3):33-39 (1969) |

VODAS    Clingan, Thomas A., Jr., and David Stang.  THE LAW AND DATA BUOYS.
         Undersea Technology 8:33-40 (1967)

IICZM    COASTAL CONTROLS IN CALIFORNIA:  WAVE OF THE FUTURE?  Harvard Jour-
         nal on Legislation 11:463-508 (1974)

IICZM    COASTAL CONTROLS IN CALIFORNIA:  WAVE OF THE FUTURE?  FEDERAL STRAT-
         EGY FOR NEIGHBORHOOD REHABILITATION AND PRESERVATION.  Harvard Jour-
         nal on Legislation 11:417-538 (1974)

IISL     COASTAL WETLANDS IN NEW ENGLAND.  Boston University Law Review
         52:724-762 (1972)

IICZM    COASTAL ZONE MANAGEMENT PROGRAM DEVELOPMENT GRANTS.  NOAA.  Federal
         Register 38(229):33043-33051 (1973)

IISL     COASTAL ZONE MANAGEMENT - THE TIDELANDS:  LEGISLATIVE APATHY VS.
         JUDICIAL CONCERN.  San Diego Law Review 8:695-733 (1971)

IICZM    COASTLINE CRISIS.  Pacific Law Journal 2:226-244 (1971)

IVM      Coates, J.  RIG ACTIVITY INCREASING.  Ocean Industry 8(2):67-70
         (1973)

IIP      Cocomos, T.J.  MOVEMENT OF SPILLED OIL AS PREDICTED BY ESTUARINE
         NONTIDAL DRIFT.  Limnology and Oceanography 20(2):159-173 (1975)

IIIAFF   Coffey, Burton T.  AQUACULTURE SUSTAINS L. I. SOUND SHELLFISHERY.
         National Fisherman 52(10):A12,A426 (1972)

IIIF     _____ _____ U.S. REVISES STAND ON LIMITS:  FISHERMEN'S INTERESTS
         REFLECTED.  National Fisherman 53(2):A3,A2 (1972)

IIIMM    Coggins, George C.  LEGAL PROTECTION FOR MARINE MAMMALS:  AN OVER-
         VIEW OF INNOVATIVE RESOURCE CONSERVATION LEGISLATION.  Environ-
         mental Law 6:1-59 (Fall, 1975)

IVM      Cole, A.R.  INDONESIA MARKS UP BIG GAIN IN OFFSHORE CRUDE PRODUCTION.
         Offshore 33(7):186-   (1973)

VP       Cole, H.A.  MARINE POLLUTION IN THE NORTHEAST ATLANTIC.  Nature in
         Focus 17:10-13 (1973)

IVMMR    Collis, D.S.  BRITAIN'S INVOLVEMENT IN THE FINANCE OF OFFSHORE OPER-
         ATIONS.  Offshore Services 7(8):  (1974)

VP       COLLISION AVOIDANCE:  NEW COMPUTERIZED SYSTEMS TO HELP AVOID CATAS-
         TROPHE.  Marine Engineering/Log 79(7):25-29,84 (1974)

IVOSTR   Colvin, W.B.  REPORT ON 89 SUBSEA COMPLETIONS.  Ocean Industry
         8(6):51-59 (1973)

VOR      Comitini, S.  MARINE RESOURCES EXPLOITATION AND MANAGEMENT IN THE
         ECONOMIC DEVELOPMENT OF JAPAN.  Economic Development and Cultural
         Change 14:414-427 (1966)

IIICONS  COMMENTARY UPON THE IUCN DRAFT CONVENTION ON THE EXPORT, IMPORT AND
         TRANSIT OF CERTAIN SPECIES OF WILD ANIMALS AND PLANTS.  Catholic
         University Law Review 21:665-682 (1972)

IIICONS COMMISSION RECOMMENDS A CENTRAL FISHERIES BOARD FOR CONTROL OF LIVING MARINE RESOURCES. South African Shipping News and Fishing Industry Review 27(7):48-49,51,53 (1972)

VLOS COMMITTEE ON PEACEFUL USES OF THE SEA-BED. SPECIAL SESSION HELD. United Nations Monthly Chronicle 6(11):78-80 (1969)

VP Commoner, Barry. CURRENT PROBLEM IN THE ENVIRONMENTAL CRISIS, MERCURY POLLUTION, AND ITS LEGAL IMPLICATIONS. Natural Resources Lawyer 4:139-152 (1971)

VP THE COMMON SEA. The New York Times :4 (February 13, 1975)

VB COMMUNIST CHINA'S TERRITORIAL WATERS. Union Research Service. Hong Kong 8(20) (1957)

VP COMPENSATION FOR OIL POLLUTION AT SEA: AN INSURANCE APPROACH. Federation of Insurance Counsel Quarterly 26:3-26 (1975)

VP COMPULSORY SELF-DISCLOSURE AND PENALTY PROVISIONS OF THE 1972 AMENDMENTS TO THE FEDERAL WATER POLLUTION CONTROL ACT: CATCH-22 AT SEA? Tulane Law Review 49:1124-38 (1975)

IVOSTR CONCRETE PLATFORM DOES NOT NEED DEEPWATER SITE. Offshore Services 8(3):52-52 (1975)

IVMMR CONCURRENT RIGHT TO SURFACE USE IN CONJUNCTION WITH OIL AND GAS DEVELOPMENT IN Louisiana. Louisiana Law Review 33:655-671 (1973)

VP Cone, S.M.,III, et al. JURISDICTION OVER VESSEL-SOURCE POLLUTION. Record of the Association of the Bar of the City of New York 30:231-254 (1975)

VP CONGESTION IN THE CHANNEL. Surveyor 6(3):12-17 (1972)

IIIF CONGRESSIONAL HOPPERS FILLED WITH BILLS, MOST OF THEM REPEATS FROM PAST SESSIONS. Fish Boat 18(3):29,64-65 (1973)

IISL Connally, J. GOVERNMENTAL REGULATION OF OPERATIONS ON SUBMERGED LANDS. Oil and Gas Institute 21:31-46 (1970)

IIIMM CONSERVATION OF WHALES. Cornell International Law Journal 5:99-112 (1972)

IIP&H CONSTITUTIONAL CONSIDERATIONS IN THE STRUGGLE FOR OWNERSHIP AND CONTROL OF BRITISH COLUMBIA'S "SUPERPORT". Manitoba Law Journal 3:27-39 (1969)

VB CONSTITUTIONAL LAW - RIGHTS TO SEABED BEYOND THREE MILE LIMIT - UNITED STATES HAS SOVEREIGN RIGHTS OVER SEABED UNDERLYING ATLANTIC OCEAN MORE THAN THREE MILES FROM COAST LINE. Virginia Journal of International Law 15:1009-1116 (1975)

IIIF CONSTITUTIONALITY OF A PROGRAM RESTRICTING THE NUMBER OF COMMERCIAL FISHERMEN IN THE COASTAL WATERS OF THE UNITED STATES. Louisiana Law Review 34:801-819 (1974)

IIIB CONSTITUTIONALITY OF STATE FISHING ZONES IN THE HIGH SEAS: THE OREGON FISHERIES CONSERVATION ZONE ACT. Oregon Law Review 55(1):141-153 (1976)

| | |
|---|---|
| IVOSTR | CONSTRUCTION DESIGNS FOR VALDEZ TERMINAL DESCRIBED. World Dredging and Marine Construction 11(3):28-30 (1975) |
| VMT | CONSTRUCTION OF TANKERS. Computation of foreign cost. Federal Register 38(27):4003-4003 (February 9, 1973) |
| VP | LA CONTAMINACION DEL MAR POR EL PETROLEO. Oilgas(Spain:5-14 (1974) |
| VCS | CONTINENTAL SHELF AND THE UNITED STATES. South Carolina Law Review 22:34-49 (1970) |
| VCS | CONTINENTAL SHELF (NORTH SEA). International and Comparative Law Quarterly 21(3):563-564 (1972) |
| VCS | CONTINENTAL SHELF (U.K.) International and Comparative Law Quarterly 21(2):376-377 (1972) |
| VCS | CONTINENTAL SHELF (U.K.) International and Comparative Law Quarterly 21(4):793-794 (1972) |
| VCS | CONTINENTAL SHELVES. MORE COAST - MORE SEA BED? Nature 221:795-795 (1969) |
| VENV | CONTROLLING THE ENVIRONMENTAL HAZARDS OF INTERNATIONAL DEVELOPMENT. Ecology Law Quarterly 5:321-376 (1976) |
| VP | CONVENTION FOR THE PREVENTION OF MARINE POLLUTION FROM LAND-BASED SOURCES. International Legal Materials 13:352-376 (1972) |
| VP | CONVENTION FOR THE PREVENTION OF MARINE POLLUTION FROM LAND-BASED SOURCES: AN EFFECTIVE METHOD FOR ARBITRATING INTERNATIONAL EFFLUENT POLLUTION DISPUTES. California Western International Law Journal 5:350-375 (1975) |
| IIIT&L | CONVENTION ON THE CONDUCT OF FISHING OPERATIONS IN THE NORTH ATLANTIC. International Legal Materials 6:760-775 (1967) |
| VINTL | CONVENTION ON THE INTERNATIONAL MARITIME SATELLITE ORGANIZATION. OPERATING AGREEMENT ON THE INTERNATIONAL MARITIME SATELLITE ORGANIZATION. IMCO DOCUMENT MARSAT/CONF/29, FEBRUARY 28, 1976. International Legal Materials XV(2):233-248 (March, 1976) |
| VOD | CONVENTION ON THE PREVENTION OF MARINE POLLUTION BY DUMPING OF WASTES AND OTHER MATTER. Law and Policy in International Business 6:575-586 (1974) |
| VOD | CONVENTION SIGNED TO PREVENT DUMPING OF WASTES, OTHER MATTER IN OCEAN. Environment Reporter 3(36):1020,1039-1044 (1973) |
| IIP | Cooper, Hal B.H., Jr., et al. AIR POLLUTION IMPACT OF MARITIME SHIPPING OPERATIONS IN THE PORT OF HOUSTON. Coastal Zone Management Journal 1:415-432 (1974) |
| IIOR | Cooper, Larry M. ICEBERG FARMING; A NEW SUPPLY OF FRESH WATER? Ocean Industry 8:28-31 (1973) |
| VOR | Cooper, R.N. AN ECONOMIST'S VIEW OF THE OCEANS. Journal of World Trade Law 9:357-377 (1975) |

| | |
|---|---|
| IICONS | COOPERATION ENTRE LA 'NATIONAL OCEANIC AND ATMOSPHERIC ADMINISTRATION' DES ETATS-UNIS, ET LE CENTRE NATIONAL POUR L'EXPLOITATION DES OCEANS: REUNIONS DE TRAVAIL A PARIS ET A BREST, DU 30 MAI AU 2 JUIN 1972. France. Centre National pour l'Exploitation des Oceans. Bulletin d'information 41:1-2 (1972) |
| IICR | Cooter, Paul A. ON SHORE OIL AND GAS RECOMMENDATIONS. Natural Resources Lawyer 4:204-215 (1971) |
| IIIFP | Copes, Parzival. THE BACKWARD-BENDING SUPPLY CURVE OF THE FISHING INDUSTRY. Scottish Journal of Political Economy 17:69-77 (1970) |
| IIB | Corker, Charles. WHERE DOES THE BEACH BEGIN AND TO WHAT EXTENT IS THIS A FEDERAL QUESTION? Washington Law Review 42:33-118 (1966) |
| IIP&H | CORPS LISTS PORT ALTERNATIVES. World Dredging and Marine Construction 10(3):33-34 (1974) |
| VENV | CORPS OF ENGINEERS - NEW GUARDIANS OF ECOLOGY. Louisiana Law Review 31:666-681 (1971) |
| VINTL | Corredor Serrano, A. DEL MAR TERRITORIAL Y OTROS ESPACIOS MARITIMOS. (Tesis- Bogata). Bogata, 1973. 77,18p. |
| IVMMR | Cortesini, A., and J.R. Minner. PETROLEUM DEVELOPMENTS IN CENTRAL AND SOUTHERN AFRICA IN 1972. The American Association of Petroleum Geologists Bulletin 57:2008-2056 (1973) |
| VENE | Cotillon, J. LA RANCE: SIX YEARS OF OPERATING A TIDAL POWER PLANT IN FRANCE. Water Power 26(10):314-322 (1974) |
| VCS | Coulter, Raymond C., et al. OUTER CONTINENTAL SHELF LANDS ACT - ITS ADEQUACIES AND LIMITATIONS: A PANEL DISCUSSION. QUESTIONS AND DISCUSSION. Natural Resources Lawyer 4:725-731 (1971) |
| VLOS | Cousy, H. NAAR EEN NIEUWE INTERNATIONALE ZEERECHTCONFERENTIE. Jura Falconis 10:93-107 (1973/1974) |
| IVOSTR | Covey, Charles W. FLATTOP - THE VERSATILE MARINE PLATFORM. Undersea Technology and Oceanology International Offshore Technology 13(12):21,29 (1972) |
| VINTL | Coyle, R.E. SURVEILLANCE FROM THE SEAS. Military Law Review 60:75-97 (1973) |
| VP | Cox, J.L. DDT RESIDUES IN MARINE PHYLOPLANKTON. Residue Reviews ... 44:23-38 (1972) |
| IICZM | Craine, L. INSTITUTIONS FOR MANAGING LAKES AND BAYS. Natural Resources Journal 519-546 (1971) |
| VP | Cramer, J. MODEL OF THE CIRCULATION OF DDT ON EARTH. Atmospheric Environment 7(3):241-256 (1973) |
| VENV | Cramton, Roger C., and R.K. Berg. ENFORCING THE NATIONAL ENVIRONMENTAL POLICY ACT IN FEDERAL AGENCIES. Practical Lawyer 18:79- (1972) |

IVMMR    Crauciuc, O.A.G. L'EXPLORATION ET L'EXPLOITATION DES RESSOURCES
         MINÉRALES MARINES. Revue Roumaine des Sciences Sociales 19:211-221
         (1975)

VOCET    Craven, J. THE CHALLENGE OF OCEAN TECHNOLOGY TO THE LAW OF THE SEA.
         JAG Journal 22:31-39 (1967)

VAC      _____  _____ OCEAN TECHNOLOGY AND SUBMARINE WARFARE. Astronautics
         and Aeronautics 7(4):66-70 (1969)

IIOSTR   Craven, John P. PRESENT, FUTURE USES OF FLOATING PLATFORMS. Sea
         Grant Newsletter(Hawaii) 6(3)(4): (1976)

VOR      Creamer, R. TITLE TO THE DEEP SEABED: PROSPECTS FOR THE FUTURE.
         Harvard International Law Journal 9:205-231 (1968)

IVOL     Crews, R. THE ADMINISTRATION OF OFFSHORE MINERAL LEASING STATUTES
         IN THE PACIFIC NORTHWEST (ALASKA AND WASHINGTON). Natural Resources
         Lawyer 1(3):49-59 (1968)

VINTL    CRIMINAL JURISDICTION OVER ARCTIC ICE ISLANDS: UNITED STATES v.
         ESCAMILLA (467 F.2d 341). UCLA-Alaska Law Review 4:419-440 (1975)

IVMMR    Cronan, D.S. MANGANESE NODULES AND OTHER FERROMANGANESE OXIDE DE-
         POSITS FROM THE ATLANTIC OCEAN. Journal of Geophysical Research
         80:3831-3837 (1975)

IVOSTR   Crooke, J.O., and Ray Lacy. NOTES ON OFFSHORE RIG DESIGN. Ocean
         Industry 5:41-43 (1970)

VP       Crow, S.A., et al. MICROBIOLOGICAL ASPECTS OF PETROLEUM DEGRADATION
         IN THE AQUATIC ENVIRONMENT. Bulletin Societe Franco-Japonaise
         d'oceanographie 12(2):95-112 (1974)

IVDR     Cruickshank, Michael J. ECONOMIC FACTORS INVOLVED IN NON-PETROLEUM
         DRILLING. Ocean Industry 5:51-52 (1970)

IVM      Cruickshank, Michael J., et al. OFFSHORE MINING - PRESENT AND FU-
         TURE. Engineering and Mining Journal 169:84-91 (1968)

IIIOR    Crutchfield, J.A. THE CONVENTION OF FISHING AND LIVING RESOURCES OF
         THE HIGH SEAS. Natural Resources Lawyer 1(2):114-124 (1968)

IIIINTL  _____ _____ MANAGEMENT OF THE NORTH PACIFIC FISHERIES: ECONOMIC
         OBJECTIVES AND ISSUES. Washington Law Review 43:283-307 (1967)

IIIINTL  _____ _____ THE MARINE FISHERIES; A PROBLEM IN INTERNATIONAL
         COOPERATION. American Economic Review 54:207-218 (1964)

IIIINTL  Crutchfield, J.A., and G. Pontecorvo. CRISIS IN THE FISHERIES.
         Bulletin of the Atomic Scientists 18:18-20 (1962)

IIIF     Culp, M.S. DUE PROCESS ... FISHING RIGHTS IN THE PUBLIC WATERS OF
         MICHIGAN. Michigan Law Review 32:858-861 (1934)

VP       Cummins, P.A., et al. OIL TANKER POLLUTION CONTROL: DESIGN VS.
         EFFECTIVE LIABILITY ASSESSMENT. Journal of Maritime Law and Com-
         merce 7(1):169-206 (1975)

| | |
|---|---|
| VP | Cummins, Phillip A., et al. OIL TANKER POLLUTION CONTROL: DESIGN CRITERIA VS. EFFECTIVE LIABILITY ASSESSMENT. Journal of Maritime Law 7:169-206 (1975) |
| VP | Cumont, G., et al. CONTAMINATION DES POISSONS DE MER PAR LE MERCURE. Revue Internationale d'Oceanographie Medicale 28:95-127 (1972) |
| VOD | Cundick, R.P. ARMY NERVE GAS DUMPING: INTERNATIONAL ATROPINE. Military Law Review 56:165-209 (1972) |
| VINTL | Cundick, Palmer R. HIGH SEAS INTERVENTION: PARAMETERS OF UNILATERAL ACTION. San Diego Law Review 10:514-558 (1973) |
| VOD | Cundick, Ronald P. ARMY NERVE GAS DUMPING: INTERNATIONAL ATROPINE. Military Law Review 56:165- (1972) |
| VMT | _____ _____ INTERNATIONAL STRAITS: THE RIGHT OF ACCESS. Georgia Journal of International and Comparative Law 5:107-140 (1975) |
| VP | _____ _____ OIL POLLUTION: NEGOTIATION - AN ALTERNATIVE TO INTERVENTION? The International Lawyer 6:34-41 (1972) |
| IVM | Curle, C. HAMILTON BROTHERS TAKE CHARGE FAST. Offshore 33(2):77-78,80,83-85 (1973) |
| IVM | _____ _____ IN BARELY 10 YEARS, NORTH SEA SOARS TO TOP OF LIST. Offshore 33(7): 142- (1973) |
| VP | Curlin, James W. INTERSTATE WATER POLLUTION COMPACT - PAPER TIGER OR EFFECTIVE REGULATORY DEVICE? Ecology Law Quarterly 2:333-355 (1972) |
| VOR | CURRENT LEGAL DEVELOPMENTS - RESOURCES OF THE SEA-BED. International and Comparative Law Quarterly 17:527-529 (1968) |
| IIIINTL | CUSTODIAN PRINCIPLE GAINS FAVOR IN FISHING LIMITS WRANGLE. South African Shipping News and Fishing Industry Review 27(12):61,63,65 (1972) |
| IIICONS | Cutting, Charles L. FISH SAVING. New York, Philosophical Library, Inc., 1956 |
| IIIF | Dagget, A. THE REGULATION OF MARITIME FISHERIES BY TREATY. American Journal of International Law 28:693-717 (1934) |
| IVOSTR | Dailey, James E. FIXED OFFSHORE PLATFORM DESIGN. Ocean Industry 8:31-35 (1973) |
| IIIP | Dale, I.M., et al. MERCURY IN SEABIRDS. Marine Pollution Bulletin 4(5):77-79 (1973) |
| IVOSTR | Dalley, J.E. FIXED OFFSHORE PLATFORM DESIGN. Ocean Industry 8(1):31-35 (1973) |
| IVOL | Dam, K.W. OIL AND GAS LICENSING AND THE NORTH SEA. Journal of Law and Economics 8:51-75 (1965) |
| IVP | Daniels, J.T. OIL SPILL CONTINGENCY PLANNING IN THE NORTH SEA. Journal of Petroleum Technology 25:1153-1154 (1973) |

VLOS     Danzig, A.L. DRAFT TREATY PROPOSALS BY THE UNITED STATES, THE UNITED KINGDOM AND FRANCE ON THE EXPLOITATION OF THE SEABED AN ANALYSIS. Ocean Management 1:55-82 (1973)

VLOS     Danzig, A. A VIABLE REGIME TO GOVERN EXPLOITATION OF OCEAN BED. New York Law Journal 160(93):4-4; 160(94):4-4 (1968)

VOR     _____ WHO SHALL OWN THE RICHES OF THE SEA? Vista of the United Nations 3(5):10-19 (1968)

VLOS     Danzig, Aaron L. A FUNNY THING HAPPENED TO THE COMMON HERITAGE ON THE WAY TO THE SEA. San Diego Law Review 12:655-664 (1975)

VP     _____ MARINE POLLUTION - A FRAMEWORK FOR INTERNATIONAL CONTROL. Ocean Management 1:347-379 (1973)

VOCET     Dar, V., and M. Levis. EFFECTIVE COMMUNICATION IN TECHNOLOGY SHARING. Ocean Development and International Law Journal 2:379-401 (1974)

VP     D'arge, R.C., and E.K. Hunt. ENVIRONMENTAL POLLUTION, EXTERNALITIES, AND CONVENTIONAL ECONOMIC WISDOM: A CRITIQUE. Environmental Affairs 1:266- (1971)

VENE     Darmstadter, Joel. LIMITING THE DEMAND FOR ENERGY: POSSIBLE? PROBABLE? Environmental Affairs 2:717-731 (1973)

VP     David George, J. CAN THE SEAS SURVIVE? LONG-TERM EFFECTS OF POLLUTION ON MARINE LIFE. Ecologist (London) 1:4-13 (March, 1971)

IIB     Davidson-Arnott, R., et al. INTRODUCTORY NOTES ON THE COASTLINE OF THE MARITIME PROVINCES OF CANADA: A SYMPOSIUM. Maritime Sediments 8(3):87-122 (1972)

IIP&H     Davies, C.M., and R.J. Webb. NEWPORT - THE REALITY BEHIND A LARGE SHIP TERMINAL. Dock and Harbour Authority 55(645):84-88 (1974)

IIIMM     Davis, Bud. GIVING THE WHALE A FIGHTING CHANCE. Our Sun. Philadelphia 1972:14-17 (Winter, 1972)

IVMMR     Davis, J.C. OILMEN LOOK OFFSHORE. Chemical Engineering 81:74-76 (1974)

VENV     Davis, Joyce P. TAMING THE TECHNOLOGICAL TYGER - THE REGULATION OF THE ENVIRONMENTAL EFFECTS OF NUCLEAR POWER PLANTS - A SURVEY OF SOME CONTROVERSIAL ISSUES. Fordham Urban Law Journal 1:19-47 (1973)

VP     Davis, Joyce P., and Robert J. Glasser. DISCHARGE PERMIT PROGRAM UNDER THE FEDERAL WATER POLLUTION CONTROL ACT OF 1972 - IMPROVEMENT OF WATER QUALITY THROUGH THE REGULATION OF DISCHARGES FROM INDUSTRIAL FACILITIES. Fordham Urban Law Journal 2:179-243 (1974)

IIP&H     Davis, M.S. THE PORTS AND WATERWAYS SAFETY ACT OF 1972: AN EXPANSION OF THE FEDERAL APPROACH TO OIL POLLUTION. Journal of Maritime Law and Commerce 6(2):249-257 (1975)

VP     Davis, P. THEORIES OF WATER POLLUTION LITIGATION. Wisconsin Law Review 738-816 (1971)

| | |
|---|---|
| VOCET | Dawson, Camille J. SLICING HISTORY FROM THE OCEAN FLOOR. Our Sun 21:26-26 (1972) |
| VINTL | Day, J.C. URBAN WATER MANAGEMENT OF AN INTERNATIONAL RIVER: THE CASE OF EL PASO-JUAREZ. Natural Resources Journal 15:435-470 (1975) |
| VENE | Deal, David T. THE DURHAM CONTROVERSY: ENERGY FACILITY SITING AND THE LAND USE PLANNING AND CONTROL PROCESS. Natural Resources Lawyer VIII(3):437-453 (1975) |
| VCS | Dean, Arthur H. GENEVA CONVENTION ON THE CONTINENTAL SHELF. Tulane Law Review XLI:419-432 (1967) |
| VLOS | _____  _____ SECOND GENEVA CONFERENCE ON THE LAW OF THE SEA: THE FIGHT FOR FREEDOM OF THE SEAS. American Journal of International Law 54:751-789 (1960) |
| IVOSTR | Dean, Joel, et al. PIPELINE CONSTRUCTION AT KHARG ISLAND ENDS UP QUICKLY. Offshore 32(12):61-62,64,69 (1972) |
| IICZM | A DECISION-MAKING PROCESS FOR THE CALIFORNIA COASTAL ZONE. Southern California Law Review 46:513-564 (1973) |
| VLOS | THE DECLARATION OF MONTEVIDEO ON LAW OF THE SEA. International Legal Materials 9:1081-1083 (1970) |
| IIIP | De Clerck, R., et al. MERCURY CONTENT OF FISH AND SHRIMPS CAUGHT OFF THE BELGIAN COAST. Ocean Management 2:117-126 (1974) |
| IIIP | De Coursey, and W.B. Vernberg. THE EFFECT OF DREDGING IN A POLLUTED ESTUARY ON THE PHYSIOLOGY OF LARVAL ZOOPLANKTON. Water Research 9(2):149-154 (1975) |
| VMT | Deddish, M. RIGHT OF PASSAGE BY WARSHIPS THROUGH INTERNATIONAL STRAITS. JAG Journal 24:79-86 (1970) |
| IVLOS | DEEPSEA VENTURES: EXCLUSIVE MINING RIGHTS TO THE DEEP SEABED AS A FREEDOM OF THE SEA. Baylor Law Review 28(1):170-186 (1976) |
| VINTL | DEEPSEA'S ADVENTURES: GROTIUS REVISITED. The International Lawyer 9:271-281,751-753 (1975) |
| IIOSTR | DEEP-WATER OIL TERMINAL OFF DELAWARE STUDIED. Petroleum Engineer 44(10):15-16 (1972) |
| IIP&H | DEEPWATER PORT SITE EVALUATION: PROPOSED REQUIREMENTS. Federal Register 40(217):52581-52582 (1975) |
| IIP&H | DEEPWATER PORTS. Federal Register 40(89):19955-19978 (1975) |
| IIP&H | DEEPWATER PORTS: LICENSING PROCEDURES AND DESIGN CONSTRUCTION, EQUIPMENT AND OPERATIONS. Federal Register 40(217):52540-52580 (1975) |
| VLOS | Defensor Santiago, M. THE ARCHIPELAGO CONCEPT IN THE LAW OF THE SEA. Philippine Law Journal 49:315-386 (1974) |

| | |
|---|---|
| VOCET | Degens, E.T., and D.A. Ross. THE RED SEA HOT BRINES. <u>Scientific American</u> 222:32-42 (1970) |
| IIICONS | de Klemm, Cyrille. THE CONSERVATION OF MIGRATORY ANIMALS THROUGH INTERNATIONAL LAW. <u>Natural Resources Journal</u> 12:271-277 (1972) |
| VCONS | \_\_\_\_\_ \_\_\_\_\_ SPECIES AND HABITAT PRESERVATION: AN INTERNATIONAL TASK. <u>Environmental Policy and Law</u> 1(1):10-15 (1975) |
| VB | DELIMITATIONS OF THE CONTINENTAL SHELF TO BE MADE ON EQUITABLE PRINCIPLES IN ACCORDANCE WITH THE NATURAL PROLONGATION OF THE LAND IN ABSENCE OF BILATERAL AGREEMENT OR APPLICATION OF INTERNATIONAL CONVENTION. <u>Journal of Maritime Law and Commerce</u> 1:325-333 (1970) |
| VB | Delin, L. SHALL ISLANDS BE TAKEN INTO ACCOUNT WHEN DRAWING THE MEDIAN LINE ACCORDING TO ART. 6 OF THE CONVENTION ON THE CONTINENTAL SHELF? <u>Nordisk Tidsskrift for International Ret</u> 41:205-219 (1971) |
| VB | Dellapenna, Joseph W. CANADIAN CLAIMS IN ARCTIC WATERS. <u>Land and Water Law Review</u> 7:383-420 (1972) |
| IICZM | Delogu, O. LAND USE CONTROL PRINCIPLES APPLIED TO OFFSHORE COASTAL WATERS. <u>Kentucky Law Journal</u> 59:606-628 (1971) |
| VLOS | Delupis, I. LAND-LOCKED STATES AND THE LAW OF THE SEA. <u>Scandinavian Studies in Law</u> 19:101-120 (1975) |
| VP | De Mestral, Armand L.C. LA CONVENTION INTERNATIONALE DE 1973 SUR LA PRÉVENTION DE LA POLLUTION PAR LES NAVIRES. <u>Canadian Yearbook of International Law</u> 12:239-254 (1974) |
| VP | \_\_\_\_\_ \_\_\_\_\_ LA CONVENTION SUR LA PRÉVENTION DE LA POLLUTION RÉSULTANT DE L'IMMERSION DE DÉCHETS. <u>Canadian Yearbook of International Law</u> 11:226-243 (1973) |
| VLOS | \_\_\_\_\_ \_\_\_\_\_ LE RÉGIME JURIDIQUE DU FOND DES MERS: INVENTAIRE ET SOLUTIONS POSSIBLES. <u>Revue Générale de Droit International Public</u> 74:641-667 (1970) |
| VLOS | DEN DIPLOMATISKE SJØRETTSKONFERANSE: BRUSSEL 1971: INNBERETNING FRA DEN NORSKE DELEGASJON. <u>Arkiv for Sjørett</u> 12(1):97-115 (1972) |
| IIOSTR | Denis, M.St. THE WINDS, CURRENTS AND WAVES AT THE SITE OF THE FLOATING CITY OFF WAIKIKI. UNIHI SEAGRANT-CR-75-01. Honolulu, University of Hawaii 93p (1974) |
| VCS | DENMARK/UNITED KINGDOM: CONTINENTAL SHELF. <u>Bulletin of Legal Developments</u> 2:20-20 (January 29, 1975) |
| IIIMM | Dent, F.B. MARINE MAMMAL PROTECTION ACT. <u>Federal Register</u> 38(147):20563-20601 (1973) |
| VB | de Passalacqua, J.L.A. LA EXTENSIÓN DE LA MAR TERRITORIAL Y LOS DERECHOS HUMANOS. <u>Revista de Derecho Puertorriqueno</u> 12:425-428 (1975) |
| IIIF | de Rango, M. METHODE DE RATIONALISATION DES CHOIX BUDGETAIRES. <u>France Peche</u> 166:100-103 (1971/1972) |

IIIF      DESENVOLVIMENTO PESQUEIRO E META DE CONVENIO DA SUDEPE COM A FAO.
          Revista Nacional da Pesca 12(105):(1971)

VLOS      De Soto, Alvaro. THE LATIN AMERICAN VIEW OF THE LAW OF THE SEA.
          India Quarterly XXIX(2):126-137 (1973)

IVMMR     Deter, D.R. HALBTAUCHER FUER DIE OFFSHORE-EXPLORATION. Erdoel-
          eragas Zeitschrift 89(1):31-38 (1973)

IVMMR     Devaux-Charbonnel, J. TODAY'S TRENDS IN OFFSHORE OIL AND GAS LEGIS-
          LATION. World Petroleum 38(4):242-249 (1967)

VP        DEVELOPMENT OF THE CALIFORNIA AND FEDERAL WATER POLLUTION CONTROL
          PROGRAMS. U.C.D. Law Review 5:234-    (1972)

VENV      Devine, D.J. PROTECTION OF MARITIME ENVIRONMENT BY THE COURTS OF
          THIRD STATES: SOME DIFFICULTIES. McGill Law Journal 19:279-283
          (1973)

IVMMR     Devine, S.B., et al. MINERAL DISTRIBUTION PATTERNS, DEEP GULF OF
          MEXICO. American Association of Petroleum Geologists Bulletin
          57:28-41 (1973)

IIOSTR    de WERK, Ir.K.J.C. FLOATING STORAGE AND PRODUCTION SYSTEM. Off-
          shore Services 5(6):33-35 (1972)

VMLAD     De Zwijger, F. FRANCE'S MARITIME POLICY: 1713-1869. Dock and
          Harbour Authority 55(652):402-404 (1975)

IIICONS   Dickens, James R. LAW AND ENDANGERED SPECIES OF WILDLIFE. Gonzaga
          Law Review 9:57-115 (1973)

VB        Dickenson, Edwin D. JURISDICTION AT THE MARITIME FRONTIER. Harvard
          Law Review 40:1-29 (1926)

IIIP      Dicks, P. SOME EFFECTS OF KUWAIT CRUDE OIL ON THE LIMPET, PATELLA
          VULGATA. Environmental Pollution 5:219-229 (1973)

VP        Dickstein, H.L. INTERNATIONAL LAKE AND RIVER POLLUTION CONTROL:
          QUESTIONS OF METHOD. Columbia Journal of Transnational Law 12:487-
          519 (1973)

VENV      _____ _____ NATIONAL ENVIRONMENTAL HAZARDS AND INTERNATIONAL LAW.
          International and Comparative Law Quarterly 23:426-446 (1974)

IVOSTR    Dicky, L. TURBO-DRILLING FROM FLOATING RIGS. Petroleum Engineer
          45(6):58,60,63 (1972)

VENE      DIESEL ENGINE FOR SEA FLOOR POWER. Ocean Industry 9:31-32,39 (1974)

IVMMR     Dillon, John. OFFSHORE OIL: AMEXICALE TRILLION-DOLLAR DECISION.
          A series of five articles. Christian Science Monitor April 15, 1974,
          p.1,F4; April 16, p.Fb; April 17, p.F5; April 18, p.7; April 19,
          p.F1.

IIB       Dinkins, Carol E. TEXAS SEASHORE BOUNDARY LAW: THE EFFECT OF NAT-
          URAL AND ARTIFICIAL MODIFICATIONS. Houston Law Review 10:43-83
          (1972)

VP          Dinstein, Y. OIL POLLUTION BY SHIPS AND FREEDOM OF THE HIGH SEAS. Nordisk Tidskrift for International Ret 41:220-228 (1971)

VP          Dinstein, Yoram. OIL POLLUTION BY SHIPS AND FREEDOM OF THE HIGH SEAS. Journal of Maritime Law and Commerce 3:363-374

IIP&H       DISCHARGING NEW WINE INTO OLD WINESKINS: THE METAMORPHOSIS OF THE RIVERS AND HARBORS ACT OF 1899. University of Pittsburgh Law Review 33:483-531 (1972)

IVB         "DISTANCE PLUS JOINT DEVELOPMENT ZONE" FORMULA: A PROPOSAL FOR THE SPEEDY AND PRACTICAL RESOLUTION OF THE EAST CHINA AND YELLOW SEAS CONTINENTAL SHELF OIL CONTROVERSY. Cornell International Law Journal 7:49-71 (1973)

IIIF        THE DISTRESSED STATE OF THE FISHERIES. Fish Boat 20(4):16-17 (1975)

VENV        Ditzen, Ulrich. ENVIRONMENTAL PROTECTION IN WEST GERMANY. Business Lawyer 27:833-835 (1972)

VLOS        Dixit, R.K. FREEDOM OF SCIENTIFIC RESEARCH IN AND ON THE HIGH SEAS. Indian Journal of International Law 11:1-8 (1971)

IIIFV&G     DO ARTESANATO A INDUSTRIZALIACAO. Revista Nacional da Pesca 12(105): 13-14 (1971)

IVOCET      Dobrin, M.B. GEOPHYSICS OFFSHORE IS A MUST. Oil and Gas Journal 65:77-81 (1967)

IVLOS       Dole, Hollis M. OCEAN MINERALS AND THE LAW. Natural Resources Lawyer 2(4):352-359 (1969)

VORM        Dole, Hollis M., and David P. Stang. OCEAN POLITICS AT THE UNITED NATIONS. Oregon Law Review 50:378-397 (1971)

IVMMR       Dombrovski, John. EXPLOITATION OF SEABED MINERAL RESOURCES - CHAOS OR LEGAL ORDER? Cornell Law Review 58:575-601 (1973)

IVP         Dominick, Peter H., and David E. Brody. ALASKA PIPELINE: WILDERNESS SOCIETY v. MORTON (479 F.2d 842) AND THE TRANS-ALASKA PIPELINE AUTHORIZATION ACT. American University Law Review 23:337-389 (1973)

VP          Donnier, B. ETUDE DE LA TOXICITE D'EFFLUENTS DE PAPETERIE EN MILIEU MARIN. Revue Internationale d'Oceanographic Medicale 28:53-93 (1972)

VLOS        Doorn, H.R.V., and A.C.J. de Rouw. REPORT OF THE DISCUSSION ON THE INTERNATIONAL LAW ASPECTS OF ARTIFICIAL ISLANDS. Nederlands Tijdschrift voor Internationalen Recht 21:163-169 (1974)

VENV        Doran, Charles F. CAN NATO DEFEND THE ENVIRONMENT? Environmental Affairs 2:667-684 (1973)

VLOS        _____. MULTIPLE JURISDICTION - WILL IT SAVE OR DESTROY THE OCEANS? POLITICAL ANALYSIS OF A LEGAL PROBLEM. Vanderbilt Journal of Transnational Law 7:631-685 (1974)

IIIB        LE DOSSIER EXPLOSIF DES LIMITES TERRITORIALES. France Peche 170:20-21 (1972)

VENE       Doub, William O.  MEETING THE CHALLENGE TO NUCLEAR ENERGY HEAD-ON. Atomic Energy Law Journal 15:238-264 (1974)

VMT        DOUBLE HULL AIDS SALVAGING OF SWAZI.  World Dredging and Marine Construction 8:11:38-38 (1972)

VP         Doud, Alden L.  COMPENSATION FOR OIL POLLUTION DAMAGE:  FURTHER COMMENT ON THE CIVIL LIABILITY AND COMPENSATION FUND CONVENTIONS.  Journal of Maritime Law and Commerce 4(4):525-542 (1973)

VENV       _____ _____  INTERNATIONAL DEVELOPMENTS, PERCEPTIONS OF DEVELOPING AND DEVELOPED COUNTRIES.  Natural Resources Journal 12:520-529 (1972)

IICZM      Douglas, P.M.  COASTAL ZONE MANAGEMENT - A NEW APPROACH IN CALIFORNIA.  Coastal Zone Management Journal 1:1-25 (1973)

VENV       Douglas, William O.  ENVIRONMENTAL PROBLEMS OF THE OCEANS:  THE NEED FOR INTERNATIONAL CONTROLS.  Environmental Law 1:149-166 (1971)

VOR        Douvry, Robert.  WORLD'S LARGEST DESALINATION PLANT.  Ocean Industry 5:43-44 (1970)

IVMMR      Down, A.F.  NORTH SEA OIL NEEDS TO BE PUT IN PERSPECTIVE BEFORE OVERESTIMATING.  OFFSHORE 33(4):99-100 (1973)

VEEZ       DRAFT ARTICLES ON EXCLUSIVE ECONOMIC ZONE CONCEPT (PRESENTED BY KENYA).  Indian Journal of International Law 13(1):121-122 (1973)

IIIF       Draganik, B.  BARENTS SEA FISHERY RESOURCES AND THEIR EXPLOITATION.  National Marine Fisheries Service, Division of Foreign Fisheries Trans. of Technika i Gospodarka Morska 20(5):205-207 (1970)

IVMMR      Drechsler, H.D.  EXPLOITATION OF THE SEA:  A PRELIMINARY COST-BENEFIT ANALYSIS OF NODULE MINING AND PROCESSING.  Maritime Studies and Management 1:53-66 (1973)

IICZM      DREDGE SPOIL TO FORM TORONTO'S AQUATIC PARK.  World Dredging and Marine Construction 8(9):21-21 (1972)

IIP&H      DREDGING BEGINS AT SALDANHA BAY.  World Dredging and Marine Construction 10(5):21-23 (1974)

IIP&H      DREDGING UNDERWAY FOR FRENCH SUPERPORT.  World Dredging and Marine Construction 10(3):26-29 (1974)

IIDR       DREDGING VO2 - YOUTH AND EXPERIENCE.  World Dredging and Marine Construction 10(1):15-16 (1974)

VENV       Dreyfus, D.A.  INFLUENCE OF THE ENERGY CRISIS UPON THE FUTURE OF ENVIRONMENTAL POLICY.  Environmental Affairs 3:252-274 (1974)

IVDRIL     DRILLING TO TEST NORTH EUROPE'S SHELF.  Oil and Gas Journal 71:69-72 (1973)

IIOSTR     DUBAI SETS THREE UNDERWATER TANKS.  Offshore 32(1):125-126 (1972)

IVP        Dubais, Bernard A.  COMPENSATION FOR OIL POLLUTION DAMAGE RESULTING FROM EXPLORATION AND EXPLOITATION OF HYDROCARBONS IN THE SEA BED.  Journal of Maritime Law and Commerce 6:549-573 (1975)

| | |
|---|---|
| VINTL | Dubner, B.H. PROPOSAL FOR ACCOMMODATING THE INTERESTS OF ARCHIPELAGIC AND MARITIME STATES. New York University Journal of International Law and Politics 8:39-61 (1975) |
| VOD | Dugan, G.L., and R.H.F. Young. EFFECTS OF COASTAL WATER DISPOSAL IN HAWAII. Journal of the American Society of Civil Engineers 99:691-701 (1973) |
| IIIP | Duke, T.W. CRITERIA FOR DETERMINING IMPORTANCE AND EFFECTS OF PESTICIDES ON THE MARINE ENVIRONMENT: A BRIEF OVERVIEW. Marine Technology Society Journal 8:21-22 (1974) |
| VOD | Duncan, Rodney N. 1972 CONVENTION ON THE PREVENTION OF MARINE POLLUTION BY DUMPING OF WASTES AT SEA. Journal of Maritime Law and Commerce 5:299-315 (1974) |
| IIWQ | Dunkel, H. FEDERAL-STATE RELATIONSHIP IN THE ADOPTION OF WATER QUALITY STANDARDS UNDER THE FEDERAL POLLUTION CONTROL ACT. Natural Resources Lawyer 2(1)47-61 (1969) |
| IIIFP | Dunlop, John T., and Benjamin Higgins. 'BARGAINING POWER' AND MARKET STRUCTURES. Journal of Political Economy 50(1):1- (1942) |
| IVMMR | Dunn, W.W., S. Eha, and H.H. Heikkila. NORTH SEA IS A TOUGH THEATER FOR THE OIL-HUNGRY INDUSTRY TO EXPLORE. Oil and Gas Journal 71:122-128 (1973) |
| IIP | Dunne, James D., and John A. Hargrave. OIL POLLUTION ON THE PACIFIC COAST. University of British Columbia Law Review 6:137-165 (1971) |
| VLOS | Dupuy, R.L. THE LAW OF THE SEA CONFERENCE. International Perspective :63-72 (March/April, 1974) |
| IVMMR | Durkee, E.F. PETROLEUM DEVELOPMENTS IN AUSTRALIA IN 1970. American Association of Petroleum Geologists Bulletin 55:1662-1675 (1971) |
| IVMMR | ———— ———— PETROLEUM DEVELOPMENTS IN AUSTRALIA AND OCEANIA IN 1972. American Association of Petroleum Geologists Bulletin 57:2114-2125 (1973) |
| IIIAFF | Durston, P.H. THE SEA FARM. Vista of the United Nations Associations 1:31-41 (1966) |
| IIIFV&G | DUTCH FISHERY DEVELOPMENTS - BOATS AND GEAR. World Fishing 23:33,35 (1974) |
| VINTL | Dworsky, Leonard B., et al. MANAGEMENT OF THE INTERNATIONAL GREAT LAKES. Natural Resources Journal 14:103-138 (1974) |
| VP | Dybern, B.I. WATER POLLUTION: A PROBLEM WITH GLOBAL DIMENSIONS. Ambio 3:139-145 (1974) |
| VOR | Dyck, S. EINE NEVE ETAPPE DER MEERWASSERENTSALZUNG BEGANN. Wasserwirtschaft-Wassertechnik 22:178-179 (1972) |
| VOR | Dyment, Robert. DESALTING WATER; A GROWING TREND. Ocean Industry 5:41-42 (1970) |
| VINTL | EAST CHINA SEA: THE ROLE OF INTERNATIONAL LAW IN THE SETTLEMENT OF DISPUTES. Duke Law Journal 1973:823-865 (1973) |

IIIF    EASTERN PACIFIC TUNA FISHERIES. Yellowfin Tuna. *Federal Register* 38(9):1521-1522 (January 15, 1973)

VOCET    Eaton, S.K., Jr., and J. Judy. SEAMOUNTS AND GUYOTS: A UNIQUE RESOURCE. *San Diego Law Review* 10(3):599-637 (1973)

IVMMR    Eckert, Ross D. EXPLOITATION OF DEEP OCEAN MINERALS: REGULATORY MECHANISMS AND UNITED STATES POLICY. *Journal of Law and Economics* 17:143-177 (1974)

VCS    Eckhardt, Sherry. INTERNATIONAL LAW - CONTINENTAL SHELF - PROPRIETARY INTEREST OF UNITED STATES IN CONTINENTAL SHELF PRECLUDES CLAIMED ACQUISITION BY PRIVATE ENTREPENEURS. UNITED STATES v. RAY (S.D. Fla.1969) *San Diego Law Review* 6:487-501 (1969)

IVMMR    ECONOMIC SIGNIFICANCE IN TERMS OF SEA-BED MINERAL RESOURCES, OF THE VARIOUS LIMITS PROPOSED FOR NATIONAL JURISDICTION. *Ocean Management* 2:249-259 (1975)

IVDRIL    ECONOMIST FORECASTS IMPACT OF OFFSHORE OIL DRILLING. *Ocean Industry* 8(4):153-154 (1973)

IIIB    ECUADOR: FISHING LIMITS. *Bulletin of Legal Developments* 2:15-15 (January 29, 1975)

VOR    Edelman, P. LIABILITY PROBLEMS IN THE EXPLOITATION OF THE SEAS. *Trial Lawyer's Quarterly* 5:43-66 (1968)

IIIB    Edeson, W. THE IMPACT ON FISHERIES OF TWO-HUNDRED-MILE ZONES. *Maritime Studies and Management* 2(3):138-143 (1975)

IIB    Edeson, W.R. AUSTRALIAN BAYS. *Australian Yearbook of International Law* 5:1968-1969

VB    _____ _____ PREROGATIVE OF THE CROWN TO DELIMIT BRITAIN'S MARITIME BOUNDARY. *Law Quarterly Review* 89:364-386 (1973)

VINTL    _____ _____ VALIDITY OF AUSTRALIA'S POSSIBLE MARITIME HISTORIC CLAIMS IN INTERNATIONAL LAW. *Australian Law Journal* 48:295-305 (1975)

IVP    Edmiston, Ken. CHEVRON'S FIGHT AGAINST POLLUTION FROM MAIN PASS PLATFORM. *Ocean Industry* 5:107-111 (1970)

IVMMR    _____ _____ SHELL FIRE DYING PEACEFULLY. *Ocean Industry* 6:36-39 (1971)

IVOL    Edsall, Thomas B. STATE NOT READY FOR ONSHORE UPHEAVAL AN OFFSHORE STRIKE WOULD BRING. In Extensions of remarks of Robert E. Bauman, *Congressional Record* (daily ed.) 121:E525-E528 (February 13, 1975)

VENE    Edwards, Richard W., Jr. MANY SPLENDORED POSSIBILITIES OR HOBSON'S CHOICE? - WHO MADE THE POLICIES AND WHAT ARE THE ASSUMPTIONS. *Case Western Reserve Journal of International Law* 5:39-51 (1972)

VLOS    Eichelberger, Clark M. CAN U. N. PARCEL OUT THE SEA-BED? *Business Week* 66-68 (Nov. 11, 1967)

VLOS      Eichelberger, Clark M. A CASE FOR THE ADMINISTRATION OF MARINE RE-
SOURCES UNDERLYING THE HIGH SEAS BY THE UNITED NATIONS. Natural
Resources Lawyer 1(2):85-94 (1968)

VLOS      _____ _____ THE SEABED QUESTION IN CONTEXT: ONE OF THE MANY
ISSUES MASSING FOR THE 1973 CONFERENCE. San Diego Law Review
8:653-657 (1971)

VOR       _____ _____ SHARING THE SEAS' RICHES. Saturday Review 49:18-18
(Aug. 13, 1966)

VLOS      _____ _____ UNITED NATIONS AND THE BED OF THE SEA. San Diego Law
Review 6:339-353 (1969)

VLOS      _____ _____ THE U.N. AND THE SEA. Saturday Review 50:22,114
(Oct. 14, 1967)

IICZM     Eikel, M.A., et al. PUBLIC TRUST DOCTRINE AND THE CALIFORNIA COAST-
LINE. The Urban Lawyer 6:519-571 (1975)

IVDRIL    Eickelberg, H.D. OFFSHORE DRILLING RIGS IN THE NORTH SEA. Marine
Technology 6(2):37-46 (1975)

IVP       Eiling, Rolf. DAS SYSTEM DER BEKAEMPFUNG VON MINERALOELNAVARIEN IN
DER WASSERWIRTSCHAFT. Wasserwirtschaft-Wassertechnik 22(1):3-8
(1972)

IIILOS    Eisenbud, Robert. UNDERSTANDING THE INTERNATIONAL FISHERIES DEBATE.
Natural Resources Lawyer 4:19-46 (1971)

IVOSTR    EKOFISK - HISTORY AND FUTURE. Northern Offshore 2:70,73-74 (1973)

IVOSTR    EKOFISK ONE BECOMES AN ISLAND IN THE NORTH SEA. Ocean Industry
8(8):21-24 (1973)

IVOSTR    EKOFISK I: THE TRANSPORT OF AN ISLAND. Ship and Boat International
27:16-18 (1974)

VINTL     el-Enani, I.M. ORGANISATION LÉGALE DU FOND DE LA MER. Revue Egypt-
ienne de Droit International 29:93-164 (1973)

IIIB      ELEVENTH HOUR FOR ALASKA'S SALMON FISHERY: A PROPOSED REGULATORY
SOLUTION. Ecology Law Quarterly 3:391-423 (1973)

VENV      Elliott, John M. ENVIRONMENTAL ASPECTS OF NUCLEAR POWER. The Urban
Lawyer 4:33-58 (1972)

IVCS      Ellis, Frederick W. ANOTHER LOOK AT LOUISIANA WATERBOTTOM PROBLEMS.
Institute on Mineral Law (La SU) 19:113- (1972)

IVMMR     Ely, Northcutt. AMERICAN POLICY OPTIONS IN THE DEVELOPMENT OF UNDER-
SEA MINERAL RESOURCES. The International Lawyer 2:215-223 (1968)

IVLOS     _____ _____ A CASE FOR THE ADMINISTRATION OF MINERAL RESOURCES
UNDERLYING THE HIGH SEAS BY NATIONAL INTERESTS. Natural Resources
Lawyer 1(2):78-84 (1968)

VLOS      _____ _____ DRAFT UNITED NATIONS CONVENTION ON THE INTERNATIONAL
SEABED AREA - AMERICAN BAR ASSOCIATION POSITION. Natural Resources
Lawyer 4:60-72 (1971)

VB        Ely, Northcutt. SEABED BOUNDARIES BETWEEN COASTAL STATES: THE
          EFFECT TO BE GIVEN ISLETS AS "SPECIAL CIRCUMSTANCES". The International Lawyer 6:219-236 (1972)

VB        Ely, Northcutt, and Robert F. Pietrowski, Jr. BOUNDARIES OF SEABED
          JURISDICTION OFF THE PACIFIC COAST OF ASIA. Natural Resources Lawyer 8:611-629 (1976)

VLOS      Emanuelli, Claude C. CANADIAN APPROACH TO THE THIRD LAW OF THE SEA
          CONFERENCE. University of New Brunswick Law Review 24:3-28 (1975)

VP        _____ _____ LA POLLUTION MARITIME ET LA NOTION DE PASSAGE INOFFENSIF. Canadian Yearbook of International Law 11:13-36 (1973)

VP        _____ _____ LE DROIT INTERNATIONAL ET LA RESPONSABILITÉ CIVILE
          POUR LES DOMMAGES DUS À LA POLLATION DES MERS PAR LES HYDROCARBURES:
          LA CONVENTION DE BRUXELLES DE 1969 ET SES DÉVELOPEMENTS ULTÉRIEURS.
          Revue de Droit Univerisité de Sherbrooke 4:25-54 (1973)

IIWQ      Emerson, Frank C. RIVER QUALITY AND INDUSTRIAL ADJUSTMENT: A CASE
          STUDY. Environmental Affairs 3:188-197 (1974)

IVMMR     Emery, K.O. CONTINENTAL RISES AND OIL POTENTIAL. Oil and Gas
          Journal 67:231-243 (1969)

VCS       _____ _____ THE CONTINENTAL SHELVES; THEY ARE ALTERNATELY EXPOSED
          AND SUBMERGED AS THE GLACIERS ADVANCE AND RETREAT. Scientific American 221:106-114 (1969)

IVLOS     _____ _____ LATIDUNAL ASPECTS OF THE LAW OF THE SEA AND OF PETROLEUM PRODUCTION. Ocean Development and International Law 2:137-149
          (1974)

IVMMR     Emery, K.O., and Elazar Uchipi. CARIBE'S OIL POTENTIAL IS BOUNDLESS.
          Oil and Gas Journal 70(50):156-   (1972)

VP        Emond, Paul. CASE FOR A GREATER FEDERAL ROLE IN THE ENVIRONMENTAL
          PROTECTION FIELD: AN EXAMINATION OF THE POLLUTION PROBLEM AND THE
          CONSTITUTION. Osgoode Hall Law Journal 10:647-680 (1972)

VENE      ENERGY AND THE LAW: A SYMPOSIUM. Oregon Law Review 54:503-679
          (1975)

IIIFV&G   DIE ENTWICKLUNG DER SOWJETISCHEN FISCHEREI-FANGSCHIFFFLOTTE. Seewirtschaft 4(6):422-424 (1972)

VENV      ENVIRONMENTAL IMPACT STATEMENTS - A DUTY OF INDEPENDENT INVESTIGATION BY FEDERAL AGENCIES. University of Colorado Law Review
          44:161-   (1972)

IIENV     ENVIRONMENTAL LAND-USE CONTROL: COMMON LAW AND STATUTORY APPROACHES.
          University of Miami Law Review 28:135-208 (1974)

VENV      ENVIRONMENTAL LAW - ADMINISTRATIVE REVIEW - NATIONAL ENVIRONMENTAL
          POLICY ACT OF 1969 REQUIRES THE FEDERAL AGENCY CHARGED WITH ULTIMATE
          RESPONSIBILITY FOR A PROJECT TO CONDUCT COMPREHENSIVE ENVIRONMENTAL
          IMPACT STUDIES IN EVERY IMPORTANT STAGE OF ITS DECISION MAKING PROCESS. Georgetown Law Journal 60:1353-1374 (1972)

IVP    ENVIRONMENTAL LAW - ADMIRALTY LAW - VALIDITY OF STATES' OIL POLLUTION SANCTIONS. Boston College Industrial and Commercial Law Review 15:829-847 (1974)

VP     ENVIRONMENTAL LAW - APPLICATION OF THE NATIONAL ENVIRONMENTAL POLICY ACT OF 1969 TO FEDERAL PROJECTS WHICH WERE ONGOING BEFORE ITS ENACTMENT DATE. Ohio State Law Journal 35:715-723 (1975)

VP     ENVIRONMENTAL LAW - A SURVEY OF INTERNATIONAL MARINE POLLUTION CONTROLS: PRELUDE TO GENEVA. Vanderbilt Journal of Transnational Law 8:477-492 (1975)

VP     ENVIRONMENTAL LAW - ATOMIC ENERGY - FEDERAL PREEMPTION PRECLUDES MORE STRINGENT STATE REGULATION. Tulane Law Review 46:1016-1023 (1972)

VP     ENVIRONMENTAL LAW - CAUSE OF ACTION UNDER FEDERAL COMMON LAW FOR POLLUTION OF INTERSTATE WATERS. Dickinson Law Review 77:451-458 (1973)

IIP    ENVIRONMENTAL LAW - COMMERCE CLAUSE - CONGRESS MAY PROHIBIT THE DISCHARGE OF OIL INTO NONNAVIGABLE TRIBUTARY OF NAVIGABLE WATER ABSENT SHOWING THAT OIL REACHED AND POLLUTED NAVIGABLE WATER. Alabama Law Review 27:227-248 (Spring, 1975)

VP     ENVIRONMENTAL LAW - CORPORATE IMMUNITY FROM PROSECUTION UNDER THE FEDERAL WATER POLLUTION CONTROL ACT. Texas Law Review 51:155-163 (1972)

IIP&H  ENVIRONMENTAL LAW: ECOLOGICAL CONSIDERATIONS IN GRANTING PERMITS UNDER THE RIVERS AND HARBOURS ACT. Loyola Law Review 17:749-757 (1971)

VENV   ENVIRONMENTAL LAW - EXPANDING THE DEFINITION OF PUBLIC TRUST USES. North Carolina Law Review 51:316-325 (1972)

VP     ENVIRONMENTAL LAW - FEDERAL COMMON LAW APPLICABLE TO INTERSTATE POLLUTION CASES. Suffolk University Law Review 7:790-805 (1973)

VP     ENVIRONMENTAL LAW - IMPLIED FEDERAL PREEMPTION - STATES PRECLUDED FROM REGULATING RADIOACTIVE EMISSIONS FROM NUCLEAR POWER PLANTS. Missouri Law Review 37:106-119 (1972)

IIP    ENVIRONMENTAL LAW: MARITIME UNIFORMITY VERSUS COMPELLING STATE INTEREST IN CONTROLLING OIL POLLUTION OF NAVIGABLE WATERS. University of Florida Law Review 24:789-795 (1972)

VENV   ENVIRONMENTAL LAW - NATIONAL ENVIRONMENTAL POLICY ACT - FEDERAL AGENCIES MUST EVALUATE POSSIBLE ENVIRONMENTAL DAMAGE FROM PROPOSED ACTIVITIES. University of Illinois Law Forum 1971:531-    (1971)

VP     ENVIRONMENTAL LAW - NATIONAL ENVIRONMENTAL POLICY ACT OF 1969 - ATOMIC ENERGY COMMISSION FAILS TO MEET THE REQUIREMENTS OF THE NEPA. University of Kansas Law Review 20:501-512 (1972)

VENV   ENVIRONMENTAL LAW - NEW JERSEY SPORTS AND EXPOSITION AUTHORITY ACT - APPLICABILITY OF PUBLIC TRUST DOCTRINE TO PROPOSED SPORTS COMPLEX - ACT HELD TO MANDATE HEARING ON ENVIRONMENTAL IMPACT OF PROJECT. Rutgers Law Review 26:868-887 (1973)

| | |
|---|---|
| VENV | ENVIRONMENTAL LAW - NEPA - SECTION 102 OF THE NATIONAL ENVIRONMENTAL POLICY ACT OF 1969 IMPOSES ON FEDERAL AGENCIES A JUDICIALLY ENFORCE-ABLE DUTY TO CONSIDER AT EVERY DISTINCTIVE AND COMPREHENSIVE STAGE OF AN AGENCY REVIEW PROCESS ALL ENVIRONMENTAL VALUES EXCEPT THOSE EXPRESSLY WITHIN THE EXCLUSIVE JURISDICTION OF ANOTHER AGENCY. George Washington Law Review 40:558-570 (1972) |
| IVP | ENVIRONMENTAL LAW - OIL POLLUTION CONTROL - IN THE ABSENCE OF FEDERAL PREEMPTION AND ANY FATAL CONFLICT BETWEEN STATUTORY SCHEMES, A STATE MAY CONSTITUTIONALLY EXERCISE ITS POLICE POWER TO PROVIDE FOR CLEANUP OF OIL, SPILLAGE AND FOR RECOUPEMENT OF COSTS CONCURRENTLY WITH THE FEDERAL GOVERNMENT. Georgia Journal of International and Comparative Law 4:216-224 (1974) |
| IIENV | ENVIRONMENTAL LAW - PRESERVATION OF THE ESTUARINE ZONE. North Carolina Law Review 49:964-973 (1971) |
| IIP&H | ENVIRONMENTAL LAW - PRIVATE CAUSE OF ACTION UNDER THE RIVERS AND HARBORS APPROPRIATION ACT OF 1899 FOR INJURY TO THE ECOLOGY OF NAVIGABLE WATERS. Texas Law Review 50:1255-1264 (1972) |
| IIP&H | ENVIRONMENTAL LAW - PRIVATE REMEDIES FOR POLLUTION OF NAVIGABLE WATERS. North Carolina Law Review 50:153-162 (1971) |
| IIP&H | ENVIRONMENTAL LAW - RIVERS AND HARBORS ACT OF 1899 - CONSTRUCTION ACTIVITIES IN VIOLATION OF ACT ENJOINED BY WAY OF ABATEMENT. Seton Hall Law Review 5:121-133 (1973) |
| IIP&H | ENVIRONMENTAL LAW - RIVERS AND HARBORS APPROPRIATIONS ACT - PRIVATE PERSONS MAY NOT SUE IN QUI TAM WITHOUT EXPLICIT LEGISLATIVE GRANT OF PERMISSION FOR CITIZEN SUITS. Fordham Urban Law Journal 1:480-492 (1973) |
| IIENV | ENVIRONMENTAL LAW: STATE LAND USE STATUTES. Washburn Law Journal 13:232-237 (1974) |
| VENV | ENVIRONMENTAL LAW SYMPOSIUM - LAND USE, AESTHETICS AND THE STATE LEGISLATURE. Wayne Law Review 19:73-219 (1972) |
| VENV | ENVIRONMENTAL LAW - THE NATIONAL ENVIRONMENTAL POLICY ACT. West Virginia Law Review 76:522-542 (1974) |
| VENV | ENVIRONMENTAL LAW - THE NATIONAL ENVIRONMENTAL POLICY ACT OF 1969 - THE INFLUENCE OF AGENCY DIFFERENCES ON JUDICIAL ENFORCEMENT. Texas Law Review 52:1127-1244 (1975) |
| IIENV | ENVIRONMENTAL LAW - THE REFUSE ACT AND THE QUI TAM ACTION. Tulane Law Review 46:1023-1030 (1972) |
| VENV | ENVIRONMENTAL LAW - THE REQUIREMENT FOR AN IMPACT STATEMENT: A SUGGESTED FRAMEWORK FOR ANALYSIS. Washington Law Review 49:939-971 (1974) |
| IIP&H | ENVIRONMENTAL LAW: THE RIVERS AND HARBORS ACT OF 1899 - A NEW REMEDY FOR ILLEGAL DREDGE AND FILL OPERATIONS. University of Florida Law Review 24:795-801 (1972) |
| IISL | ENVIRONMENTAL LAW - WETLAND FILL-RESTRICTIONS DO NOT CONSTITUTE A COMPENSABLE "TAKING" WITHIN THE MEANING OF THE FIFTH AMENDMENT. Seton Hall Law Review 4:662-682 (1973) |

IISL    ENVIRONMENTAL LAW - ZONING - ORDINANCE PROHIBITING FILLING OF WET-
        LANDS ADJACENT TO NAVIGABLE WATERS WITHOUT PERMIT IS CONSTITUTIONAL
        EXERCISE OF POLICE POWER NOT REQUIRING PAYMENT OF COMPENSATION.
        Harvard Law Review 86:1582-1592 (1973)

IICZM   ENVIRONMENTAL PROTECTION AGENCY AND COASTAL ZONE MANAGEMENT:
        STRIKING A FEDERAL-STATE BALANCE OF POWER IN LAND USE MANAGEMENT.
        Houston Law Review 11:1152-1193 (1974)

IIENV   ENVIRONMENTAL PROTECTION - NATIONAL ENVIRONMENTAL POLICY ACT -
        FEDERAL AGENCIES MUST GIVE FULL AND IMMEDIATE CONSIDERATION TO EN-
        VIRONMENTAL FACTORS IN THEIR PROJECT PLANS, REGARDLESS OF COMPLIANCE
        WITH SPECIFIC QUALITY STANDARDS IN OTHER STATUTES. Vanderbilt Law
        Review 25:258-271 (1972)

VENV    ENVIRONMENTAL PROTECTION - NEPA - THE SECOND CIRCUIT CREATES NEW
        SUBSTANTIVE AND PROCEDURAL GUIDELINES TO AID AGENCIES IN MAKING
        THRESHOLD DETERMINATIONS OF THE NEED FOR AN IMPACT STATEMENT. Texas
        Law Review 51:1016-1022 (1973)

IIP&H   ENVIRONMENTAL PROTECTION - RIVERS AND HARBORS ACT OF 1899 - ANY IND-
        USTRIAL DISCHARGE INTO A NAVIGABLE WATER WITHOUT A PERMIT IS PRO-
        HIBITED. Dickinson Law Review 76:375-384 (1972)

IVENV   ENVIRONMENTAL STATEMENTS FOR OFFSHORE OPERATIONS. Sea Technology
        16:25-26,29-30 (1975)

IIF     EQUILIBRES DYNAMIQUES DANS LES ESTUAIRES: ASPECTS PHYSIQUES ET
        ECOLOGIQUES. Revue Internationale de l'Eau 102:21-154 (1974)

IISL    Ereli, Eliezer. THE SUBMERGED LANDS ACT AND THE GENEVA CONVENTION
        ON THE TERRITORIAL SEA AND THE CONTIGUOUS ZONE. Tulane Law Review
        XLI(3):555-578 (1967)

VC      Erickson, O.P. SUEZ CANAL - A BRIEF HISTORY. World Dredging and
        and Marine Construction 11(3):16-17 (1975)

IVOSTR  ESCAPE BOOMS FOR PLATFORMS AT SEA. Ocean Industry 8:40-41 (1973)

VLOS    Essen, A. van der. LA BELGIQUE ET LE DROIT DE LA MER. Revue Belge
        de Droit International 11:103-119 (1975)

IIILOS  THE ESTABLISHMENTS OF INTERNATIONAL FISHERIES CLAIMS BOARDS FOR THE
        RESOLUTION OF FISHERY-RELATED DISPUTES. American University Law
        Review 24:1333-1371 (1975)

VMT     ESTABLISHMENT OF MANDATORY SEALANES BY UNILATERAL ACTION. Catholic
        University Law Review 22:108-130 (1972)

IIIFV&G ESTALEIRO CONSTROI BARCOS DE PESCA COM TECHNOLOGIA PROPRIA. Revista
        Nacional da Pesca 13(109):12-12 (1971)

IVP     Estes, J.E., and Berl Golomb. OIL SPILLS; METHOD FOR MEASURING
        THEIR EXTENT ON THE SEA SURFACE. Science 169:676-678 (1970)

IIIP    ESTUARINE POLLUTION: THE DETERIORATION OF THE OYSTER INDUSTRY IN
        NORTH CAROLINA. North Carolina Law Review 49:921-943 (1971)

IIE     ESTUARINE SANCTUARY GUIDELINES. Federal Register 39(108):19921-
        19927 (June 4, 1974)

VOD THE EURALLUMINA CASE - INDUSTRIAL WASTE DUMPING ON THE HIGH SEAS OFF SARDINIA. Rivista di Diritto Internazionale 57:826 (1974)

IIP&H EUROPE AND NORTH ATLANTIC. World Dredging and Marine Construction 10(1):26-28 (1974)

IIIF EUROPEAN COMMUNITIES: COMMON FISHERIES POLICY. Aftenposten ;6(September 8, September 22, 1973)

VENV EUROPEAN COMMUNITIES: ENVIRONMENTAL PROTECTION. Guardian :2(July 21, 1973)

VCS EUROPEAN CONTINENTAL SHELF Common Market 5:148-150 (1965)

VENE Evans, Brock. SIERRA CLUB INVOLVEMENT IN NUCLEAR POWER: AN EVOLUTION OF AWARENESS. Oregon Law Review 54:607-621 (1975)

IVMMR EVANS, JACKSON, MAGNUSON. THREE ON OIL. Pacific Northwest Sea 8(4): (1975); 9(1):26-30 (1976)

IIIMM Evans, W.E. THE CALIFORNIA GRAY WHALE. Marine Fisheries Review 36(4):1-64 (1974)

IVMT Everett, John L., et al. OPTIMIZATION OF A FLEET OF LARGE TANKERS AND BULKERS: A LINEAR PROGRAMMING APPROACH. Marine Technology 9(4): 430-438 (1972)

VOI Everett, John P. CURRENT PROBLEMS IN OFFSHORE OPERATIONS. Institute on Mineral Law (La SU) 19:67- (1972)

IIIF Everman, B.W. CAN THE ALASKA FISHERIES BE SAVED? Scientific Monthly 12:163-184 (Feb., 1921)

IIENV EXCLUSIONARY ZONING: A QUESTION OF BALANCING DUE PROCESS, EQUAL PROTECTION AND ENVIRONMENTAL CONCERNS. Suffolk University Law Review 8:1190-1216 (1974)

VP EXPANSION OF FEDERAL COMMON LAW AND FEDERAL QUESTION JURISDICTION TO INTERSTATE POLLUTION. Houston Law Review 10:121-130 (1972)

IIIFV&G EXPERIMENTAL DRUM SEINING FOR WETFISH IN CALIFORNIA. Commercial Fisheries Review 34(1-2):23-32 (1972)

IIP&H EXPERTS CALL U.S. OIL SUPERPORTS VITAL. Oil and Gas Journal 70(43): 48-49 (1972)

IVMMR EXPLOITATION OF SEABED MINERAL RESOURCES - CHAOS OR LEGAL ORDER? Cornell Law Review 58:575-601 (1973)

VP Ezediaro, Samuel O. REVIEW OF THE LEGAL ASPECTS OF INTERNATIONAL WATER POLLUTION CONTROL. Howard Law Journal 17:69-90 (1971)

VENV Falk, Richard A. GLOBAL ENVIRONMENT AND INTERNATIONAL LAW: CHALLENGE AND RESPONSE. Kansas Law Review 23:385-420 (1975)

VENV _____ _____ TOWARD A WORLD ORDER RESPECTFUL OF THE GLOBAL ECOSYSTEM. Environmental Affairs 1:251- (1971)

IVMMR    FAR EAST OIL PROSPECTS. Ocean Industry 4:42-43 (1969)

IIISF    FARINHA DE PEIXE FABRICADA NO PROPRIO BARCO. Revista Nacional da Pesca 12(96): (1970)

IIIF     Fasten, M. NEED FOR GAME FISHERY INVESTIGATIONS. Scientific Monthly 24:81-83 (Jan. 1927)

VLOS     Fawcett, J.E.S. HOW FREE ARE THE SEAS? International Affairs 49:14-22 (1973)

VLOS     _____  _____ THE LAW OF THE SEA: ISSUES AT CARACAS. World Today 30:329-246 (1974)

VLOS     _____  _____ PROBLEME DES SEERECHTS: AUSBLICK AUF DIE KONFERENZ VON CARACAS. Europa Archiv 29:365-372 (1974)

VLOS     Fay, F.M. LA NATIONALITÉ DES NAVIRES EN TEMPS DE PAIX. Revue Générale de Droit International Public 77:1000-1080 (1973)

VLOS     Fedeli, M. PROFILI NORMATIVI DELL'INQUINAMENTO DEL MARE E RIFLESSI INTERNAZIONALE. Corti di Brescia Venezia e Trieste 25:458-473 (1972)

IICONS   FEDERAL AND STATE PROTECTION AGAINST COMMERCIAL EXPLOITATION OF ENDANGERED WILDLIFE. Catholic Lawyer 17:241-254 (1971)

VP       FEDERAL AND STATE RESPONSIBILITIES IN THE ENVIRONMENTAL CONTROL OF NUCLEAR POWER PLANTS. New York University Review of Law and Social Change 2:20-43 (1972)

VP       FEDERAL COMMON LAW AND INTERSTATE POLLUTION. Harvard Law Review 85:1439-1459 (1972)

IISL     FEDERAL CONTROL OF WETLANDS: THE EFFECTIVENESS OF CORPSI REGULATIONS UNDER SECT. 404 OF THE FWPCA. Notre Dame Lawyer 51(3):505-521 (1976)

IIP&H    FEDERAL GOVERNMENT'S ROLE IN SUPERPORTS ANALYZED. World Dredging and Marine Construction 10(3): (1974)

IVB      FEDERAL INCOME TAXATION - JURISDICTION OVER MINERAL OPERATIONS IN CONTINENTAL SHELF AREAS. Treas. Reg. Sect. 1.638 (1973). Texas International Law Journal 9:102-107 (1974)

VP       FEDERAL JURISDICTION AND FEDERAL COMMON LAW - ENVIRONMENTAL LAW - PUBLIC NUISANCE SUITS CONCERNING INTERSTATE WATER POLLUTION. Denver Law Journal 49:609-618 (1973)

IIP      FEDERAL JURISDICTION - WATER POLLUTION CONTROL - FEDERAL WATER POLLUTION CONTROL ACT AMENDMENTS OF 1972 REACH POLLUTING ACTIVITIES OCCURRING ABOVE MEAN HIGH-WATER LINE. Florida State University Law Review 2:799-806 (1975)

IVOL     FEDERAL LEASE SALES: OFFSHORE PRODUCERS DON'T ALWAYS FOLLOW PRE-SALE ESTIMATES. Offshore 33(6):27-28 (1973)

IIP      FEDERAL MARITIME JURISDICTION AND STATE MARINE POLLUTION LEGISLATION: THE FLORIDA ACT NOT PREEMPTED PER SE. University of Miami Law Review 28:209-218 (1974)

| | |
|---|---|
| VCS | FEDERAL REPUBLIC OF GERMANY; CONTINENTAL SHELF. Financial Times :7-7 (November 8, 1972) |
| IIIT&L | FEDERAL REPUBLIC OF GERMANY-ICELAND: FISHERIES AGREEMENT ON THE EXTENSION OF THE ICELANDIC FISHERY LIMITS TO 200 MILES. (Done at Reykjavik, November 28, 1975). International Legal Materials Current Documents XV(I):43-47 (January, 1976) |
| IICONS | FEDERAL RULE OF ACCRETION AND CALIFORNIA COASTAL PROTECTION. Southern California Law Review 48:1457-1476 (1975) |
| VP | FEDERAL WATER POLLUTION CONTROL ACT AMENDMENTS OF 1972. Wisconsin Law Review 1973:893-907 (1973) |
| VP | FEDERAL WATER POLLUTION LEGISLATION: CURRENT PROPOSALS TO ACHIEVE MORE EFFECTIVE ENFORCEMENT. Boston College Industrial and Commercial Law Review 13:749-781 (1972) |
| IVOL | FEDERAL WATERS: LOUISIANA OFFSHORE GULF OF MEXICO SHOWING LEASES AND PLATFORMS. Offshore 33(2): (1973) |
| IVOL | FEDERAL WATERS: TEXAS OFFSHORE, GULF OF MEXICO SHOWING LEASES AND PLATFORMS. Offshore 33(9): (1973) |
| IISL | Feess, Gary. THE TIDELAND TRUST: ECONOMIC CURRENTS IN A TRADITIONAL LEGAL DOCTRINE. UCLA Law Review 21:826-891 (1974) |
| VB | Fell, Lloyd C. MARITIME CONTIGUOUS ZONES. Michigan Law Review 62(5):848-864 (1964) |
| VLOS | Ferone, A. LE CONVENZIONI INTERNAZIONALI SULL'INQUINAMENTO DEL MARE DA IDROCARBURI. Rivista di Diritto Internazionale 55:94-118 (1972) |
| IIP | Ferrar, Terry A., and A. Whinston. TAXATION AND WATER POLLUTION CONTROL. Natural Resources Journal 12:307-317 (1972) |
| IIIF | Fidell, Eugene R. CASE OF THE INCIDENTAL LOBSTER: UNITED STATES REGULATION OF FOREIGN HARVESTING OF CONTINENTAL SHELF FISHERY RESOURCES. The International Lawyer 70:95-101 (January, 1976) |
| IIIF | _____ _____ FISHERIES LEGISLATION: NAVAL ENFORCEMENT. Journal of Maritime Law 7:351-366 (1976) |
| IIIINTL | _____ _____ HOT PURSUIT FROM A FISHERIES ZONE. UNITED STATES v. FISHING VESSEL TAIYO MARU NO. 28; UNITED STATES v. KAWAGUCHI. American Journal of International Law 70(1):95-101 (1976) |
| IIIF | _____ _____ TEN YEARS UNDER THE BARTLETT ACT: A STATUS REPORT ON THE PROHIBITION ON FOREIGN FISHING. Boston University Law Review 54:703-756 (1974) |
| VOD | FIGHTING POLLUTION: HOW TO CURTAIL OR END DISCHARGES OF SEWAGE FROM SHIPS. Marine Engineering/Log 79:34-37,119 (1974) |
| IVOD | FIGHTING POLLUTION: LATEST GOVERNMENT ACTION IS AIMED AT REDUCING OIL SPILLS AND DISCHARGES. Marine Engineering/Log 79:29-33,116,118 (1974) |

VLOS Filipović, V. NOVI MEĐUNARODNI SPORAZUM O POMORSKOM PRIJEVOZU NUK-LEARNOG MATERIJALA. <u>Zbornik Pravnog Fakulteta u Zagrebu</u> 22:123-132 (1972)

VLOS THE FINAL ACT AND ANNEXES OF THE U.N. CONFERENCE ON THE LAW OF THE SEA, GENEVA, 1958, TOGETHER WITH A SYNTOPICAL TABLE OF CLAIMS TO JURISDICTION OVER THE TERRITORIAL SEA, THE CONTIGUOUS ZONE AND THE CONTINENTAL SHELF. <u>International and Comparative Law Quarterly</u> 7:Special Supp.(1958) 42p.

VLOS FINAL REPORT OF THE U.N. AD HOC COMMITTEE ON PEACEFUL USES OF THE SEABED TO THE GENERAL ASSEMBLY. <u>United Nations Monthly Chronicle</u> 5(8): 97-100 (1968)

VLOS Finlay, Luke W. DRAFT UNITED NATIONS CONVENTION ON THE INTERNATIONAL SEABED AREA - AMERICAN PETROLEUM INSTITUTE POSITION. <u>Natural Resources Lawyer</u> 4:73-83 (1971)

VB _____ THE OUTER LIMIT OF THE CONTINENTAL SHELF - A REJOINDER TO PROFESSOR LOUIS HENKIN. <u>American Journal of International Law</u> 64:42-62 (1970)

VLOS Finlay, L.W., and M.S. McKnight. LAW OF THE SEA: ITS IMPACT ON THE INTERNATIONAL ENERGY CRISIS. <u>Law and Policy in International Business</u> 6:639-676 (1974)

VOR Finlay, Luke W., et al. MARINE RESOURCES COMMITTEE. <u>Natural Resources Lawyer</u> 8(1):109-115 (1975)

VENE THE FIRST ENERGY CRISIS. <u>Surveyor</u> 9(1):2-7 (1975)

IVDRIL FIRST OF THE SUPER-RIGS. <u>Offshore Services</u> 5(6):29-32 (1972)

VOR Fischer, David W. SOME SOCIAL AND ECONOMIC ASPECTS OF MARINE RESOURCE DEVELOPMENT. <u>American Journal of Economics and Sociology</u> 32:113-127 (1973)

IIIF FISH. TARIFF RATE QUOTA FOR CALENDAR YEAR 1973. <u>Federal Register</u> 38(26):3612-3612 (February 8, 1973)

VAC Fisher, A. U.S. SUBMITS DRAFT TREATY BANNING EMPLACEMENT OF NUCLEAR WEAPONS ON THE SEABED. <u>U.S. Department of State Bulletin</u> 60:520-524 (1969)

IIP Fisher, Adam, Jr., and Clark Gaston, Jr. POLLUTION CONTROL PRACTICE IN SOUTH CAROLINA - AN OVERVIEW. <u>South Carolina Law Review</u> 23:723-747 (1971)

IVMMR Fisher, David E., and Kurt Bostrom. URANIUM RICH SEDIMENTS ON THE EAST PACIFIC RISE. <u>Nature</u> 224:64-65 (1969)

IIIP Fisher, H.I. POLLUTANTS IN NORTH PACIFIC ALBATROSSES. <u>Pacific Science</u> 27:220-225 (1973)

IIIB FISHERIES JURISDICTION BEYOND THE TERRITORIAL SEA - WITH SPECIAL REFERENCE TO THE POLICY OF THE UNITED STATES. <u>Washington Law Review</u> 44:307-334 (1968)

IIIB FISHERY LIMIT TO 50 MILES. <u>Atlantica Iceland Review</u> 9(4): (1971), 10(1): (1972)

| | |
|---|---|
| IIIFV&G | FISHING BOATS OF AUSTRALIA: TASMANIAN PATROL-RESEARCH VESSEL; KING PRAWN RESEARCH VESSEL. Australian Fisheries 31(8):12-14 (1972) |
| IIIF | FISHING RIGHTS. Law Journal 76:387-387 (1933) |
| IIIF | FISHING TREATY; SIX MAN COMMISSION MAY END BICKERING AMONG FISHERMEN OF LAKE STATES AND ONTARIO. Business Week 46-48 (January 12, 1946) |
| IIIFV&G | FISHING VESSELS FROM HOLLAND. World Fishing 23:28-29 (1974) |
| IIIFP | FISHMEAL AND FPC - BIG NORWAY EXPORT. World Fishing 23(5):49-50 (1974) |
| VLOS | Fitzmaurice. REGIME OF THE HIGH SEAS, (1956). Yearbook of the International Law Commission 2:1-103. U.N. Document A/CN. 4.101 (1956) |
| IIIMM | A FIVE YEAR REPRIEVE. Nature 236(5342):93-94 (March 17, 1972) |
| IVDRIL | FIXED RIGS ARE VITAL TO OFFSHORE DRILLING. Offshore 35:38-39- (1975) |
| VB | Flaherty, David H. VIRGINIA AND THE MARGINAL SEA: AN EXAMPLE OF HISTORY IN THE LAW. Virginia Law Review 58:694-725 (1972) |
| VINTL | FLAK AROUND THE "FREE FLAGS". Tanker and Bulker International 1(1):23-25 (1975) |
| IIP&H | Fleck, M.W. THE CASE FOR DEEPWATER PORTS. Exxon USA 12:12-15 (1973) |
| VLOS | Fleischer, Carl A. INTERNATIONAL STRAITS: A KEY ISSUE AT THE LAW OF THE SEA CONFERENCE. Environmental Policy and Law 1(3):120-126 (1975) |
| VLOS | Flemming, B. THE LEGAL FUTURE OF THE OCEANS. Canadian Bar Journal 4:4-8 (1973) |
| VLOS | Flemming, N. DEEP OCEAN FLOOR OWNERSHIP: U.N. CAPITALISM OR FREE-FOR-ALL? Hydrospace 1:19-21,41 (1968) |
| IIOSTR | FLOATING BASE FOR SUPPLY VESSELS IN THE NORTH SEA. Ocean Industry 9(7): (1974) |
| IIOSTR | FLOATING NUCLEAR PLANTS ARE A REALITY. Offshore 33(9):78,83 (1973) |
| IVOSTR | FLOATING OIL WELLS: HOW DEEP CAN MAN GO? Marine Engineering/Log 77(9):19-25 (1972) |
| IIP | FLORIDA COURTS AND WATER POLLUTION: A FLOATING CRAP GAME? Environmental Law 2:189-195 (1971) |
| IIENV | FLORIDA ENVIRONMENTAL PROTECTION ACT OF 1971: THE CITIZEN'S ROLE IN ENVIRONMENTAL MANAGEMENT. Florida State University Law Review 2:736-765 (1975) |
| IVP | FLORIDA OIL SPILL AND POLLUTION CONTROL ACT, AN INTRUSION INTO THE FEDERAL MARITIME DOMAIN. Natural Resources Journal 12:615-626 (1972) |
| VP | FLORIDA POLLUTION STATUTE INFRINGES UPON EXCLUSIVE FEDERAL MARITIME LEGISLATIVE DOMAIN. Journal of Maritime Law and Commerce 4(1):163-165 (1972) |

| | |
|---|---|
| IISL | FLORIDA'S SOVEREIGNTY SUBMERGED LANDS: WHAT ARE THEY, WHO OWNS THEM AND WHERE IS THE BOUNDARY? <u>Florida State University Law Review</u> 1: 596-644 (1973) |
| VP | Florio, Franco. SOME REFLECTION ON MARINE POLLUTION AND THE GENERAL PRINCIPLES OF INTERNATIONAL LAW. <u>Water, Air and Soil Pollution; an International Journal of Environmental Pollution</u> 1(3):303-313 (1972) |
| VP | Folker. INTERNATIONALE KONFERENZ UEBER MEERESVERSCHMUTZUNG: LONDON 8.10. BIS 2.11, 1973. <u>Hansa</u> 110:2103-2108 (1973) |
| IIIF | Folsom, William B. THE JAPANESE FISHING INDUSTRY: 1971 HIGHLIGHTS. <u>Commercial Fisheries Review</u> 34:36-40 (1972) |
| VOR | Fonselius, S.H. STAGNANT SEA. <u>Environment</u> 12:2-11 (July, 1970); 12:40-48 (August, 1970) |
| VOD | Forster, Malcolm. CIVIL LIABILITY OF SHIPOWNERS FOR OIL POLLUTION. <u>Journal of Business Law</u> 1973:23-31 (1973) |
| VP | Forster, Malcolm J. THE PREVENTION OF OIL POLLUTION, ACT 1971. <u>The International and Comparative Law Quarterly</u> 21(4):771-774 (1972) |
| IIB | Foster, William A. NEW ZEALAND'S COASTAL JURISDICTION. <u>California Western International Law Journal</u> 1:13-32 (1970) |
| IIIFV&G | FOUR 87-FOOT LOBSTER BOATS INAUGURATE MOST SOUTHERLY LOBSTER FISHERY. <u>Fish Boat</u> 17(14):44-45,63,66 (1972) |
| IIIAFF | Fournier, F. INSTITUTIONAL CONSTRAINTS TO THE DEVELOPMENT OF AQUACULTURE. <u>Marine Fisheries Review</u> 37(1):31-32 (1975) |
| IIIOI | Foussat, P. L'INTERACTION DES ACTIVITIES "OFFSHORE" ET DE PECHE. <u>France Peche</u> 175:30-32 (1972) |
| VLOS | Franck, T.M., et al. AN EQUITABLE REGIME FOR SEABED AND OCEAN SUBSOIL RESOURCES. <u>Denver Journal of International Law and Policy</u> 4:161-186 (1974) |
| VINTL | Franck, Thomas M. "TO DEFINE AND PUNISH PIRACIES" - THE LESSON OF THE SANTA MARIA: A COMMENT. <u>New York University Law Review</u> 36:839-844 (1961) |
| VINTL | Franck, Thomas M., et al. NEW POOR: LAND-LOCKED, SHELF-LOCKED AND OTHER GEOGRAPHICALLY DISADVANTAGED STATES. <u>New York University Journal of International Law and Politics</u> 7:33-57 (1974) |
| VINTL | _____ _____ WORLD MADE LAW: THE DECISION OF THE INTERNATIONAL COURT OF JUSTICE IN THE NUCLEAR TEST CASES. <u>American Journal of International Law</u> 69:612-620 (1975) |
| IVMMR | Franco, A. ARGENTINA PREPS FOR NEW OFFSHORE CAMPAIGN. <u>Oil and Gas Journal</u> 72:103-103 (1974) |
| IVM | Franco, Alvaro. BRAZILIAN FIELD TO BE WATERFLOODED FROM THE BEGINNING. <u>Oil and Gas Journal</u> 70(40):57-61 (1972) |
| IVM | _____ _____ LATIN AMERICA PURSUES MORE OIL SUPPLIES IN COASTAL WATERS. <u>Offshore</u> 33(7):107-108,110,115-116 (1973) |

| | |
|---|---|
| IVMMR | Franco, Alvaro. SUCCESSES SPUR EXPLORATION IN MEXICO. Oil and Gas Journal 70(49):26-27 (1972) |
| IVENV | Frank, Richard A. ENVIRONMENTAL ASPECTS OF DEEPSEA MINING. Virginia Journal of International Law 15:815-826 (1975) |
| VLOS | Franklin, Carl M. THE LAW OF THE SEA: SOME RECENT DEVELOPMENTS. Southern California Law Review 33(4):357-368 (1960) |
| VENV | Franson, R.T., and P.T. Burns. ENVIRONMENTAL RIGHTS FOR THE CANADIAN CITIZEN: A PRESCRIPTION FOR REFORM. Alberta Law Review 12:153-157 (1974) |
| IVMMR | Franssen, Herman T. OIL AND GAS IN THE OCEAN. U.S. Naval War College Review 26:50-66 (1974) |
| VOCET | _____ _____ RESEARCH vs. REGULATION. Oceanus 17:18-23 (1973) |
| VOCET | _____ _____ UNDERSTANDING THE OCEAN SCIENCE DEBATE. Ocean Development and International Law 2:187-202 (1974) |
| VINTL | FRANSSEN, M.K.T. THE ARCHIPELAGIC PRINCIPLE. Oceanus 17:14-17 (1973) |
| VENV | Fraser, J.C. ENVIRONMENT PROTECTION ACT 1970. Law Institute Journal 45:393- (1971) |
| VMT | FREE TRANSIT IN TERRITORIAL STRAITS: JURISDICTION ON AN EVEN KEEL? California Western International Law Journal 3:375-396 (1973) |
| VEZ | Freeman, Robert O. POSSIBLE SOLUTIONS TO THE 200-MILE TERRITORIAL LIMIT. International Lawyer 7:387-395 (1973) |
| IICZM | Freilich, Robert H. MISSOURI LAW OF LAND USE CONTROLS: WITH NATIONAL PERSPECTIVES. University of Missouri at Kansas City Law Review 42:1-132 (1973) |
| VENV | Freimueller, Hans-Ulrich. ENVIRONMENTAL PROTECTION IN SWITZERLAND. Business Lawyer 27:837-840 (1972) |
| IVMMR | French, J.J., Jr. RECENT DEVELOPMENTS IN OIL AND GAS OPERATIONS. Tulane Tax Institute 23:136-162 (1974) |
| IIIF | FRENCH TUNA LOOKS TO AN UNCERTAIN FUTURE. World Fishing 23(6):14-15, 17-18 (1974) |
| VOR | Frey, F. LA 'BATAILLE' DU DROIT DE LA MER. France Peche 167:56-58 (1972) |
| VORM | Friedheim, Robert J., and Joseph B. Kadane. OCEAN SCIENCE IN THE UN POLITICAL ARENA. Journal of Maritime Law and Commerce 3:473-502 (1972) |
| VINTL | Friedheim, Robert L. SATISFIED AND DISSATISFIED STATES NEGOTIATE INTERNATIONAL LAW; A CASE STUDY. World Politics 18:20-41 (1965) |
| IVLOS | Friedmann, W. THE RACE TO THE BOTTOM OF THE SEA. Columbia Forum 12(1):18-21 (1969) |

| | |
|---|---|
| VLOS | Friedmann, W. "SELDEN REDIVIVUS - TOWARDS A PARTITION OF THE SEAS?" American Journal of International Law 65:757-770 (1971) |
| IVINTL | Friedmann, Wolfgang. NORTH SEA CONTINENTAL SHELF CASES: A CRITIQUE. American Journal of International Law 64(3):229-240 (1970) |
| VLOS | Frohnmayer, John E. THE NIXON PROPOSAL FOR AN INTERNATIONAL SEABED AUTHORITY. Oregon Law Review 50:599-618 (1971) |
| IIIFV&G | FROM A GULF YARD, BOATS FOR THE PACIFIC AND ATLANTIC TUNA FLEETS. Fish Boat 19(3):22-23 (1974) |
| IVMMR | Frosch, R.A. MARINE MINERAL RESOURCES: NATIONAL SECURITY AND NATIONAL JURISDICTION. Naval War College Review 21(2):53-60 (1968) |
| VP | Frye, John. TOMORROW'S NUCLEAR POWER PLANTS. NUKES: ALL THINGS TO ALL MEN IN THE 70'S. National Fisherman 52(13):12-15 (1972) |
| VOR | Fukuoka, J. A CONSIDERATION ABOUT PRODUCTIVITY IN THE SUBARCTIC ZONE OF THE NORTH PACIFIC OCEAN. Hokkaido Diagaku, Sapporo, Japan, Suisangakubu, Kenkyu Ino 25(3):230-237 (1974) |
| IVOSTR | FULL SCALE DEVELOPMENT UNDERWAY AT EKOFISK. World Oil 178:114,116 (1974) |
| VENE | Furlong, David B. BILATERAL EXPLOITATION OF NORTH AMERICAN ENERGY RESOURCES - AN INTRODUCTION. Case Western Reserve Journal of International Law 5:36-38 (1972) |
| VINTL | FUTURE OF SCIENTIFIC RESEARCH IN CONTIGUOUS RESOURCE ZONES: LEGAL ASPECTS. The International Lawyer 8:242-261 (1974) |
| IIIF | GABON; NEW FISHING LIMITS. West Africa :1636-1636 (December 4, 1972) |
| VOR | Gadda, David G. TAXATION AS A TOOL OF NATURAL RESOURCE MANAGEMENT: OIL AS A CASE STUDY. Ecology Law Quarterly 1:749-772 (1970) |
| VCS | Gaither, W.S. A PUBLIC AUTHORITY TO MANAGE THE ATLANTIC OUTER CONTINENTAL SHELF. Coastal Zone Management Journal 2(1):59-64 (1975) |
| VORM | Gallup, E.L. SOVEREIGNTY OF THE SEAS AND THE EFFECT UPON NAVAL STRATEGY. Marine Affairs Journal 1:1-8 (1973) |
| IIP&H | GALVESTON'S SUPERPORT PLAN. World Dredging and Marine Construction 10(3):22-25 (1974) |
| VENE | Galway, Michael A. CURRENT VIEWS CONCERNING BILATERAL EXPLOITATION OF NORTH AMERICA ENERGY RESOURCES; A CONTINENTAL ENERGY POLICY - AN EXAMINATION OF SOME OF THE CURRENT ISSUES. Case Western Reserve Journal of International Law 5:65-80 (1972) |
| IIIMM | Gambell, Ray. A SHORT HISTORY OF MODERN WHALING OFF NATAL. Mercurius 14: (1971) |
| VENV | Gammelgard, P.N. OIL AND ENVIRONMENT; THE CHALLENGES OF OUR TIMES. Petroleum Today 12:6-17 (1971) |
| VINTL | Garcia, J. Jorge. EL MAR PATRIMONIAL EN EL CARIBE. Revista de Derecho Puertorriqueno 12:413-425 (1973) |

| | |
|---|---|
| VLOS | Garcia-Amador, F.V. LATIN AMERICAN CONTRIBUTION TO THE DEVELOPMENT OF THE LAW OF THE SEA. <u>American Journal of International Law</u> 68:33-50 (1974) |
| VLOS | Garcia-Robles, Alfonso. SECOND UNITED NATIONS OF THE LAW OF THE SEA - A REPLY. <u>American Journal of International Law</u> 55:669-675 (1961) |
| IVP | Gardner, D., and J.P. Riley. DISTRIBUTION OF DISSOLVED MERCURY IN THE IRISH SEA. <u>Nature</u> 241:526-527 (1973) |
| IVMMR | Gardner, F.J. INTEREST IN OFFSHORE SPAIN REVIVES. <u>Oil and Gas Journal</u> 71:129-129 (1973) |
| IVOI | \_\_\_\_\_ \_\_\_\_\_ NORTH SEA OPERATORS BACK OPTIMISM WITH ACTIVITY. <u>Oil and Gas Journal</u> 71:70-72 (1973) |
| IVMMR | \_\_\_\_\_ \_\_\_\_\_ THE SEARCH NOW SPANS THE GLOBE. <u>Oil and Gas Journal</u> 64:109-120 (1966) |
| IVDRIL | Gardner, Frank J. OFFSHORE OIL INDUSTRY BIG, BETTING BIGGER. <u>Oil and Gas Journal</u> 66:133-138 (1968) |
| IVP | Garner, D., and J.P. Riley. MERCURY IN THE ATLANTIC AROUND ICELAND. <u>International Council for the Exploration of the Sea. Journal du Conseil</u> 35(2):202-204 (1974) |
| VINTL | Garrett, M. ISSUES IN INTERNATIONAL LAW CREATED BY SCIENTIFIC DEVELOPMENT OF THE OCEAN FLOOR. <u>Southwestern Law Journal</u> 19:97-115 (1965) |
| IIIF | Garrod, D.J., and J.G. Pope. STOCKS ET PREVISIONS: L'EVALUATION DES RESSOURCES COMPLEXES DE LA PECHE. <u>France Peche</u> 166:73-75 (1971/1972) |
| VOR | Garron, R. LA RÉPARTITION DES RICHESSES DE LA MER. <u>Droit Maritime Française</u> 25:579-587 (1973) |
| IIIF | Garroz, J.E., and Roche, A.G. THE INTERNATIONAL POLICING OF HIGH SEA FISHERIES. <u>The Canadian Yearbook of International Law</u> 6:61-90 (1968) |
| VLOS | Garruccio, L. KISSINGER L'OSCURO. <u>Affari Esteri</u> 6(23):13-33 (1974) |
| VP | Garton, William A. STATE VERSUS EXTRATERRITORIAL POLLUTION - STATES' "ENVIRONMENTAL RIGHTS" UNDER FEDERAL COMMON LAW. <u>Ecology Law</u> 2:313-332 (1972) |
| IVDRIL | Gascoigne, P. OIL RECOVERY SYSTEM OPERATES EFFECTIVELY IN ROUGH WATER. <u>World Oil</u> 178(7):93-94 (1974) |
| VCS | Gass, James D. THE FRENCH CLAIM TO THE EASTERN NORTH AMERICAN CONTINENTAL SHELF. <u>JAG Journal</u> 27(3):367-391 (1973) |
| VLOS | Gastines, L. de. LA MER PATRIMONIALE. <u>Revue Générale de Droit International Public</u> 79:447-457 (1975) |

| | |
|---|---|
| IIIF | Gates, J.M. DEMAND PRICE, FISH SIZE AND THE PRICE OF FISH. Canadian Journal of Agriculture and Economics 22(3):1-12 (1974) |
| VOR | Gauchi, V. and A. Pardo. THE SEABED: COMMON HERITAGE OF MANKIND. War/Peace Report 8(7):3-6 (1968) |
| IIIF | Gaudilliere, J. LA PECHE FRANCAISE NE DEMANDE QUE L'EGALITÉ DES CHANCES. France Peche 171:41-44 (1972) |
| IIB | Gay, N. THE HIGH WATER MARK: BOUNDARY BETWEEN PUBLIC AND PRIVATE LANDS. University of Florida Law Review 18:553-576 (1966) |
| IVDRIL | Geary, John A. PLANNING FOR SAFETY IN OFFSHORE DRILLING. Petroleum Engineer 44(11):32-35 (1972) |
| VINTL | Gehring, Robert W. DEFENSE AGAINST INSURGENTS ON THE HIGH SEAS: THE LYLA EXPRESS AND JOHNNY EXPRESS. JAG Journal 27:317-348 (1973) |
| VAC | _____ _____ LEGAL RULES AFFECTING MILITARY USES OF THE SEABED. Military Law Review 54:168- (1971) |
| IIIF | GENEROS ALIMENTICIOS E PESCA NO JAPAO. Revista Nacional da Pesca 1971:46-47 (1971) |
| VAC | GENEVA DISARMAMENT CONFERENCE AGREES ON TEXT OF TREATY BANNING EMPLACEMENT OF NUCLEAR WEAPONS ON THE SEABED. Statement by Mr. Leonard. U.S. Department of State Bulletin LXIII:362-366 (September 28, 1970) |
| VOR | Gerard, R.D., and O.A. Roels. DEEP OCEAN WATER AS A RESOURCE FOR COMBINED MARICULTURE, POWER AND FRESH WATER PRODUCTION. Journal of the Marine Technology Society 4:69-70 (1970) |
| VP | Gerks, E.B. NEW HAVEN SUFFERS A SPREADING AILMENT. World Ports 35(4):26-29 (1973) |
| IIIFV&G | GERMANS BUILD 14 SUPER TRAWLERS - BUT WHERE WILL THEY FISH? South African Shipping News and Fishing Industry Review 28(2):63,65 (1973) |
| VLOS | Gerstle, M. THE U.N. AND THE LAW OF THE SEA: PROSPECTS FOR THE UNITED STATES SEABED TREATY. San Diego Law Review 8:573-583 (1971) |
| IIOSTR | Gerwick, B.C., Jr., and E. Hognestad. CONCRETE OIL STORAGE TANK PLACED ON NORTH SEA FLOOR. Civil Engineering 43(8):81-85 (1973) |
| VOSTR | Getchell, D. TREND IS TOWARD INTERNATIONAL CONTROL OF THE SEAS. National Fisherman 49(3):4A-19A |
| VB | GHANA: TERRITORIAL SEA. Svenska Dagbladet :6 (March 29, 1973) |
| IVOSTR | GIANT FLOATING CAPSULE TO STORE OIL ON NORTH SEA. Marine Engineering/Log 78:64-64 (1973) |
| IISL | Gibbs, H. SUBMERGED LANDS. Virgin Islands Bar Journal 2:1-13 (1968) |
| IIIAFF | Gibson, A. A FUTURE IN MARICULTURE FOR IRELAND TECHNOLOGY IRELAND. Technology Ireland 6:7-10 (1975) |

IVMMR    Gibson, J.P.  BOOSTING THE BRITISH EFFORT.  Offshore Services 7(8): 28-30 (1974)

IICZM    Gifford, K. Dun.  SYMPOSIUM: LAND USE REGULATION.  ISLANDS TRUST: LEADING EDGES IN LAND USE LAWS.  Harvard Journal on Legislation 11: 417-461 (1974)

IIIF     Gilbert, DeWitt.  THE CITY-BRED SALMON OF SEATTLE, WASHINGTON.  National Fisherman 52(13):119-120 (1972)

IIIF     _____ _____ INDIAN OCEAN'S ENTRANCING FISHERIES FUTURE.  National Fisherman 52(13):104-105 (1972)

IIIF     _____ _____ SALMON HARVESTING RULES: BONES IN CANADA – U.S. FISHERIES THROAT.  National Fisherman 52(13):28-30 (1972)

IIILOS   _____ _____ U.S. FISHERIES STAKE IN LAW OF SEA CONFERENCE.  National Fisherman 52(13):3-5 (1972)

IIP      Gilbert, J. and R. Robie.  CONTROL OF ESTUARINE POLLUTION.  Natural Resources Journal 11:256-273 (1971)

IIIINTL  Ginsburgs, George, and Scott Shrewsbury.  THE POSTWAR SOVIET-JAPANESE FISHERIES DISPUTE.  Orbis VIII(3):   (1963)

VENV     Giroux, L.  LE DROIT QUÉBÉCOIS DE LA PROTECTION ET DE LA QUALITÉ DE L'ENVIRONNEMENT.  Les Cahiers de Droit 15:5-71 (1975)

IIIAFF   Gitay, A.  MARINE FARMING PROSPECTS ON THE SOUTH AFRICAN WEST COAST.  South African Shipping News and Fishing Industry Review 27(5):50-51, 53 (1972)

VP       Gjoerr, O.E.  CONCRETE IN THE OCEANS.  Marine Science Communication 1(1):51-74 (1975)

IVMMR    Glasby, G.P.  THE MINERALOGY OF MANGANESE NODULES FROM A RANGE OF MARINE ENVIRONMENTS.  Marine Geology 13:57-72 (1972)

VOR      Glaser, E.  LA VALORISATION DES RESSOURCES NATURELLES: DROIT SOUVERAIN D L'ETAT INDÉPENDANT.  Studii şi Cercetări Juridice 19: 63-70 (1974)

VOR      Glassner, Martin I.  DEVELOPING LAND-LOCKED STATES AND THE RESOURCES OF THE SEABED.  San Diego Law Review 11:633-655 (1974)

VOR      _____ _____ THE ILLUSORY TREASURE OF DAVY JONES' LOCKER.  San Diego Review 13(3):533-551 (1976)

VINTL    _____ _____ THE RIO LAUCA: DISPUTE OVER AN INTERNATIONAL RIVER.  Geographical Review 1970:192-207

IIB      Glassner, Martin I., and Michael Unger.  ISRAEL'S MARITIME BOUNDARIES.  Ocean Development and International Law Journal 1(4):303-314 (1974)

VLOS     Goerner, G., and H. Wuensche.  ENTWICKLUNGS TENDENZEN BEI DER KODIFIZIERUNG DES SEEVOELKERRECHTS.  Neue Justiz 29:673-676 (1975)

VAC     Gofman, John W. EXISTENCE OF NUCLEAR WEAPONS: A PRIME ENVIRONMENTAL THREAT. Environmental Affairs 1:782-  (1972)

VENV    Gofman, John W., and Arthur R. Tamplin. NUCLEAR POWER, TECHNOLOGY AND ENVIRONMENTAL LAW. Environmental Law 2:57-73 (1971)

IIOSTR  Golay, M.W. OFFSHORE NUCLEAR POWER STATIONS. Oceanus 17:46-52 (1974)

VP      Gold, Edgar. POLLUTION OF THE SEA AND INTERNATIONAL LAW: A CANADIAN PERSPECTIVE. Journal of Maritime Law and Commerce 3:13-44 (1971)

VLOS    Goldberg, A. U.N. ESTABLISHES AD HOC COMMITTEE TO STUDY USE OF OCEAN FLOOR. American Journal of International Law 62:485-488 (1968)

VLOS    _____ _____ U.S. CALLS FOR U.N. COMMITTEE TO DEVELOP PRINCIPLES FOR COOPERATIVE EXPLORATION AND USE OF THE OCEAN FLOOR. U.S. Department of State Bulletin 58:723-725 (1967)

VP      Goldberg, Edward D. THE SURPRISE FACTOR IN MARINE POLLUTION STUDIES. Journal of the Marine Technology Society 8:29-34 (1974)

IVM     Golden, Paul C. OIL REMOVAL TECHNIQUES IN AN ARTIC ENVIRONMENT. Journal of the Marine Technology Society 8:38-43 (1974)

VINTL   Goldie, D. INTERNATIONAL LAW AND THE DEVELOPMENT OF INTERNATIONAL RIVER BASINS. University of British Columbia Law Review 1:763-776 (1963)

VLOS    Goldie, Louis F. E. CONTENTS OF DAVY JONES' LOCKER - A PROPOSED REGIME FOR THE SEABED AND SUBSOIL. Rutgers Law Review 22:1-66 (1967)

VB      _____ _____ THE CONTINENTAL SHELF'S OUTER BOUNDARY - A POSTSCRIPT. Journal of Maritime Law and Commerce 2(1):173-177 (1970)

VOR     _____ _____ THE EXPLOITABILITY TEST - INTERPRETATION AND POTENTIALITIES. Natural Resources Journal 8:434-477 (1968)

VLOS    _____ _____ A GENERAL INTERNATIONAL LAW DOCTRINE FOR SEABED REGIMES. International Lawyer 7:796-824 (1973)

VCS     _____ _____ THE INTERNATIONAL COURT OF JUSTICE'S "NATURAL PROLONGATION" AND THE CONTINENTAL SHELF PROBLEM OF ISLANDS. Netherlands Yearbook of International Law :237-261 (1973)

VCONS   _____ _____ INTERNATIONAL IMPACT REPORTS AND THE CONSERVATION OF THE OCEAN ENVIRONMENT. Natural Resources Journal 13(2):256-281 (1973)

VP      _____ _____ LIABILITY FOR OIL POLLUTION DISASTERS: INTERNATIONAL LAW AND THE DELIMITATION OF COMPETENCES IN A FEDERAL POLICY. Journal of Maritime Law and Commerce 6:303-329 (1975)

IVINTL  _____ _____ NORTH SEA CONTINENTAL SHELF CASES: A POST-SCRIPT. New York Law Forum 18:411-434 (1972)

IVINTL      Goldie, Louis F. E. NORTH SEA CONTINENTAL SHELF CASES - A RAY OF HOPE FOR THE INTERNATIONAL COURT? New York Law Forum 16:325-377 (1970)

VINTL       _____ _____ NUCLEAR TESTS CASES (AUSTRALIA v. FRANCE 1973 ICJ 99); (NEW ZEALAND v. FRANCE 1973 ICJ 135): RESTRAINTS ON ENVIRONMENTAL HARM. Journal of Maritime Law and Commerce 5:491-505 (1974)

IIIF        _____ _____ OCCUPATION OF THE SEDENTARY FISHERIES OFF THE AUSTRALIAN COASTS. Sidney Law Review 1:34-95 (April, 1953)

IIIINTL     _____ _____ THE OCEAN'S RESOURCES AND INTERNATIONAL LAW - POSSIBLE DEVELOPMENTS IN REGIONAL FISHERIES MANAGEMENT. Columbia Journal of Transnational Law 8:1-53 (1969)

IVP         _____ _____ POLLUTION AND LIABILITY PROBLEMS CONNECTED WITH DEEP-SEA MINING. Natural Resources Journal 12:172-181 (1972)

IIILOS      _____ _____ SEDENTARY FISHERIES AND ARTICLE 2 (4) OF THE CONVENTION ON THE CONTINENTAL SHELF - A PLEA FOR A SEPARATE REGIME. American Journal of International Law 63:86-97 (1969)

IIIINTL     _____ _____ SEDENTARY FISHERIES AND THE NORTH SEA CONTINENTAL SHELF CASES - A PARADOX REVEALED. American Journal of International Law 63:536-541 (1969)

VLOS        _____ _____ TWO NEGLECTED PROBLEMS IN DRAFTING REGIMES FOR DEEP OCEAN RESOURCES. American Journal of International Law 64:905-919 (1970)

VINTL       Goldsworthy, Peter J. COMMISSION OF CUSTOMS OFFENCES IN THE AUSTRALIAN TERRITORIAL SEA: AN ANALYSIS AND SYNTHESIS OF R. v. BULL (1974) 48 ALJR 232. Australian Law Journal 49:16-21 (1975)

IVLOS       Gombos, L. CONTINENTAL SHELF ACT, 1964: OIL SEARCH AND PRODUCTION IN THE NORTH SEA. Law Society's Gazette 61:475-479 (1964)

IIP&H       Goodier, J.L. DEEPWATER PORTS FOR SUPERSHIPS. Civil Engineering 43:45-49 (1973)

VLOS        Góralczyk, W. LEGAL PROBLEMS OF THE PEACEFUL USES OF THE SEA-BED AND THE OCEAN FLOOR BEYOND THE LIMITS OF NATIONAL JURISDICTION. Polish Yearbook of International Law 4:147-170 (1972)

VLOS        _____ _____ LEGAL PROBLEMS OF THE PEACEFUL USES OF THE SEA-BED AND THE OCEAN FLOOR: DENUCLEARIZATION. Polish Yearbook of International Law 5:43-60 (1972/1973)

VP          Gordon, D.C., and A. Walton. MARINE POLLUTION RESEARCH. Dartmouth, Nova Scotia, Bedford Institute of Oceanography. Ocean Science Review 1971-1972:67-74

IIIAFF      Gordon, H.S. MARICULTURE COMES OF AGE. Chemical Engineering 79: 26-28 (1972)

VOI         _____ _____ OFFSHORE INDUSTRY AHOY! Chemical Engineering 80(17): 62-64,66 (1973)

VP          Gordon, Michael M. PRIVATE ACTIONS FOR DAMAGES RESULTING FROM OFF-SHORE OIL POLLUTION. Columbia Journal of Environmental Law 2(1)(1975)

IVMMR       Gordon, R.L. OCEAN RESOURCES AND WORLD MINERAL SUPPLIES. Annalog d'Etudes Internationales 4:109-125 (1973)

IIIF        Gorelick, Jeffrey A. THE ELEVENTH HOUR FOR ALASKA'S SALMON FISHERY: A PROPOSED REGULATORY SOLUTION. Ecology Law Quarterly 3:391-424 (1973)

VINTL       Gormley, W. Paul. THE DEVELOPMENT AND SUBSEQUENT INFLUENCE OF THE ROMAN LEGAL NORM OF "FREEDOM OF THE SEAS". University of Detroit Law Journal 40(5):34p. (1963)

VB          _____ _____ UNILATERAL EXTENSION OF TERRITORIAL WATERS. University of Detroit Law Journal 43(5): 35p. (1966)

VLOS        Gorove, Stephen. THE CONCEPT OF 'COMMON HERITAGE OF MANKIND': A POLITICAL, MORAL OR LEGAL INNOVATION? San Diego Law Review 9:390-403 (1972)

VINTL       _____ _____ INTERNATIONALIZATION OF THE DANUBE: A LESSON IN HISTORY. Journal of Public Law 8(1): (1959)

VP          _____ _____ POLLUTION AND OUTER SPACE: A LEGAL ANALYSIS AND APPRAISAL. New York University Journal of International Law and Politics 5:53-65 (1972)

VINTL       _____ _____ TOWARD DENUCLEARIZATION OF THE OCEAN FLOOR. San Diego Law Review 7:504-518 (1970)

VOCET       Gorshkov, A.S., et al. O VOZMOZHNOSTI ISPOL'ZOVANIIA SOVREMENNYKH AVTONOMNYKH BUIKOVYKH STANTSII DLIA OKEANOLOGICHESKIKH ISSLEDOVANII V RAIONAKH S SIL'NYMI TECHENIIAMI. Meteorologiia i gidrologiia (Moskva) 11:67-74 (1972)

IIIB        Gotlieb, Allan. THE CANADIAN CONTRIBUTION TO THE CONCEPT OF A FISHING ZONE IN INTERNATIONAL LAW. Canadian Yearbook of International Law 2:55-76 (1964)

VINTL       Gotlieb, Allan and Charles Dalfe. NATIONAL JURISDICTION AND INTERNATIONAL RESPONSIBILITY: NEW CANADIAN APPROACHES TO INTERNATIONAL LAW. American Journal of International Law 67:229-258 (1973)

VOR         Gotlieb, Allan E. RECENT DEVELOPMENTS CONCERNING THE EXPLORATION AND EXPLOITATION OF THE OCEAN FLOOR. McGill Law Journal 15(2):260-278 (1969)

IVMMR       Gould, H.R. OFFSHORE PETROLEUM DEVELOPMENT AND POTENTIAL. Maritime Studies and Management 2(3):181-189 (1975)

VINTL       Govindraj. V.C. LAND-LOCKED STATES: THEIR RIGHT TO THE RESOURCES OF THE SEA-BED AND THE OCEAN FLOOR. Indian Journal of International Law 14:409-424 (1974)

IIIINTL     Goy, R. LA NOUVELLE AFFAIRE DES PÊCHERIES ISLANDAISES: LA PROCÉDURE DEVANT LA COUR. Journal du Droit International 101:279-322 (1974)

IIP&H       Graham, Katherine A. THE REGULATION OF DEEPWATER PORTS. Virginia Journal of International Law 15(4):928-957 (1975)

| | |
|---|---|
| VMT | Grandison, W. George, and Virginia J. Meyer. INTERNATIONAL STRAITS, GLOBAL COMMUNICATIONS, AND THE EVOLVING LAW OF THE SEA. Vanderbilt Journal of Transnational Law 8:393-449 (1975) |
| IIIREFS | GRANT-IN-AID. Fish Boat 19(4):39-49 (1974) |
| VREFS | GRANT-IN-AID. Fish Boat 20(4):26-26 (1975) |
| IVM | Gray, A.D., Jr. NORTH SEA: FOREIGN TAX PLANNING FOR OIL AND GAS PRODUCING AND SERVICE OPERATIONS. Tulane Tax Institute 24:354-371 (1975) |
| VCS | GREECE-TURKEY: CONTINENTAL SHELF. Bulletin of Legal Developments 5:49-49 (March 19, 1975) |
| VOI | Green, A.H. SIGNS OF GROWTH AHEAD FOR MARINE INDUSTRIES? Canadian Fishermen and Ocean Science 58(6):19,22 (1972) |
| VP | Green, Harold P. RADIOACTIVE WASTE AND THE ENVIRONMENT. Natural Resources Journal 11:281-295 (1971) |
| VCS | Green, L.C. THE CONTINENTAL SHELF. Current Legal Problems (1951) |
| VP | _____ _____ INTERNATIONAL LAW AND CANADA'S ANTI-POLLUTION LEGISLATION. Oregon Law Review 50:462-503 (1971) |
| VLOS | Greenblatt, G.D., et al. RECENT DEVELOPMENTS IN THE LAW OF THE SEA IV: A SYNOPSIS. San Diego Law Review 10(3):559-598 (1973) |
| VLOS | Greenwald, D.L., et al. RECENT DEVELOPMENTS IN THE LAW OF THE SEA V: A SYNOPSIS. San Diego Law Review 11:691-732 (1974) |
| VP | Greer, E. OBSTACLES TO TAMING CORPORATE POLLUTERS: WATER POLLUTION POLITICS IN GARY, INDIANA. Environmental Affairs 3:199-220 (1974) |
| IIIFP | Gregory, Homer E. SALMON INDUSTRY OF THE PACIFIC COAST. Economic Geography XVI:407-415 (1940) |
| IVOL | Gremillion, C.C. OFFSHORE LEASES IN THE GULF OF MEXICO - JOINT VENTURE AGREEMENTS AND RELATED MATTERS. Oil and Gas Law and Taxation Institute (Southwestern Legal Foundation) 25:205-232 (1974) |
| IISL | Gremillion, J. CURRENT VIEW OF THE TIDELANDS DISPUTE. Institute of Mineral Law 12:17-38 (1965) |
| IISL | _____ _____ TIDELANDS CONTROVERSY AND LOUISIANA'S EXPERIENCE IN THE DISPUTE. Tulane Tidelands Institute 7:77-100 (1963) |
| VENV | Grendon, Alexander. NUCLEAR POWER AND THE ENVIRONMENT. The Forum 8:70-92 (1972) |
| IVP | Greve, P.A. CHEMICAL WASTES IN THE SEA; NEW FORMS OF MARINE POLLUTION. Science 173:1021-1022 (1971) |
| VENV | Grieves, Forest. INTERNATIONAL LAW AND THE ENVIRONMENTAL ISSUE. Environmental Affairs 1:826- (1972) |
| VLOS | Griffin, W. EMERGING LAW OF OCEAN SPACE. The International Lawyer 1:548-587 (1967) |

| | |
|---|---|
| IIIMM | Griffis, Hughes. THE CONSERVATION OF WHALES. <u>Cornell International Law Journal</u> 5(1):99-112 (1972) |
| VP | Grindley, J.R. POLLUTION OF THE SEA. <u>South African Journal of Science</u> 68(6):162-170 (1972) |
| IVINTL | Grisel, Etienne. THE LATERAL BOUNDARIES OF THE CONTINENTAL SHELF AND THE JUDGEMENT OF THE INTERNATIONAL COURT OF JUSTICE IN THE NORTH SEA CONTINENTAL SHELF CASES. <u>American Journal of International Law</u> 64(3):562-593 (1970) |
| VMT | Gross, A. PASSAGE THROUGH THE STRAIT OF TIRAN AND IN THE GULF OF AQABA. <u>Law and Contemporary Problems</u> 33:125-146 (1968) |
| VB | Gross, Avrum M. THE MARITIME BOUNDARIES OF THE STATES. <u>Michigan Law Review</u> 64(4):639-670 (1966) |
| IIIF | GROUNDFISH FISHERIES. CLOSURE OF SEASON. <u>Federal Register</u> 38(39):5357-5357 (February 28, 1973) |
| IVDRIL | GROUPS WILL DRILL 18 PORTUGUESE WELLS. <u>Offshore</u> 33:62-62 (1973) |
| IVP | GROWING PROBLEM OF OIL SPILLS; REASONS AND REMEDIES. <u>U.S. News and World Report</u> 70:52-54 (1971) |
| VINTL | Gruber, M. ON OWNING THE OCEAN. <u>Sea Frontiers</u> 15(3):170-179 (1969) |
| VINTL | Grunawalt, R. ACQUISITION OF THE RESOURCES OF THE BOTTOM OF THE SEA - A NEW FRONTIER OF INTERNATIONAL LAW. <u>Military Law Review</u> 34:101-133 (1966) |
| IVMMR | GUARDING THE TREASURES OF THE DEEP: THE DEEP SEABED HARD MINERAL RESOURCES ACT. <u>Harvard Journal on Legislation</u> 10:596-620 (1973) |
| IVOI | GUIDE TO BRITISH INDUSTRY AT OFFSHORE NORTH SEA. <u>Offshore Services</u> 7(8): (1974) |
| IVMMR | "GUIDELINES FOR NORWAY'S OIL POLICY STILL OBSCURE." <u>Northern Offshore</u> 2:6,9-10,13 (1973) |
| IVOI | GUIDELINES FOR OIL AND GAS EXPLORATION AND DEVELOPMENT ACTIVITIES IN TERRITORIAL AND NAVIGABLE WATERS AND WETLANDS: PROPOSED ADOPTION. <u>Federal Register</u> 40(137):30019-30024 (July 16, 1975) |
| IVDRIL | Guidry, M.J., and C.S. Budnik. ZEPHYR I USES HONEYWELL SYSTEM IN HOSTILE WATERS. <u>Offshore</u> 33(2):119,121 (1973) |
| IVOL | GULF OF MEXICO LEASE SALE. <u>Ocean Industry</u> 8(1):30-30 (1973) |
| IIIF | Gulland, M. LE THON POISSON INTERNATIONAL PAR EXCELLENCE. POUR UNE QUESTION MONDIALE DE LA RESSOURCE. <u>France Peche</u> 166:82-85 (1971/1972) |
| VLOS | Gureev, A.A., and R.S. Kangun. LEGAL POSITION OF SOVIET SHIPOWNERS AND IMMUNITY OF STATE SEA-GOING MERCHANT VESSELS. Translation of <u>Rybnoe Khozyaistvo</u> 8:43-46 (1971) |
| IVSL | Guste, William J., Jr., and Frederick W. Ellis. LOUISIANA TIDELANDS PAST AND FUTURE. <u>Loyola</u> 21(4):817-833 (1975) |

VLOS    Gutiérrez Posse, H. LOS FONDOS MARINOS Y OCEANICOS FUERA DE LOS LIM-
ITES DE LA JURISDICCION NACIONAL Y EL DERECHO INTERNACIONAL CONTEMP-
ORANEO. Federación Argentina de Colegios de Abogados 22:5-13 (1972)

VLOS    _____ LOS FONDOS MARINOS Y OCEÁNICOS FUERA DE LOS LÍMITES DE
LA JURICCIÓN NACIONAL Y L DERECHO INTERNACIONAL CONTEMPORÁNEO. Jus-
tica 32:43-54 (1973)

VB      Gutteridge, Joyce A.C. BEYOND THE THREE-MILE LIMIT: RECENT DEVELOP-
MENTS AFFECTING THE LAW OF THE SEA. Virginia Journal of International Law 14:195-219 (1974)

VLOS    Hafner, G. DIE DRITTE SEERECHTSKONFERENZ DER VEREINTEN NATIONEN.
Oesterreichische Zeitschrift fuer Aussenpolitik 15:3-36 (1975)

VINTL   HAGUE. INTERNATIONAL COURT OF JUSTICE: THE NUCLEAR TESTS CASES.
Harvard International Law Journal 16:614-637 (1975)

VLOS    Haight, G. DEVELOPMENTS IN THE UNITED NATIONS RELATING TO SEA-BED
AND OCEAN FLOOR. Natural Resources Lawyer 2(2):119-130 (1969)

VLOS    _____ SEA-BED AND THE OCEAN FLOOR. The International Lawyer
3:642-681 (1969)

VLOS    _____ SEA-BED DISCUSSIONS IN THE TWENTY-FOURTH GENERAL ASSEM-
BLY. Natural Resources Lawyer 3:405-429 (1970)

VLOS    _____ UNITED NATIONS AFFAIRS: AD HOC COMMITTEE ON SEA-BED
AND OCEAN FLOOR. The International Lawyer 3:22-30 (1968)

VLOS    Haight, G.W. INTERNATIONAL DEVELOPMENTS IN THE LAW OF THE SEA. Private Investors Abroad pp.353-386 (1972)

VINTL   Hale, Richard W. TERRITORIAL WATERS AS A TEST OF CODIFICATION.
American Journal of International Law: Supplement 24:65-68 (1930)

IICR    Hale, S.O. ONE STATE'S WAY TO MEET THE COASTAL RESOURCES CRISIS.
Maritimer 18(2):8-10 (1974)

IIIF    HALIBUT PRICES LEAP UPWARD AS BERING LONGLINERS RETURN. National
Fisherman 53(2):A2 (1972)

IICZM   Hall, Glenna S. ADMINISTRATIVE LAW - SHORELINES MANAGEMENT - JUDI-
CIAL REVIEW OF SHORELINES HEARINGS BOARD DECISIONS. Department of
Ecology v. Ballard Elks Lodge No. 827, 84 Wn.2d 551, 527 P.2d 1121
(1974). Washington Law Review 51:405-424 (1976)

IISL    Hall, Ridgeway M., Jr. INLAND WETLANDS ACT: RECONCILING A COLLISION
OF INTERESTS. Connecticut Bar Journal 48:3-29 (1974)

VENE    Hall, William. THE COMING CRISIS IN NORTH SEA FINANCE. Banker 125:
125-130 (1975)

VINTL   Hambro, Edvard. SOME NOTES ON THE FUTURE OF THE ANTARCTIC TREATY
COLLABORATION. The American Journal of International Law 68:217-226
(1974)

IVDRIL  HAMILTON BROS. FIELD IN NORTH SEA APPEARS TO BE GOOD STRIKE. Offshore 32(11):80-80 (1972)

| | |
|---|---|
| IVDRIL | Hamm, B. LOUISIANA OFFSHORE REVIVED WITH NEW TRACTS TO DRILL. Offshore 33(7):92-92 (1973) |
| IVDRIL | Hammet, D.S. DRILLING IN ULTRADEEP WATER WITHOUT ANCHORS OR GUIDELINES. Petroleum Engineering 46(5):60,62,66,71,74 (1974) |
| IVMMR | Hammond, A.L. MANGANESE NODULES (I): MINERAL RESOURCES ON THE DEEP SEABED. Science 183:502-503 (1974) |
| IVMMR | _____ _____ MANGANESE NODULES (II): PROSPECTS FOR DEEP SEA MINING. Science 183:644-646 (1974) |
| VP | Handl, Guenther. TERRITORIAL SOVEREIGNTY AND THE PROBLEM OF TRANSNATIONAL POLLUTION. American Journal of International Law 69:50-76 (1975) |
| IIIFV&G | HANDLING THE CATCH. World Fishing 23:19-20,23 (1974) |
| IVMMR | Hanreck, R.G.S. PETROLEUM DEVELOPMENTS IN ISRAEL IN 1972. Bulletin of the American Association of Petroleum Geologists 57:2136-2136 (1973) |
| VINTL | Harben, W. SOVIET ATTITUDES AND PRACTICES CONCERNING MARITIME WATERS - A RECENT HISTORICAL SURVEY. JAG Journal 15:149-154 (1961) |
| IVOI | Harbonn, J. SEA FLOOR PRODUCTION SYSTEM WORKS OUT IN PERSIAN GULF. Ocean Industry 7:41-44 (1972) |
| IVMMR | Harders, C. AUSTRALIA'S OFFSHORE PETROLEUM LEGISLATION: A SURVEY OF ITS CONSTITUTIONAL BACKGROUND AND ITS FEDERAL FEATURES. Melbourne University Law Review 6:415-428 (1968) |
| IIIF | Hardy, E. OFFSETTING THE WORLD SHORTAGE OF SALMON: SURPLUS KRILL COULD SUPPORT ANTARCTIC SALMON FISHERY. World Fishing 24(3):72-72 (1975) |
| IVOL | Hardy, G. THE ADMINISTRATION OF OFFSHORE MINERAL LEASING STATUTES IN THE GULF OF MEXICO (LOUISIANA AND TEXAS). Natural Resources Lawyer 1(3):70-104 (1968) |
| VP | Hardy, J.T., and S.A. Hardy. TIDAL CIRCULATION AND SEWAGE POLLUTION IN A TROPICAL MARINE LAGOON. Environmental Pollution 3(3):195-203 (1972) |
| VP | Hardy, Michael. INTERNATIONAL CONTROL OF MARINE POLLUTION. Natural Resources Journal 11:296-348 (1971) |
| VP | _____ _____ OFFSHORE DEVELOPMENT AND MARINE POLLUTION. Ocean Development and International Law Journal 1(3):239-274 (1973) |
| VLOS | _____ _____ REGIONAL APPROACHES TO LAW OF THE SEA PROBLEMS: THE EUROPEAN COMMUNITY. International and Comparative Law Quarterly 24:336-348 (1975) |
| VENV | _____ _____ THE UNITED NATIONS ENVIRONMENT PROGRAMME. Natural Resources Journal 13:177-390 (1973) |
| IIOD | Harger, J.R.E., et al. MARINE INTERTIDAL COMMUNITY RESPONSES TO KRAFT PULP MILL EFFLUENT. Water, Air, and Soil Pollution 3(1):107-122 (1974) |

VLOS      Hargrove, John L. NEW CONCEPTS IN THE LAW OF THE SEA. *Ocean Development and International Law Journal* 1:4-12 (1973)

IVMMR     Hark, Hans-Ulrich and Hubertis Schoeneich. DIE NEUEN ERDOEL-UND ERDGASFUNDE IN DER NORDSEE: STAND UND ENTWICKLUNG DER KW-EXPLORATION IN DEN JAHREN 1971/1972. *Erdoel-Erdgas Zeitschrift* 89(1):3-11 (1973)

IIB       Harlow, B. LEGAL ASPECTS OF CLAIMS TO JURISDICTION IN COASTAL WATERS. *JAG Journal* 23(3):81-95 (1969)

VENE      HARNESSING THE ATOMIC JUGGERNAUT: THE NEED FOR MULTI-LATERAL INPUT IN NUCLEAR ENERGY DECISION-MAKING. *National Resources Journal* 14:411-422 (1975)

IVOI      Harrison, D.S. NEW CONCEPT SPEEDS OFFSHORE DEVELOPMENT. *Petroleum Engineer* 46(5):40,42-43,46 (1974)

IICZM     Harrison, Peter. SPATIAL ASPECTS OF THE PRESSURE FOR SHORELINE DEVELOPMENT: THE EXAMPLE OF PUGET SOUND. *Coastal Zone Management Journal* 2(2):125-148 (1975)

IVOI      Harrison, Rowland J., et al. CANADIAN ARCTIC AND NORTHERN REGIONS AND OTHER SELECTED MATTERS OF CURRENT INTEREST TO THE OIL AND GAS INDUSTRY. SELECTED CASES, LEGISLATION AND DEVELOPMENTS IN OIL AND GAS LAW. *Alberta Law Review* 10:391- (1972)

VMT       HAS WORLD ORDERBOOK TOPPED OUT? *Marine Engineering/Log* 79(7): (1974)

VINTL     Haubert, W.H. TOWARD PEACEFUL SETTLEMENT OF OCEAN DISPUTES: A WORKING PAPER. *San Diego Law Review* 11:733-756 (1974)

IISL      Haueisen, A.J. AN EXAMINATION OF LEGISLATION FOR THE PROTECTION OF THE WETLANDS OF THE ATLANTIC AND GULF STATES. *Gulf Search Reports* 4:233-263 (1973)

IVMMR     Haughton, Daniel J. A PARTNERSHIP FOR THE SEA; PETROLEUM AND SPACE. *World Petroleum* 38:28 (1967)

VENV      Hay, Keith G. OIL AND THE SEA; THE ECOLOGICAL IMPLICATIONS OF A CONTROVERSIAL INVASION. *Journal of the Marine Technology Society* 8:19-20 (1974)

VLOS      Hayashi, M. AN INTERNATIONAL MACHINERY FOR THE MANAGEMENT OF THE SEABED: BIRTH AND GROWTH OF AN IDEA. *Annales d'Etudes Internationales* 4:251-279 (1973)

IIIINTL   Hayashi, Moritaka. SOVIET POLICY ON INTERNATIONAL REGULATION OF HIGH SEAS FISHERIES. *Cornell International Law Journal* 5(2):131-160 (1972)

IVDRIL    Hayward, T. CELTIC SEA: PEMBROKE WAITS FOR RIGS TO MOVE IN. *Offshore Services* 6(1):48-51,59 (1973)

IVDRIL    _____ NO MORE DRILLING UNTIL GAS PRICES RISE? *Offshore Services* 7:27-28 (1974)

IVMMR     Hazzard, J.C., A.E.L. Morris, and S.G. Wissler. DEVELOPMENTS IN CENTRAL AND SOUTHERN AFRICA IN 1970. *American Association of Petroleum Geologists Bulletin* 55:1559-1602 (1971)

| | |
|---|---|
| IVMMR | Head, I. LEGAL CLAMOUR OVER CANADIAN OFF-SHORE MINERALS. Alberta Law Review 5:312-327 (1967) |
| IVMMR | Head, Ivan L. THE CANADIAN OFFSHORE MINERALS REFERENCE. University of Toronto Law Journal XVIII:131-157 (1968) |
| IIE | Health, M. ESTUARINE CONSERVATION LEGISLATION IN THE STATES. Land and Water Law Review 5:351-390 (1970) |
| VP | Healy, Nicholas J., et al. FEDERAL LEGISLATION REGARDING MARINE POLLUTION. American Bar Association Section of Insurance, Negligence and Compensation Law 1971:251- (1971) |
| VP | Healy, Nicholas J. WATER POLLUTION LIABILITY FROM AN INSURANCE STANDPOINT. Houston Law Review 9:662-668 (1972) |
| IIOSTR | Heaney, J. SHELL OUTLINES BRENT, AUK PRODUCTION PLANS. World Oil 176(7):55-57 (1973) |
| IVOI | Heard, J. TAX ASPECTS OF TIDELANDS OPERATIONS. Oil and Gas Institute 15:577-589 (1964) |
| VORM | Hearn, W. THE ROLE OF THE UNITED STATES NAVY IN THE FORMULATION OF FEDERAL POLICY REGARDING THE SEA. Natural Resources Lawyer 1(2):23-31 (1968) |
| IIP&H | Heathcote, K.A. IMPACT OF NORTH SEA OIL ON UK PORTS. Tanker and Bulk Carrier 19(6):28-28 (1972) |
| IIIF | Heck, C.B. COLLECTIVE ARRANGEMENTS FOR MANAGING OCEAN FISHERIES. International Organization 29:711-743 (1975) |
| VOD | Heckroth, C.W. SPECIAL REPORT: OCEAN DISPOSAL - GOOD OR BAD? Water and Wastes Engineering 10:32-38 (1973) |
| IVLOS | Hedberg, Hollis D., et al. LEGAL ASPECTS OF SEABED PETROLEUM AND MINERAL RESOURCE DEVELOPMENT - THE DRAFT UNITED NATIONS CONVENTION ON THE INTERNATIONAL SEABED AREA AND THE UNITED STATES WORKING PAPER SUBMITTED TO THE UNITED NATIONS SEABED COMMITTEE: A SYMPOSIUM. OPENING REMARKS. Natural Resources Lawyer 4:681-682 (1971) |
| VB | Hedberg, Hollis D. THE NATIONAL-INTERNATIONAL JURISDICTIONAL BOUNDARY ON THE OCEAN FLOOR. Ocean Management 1:83-118 (1973) |
| VOCET | Hedgpeth, J.W. THE IMPACT OF IMPACT STUDIES. Helgolaender Wissenschaftliche Meeresuntersuchungen 24(1-4):436-445 (1973) |
| VP | _____ _____ THE OCEANS; WORLD SUMP. Environment 12:40-47 (1970) |
| IIIMM | Heg, James E. CONFERENCE ON THE CONSERVATION OF ANTARCTIC SEALS. Antarctic Journal of the United States 7(3):45-46 (1972) |
| VINTL | Heijmans, A.M.J. ARTIFICIAL ISLANDS AND THE LAW OF NATIONS. Nederlands Tijdschrift voor International Recht 21:139-161 (1974) |
| IVORM | Heinz, R.A. NORTH SEA OIL-WATER MIX. Civil Engineering 45(4):70-74 (1975) |
| VB | Heinzen, B. THREE-MILE LIMIT: PRESERVING THE FREEDOM OF THE SEAS. Stanford Law Review 11:597-664 (1959) |

IIIAFF    Hendricks, Pete. AQUACULTURE: AN OVERVIEW. Hawaii Sea Grant Newsletter 5(12):4-4 (December, 1975)

IVLOS    Henkin, L. THE CHANGING LAW OF SEA-MINING. Annales d'Etudes Internationales 4:281-305 (1973)

VLOS    \_\_\_\_\_ \_\_\_\_\_ A CLOSER LOOK AT SOME ISSUES FOR GENEVA: OCEANS POLICY, MARINE ENVIRONMENT, AND FISHERIES. Columbia Journal of Transnational Law 14:56-79 (1975)

VP    Henkin, Louis. ARCTIC ANTI-POLLUTION: DOES CANADA MAKE - OR BREAK - INTERNATIONAL LAW? American Journal of International Law 65:131-136 (1971)

VLOS    \_\_\_\_\_ \_\_\_\_\_ INTERNATIONAL LAW AND "THE INTERESTS": THE LAW OF THE SEABED. American Journal of International Law 63:504-510 (1969)

VB    \_\_\_\_\_ \_\_\_\_\_ OUTER LIMIT OF THE CONTINENTAL SHELF L.W. FINLAY; A REPLY TO MR. FINLAY. American Journal of International Law 64:62-72 (1970)

VLOS    \_\_\_\_\_ \_\_\_\_\_ POLITICS AND THE CHANGING LAW OF THE SEA. Political Science Quarterly 89:46-47 (1974)

IVOL    Henri, William F. THE ATLANTIC STATES' CLAIM TO OFFSHORE OIL RIGHTS: UNITED STATES v. MAINE. Environmental Affairs 2:827-839 (1973)

IVOL    Henriques, D. THE IMPACT OF RECENT DEVISIONS AND ADMINISTRATIVE PROCEDURES OF THE DEPARTMENT OF THE INTERIOR ON OIL AND GAS LEASING BY THE BUREAU OF LAND MANAGEMENT. Rocky Mountain Mineral Law Institute 14:33-87

IVMMR    Hering, N. NEW KNOWLEDGE ON PROSPECTING AND EXPLORATION OF ORE NODULES DEPOSITS. Meerestechnik 4(1):1-11 (1973)

VB    Hermoso, J. TERRITORIAL SEA. Decision Law Journal 14:723-742 (1958)

VENE    Heronemus, William E. ALTERNATE ENERGY SOURCES FROM THE OCEAN. Journal of the Marine Technology Society 8:35-38 (1974)

VCS    Herpin, E.J., and L.S. Bartlett. TAXATION OF THE EUROPEAN CONTINENTAL SHELF. European Taxation 15:220-241 (1975)

IIIMM    Herrington, Alice, and Lewis Regenstein. PLIGHT OF OCEAN MAMMALS. Environmental Affairs 1:792    (1972)

IIIF    Herrington, W. INTERNATIONAL ISSUES OF PACIFIC FISHERIES. U.S. Department of State Bulletin 55:500-504 (1966)

IIIF    \_\_\_\_\_ \_\_\_\_\_ TRIPARTITE FISHERIES CONFERENCE, TOKYO, 1951 - PROBLEMS AFFECTING NORTH PACIFIC FISHERIES; WITH TEXT OF DOCUMENTS. U.S. Department of State Bulletin 26:340-346 (1952)

VAC    Hersh, S. AN ARMS RACE ON THE SEABED. War/Peace Report 8(7):8-9 (1968)

IICR    Hershmann, Marc J. ACHIEVING FEDERAL-STATE COORDINATION IN COASTAL RESOURCES MANAGEMENT. William and Mary Law Review 16(4):747-772 (1975)

| | |
|---|---|
| IICZM | Hershmann, Marc J., and J.C. Folkenroth. COASTAL ZONE MANAGEMENT AND INTERGOVERNMENTAL COORDINATION. Oregon Law Review 54:13-33 (1975) |
| IVM | Hess, H.D. THE OCEAN; MINING'S NEWEST FRONTIER. Engineering and Mining Journal 166:79-96, no. 8 (1965) |
| VENV | Heyman, Ira M., and R.H. Twiss. ENVIRONMENTAL MANAGEMENT OF THE PUBLIC LANDS. Ecology Law Quarterly 1:94-141 (1971) |
| VOR | Hiatt, B. UNDERWATER MEDICINE. Research News 15(8):20-22 (1975) |
| IIIF | Higgins, E. COOPERATIVE FISHERY INVESTIGATION IN LAKE ERIE. Scientific Monthly 27:301-306 (October, 1928) |
| VP | Higgins, James J. OIL POLLUTION AND THE BRUSSELS CONVENTION. American Bar Association Section of Insurance, Negligence and Compensation Law 1971:266-   (1971) |
| IIIP | HIGH MERCURY LEVELS IN FISH NOT MAN-MADE. Australian Fisheries 32:3-3 (1973) |
| VENV | HIGHWAYS, ENVIRONMENTAL LEGISLATION, AND JUDICIAL REVIEW: THE CHANGING NOTION OF NECESSITY. North Dakota Law Review 50:483-501 (1974) |
| IIENE | Hildreth, Richard G. COAST: WHERE ENERGY MEETS THE ENVIRONMENT. San Diego Law Review 13:253-305 (February, 1976) |
| IICZM | _____ _____ COASTAL LAND USE CONTROL IN SWEDEN. Coastal Zone Management Journal 2(1):1-29 (1975) |
| VP | _____ _____ FEDERAL CONTROL OF WATER POLLUTION: THE REFUSE ACT PERMIT PROGRAM. Business Lawyer 27:567-579 (1972) |
| VMT | Hinz, C. NEUE ZWISCHENSTAATLICHE SCHIFFFAHRTSVEREINBARUNGEN DER BUNDESREPUBLIK DEUTSCHLAND. Hansa 110:1614-1617 (1973) |
| IICONS | Hiscock, K. CONFLICT AND CONSERVATION AT THE COAST OF GREAT BRITAIN. Nature in Focus 17:21-22 (1973) |
| IIIREFS | Hitz, Charles R. CATALOGUE OF THE SOVIET FISHING FLEET. National Fisherman Yearbook 48(13):   (March 13, 1968) |
| VOD | Hodges, J.W. INTERNATIONAL LAW AND RADIOACTIVE POLLUTION BY OCEAN DUMPING: "WITH ALL THEIR GENIUS AND WITH ALL THEIR SKILL ... ". San Diego Law Review 11:757-775 (1974) |
| VLOS | Hodgson, Robert D., and Robert W. Smith. THE INFORMAL SINGLE NEGOTIATING TEXT (COMMITTEE II): A GEOGRAPHICAL PERSPECTIVE. Ocean Development and International Law Journal 3:225-259 (1976) |
| VINTL | Hoeffel, J.M. LA ZONE MARITIME PÉRUVIENNE DE SOUVERAINETÉ ET DE JURIDICTION NATIONALES. Revue Générale de Droit International Public 79:442-446 (1975) |
| VLOS | Hoffman, B. THE SIERRA CLUB AND THE LAW OF THE SEA. Marine Pollution Bulletin 4(4):56-59 (1973) |
| VOSTR | Hoffman, John F. MAN-MADE ISLANDS CAN SOLVE MANY OF OUR PROBLEMS. Ocean Industry 5:48-51 (1970) |

VENV      Hoffman, Kenneth F. ENVIRONMENTAL POLITICS - THE DECIDING FACTOR. Florida Bar Journal 46:576- (1972)

VORM      Hollick, Anne L. THE CLASH OF U.S. INTERESTS: HOW U.S. POLICY EVOLVED. Marine Technology Society Journal 8(6):15-28 (1974)

VLOS      _____ _____ LOS III: PROSPECTS AND PROBLEMS. Columbia Journal of International Law 14:102-111 (1975)

VOCET     _____ _____ NATIONAL OCEAN INSTITUTIONS: RESEARCH NEEDS. Ocean Development and International Law 3:155-170 (1975)

VORM      _____ _____ UNITED STATES OCEANS POLITICS. San Diego Law Review 10:467-499 (1973)

VLOS      _____ _____ WHAT TO EXPECT FROM A SEA TREATY. Foreign Policy 18:68-78 (1975)

IICZM     Hollings, E.F. CONGRESS AND COASTAL ZONE MANAGEMENT. Coastal Zone Management Journal 1:115-118 (1973)

VINTL     Holstein, Thomas O. STATE RESPONSIBILITY AND THE LAW OF INTERNATIONAL WATERCOURSES. Lawyer of the Americas 7:535-555 (1975)

VP        Holt, S.J. POLLUTION IN THE MEDITERRANEAN. Nature in Focus 17:5-9 (1973)

IIIFP     _____ _____ THE FOOD RESOURCES OF THE OCEAN: THE ANNUAL HARVEST IS 55 MILLION TONS, HALF OF WHICH IS CONVERTED INTO FISH MEAL. Scientific American 221:178-194 (1969)

VB        Hood, Peter. SEA-FLOOR SPREADING AND CONTINENTAL DRIFT. Canadian Geographical Journal 80:32-36 (1970)

IIIF      Hoon, C.J. A STUDY OF NORTH PACIFIC FISHERIES CONVENTIONS. Pusan National University Law Review 11(1):35-72 (1969)

IVOI      Hope-Ross, W.J. INSURANCE AND INDEMNITY PROBLEMS IN OFFSHORE DRILLING OPERATIONS. Alberta Law Review 11: (1973)

IVINTL    Horigan, J.E. UTILIZATION OF PETROLEUM RESERVOIRS EXTENDING ACROSS SUB-SEA BOUNDARY LINES OF BORDERING STATES IN THE NORTH SEA. Natural Resources Lawyer 7(1):67-76 (1974)

IVMMR     Horn, D.R., et al. WORLDWIDE DISTRIBUTION OF MANGANESE NODULES. Ocean Industry 7:26-29 (1972)

IVOI      Horning, J.I., and Gerald L. McCurry. DUBAI EXPANDS PRODUCTION SYSTEM. Oil and Gas Journal 70(35):53-57 (1972)

IIICONS   Houghton, A. WILDLIFE AND THE FLORIDA CONSTITUTION. Florida Law Journal 19:247-250 (1945)

IVOI      HOW DANISH NORTH SEA OIL WILL BE PRODUCED. World Oil 175:33-35 (1972)

IVOI      HOW HUMBLE PLANES TO PRODUCE OIL IN THE SANTA BARBARA CHANNEL. Ocean Industry 6:23-28 (1971)

| | |
|---|---|
| IVMMR | Hudson, Luther. SALT WATER IS A MINERAL: OWNERSHIP OF A NATURAL RESOURCE OF INCREASING IMPORTANCE IN OIL PRODUCING STATES. Texas Law Review 50:448-461 (1972) |
| VORM | Hughes, C. RECENT QUESTIONS AND NEGOTIATIONS. American Journal of International Law 18:229-245 (1924) |
| IIIFV&G | Hughes, W.D. AUSTRALIAN LOBSTER FISHERY: GEAR AND METHODS. Australian Fisheries 30(7):4-11 (1971) |
| VENV | Hull, A.R. ENVIRONMENTAL INFLUENCES ON OFFSHORE FACILITIES. Marine Technology Society Journal 8(4):15-21 (1974) |
| VORM | Hull, E.W. Seabrook. THE POLITICAL OCEAN. Foreign Affairs 45:492-502 (1967) |
| VENV | Hull, E.W. Seabrook, and Albert W. Koers. CONVENTION ON THE INTERNATIONAL ENVIRONMENT PROTECTION AGENCY: A PROPOSAL. Boston University Law Review 52:690-701 (1972) |
| IIB | Humbach, John A. TIDAL TITLE AND THE BOUNDARIES OF THE BAY: THE CASE OF THE SUBMERGED "HIGH WATER" MARK. Urban Law Journal 4:91-128 (1975) |
| IIIFP | Hume, R.D. THE FIRST SALMON CANNERY. Pacific Fisherman 11(1):19-21 (1904) |
| IIIMM | HUMPBACK WHALES ARE PROTECTED BY LAW. Hawaii Sea Grant Newsletter 6(2):1,6 (February, 1976) |
| IVLOS | Humphreys, Donald L. INTERNATIONAL REGIME FOR THE EXPLORATION FOR AND EXPLOITATION OF THE RESOURCES OF THE DEEP SEABED - THE UNITED STATES HARD MINERALS INDUSTRY POSITION. Natural Resources Lawyer 5:731-758 (1972) |
| VLOS | _____ _____ LAW OF THE SEA - WILL THERE BE ANY? In Re 5:2,8 (October, 1974) |
| IIP | Hung, T.C. WATER POLLUTION OF KEELUNG - PATOUTZU COASTAL AREA. Acta Oceanographica Taiwanica 3:65-76 (1973) |
| VORM | Hunnings, N. PIRATE BROADCASTING IN EUROPEAN WATERS. International and Comparative Law Quarterly 14:410-436 (1965) |
| IIIAFF | Hunter, C.J. EDIBLE SEAWEEDS - A SURVEY OF THE INDUSTRY AND PROSPECTS FOR FARMING THE PACIFIC NORTHWEST. Marine Fisheries Review 37(2):19-26 (1975) |
| VP | Hunter, Lawson A.W. POSSIBILITIES AND PROBLEMS OF PREVENTING OIL POLLUTION OF THE OCEANS. Transportation Law Journal 4:21-56 (1972) |
| VP | _____ _____ THE PROPOSED INTERNATIONAL COMPENSATION FUND FOR OIL POLLUTION DAMAGE. Journal of Maritime Law and Commerce 4(1):117-139 (1972) |
| VOD | Hunzinger, W. SICHERHEITSASPEKTE DER MEERVERSENKUNG RADIOAKTIVER ABFAELLE. Meerestechnik 6(1):23-27 (1975) |

VOR       Hurst, C. WHOSE IS THE BED OF THE SEA? British Yearbook of International Law 4:34-43 (1923-1924)

VP        Ianni, Ronald W. INTERNATIONAL AND PRIVATE ACTIONS IN TRANSBOUNDARY POLLUTION. Canadian Yearbook of International Law 11:258-270 (1973)

VLOS      Ibler, Vladimar. THE INTERESTS OF SHELF-LOCKED STATES AND THE PROPOSED DEVELOPMENT OF THE LAW OF THE SEA. Indian Journal of International Law 11:389-410 (1971)

VINTL     _____ _____ THE LAND-AND SHELF-LOCKED STATES AND THE DEVELOPMENT OF THE SEA. Annales d'Études Internationales 4:55-65 (1973)

IVDRIL    ICE PLATFORM, SUBSEA METHODS USED FOR ARCTIC OCEAN WELL. World Oil 179(1):79-82 (1974)

VINTL     ICELAND: FISHERIES. Aftenposten :12-12 (August 17, 1972)

IIIT&L    ICELAND; FISHERIES AGREEMENT WITH BELGIUM. International Herald Tribune :3-3 (September 8, 1972)

IIIB      ICELAND; FISHING LIMITS. Financial Times 17: (July 15, 1972)

IIIB      ICELAND/NORWAY: FISHING LIMITS. Aftenposten :1 (June 27, 1973)

IIIINTL   ICELANDIC FISHERIES DISPUTE (FISHERIES JURISDICTION CASE (UNITED KINGDOM v. ICELAND) 1974 ICJ 3): A DECISION IS FINALLY RENDERED. Georgia Journal of International and Comparative Law 5:248-256 (1975)

IIIB      THE ICELANDIC FISHING LIMITS; A SCIENTIFIC STUDY. EFTA Bulletin 14:17-19 (1973)

IIIF      ICNAF PROPOSES 1973 QUOTA LEVELS. Marine Fisheries Review 34:43-44 (1972)

VINTL     Iglesias Buigues, J.L. EL DERECHO AL PABELLÓN DE LAS ORGANIZACIONES INTERNACIONALES. Revista Espanola de Derecho Internacional :339-352 (1971)

IVOL      Ikard, Frank N. OIL INDUSTRY URGES MORE OFFSHORE LEASES. Undersea Technology 14:21 (1973)

IVMMR     AN ILLUSION OF CAMELOT, THE VALIDITY OF A CLAIM, AND THE CONSEQUENCES OF THE NEGOTIATIONS: THE GREAT NODULE SPECTACLE. San Diego Law Review 13(3):667-706 (1976)

VP        IMCO - SECRETARIAT'S DRAFT RESOLUTIONS FOR SUBMISSION TO THE INTERNATIONAL CONFERENCE ON MARINE POLLUTION, 1973 ON THE SUBJECT OF PREVENTION AND CONTROL OF MARINE POLLUTION. Journal of Maritime Law and Commerce 5:151-156 (1973)

IIOSTR    IMPERIAL'S DRILLING ISLAND - SO FAR SO GOOD. Oil and Gas Journal 70(43):67-68 (1972)

IICZM     IMPLEMENTATION OF THE COASTAL ZONE MANAGEMENT ACT OF 1972: A SYMPOSIUM. THE CONCEPT OF STATE AND LOCAL RELATIONS UNDER THE CZMA. William and Mary Law Review 16:717-822 (1975)

| | |
|---|---|
| IVORM | THE IMPLICATIONS OF NORTH SEA OIL AND GAS IN RELATION TO THE U.K. ENERGY AND ECONOMIC POLICIES AND TO BRITISH INDUSTRY. Proceedings. <u>Society for Underwater Technology</u> 3(2):16-20 (1974) |
| VP | IMPORT-EXPORT CLAUSE AND THE CONTROL OF OIL POLLUTION: REGULATORY FEES IMPOSED PURSUANT TO THE POLICE POWER. <u>Boston University Law Review</u> 54:610-636 (1974) |
| IIIOR | THE IMPORTANCE OF OCEAN UPWELLING. <u>Marine Technology Society Journal</u> 8(8):10-16 (1974) |
| VP | IMPROVING THE CAPABILITY TO CLEANUP OIL SPILLS IN U.S. WATERS. <u>Undersea Technology and Oceanology International Offshore Technology</u> 14(2):14-16 (1973) |
| IIP&H | INDIA ENLARGES ORE PORT FACILITIES FOR INCREASED JAPANESE TRADE. <u>Tanker and Bulk Carrier</u> 20(9-10):21,28 (1974) |
| IIIFV&G | INDUSTRIA DE CONSTRUCAO NAVAL. <u>Revista Nacional da Pesca</u> 12(105): (1971) |
| IVDRIL | INDUSTRY ADDS MORE PLATFORM RIGS. <u>Offshore</u> 33(1):52-53,56,58 (1973) |
| VLOS | INFORMATION REPORT ON THE LAW OF THE SEA: UNDERSTANDING THE DEBATE ON THE LAW OF OCEAN SPACE. <u>International Lawyer</u> 8:688-723 (1974) |
| VP | Ingram, G.E., and P.A. Dee. ANALYTICAL TECHNIQUE MAY CUT OIL SPILLS. <u>Oil and Gas Journal</u> 70:75-76 (1972) |
| IIIFP | IN SEARCH OF DIVERSIFIED FISH PRODUCTS TO SATISFY FUTURE NEEDS. <u>South African Shipping News and Fishing Industry Review</u> 28:61,63,65 (1973) |
| IIIFP | INSTANT FISHMEAL FROM MEXICAN INVENTION. <u>Australian Fisheries</u> 31 (10):17-17 (1972) |
| VLOS | INTEGRATIVE POTENTIAL OF THE PROPOSED INTERNATIONAL REGIME FOR THE SEABED. <u>Iowa Law Review</u> 60:148-173 (1974) |
| VINTL | THE INTERESTS OF LAND-LOCKED STATES IN LAW OF THE SEAS. <u>San Diego Law Review</u> 9:701-732 (1972) |
| VINTL | Intergovernmental Maritime Consultative Organization: International Conference on the Establishment of an International Maritime Satellite System. SESSIONAL ACT OF THE SECOND SESSION OF THE INTERNATIONAL CONFERENCE ON THE ESTABLISHMENT OF AN INTERNATIONAL MARITIME SATELLITE SYSTEM, 9-28 FEBRUARY, 1976. IMCO DOCUMENT MARSAT/CONF/27. <u>International Legal Materials</u> XV(2):219-233 (March, 1976) |
| VP | INTERGOVERNMENTAL MARITIME CONSULTATIVE ORGANISATION: MARINE POLLUTION. <u>Guardian</u> :6-6 (October 9, 1973) |
| VP | INTERGOVERNMENTAL MARITIME CONSULTATIVE ORGANISATION: MARINE POLLUTION. <u>Aftenposten</u> (Evening Edition):1-1 (November 3, 1973); <u>Guardian</u> :6-6 (November 3, 1973); <u>Times</u> :4-4 (November 3, 1973) |
| IVOL | INTERIOR GEARING UP FOR DECEMBER SALE. <u>Oil and Gas Journal</u> 70(31): 70-70 (1972) |

| | |
|---|---|
| VINTL | INTERNATIONAL CONFERENCE ON MARINE POLLUTION PROTOCOL RELATIVE TO INTERVENTION ON THE HIGH SEAS IN CASES OF MARINE POLLUTION BY SUBSTANCES OTHER THAN OIL, 1973. American Journal of International Law 68:577-580 (1974) |
| VP | INTERNATIONAL COUNCIL FOR THE EXPLORATION OF THE SEA; POLLUTION. Aftenposten :7-7 (October 5, 1972) |
| IIIINTL | INTERNATIONAL COURT OF JUSTICE: FISHERIES JURISDICTION CASES. International Court of Justice Communique 15:13 (August 4, 1973) |
| VINTL | INTERNATIONAL COURT OF JUSTICE - PROCEDURE - TEMPORARY RELIEF IN THE FORM OF INTERIM MEASURES GRANTED ON PRIMA FACIE EVIDENCE OF JURISDICTION AND JURISDICTION OF THE MERITS FOUND ON BASIS OF PRIOR AGREEMENT TO COMPULSORY ICJ JURISDICTION. Vanderbilt Journal of Transnational Law 7:512-520 (1974) |
| IIIF | INTERNATIONAL FISHERIES: FAEROS. Guardian :2-2 (September, 1973); Aftenposten :7 (September 26, 1973) |
| IIIINTL | INTERNATIONAL FISHERIES REGULATION. Georgia Journal of International and Comparative Law 3:387-407 (1973) |
| IIIINTL | INTERNATIONAL LAW; AFRICA FISHERIES. West Africa :1056-1056 (August 11, 1972) |
| VP | INTERNATIONAL LAW AND CANADIAN ARCTIC POLLUTION CONTROL. Albany Law Review 38:921-942 (1974) |
| VOD | INTERNATIONAL LAW AND RADIOACTIVE POLLUTION BY OCEAN DUMPING: "WITH ALL THEIR GENIUS AND WITH ALL THEIR SKILL..." San Diego Law Review 11:757-775 (1974) |
| IIIMM | INTERNATIONAL LAW; ANTARCTIC WHALING. Financial Times :25-25 (August 2, 1972) |
| VOD | INTERNATIONAL LAW - DISPOSAL OF RADIOACTIVE WASTES IN THE OCEANS. North Carolina Law Review 49:985- (1971) Special Issue |
| VINTL | INTERNATIONAL LAW; ENGLISH CHANNEL POLLUTION. Guardian :7-7 (August 10, 1972) |
| VMT | INTERNATIONAL LAW: IMPLICATIONS OF THE OPENING OF THE NORTHWEST PASSAGE. Dickenson Law Review 74:678-690 (1970) |
| VINTL | INTERNATIONAL LAW; MARINE JURISDICTION - EASTERN EUROPEAN COUNTRIES. Financial Times :6-6 (August 24, 1972) |
| VP | INTERNATIONAL LAW - OIL SPILLS AND THEIR LEGAL RAMIFICATIONS. North Carolina Law Review 49:996 (1971) Special Issue |
| IIIINTL | INTERNATIONAL LAW; SALMON FISHERIES. Aftenposten :6-6 (July 8, 1972) |
| VINTL | INTERNATIONAL LAW SYMPOSIUM. Indiana Law Review 6:172-219 (1972) |
| IIIINTL | INTERNATIONAL LAW - TWELVE-MILE FISHERIES ZONE. Louisiana Law Review 27:625-634 (1967) |

IIIMM      INTERNATIONAL LAW; WHALING QUOTAS. Aftenposten :6-6 (June 11, 1972)

IVINTL     INTERNATIONAL LEGAL IMPLICATIONS OF OFF-SHORE TERMINAL FACILITIES. Texas International Law Journal 9:205-223 (1974)

IVREFS     INTERNATIONAL OFFSHORE DRILLING CONTRACTORS. Petroleum Engineers 47(10):R-34,R-36-R-38,R-40-R-42,R-46 (1975)

IVREFS     INTERNATIONAL OFFSHORE RIG REGISTER. Petroleum Engineer 45:19,21, 23,25 (1973)

IVREFS     INTERNATIONAL OFFSHORE RIG REGISTER. Petroleum Engineer 46:17,19, 21,24 (1974)

IVREFS     INTERNATIONAL OFFSHORE RIG REGISTER. Petroleum Engineer 46(5):21, 23,25,27,29,31,33,35 (1974)

VLOS       INTERNATIONAL REGULATION OF THE OCEANS AND THEIR RESOURCES. Brooklyn Law Review 37:402-425 (1971)

VOR        INTERNATIONAL SEABED RESOURCES: THE U.S. POSITION. Virginia Journal of International Law 15:903-925 (1975)

IIIF       INVESTIMENTOS CRESCEM NE SETOR DA PESCA. Revista Nacional da Pesca 13(108):   (1971)

VORM       IRAN/OMAN: NAVAL OPERATIONS. Bulletin of Legal Developments 3:32-32 (February 12, 1975)

IIIF       Ireland, G. THE NORTH PACIFIC FISHERIES. American Journal of Innational Law 36:400-424 (1942)

IICZM      Irland, Lloyd C. FEDERAL RIVERBASIN PLANNING IN THE COASTAL ZONE: THE LONG ISLAND SOUND STUDY. Coastal Zone Management Journal 2(3): 247-272 (1976)

VENV       Irwin, Frances. LAW SCHOOL AND THE ENVIRONMENT. Natural Resources Journal 12:278-285 (1972)

IVP        Irwin, William A., and Wolfgang E. Burhenne. MODEL WASTE OIL DISPOSAL PROGRAM IN THE FEDERAL REPUBLIC OF GERMANY. Ecology Law Quarterly 1:471-494 (1971)

VP         IS THE MEDITERRANEAN DYING? The New York Times :24 (February 21, 1971)

VOCET      Ishikura, Hidetsugu. MARINE TECHNOLOGY IN JAPAN. Nature 240:209-211 (1972)

VINTL      Ito, F. ANALYSIS OF HUGO GROTIUS' MARE LIBERUM. Hōsei-Kenkyu 2/4: 201-248 (1975)

VINTL      _____ ____ THE THOUGHT OF HUGO GROTIUS IN THE MARE LIBERUM. Japanese Annual of International Law 18:1-15 (1974)

IVOC       Ives, G. ICE PLATFORMS CONCEPT PROVEN FOR ARCTIC OFFSHORE DRILLING. Petroleum Engineer 46:10-11 (1974)

| | |
|---|---|
| VP | Jackson, C.I., et al. DIMENSIONS OF INTERNATIONAL POLLUTION. <u>Oregon Law Review</u> 50:223-258 (1971) Part I |
| IVMMR | Jackson, Henry M. RATIONAL DEVELOPMENT OF OUTER CONTINENTAL SHELF OIL AND GAS. <u>Oregon Law Review</u> 54:567-581 (1975) |
| IVM | JACK-UPS - A FUTURE IN THE NORTH SEA. <u>Northern Offshore</u> 3(4):33-34, 37-38,41-42 (1974) |
| IVMMR | Jacobs, M.B. and M. Ewing. MINERAL SOURCE AND TRANSPORT IN WATERS OF THE GULF OF MEXICO AND CARIBBEAN SEA. <u>Science</u> 163:805-809 (1969) |
| IIIINTL | Jacobs, Michael J. UNITED STATES PARTICIPATION IN INTERNATIONAL FISHERIES AGREEMENTS. <u>Journal of Maritime Law</u> 6:471-529 (1975) |
| IVMMR | Jacobsen, P., Jr., and C.H. Neff. PETROLEUM DEVELOPMENTS IN SOUTH AMERICA, CENTRAL AMERICA, AND CARIBBEAN IN 1972. <u>American Association of Petroleum Geologists Bulletin</u> 57:1868-1933 (1973) |
| IIIF | Jacobson, Jon L. BRIDGING THE GAP TO INTERNATIONAL FISHERIES AGREEMENT: A GUIDE FOR UNILATERAL ACTION. <u>San Diego Law Review</u> 9:454-490 (1972) |
| IIILOS | _____ _____ INTERNATIONAL FISHERIES LAW DEBATED IN CARACAS. <u>Ocean Law Memo</u> 1(4): (August 23, 1974) |
| VLOS | _____ _____ STAKING OUT THE OCEANS. <u>The New Pacific</u> 13-21 (April/May 1974) |
| VLOS | _____ _____ THE THIRD LAW OF THE SEA CONFERENCE: A PESSIMISTIC PREVIEW OF THE UPCOMING GENEVA SESSION. <u>Ocean Law Memo</u> 2(1): (March 15, 1975) |
| IIIB | _____ _____ THE 200-MILE LIMIT CONTROVERSY. <u>Ocean Law Memo</u> 1(2): (July 8, 1974) |
| IVM | Jacobson, Jon L., and Thomas A. Hanlon. REGULATION OF HARD-MINERAL MINING ON THE CONTINENTAL SHELF. <u>Oregon Law Review</u> 50:425-461 (1971) |
| VORM | Jacoby, Neil H. CORPORATE ENTERPRISES IN AN OCEAN REGIME. <u>Columbia Journal of World Business</u> 6:7-21 (1971) |
| VENV | _____ _____ THE ENVIRONMENTAL CRISIS. <u>Center Magazine</u> 3:36-48 (1970) |
| VP | Jaenicke, G. INTERNATIONAL MARITIME LAW AND THE CONTROL OF MARINE POLLUTION. <u>Law and State</u> 4:91-96 (1971) |
| VOR | _____ _____ LEGAL PROBLEMS OF THE EXPLOITATION AND EXPLORATION OF THE SEA. <u>Law and State</u> 6:60-77 (1972) |
| IISL | Jaffee, Leonard R. PUBLIC TRUST DOCTRINE IS ALIVE AND KICKING IN NEW JERSEY TIDAL WATERS: NEPTUNE CITY v. AVON-BY-THE-SEA (BOROUGH OF NEPTUNE CITY v. BOROUGH OF AVON-BY-THE-SEA (N.J.) 294 A.2d 47) - A CASE OF HAPPY ATAVISM? <u>Natural Resources Journal</u> 14:309-305 (1974) |
| VLOS | Jagato, S.P. BASIC ISSUES FOR THE FORTHCOMING CONFERENCE ON THE LAW OF THE SEA. <u>Indian Journal of International Law</u> 14:141-159 (1974) |

VP            Jain, I.C. LEGAL CONTROL OF MARINE POLLUTION. Indian Journal of International Law 13(3):411-424 (1973)

IVOSTR        James, W.P. EFFECTS OF AN OFFSHORE CRUDE OIL UNLOADING TERMINAL ON THE MARINE ENVIRONMENT. Marine Technology Society Journal 9(1):27-31 (1975)

VINTL         Janis, Mark W. THE DEVELOPMENT OF EUROPEAN REGIONAL LAW OF THE SEA. Ocean Development and International Law Journal 1:275-289 (1973)

VORM          _____ _____ NAVAL MISSIONS AND THE LAW OF THE SEA. San Diego Law Review 13(3):583-593 (1976)

VINTL         _____ _____ THE ROLES OF REGIONAL LAW OF THE SEA. San Diego Law Review 12:553-568 (1975)

VP            Jannasch, H.W., et al. MICROBIAL DEGRADATION OF ORGANIC MATTER IN THE DEEP SEA. Science 171:672-674 (1971)

VP            JAPAN: MERCURY POLLUTION COMPENSATION. Times :7 (March 2, 1973)

VB            JAPAN: TERRITORIAL SEA. Bulletin of legal developments 5:46-46 (March 19, 1975)

IIIF          JAPANESE FISHING DISPUTE. Current History 48:54-57 (May, 1938)

IVMMR         JAPANESE INTEREST HIGH OFF SOUTH ASIA. Oil and Gas Journal 72:92-92 (1974)

IIIF          JAPANESE, U.S. AGREE ON SALMON. Business Week 127-127 (July 12, 1958)

IVDRIL        JAPAN'S FIRST FULL SCALE DRILLING AND PRODUCTION PLATFORM. Ocean Industry 9(7): (1974)

IIIF          JAPON: LIMITES LE DROIT A LA PECHE. France Peche 166:85-85 (1971/1972)

IIICONS       Jaworski, M. INTERNATIONAL PROTECTION OF BIOLOGICAL RESOURCES AND THE ENVIRONMENT OF THE BALTIC SEA. Sprawy Międzynarodowe 7:109-118 (1974)

IIENV         Jeane, G.S. ENVIRONMENTAL EFFECTS OF DREDGING AND SPOIL DISPOSAL. Water Pollution Control Federation Journal 47(3):553-561 (1975)

IIP           Jefferies, D.F., et al. DISTRIBUTION OF CAESIUM-137 IN BRITISH COASTAL WATERS. Marine Pollution Bulletin 4:118-122 (1973)

VP            Jeffers, Frederick J. A METHOD FOR MINIMIZING EFFECTS OF WASTE HEAT DISCHARGES. International Journal of Environmental Studies 3(4):321-327 (1972)

VINTL         Jenisch, U. NUCLEAR TESTS AND FREEDOM OF THE SEAS. Jahrbuch fuer Internationales Recht 17:177-194 (1974)

VLOS          _____ _____ TENDENZEN IM INTERNATIONALEN SEERECHT: POST CARACAS 1974. Europa Archiv 29:799-808 (1974)

VORL          Jenkin, P. NORWAY NO MODEL FOR U.K. POLICY. Northern Offshore 3(5): 48,51-52,54 (1974)

| | |
|---|---|
| IIIFV&G | Jenner, John. SOVIETS SUCCESSFULLY TRAWL AT MORE THAN 700 FATHOMS. National Fisherman 53(2):C4 (1972) |
| IVOCET | Jennings, Feenan D. IDOE STARTS MAJOR OCEAN RESEARCH PROJECTS. Undersea Technology 14:23-24 (1973) |
| VLOS | Jennings, R.Y. A CHANGING INTERNATIONAL LAW OF THE SEA. Cambridge Law Journal 31(1):32-49 (1972) |
| VB | _____ _____ THE LIMITS OF CONTINENTAL SHELF JURISDICTION: SOME POSSIBLE IMPLICATIONS OF THE NORTH SEA CASE JUDGMENT. International and Comparative Law Quarterly 18:819-832 (1969) |
| VLOS | _____ _____ THE UNITED STATES DRAFT TREATY ON THE INTERNATIONAL SEABED AREA; BASIC PRINCIPLES. International and Comparative Law Quarterly 20:433-452 (1971) |
| IIIP | Jensen, A.C. SPORT FISHERIES AND OFFSHORE OIL. New York Fish and Game Journal 21(2):105-116 (1974) |
| IIIMM | Jessup, Philip C. THE INTERNATIONAL PROTECTION OF WHALES. American Journal of International Law: Supplement 24:751-752 (1930) |
| VLOS | _____ _____ THE LAW OF THE SEA AROUND US. American Journal of International Law 55:104-109 (1961) |
| IIIF | _____ _____ THE PACIFIC COAST FISHERIES. American Journal of International Law 33:129-138 (1939) |
| VLOS | _____ _____ UNITED NATIONS CONFERENCE ON THE LAW OF THE SEA. Columbia Law Review 59:234-268 (1959) |
| VP | Joelson, Mark R., and Marc L. Fleischaker. WATER POLLUTION CONTROL ACT. Practical Lawyer 20:29-40 (1974) |
| IIIP | Joensen, A.H. DANISH SEABIRD DISASTERS IN 1972. Marine Pollution Bulletin 4:117-118 (1973) |
| IVMMR | Johannessen, K.S. EFFECTS OF OIL AND GAS DISCOVERIES ON THE NORWEGIAN CONTINENTAL SHELF. Northern Offshore 2(1):10,13-14 (1973) |
| IVM | _____ _____ NORWAY MEETS THE OIL AGE. Northern Offshore 3(4):14, 17-18 (1974) |
| IVMMR | _____ _____ WHITE PAPERS AND CONTROVERSY. Northern Offshore 2:14-14 (1973) |
| IIP | John, James E.A. THERMAL POLLUTION: A POTENTIAL THREAT TO OUR AQUATIC ENVIRONMENT. Environmental Affairs 1:287-   (1971) |
| IIIF | Johnson, B. TECHNOCRATS AND THE MANAGEMENT OF INTERNATIONAL FISHERIES. International Organization 29:745-770 (1975) |
| IIWQ | Johnson, Corwin W. LEGAL ASSURANCES OF ADEQUATE FLOWS OF FRESH WATER INTO TEXAS BAYS AND ESTUARIES TO MAINTAIN PROPER SALINITY LEVELS. Houston Law Review 10:598-640 (1973) |
| VMT | Johnson, D. SOME LEGAL PROBLEMS OF INTERNATIONAL WATERWAYS, WITH PARTICULAR REFERENCE TO THE STRAITS OF TIRAN AND THE SUEZ CANAL. Modern Law Review 31:153-164 (1968) |

VOR      Johnson, D. WHO OWNS THE SEA-BED? New Scientist 41:394-395 (February 20, 1969)

VOD      Johnson, H. HAZARDOUS WASTE DISPOSAL STUDIES. Waste Age 4(2):38,40 (March/April 3, 1973)

VMT      Johnson, Ralph W. FREEDOM OF NAVIGATION FOR INTERNATIONAL RIVERS. Michigan Law Review 62:465-484 (1964)

IIIINTL  _____ _____ THE JAPAN-UNITED STATES SALMON CONFLICT. Washington Law Review 43:1-43 (1967)

VINTL    Johnson, Ralph W., and D.M.M. Goldie. EFFECT OF EXISTING USES ON THE EQUITABLE APPORTIONMENT OF INTERNATIONAL RIVERS: I, AN AMERICAN VIEW, BY RALPH W. JOHNSON; II, A CANADIAN VIEW, BY D.M.M. GOLDIE. University of British Columbia Law Review 1(3):389-408 (1960)

IIIF     Johnson, Ralph W., et al. NORTH PACIFIC FISHERIES SYMPOSIUM. Washington Law Review 43(1):307p. (1967)

VORM     Johnson, U. DEPARTMENT REVIEWS HISTORY OF INTERNATIONAL EFFORTS GOVERNING ACTIVITIES ON THE SEABED. U.S. Department of State Bulletin 61:191-194 (1969)

VINTL    Johnston, D. NEW USES OF INTERNATIONAL LAW IN THE NORTH PACIFIC. Washington Law Review 43:77-114 (1967)

VEZ      Johnston, Douglas M. THE ECONOMIC ZONE IN NORTH AMERICA: SCENARIOS AND OPTIONS. Ocean Development and International Law 3:53-68 (1975)

IVOI     JOINT OFFSHORE VENTURES: HOW THEY WORK. AN OILMAN'S VIEW. Marine Engineering/Log 79(4):40,149,151-152 (1974)

VB       Jones, L. INTERNATIONAL LAW - THE THREE MILE LIMIT OR MORE - IT'S ANYONE'S GUESS. Journal of Air Law and Commerce 33:356-361 (1967)

IVP      Jones, Laurence G., et al. JUST HOW SERIOUS WAS THE SANTA BARBARA OIL SPILL? Ocean Industry 4:53-56 (1969)

VP       Jones, T.B. WATER POLLUTION CONTROL LAW IN SWEDEN. The International Lawyer 8:478-491 (1974)

VMLAD    Jones, W.Jay PERSONAL INJURY - OFFSHORE OIL OPERATIONS. Natural Resources Lawyer 5:681-730 (1972)

VP       Jordan, F.J.E. GREAT LAKES POLLUTION: A FRAMEWORK FOR ACTION. Ottawa Law Review 5:65-83 (1971)

VINTL    Jorge García, J. LA MAR PATRIMONIAL EN EL CARIBE. Revista de Derecho Puertorriqueño 48:413-423 (1973)

IVMMR    Joseph, William. OFFSHORE PETROLEUM; WHERE THE INDUSTRY IS HEADED. Undersea Technology 11:22 (1970)

VENV     Joyner, Christopher C. STOCKHOLM IN RETROSPECT: PROGRESS IN THE INTERNATIONAL LAW OF ENVIRONMENT. World Affairs 136:347-463 (1974)

VLOS     _____ _____ TOWARDS A LEGAL REGIME FOR THE INTERNATIONAL SEA-BED: THE SOVIET UNION'S EVOLVING PERSPECTIVE. Virginia Journal of International Law 15(4):871-901 (1975)

| | |
|---|---|
| VLOS | Joyner, Nancy D., and Christopher C. Joyner. PRESCRIPTIVE ADMINISTRATIVE PROPOSAL: AN INTERNATIONAL MACHINERY FOR CONTROL OF THE HIGH SEAS. The International Lawyer 8:57-73 (1974) |
| IIIAFF | Joyner, Timothy. FARMING THE OCEAN RANGE. Pacific Northwest Sea. 8(4): (1975); 9(1):12-15 (1976) |
| IIIF | _____ _____ SALMON FOR NEW ENGLAND FISHERIES. PARTS I - III. Marine Fisheries Review 35:1-13 (1973) |
| IIIINTL | JUDGMENT BY COURT IN ANGLO-NORWEGIAN CASE. U.N. Bulletin 12:19-19 (January 1, 1952) |
| VP | JUDICIAL ALTERATION OF ADMINISTRATIVE WATER POLLUTION STANDARDS. Urban Law Annual 7:362-369 (1974) |
| VP | JUDICIAL REVIEW AND THE 1972 AMENDMENTS TO THE FEDERAL WATER POLLUTION CONTROL ACT: AND WHO SHALL GUARD THE GUARDS? Northwestern University Law Review 68:770-809 (1973) |
| VP | Juergensmeyer, Julian C. AMERICAN LEGAL SYSTEM AND ENVIRONMENTAL POLLUTION. University of Florida Law Review 23:439-450 (1971) |
| IIWQ | _____ _____ TENNESSEE WATER QUALITY CONTROL ACT OF 1971: A SIGNIFICANT NEW ENVIRONMENTAL STATUTE. Vanderbilt Law Review 25:323-330 (1972) |
| VP | Jurick, Fred. TACKLING WASTE PROBLEMS. Sea Grant '70s 5(11):5-5 (1975) |
| IIIINTL | JURISDICTION OF THE INTERNATIONAL COURT OF JUSTICE UNDER COMPROMISSORY CLAUSE IN EXCHANGE OF NOTES. FISHERIES JURISDICTION CASE (UNITED KINGDOM v. ICELAND ICJ REPORTS 1973). American Journal of International Law 67:563-678 (1973) |
| VOD | JURISDICTION OVER VESSEL-SOURCE POLLUTION. Record of the Association of the Bar of the City of New York 30:231-254 (1975) |
| VORM | Kadane, Joseph B., and Robert L. Friedheim. OCEAN SCIENCE IN THE UN POLITICAL ARENA. Journal of Maritime Law and Commerce 3:473-502 (1972) |
| IIIFP | Kahn, Leslie N. SQUID PROTEIN CONCENTRATES. Lebensmittelwissenschaft- und Technologie 8:64-69,70-74 (1975) |
| VAC | Kalinkan, G. MILITARY USE OF THE SEA-BED SHOULD BE BANNED. International Affairs (Moscow) 45-48 (1969) |
| VINTL | Kalinkan, G.F. PROBLEMS OF LEGAL REGULATION OF SEABED USES BEYOND THE LIMITS OF THE CONTINENTAL SHELF. Ocean Development and International Law 3:69-86,127-153 (1975) |
| IVP | Kalman, Paul. OIL AND WATER: CAN THEY MIX? Field and Stream 79:55, 149-150,152,154-156 (1975) |
| IVP | Kalsi, Swadesh S. OIL IN NEPTUNE'S KINGDOM: PROBLEMS AND RESPONSES TO CONTAIN ENVIRONMENTAL DEGRADATION OF THE OCEANS BY OIL POLLUTION. Environmental Affairs 3:79-108 (1974) |

VLOS    Kalsi, Swadesh S. PROBLEMS IN NEGOTIABILITY OF THE U.S. DRAFT CONVENTION ON THE SEABED. International Bar Journal :70-83 (November, 1973)

IVOL    Kalter, Robert J., et al. THE ECONOMICS OF OUTER CONTINENTAL SHELF LEASING. American Journal of Agricultural Economics 57:251-258 (1975)

VLOS    Kamat, D.A. RECENT DEVELOPMENTS IN THE LAW RELATING TO THE SEA-BED. Indian Law Journal 11:9-19 (1971)

IVMMR   Kamer, Hansrudolf. NORWAY AND THE USSR SQUARE OFF IN THE ARCTIC. Swiss Review of World Affairs 24:4-7 (1974)

VINTL   Kamminga, M. CHINA'S MARITIME POLICY. International Spectator 28:222-226 (1974)

VOR     Kanenas (pseudonym) WIDE LIMITS AND 'EQUITABLE' DISTRIBUTION OF SEA-BED RESOURCES. Ocean Development and International Law Journal 1:137-158 (1973)

VLOS    Kapoor, S.K. SUGGESTIONS FOR AN APPROPRIATE AND VIABLE INTERNATIONAL LEGAL REGIME INCLUDING AN INTERNATIONAL MACHINERY OVER THE DEEP SEA FLOOR. Lawyer Madras 5:8-17 (1973)

IIP     Karpuzcu, M. POLLUTION PROBLEM OF THE GOLDEN HORN. Marine Pollution Bulletin 5:26-27 (1974)

VP      Kashiwa, Shiro, et al. REFUSE ACT OF 1899 - WILL IT CURB INDUSTRIAL WASTES? A PANEL. Federal Bar Journal 30:327-342 (1971)

VOI     Katz, H. PRODUCTIVITY IN THE MARITIME INDUSTRY. Journal of Maritime Law and Commerce 6:449-459 (1975)

IVMMR   Katz, H.R. PETROLEUM DEVELOPMENTS IN NEW ZEALAND DURING 1970. American Association of Petroleum Geologists Bulletin 55:1657-1661 (1971)

IVMMR   _____ _____ PETROLEUM DEVELOPMENTS IN NEW ZEALAND DURING 1972. American Association of Petroleum Geologists Bulletin 57:2109-2113 (1973)

IIIEZ   Katz, S.R. CONSEQUENCES OF THE ECONOMIC ZONE FOR CATCH OPPORTUNITIES OF FISHING NATIONS. Maritime Studies and Management 2(3):144-153 (1975)

VOCET   Kaufmann, Sidney. SEABED TECHNOLOGY. Texas International Law Forum 5:195-203 (1970)

VOCET   Kay, D. INTERNATIONAL TRANSFER OF MARINE TECHNOLOGY: THE TRANSFER PROCESS AND INTERNATIONAL ORGANIZATIONS. Ocean Development and International Law Journal 2:351-377 (1974)

IIIF    Kearney, R.E. SKIPJACK TUNA FISHING IN PAPUA NEW GUINEA, 1970-1973. Marine Fisheries Review 37(2):5-8 (1975)

IVP     Keener, Kenneth C. FEDERAL WATER POLLUTION LEGISLATION AND REGULATIONS WITH PARTICULAR REFERENCE TO THE OIL INDUSTRY. Natural Resources Lawyer 4:484-504 (1971)

| | |
|---|---|
| IIOSTR | Kehnemuyi, M. FLOATING NUCLEAR ELECTRIC GENERATING PLANTS. Society for Underwater Technology Journal 1(1):23-26 (1975) |
| IVMMR | Kennedy, J.L. NORTH SEA PLANS TURNED INTO TANGIBLES. Oil and Gas Journal 71:65-69 (1973) |
| IVDRIL | Kennedy, John L. OP DRILLING PASSES SATELLITE TEST, GEARS FOR EXPANSION. Oil and Gas Journal 70(35):84,87-88 (1972) |
| VMT | _____ _____ SUB DEVELOPED FOR HOSTILE WATERS. Oil and Gas Journal 71:51-55 (June 4, 1973) |
| IVMMR | Kennedy, T. SOUTH EAST ASIA: POTENTIAL OF THE PACIFIC. Petroleum Engineer 46:68,71-72 (1974) |
| IIIAFF | Kennedy, W.A. PRELIMINARY STUDY OF SABLEFISH CULTURE; A POTENTIAL NEW INDUSTRY. Canada Fisheries Research Board Journal 29(2):207-210 (1972) |
| VENV | Kennedy, William F. NUCLEAR ELECTRIC POWER AND THE ENVIRONMENT - NEW REGULATORY STRUCTURES AND PROCEDURES. Atomic Energy Law Journal 13:293-304 (1972) |
| VENV | Kennedy, W.V., and B.B. Hanshaw. EFFECTIVENESS OF IMPACT STATEMENTS; THE U.S. ENVIRONMENTAL POLICY ACT OF 1969. Ekistics 37:19-22 (1974) |
| IVMMR | Kennett, W.E. PETROLEUM DEVELOPMENTS IN FAR EAST IN 1972. American Association of Petroleum Geologists Bulletin 57:2085-2108 (1973) |
| IICONS | Kenney, Nathaniel T. OUR CHANGING ATLANTIC COASTLINE. National Geographic Magazine 112:860-867 (1962) |
| VOR | Kenny, J. OWNERSHIP OF THE TREASURES OF THE SEA. William and Mary Law Review 9:383-401 (1967) |
| VP | Kenward, M. GOODBYE TO EXPLODING OIL TANKERS. Canadian Shipping and Marine Engineering 46:23,29 (1975) |
| VMT | Kestermann, Frank. SHIPPING AND PORT OPERATIONS IN THE PERSIAN GULF. Journal of Maritime Law 7:315-326 (1975) |
| IVOI | Kesterman, Frank, and E.L. Towle. CARIBBEAN WEIGHS IMPACT OF STEPPED UP OIL INDUSTRY ACTIVITY. Journal of Maritime Law and Commerce 4:517-523 (1973) |
| IVDRIL | Kesterman, Frank R., and Keith G. Hay. DOMESTIC OFFSHORE DRILLING AND U.S. ENERGY OPTIONS. Journal of Maritime Law and Commerce 5:701-710 (1974) |
| VP | Ketchum, B. A REALISTIC LOOK AT OCEAN POLLUTION. Marine Technology Society Journal 7:8-15 (1973) |
| IVOI | KEY NORTH SEA OILFIELDS TO WATCH THIS SUMMER. Offshore Services 7(5):39-39 (1974) |
| VC | Khadduri, M. CLOSURE OF THE SUEZ CANAL TO ISRAELI SHIPPING. Law and Contemporary Problems 33:147-157 (1968) |
| IIIINTL | Khan, R. THE FISHERIES JURISDICTION CASE. Indian Journal of International Law 15:1-16 (1975) |

VP          Khan, Rahmatullah. MARINE POLLUTION AND INTERNATIONAL LEGAL CONTROLS. Indian Journal of International Law 13(3):389-410 (1973)

IIIOR       _____ ON THE FAIRER AND EQUITABLE SHARING OF THE FISHERY RESOURCES OF THE OCEANS. Indian Journal of International Law 13:87-95 (1973)

VLOS        Khslestov, O. INTERNATIONAL-LEGAL PROBLEMS OF THE WORLD OCEAN. International Affairs (Moscow) 49:34-44 (1973)

VOR         Kierr, R. BEYOND THE BLUE HORIZON. Louisiana Bar Journal 15:105-116 (1967)

IICONS      Kifer, Robert R. NOAA'S MARINE SANCTUARY PROGRAM. Coastal Zone Management Journal 2(2):177-188 (1975)

VB          Kikuchi, T. DELIMITATION OF THE CONTINENTAL SHELF OF THE EAST CHINA SEA. Meijo Law Review 22(3/4):1-51 (1973)

VLOS        Kildow, J.T. THE LAW OF THE SEA: ALLIANCES AND DIVISIVE ISSUES IN INTERNATIONAL OCEAN NEGOTIATIONS. San Diego Law Review 11:558-578 (1974)

IVDRIL      Killey, J.M. DRILLING AND SERVICE CONTRACTS IN OFFSHORE OIL AND GAS OPERATIONS. Alberta Law Review 11:    (1973)

VP          Kimball, J.D. POLLUTION - RIGHT OF SHIPOWNER TO CONTRIBUTION FROM UNITED STATES WHERE NEGLIGENCE OF COAST GUARD WAS A CAUSE OF CASUALTY AND ENSUING SPILL. BURGESS v. THE TAMANO, 373 F.Supp. 839 (D.ME. 1974). Journal of Maritime Law and Commerce 6(4):665-667 (1975)

VP          _____ POLLUTION - SHIPOWNER'S LIABILITY NOT LIMITED BY LIMITATION OF LIABILITY ACT. THE OCEAN EAGLE, 1974 A.M.C. 1629 (D.P.R. 1974) (DICTUM). Journal of Maritime Law and Commerce 6(4):661-664 (1975)

IIB         King, A. THE FORESHORE: HAVE THE PUBLIC ANY RIGHTS OVER IT? New Zealand Law Journal 44:254-258 (1968)

IVMMR       King, R.E. INTEREST FOCUSES ON NORTH SEA, GULF OF MEXICO, FAR EAST. World Oil 177(1):75-80 (1973)

IVMMR       _____ LOUISIANA OFFSHORE HAS TOP DISCOVERY POTENTIAL IN 1973. World Oil 176(5):59-62,75 (1973)

IVMMR       _____ NORTH SEA GEOLOGY FAVORS MORE GIANT GAS/OIL FINDS. World Oil 175(4):35-39 (1972)

IVMMR       _____ PETROLEUM EXPLORATION AND PRODUCTION IN EUROPE DURING 1970. American Association of Petroleum Geologists Bulletin 55:1483-1530 (1971)

IVMMR       _____ PETROLEUM EXPLORATION AND PRODUCTION IN EUROPE IN 1972. American Association of Petroleum Geologists Bulletin 57:1934-1983 (1973)

IVMT        Kirby, J.H. SVILUPPI NEI TRASPORTI OCEANICI DEL PETROLIO. Mondo Economico 24:29-32 (1969)

| | |
|---|---|
| VENV | Kirchner, John E. LAW OF ENVIRONMENTAL RESPONSIBILITY: A NEW FIELD FOR THE MILITARY LAWYER. Military Law Review 58:137- (1972) |
| VP | Kirgis, Frederic L., Jr. EFFECTIVE POLLUTION CONTROL IN INDUSTRIAL-IZED COUNTRIES: INTERNATIONAL ECONOMIC DISINCENTIVES, POLICY RESPONSES, AND THE GATT. Michigan Law Review 70:859-918 (1972) |
| VP | Kiss, A.C. UN CAS DE POLLUTION INTERNATIONALE: L'AFFAIRE DES BOUES ROUGES. Journal du Droit International 102:207,237 (1975) |
| IVOSTR | Kitchen, J.S. LESSONS FROM THE "SEA GEM": LEGAL ASPECTS OF SAFETY AND DISCIPLINE ON OFFSHORE OIL RIGS. Maritime Studies and Management 1:232-242 (1974) |
| VB | Klein, Carl B. THE TERRITORIAL WATERS OF ARCHIPELAGOS. Federal Bar Journal 26(4):317-323 (1966) |
| VINTL | Klemm, U.D. DER STREIT UM DEN FESTLAND-SOCKEL IN DER AGAEIS. Recht der Internationalen Wirtschaft 21:568-574 (1975) |
| IIIF | Klima, E.F. DEVELOPMENT OF AN ADVANCED HIGH SEAS FISHERY AND PROCESSING SYSTEM. Journal of the Marine Technology Society 4:80-87 (1970) |
| VOR | Klima, O.F. THE OCEAN; UNEXPLOITED OPPORTUNITIES. Harvard Business Review 46:140-156 (1968) |
| VOR | Klima, Otto, and Gibson M. Wolfe. THE OCEANS; ORGANIZING FOR ACTION. Harvard Business Review 46:98-112 (1968) |
| VP | Kline, Jerome N. INTERGOVERNMENTAL RELATIONS IN THE CONTROL OF WATER POLLUTION. Natural Resources Lawyer.4:505-536 (1971) |
| VP | Klotz, John C. ARE OCEAN POLLUTERS SUBJECT TO UNIVERSAL JURISDICTION - CANADA BREAKS THE ICE. The International Lawyer 6:706-717 (1972) |
| VLOS | Knauss, John A. DEVELOPMENTS OF THE FREEDOM OF SCIENTIFIC RESEARCH ISSUE OF THE THIRD LAW OF THE SEA CONFERENCE. Ocean Development and International Law Journal 1:93-120 (1973) |
| VLOS | _____ _____ MARINE SCIENCE AND THE 1974 LAW OF THE SEA CONFERENCE. Science 184:1335-1341 (1974) |
| IICZM | Knecht, R.W. COASTAL ZONE MANAGEMENT ACT: A BROADER SCOPE FOR STATE INITIATIVE. Water Spectrum 5(1):32-36 (1973) |
| IICZM | _____ _____ COASTAL ZONE MANAGEMENT - A FEDERAL PERSPECTIVE. Coastal Zone Management Journal 1:123-128 (1973) |
| IVMMR | Knight, H. Gary. THE DEEP SEABED HARD MINERAL RESOURCES ACT - A NEGATIVE VIEW. San Diego Law Review 10:446-466 (1973) |
| VLOS | _____ _____ DRAFT UNITED NATIONS CONVENTIONS ON THE INTERNATIONAL SEABED AREA: BACKGROUND, DESCRIPTION, AND SOME PRELIMINARY THOUGHTS. San Diego Law Review 8:459-550 (1971) |
| IIIINTL | _____ _____ INTERNATIONAL LAW OF FISHERIES. LSU Marine Science Teaching Aid 2: (January, 1973) |

IIP&H    Knight, H. Gary. INTERNATIONAL LEGAL ASPECTS OF DEEP DRAFT HARBOR FACILITIES. Journal of Maritime Law and Commerce 4(3):367-395 (1973)

IIILOS    _____ _____ ISSUES BEFORE THE THIRD UNITED NATIONS CONFERENCE ON THE LAW OF THE SEA. Louisiana Law Review 34:155-196 (1974)

VINTL    _____ _____ JURISDICTIONAL ISSUES IN OCEAN MANAGEMENT. The Columbia Journal of World Business 10:5-14 (1975)

VLOS    _____ _____ LAW OF THE SEAS NEGOTIATIONS 1971-1972. San Diego Law Review 9:383-389 (1972)

VB    _____ _____ THE 1971 UNITED STATES PROPOSALS ON THE BREADTH OF THE TERRITORIAL SEA AND PASSAGE THROUGH INTERNATIONAL STRAITS. Oregon Law Review 51(4):759-787 (1972)

IICZM    _____ _____ PROPOSED SYSTEMS OF COASTAL ZONE MANAGEMENT: AN INTERIM ANALYSIS. Natural Resources Lawyer 3(4):599-619 (1970)

VOR    _____ _____ A REPLY TO "DEEP SEA'S ADVENTURES: GROTIUS REVISITED." International Lawyer 9:751-753 (1975)

VORM    _____ _____ UNITED STATES OCEANS POLICY: PERSPECTIVE 1974. Notre Dame Lawyer 49:241-275 (1973)

VINTL    Knijff, D. VAREN ONDER VREEMDE VLAG. Tijdskrift Voor Venootschappen, Verenigingen en Stichtingen 16:302-310 (1973)

VMMR    Knodell, John D., Jr. PROBLEMS OF DEVELOPMENT OF OIL AND GAS RESOURCES IN ALASKA. Rocky Mountain Mineral Law Institute 17:525- (1972)

IVDRIL    Knutsen, O. POWER SYSTEMS FOR OFFSHORE RIGS. Northern Offshore 3:51-52,55-56 (1974)

VSUB    Koblick, Ian, et al. UNDERSEA LABS FOR MARINE RESOURCE INVENTORY. Journal of the Marine Technology Society 8:12-18 (1974)

VP    Koburger, C.W., Jr. THE SHADOW OF TORREY CANYON: A STATUS REPORT ON THE U.S. COAST GUARD'S POLLUTION R & D. Naval Engineers Journal 86(1):28-30 (1974)

IIIP    Koemann, J.H. MERCURY AND SELENIUM IN MARINE MAMMALS AND BIRDS. Science of the Total Environment 3:279-287 (1975)

IIIP    Koemann, J.H., et al. PERSISTENT CHEMICALS IN MARINE MAMMALS. T.N.O. - Nieuws 27(10):570-578 (1972)

IIIINTL    Koers, Albert W. THE ENFORCEMENT OF INTERNATIONAL FISHERIES AGREEMENTS. Netherlands Yearbook of International Law :1-31 (1970)

IIILOS    _____ _____ FISHERY PROPOSALS IN THE UNITED NATIONS SEABED COMMITTEE: AN EVALUATION. Journal of Maritime Law and Commerce 5:183-209 (1974)

IIIINTL    _____ _____ THE INTERNATIONAL REGULATION OF MARINE FISHERIES; SOME PROBLEMS AND PROPOSALS. Annales d'Études Internationales 4:191-211 (1973)

VORM      Kolb, Kenneth H.  CONGRESS AND THE OCEAN POLICY PROCESS.  Ocean Development and International Law Journal 3:261-286 (1976)

VINTL     Kolodkin, A.L., and V.D. Pisarev.  PROBLEM OF SEABED IN THE US INTERNATIONAL LAW DOCTRINE.  Soviet Yearbook of International Law 1971:143-152 (1973)

IIB       Komar, Paul D., et al.  OREGON COAST SHORELINE CHANGES DUE TO JETTIES.  Journal of the Waterways, Harbors and Coastal Engineering Division, ASCE 102(WWI):13-30 (1976)

VLOS      Kopal, V.  FUNDAMENTAL QUESTIONS OF THE LEGAL REGIME OF THE SEABED.  Pravnik 112:493-519 (1973)

IIIF      Kostyuchenko, V.A.  REGULATION OF THE GOBIIDAE FISHERY IN THE AZOV SEA.  Canada Fisheries Research Board Trans. of Trudy Vsesoyuznogo Nauchno-Issledovatel'skogo Instituta Morskogo Rynogo Kozaistva i Okeanogrifii 71(2):51-67 (1970)

VB        Koulouris, M.  LES DROITS SOUVERAINS SUR LE PLATEAU CONTINENTAL.  Revue Hellénique de Droit International 24:292-308 (1971)

VOR       _____ _____ LES DROITS SOUVERAINS SUR LE PLATEAU CONTINENTAL EN VUE DE L'EXPLORATION ET D L'EXPLOITATION.  Egypte Contemporaine 64(352):87-101 (1973)

VB        Kovalyov, F.  TERRITORIAL WATERS AND INTERNATIONAL LAW.  International Affairs (Moscow) 6:41-46 (1974)

IISL      Kramon, James M.  SECTION 10 OF THE RIVERS AND HARBORS ACT:  THE EMERGENCE OF A NEW PROTECTION FOR TIDAL MARSHES.  Maryland Law Review 33:229-264 (1973)

VLOS      Krieger, K.F.  DIE ENTWICKLUNG DES SEERECHTS IM MITTELMEERRAUM VON DER ANTIKE BIS ZUM CONSOLAT DE MAR.  Jahrbuch fuer Internationales Recht 16:179-208 (1973)

VAC       Krieger, Walter W., Jr.  UNITED NATIONS TREATY BANNING NUCLEAR WEAPONS AND OTHER WEAPONS OF MASS DESTRUCTION ON THE OCEAN FLOOR.  Journal of Maritime Law and Commerce 3:107-128 (1971)

IIIOR     Krueger, P.  MIT DEM TAUCHBOOT ZUR KORALLENERNTE.  Meerestechnik 4(1):12-15 (1973)

VCS       Krueger, R.  BACKGROUND OF THE DOCTRINE OF THE CONTINENTAL SHELF AND THE OUTER CONTINENTAL SHELF LANDS ACT.  Natural Resources Journal 10:442-494 (1970)

VCS       _____ _____ THE CONVENTION ON THE CONTINENTAL SHELF AND THE NEED FOR ITS REVISION AND SOME COMMENTS REGARDING THE REGIME FOR THE LANDS BEYOND.  Natural Resources Lawyer 1(3):1-18 (1968)

VOR       _____ _____ DEVELOPMENT AND ADMINISTRATION OF THE OUTER CONTINENTAL SHELF LANDS OF THE UNITED STATES.  Rocky Mountain Mineral Law Institute 14:643-721 (1968)

VORM      Krueger, Robert B.  AN EVALUATION OF UNITED STATES OCEANS POLICY.  McGill Law Journal 17(4):603-698 (1971)

IVP        Krueger, Robert B. INTERNATIONAL AND NATIONAL REGULATION OF POLLU-
           TION FROM OFFSHORE OIL PRODUCTION. San Diego Law Review 7:541-573
           (1970)

VOI        _____  _____ LEGAL COMMENTS ON ROCKS AND SHOALS FOR OCEAN INDUSTRY
           GROWTH. Shore and Beach 36(2):23-25 (1968)

IVMMR      _____  _____ MINERAL DEVELOPMENT ON THE CONTINENTAL SHELF AND BE-
           YOND. Journal of the State Bar of California 42:515-533 (1967)

VLOS       _____  _____ WHERE ARE WE ON THE LAW OF THE SEA. San Diego Law Re-
           view 13(3):552-557 (1976)

IIP        Kuchenbecker, David J., and D.E. Long. WILL MUNICIPAL SEWAGE CON-
           TINUE TO THREATEN PRIMARY WATER-CONTACT RECREATION?: AN APPRAISAL
           OF THE 1972 WATER POLLUTION CONTROL ACT. Rutgers Camden Law Journal
           4:260-288 (1973)

IIIB       Kuebler, J. FISHING RIGHTS AND TERRITORIAL WATERS. Editorial Re-
           search Reports :645-662 (1963)

VOD        Kullenberg, G.E.B. OCEAN DUMPING SITES. Ocean Management 2:189-
           209 (1975)

IIIF       Kury, C. THE FISHERIES PROPOSALS. San Diego Law Review 12:644-
           654 (1975)

IIIF       Kury, C.R. THE APPLICATION OF A MARKET THEORY TO THE REGULATION OF
           INTERNATIONAL FISHERIES. Ocean Development and International Law
           1:355-368 (1974)

IIREC      Kusler, Jon A. CARRYING CAPACITY CONTROLS FOR RECREATION WATER
           USES. Wisconsin Law Review 1973:1-36 (1973)

VLOS       Kutner, Luis. HABEAS MARINUS: A PROPOSAL IN OCEAN LAW. Lawyer of
           the Americas 1:1-24 (1969)

IIP&H      Kuzenski, Sally. SUPERPORTS - A CANDID LOOK. Sea Grant '70s 6(2):
           4-5 (1975)

IVDRIL     Laborde, A.J. AMERICAN DRILLERS CAN NO LONGER COUNT ON A DOMINANT
           POSITION IN THE OFF SHORE DUE TO NEW COMPETITION. Offshore 33:80,
           82-84,86 (1973)

IIIF       Lagarde, R.A. METHODES DE CONTROLE DE LA PECHE A'LECHELLE INTER-
           NATIONALE. France Peche 166:62-64 (1971/1972)

VCS        LAGGING LAW OF THE CONTINENTAL SHELF: SOME PROBLEMS AND PROPOSALS.
           Catholic University Law Review 22:131-155 (1972)

IIDR       LAKE ERIE HARBOR DREDGE DISPOSAL PROGRAM. Lake Erie Shore Zone Man-
           agement Newsletter 1(3):   (January-March, 1975)

VINTL      Lakhtine, W. RIGHTS OVER THE ARCTIC. American Journal of Interna-
           tional Law: Supplement 24:703-717 (1930)

IIIF       Lakshmanan, R. INTERNATIONAL REGULATION OF FISHERIES. Indian Jour-
           nal of International Law 13(3):367-388 (1973)

| | |
|---|---|
| IVMMR | Lalou, Claude, and Evelyne Brichet. SIGNIFICATION DES MESURES RADIOCHIMIQUES DANS L'EVALUATION DE LA VITESSE DE CROISANCE DES NODULES DE MANGANESE. Sciences Naturelles 275(7):815-818 (1972) |
| IVM | La Motte, C. HOW THE ENERGY CRISIS WILL SPUR OCEAN-RELATED ACTIVITIES. Ocean Industry 8(6):75-76 (1973) |
| VOR | _____ _____ WHO CONTROLS THE DEEP SEA. Ocean Industry 4(5):78-80 (1969) |
| IVMMR | LaMotte, Clyde. DEEPSEA VENTURES PILOT RUN IS SUCCESSFUL. Ocean Industry 5:7-14 (1970) |
| IVOI | _____ _____ GAS-OIL ACTIVITY WILL SOAR IN 1970s. Ocean Industry 5:7-9 (1970) |
| VLOS | Lampe, Wilhelm H., Max I. Kehden. DIE DRITTE SEERCHTSKONFERENZ DER VEREINTEN NATIONEN UND DIE FREIHEIT DES SEEVERKEHRS. Hansa 111: 347-351 (1971) |
| VP | Lanctot, Lawrence R. MARINE POLLUTION: A CRITIQUE OF PRESENT AND PROPOSED INTERNATIONAL AGREEMENTS AND INSTITUTIONS - A SUGGESTED GLOBAL OCEAN'S ENVIRONMENTAL REGIME. Hastings Law Journal 24:67-110 (1972) |
| VSUB | Land, T. DEADLIER THAN SPACE TRAVEL. Canadian Shipping and Marine Engineering 45:26-28 (1973) |
| IIP&H | LAND FROM THE SEA. Engineering 212(9):844-848 (1974) |
| IVP | Landes, K.K. MOTHER NATURE AS AN OIL POLLUTER. American Association of Petroleum Geologists Bulletin 57:637-641 (1973) |
| IVP | Landner, L. OIL SPILL PROTECTION IN THE BALTIC SEA. Water Pollution Control Federation Journal 47:796-809 (1975) |
| IICZM | LAND-USE MANAGEMENT IN DELAWARE'S COASTAL ZONE. University of Michigan Journal of Law Reform 6:251-267 (1972) |
| IISL | LAND USE - WETLANDS REGULATION. Arkansas Law Review 27:527-538 (1973) |
| IIIAFF | Landy, B.A. CONSTRAINTS ON AQUACULTURE PROJECTS. Marine Fisheries Review 37(1):33-35 (1975) |
| VLOS | Langeraar, W. THOUGHTS ON AN INTERNATIONAL REGIME AND ADMINISTRATIVE AGENCY FOR THE SEABED AND OCEAN FLOOR BEYOND THE LIMITS OF NATIONAL JURISDICTION. Journal of Maritime Law and Commerce 1:123-130 (1969) |
| IIP&H | Langlois, A.E. CLEANER PORTS FOR THE AMERICAS. World Ports 36(5): 15-16 (1974) |
| IICZM | Langlois, Edward. PORT AUTHORITIES VIEW STATE COASTAL MANAGEMENT PROGRESS. Coastal Zone Management Journal 2(2):171-176 (1975) |
| VINTL | Lapidoth, R. FREEDOM OF NAVIGATION AND THE NEW LAW OF THE SEA. Israel Law Review 10:456-502 (1975) |

| | |
|---|---|
| VINTL | Lapidoth, R. FREEDOM OF NAVIGATION - ITS LEGAL HISTORY AND ITS NORMATIVE BASIS. <u>Journal of Maritime Law and Commerce</u> 6(2):259-272 (1975) |
| VLOS | Lapointe, P.A. LAW OF THE SEA CONFERENCE: THE PROGRESS MADE AT CARACAS. <u>International Perspectives</u> :19-24 (November/December, 1974) |
| IVOCET | LaPrairie, Yves. RECENT ACHIEVEMENTS OF THE FRENCH IN OFFSHORE TECHNOLOGY. <u>Ocean Industry</u> 7:115-120 (1972) |
| IIIINTL | LA CHASSE À LA BALEINE DANS LE DROIT INTERNATIONAL PUBLIC ACTUEL. <u>Revue Générale de Droit International Public</u> 79:92-124 (1975) |
| IVMT | LARGEST ORE/OIL CARRIER. <u>Tanker and Bulk Carrier</u> 19(11):26-26 (1973) |
| IIIINTL | Lascu, I. CU PRIVIRE LA UNELE CAZURI DE EX ONERARE DE RĂSPUNDERE IN PESCUITUL OCEANIC. <u>Arbitrajul de Stat</u> 19(3):30-37 (1973) |
| VP | Laska, Lewis L. WATER POLLUTION CONTROL IN ALASKA: THE ALASKA ENVIRONMENTAL CONSERVATION ACT OF 1971. <u>UCLA-Alaska Law Review</u> 4: 263-293 (1975) |
| VENE | Lasúrtegui, A. de los S. PROBLEMAS LEGALES EN RELACIÓN CON LA NAVEGACIÓN Y LA ENERGIA NUCLEAR. <u>Arquivos do Ministério da Justiça</u> 29(122):115-133 (1972) |
| IIIF | LATIN AMERICA: FISHING. <u>Bulletin of Legal Developments</u> 3:32-32 (February 12, 1975) |
| VB | LATIN AMERICA: TERRITORIAL WATERS. <u>Latin America Newsletter</u> :56 (February, 1973) |
| IIP&H | LATIN AMERICA. <u>World Dredging and Marine Construction</u> 10(1):20-24 (1974) |
| IIIFV&G | Lau, K. SEEVERHALTEN AUSGEWAEHLTER GROSS HECKTRAWLER. <u>Seewirtschaft</u> 4(5):358-362 (1972) |
| IICZM | Lauf, Ted. SHORELAND REGULATION IN WISCONSIN. <u>Coastal Zone Management Journal</u> 2(1):47-58 (1975) |
| VENE | Lavi, A., and C. Zener. PLUMBING THE OCEAN DEPTHS: A NEW SOURCE OF POWER. <u>IEEE Spectrum</u> 10(10):22-27 (1973) |
| VP | LAW COURT RULINGS OF MAJOR IMPORTANCE IN 1974. <u>Shipping World and Shipbuilder</u> 168:55-56 (1975) |
| VLOS | LAW-OF-THE-SEA AGREEMENT NOW APPEARS POSSIBLE. <u>Sea Technology</u> 16 (1):25-26 (1975) |
| VLOS | LAW OF THE SEA. <u>Asian African Legal Consultative Committee. Report</u>. 12:195-305 (1971) |
| VLOS | LAW OF THE SEA. <u>Asian African Legal Consultative Committee. Report</u>. 13:87-128 (1972) |
| VLOS | THE LAW OF THE SEA. <u>International and Comparative Law Quarterly</u> (1958) Special Supplement |

| | |
|---|---|
| IIIEZ | LAW OF THE SEA - EXCLUSIVE ECONOMIC ZONE - ICELAND ACCORDED PREFERENTIAL FISHING RIGHTS IN WATER ADJACENT TO ITS COAST - DUTY TO NEGOTIATE IMPOSED UPON DISPUTING PARTIES TO DEFINE ICELAND'S RIGHTS AGAINST THE UNITED KINGDOM AND ITS HISTORIC RIGHTS. Harvard International Law Journal 16:474-490 (1975) |
| VLOS | LAW OF THE SEA: FROM CARACAS TO GENEVA - A TIME FOR DECISION. The Friedman Series in International Law. Columbia Journal of Transnational Law 14:1-79 (1975) |
| VB | LAW OF THE SEA - HISTORIC BAYS - A BODY OF WATER IS A HISTORIC BAY WHEN CONTINUOUS AUTHORITY IS EXERCISED BY THE COASTAL STATE AND RECOGNIZED BY FOREIGN NATIONS, DESPITE UNITED STATES GOVERNMENT DISCLAIMERS. Vanderbilt Journal of Transnational Law 7:225-234 (1973) |
| VINTL | LAW OF THE SEA; INTERNATIONAL SEA LANE SAFETY CONVENTION. Times :2-2 (October 21, 1972) |
| VP | LAW OF THE SEA; MARINE POLLUTION. Financial Times :1-1 (November 13, 1972) |
| VP | LAW OF THE SEA: NORTHEAST ATLANTIC POLLUTION. Aftenposten :1-1 (October 20, 1972) |
| VOD | LAW OF THE SEA: OCEAN DUMPING. Bulletin of Legal Developments 17: 9-9 (1973) |
| VLOS | LAW OF THE SEA VI: A SYMPOSIUM. San Diego Law Review 11:535-722 (1974) |
| VCS | LAW OF THE SEA - THE CONTINENTAL SHELF - UNITED STATES PROPRIETARY CLAIM TO THE CONTINENTAL SHELF GIVES RISE TO A NEW PUBLIC DOMAIN. Land and Water Law Review 5:509-516 (1970) |
| IIIINTL | LAW PROHIBITING FOREIGN VESSELS FROM FISHING IN TERRITORIAL WATERS AND ON CONTINENTAL SHELF. International Legal Materials 3:642-648 (1964) |
| VB | Lawrence, Keith D. MILITARY-LEGAL CONSIDERATIONS IN THE EXTENSION OF TERRITORIAL SEAS. Military Law Review 29: (1965) |
| IIOSTR | Lawrence, W.H. SUPERPORTS, AIRPORTS AND OTHER FIXED INSTALLATIONS ON THE HIGH SEAS. Journal of Maritime Law 6:575-591 (1975) |
| IVLOS | Laylin, John G. THE LAW TO GOVERN DEEPSEA MINING UNTIL SUPERSEDED BY INTERNATIONAL AGREEMENT. San Diego Law Review 10:433-445 (1973) |
| IVLOS | _____ THE LEGAL REGIME OF THE DEEP SEABED PENDING MULTINATIONAL AGREEMENT. Virginia Journal of International Law 13:319-330 (1973) |
| VINTL | _____ PAST, PRESENT AND FUTURE DEVELOPMENT OF THE CUSTOMARY INTERNATIONAL LAW OF THE SEA AND DEEP SEABED. The International Lawyer 5:442-451 (1971) |
| VLOS | Lazarev, M.I. SCIENTIFIC - TECHNOLOGICAL PROGRESS AND THE SEARCH FOR LEGAL REGULATION OF POSSIBLE SEABED USES. Ocean Development and International Law 3:75-86 (1975) |

VINTL     Lazarev, M.I.  SOME PROBLEMS OF THE INTERNATIONAL LAW OF THE SEA IN PERSPECTIVE.  Soviet Yearbook of International Law 1971:162-172 (1973)

IIIF      LEADING FISH TO AN AUTOMATED HARVEST.  Ocean Industry 6:65-67 (1971)

VLOS      Leanza, U.  LA NUOVA CONFERENZA DI CODIFICAZIONE DEL DIRITTO DEL MARE.  Diritto Marittimo 76:714-732 (1974)

IIIP      Leathem, W., et al.  EFFECT OF SPOIL DISPOSAL ON BENTHIC INVERTEBRATES.  Marine Pollution Bulletin 4:122-125 (1973)

VINTL     Lebedev, S.N.  MARITIME ARBITRATION IN THE USSR.  Soviet Yearbook of International Law 1971:226-243 (1973)

IIIINTL   Lecuona, D.  ECUADOR FISHERIES DISPUTE (A NEW APPROACH TO AN OLD PROBLEM).  Journal of Maritime Law and Commerce 2:91-114 (1970)

IVMT      Ledbetter, B.G.  STEPS TOWARDS A STATE OIL TRANSPORTATION POLICY. Remarks made at a U.S. Coast Guard Maritime Conference Luncheon, held in Seattle, May 6, 1975.  Pacific Northwest Sea 8(1):8-12 (1975)

IIIINTL   Ledun, M.  COMITE INTERPROFESSIONEL DE LA GRANDE PECHE.  LE DEVELOPEMENT DU SURGELE NE RESOUT PAS FOUS LES PROBLEMES.  France Peche 171:58-61 (1972)

IIIOR     Lee, G.  THE RIGHT TO TAKE SEAWEED FROM THE FORESHORE.  Northern Ireland Legal Quarterly 18:33-43 (1967)

VINTL     Lee, H.C.  AN ARCHIPELAGIC CLAIM FOR PAPUA NEW GUINEA.  Melanesian Law Journal 2(1):91-107 (1974)

IIOL      Lee, Henry.  DECISION TO LEASE OUTER CONTINENTAL SHELF LANDS.  Coastal Zone Management Journal 2(1):31-46 (1975)

VC        Lee, L.  LEGAL ASPECTS OF INTERNATIONALIZATION OF INTEROCEANIC CANALS.  Law and Contemporary Problems 33:158-168 (1968)

VINTL     Lee, Luke T.  JURISDICTION OVER FOREIGN MERCHANT SHIPS IN THE TERRITORIAL SEA.  American Journal of International Law 55:77-96 (1961)

IVM       Leenhardt, Oliver.  OIL PRODUCTION PROSPECTS FOR WESTERN MEDITERRANEAN.  Ocean Industry 8(2):41-42 (1973)

VOSTR     _____  _____  Structures in the Mediterranean.  Ocean Industry 4:50-54 (1969)

IISL      Lefkowitz, Louis J.  JAMAICA BAY:  AN URBAN MARSHLAND IN TRANSITION. Fordham Urban Law Journal 1:1-18 (1972)

IVLOS     LEGAL ASPECTS OF SEABED PETROLEUM AND MINERAL RESOURCE DEVELOPMENT - THE DRAFT UNITED NATIONS CONVENTION ON THE INTERNATIONAL SEABED AREA AND THE UNITED STATES WORKING PAPER SUBMITTED TO THE UNITED NATIONS SEABED COMMITTEE.  UNITED STATES PROPOSAL FOR LEGAL REGULATION OF SEABED MINERAL EXPLOITATION BEYOND NATIONAL JURISDICTION.  Natural Resources Lawyer 4:569-    (1971)

IVMMR     LEGAL ISSUES OF THE OFFSHORE MINERAL RIGHTS DISPUTE IN CANADA.  McGill Law Journal 14:475-493 (1968)

| | |
|---|---|
| VENE | LEGAL SETTING OF NUCLEAR POWERPLANT SITING DECISIONS: A NEW YORK STATE CONTROVERSY. Cornell Law Review 57:80-104 (1971) |
| VP | Legault, L. FREEDOM OF THE SEAS: A LICENSE TO POLLUTE? University of Toronto Law Journal 21:211-221 (1971) |
| VLOS | Legault, L.H.J. CANADA AND THE LAW OF THE SEA. World Fishing 23(5): 23-24 (1974) |
| IIIF | LEGISLATION. Fish Boat 19(4):29,31,35,62-63 (1974) |
| IIIB | LEGISLATION: FISHERY JURISDICTION BILLS LEAD THE PACK. Fish Boat 20(4):18-19,21,53-54 (1975) |
| IICZM | LEGISLATION - THE DELAWARE COASTAL ZONE ACT. Buffalo Law Review 21:481- (1972) |
| VP | Lehr, William E. MILESTONES ACCOMPLISHED IN OIL POLLUTION CONTROL. Undersea Technology 14:22 (1973) |
| VINTL | Leifer, Michael, and Dolliver Nelson. CONFLICT OF INTEREST IN THE STRAITS OF MALACCA. International Affairs 49:190-203 (1973) |
| VOD | Leitzell, Terry L. THE OCEAN DUMPING CONVENTION - A HOPEFUL BEGINNING. San Diego Law Review 10:502-513 (1973) |
| IIIOL | LE LEASING. UN FINANCEMENT SUR MESURE: LE LEASING DE CHALUTIERS. France Peche 168:22-23 (1972) |
| IVOR | Le Leuch, H., and J. Masseron. ECONOMIC ASPECTS OF OFFSHORE HYDROCARBON EXPLORATION AND PRODUCTION. Ocean Management 1:287-325 (1973) |
| IIIFV&G | Le Morgat. UN ECHELON DANS LA CONSTRUCTION FRANCAISE DE THONIERS OCEANIQUES. France Peche 171:98-99,101-102 (1972) |
| IVMMR | Lennard, D.E. COORDINATION IS KEY TO NORWEGIAN SUCCESS. Offshore Services 6:23-25 (1973) |
| IVMMR | Lense, A.H. SAMPLING MINERALS OF THE OCEAN FLOOR. Mining Engineering 20(8):54-57 (1968) |
| VAC | Leonard, J. U.S. AND U.S.S.R. AGREE ON DRAFT TREATY BANNING EMPLACEMENT OF NUCLEAR WEAPONS ON THE SEABED. U.S. Department of State Bulletin 61:365-368 (1969) |
| VAC | _____ _____ UNITED STATES COMMENTS ON REVISION OF DRAFT TREATY BANNING EMPLACEMENT OF NUCLEAR WEAPONS ON THE SEABED. U.S. Department of State Bulletin 61:480-484 (1969) |
| VAC | _____ _____ U.S. DISCUSSES VERIFICATION PROCEDURES UNDER THE DRAFT TREATY BANNING EMPLACEMENT OF NUCLEAR WEAPONS ON THE SEABED. U.S. Department of State Bulletin 61:425-429 (1969) |
| IVM | Leopola, L.C. A REVIEW OF THE PRESENT, AND ANNOUNCED FUTURE, CAPABILITIES FOR COMMERCIAL OIL RECOVERY BEYOND THE 656-FOOT ISOBATH. Marine Affairs Journal 1:91-97 (1973) |
| VP | Leppakoski, E. EFFECTS ON AN OIL SPILL IN THE NORTHERN BALTIC. Marine Pollution Bulletin 4:93-94 (1973) |

VP            Lesaca, Reynaldo, M. POLLUTION CONTROL LEGISLATION AND EXPERIENCE IN A DEVELOPING COUNTRY: THE PHILIPPINES. The Journal of Developing Areas 8:537-556 (1974)

VP            Leslie, H.A. WATER POLLUTION PERMITTING SYSTEM. Alabama Lawyer 35:192-201 (1974)

IIIF          LES MEILLEURES PRODUCTIONS DE LA PECHE HAUTURIERE. France Peche 167:42-42 (1972)

IIIFV&G       LES NOUVEAUX THONIERS AMERICAINS: LE GIGANTISME PAIE. France Peche 168:38-38 (1972)

IIIFV&G       LES PROGRES TECHNIQUES DE LA FLOTTE DE PECHE SOVIETIQUE ET SON DEVELOPEMENT FUTUR. France Peche 167:60-62 (1972)

IVOSTR        LESS FIXED PLATFORM RIGS ARE SEEN OFFSHORE. Offshore 33(8):50,52- (1973)

VP            Lester, A. RIVER POLLUTION IN INTERNATIONAL LAW. American Journal of International Law 57:828-853 (1963)

IVP           Lester, T.E., and L.R. Beynon. POLLUTION AND THE OFFSHORE OIL INDUSTRY. Marine Pollution Bulletin 4(2):23-25 (1973)

VLOS          Levy, J.P. OCEAN MANAGEMENT AND A NEW LAW OF THE SEA. Ocean Management 1:129-143 (1973)

VLOS          Lévy, Jean-Pierre. LA IIIe CONFÉRENCE SUR LE DROIT DE LA MER. Annuaire Française de Droit International 17:784-832 (1971)

IVMMR         _____ _____ LES RESSOURCES MINÉRALES DES FONDS MARINS INTERNATIONAUX. Revue française de Pénergie 23:417-427 (1972)

IISL          Lewis, A. CAPSULE HISTORY AND THE PRESENT STATUS OF THE TIDELANDS CONTROVERSY. Natural Resources Lawyer 3(4):620-636 (1970)

IVOI          Lewis, A., and W. Meyers. OFFSHORE OPERATIONS. Rocky Mountain Mineral Law Institute 16:421-462 (1971)

IVP           Lewis, D.E. LEGAL LIABILITY IN THE CANADIAN ARCTIC RELATING TO OIL SPILLS AND BLOWOUTS. Alberta Law Review 10:440-    (1972)

VOR           Lewis, J. THE DEEP-SEA RESOURCES. Naval War College Review 21(10):130-151 (1969)

IVMMR         Li, V.H. CHINA AND OFF-SHORE OIL. Stanford Journal of International Studies 10:143-162 (1975)

VLOS          Liang, Y.-I. THE REPUBLIC OF CHINA AND A FUTURE CONFERENCE ON THE LAW OF THE SEA. Chung-Kuo Kuo Chi Fa Hsueh Hui 8/9:99-120 (1971/1972)

VOR           Lillich, R. WHOSE IS THE BED OF THE SEA? New York State Bar Journal 40:601-604 (1968)

VLOS          Lillich, Richard B. THE GENEVA CONFERENCE ON THE LAW OF THE SEA AND THE IMMUNITY OF FOREIGN STATE-OWNED COMMERCIAL VESSELS. George Washington Law Review 28(2):408-420 (1960)

VCS    Limitone, A. THE INTERACTION OF LAW AND TECHNOLOGY: THE CONTINENTAL SHELF PROBLEM. Cornell International Law Journal 1:49-65 (1968)

IIIEZ   LIMITS AND STATUS OF THE TERRITORIAL SEA, EXCLUSIVE FISHING ZONES, FISHERY CONSERVATION ZONES AND THE CONTINENTAL SHELF. International Legal Materials 8:516-539 (1969)

VCS    Linares, A. PROBLEMAS DE LA PLATA FORMA CONTINENTAL. Boletin de la Facultad de Derecho y C Sociales 1/5:305-349 (1973)

IIE    Lindall, W.N., Jr. ALTERATIONS OF ESTUARIES OF SOUTH FLORIDA: A THREAT TO ITS FISH RESOURCES. Marine Fisheries Review 35:26-33 (1973)

IVENV  Lindberg, Charles S. ENVIRONMENTAL DELAYS AFFECTING MINERAL LESSEES ON PUBLIC LANDS. Rocky Mountain Mineral Law Institute 18:45-86 (1973)

IVDRIL Linden, William M. REVIEW OF OFFSHORE DRILLING - WHAT ARE INTANGIBLES? Oil and Gas Institute 26:441-480 (1975)

VP     Lindholm, Robert M. FEDERAL WATER POLLUTION CONTROL ACT AMENDMENTS OF 1972 ... THE GREAT CLEANSING OR BEING TAKEN TO THE CLEANERS? Journal of the Missouri Bar 30:23-36 (1974)

VP     Lindner, H., and K.H. Zilm. NUTZUNG UND REINHALTUNG DER KUESTENGEWAESSER - EIN BETRAG ZUR REINHALTUNG DER OSTSEE. Wasserwirtschaft-Wassertechnik 22:134-137 (1972)

VLOS   Lissitzyn, O.J. A NEW INTERNATIONAL LAW FOR THE DEEP SEABED REGIME. Columbia Journal of Transnational Law 14:30-55 (1975)

IIIOCET Liston, J., and L. Smith. FISHING AND THE FISHING INDUSTRY. AN ACCOUNT WITH COMMENTS ON OVERSEAS TECHNOLOGY TRANSFER. Ocean Development and International Law Journal 2:285-312,213-349 (1974)

IVMMR  Little, C.H. OFF-SHORE EXPLORATION FOR GAS AND OIL. Canadian Geographical Journal 77:108-115 (1968)

IIIF   LITTLE LEGISLATION AFFECTING FISHERIES EXPECTED TO EMERGE INTO LAW. Fish Boat 17(3):39-40 (1972)

IIIFV&G LOBSTER/FREIGHT/SHRIMP BOAT IS FIRST OF ITS TYPE FROM YARD. Fish Boat 17(10):54-55 (1972)

IISL   Logan, W., and R. Williams TIDELANDS IN SOUTH CAROLINA: A STUDY IN THE LAW OF REAL PROPERTY. South Carolina Law Review 15:657-676 (1963)

IIP    Lohne, A. OIL POLLUTION OF COASTAL AND INLAND WATERS OF THE UNITED STATES UNDER THE WATER QUALITY IMPROVEMENT ACT OF 1970. Insurance Counsel Journal 38:49-62 (1971)

IIIP   Lollock, Donald L. TEMPERATURE - BIOLOGICAL ASPECTS RELATED TO NUCLEAR POWER PLANT SITING, OPERATION, AND OTHER CONSIDERATIONS. The Forum 8:381-410 (1972)

IVOSTR Londenberg, R. ARE RIGS STARTING TO COME BACK TO U.S.? Offshore 33(5):45-47 (1973)

IVOL       Londenberg, R. DEEP WATER LEASES MAY BE OFFERED IN GULF BY U.S. GOVERNMENT. Offshore 33(3):31-34 (1973)

IVMMR      _____ _____ DIFFERENCES IN OPERATING RULES FOR VARIOUS NATIONS AROUND THE NORTH SEA COULD HAMPER RAPID DEVELOPMENT. Offshore 33(2): 98,100 (1973)

VDRIL      _____ _____ DRILLING SEEMS DUE TO PICK UP SOMETIME THIS YEAR OR NEXT. Offshore 33(7):84,86 (1973)

IVOL       _____ _____ LOUISIANA SALE BREAKS MOST OFFSHORE RECORDS. Offshore 33(1):31-34 (1973)

IVM        _____ _____ MAN, OIL AND THE SEA. Offshore 32(1):54-56- (1972)

IVM        _____ _____ OFFSHORE CRUDE FLOW RISES BY 8.4% LAST YEAR AND GAS IS UP 5%. Offshore 33(7):51-54 (1973)

IVOL       _____ _____ TEXAS SALE ALMOST SETS RECORD FOR HIGH BIDDING. Offshore 33(8):31-33 (1973)

VENV       Long, B.L. IMPLEMENTING OUR NATIONAL POLICY FOR THE MARINE ENVIRONMENT. Journal of Environmental Science 13:21-25 (1970)

IIODAS     Long. F. Vinton. A STEADY OCEAN BUOY. Ocean Industry 6:29-34 (1971)

IVM        Longworth, Richard C. THE NORTH SEA OIL RUSH IS ON BUT BRITAIN AND NORWAY'S EUROPEAN NEIGHBORS SHOULDN'T COUNT ON AN ENERGY BONANZA. European Community 185:3-6 (1975)

IIIB       Lonsdale, A.L. COAST GUARD - NMFS TEAMS STEP-UP PATROLS. National Fisherman 52(13):6-8 (1972)

IVMMR      THE LOOMING OIL BATTLE OFF THE EAST COAST. Business Week 2328:80, 83-84 (1974)

IIIINTL    Looney, W.F. IMPLEMENTING THE GREAT LAKES FISHERIES CONVENTION WITH CANADA. U.S. Department of State Bulletin 34:890-893 (1956)

VINTL      Łopuski, J. LEGAL PROBLEMS OF CO-OPERATION IN THE UTILIZATION OF THE BALTIC SEA. In Polish. Sprawy Miedzynarodowe 6:110-118 (1975)

IIILOS     L'ORGANISATION MONDIALE DES PECHES: LES PECHES MARITIMES ET LE DROIT DE LA MER. France Peche 166:54-58 (1971/1972)

IIIF       Loring, D. UNITED STATES - PERUVIAN "FISHERIES" DISPUTE. Stanford Law Review 23:391-453 (1971)

IIILOS     Loris, W.T. PREPARATIONS FOR THE THIRD UNITED NATIONS CONFERENCE ON THE LAW OF THE SEA: MARITIME JURISDICTION OVER FISHERIES. Nederlands Tijdschrift voor Internationaal Recht 20:233-265 (1973)

IIP&H      LOUISIANA OIL SUPERPORT A STEP NEARER. Oil and Gas Journal 70(49): 30-32 (1972)

IIP&H      LOUISIANA SUPERPORT. World Dredging and Marine Construction 10(3): 30-31 (1974)

VLOS    Løvald, J.L. IN SEARCH OF AN OCEAN REGIME: THE NEGOTIATIONS IN THE GENERAL ASSEMBLY'S SEA-BED COMMITTEE, 1968-1970. International Organization 29:681-709 (1975)

VP      Lowe, A.V. THE ENFORCEMENT OF MARINE POLLUTION REGULATIONS. San Diego Law Review 12:624-643 (1975)

IVLOS   _____ _____ THE INTERNATIONAL SEABED AND THE SINGLE NEGOTIATING TEXT. San Diego Law Review 13(3):489-532 (1976)

VP      Lowry, P.D. SHIPOWNER AND OIL POLLUTION LIABILITY. McGill Law Journal 18:577-591 (1972)

VLOS    Luard, E. WHO GETS WHAT ON THE SEABED? THE NEXT CONFERENCE ON THE LAW OF THE SEA AND THE INTERNATIONAL REGIME. Foreign Policy 132-147 (1972-73)

VP      Lucas, Alastair R. LEGAL TECHNIQUES FOR POLLUTION CONTROL: THE ROLE OF THE PUBLIC. University of British Columbia Law Review 6:167-191 (1971)

VP      Lucchini, L. LE RENFORCEMENT DU DISPOSITIF CONVENTIONNEL DE LUTTA CONTRE LA POLLUTION DES MERS. Journal du Droit International 101:755-793 (1974)

IVLOS   Luce, Charles F. THE DEVELOPMENT OF OCEAN MINERALS AND THE LAW OF THE SEA. Natural Resources Lawyer 1(3):29-35 (1968)

VENE    _____ _____ POWER FOR TOMORROW: THE SITING DILEMMA. Environmental Law 1:60-71 (1970)

VLOS    Ludwigson, J. LAW COMES TO THE SEA FLOOR. Science News 91:474-474 (May 20, 1967)

IISL    Luken, Ralph A. PRESERVATION OF WETLANDS: THE CASE OF SAN FRANCISCO BAY. Natural Resources 14:139-152 (1974)

VB      Lumb, R. AUSTRALIAN OFF-SHORE JURISDICTION. World Review 3:39-46 (1964)

VCS     _____ _____ THE CONTINENTAL SHELF. Melbourne University Law Review 6:357-369 (1968)

IVMMR   _____ _____ OFFSHORE PETROLEUM AGREEMENT AND LEGISLATION. Australian Law Journal 41:453-461 (1968)

VLOS    Lumb, R.D. 1973 LAW OF THE SEA CONFERENCE: SIGNIFICANT ISSUES. University of Queensland Law Journal 7:256-279 (1971)

IIIT&L  Lundy, B. U.S. AND U.S.S.R. AGREE ANEW ON SOVIET FISHING OFF U.S. MID-ATLANTIC COAST. Commercial Fisheries Review 31:38-41 (1969)

VOCET   Luther, G. UWL HELGOLAND - AN UNDERWATER LABORATORY FOR ROUGH SEA CONDITIONS. Helgolaender Wissenschaftliche Meeresuntersuchungen 24(1-4):45-53 (1973)

VINTL   Luther, R., und K. Mann. DAS PRINZIP DER FREIHEIT DER MEERE: EINE NORM DES JUS COGENS DER ALLGEMEIN-DEMOKRATISCHEN VOELKERRECHTS. Staat und Recht 23:419-428 (1974)

| | |
|---|---|
| VOR | Lynch, William C. THE SHRINKING OCEANS. Sea Power 15(11): 24-28 (1972) |
| IIWQ | Lynch, Thomas C., et al. COORDINATED RESOURCES DEVELOPMENT: LEGAL CONTROLS OF WATER QUALITY AND OIL POLLUTION IN A MARINE ENVIRONMENT. Los Angeles Bar Bulletin 44:154-157,180-184 (1968) |
| VOCET | Lythall, B.W. UNDERWATER TECHNOLOGY IN DEFENCE. PROCEEDINGS. Society for Underwater Technology 3(2):33-46 (1974) |
| VP | McCaffrey, Stephen C. TRANS-BOUNDARY POLLUTION INJURIES: JURISDICTIONAL CONSIDERATIONS IN PRIVATE LITIGATION BETWEEN CANADA AND THE UNITED STATES. California Western International Law Journal 3:191-259 (1973) |
| IVMMR | McCashin, J.C. EUROPE'S NORTH SEA BASIN HAS INTERESTING NEIGHBOURS. Oil and Gas Journal 70:155 (1972) |
| IVMMR | McCaslin, J.C. INDUSTRY NEEDS TO LOOK AT OFFSHORE LIBERIA. Oil and Gas Journal 71(35):131-131 (1973) |
| IVMMR | _____ _____ WORLD OFFSHORE-OIL PRODUCTION SOARS. Oil and Gas Journal 71:126,130,135 (1973) |
| IVMMR | McCaslin, John C. OFFSHORE EXPLORATION IS MOVING AROUND THE GLOBE. Oil and Gas Journal 70(50):106- (1972) |
| IVMMR | _____ _____ WHAT THEY'VE FOUND IN THE ARCTIC. Oil and Gas Journal 70(43):69-70,75-78 (1972) |
| IVM | McCaslin, John G. ATLANTIC WELL LIST GROWS. Oil and Gas Journal 70(37):127-127 (1972) |
| IVDRIL | McCaslin, John G., and Jim West. U.S. STILL DOMINATES THE FREE-WORLD DRILLING SCENE. Oil and Gas Journal 70(49):21-25 (1972) |
| IIIB | McClosky, William B., Jr. BOARD AND SEIZE; SUPEREFFICIENT FOREIGN FLEETS DEPLETE STOCKS OF FISH OFF U.S. SHORES, AND COAST GUARD CUTTERS PLUNGE THROUGH LONESOME SEAS TO PATROL THE 12-MILE PERIMETER FORBIDDEN TO FOREIGN FISHING. WHAT WILL HAPPEN IF THE LIMIT IS EXTENDED TO 200 MILES? New York Times Magazine :13,81,84-86 (March 7, 1976) |
| IVMT | McClure, A. SEMI-SUBMERSIBLE SUPPLY VESSEL DESIGN FOR NORTH SEA OPERATIONS. Ocean Industry 10(2):70-72,74 (1975) |
| VMT | McClure, Alan C. DESIGN FOR A SEMI-SUBMERSIBLE SHIP. Ocean Industry 7:19-23 (1972) |
| IVP | McCoy, Francis T. OIL SPILL AND POLLUTION CONTROL: THE CONFLICT BETWEEN STATE AND MARITIME LAW. George Washington Law Review 40:97-122 (1971) |
| IIIAFF | McCutcheon, Ross C. AQUACULTURE: PROBLEMS OF IMPLEMENTATION UNDER EXISTING LAW. University of British Columbia Law Review 10(2):289-319 (1976) |
| IIIF | McDonagh, M. EEC FISHERIES POLICY. Technology Ireland 7:35-37 (1975) |

IVM      McDonald, John G. FEDERAL INCOME TAX AFFECTING THE MINING AND PETRO-
         LEUM INDUSTRIES. Alberta Law Review II: (1973)

IVP      McDonald, Ross, and Easton Robert. SANTA BARBARANS CITE AN 11TH COM-
         MANDMENT: 'THOU SHALT NOT ABUSE THE EARTH.' New York Times Magazine
         32-33, 142-149,151,156 (October 12, 1969)

IVMMR    McDonald, Stephen L. UNIT OPERATION OF OIL RESERVOIRS AS AN INSTRU-
         MENT OF CONSERVATION. Notre Dame Lawyer 49:305-316 (1973)

IICZM    MacDonald, W.E. SHORELAND ZONING IN MAINE. Coastal Zone Management
         Journal 1:109-114 (1973)

VLOS     McDougal, Myres S. THE LAW OF THE HIGH SEAS IN TIME OF PEACE. U.S.
         Naval War College 25(3):35-47 (1973)

VLOS     _____ _____ REVISION OF THE GENEVA CONVENTIONS ON THE LAW OF THE
         SEA - THE VIEWS OF A COMMENTATOR. Natural Resources Lawyer 1(3):19-
         28 (1968)

VB       McDougal, Myres S., and William T. Burke. COMMUNITY INTEREST IN A
         NARROW TERRITORIAL SEA; INCLUSIVE VERSUS EXCLUSIVE COMPETENCE OVER
         THE OCEANS. Cornell Law Quarterly 45:171-253 (1960)

VLOS     _____ _____ CRISIS IN THE LAW OF THE SEA; COMMUNITY PERSPECTIVES
         VERSUS NATIONAL EGOISM. Yale Law Journal 67:539-589 (1958)

IVOI     McFarlane, James R., and Allan R. Trice. HUDSON BAY ACTIVITIES OUT-
         LINED. Offshore 32(1):86- (1972)

IVDRIL   McGhee, Ed. SUN LAYS BASE FOR SVERDRUP DRILLING. Oil and Gas Jour-
         nal 70(43):120-123 (1972)

IVMMR    McGhee, E., and C.D. Johnston. NORTH AMERICAN ARCTIC AREAS. Oil and
         Gas Journal 71: (1973)

IVDRIL   McGinnis, L.D., et al. DRY VALLEY DRILLING PROJECT. Antarctic Jour-
         nal of the United States 7(3):53-56 (1972)

VENE     McGowan, J.G., and W.E. Heronemus. OCEAN THERMAL AND WIND POWER:
         ALTERNATIVE ENERGY SOURCES BASED ON NATURAL SOLAR COLLECTION. Envi-
         ronmental Affairs 4:629-660 (1975)

IIIF     McGrath, P. ATLANTIC FISHERIES QUESTION. Atlantic 90:741-748 (1902)

IICONS   McHarg, Ian. BEST SHORE PROTECTION: NATURE'S OWN DUNES. Civil En-
         gineering 42(9):66-70 (1972)

VP       McHose, John C., et al. DOMESTIC AND FOREIGN ASPECTS OF MARINE POLLU-
         TION. American Bar Association Section of Insurance, Negligence and
         Compensation Law 1971:251- (1971)

VP       McHose, John C. MARINE POLLUTION - LEGISLATION, LITIGATION, UNDER-
         WRITING - WHERE ARE WE? WHERE AWAY? The Forum 10:251-298 (1974)

VOCET    MacInnis, J.B. LIVING UNDER THE SEA. Scientific American 214:20,
         24-33 (1966)

IVMMR    MacKay, John R. CONSIDERATIONS IN THE SEARCH AND EXPLORATION FOR
         MINERALS IN BRITISH COLUMBIA. Alberta Law Review II: (1973)

VLOS      McKelvey, V., and C. Philips. AUGUST SESSION OF U.N. SEA-BED COMMIT-
          TEE HELD AT NEW YORK. U.S. Department of State Bulletin 61:285-294
          (1969)

IVP       McKelvey, V.E. ENVIRONMENTAL PROTECTION IN OFFSHORE PETROLEUM OPER-
          ATIONS. Ocean Management 1:119-128 (1973)

VENE      _____ _____ WORLD ENERGY RESERVES AND RESOURCES. Public Utilities
          Fortnightly 7:27-33 (1975)

IVMMR     McKenna, F.J. NEW BRUNSWICK AND OFFSHORE MINERAL RIGHTS. University
          of New Brunswick Law Journal 22:69-88 (1973)

VENE      McKnight, M.S., et al. LAW OF THE SEA: ITS IMPACT ON THE INTERNA-
          TIONAL ENERGY CRISIS. Law and Policy in International Business
          6:639-676 (1974)

IVOI      McKnight, M.S. THE OIL INDUSTRY GOES TO SEA. Marine Technology Soci-
          ety Journal 8(6):44-55 (1974)

IIREC     McLennan, Janet. PUBLIC PATRIMONY: AN APPRAISAL OF LEGISLATION AND
          COMMON LAW PROTECTING RECREATIONAL VALUES IN OREGON'S STATE-OWNED
          LANDS AND WATERS. Environmental Law 4:317-381 (1974)

IVMMR     MacLeod, Greig, and Robert Boardman. NATIONALISM COMES OF AGE WITH
          DISCOVERY OF NORTH SEA OIL. International Perspectives :36-39
          (March-April, 1975)

VLOS      McLoughlin, D. THE APPROACH BY FIJI, A MID-OCEAN ARCHIPELAGO, TO THE
          CONFERENCE ON THE LAW OF THE SEA. Melanesian Law Journal 1(3):37-46
          (1972)

VP        McMahon, J.P. POLLUTION - NO PRIVATE COMPENSATION FOR INVASION OF
          PUBLIC RIGHTS ABSENT PARTICULAR DAMAGES. BURGESS v. THE TAMANO, 1973
          A.M.C. 1939 (D.ME.1973). Journal of Maritime Law and Commerce 5:539-
          544 (1974)

IIIF      McMilan, Hollis K. INDIAN FISHING RIGHTS - UNITED STATES v. WASHING-
          TON. Ocean Law Memo 1(3): (August 16, 1974)

VMT       McNees, R.B. FREEDOM OF TRANSIT THROUGH INTERNATIONAL STRAITS.
          Journal of Maritime Law and Commerce 6(2):175-211 (1975)

IIIMM     McNulty, Faith. PROFILES (THE WHALE). The New Yorker August 6 (1973)

VINTL     McRae, D.M. INTERNATIONAL COURT OF JUSTICE - INTERIM MEASURES OF
          PROTECTION - JURISDICTION - NUCLEAR TESTS CASES (NEW ZEALAND v.
          France (1973) I C J 135). University of British Columbia Law Review
          8:375-382 (1973)

IVOI      MacWilliam, D.A., and R.C. Muir. OFFSHORE OPERATING AGREEMENTS. Al-
          berta Law Review 11:(1973); PUBLIC LAND AND RESOURCES. Law Digest
          12:90-103 (1975)

VLOS      Maciel Filho, É. CONSIDERAÇÕES SOBRE OS ATUAIS MÉTODOS DE ESTUDO E
          DE ENSINO DO DIREITO INTERNACIONAL MARÍTIMO. Arquivos do Ministério
          da Justiça 29(122):223-238 (1972)

VINTL     Maechling, Charles, Jr. FREEDOM OF SCIENTIFIC RESEARCH: STEPCHILD
          OF THE OCEANS. Virginia Journal of International Law.15:539-559(1975)

| | |
|---|---|
| VORM | Maechling, Charles, Jr. THE POLITICS OF THE OCEAN; NEW ECONOMIC AND STRATEGIC SIGNIFICANCE OF THE OCEANS. Virginia Quarterly Review 47:505-517 (1971) |
| IVOL | Magida, Arthur J. COASTAL STATES SEEK CHANGES IN OCS LEASING POLICY. National Journal Reports 7:229-239 (1975) |
| VORM | Magnuson, Warren G. U.S. OCEANS POLICY: THE CONGRESSIONAL VIEW. The Columbia Journal of World Business 10:20-28 (1975) |
| VINTL | Maidment, S. HISTORICAL ASPECTS OF THE DOCTRINE OF HOT PURSUIT. British Yearbook of International Law 46:365-381 (1975) |
| IVMT | MAINE'S COASTAL CONVEYANCE OF OIL ACT: JURISDICTIONAL CONSIDERATIONS. Maine Law Review 24:299-315 (1972) |
| VOR | Malley, Diane F. OCEAN RESOURCES. Ecology Today 2(2):2-5,47-48 (1972) |
| VLOS | Mallon, L.G. THE OCEANS. Lawyer of the Americas 6:574-584 (1974) |
| IIB | Maloney, Frank E., and Richard C. Ausness. THE USE AND LEGAL SIGNIFICANCE OF THE MEAN HIGH WATER LINE IN COASTAL BOUNDARY MAPPING. North Carolina Law Review 53:186-273 (1974) |
| VOCET | MAN IN THE SEA - IN SITU STUDIES ON LIFE IN OCEANS AND COASTAL WATERS. Wissenschaftliche Meeresuntersuchungen 24(1-4): (1973) |
| VOR | Mani, V.S. RESOURCES OF THE SEA-BED BEYOND NATIONAL JURISDICTION: WHO SHALL EXPLOIT AND HOW? Indian Journal of International Law 14: 245-260 (1974) |
| VINTL | Mani, V.S., and S. Balupuri. MALACCA STRAITS AND INTERNATIONAL LAW. Indian Journal of International Law 13(3):455-467 (1973) |
| IIP&H | Mankabady, S. CONCEPT OF SAFE PORT. Journal of Maritime Law and Commerce 5:633-643 (1974) |
| VLOS | Manley, Robert H. THE GENEVA CONFERENCES ON THE LAW OF THE SEA AS A STEP IN THE INTERNATIONAL LAW-MAKING PROCESS. Albany Law Review 25(1)21p. (1961) |
| IIIF | Mann, A. FRAFFEN v. BLACK - THE STATE'S POWER TO REGULATE FISHING IN PRIVATE PONDS. Kentucky Law Journal 36:225-239 (1948) |
| IIIEZ | MANY ANOMALIES IN INTERNATIONAL FISHING ZONE POLICIES. South African Shipping News and Fishing Industry Review 24:83-84 (1969) |
| IVOSTR | MANY IMPORTANT TASKS FOR THE NORWEGIAN DEEP WATER PIPELINE PROJECT COMMITTEE. Northern Offshore 2:63-64,67 (1973) |
| IIOSTR | MAPLIN OFFSHORE AIRPORT SITE SELECTED. World Dredging and Marine Construction 8(13):64-67 (1972) |
| VB | Marcílio, F. FIXAÇÃO DOS LIMITES DO MAR TERRITORIAL BRASILEIRO. Revista de Informação Legislativa 8(30):45-62 (1971) |
| IIB | Marcin, Raymond B. HISTORY OF CONNECTICUT'S LONG ISLAND SOUND BOUNDARY. Connecticut Bar Journal 46:506- (1972) |

| | |
|---|---|
| IVOI | Marcoux, Michel J. SEABED MINERAL RESOURCE PRODUCTION AND THE FREE MARKET. <u>Natural Resources Lawyer</u> 6:217-248 (1973) |
| VINTL | MARE NOSTRUM, VOSTRUM ET CLAUSUM: JURISDICTION OVER SEA, SEABED AND SUBSOIL. <u>University of San Fernando Valley Law Review</u> 4:131-145 (1975) |
| VOR | Marinho Júnior, I.P. A PLATAFORMA CONTINENTAL E AS ATIVIDADES DE PESQUISA E LAVRA DE PETROLEO. <u>Arquivos do Ministerio da Justiça</u> 29(122):191-219 (1972) |
| VOR | \_\_\_\_\_ \_\_\_\_\_ O MAR TERRITORIAL E O MONOPÓLIO ESTATAL DO PETROLEO. <u>Arquivos do Ministério da Justiça</u> 29(122):82-122 (1972) |
| VOCET | MARINE ARCHELOGY AND INTERNATIONAL LAW: BACKGROUND AND SOME SUGGESTIONS. <u>San Diego Law Review</u> 9:668-700 (1972) |
| IIIMM | MARINE MAMMAL PROTECTION ACT: REPORT OF SECRETARY OF COMMERCE. <u>Federal Register</u> 39(122):22895-22932 (1974) |
| IIIMM | MARINE MAMMALS. NOTICE OF INTENT TO ISSUE EXEMPTIONS. <u>Federal Register</u> 38(16):2340-2340 (January 24, 1973) |
| IIIMM | MARINE MAMMALS: PROTECTION. USDI. <u>Federal Register</u> 39(38):7261-7267 (February 25, 1974) |
| VP | MARINE MONITORING OFF THE COAST OF SOUTH AFRICA. <u>South African Journal of Science</u> 68(5):113-142 (1972) |
| VOD | MARINE POLLUTION: DUMPING. <u>Aftenposten</u> :3 (December 30, 1972) |
| VP | MARINE POLLUTION. <u>International and Comparative Law Quarterly</u> 21(2): 382-383 (1972); 2(3):572-573 (1972); 21(4):800-802 (1972) |
| VP | MARINE POLLUTION SYMPOSIUM. INTERNATIONAL LAW AND MARINE POLLUTION: RADIOACTIVE WASTE AND "OTHER HAZARDOUS SUBSTANCES." <u>Natural Resources Journal</u> 11:221-255 (1971) |
| VOD | MARINE SANITATION DEVICES: CERTIFICATION PROCEDURES AND DESIGN AND CONSTRUCTION REQUIREMENTS. <u>Federal Register</u> 40(21):4621-4630 (January 30, 1975) |
| VMT | MARINE TRAFFIC REQUIREMENTS: ADVANCE NOTICE OF PROPOSED RULEMAKING. <u>Federal Register</u> 39(126):24157-24159 (June 28, 1974) |
| IIP&H | MARITIME ACTIVITIES BOOMING IN SOUTH AFRICA. <u>Marine Engineering/Log</u> 77(12):43-45,128-129 (1972) |
| IIP&H | MARITIME BACKS TERMINAL OFF DELAWARE. <u>Oil and Gas Journal</u> 70(31): 68-69 (1972) |
| VB | MARITIME CONTIGUOUS ZONES. <u>Michigan Law Review</u> 62:848-864 (1964) |
| VB | MARITIME JURISDICTION (BRAZIL-USA). <u>International and Comparative Law Quarterly</u> 21(4):802-803 (1972) |
| IIIB | MARITIME JURISDICTION OVER FISHERY RESOURCES. <u>Vanderbilt International</u> 4:109-119 (1971) |

| | |
|---|---|
| VP | MARITIME POLLUTION: THE CANADA SHIPPING ACT AMENDED. University of British Columbia Law Review 8:197-204 (1973) |
| IVMMR | MARKET GROWTH AND FUTURE DEVELOPMENTS. Tanker and Bulk Carrier 20(20):11-13,15 (1975) |
| VP | Markow, Herbert L. BURNING WATERS. Florida Bar Journal 50:20-23 (1976) |
| IVP | Marks, Ronald A. POLLUTION OF THE SEAS BY CRUDE OIL - A PROPOSAL FOR EFFECTIVE REMEDIAL ACTION. Ohio State Law Journal 33:80-101 (1972) |
| IVOCET | Marriott, J. EXPLORATION OFF U.K. COAST STARTS TO MOVE TOWARD NORTH. Offshore 33(7):180-182,184 (1973) |
| VLOS | Marston, Geoffrey. THE DEVELOPMENT OF THE LAW OF THE SEA WITH SPECIAL REFERENCE TO THE EXCLUSIVE ECONOMIC ZONE. Úlfljótur 27:297-307 (1974) |
| VINTL | _____ _____ INTERNATIONAL LAW AND MID-OCEAN ARCHIPELAGOES. Annales D'ETUDES INTERNATIONALES 4:171-190 (1973) |
| VORM | Marti, Iu. Iu. PLANETA-OKEAN-RYBA. Priroda (Moskva) 2:30-36 (1970) |
| IVMMR | Martin, C. NEWFOUNDLAND'S CASE ON OFFSHORE MINERALS. Ottawa Law Review 7:34-61 (1975) |
| VLOS | Martin, H.J. DIE WIRTSCHAFTLICHE NUTZUNG MARINER RESSOURCEN NACH DEM NEVEN MEERESVOELKERRECHT. Recht der Internationalen Wirtschaft 21:240-246 (1975) |
| VLOS | _____ _____ UMWELT UND RECHT: DAS NEUE SEE VOELKERRECHT. Neue Juristische Wochenschrift 28:722-726 (1975) |
| VOD | Martin, J.J. RADIOLOGICAL PROBLEMS OF LIQUID WASTE DISPOSAL INTO THE SEA. Transactions 20:423-426 (1975) |
| IIOSTR | Martin, M. Rod. WHAT TO EXPECT IN THE WAY OF MARINE PLATFORMS TO COME. Offshore 32(12):49-50,53-55 (1972) |
| VB | Martinez, Arthur D. THE POLITICS OF TERRITORIAL WATERS; 12 MILES OR 200? Studies in Comparative International Development 8:213-223 (1973) |
| VLOS | _____ _____ THIRD UNITED NATIONS CONFERENCE ON THE LAW OF THE SEA; PROSPECTS, EXPECTATIONS AND REALITIES. Journal of Maritime Law 7:253-274 (1975) |
| IVOCET | Martison, N.W., et al. EXPLORATION ON CONTINENTAL SHELF OFF NORTHWEST AUSTRALIA. American Association of Petroleum Geologists Bulletin 57:972-989 (1973) |
| VENV | Marty-Lavauzelle, Jean P. ENVIRONMENTAL PROTECTION IN FRANCE. Business Lawyer 27:841-843 (1972) |
| VCONS | Martz, Clyde O. CONSERVATION OF THE ENVIRONMENT AS A PUBLIC RESOURCE. Rocky Mountain Mineral Law Institute 18:225-251 (1973) |

| | |
|---|---|
| IVP | Marumo, R., and K. Kamada. OIL GLOBULES AND THEIR ATTACHED ORGANISMS IN THE EAST CHINA SEA AND THE KUROSHIO AREA. Nippon Kaiyo Gakkai-shi 29(4):155-158 (1973) |
| IISL | MARYLAND'S WETLANDS: THE LEGAL QUAGMIRE. Maryland Law Review 30: 240-266 (1970) |
| IVOSTR | Mason, B.N. ARCTIC SUBSEA COMPLETIONS. Petroleum Engineer 1:40- (1975) |
| IVMMR | Mason, J.F., et al. PETROLEUM DEVELOPMENTS IN MIDDLE EAST COUNTRIES IN 1972. American Association of Petroleum Geologists Bulletin 57: 2057-2084 (1973) |
| IIIB | MASSACHUSETTS COMMERCIAL FISHING AND THE 200-MILE FISHERIES ZONE. Coastlines 2(2): (February/March, 1976) |
| VP | Masuda, Melvin M.M. EFFLUENT CHARGE TAX: WHAT IT CAN AND CANNOT DO. Hawaii Bar Journal 9:40- (1972) |
| VAC | Mattes, Martin A., and Michael Bothe. DRAFT CONVENTION ON ENVIRONMENTAL WARFARE OFFERED AT DISARMAMENT CONFERENCE. Environmental Policy and Law 1(3):136-137 (December, 1975) |
| VP | Matthews, Gwenda. POLLUTION OF THE OCEANS; AN INTERNATIONAL PROBLEM? Ocean Management 1:161-170 (1973) |
| IVMMR | MAUI NATURAL GAS/OIL - NEW ZEALAND'S BIG INVESTMENT. Dock and Harbour Authority 55(644):54-57 (1974) |
| IVDRIL | Maxwell, A.E., et al. DEEP SEA DRILLING IN THE SOUTH ATLANTIC. Science 168:1047-1059 (1970) |
| IISL | Maxwell, R. THE DEVELOPMENT OF OWNERSHIP TO CALIFORNIA TIDELANDS. Los Angeles Bar Bulletin 41:552-557 (1966) |
| IISL | Maxwell, Richard C. THE DEVELOPMENT OF OWNERSHIP TO CALIFORNIA TIDELANDS. Los Angeles Bar Bulletin 41:552-557 (1966) |
| VINTL | THE MAYAGUEZ: THE RIGHT OF INNOCENT PASSAGE AND THE LEGALITY OF REPRISAL. San Diego Law Review 13(3):765-778 (1976) |
| VP | MEDITERRANEAN: MAKING THE GREEN ONE RED. The Economist :32 (March 31, 1973) |
| IIOSTR | MEDITERRANEAN-LINE STUDY NEARS FINISH. Oil and Gas Journal 70(41): 57-57 (1972) |
| IVMMR | Meiser, H.J., and E. Mueller. MANGANESE NODULES - A FURTHER RESOURCE TO COVER THE MINERAL REQUIREMENTS? Meerestechnik 4:145-150 (1973) |
| IVMMR | Meister du Bourg, H. de. DROIT PÉTROLIER ET PLATEAU CONTINENTAL. Revue de Droit (Université de Sherbrooke) 1:1-53 (1970) |
| VLOS | Melkov, G.M. THE LEGAL SIGNIFICANCE OF THE TERM EXCLUSIVELY FOR PEACEFUL PURPOSES. Soviet Yearbook of International Law 1971:153-161 (1973) |

VOR       Menard, H.  THE DEEP OCEAN FLOOR.  Scientific American :126-142
          (September, 1969)

VB        Menchaca, A., et al.  EXTENSÃO DO MAR TERRITORIAL E SUAS IMPLICAÇÕES.
          Arquivos da Justiça 29(122):29-54 (1972)

VP        Mendelsohn, Allan I.  OCEAN POLLUTION AND THE 1972 UNITED NATIONS
          CONFERENCE ON THE ENVIRONMENT.  Journal of Maritime Law and Commerce
          3:385-398

VB        Mendoza, E.P.  THE BASELINES OF THE PHILIPPINE ARCHIPELAGO.  Philippine Law Journal 46:628-639 (1971)

VCS       Mengozzi, P.  ESECUTIVO ED AUTORITÀ GIUDIZIARIA NELLA DETERMINAZIONE
          DEI POTERI DELLO STATO SULLA PIATTAFORMA CONTINENTALE.  Revista di
          Diritto Internazionale 55:609-660 (1972)

VLOS      Mensbrugghe, Y. van der.  HET INTERNATIONAAL ZEERECHT TUSSEN CARACAS
          EN GENÈVE.  Rechtskundig Weekblad 38:1281-1300 (1975)

VLOS      _____ _____ LE POUVIER DE POLICE DES ÉTATS EN HAUTE MER.  Revue
          Belge de Droit International 11:56-102 (1975)

IVLOS     Mero, John L.  A LEGAL REGIME FOR DEEP SEA MINING.  San Diego Law
          Review 7:488-503 (1970)

IIIF      Meron, Theodor.  THE FISHERMEN'S PROTECTIVE ACT:  A CASE STUDY IN
          CONTEMPORARY LEGAL STRATEGY OF THE UNITED STATES.  American Journal
          of International Law 69:290-309 (1975)

IIILOS    Meseguer Sanchez, J.L.  VERS UN NOUVEAU RÉGIME INTERNATIONAL DES
          ENTREPRISES COMMUNES DE PÊCHE.  Annuaire Français de Droit Internationale 20:860-874 (1974)

VLOS      Metcalf, Lee.  FOREWORD TO FIFTH ANNUAL LAW OF THE SEA SYMPOSIUM.
          San Diego Law Review 10:425-432 (1973)

VP        METHOD OF ANALYSIS AND PRECEDENTS IN THE INTERNATIONAL LITIGATION
          OF MARINE POLLUTION CLAIMS.  Columbia Journal of Law and Social Problems 9:537-574 (1973)

VENE      Metz, W.D.  OCEAN TEMPERATURE GRADIENTS;  SOLAR POWER FROM THE SEA.
          Science 180:1266-1267 (1973)

IVCONS    Meurs, L.V.  PRESERVATION OF THE OCEAN ENVIRONMENT WITH SPECIAL
          REFERENCE TO EXPLORATION AND EXPLOITATION OF THE SEABED AND SUBSOIL.
          International Business Lawyer :70-79 (July, 1974)

VEZ       MEXICO:  DECREE ON CONSTITUTIONAL CHANGE TO ACCOUNT FOR EXCLUSIVE
          ECONOMIC ZONE BEYOND LIMITS OF TERRITORIAL SEA;  LAW ON EXCLUSIVE
          ECONOMIC ZONE;  DECREE AMENDING LAW ON FISHERIES DEVELOPMENT.  International Legal Materials XV(2):380-387 (March, 1976)

VOCET     MEXICO/ROMANIO:  SEABED TECHNOLOGY.  Bulletin of Legal Developments
          3:32-32 (February 12, 1975)

IVMMR     Meyer, Galow, E., et al.  THE MARINE NODULES PROJECT:  SPOTLIGHTS
          FROM THE VIEW OF PROCESS ENGINEERING.  Meerestechnik 4:155-157
          (1973)

IVMMR    Meyerhoff, A.A.  RUSSIANS LOOK HARD AT THE ANADYR' BASIN.  PART I. Oil and Gas Journal 70(43):124,129 (1972)

IICONS   MIAMI BEACH RESTORATION STUDY.  World Dredging and Marine Construction 10(6):43-44 (1974)

IIP&H    MIDDLE EAST.  World Dredging and Marine Construction 10(1): (1974)

VLOS     Miles, Edward.  AN INTERPRETATION OF THE GENEVA PROCEEDINGS - PART I. Ocean Development and International Law Journal 3:187-224 (1976)

VINTL    Milić, Milenko.  OSNOVE PRAVNOG PORETKA NA OTVORENOM MORU.  (BASIC PRINCIPLES OF THE REGIME OF HIGH SEAS.)  Pomorskog z bornikaj Knj 1965(3):633-639

VINTL    _____  _____ PRAVNA PROBLEMATIKA NOVIH PROSTORA PODMORJA.  (LEGAL PROBLEMS OF THE OCEAN FLOOR AREAS.)  Pomorskog z bornikaj knj 1968(6):314-315

VAC      MILITARY USE OF THE OCEAN SPACE AND THE CONTINENTAL SHELF.  Columbia Journal of Transnational Law 7:279-301 (1968)

VLOS     Miljan, T.  MARE CLAUSUM BALTICUM AND THE LAW OF THE SEA.  Osteuropa Recht 21:103-118 (1975)

VOR      Miller, E.F.  DESALTING AS A SOURCE OF WATER SUPPLY.  Journal of the American Water Works Association 64(12):804-807 (1972)

VOD      Miller, H. Crane.  OCEAN DUMPING - PRELUDE AND FUGUE.  Journal of Maritime Law and Commerce 5:51-75 (1973)

VOCET    Miller, J.W., and D.C. Beaumariage.  NOAA'S MANNED UNDERSEA SCIENCE AND TECHNOLOGY PROGRAM.  Wissenschaftliche Meeresuntersuchungen 24(1-4):7-15 (1973)

IIIFP    Miller, M.M.  FACTORS IN THE FISH PICTURE OF CONCERN TO INDUSTRY AND CONSUMERS.  Marine Fisheries Review 35:20-25 (1973)

IIP&H    Miller, Stanton S.  THE CASE FOR DEEP PORT CONSTRUCTION.  Environmental Science and Technology 6(9):778-779 (1972)

VINTL    Miller, W.  A NEW INTERNATIONAL LAW FOR THE SUBMARINE?  U.S. Naval Institute Proceedings 92:96-103 (October, 1966)

IIIMM    Miller, William C.  KILLER WHALE MAY SAVE NET-BOUND PORPOISE.  National Fisherman 52(10):A15 (1972)

VP       Millett, Francis N., Jr.  POLLUTION AND THE FEDERAL REVENUE CODE. Wake Forest Law Review 8:535-551 (1972)

IVINTL   Milsten, D.E.  ENFORCING INTERNATIONAL LAW:  U.S. AGENCIES AND THE REGULATION OF OIL POLLUTION IN AMERICAN WATERS.  Journal of Maritime Law and Commerce 6(2):273-283 (1975)

VP       Milz, E.A.  EVALUATING OIL SPILL CONTROL EQUIPMENT AND TECHNIQUES. Ocean Industry 5:40-44 (1970)

VLOS     Mircea, T.  LA CONFÉRENCE DE L'O.N.U. SUR LE DROIT DE LA MER.  Revue Roumaine d'Etudes Internationales :21-34 (1975)

VCS	Miron, G. OUTER CONTINENTAL SHELF - MANAGING (OR MISMANAGING) ITS RESOURCES. Journal of Maritime Law 2:267-288 (1971)

IVMMR	Mirvahabi, Farin. CLAIMS TO THE OIL RESOURCES IN THE PERSIAN GULF: WILL THE WORLD ECONOMY BE CONTROLLED BY THE GULF IN THE FUTURE? Texas International Law Journal 11:75-112 (1976)

VP	Mizukami, C. IMCO AND MARINE POLLUTION. Journal of International Law and Diplomacy 72:642-662 (1974)

IIIOR	Moal, R.A. POUR UNE COOPERATION INTERNATIONALE DANS L'EXPLOITATION DES THONS TROPICAUX. France Peche 166:90-93 (1971/1972)

IVOSTR	MOBILE UNITS: RIGS UNDER CONSTRUCTION. Offshore 33(1):87-89,91, 94-100 (1973)

IVREFS	MOBILE UNITS - WORLDWIDE RIG LOCATION. Offshore 33:159,161-162- (1973)

IIIFP	Molteno, C.J. FULL UTILIZATION OF RAW MATERIAL ESSENTIAL IN S.A. TRAWL INDUSTRY. South African Shipping News and Fishing Industry Review 30(2):50-51 (1975)

IIILOS	Momtaz, D. LA QUESTION DES DETROITS À LA IIIE CONFERENCE DU DROIT DE LA MER. Annuaire Français de Droit International 20:860-874 (1974)

IIILOS	_____ _____ VERS UN NOUVEAU RÉGIME JURIDIQUE DES PECHERIES ADJA- CENTES. Revue Générale de Droit Internationale Public 78:228-245 (1974)

IIP&H	Monney, N.T. ENVIRONMENTAL PROTECTION FOR HARBORS. Journal of Environmental Sciences 16:17-21 (1973)

VCS	Montgomery, John E. MULTIPLE USE CONCEPT AS THE BASIS OF A NEW OUTER CONTINENTAL SHELF LEGISLATIVE POLICY. Kentucky Law Journal 62: 327-365 (1973-1974)

VP	Montgomery, Suzanne. COAST GUARD HAS NEW TOOL TO COUNTER TANKER OIL SPILLS. Undersea Technology 11:32-34 (1970)

VP	Moore, James B. ENVIRONMENTALIST AND RADIOACTIVE WASTE. Chicago-Kent Law Review 49:55-80 (1972)

VLOS	Moore, John Norton. THE LAW OF THE SEA: A CHOICE AND A CHALLENGE. Virginia Journal of International Law 15:791-793 (1975)

VOCET	Moore, J.R. THE FUTURE OF SCIENTIFIC RESEARCH IN CONTIGUOUS RESOURCE ZONES: LEGAL ASPECTS. International Lawyer 8:242-261 (1974)

VP	Moore, N.W. MARINE POLLUTION BY PESTICIDES AND POLYCHLORINATED BIPHENYLS. Journal of the Marine Biological Association of India 13(1-2):61-65 (1972)

VLOS	Morales Barria, F. y B Nun Peicihovici. MECANISMOS DEL ACUERDO DE CARTAGENA PARA LA ELABORACION DE UNA POLITICA DEL MAR. Boletin del Instituto de Docencia e Investigaciones Juridicas 19:129-142 (1973)

IVOSTR    Moreland, Douglas H. RECOVERY FOR INJURIES OR DEATH ON OFFSHORE DRILLING PLATFORMS: A PROBLEM OF APPLICABLE LAW UNDER THE LANDS ACT. Oregon Law Review 51(4):813-825 (1972)

IICZM     Morgan, R. ON THE LEGAL ASPECTS OF NORTH CAROLINA COASTAL PROBLEMS. North Carolina Law Review 49:857-865 (1971)

IVMMR     Morgenstein, M. A STUDY OF THE GROWTH MORPHOLOGIES OF TWO DEEP-SEA MANGANESE NODULES. Pacific Science 25(3):308-312 (1971)

IVMMR     Morgenstein, M., and J. Andrews. MANGENESE RESOURCES IN THE HAWAIIAN REGION. Marine Technological Society Journal 5(6):27-30 (1971)

VP        Morgenstern, Ann. RELATIONSHIP BETWEEN FEDERAL AND STATE LAWS TO CONTROL AND PREVENT POLLUTION. Environmental Law 1:238-256 (1971)

IIIEZ     Morin, Jacques-Yvan. LA ZONE DE PÊCHE EXCLUSIVE DU CANADA. Canadian Yearbook of International Law 2:77-106 (1964)

VLOS      _____ _____ LES NOUVELLES UTILISATIONS DU MILIEU MARIN ET L'AVENIR DU DROIT DE LA MER. Canadian Bar Review 51:333-388 (1973)

VP        Morley, C.G. POLLUTION AS A CRIME: THE FEDERAL RESPONSE. Manitoba Law Journal 5:297-311 (1973)

IVCS      Morris, J. NORTH SEA CONTINENTAL SHELF: OIL AND GAS LEGAL PROBLEMS. The International Lawyer 2:191-214 (1968)

VCS       _____ _____ OIL AND GAS LEGAL PROBLEMS ON THE NORTH SEA CONTINENTAL SHELF. Washburn Law Journal 7:245-269 (1968)

VB        Morris, Richard B. THE FORGING OF THE UNION RECONSIDERED: A HISTORICAL REFUTATION OF STATE SOVEREIGNTY OVER SEABEDS. Columbia Law Review 74:1056-1093 (1974)

IIIFP     Morris, Robert F., and James R. Stouffer. NEW FOOD PRODUCTS FROM SHARKS. New York's Food and Life Sciences Quarterly 8:3-7 (April-June, 1975)

IIIFV&G   Morris, Sam W. CAPTURA DO PEIXE POR MEIO DA ELECTRICIDADE. Revista Nacionale da Pesca 1971:26-28 (1971)

IIIP      Morrow, J.E. OIL-INDUCED MORTALITIES IN JUVENILE COHO AND SOCKEYE SALMON. Journal of Marine Research 31:135-143 (1973)

IIP&H     Mosely, J.C. ONE APPROACH TO THE SUPERPORT/REFINERY QUESTION. Marine Technology Society Journal 8(8):3-9 (1974)

IIP&H     Moss, Mitchell L. THE URBAN PORT: A HIDDEN RESOURCE FOR THE CITY AND THE COASTAL ZONE. Coastal Zone Management Journal 2(3):223-246 (1976)

VMT       Mostert, Noël. SUPERTANKERS. New Yorker :45-100 (13 May, 1974); 46-99 (20 May, 1974)

VLOS      Moya Dominguez, M.T. ESTUDIO PRELIMINAR COMO APORTE PARA LA REDACCIÓN DE ESTATUTO DE LOS PAÍSES SIN LITORAL MARÍTIMO. Arquivos do Ministério da Justiça 32:22-23 (1975)

| | |
|---|---|
| VP | Mrachek, L.L. METHOD OF ANALYSIS AND PRECEDENTS IN THE INTERNATIONAL LITIGATION OF MARINE POLLUTION CLAIMS. <u>Columbia Journal of Law and Social Problems</u> 9:537-574 (1973) |
| IVOCET | Mueller, C. ELEKTROTECHNISCHE ANLAGEN AUF OFFSHORE SYSTEMEN. <u>Meerestechnik</u> 5(2):53-56 (1974) |
| VENE | Muir, J.D. CHANGING LEGAL FRAMEWORK OF INTERNATIONAL ENERGY MANAGEMENT. <u>The International Lawyer</u> 9:605-614 (1975) |
| VENE | Muntzing, L.M. STANDARDIZATION IN NUCLEAR POWER. <u>Atomic Energy Law Journal</u> 15:21-33 (1973) |
| VOS | Murdoch, Joseph B. OCEAN PROJECTS COURSE. <u>Sea Grant '70s</u> 5(11):6-7 (1975) |
| VENE | Murphy, Earl F. THE EFFECT OF LAW, ECONOMICS, AND POLITICS ON ENERGY RESOURCES DEVELOPMENT. <u>Case Western Reserve Journal of International Law</u> 5:81-86 (1972) |
| IIIFV&G | Murray, J.A. BOATBUILDING FOR THE FISHING INDUSTRY. <u>Technology Ireland</u> 7:26-30 (1975) |
| VINTL | Murray, S. DISCUSSION OF THE WORLD COURT'S NORTH SEA JUDGMENT. <u>American University Law Review</u> 19:470-493 (1970) |
| VINTL | _____ _____ NORTH SEA CONTINENTAL SHELF CASES: A CRITIQUE. <u>JAG Journal</u> 24:87-98 (1969-1970) |
| VP | Murray, Stephen P. TURBULENT DIFFUSION OF OIL IN THE OCEAN. <u>Limnology and Oceanography</u> 17:651-660 (1972) |
| VINTL | Murty, B. THE INTERNATIONAL REGULATION OF THE USES OF THE SEA-BED AND OCEAN FLOOR. <u>The Indian Journal of International Law</u> 9:72-77 (1969) |
| VENV | Muskie, Edmund S. ENVIRONMENTAL PROGRAM FOR AMERICA. <u>Environmental Law</u> 1:2-7 (1970) |
| IIIF | Nagasaki, F. SOME JAPANESE FAR-SEA FISHERIES. <u>Washington Law Review</u> 43:197-229 (1967) |
| VB | Nakamura, K. THE BREADTH OF THE TERRITORIAL SEA IN A CHANGING INTERNATIONAL LAW: IN CONNECTION WITH THE DRAFT ARTICLES SUBMITTED BY THE UNITED STATES IN 1971. <u>Hogaku Kenkyu</u> 45(2):105-130 (1972) |
| VINTL | Nanda, V. SOME LEGAL QUESTIONS ON THE PEACEFUL USES OF OCEAN SPACE. <u>Virginia Journal of International Law</u> 9:343-407 (1969) |
| VP | Nanda, Ved P. THE "TORREY CANYON" DISASTER: SOME LEGAL ASPECTS. <u>Denver Law Journal</u> 44(3):400-425 (1967) |
| VP | Nanda, Ved P., and Kenneth R. Stiles. OFFSHORE OIL SPILLS: AN EVALUATION OF RECENT UNITED STATES RESPONSES. <u>San Diego Law Review</u> 7:519-540 (1970) |
| VENV | NATIONAL ENVIRONMENTAL POLICY ACT OF 1969 AND THE ENERGY CRISIS: THE ROAD TO ALASKA. <u>Columbia Journal of Law and Social Problems</u> 10:265-327 (1974) |

| | |
|---|---|
| IIIF | NATIONAL FISHERIES SEMINAR. HELD IN CANBERRA, AUSTRALIA, DECEMBER 6-10, 1971. Australian Fisheries 31(1):1-31 (1972) |
| VP | NATIONAL OIL AND HAZARDOUS SUBSTANCES POLLUTION CONTINGENCY PLAN. Federal Register 38(155):21887-21909 (1973); 40(28):6281-6302 (February 10, 1975) |
| IVP | National Petroleum Council. PROTECTION OF THE MARINE ENVIRONMENT. Natural Resources Lawyer VIII(3):511-543 (1975) |
| IIICONS | NATIONAL SHELLFISH SAFETY PROGRAM: PROPOSED RULEMAKING. Federal Register 40(119):25915-25935 (June 19, 1975) |
| VB | NATIONAL SOVEREIGNTY AND THE TWO HUNDRED MILE LIMIT: THE CASE FOR THE LITTORAL STATE. American University Law Review 21:593-608 (1972) |
| IIIFV&G | NAVIO-FABRICA-O FUTURO E SEU OS NOVOS CAMINHOS DA PESCA EM ALTOMAR. Revista Nacional da Pesca 1971:62-63 (1971) |
| VB | Nawaz, M.K. ALTERNATIVE CRITERIA FOR DELIMITING THE CONTINENTAL SHELF. Indian Journal of International Law 13:25-40 (1973) |
| VINTL | _____ _____ CHINESE VIEW ON THE LAW OF THE SEA; SELECTED ASPECTS. Indian Journal of International Law 12:606-614 (1972) |
| VEZ | _____ _____ THE LIMITS OF THE COASTAL STATE JURISDICTION: CONTINENTAL SHELF, FISHERIES AND ECONOMIC ZONE. Indian Journal of International Law 14:261-279 (1974) |
| IIIINTL | Nawaz, M.K., and Lakshmi Jambholkar. THE SHANK FISHERIES CASE REVISITED. Indian Journal of International Law 13(3):494-510 (1973) |
| IVMMR | Neff, C.H. REVIEW OF 1970 PETROLEUM DEVELOPMENTS IN SOUTH AMERICA, CENTRAL AMERICA AND THE CARIBBEAN AREA. American Association of Petroleum Geologists Bulletin 55:1418-1482 (1971) |
| IIENV | Nehman, G., et al. LAND USE AND ENVIRONMENTAL PLANNING: AN APPLICATION IN THE SOUTH CAROLINA COASTAL ZONE. Water Resources Bulletin 11:759-769 (1975) |
| IISL | Nelson, D. STATE DISPOSITION OF SUBMERGED LANDS VERSUS PUBLIC RIGHTS IN NAVIGABLE WATERS. Natural Resources Lawyer 3(3):491-511 (1970) |
| IIE | Nelson, J.C. THE EFFECTS OF WATER RESOURCES DEVELOPMENT ON ESTUARINE ENVIRONMENTS. Water Resources Bulletin 9:1249-1257 (1973) |
| VINTL | Nelson, L.D.M. NORTH SEA CONTINENTAL SHELF CASES AND LAW-MAKING CONVENTIONS. Modern Law Review 35:52-56 (1972) |
| VINTL | _____ _____ THE PATRIMONIAL SEA. International and Comparative Law Quarterly 22:668-686 (1973) |
| IVOL | NETHERLANDS AWARDS 26 NORTH SEA BLOCKS. Oil and Gas Journal 70(50):64-65 (1972) |
| VP | NETHERLANDS; MARINE POLLUTION. Financial Times 6: (July 18, 1972) |
| IVMMR | NEW BRUNSWICK AND OFFSHORE MINERAL RIGHTS. University of New Brunswick Law Journal 22:69-88 (1973) |

| | |
|---|---|
| IVOSTR | NEW DEEPWATER PLATFORM FOR THE NORTH SEA. Ocean Industry 10:21-24 (1975) |
| IVDRIL | NEW DRILLING SHIP FOR GULF. Northern Offshore 3(4): (1974) |
| IIP&H | NEW ERA FOR WORLD PORTS. Surveyor 8(2):14-24 (1974) |
| IIIF | NEW FISHING LAWS FOR NORTHERN TERRITORY. Australian Fisheries 32:4-5 (1973) |
| VOCET | NEW FRENCH EXPERIMENTAL SUBMARINE. Ocean Industry 5(2):39-39 (1970) |
| IVDRIL | NEW GENERATION JACKUP DRILLS IN 300-FOOT WATER. World Oil 175(1):36-36 (1972) |
| VP | NEW LAB METHODS IDENTIFY OIL SPILL ORIGINS. World Oil 180:111-112, 114 (1972) |
| VP | NEW OPPORTUNITIES FOR STATE PARTICIPATION IN THE CONTROL OF RADIOACTIVE POLLUTION. Chicago-Kent Law Review 52:157-168 (1975) |
| VENV | NEW PERSPECTIVES ON INTERNATIONAL ENVIRONMENTAL LAW. Yale Law Journal 82:1659-1680 (1973) |
| IIP&H | NEW TEESIDE BULK TERMINAL. Shipping World and Shipbuilder 168:65, 67 (1975) |
| IIIFV&G | NEW TRAWLING AID IN WEST GERMAN FACTORY SHIP. Fishing News International 12(1):52,55 (1973) |
| VOCET | NEW TYPE OCEAN RESEARCH VESSEL. Marine Engineering/Log 79(3):63-65 (1974) |
| IIIFV&G | NEW VESSELS: THREE FROM NORTH AMERICA. World Fishing 23:15-16 (1974) |
| VP | NEW ZEALAND: MARINE POLLUTION. New Zealand High Commission News Bulletin (March 7, 1973) |
| VINTL | NEWFOUNDLAND FORMULATES OFFSHORE RESOURCE POLICY. World Oil 175(4):80-81 (1972) |
| VOR | Newton, W. THE NEW QUEST FOR ATLANTIS: PROPOSED REGIMES FOR SEABED RESOURCES. JAG Journal 25:79-92 (1970-1971) |
| VOR | _____ SEABED RESOURCES: THE PROBLEMS OF ADOLESCENCE. San Diego Law Review 8:551-572 (1971) |
| IICZM | NFI TALKS COASTAL ZONES, LIMITS, MANAGEMENT. Fish Boat 19(7):22-25, 51-55 (1974) |
| VINTL | Niblock, R. BAR ASSOCIATION PROBES U.N. UNDERSEA ROLE. Technology Week 20:39-40 (June 19, 1967) |
| IIOSTR | Nichols, A.R., and R.C. Nichols. FLOATING NUCLEAR POWER PLANTS FOR OFFSHORE SITING. Combustion 44(12):10-16 (1973) |
| IIIF | Nichols, J.P. TRENDS IN CATCH-EFFORT RELATIONSHIPS WITH ECONOMIC IMPLICATIONS: GULF OF MEXICO SHRIMP FISHERY. Marine Fisheries Review 37(2):1-4 (1975) |

| | |
|---|---|
| VOR | Nicholson, William N. A NAVY VIEW OF OCEAN RESOURCES. <u>Natural Resources Lawyer</u> 1:77-81 (1968) |
| IISL | Niering, William A. THE WETLANDS. <u>Ecology Today</u> 2(2):32-36,50 (1972) |
| IVDRIL | NIGERIA HOGS SPOTLIGHT IN DRILLING ACTIVITY OFF AFRICA. <u>Offshore</u> 33(7):121,123 (1973) |
| VLOS | 1958 GENEVA CONVENTIONS ON THE LAW OF THE SEA. <u>Record</u> 14:464-474 (1959) |
| VENV | 1974 AMENDMENTS TO WASHINGTON'S STATE ENVIRONMENTAL POLICY ACT. <u>Gonzaga Law Review</u> 10:787-802 (1975) |
| VORM | NIXON PROPOSAL FOR AN INTERNATIONAL SEABED AUTHORITY. <u>Oregon Law Review</u> 50:599-618 (1972) Part II |
| VOCET | NOAA RESEARCH SHIPS PROBE THE WORLD OCEANS. <u>International Offshore Technology</u> 13(12):18-19 (1972) |
| IVMMR | Noakes, John E., et al. LOCATING OFFSHORE MINERAL DEPOSITS BY NATURAL RADIOACTIVE MEASUREMENTS. <u>Marine Technical Society Journal</u> 8:36-39 (1974) |
| IIICONS | Noble, J. OVERFISHED OR UNDERUTILIZED? <u>Fish Boat</u> 19(3):27,52-53 (1974) |
| VOD | NO DUMPING IN THIS OCEAN: NEARING THE END OF SHIP-GENERATED POLLUTION. <u>New York University Journal of International Law and Politics</u> 7:545-573 (1974) |
| VMT | Nolta, F. PASSAGE THROUGH INTERNATIONAL STRAITS: FREE OR INNOCENT? <u>San Diego Law Review</u> 11:815-833 (1974) |
| IIIB | Nomura, L. FISHERIES JURISDICTION BEYOND THE TERRITORIAL SEA, WITH SPECIAL REFERENCE TO THE POLICY OF THE UNITED STATES. <u>Washington Law Review</u> 44:307-334 (1968) |
| IVMMR | NON-LIVING RESOURCES OF THE SEA. A CRITIQUE. <u>Natural Resources Lawyer</u> 2(4):409-439 (1969) |
| IICZM | NON-RESIDENT RESTRICTIONS IN MUNICIPALLY OWNED BEACHES: APPROACHES TO THE PROBLEM. <u>Columbia Journal of Law and Social Problems</u> 10:177-227 (1974) |
| IVDRIL | NORDIC COOPERATION ON NEW DRILLING VESSEL. <u>Northern Offshore</u> 2(1):25-26,29-30 (1973) |
| VINTL | Nordquist, Myron H. LEGAL STATUS OF ARTICLES 1-3 OF THE CONTINENTAL SHELF CONVENTION ACCORDING TO THE NORTH SEA CASES. <u>California Western International Law Journal</u> 1:60-79 (1970) |
| VLOS | Nordquist, Myron H., and Amanda Lee Moore. EMERGING LAW OF THE SEA: ISSUES IN THE MARIANA ISLANDS. <u>Journal of International Law and Economics</u> 7:43-59 (1972) |
| IVMMR | Norgaard, Richard B. PETROLEUM DEVELOPMENT IN ALASKA: PROSPECTS AND CONFLICTS. <u>Natural Resources Journal</u> 12:83-107 (1972) |

| | |
|---|---|
| IVMMR | Norris, J. THE NORTH SEA CONTINENTAL SHELF: OIL AND GAS PROBLEMS. The International Lawyer 2:191-214 (1968) |
| IIIOR | Norris, Russel T. THE FUTURE OF NEW ENGLAND'S MARINE RESOURCES. Commercial Fisheries Review 34:12-18 (1972) |
| IIIINTL | NORTH PACIFIC FISHERIES TREATIES AND INTERNATIONAL LAW OF THE SEAS. Washington Law Review 38:223-248 (1963) |
| IVOCET | NORTH SEA: A WORKSITE FOR MANNED SUBMARINES. Petroleum Engineers 46:11-12 (1974) |
| IVMMR | NORTH SEA ACTION TAKES LEAD FROM GULF OF MEXICO. Offshore 32(12): 33-37 (1972) |
| IVMMR | NORTH SEA MAJORS - WHO BUYS WHAT? Offshore Services 7(8):42-44 (1974) |
| IVM | NORTH SEA RIG CONTRACTS, 1973/1974. Offshore Services 6(1):13,15 (1973) |
| IVREFS | NORTH SEA RIGS - WHO DOES WHAT. Offshore Services 6(1):38-39 (1972); 8:34-37 (1975) |
| IVOCET | NORTH SEA TO GET FIRST MANNED SEAFLOOR COMPLETION. World Oil 176(5): 139-139 (1973) |
| IIIF | NORTH-EAST ATLANTIC FISHERIES COMMISSION: RECOMMENDATIONS. Aftenposten :18 (May 16, 1973) |
| IIF | NORTHWEST ATLANTIC COMMERCIAL FISHERIES. NOTICE OF PROPOSED RULE MAKING. 50 CFR PART 240. Federal Register 38(25):3517-3523 (February 7, 1973) |
| IIIOSTR | NORWAY BUILDS FLOATING FISH MEAL AND OIL FACTORY. Commercial Fisheries Review 34(3-4):40-41 (1972) |
| IVCS | NORWAY; CONTINENTAL SHELF. Aftenposten (Evening Edition):20-20 (December 8, 1972) |
| IIIAFF | NORWAY: FISH FARMS. Aftenposten :2-2 (May 19, 1973); :20-20 (June 9, 1973) |
| IIIF | NORWAY: FISHERIES. Aftenposten :7-7 (June 13, 1973) |
| IIIINTL | NORWAY; FISHING LIMITS. Aftenposten :3-3 (August 4, 1972); Guardian :4-4 (August 15, 1972) |
| VLOS | NORWAY; LAW OF THE SEA. Aftenposten :1-1 (June 22, 1973); :18-18 (June 26, 1973) |
| VP | NORWAY; OIL POLLUTION. Aftenposten :12-12 (September 26, 1972); :8-8 (March 22, 1973) |
| VP | NORWAY: POLLUTION. Aftenposten :20-20 (December 19, 1972); :8-8 (April 16, 1973) |
| IVOSTR | NORWAY SPREADS THE NET. Offshore Services 7:15-16 (1974) |

| | |
|---|---|
| IIIF | NORWAY/USSR/UK: ARCTIC COD. Aftenposten :27-27 (1973) |
| IVM | NORWEGIAN EXPERTISE PREPARING TO MEET THE NORTH SEA CHALLENGE. Northern Offshore 2(1):6,9-10 (1973) |
| IIIF | NORWEGIAN FLEET ACTIVITIES: 1972. Tanker and Bulk Carrier 19(8): 18-19,26 (1972) |
| IIIF | Nosov, N. THE OCEAN CAN PROVIDE MORE. National Fisherman 52(13): 74-75 (1972) |
| IIIF | A NOSSA FROTA PESQUEIRA E SUA PRODUCAO ANNUAL. Revista Nacional da Pesca 13(110):14-15 (1971) |
| VENV | NUISANCE ACTION: A USEFUL TOOL FOR THE ENVIRONMENTAL LAWYER. University of New Brunswick Law Journal 23:21-29 (May, 1974) |
| IIB | Nunez, Peter K. FLUCTUATING SHORELINES AND TIDAL BOUNDARIES: AN UNRESOLVED PROBLEM. San Diego Law Review 6:447-469 (1969) |
| VINTL | Nweihed, Kaldone G. VENEZUELA'S CONTRIBUTION TO THE CONTEMPORARY LAW OF THE SEA. San Diego Law Review 11:603-632 (1974) |
| VB | Nwogugu, E.I. PROBLEMS OF NIGERIAN OFF-SHORE JURISDICTION. International and Comparative Law Quarterly 22:349-363 (1973) |
| VLOS | Nye, J.S. OCEAN RULE MAKING FROM A WORLD POLITICS PERSPECTIVE. Ocean Development and International Law 3:29-52 (1975) |
| VLOS | Nyhart, J.D. THE INTERPLAY OF LAW AND TECHNOLOGY IN DEEP SEABED MINING ISSUES. Virginia Journal of International Law 15:825-868 (1975) |
| IVINTL | NORTH SEA CONTINENTAL SHELF CASE. VARIOUS DOCUMENTS. International Legal Materials 8:340,343 (1969); 10:600 (1971) |
| IVMMR | Oakley, S.D. SOLVING THE PROBLEMS OF OFFSHORE EXPLORATION. Meerestechnik 4:A12-A14 (1973) |
| VLOS | O'Brien, William V., and A.C. Chapelli. LAW OF THE SEA IN THE "CANADIAN" ARCTIC: THE PATTERN OF CONTROVERSY. McGill Law Journal 19: 322-366 (1973) |
| VOD | OCEAN DUMPING: FINAL REGULATIONS AND CRITERIA. EPA. Federal Register 38(198):28609-29621 (October 15, 1973) |
| VOCET | OCEANOLOGICAL RESEARCH FROM MANNED UNDERWATER LABORATORIES. Oceanology 12(1):120-130 (1972) |
| VP | OCEAN POLLUTION: AN EXAMINATION OF THE PROBLEM AND AN APPEALS FOR INTERNATIONAL COOPERATION. San Diego Law Review 7:574-604 (1970) |
| VOR | OCEAN RESOURCES. Stanford Journal of International Studies IV:142p. (1969) |
| VB | O'Connell, D. PROBLEMS OF AUSTRALIAN COASTAL JURISDICTION. Australian Law Journal 42:39-51 (1968) |
| VB | _____ _____ PROBLEMS OF AUSTRALIAN COASTAL JURISDICTION. British Yearbook of International Law 34:199-259 (1958) |

| | |
|---|---|
| IIIF | O'Connell, D. SEDENTARY FISHERIES AND THE AUSTRALIAN CONTINENTAL SHELF. American Journal of International Law 49:185-209 (1955) |
| IVP | O'Connell, Dennis M. CONTINENTAL SHELF OIL DISASTERS: CHALLENGE TO INTERNATIONAL POLLUTION CONTROL. Cornell Law Review 55(1):113-128 (1969) |
| VB | O'Connell, D.P. JURIDICAL NATURE OF THE TERRITORIAL SEA. British Yearbook of International Law 45:303-383 (1971) |
| VOR | _____ _____ LEGAL PROBLEMS OF THE EXPLOITATION OF THE OCEAN FLOOR. Impact of Science on Society 21(3):253-264 (1971) |
| VAC | _____ _____ LEGALITY OF NAVAL CRUISE MISSILES. American Journal of International Law 66:785-794 (1972) |
| VINTL | _____ _____ MID-OCEAN ARCHIPELAGOS IN INTERNATIONAL LAW. British Yearbook of International Law 45:1-77 (1971) |
| VOCET | O'Connor, Dennis M. DECADE OF OCEAN EXPLORATION. Lawyer of the Americas 1(2):100-106 (1969) |
| VOR | _____ _____ THE OCEANS. Lawyer of the Americas 1(1):93-100 (1969) |
| VB | Oda, Shigeru. BOUNDARY OF THE CONTINENTAL SHELF. Japanese Annual of International Law :264-284 (1968) |
| VB | _____ _____ THE DELIMITATION OF THE CONTINENTAL SHELF IN SOUTHEAST ASIA AND THE FAR EAST. Ocean Management 1:327-346 (1973) |
| VLOS | _____ _____ THE GENEVA CONVENTIONS ON THE LAW OF THE SEA: SOME SUGGESTIONS FOR THEIR REVISION. Natural Resources Lawyer 1(2):103-113 (1968) |
| VINTL | _____ _____ THE INTERNATIONAL LAW OF THE OCEAN DEVELOPMENT: BASIC DOCUMENTS (COMPILED AND EDITED). Harvard International Law Journal 14(2):409-411 (1973) |
| IIIINTL | _____ _____ JAPAN AND INTERNATIONAL CONVENTIONS RELATING TO NORTH PACIFIC FISHERIES. Washington Law Review 43:63-75 (1967) |
| VP | _____ _____ MARINE POLLUTION AND INTERNATIONAL LAW. Journal of International Law and Diplomacy 72:599-622 (1974) |
| VLOS | _____ _____ NEW DEVELOPMENTS IN THE UNITED NATIONS SEABED COMMITTEE. Journal of Maritime Law and Commerce 4:577-598 (1973) |
| VCS | _____ _____ PROPOSALS FOR REVISING THE CONVENTION ON THE CONTINENTAL SHELF. Columbia Journal of Transnational Law 7:1-31 (1968) |
| VINTL | _____ _____ SOME OBSERVATIONS ON THE INTERNATIONAL LAW OF THE SEA. Japanese Annual of International Law :37-50 (1967) |
| VOR | _____ _____ TOWARDS A NEW REGIME FOR OCEAN DEVELOPMENT. Ocean Development and International Law 1:291-302 (1973) |
| IVDRIL | ODECO TAKES DELIVERY ON NEW RIG, A SEMISUBMERSIBLE. OCEAN VICTORY. Offshore 32(13):92-92 (1972) |

VINTL      Odnopozov, P.S.  INTERNATIONAL LEGAL REGIME OF ARCTIC SEAS' SPACES.
           Pravovedenie 4:78-82 (1973)

IVM        O'Donnell, John.  HUMBLE EXTENDS OFFSHORE OIL LINE.  Oil and Gas
           Journal 70(43):60-63 (1972)

IIOSTR     O'Donnell, J.P.  MULTIPLATFORM COMPLEX SERVES OFFSHORE GAS LINE.  Oil
           and Gas Journal 71(38):93-95 (1973)

IIIINTL    O'Donovan, Vincent.  ICELANDIC FISHERIES DISPUTE - LEGAL IMPLICATIONS.
           New Law Journal 123:527-529 (1973)

VINTL      OECD STUDY ON FLAGS OF CONVENIENCE.  Journal of Maritime Law and Commerce 4:231-254 (1973)

VP         Oesterling, J.F., and L.A. Spano.  WASTE PAPER USED FOR THE CLEANUP
           OF OIL SPILLS.  Science 181:775-775 (1973)

IVOSTR     OFFSHORE CONSTRUCTION REFLECTS BOOM.  Offshore 31(12):70- (1972)

IVDRIL     OFFSHORE DRILLING PRACTICES.  World Oil 160:110-115 (1965)

IVM        OFFSHORE GERMANY.  Northern Offshore 3(4):92,95-96 (1974)

IVM        OFFSHORE MINING PAVES THE WAY TO OCEAN MINERAL WEALTH.  Engineering
           and Mining Journal 5:124-132 (1965)

IVDRIL     OFFSHORE OIL DRILLING: A QUESTION OF PACE.  Congressional Quarterly
           Weekly Report 32:1967-1970 (July 27, 1974)

IVMLAD     OFFSHORE OIL PLATFORMS AND ADMIRALTY LAW:  RODRIGUE IN RETROSPECT.
           Tulane Law Review 49:658-677 (1975)

IVOI       OFFSHORE OIL'S MARINE SERVICES:  THE PROBLEM AND POSSIBLE SOLUTIONS.
           Ocean Industry 8(6):43-45 (1973)

IVOSTR     OFFSHORE PLATFORM HANDLES 450,000 B/D.  Petroleum Engineer.  45:55-55
           (1973)

IVOI       OFFSHORE PRODUCTION PRACTICES.  World Oil 160:124-140 (1965)

IVOSTR     OFFSHORE WORKING PLATFORMS COMBINED WITH VESSELS.  Northern Offshore
           2:92,95-96,99-100 (1973)

VLOS       Ogley, R.C.  BIRTH-PANGS OR DEATH RATTLE?:  THE COMMON HERITAGE AT
           GENEVA.  International Relations 5:876-896 (1975)

VLOS       _____ _____ CARACAS AND THE COMMON HERITAGE.  International Relations (London) 4:604-628 (1974)

VINTL      Ogundere, J.G.  DEVELOPMENT OF INTERNATIONAL ENVIRONMENTAL LAW AND
           POLICY IN AFRICA.  Natural Resources Journal 12:255-270 (1972)

VINTL      O'Higgins, P.  IRISH MARITIME JURISDICTION ACT, 1959.  International
           and Comparative Law Quarterly 9:325-334 (1960)

IIIINTL    Ohiro, Z.  FISHERY PROBLEMS BETWEEN SOVIET RUSSIA AND JAPAN.  Japanese Annual of International Law 2:1-18 (1958)

| | |
|---|---|
| IVMMR | Ohly, D. Christopher. INTERNATIONAL SEABED RESOURCES: THE U.S. POSITION. Virginia Journal of International Law 15(4):903-925 (1975) |
| VOI | Ohmura, T. THE STATUS OF MARINE DEVELOPMENT IN JAPAN. Marine Technology Society Journal 8:29-33 (1974) |
| VP | Ohya, M., et al. OIL POLLUTION IN THE IZU ISLAND WATERS. Nippon Kaiyo Gakki-Shi 29: (1973) |
| IIP | OIL AND ESTUARY POLLUTION CONTROL: A QUICK LOOK AT SOME DEVELOPMENTS. Water and Waste Treatment Journal 18:24-28 (1975) |
| IVOL | OIL AND GAS - AN OIL AND GAS LESSEE OWES THE DUTY TO REFRAIN FROM INTENTIONALLY INJURING SURFACE LESSEE'S LIVESTOCK WITHIN THE LEGITIMATE OPERATING AREA OF THE OIL AND GAS LEASE. Texas Tech Law Review 5: 195-199 (1973) |
| IVOL | OIL AND GAS - MINERAL LESSEE CANNOT USE SALT WATER EXTRACTED FROM THE LEASED TRACT TO IMPROVE MINERAL RECOVERY ON OTHER TRACTS. Texas Law Review 52:781-789 (1974) |
| IVP | OIL AND GAS WELL OPERATOR'S LIABILITY TO LESSOR-SURFACE OWNER FOR SLUSH PIT OVERFLOW OR SEEPAGE. Mississippi Law Journal 44:980-995 (1973) |
| IVMMR | OIL CHANGING THE FACE OF SCOTLAND. Northern Offshore 3(5):21-22,25-26, 29 (1974) |
| IVMMR | OIL-EXPLORATION AND PRODUCTION. Dock and Harbour Authority 55(644): 58-60 (1974) |
| IVMMR | OIL MAKES DEEP WATER PLANS. Oil and Gas Journal 62:81-85 (1964) |
| IVOL | OIL MEN AND THE SEA: THE FUTURE OF OCEAN RESOURCE DEVELOPMENT IN LIGHT OF SANTA BARBARA - SOME PROPOSALS TO RECTIFY CONTINUING INADEQUATE FEDERAL REGULATION OF OFFSHORE LEASING. Arizona Law Review 11:677-730 (1969) |
| IVOSTR | OIL PIPELINES LAID IN TRENCH ACROSS CANAL. World Dredging and Marine Construction 10(3): (1974) |
| IVMMR | AN OIL POLICY PROPOSED. Pacific Northwest Sea 8(4) 1975; 9(1):3-4 (1976) |
| VP | OIL POLLUTION ACT AMENDMENTS OF 1973. Law and Policy in International Business 6:1251-1261 (1975) |
| IVP | OIL POLLUTION PREVENTION: NON-TRANSPORTATION-RELATED ONSHORE AND OFFSHORE FACILITIES; PROPOSED RULE-MAKING. EPA. Federal Register 38 (138):19333-19339 (July 19, 1973) 38(237:34163-34170 (1973) |
| VP | OIL POLLUTION REGULATIONS. Work Boat 30(7):23-23 (1973) |
| VP | OIL POLLUTION: WHAT'S AVAILABLE TO PREVENT OR CONTROL SPILLS. Marine Engineering/Log 77:25-29 (1973) |
| IVOI | OIL SUPPLIER - A SERVICE VESSEL FOR OFFSHORE RIGS. Shipbuilding and Marine Engineering International 95(1158):424-427 (1972) |

| | |
|---|---|
| IVMMR | OIL UPDATE '76. Pacific Northwest Sea 8(4): (1975); 9(1):16-21 (1976) |
| VP | OILY BALLAST DISCHARGE REQUIREMENTS. Notice of proposed rule making. 46 CFR parts 35, 56, 74, 93, 191. Federal Register 38(31):4516-4517 (February 15, 1973) |
| IIIF | Okamoto, Issamul. O EMPRESARIO DA PESCA. Revista Nacional da Pesca 12(96): (1970) |
| VB | Okuhara, T. THE TERRITORIAL SOVEREIGNTY OVER THE SENKAKU ISLANDS AND PROBLEMS ON THE SURROUNDING CONTINENTAL SHELF. Japanese Annual of International Law 15:97-106 (1971) |
| IIIOR | Olds, N.V., and H.W. Glassen. DO STATES STILL OWN THEIR FISH AND GAME? Michigan State Bar Journal 30:16-23 (1951) |
| IIIF | Oliver, Edward F. WET WAR - NORTH PACIFIC. San Diego Law Review 8:621-638 (1971) |
| VOD | Olivier, J.P. SEA DISPOSAL OF PACKAGED RADIOACTIVE WASTES. Transactions 20:693-695 (1975) |
| IIIFV&G | Oliveira, Helena P.de. PESCA DA LAGOSTA - TIPOS DE COVOS. Revista Nacional da Pesca 1971:88-91 (1971) |
| IVMMR | Olson, W.S. ATLANTIC OFFSHORE - THE LAST FRONTIER FOR U.S. OIL. Oil and Gas Journal 71(25):106-108 (1973) |
| VOR | O'Meara, J.W. CURRENT STATUS OF THE DESALTING PROGRAM IN THE UNITED STATES OF AMERICA. Desalination 14(2):239-247 (1974) |
| VP | Ono, S. THERMAL POLLUTION. Kagaku 44(2):110-116 (1974) |
| IVOL | OPERATORS TO TAKE ON A BIG CHUNK OF GULF OF MEXICO. Offshore 33:53-55 (1973) |
| VLOS | Opoku, K. THE LAW OF THE SEA AND THE DEVELOPING COUNTRIES. Revue de Droit International de Sciences Diplomatiques et Politiques 51:28-45 (1973) |
| IIILOS | Opsahl, T. TOWARD THE RULE OF INTERNATIONAL LAW IN HIGH SEAS FISHERIES. Nordisk Tidsskrift 27:265-322 (1957) |
| IIIFP | Oren, O.H. MULLET AS A WORLD PROTEIN SOURCE. Australian Fisheries 34:19-20 (1975) |
| VB | ORGANISATION OF AFRICAN UNITY: TERRITORIAL WATERS. Irish Times :6 (February 8, 1973) |
| VB | Orlin, Hyman. OFFSHORE BOUNDARIES: ENGINEERING AND ECONOMIC ASPECTS. Ocean Development and International Law 3(1):87-96 (1975) |
| IVMMR | Osberger, R., and C.M. Romanowitz. HOW THE OFF-SHORE INDONESIAN TIN PLACERS ARE EXPLORED AND SAMPLED. World Mining 20:52-58 (1967) |
| VORM | Osgood, R.E. U.S. SECURITY INTERESTS IN OCEAN LAW. Ocean Development and International Law Journal 2:1-36 (1974) |

| | |
|---|---|
| VLOS | Ostroviskii, Ia. A. INTERNATIONAL LEGAL PROTECTION OF THE SEAS FROM POLLUTION. Ocean Development and International Law Journal 3:287-302 (1976) |
| VP | O'Sullivan, A.J. COASTAL WATERS - PROTECTION OR POLLUTION? Environment this Month. The International Journal of Environmental Science 1(2):55-61 (1972) |
| IIIINTL | Ottenheimer, Gerald R. PATTERNS OF DEVELOPMENT IN INTERNATIONAL FISHERY LAW. Canadian Yearbook of International Law 11:37-47 (1973) |
| VCS | Oxman, Bernard H. PREPARATION OF ARTICLE 1 OF THE CONVENTION ON THE CONTINENTAL SHELF. Journal of Maritime Law and Commerce 3:245,445,683 (1972) |
| VLOS | Oxman, Bernard H., and Mary B. West. ISSUES TO BE RESOLVED IN THE SECOND SUBSTANTIVE SESSION OF THE THIRD UNITED NATIONS CONFERENCE ON THE LAW OF THE SEA. Columbia Journal of Transnational Law 14:87-101 (1975) |
| IVM | OXY SCORES 9,200-B/D STRIKE OFF NIGERIA. Oil and Gas Journal 70(29):67-67 (1972) |
| IVM | OXY'S FIND IS CURTAIN-RAISER TO NORTH SEA'S BUSIEST YEAR. Offshore Services 6(1):19-122 (1973) |
| VB | Oyarce Y., P.E. LAS 200 MILLAS Y LOS PAÍSES LATINO-AMERICANOS. Anales de la Facultad de Ciencias Juridicas y Sociales (Chile) :111-163 (1971) |
| VMT | Padelford, Norman J. OCEAN COMMERCE AND THE PANAMA CANAL. Journal of Maritime Law and Commerce 4(3):397-423 (1973) |
| VB | Padwa, D.J. SUBMARINE BOUNDARIES. International and Comparative Law Quarterly 9:628-652 (1960) |
| IIIFV&G | PAIR OF FAST NEW TUNA SUPERSEINERS DESIGNED TO FISH ANYWHERE IN WORLD. Fish Boat 17(8):22-23 (1972) |
| IIIF | PAKISTAN: FISHING LIMITS. Svenska Dagbladet :8 (March 23, 1973) |
| VB | Palmer, William R. TERRITORIAL SEA AGREEMENT - KEY TO PROGRESS IN THE LAW OF THE SEA. JAG Journal XXV(3):69-78 (1970/1971) |
| VC | PANAMA: THE PROPOSED TRANSFER OF THE CANAL AND CANAL ZONE BY TREATY. Georgia Journal of International and Comparative Law 5:195-215 (1975) |
| VC | PANAMA-USA: WATERWAYS. ABC :35 (February 23, 1973) |
| VLOS | Paolillo, F.H. REVOLUCION EN LOS OCÉANOS. Revista Uruguaya de Derecho Internacional 1:49-96 (1972) |
| VODAS | Papadakis, N. SOME LEGAL PROBLEMS ASSOCIATED WITH THE OCEAN DATA ACQUISITION SYSTEMS, AIDS AND DEVICES, ODAS. International Relations 5:825-837,856 (1975) |

IIIINTL  Papandreou, Alexandre. LA SITUATION JURIDIQUE DES PÊCHERIES SEDEN-
TAIRES EN HAUTE-MER; CONTRIBUTION À L'ETUDE DU DROIT INTERNATIONAL
MARITIME. Revue Hellenique de Droit International, Athens, 1958
Llème Année 1-2:1-148 (1958)

VOR  PARCELLING OUT THE SEA. New Scientist 41:494-494 (1969)

VB  Pardo, A. SOVEREIGNTY UNDER THE SEA. Round Table :341-355 (1968)

VLOS  _____ _____ A STATEMENT ON THE FUTURE LAW OF THE SEA IN LIGHT OF
CURRENT TRENDS IN NEGOTIATIONS. Ocean Development and International
Law Journal 1:315-335 (1974)

VOR  _____ _____ WHO WILL CONTROL THE SEABED. Foreign Affairs 47:123-
137 (1968)

VOR  _____ _____ WHOSE IS THE BED OF THE SEA? American Society of International Legal Proceedings 62:216-229 (1968)

VLOS  Pardo, H.E. Arvid. A STATEMENT ON THE FUTURE LAW OF THE SEA IN
LIGHT OF CURRENT TRENDS IN NEGOTIATIONS. Ocean Development and International Law Journal 1(4):315-336 (1974)

IIIINTL  Park, Choon-ho. FISHING UNDER TROUBLED WATERS: THE NORTHEAST ASIA
FISHERIES CONTROVERSY. Ocean Development and International Law 2:
93-135 (1974)

IVINTL  _____ _____ OIL UNDER TROUBLED WATERS: THE NORTH EAST ASIA SEA-
BED CONTROVERSY. Harvard International Law Journal 14(2):212-260
(1973)

VEZ  _____ _____ THE SINO-JAPANESE-KOREAN SEA RESOURCES CONTROVERSY AND
THE HYPOTHESIS OF A 200-MILE ECONOMIC ZONE. Harvard International
Law Journal 16:27-46 (1975)

IVMMR  Park, Choon-ho, and J.A. Cohen. THE POLITICS OF CHINA'S OIL WEAPON.
Foreign Policy 20:28-49 (1975)

VLOS  Parks, L. THE LAW OF - AND UNDER - THE SEA. U.S. Naval Institute
Proceedings 92:54-59 (1966)

VOR  Parks, L., and S. Dye. OCEAN RESOURCE DEVELOPMENT AND LAW OF THE
SEA. Lex Et Scientia 3:107-116 (1966)

VINTL  _____ _____ WORLD LAW OPENS NEW SEA FRONTIER. Undersea Technology
7:53-58 (1966)

IIIF  Parres, Alain. L'ENTREPRISE DE PECHE. VUES COMME UN SERVICE PUBLIC
ALIMENTAIRE, LES PECHE DOIVENT ETRE AIDEES. France Peche 166:95-96
(1971/1972)

VSUB  Parrish, B.B., et al. SUBMERSIBLES AND UNDERWATER HABITATS: A RE-
VIEW. Underwater Journal 4(4): (1972)

IIIP  Parslow, J.L.F. MERCURY IN WADERS FROM THE WASH. Environmental
Pollution 5:295-304 (1973)

IIICONS  Parun, E. FISHERY PRODUCTION REGULATION AND FAUNA PROTECTION IN THE
YUGOSLAV COASTAL SEA. Nasa Zakonitost 28:759-767 (1974)

| | |
|---|---|
| VMT | PASSAGE THROUGH INTERNATIONAL STRAITS: FREE OR INNOCENT. THE INTERESTS AT STAKE. San Diego Law Review 11:815-833 (1974) |
| VB | Passalacqua, John L.A. de. LA EXTENSION DE LA MAR TERRITORIAL Y LOS DERECHOS HUMANOS. Revista de Devecho Puertorrigueno 12:425-438 (1973) |
| IIP | Patel, B., et al. RADIOECOLOGY OF BOMBAY HARBOUR - A TIDAL ESTUARY. Estuarine and Coastal Marine Science 3(1):13-42 (1975) |
| IIIFV&G | Patterson, D. BOATS IN THE IRISH FISHING INDUSTRY. Technology Ireland 7:17-19 (1975) |
| IIIF | Paulsen, Trond S. THE FISHING INDUSTRY OF NORWAY. EFTA Bulletin 15:15-18 (1974) |
| IIIINTL | Payne, Richard J. INTERNATIONAL LAW AND MARITIME JURISDICTION IN RELATION TO SEA RESOURCES: THE CASE OF FISHING IN PERU. Howard Law Journal 18:361-384 (1974) |
| VLOS | PEACEFUL USES OF THE SEA-BED COMMITTEE CONCLUDES GENERAL DEBATE. U.N. Monthly Chronicle 6(11):60-66 (1969) |
| VLOS | PEACEFUL USES OF THE SEA-BED CONCLUDES THIRD SESSION. U.N. Monthly Chronicle 6(8):126-128 (1969) |
| VINTL | Pearce, Jack. MARITIME POLICY: WILL THE SEAS BE FREE OR CONTAINERIZED? Transportation Law Journal 5:23-43 (1973) |
| VOR | Pearson, C.S. EXTRACTING RENT FROM OCEAN RESOURCES: DISCUSSION OF A NEGLECTED SOURCE. Ocean Development and International Law 1:221-237 (1974) |
| IVOI | Pearson, John. FINANCING; FROM EXPLORATION TO PRODUCTION. Ocean Industry 8:65-66 (February, 1973) |
| IIIFV&G | LA PECHE THONIERE SOVIETIQUE ET L'EXPERIENCE JAPONAISE. France Peche 168:34-36 (1972) |
| VOR | Pell, Claiborne. THE OCEANS: MAN'S LAST GREAT RESOURCE. Saturday Review :19-21,62-63 (October 11, 1969) |
| VENE | Penland, Lee S. NUCLEAR POWER DEBATE: IN THIS ENVIRONMENTAL CRISIS AND ENERGY CRUNCH WE SHOULD ALWAYS REMEMBER "THERE IS NO FREE LUNCH". Women Lawyers Journal 62:6-18 (Winter, 1976) |
| IVMMR | Pennell, M.M. NORTH SEA OIL - THE GLOBAL CONTEXT. PART 2. Offshore Technology 4(4):14-16 (1972) |
| VOR | Penney, P.W. EXPLOITING OCEAN RESOURCES. Naval Architect 1:9-12 (1973) |
| IVMMR | Pequegnat, Willis E., et al. DEEP-SEA IRONSTONE DEPOSITS IN THE GULF OF MEXICO. Journal of Sedimentary Petrology 42:700-710 (1972) |
| VOI | PERMITS FOR ACTIVITIES IN NAVIGABLE WATERS OR OCEAN WATERS. Federal Register 40(144):31319-31344 (July 25, 1975) |

| | |
|---|---|
| VINTL | Perrin, G. LES MESURES CONSERVATOIRES DANS LES AFFAIRES RELATIVES À LA COMPÉTANCE EN MATIÉRE DE PÊCHERIES. Revue Générale de Droit International Public 77:16-34 (1973) |
| VOR | Perry, E.A. OCEAN RESOURCES. Current History 58:349-354 (1970) |
| VP | PERSISTENT PESTICIDES AND PCBS IN THE ENVIRONMENT. Nature 240:319-321 (December 8, 1972) |
| IVMMR | Pennell, M.M. NORTH SEA OIL - THE GLOBAL CONTEXT. PART I. Offshore Technology 4(3):14-21 (1972) |
| IVMMR | _____. THE SEARCH FOR AND PRODUCTION OF OIL AND GAS AT SEA WITH PARTICULAR REFERENCE TO THE NORTH SEA. Transactions 116:399-438 (1972-1973) |
| VMLAD | PERSONAL INJURIES - DRILLING RIG ACCIDENTS ON THE OUTER CONTINENTAL SHELF. Loyola Law Review 17:446-459 (1971) |
| IIIF | PERSPECTIVES FOR FISHERY. Revista Nacional da Pesca 1972:151-151 |
| IIIF | PERU: FISHERIES. Jornal do Brasil :2 (February 1, 1973) |
| VOCET | Pesch, Alan J. SIMULATED RESEARCH SUBMARINE HELPS DESIGN FOR OPERATOR EFFICIENCY. Ocean Industry 4:71-74 (1969) |
| IIIOCET | PESQUISAS PARA EXECUCAO DO PROJETO CABO FRIO. Revista Nacional da Pesca 13(112):12-12 (1972) |
| VP | Petaccio, Victor. WATER POLLUTION AND THE FUTURE LAW OF THE SEA. The International and Comparative Law Quarterly 21(1):15-42 (1972) |
| IIENV | Peter, Russell. CEQ'S PETERSON TAKES ON INDUSTRY. Environmental Action 5:3-7 (1974) |
| VLOS | Peters, H., und H. Wuensche. EINIGE PROBLEME DES INTERNATIONALEN SEERECHTS IN VORBEREITUNG DER III. UNO-SEERECHTSKONFERENZ. Staat und Recht 22:630-643 (1973) |
| IVMMR | Petersen, Erik. CANADIANS STRONG IN NORTH SEA. Oilweek 26:12-13- (April, 1975) |
| IVMMR | Petersen, Erik V. NEW OFFSHORE PLAYS DEVELOPING. Oilweek 26:12-14- (May, 1975) |
| VENV | Peterson, Nels. CHALLENGE OF ENVIRONMENTAL QUALITY: AN OUTLINE OF REMEDIES TO MEET IT. Environmental Law 1:72-91 (1970) |
| VP | Petrocelli, S.R., et al. DDT AND DIELDRIN RESIDUES IN SELECTED BIOTA FROM SAN ANTONIA BAY, TEXAS - 1972. Pesticides Monitoring Journal 8(3):167-172 (1974) |
| VAC | Petrowskie, Lawrence C. MILITARY USES OF THE OCEAN SPACE AND THE CONTINENTAL SHELF. Columbia Journal of Transnational Law 7:279-301 (1968) |
| IIIINTL | Peyroux, E. PROBLÈMES JURIDIQUES DE LA PÊCHE DANS LE MARCHÉ COMMUN. Revue Trimestvielle de Droit Européen 9:46-64 (1973) |

VCS        Pharand, Donat. THE CONTINENTAL SHELF REDEFINITION, WITH SPECIAL REFERENCE TO ARCTIC. McGill Law Journal 18:536-559 (1972)

VINTL      _____ _____ HISTORIC WATERS IN INTERNATIONAL LAW WITH SPECIAL REFERENCE TO THE ARCTIC. University of Toronto Law Journal 21:1-14 (1971)

VMT        _____ _____ LE PASSAGE DU NORD-QUEST, UN SOUCI DES CANADIENS. Review Générale de Droit 5:185-189 (1974)

VMT        _____ _____ SOVIET UNION WARNS UNITED STATES AGAINST USE OF NORTHEAST PASSAGE. American Journal of International Law 62:927-935 (1968)

VLOS       Philips, C. U.S. EXPLAINS VOTES ON SEA-BED RESOLUTIONS. U.S. Department of State Bulletin 62:89-95 (1970)

IVM        PHILLIPS GROUP BEGINS PERMANENT PRODUCTION. Petroleum Engineer 46 (5):76,80,82 (1974)

VINTL      Phleger, H. RECENT DEVELOPMENTS AFFECTING THE REGIME OF THE HIGH SEAS. U.S. Department of State Bulletin 32:934-940 (1955)

VP         PHOSPHATE DETERGENT REGULATIONS. Urban Law Annual 7:381-389 (1974)

VOSTR      Phylactopoulus, A. ARTIFICIAL ISLANDS AND INSTALLATIONS: A CALL FOR INTERNATIONAL LEGISLATIVE ACTION. International Relations 4:427-436 (1974)

VB         _____ _____ MEDITERRANEAN DISCORD: CONFLICTING GREEK-TURKISH CLAIMS ON THE AEGEAN SEABED. The International Lawyer 8:431-441 (1974)

VP         Pierce, Donald F. SOME OBSERVATIONS ABOUT THE FEDERAL WATER POLLUTION CONTROL ACT AMENDMENTS OF 1972. Federation of Insurance Counsel Quarterly 24:41-46 (1973)

IIIAFF     Pillay, T.V.R. LAND RECLAMATION AND FISH CULTURE IN THE DELTAIC AREAS OF WEST BENGAL, INDIA. Progressive Fish Culturist 20(3):99-103 (1958)

VP         Pilpel, Neiton. OIL POLLUTION OF THE SEA. Ecologist 2:4-7 (1972)

IVMMR      Pimlott, Douglas H. THE ARCTIC OFFSHORE GAMBLE. Living Wilderness 38:16-25 (Autumn, 1974)

IIENV      Pinhey, Thomas K., and Karen W. Paterson. ENVIRONMENTAL CONCERN AS A FACTOR IN COASTAL ZONE DEVELOPMENT: A STUDY OF LOUISIANA CITIZENS. Coastal Zone Management Journal 2(3):297-310 (1976)

IIIP       Pinon, J., and J. Pijck. MICROBIOLOGICAL SEA WATER CONTAMINATION ALONG THE BELGIAN COAST. II - TECHNIQUES - NORMS - PRELIMINARY RESULTS. Revue Internationale d'Oceanographie Medicale 27:17-40 (1972)

IIIP       Pinom, J., et al. MICROBIOLOGICAL SEA WATER CONTAMINATION ALONG THE BELGIAN COAST. I - GEOGRAPHICAL CONSIDERATIONS. Revue Internationale d'Oceanographic Medicale 27:5-15 (1972)

VLOS       Pisk, Z., and R. Král. ON THE PREPARATION OF THE REVISION OF THE LAW OF THE SEA. Mezinárodní Vztahy 5:55-63 (1975)

IVOSTR    Pitt, R.S.  ENGINEERING FOR THE NORTH SEA PLATFORMS.  Underwater Journal 5:255-265 (1974)

IIIF      PLANO NACIONAL DE PESQUISAS SOBRE RECURSOS PESQUEIROS MARINHOS E ESTUARINOS.  Revista Nacional da Pesca 1972:7-18

IVMMR     Platou, R.S. PROGRESS MADE BY BRITAIN IN NORTH SEA.  Northern Offshore 2:21-22,25-26,29-30 (1973)

VLOS      Platzroeder, R.  DIE DRITTE SEERECHTS KONFERENZ DER VEREINTEN NATIONEN.  Jahrbuch fuer Internationales Recht 17:195-224 (1974)

VB        Platzroeder, R., and W. Vitzthum.  WIRTSCHAFTZONEN UND ARCHIPELSTAATEN: ZWEI PROBLEME DER DRITTE UN-SEERECHTSKONFERENZ.  Verfassung und Recht in Uebersee 7:289-305 (1975)

VENV      Pledger, R. Harrison, Jr.  LEGAL ASPECTS OF ENVIRONMENTAL MANAGEMENT.  Law Notes 7:111- (1971)

VOCET     Poetschke, Herbert.  TECHNISCHE MOEGLICHKEITEN IN DER OZEANOLOGIE.  Wasser, Luft und Betrieb 16(6):187-189 (1972)

IIIFV&G   POLES SEND TRAWLERS AND SPACE-AGE RESEARCH SHIP TO SOUTHEAST ATLANTIC.  South African Shipping News and Fishing Industry Review 27(10):67,69 (1972)

VORM      THE POLITICS BEHIND THE NEW OIL HUNT.  Business Week 2166:104-106 (1971)

VENE      Pollack, H.  INTERNATIONAL COOPERATION IN ENERGY RESEARCH AND DEVELOPMENT.  Law and Policy in International Business 6:677-724 (1974)

VORM      _____ _____ NATIONAL INTEREST, FOREIGN AFFAIRS, AND THE MARINE SCIENCES.  U.S. Department of State Bulletin 58:211-215 (1968)

VEZ       Pollard, D.E.  THE EXCLUSIVE ECONOMIC ZONE.  San Diego Law Review 12:600-623 (1975)

VP        POLLUTION CONTROL (GERMANY, FED. REP.).  International and Comparative Law Quarterly 21(4):803 (1972)

VP        POLLUTION CONTROL IN THE MARINE INDUSTRIES.  Ocean Industry 8:42-45 (1973)

VP        POLLUTION CRACKDOWN NEARS.  Work Boat 31:39,47 (1974)

VP        LA POLLUTION DES OCÉANS.  Analyse et prévision 11:663-684 (1971)

VP        POLLUTION - NO PRIVATE COMPENSATION FOR INVASION OF PUBLIC RIGHTS ABSENT PARTICULAR DAMAGES.  Journal of Maritime Law and Commerce. 5:539-544 (1974)

VP        POLLUTION OF THE GREAT LAKES: A JOINT APPROACH BY CANADA AND THE UNITED STATES.  California Western International Law Journal 2:109-127 (1971)

IVP       POLLUTION OF THE HIGH SEAS RESULTING FROM DRILLING AND PRODUCING OPERATIONS - FEDERAL JURISDICTION AND OPERATOR LIABILITY.  Southern Texas Law Journal 12:73-91 (1970)

IVP    POLLUTION OF THE MARINE ENVIRONMENT FROM OUTER CONTINENTAL SHELF OIL OPERATIONS. South Carolina Law Review 22:228-240 (1970)

IIIFV&G    POLONIA: TENDENCIAS E PROBLEMAS TECHNICOS NA PROJECAO E CONSTRUCAO DE EMBARCACOES DE PESCA. Revista Nacional da Pesca 13(108):25-17 (1971)

VLOS    Pontecorvo, Giulio. LAW OF THE SEA. Atomic Scientists Bulletin 23:46-47 (1967)

VOCET    _____ _____ OCEAN SCIENCE AND MUTUAL ASSISTANCE: AN UNEASY BALANCE. Ocean Development and International Law Journal 1:51-64 (1973)

VOR    _____ _____ REFLECTIONS ON THE ECONOMICS OF THE COMMON HERITAGE OF MANKIND: THE ORGANIZATION OF THE DEEP-SEA MINING INDUSTRY AND THE EXPECTED BENEFITS FROM RESOURCES EXPLOITATION. Ocean Development and International Law Journal 2:203-216 (1974)

IIIOCET    Pontecorvo, Giulio, and M. Wilkinson. AN ECONOMIC ANALYSIS OF THE INTERNATIONAL TRANSFER OF MARINE TECHNOLOGY. Ocean Development and International Law Journal 2:255-283 (1974)

VLOS    Pontecorvo, Giulio, and R. Meznik. THE WEALTH OF THE OCEANS AND THE LAW OF THE SEA: SOME PRELIMINARY OBSERVATIONS. San Diego Law Review 11:679-690 (1974)

VENV    Popiela, W. THE CONVENTION ON THE PROTECTION OF THE MARINE ENVIRONMENT OF THE BALTIC SEA AREA. Panstwo i Prawo 7:96-102 (1975)

VORM    Popper, D. PRESENT U.S. AND INTERNATIONAL POLICY. U.S. Department of State Bulletin 59:171-178 (1968)

VLOS    _____ _____ U.N. SEA-BED COMMITTEE CONCLUDES SPRING SESSION. U.S. Department of State Bulletin 60:342-344 (1967)

VLOS    _____ _____ U.S. CALLS FOR BROAD INQUIRY ON PEACEFUL USE OF THE SEABED. U.S. Department of State Bulletin 58:543-545 (1968)

VCONS    _____ _____ U.S. RECOMMENDS ESTABLISHMENT OF MARINE PRESERVES. U.S. Department of State Bulletin 59:104-107 (1968)

IISL    Porro, Alfred. INVISIBLE BOUNDARY - PRIVATE AND SOVEREIGN MARSHLAND INTERESTS. Natural Resources Lawyer 3(3):512-520 (1970)

IISL    Porro, Alfred A., Jr., and L.S. Teleky. MARSHLAND TITLE DILEMMA: A TIDAL PHENOMENON. Seton Hall Law Review 3:323-348 (1972)

IIP&H    PORT MODERNIZATION CONTINUED, CARGO VOLUME ROSE DURING 1973. Marine Engineering/Log 79(7):187-188,234B-238,240,242-245,247 (1974)

IIP&H    PORTS AND WATERWAYS SAFETY: VESSEL TRAFFIC SYSTEMS. Federal Register 39:25429-25434 (1974)

VP    Post, Thomas R. PRIVATE COMPENSATION FOR INJURIES SUSTAINED BY THE DISCHARGE OF OIL FROM VESSELS ON THE NAVIGABLE WATERS OF THE UNITED STATES: A SURVEY. Journal of Maritime Law and Commerce 4(1):25-65 (1972)

| | |
|---|---|
| VP | Post, Thomas R. A SOLUTION TO THE PROBLEM OF PRIVATE COMPENSATION IN OIL DISCHARGE SITUATIONS. University of Miami Law Review 28:524-550 (1974) |
| IVOL | POTENTIAL SEEN GREAT FOR NEWLY ADDED AREA IN OFF-CALIFORNIA LEASE SALE. Oil and Gas Journal 72:20-22 (1974) |
| VP | Potter, J. Leon. USE POLLUTION TO BENEFIT MANKIND. Ocean Industry 4:94-97 (1969) |
| IISL | Pound, Roscoe, et al. SYMPOSIUM ON THE TEXAS "TIDELANDS" CASE. Baylor Law Review 3(2):335p. (1951) |
| IIP | Pounder, B. WILDFOWL AND POLLUTION IN THE TAX ESTUARY. Marine Pollution Bulletin 5:35-38 (1974) |
| VENE | POWER FROM THE OCEANS. Surveyor 9(1):8-14 (1975) |
| IIENV | Power, Garrett. WATERGATE VILLAGE: A CASE STUDY OF A PERMIT APPLICATION FOR A MARINA SUBMITTED TO THE U.S. ARMY CORPS OF ENGINEERS. Coastal Zone Management Journal 2(2):103-124 (1975) |
| VENE | POWER PLANT SITING - A REGULATORY CRISIS. Drake Law Review 22:645-656 (1973) |
| IIIF | Prabhu, M.S. MARINE FISHERIES OF GAO. Mahasagar Bulletin 5:74-79 (1972) |
| VP | Pradon, C., et al. LA CELLULE D'INTERVENTION CONTRE LA POLLUTION DANS LES ALPES-MARITIMES. Techniques et Sciences Municipales et Revue L'EAU 69(12):575-584 (1974) |
| IVMMR | Pratt, R.M., and P.F. McFarlin. MANGANESE PAVEMENTS ON THE BLAKE PLATEAU. Science 151:1080-1082 (1966) |
| IIIAFF | PREPARING TO FARM LOBSTERS. World Fishing 23(6):52,54 (1974) |
| IIIF | PRESIDENTE MEDICI REGULAMENTA A PESCA. Revista Nacional da Pesca 1972:68-71 |
| IVMMR | Preston, A. HEAVY METALS IN BRITISH WATERS. Nature 242:95-97 (1973) |
| VOR | PREVENTING A SCRAMBLE FOR THE SEAS. Australian Foreign Affairs Record 44(10):642-657 (1973) |
| IVDRIL | PREVIEW OF NEW DRILLING RIGS. Ocean Industry 9)7):44-45,47 (1974; 10(7):57-59 (1975) |
| VENE | Price, Harold L. CURRENT APPROACH TO LICENSING NUCLEAR POWER PLANTS. Atomic Energy Law Journal 15:227-237 (1974) |
| IIIEZ | PRINCIPLES OF ZONAL APPROACH TO FISHERIES. Australian Fisheries 31:24-25 (1972) |
| VP | PRIVATE COMPENSATION FOR OIL POLLUTION: FLORIDA'S PRACTICAL SOLUTION. University of Florida Law Review 27:546-559 (1975) |
| IVCONS | PRIVATE LIMITATION OF PETROLEUM PRODUCTION: CALIFORNIA'S APPROACH TO CONSERVATION. Stanford Law Review 17:942-964 (1965) |

| | |
|---|---|
| IIP | PRIVATE REMEDIES FOR BEACH-FRONT PROPERTY DAMAGE CAUSED BY OIL POLLUTION OF MISSISSIPPI COASTAL WATERS. Mississippi Law Journal 43:516- (1972) |
| VP | PRIVATE REMEDIES FOR WATER POLLUTION. Columbia Law Review 70:734-756 (1970) |
| VB | THE PROBLEMS OF DELIMITATIONS OF BASE LINES FOR OUTLYING ARCHIPELAGOES. San Diego Law Review 9:733-746 (1972) |
| IICONS | PROCEEDINGS OF THE ARCTIC INTERNATIONAL WILDLIFE RANGE CONFERENCE - OCTOBER 21 AND 22, 1970. University of British Columbia Law Review 6:3-107 (1971) |
| IIIF | LE PRODUCTION BELGE EN 1971. France Peche 168:37-37 (1972) |
| IIP&H | PROFILE OF A GREEK FISHING PORT. World Fishing 23(6):26-28 (1974) |
| IIIFP | PROJETO PROMETE EXTRAIR MAIS PROTEINAS DO MAR. Revista Nacional da Pesca 12(105): (1971) |
| IVOL | PROPER TIME LIMITATIONS ON OUTER CONTINENTAL SHELF LEASES UNDER THE NATIONAL ENVIRONMENTAL POLICY ACT. Houston Law Review 10:158-168 (1972) |
| IIP&H | PROPERTY - WHARFING OUT - RIPARIAN OWNER PERMITTED TO USE FILLED-IN SWAMP AS A WHARF TO REACH NAVIGABLE WATER. BURNES v. FORBES. San Diego Law Review 9:684-688 (1970) |
| IVENV | PROPOSAL TO PROTECT MAINE FROM THE OILBERGS OF THE 70'S. Maine Law Review 22:481-510 (1970) |
| VOCET | PROPOSALS CONCERNING A LEGAL SYSTEM FOR OCEANOGRAPHIC STATIONS. Ohio State Law Journal 28:93-118 (1967) |
| IIIF | PROPOSED FISHERIES LEGISLATION COULD GREATLY AFFECT INDUSTRY. Fish Boat 17(5):14,27-31 (1972) |
| VENV | PROTECTION OF THE MARINE ENVIRONMENT (EXCERPT FROM A STUDY BY NATIONAL PETROLEUM COUNCIL.) Natural Resources Lawyer 8:511-543 (1975) |
| VP | PROVING OUT POLLUTION CLEAN UP. Surveyor 9(1):16-19 (1975) |
| VB | Przetacznik, Franciszek. PROBLEMY ZWAIZANE Z OBECNOSCIA OKRETOW WOJENNYCH NA MORZU TERYTORIALNYM ORAZ W PORTACH OBCEGO PANSTWA. (LES PROBLÈMES LIÉS À LA PRÉSENCE DES NAVIRES DE GUERRE DANS LES EAUX TERRITORIALES ET LES PORTS D'UN ÉTAT ÉTRANGER). Ruch Prawniczy Ekonomiczny i Socjologiczny 4:61-79 (1971) |
| IICZM | PUBLIC ACCESS TO BEACHES. Stanford Law Review 22:564-586 (1970) |
| IICZM | PUBLIC LANDS - THE PUBLIC TRUST DOCTRINE INCLUDES A RIGHT TO EQUALITY OF ACCESS TO MUNICIPAL BEACH AREA. Loyola University Law Journal (Chicago) 4:603-611 (1973) |
| IVOL | PUBLIC PARTICIPATION IN RULEMAKING PROCEDURES UNDER THE OUTER CONTINENTAL SHELF LANDS ACT. Iowa Law Review 56:696-706 (1971) |
| IISL | PUBLIC TRUST IN TIDAL AREAS: A SOMETIME SUBMERGED TRADITIONAL DOCTRINE. Yale Law Journal 79:762-789 (1970) |

VMT         PUGET SOUND VESSEL TRAFFIC SYSTEM. Federal Register 38(150):21227-21235 (1973)

IIWQ        Pugh, O. DESALINATION. Water and Pollution Control 113(7):15-16 (1975)

IIP         Puro, Steven. WATER POLLUTION LEGISLATION AND THE RIVERS AND HARBORS ACT OF 1899: THE ENVIRONMENTALIST POINT OF VIEW. St. Louis University Law Journal 16:63-83 (1971)

VOD         Qasim, S.R., et al. ADVANCED WASTE TREATMENT FOR NAVAL VESSELS. Journal of the American Society of Civil Engineers 99:717-727 (1973)

VP          Quéneudec, J.P. LA POLLUTION DES MERS DEVANT LE DROIT INTERNATIONAL. Hosei Riron 5(3):1-66 (1973)

VEZ         \_\_\_\_\_  \_\_\_\_\_ LA ZONE ECONOMIQUE. Revue Genérale de Droit International Public 79:321-353 (1975)

VEZ         \_\_\_\_\_  \_\_\_\_\_ NOTION DE ZONE ÉCONOMIQUE DANS LE DROIT DE LA MER. Droit Maritime Français 26:639-648 (1974)

IIIINTL     Quintin, O. LA POLITIQUE COMMUNE DE LA PECHE DEPUIS L'ADHESION. Revue du Marche Commun 172:68-73 (1974)

IVM         Quintrelle, N. GOOD IMPROVEMENTS MADE IN MIDDLE EAST CRUDE OUTPUT. Offshore 33(7):132-133 (1973)

IVOI        \_\_\_\_\_  \_\_\_\_\_ LEASE, PRODUCTION COSTS REQUIRE BIG PRODUCTION IN THE GULF OF MEXICO. Offshore 33(2):43-45 (1973)

IVMMR       \_\_\_\_\_  \_\_\_\_\_ RESERVES LESSEN ONSHORE AND INCREASE OFFSHORE. Offshore 33(4):59-61 (1973)

VP          RADIOACTIVE WASTE: A FAILURE IN GOVERNMENTAL REGULATION. Albany Law Review 37:97-134 (1972)

IIILOS      Radovich, J. FISHERY RIGHTS AND THE LAW OF THE SEA. Commercial Fisheries Review 30:8-10 (1968)

VINTL       Ragland, T.R. A HARBINGER: THE SENKAKO ISLANDS. San Diego Law Review 10(3):664-691 (1973)

IVOSTR      Rainey, J.M. MARINE BUILDERS ARE FAST CHANGING PLATFORM DESIGN TO SUIT UNUSUAL OPERATING CONDITIONS IN THE NORTH SEA. Offshore 33(2):86- (1973)

VINTL       Rajan, H.P. THE 1973 DRAFT ARTICLES ON ARCHIPELAGOS BY FIJI, INDONESIA, MAURITIUS, AND THE PHILIPPINES ANALYZED. Indian Journal of International Law 14:230-244 (1974)

VINTL       \_\_\_\_\_  \_\_\_\_\_ TOWARDS CODIFICATION OF ARCHIPELAGOS IN INTERNATIONAL LAW. Indian Journal of International Law 13(3):468-480 (1973)

VB          Ramalhete, Clovis. PORQUE (E PARA QUE) 200 MILHAS. Revista Nacional da Pesca 13(109):24-26 (1971)

VP          Ramey, James T. ENERGY NEEDS OF THE NATION AND THE COST IN TERMS OF POLLUTION. Atomic Energy Law Journal 14:26-58 (1972)

| | |
|---|---|
| VENE | Ramey, James T. OLD AND NEW CONCEPTS IN SITING AND LICENSING NUCLEAR POWER PLANTS. The Forum 9:211-220 (1973) |
| IVMMR | Ramsay, H.J., Jr., and H.A. Nedom. EXPLORATION AND DEVELOPMENT OF A NEW PETROLEUM PROVINCE - JAVA SEA, INDONESIA. Journal of Petroleum Technology 25:395-401 (1973) |
| IVMMR | Rand, J. OIL SEARCH IN AUSTRALIA COST $60 MILLION IN 1972. Offshore 33(7):125-126,128-129 (1973) |
| VP | Ranken, M.B.F. CAN WE DELAY THE NEXT MAJOR TANKER DISASTER? Ocean Industry 6:35-39 (1971) |
| VENV | _____ THE MARINE ENVIRONMENT - USE AND ABUSE, ORDER OR CONFLICT - PART 1. Society of Environmental Engineers Journal 13:3-11 (1974) |
| VLOS | Rao, B. INNER SPACE: A NATIONAL CLAIM OR A U.N. TAKEOVER? Indian Yearbook of International Affairs 17:153-200 (1974) |
| VLOS | Rao, K. THE LEGAL REGIME OF THE SEA-BED AND OCEAN FLOOR. Indian Journal of International Law 9:1-18 (1969) |
| VCS | Rao, P. THE CONTINENTAL SHELF: THE PRACTICE AND POLICY OF INDIA. Indian Journal of International Law 3:191-198 (1963) |
| VLOS | Rao, P.S. AUTHORITY AND CONTROL OVER OFFSHORE AREAS: IN DEFENCE OF COMMON INTERESTS. Indian Journal of International Law 11:379-388 (1971) |
| VOR | _____ DEVELOPMENT AND THE SEA. Oceanus 17:6-13 (1973) |
| IICZM | Rao, P. Sreenivasa. COASTAL ZONE MANAGEMENT AND WORLD COMMUNITY. Indian Journal of International Law 13(3):511-516 (1973) |
| VAC | _____ LEGAL REGULATION OF MARITIME MILITARY USES. Indian Journal of International Law 13(3):425-454 (1973) |
| VAC | Rao, Pemmaraju S. THE SEABED ARMS CONTROL TREATY: A STUDY IN THE CONTEMPORARY LAW OF THE MILITARY USES OF THE SEAS. Journal of Maritime Law and Commerce 4(1):67-92 (1972) |
| IVMMR | Rasmussen, J.W. NORTH SEA OIL IN WORLD PERSPECTIVE. Ocean Industry 10(2):45-46 (1975) |
| IVMMR | Ratiner, Leigh S., and R.L. Wright. UNITED STATES OCEAN MINERAL RESOURCE INTERESTS AND THE UNITED NATIONS CONFERENCE ON THE LAW OF THE SEA. Natural Resources Lawyer 6:1-43 (1973) |
| VP | Rawlinson, Peter, et al. PAPERS SUBMITTED AT THE AMERICAN BAR ASSOCIATION ANNUAL MEETING, LONDON, ENGLAND. INTERNATIONAL PROBLEMS CONCERNING POLLUTION AND THE ENVIRONMENT. Natural Resources Lawyer 4:803 (1971) |
| VENV | Ray, Lucian Y., et al. ENERGY CRISIS, SUPERTANKERS, AND ECOLOGY. Insurance Counsel Journal 42:511-525 (1975) |
| IICONS | Rea, C. Cary, and Paul D. Komar. COMPUTER SIMULATION MODELS OF A HOOKED BEACH SHORELINE CONFIGURATION. Journal of Sedimentary Petrology 45(4):868-872 (1975) |

| | |
|---|---|
| IISL | REAL PROPERTY - TIDELANDS - PUBLIC TRUST DOCTRINE - CONVEYANCE OF TIDELAND TO PRIVATE OWNER FOR PRIVATE PURPOSE INVALID: STATE NOT ESTOPPED FROM ASSERTING TITLE. Mississippi Law Journal 44:322-328 (1973) |
| VP | Reath, Henry T. POLLUTION - THE RIGHT OF PRIVATE ENFORCEMENT IN THE COURTS. Pennsylvania Bar Association Quarterly 43:238 (1972) |
| VENV | RECENT DEVELOPMENTS IN ENVIRONMENTAL LAW. Boston College of Industrial and Commercial Law Review Vol. 13 (1972) Special Issue |
| VLOS | RECENT DEVELOPMENTS IN THE LAW OF THE SEA: A SYNOPSIS. Annual Issue. Symposium: Law of the Sea. San Diego Law Review 7- (1970)- |
| VENV | RECENT ENVIRONMENTAL DEVELOPMENTS IN MARITIME AND OFFSHORE ACTIVITIES: A SYMPOSIUM. Houston Law Review 9:655-708 (1972) |
| IIIFV&G | RECOGNITION OF FISHING VESSELS. Australian Fisheries 32(12):14-14 (1973) |
| IIIFV&G | RECONNAISSANCE CRAFT AND THE PROVISION OF ELECTRONIC EQUIPMENT FOR FISHING CRAFT. National Marine Fisheries Service, Division of Foreign Fisheries Trans. of Technika i Gospodarka Morska 20(5):240-240 (1970) |
| IVMMR | Record, Rush H. FINANCING OIL AND GAS EXPLORATION: RECENT DEVELOPMENTS IN EXPLORATION FINANCING. Oil and Gas Law and Taxation Institute (Southwestern Legal Foundation) 24:111- (1973) |
| VOR | Reed, L. A MARINE "COMMON MARKET". Hydrospace 2:8-10 (1969) |
| IIIINTL | Reese, K. THE MAKING OF A CASE FOR THE INTERNATIONAL COURT OF JUSTICE: ICELANDIC FISHING RIGHTS. Comparative and International Law Journal of Southern Africa 6:394-402 (1973) |
| VINTL | Reeves, Jesse S. THE CODIFICATION OF THE LAW OF TERRITORIAL WATERS. American Journal of International Law: Supplement 24:486-499 (1930) |
| VP | REFUSE ACT: ITS ROLE WITHIN THE SCHEME OF FEDERAL WATER QUALITY LEGISLATION. New York University Law Review 46:304-352 (1971) |
| VP | REFUSE ACT OF 1899: ITS SCOPE AND ROLE IN CONTROL OF WATER POLLUTION. California Law Review 58:1444-1473 (1971) |
| VP | REFUSE ACT OF 1899: ITS SCOPE AND ROLE IN CONTROL OF WATER POLLUTION. Ecology Law Quarterly 1:173-202 (1971) |
| IIWQ | REGIONAL WATER QUALITY CONTROL. U.C.D. Law Review 5:272- (1972) |
| IIIB | REGULAMENTADA A PESCA NAS 200 MILHAS. Revista Nacional da Pesca 12(105):30-33 (1971) |
| IIP&H | REGULATED NAVIGATION AREA: CHESAPEAKE BAY ENTRANCE. USCG. Federal Register 38(242):34777-34780 (December 18, 1973) |
| IISL | REGULATION AND OWNERSHIP OF THE MARSHLANDS: THE GEORGIA MARSHLAND ACT. Georgia Law Review 5:563-583 (1971) |
| IIP&H | REGULATION OF DEEPWATER PORTS. Virginia Journal of International Law 15:927-957 (1975) |

| | |
|---|---|
| IVMMR | Reid, Alastair. LETTER FROM SCOTLAND. New Yorker 50:76,81-83- (October, 1974) |
| VB | Reid, R.S. CANADIAN CLAIM TO SOVEREIGNTY OVER THE WATERS OF THE ARCTIC. Canadian Yearbook of International Law 12:111-136 (1974) |
| VORM | Reilly, P. THE POLITICS OF THE OCEAN BOTTOM. War/Peace Report 8(7): 6-7 (1968) |
| IIIP | Reimer, A.A., and R.D. Reimer. TOTAL MERCURY IN SOME FISH AND SHELL-FISH ALONG THE MEXICAN COAST. Bulletin of Environmental Contamination and Toxicology 14(1):105-111 (1975) |
| VB | Rembe, N.S. LAW OF THE SEA: CONFLICTS OVER LIMITS OF NATIONAL JURISDICTION. Eastern Africa Law Review 7:65-106 (1974) |
| IIIF | REPORT OF THE INTERNATIONAL BOARD OF INQUIRY FOR THE GREAT LAKES FISHERIES. Science 99:10-10 (1944) |
| VINTL | REPORT OF UNITED NATIONS SPECIAL COMMITTEE ON GEOGRAPHICAL DISADVANTAGE... THIRD UNITED NATIONS CONFERENCE ON THE LAW OF THE SEA: COMMITTEE II. Ocean Development and International Law 3(2):181-186 (1975) |
| VB | REPORT ON NATIONAL CLAIMS TO THE TERRITORIAL SEA, FISHING ZONES, AND THE CONTINENTAL SHELF. International Legal Materials 8:516-546 (1969) |
| IIICONS | REPUBLIC OF ICELAND; FISHERIES CONSERVATION. Financial Times :25-25 (September, 1972) |
| VOR | RESEARCH LAGS ON DRUGS FROM MARINE RESOURCES. Chemical and Engineering News 50(37):24,27-28 (1972) |
| VLOS | RESERVATION OF THE SEA-BED AND OCEAN FLOOR FOR PEACEFUL PURPOSES, ASSEMBLY SETS UP AD HOC COMMITTEE. U.N. Monthly Chronicle 5(1):28-34 (1968) |
| VLOS | RESERVATION OF THE SEA-BED AND OCEAN FLOOR FOR PEACEFUL PURPOSES (FIRST COMMITTEE). U.N. Monthly Chronicle 5(11):53-61 (1968) |
| VLOS | RESERVATION OF THE SEA-BED AND OCEAN FLOOR FOR PEACEFUL PURPOSES. U.N. Monthly Chronicle 6(1):56-62 (1969) |
| VLOS | RESERVATION OF THE SEA-BED AND OCEAN FLOOR FOR PEACEFUL PURPOSES. Standing Committee Holds First Session. U.N. Monthly Chronicle 6(3): 9-10 (1969) |
| VLOS | RESERVATION OF THE SEA-BED AND OCEAN FLOOR FOR PEACEFUL PURPOSES. Committee Holds Second Session. U.N. Monthly Chronicle 6(4):53-56 (1969) |
| VLOS | RESERVATION OF THE SEA-BED AND OCEAN FLOOR FOR PEACEFUL PURPOSES - ASSEMBLY ADOPTS FOUR RESOLUTIONS. U.N. Monthly Chronicle 7(1):72-80 (1970) |
| VLOS | RESERVATION OF THE SEA-BED AND OCEAN FLOOR FOR PEACEFUL PURPOSES. Committee Begins 1970 Work. U.N. Monthly Chronicle 7(4):40-43 (1970) |

VOR      Revelle, Roger. THE OCEAN; ITS USES AND ITS ROLE IN THE EMERGENCE OF THE NEW GEOLOGY. Scientific American 221:54-65 (1969)

IVOL     REVISED 5-YEAR OCS LEASE SCHEDULE BY INTERIOR. World Oil 177:81-81 (1973)

VCS      Rey Caro, E. LA COSTUMBRE INTERNACIONAL Y EL FALLO DE LA CORTE INTERNACIONAL DE JUSTICIA EN EL CASSO DE LA PLATAFORMA CONTINENTAL. Revista de Derecho Internacional y Ciencias Diplomaticas 39/40:67-97 (1971)

VLOS     Rey Caro, Ernesto J. ASPECTOS DE DERECHO INTERNACIONAL MARITIMO EN EL TRATADO SOBRE EL RIO DE LA PLATA. Anuario de Derecho Internacional (Pamplona) 1:317-334 (1974)

VB       _____  _____  LA EXTENSION DEL MAR TERRITORIAL. Revista Juridica (Tucanán, Argentina) 23:57-207 (1972)

VINTL    Reyner, A. THE STRAIT OF TIRAN AND THE SOVEREIGNTY OF THE SEA. Middle East Journal 21:403-408 (1967)

IVOSTR   Reynolds, Paul W., and Leo J. Marquette. COMPLETING SUBSEA WELLS AT EKOFISK. Petroleum Engineer 44(12):30-31,34,39 (1972)

VLOS     Ricaldoni, A. DERECHO DEL MAR EN AMÉRICA LATINA: SOBERANIA, RAZIONABILIDAD Y OTRAS CUESTIONES. Revista Uruguaya de Derecho Internacional 2:9-32 (1973)

IIE      Rice, D. ESTUARINE LAND OF NORTH CAROLINA: LEGAL ASPECTS OF OWNERSHIP, USE AND CONTROL. North Carolina Law Review 46:779-812 (1968)

VOR      Rich, A. A PROPOSAL FROM A U.S. AND A SOVIET SCIENTIST: OCEANIC RESOURCES AND DEVELOPING NATIONS. Bulletin for Atomic Scientists 24:2-3 (1968)

IVMMR    RICH POTENTIAL OF ARCTIC ISLANDS WILL REQUIRE HUGE EXPENDITURES TO DEVELOP. Offshore 33(2):65,68 (1973)

VP       Richard, R. Peter. THE POLLUTER MUST PAY - BILL C-2. Ansul 3(4): (1974?)

IVOL     Richey, J. COMPARISON OF OIL AND GAS LEASING AUTHORITIES IN THE GULF OF MEXICO (STATES OF ALABAMA, MISSISSIPPI, AND LOUISIANA, AND THE FEDERAL GOVERNMENT,) AND THE JURISDICTIONAL CONFLICT OVER THE BOUNDARY BETWEEN STATE AND FEDERAL AUTHORITY IN THE GULF OF MEXICO. Mississippi Law Journal 40:351-392 (1969)

VB       RIGHT, TITLE AND INTEREST IN THE TERRITORIAL SEA: FEDERAL AND STATE CLAIMS IN THE UNITED STATES. Georgia Journal of International and Comparative Law 4:463-480 (1974)

VINTL    Riley, Stewart. THE LEGAL IMPLICATIONS OF THE SEA USE PROGRAM. Marine Technology Society Journal 4(1):31-46 (1970)

IVMMR    Rinde, J.P. NORTH SEA OIL - LOOK TO NORWAY. Northern Offshore 2:45-46,49 (1973)

IIIB     Ring, Jeffery W. CONSTITUTIONALITY OF STATE FISHING ZONES IN THE HIGH SEAS: THE OREGON FISHERIES CONSERVATION ZONE ACT. Oregon Law Review 55(1):141-153 (1976)

VOCET    Rinheard, G. SCIENTIFIC RESEARCH: FROM FREEDOM TO DEONTOLOGY.
         Ocean Development and International Law Journal 1(2):121-136 (1973)

IVOL     Rintoul, B. ALASKA SALE GARNERS BIDS ON HALF OFFERED. Offshore
         33(1):36-37 (1973)

IVDRIL   _____ _____ BIGGEST DRILLING BOOM SINCE 1969 IS TAKING SHAPE IN WA-
         TERS OFF ALASKA. Offshore 35:110- (1975)

IVM      _____ _____ OPERATIONS OFF WEST COAST STAY LOCKED IN THE DOLDRUMS.
         Offshore 33(7):95-96,98,100,102,104,106 (1973)

VOSTR    Riphagen, W. INTERNATIONAL LEGAL ASPECTS OF ARTIFICIAL ISLANDS.
         International Relations IV(4):327-347,364 (1973)

VP       Risebrough, R.W., et al. PCB RESIDUES IN ATLANTIC ZOOPLANKTON. Bul-
         letin of Environmental Contamination and Toxicology 8(6):345-355
         (1972)

IIP&H    RISING INTERNATIONAL TRADE SPURS PORTS TO MODERNIZE AND EXPAND. Ma-
         rine/Engineering Log 78(7):153-158,192,194-202,204,209-226 (1973)

IIIP     Rivers, J.B., et al. TOTAL AND ORGANIC MERCURY IN MARINE FISH.
         Bulletin of Environmental Contamination and Toxicology 8(5):257-266
         (1972)

IIB      Robbins, J. Michael, and Marc J. Hershmann. BOUNDARIES OF THE
         COASTAL ZONE: A SURVEY OF STATE LAWS. Coastal Zone Management Jour-
         nal 1(3):305-331 (1974)

VINTL    Robertson, H. A LEGAL REGIME FOR THE RESOURCES OF THE SEA-BED AND
         SUBSOIL OF THE DEEP SEA: A BREWING PROBLEM FOR INTERNATIONAL LAW-
         MAKERS. Naval War College Review 21(2):61-108 (1968)

VOCET    Robinson, George S. EVOLUTION OF THE LAW OF THE SEAS DESTRUCTION OF
         THE PRISTINE NATURE OF BASIC OCEANOGRAPHIC RESEARCH. Natural Re-
         sources Journal 13:504-510 (1973)

VENV     Robinson, N.A. EXTRATERRITORIAL ENVIRONMENTAL PROTECTION OBLIGA-
         TIONS OF FOREIGN AFFAIRS AGENCIES: THE UNFULFILLED MANDATE OF NEPA.
         New York University Journal of International Law and Politics 7:257-
         270 (1975)

VLOS     Robles, A. Garcia. SECOND UNITED NATIONS CONFERENCE ON THE LAW OF
         THE SEA - A REPLY; RESPONSE, A.H. DEAN. American Journal of Inter-
         national Law 55:669-675 (1961)

IVDRIL   Robson, V.B. DRILLING ENGINEERING IN THE SEARCH FOR OFFSHORE OIL.
         South African Shipping News and Fishing Industry Review 28:33,35-36
         (1973)

IVDRIL   _____ _____ DRILLING ENGINEERING IN THE SEARCH FOR OFFSHORE OIL.
         South African Shipping News and Fishing Industry Review 29(1):28-29,
         31 (1974)

IIP      Rodgers, William H., Jr. INDUSTRIAL WATER POLLUTION AND THE REFUSE
         ACT: A SECOND CHANCE FOR WATER QUALITY. University of Pennsylva-
         nia Law Review 119:761-822 (1971)

| | |
|---|---|
| VENV | Roe, Charles B., Jr., and Charles W. Lean. STATE ENVIRONMENTAL POLICY ACT OF 1971 AND ITS 1973 AMENDMENTS. Washington Law Review 49: 509-549 (1974) |
| IIIF | Roedel, Philip M. FISHERIES SERVICE 'LAYS KEEL' IN THE FIRST YEAR. National Fisherman 52(13):10-11 (1972) |
| IIIF | \_\_\_\_\_ \_\_\_\_\_ INTERNATIONAL AND DOMESTIC ISSUES FACE U.S. FISHERIES. Undersea Technology 14:29-31 (1973) |
| IIIF | \_\_\_\_\_ \_\_\_\_\_ THREE NEW ACTS: WHAT THEY MEAN TO MARINE FISHERIES. Fish Boat 18(3):46-48,63 (1973) |
| IVM | Roels, O.E. WILL NODULE MINING DISTURB THE MARINE ENVIRONMENT. Marine Technology Society Journal 8(8):17-20 (1974) |
| IIIB | Rojahn, O. DIE FISCHEREIGRENZE ISLANDS VON 1972 IM LICHTE MARITIMER ABGRENZUNGSPRINZIPIEN DES INTERNATIONALEN GERICHTSHOFES. Archiv des Voelkerrechts 16:37-59 (1973) |
| IIDR | Romanowitz, C.M. THE DREDGE OF TOMORROW. Engineering and Mining Journal 163:84-91 (1962) |
| IIIF | Romenskii, L.L. SHRIMP RESOURCES OF THE CONTINENTAL SLOPE OF WESTERN AFRICA. National Marine Fisheries Service, Division of Foreign Fisheries Trans. of Rybnoe Khozyaistvo 10:11-12 (1970) |
| IVMMR | Rona, P.A. NEW EVIDENCE FOR SEABED RESOURCES FROM GLOBAL TECTONICS. Ocean Management 1:145-159 (1973) |
| VOR | ROOM AT THE BOTTOM; TOP U.S. FIRMS PLUNGE TO REAP IN THE DEEP. Finance 85:22-25 (1967) |
| VP | Roos, Leslie L., Jr., and Noralou P. Roos. POLLUTION, REGULATION, AND EVALUATION. Law and Society Review 6:509-529 (1972) |
| IIIF | Rose, A.D. THE TUNA EXAMPLE: IS THERE HOPE FOR INTERNATIONAL COOPERATION. San Diego Law Review 11:776-814 (1974) |
| IIILOS | Roseman, D.M. GENEVA CONFERENCE ON THE LAW OF THE SEA - CONVENTION ON FISHING AND CONSERVATION OF THE LIVING RESOURCES OF THE HIGH SEAS. Boston Bar Journal 3:28-32 (1959) |
| VB | Rosenne, S. THE CONCEPT OF TERRITORIAL SEA IN THE TALMUD. Israel Law Journal 10:503-508 (1975) |
| IICZM | Rosentraub, Mark S., and Robert Warren. INFORMATION UTILIZATION AND SELF-EVALUATING CAPACITIES FOR COASTAL ZONE MANAGEMENT AGENCIES. Coastal Zone Management Journal 2(3):193-222 (1976) |
| VENV | Ross, Charles R. NATIONAL SOVEREIGNTY IN INTERNATIONAL ENVIRONMENTAL DECISIONS. Natural Resources Journal 12:242-254 (1972) |
| VOCET | Ross, D.A., and L.J. Smith. TRAINING AND TECHNICAL ASSISTANCE IN MARINE SCIENCE: A VIABLE TRANSFER PRODUCT. Ocean Development and International Law Journal 2:219-253 (1974) |
| VOR | Ross, David A. RED SEA HOT BRINE AREA; REVISITED. Science 175: 1455-1457 (1972) |

| | | |
|---|---|---|
| VINTL | Ross, David A. WHAT COMMON HERITAGE? <u>Oceanus</u> 17:2-5 (1973) | |

IVMMR    Ross, S.G. STRUCTURING FOR INTERNATIONAL OIL AND GAS EXPLORATION. <u>Oil and Gas Law and Taxation Institute (Southwestern Legal Foundation)</u> 25:359-387 (1974)

IVMMR    Ross-Skinner, Jean. NORWEGIAN OIL: THE 'BLUE-EYED ARABS.' <u>Dun's Review</u> 104:62-64,66 (1974)

VINTL    Rothpfeffer, T. EQUITY IN THE NORTH SEA CONTINENTAL SHELF CASES. <u>Nordisk Tidsskrift for International Ret</u> 42:81-137 (1972)

IVM      Rothstein, Arnold J. DEEP OCEAN MINING; TODAY AND TOMORROW. <u>Columbia Journal of World Business</u> 6:43-50 (January-February, 1971)

VOCET    Rowe, Gilbert T. OCEAN EXPLORATION: A SHIRT-SLEEVE APPROACH. <u>Water Spectrum</u> 4(3):8-14 (1972)

VINTL    Rubin, Alfred P. SUNKEN SOVIET SUBMARINES AND CENTRAL INTELLIGENCE: LAWS OF PROPERTY AND THE AGENCY. <u>American Journal of International Law</u> 69(4):855-860 (1975)

IICZM    Rubin, Kenneth A. THE ROLE OF THE COASTAL ZONE MANAGEMENT ACT OF 1972 IN THE DEVELOPMENT OF OIL AND GAS FROM THE OUTER CONTINENTAL SHELF. <u>Natural Resources Lawyer</u> VIII(3):399-436 (1975)

VORM     Rudd, Joseph. WHO OWNS ALASKA? MINERAL RIGHTS ACQUISITION AMID RAPIDLY CHANGING LAND OWNERSHIP. <u>Rocky Mountain Mineral Law Institute</u> 20:109-162 (1975)

VLOS     Ruddick, Valley. CAN THE UN AGREE UPON UNDERSEA RIGHTS? <u>Canadian Geographical Journal</u> 90:12-21 (1975)

VB       Rudolf, D. QUESTIONS ON SEA BOUNDARIES OF COASTAL STATES. <u>Nasa Zakonitost</u> 28:705-742 (1974)

IVDRIL   Rudon, Frank M. INVESTMENT POTENTIAL OF OFFSHORE DRILLING INDUSTRY. <u>Commercial and Financial Chronicle</u> 212:3,14-15 (October 29, 1970)

IIIP     Rueness, J. POLLUTION EFFECTS ON LITTORAL AGAL COMMUNITIES IN THE INNER OSLOFJORD, WITH SPECIAL REFERENCE TO ASCOPHYLLUM NODOSUM. <u>Helgolaender Wissenschaftliche Meeresuntersuchungen</u> 24(1-4):446-454 (1973)

VINTL    Ruester, B. STAATEN- UND VERTRAGSPRAXIS ZUM FESTLANDSOCKEL IM SUEDASIASTISCHEN RAUM. <u>Jahrbuch fuer Internationales Recht</u> 17:225-252 (1974)

VCS      Ruiz Moreno, I., et al. EL PROBLEMA DE LA JURISDICCIÓN EN LA PLATAFORMA CONTINENTAL ARGENTINA. <u>Revista del Colegio de Abogados de la Ciudad de Buenos Aires</u> 36(1/2):5-30 (1972)

IICZM    Russel, C.S., and A.V. Kneese. ESTABLISHING THE SCIENTIFIC, TECHNICAL, AND ECONOMIC BASIS FOR COASTAL ZONE MANAGEMENT. <u>Coastal Zone Management Journal</u> 1:47-63 (1973)

IIIOR    RUSSIAN RESEARCH SHIP FINDS ABUNDANT FISH IN PERUVIAN WATERS. <u>Translations on Latin America</u> 631:57-60 (1971)

VOI         Ryther, John H. POTENTIAL PRODUCTIVITY OF THE SEA. Science 130:602-608 (1959)

IIIAFF      Ryther, John H., and G.C. Matthiesen. AQUACULTURE, ITS STATUS AND POTENTIAL. Oceanus 14:2-14 (1969)

VB          Sabate Lichtschein, D. LA PLATAFORMA CONTINENTAL Y LA LUCHA POR LA EXTENSION DEL MAR TERRITORIAL. Justicia 32(516):47-61 (1973)

IIIF        Saila, Saul B., and K.W. Hess. SOME APPLICATIONS OF OPTIMAL CONTROL THEORY TO FISHERIES MANAGEMENT. Marine Reprint No. 51. Transactions American Fisheries Society 104(3):620-629 (1975)

IVM         SALDANHA BAY. South African Shipping News and Fishing Industry Review 28(3):22-25,29 (1973)

VINTL       Salemi, E. I LIMITE DI NAVIGAZIONE NORVEGESI DELLE POLIZZE CORPI IN CONFRONTO AI LIMITI INGLESI ED ITALIANI. Diritto e Pratica nell'Assicurazione 15:499-534 (1973)

IIIP        SALMON CANNERY POLLUTION: SOLUTIONS? The Environmental Lawyer 2:116-144 (1971)

IIIOR       SALMON SQUAWK. Business Week :106-106 (October 15, 1955)

IVMMR       Salnikov, Ivan. PLANS AND ASPIRATIONS OF THE SOVIET UNION'S OIL INDUSTRY. World Petroleum 34:48-54 (1963)

IIIAFF      Salo, Ernest. SALT WATER SALMON AQUACULTURE SHIFTS INTO HIGH ON PUGET SOUND. National Fisherman 52(13):96-99 (1972)

VINTL       Sambrailo, Branko. CONTRIBUTION OF THE YUGOSLAV-ITALIAN AGREEMENT ON DELIMITATION OF THE CONTINENTAL SHELF IN THE ADRIATIC SEA TO THE SETTLEMENT OF DISPUTES IN THE NORTH SEA CONTINENTAL SHELF CASES. Jugoslovenska Revija za Medunarodno Pravo :2-3 (1970)

IIIORM      _____ _____ INTERNATIONAL RELATIONS IN MATTERS OF FISHING IN THE ADRIATIC SEA. Jugoslovenska Revija Za Medunarodno Pravo 15:110-120 (1968)

VCS         Samuels, A. CONTINENTAL SHELF ACT, 1964. Solicitors' Journal 108:536-538 (1964)

VP          Samuels, Alec. OIL POLLUTION. British Year Book of International Law 45:385-391 (1971)

IICONS      SAN FRANCISCO BAY: REGIONAL REGULATION FOR ITS PROTECTION AND DEVELOPMENT. California Law Review 55:728-779 (1967)

VENV        Sand, Peter H. METHODS TO EXPEDITE ENVIRONMENT PROTECTION: INTERNATIONAL ECOSTANDARDS. American Journal of International Law 66:37-59 (1972)

IIIP        _____ _____ PROTECTION OF THE MARINE ENVIRONMENT AGAINST POLLUTION IN THE MEDITERRANEAN. Environmental Policy 1(4):154-159 (February, 1976)

VP          _____ _____ SOCIALIST RESPONSE: ENVIRONMENTAL PROTECTION LAW IN GERMAN DEMOCRATIC REPUBLIC. Ecology Law Quarterly 3:451-505 (1973)

| | |
|---|---|
| VP | Sand, Peter H. SPACE PROGRAMMES AND INTERNATIONAL ENVIRONMENT PROTECTION. International and Comparative Law Quarterly 21:43-60 (1972) |
| IVP | Sanders, Norman. NORTH SEA OIL: CAN THE TECHNOLOGY COPE? New Scientist 56:380-382 (November 16, 1972) |
| VENV | Sanders, W. James. ENVIRONMENTAL PROTECTION IN THE UNITED KINGDOM. Business Lawyer 27:845-849 (1972) |
| IIIF | Sandiford, Roberto. IL PROBLEMA DELLE ZONE DI PESCA. Il Diritto Marittimo 1964:19p. Special Issue. |
| VINTL | _____ _____ LES CONVENTIONS INTERNATIONALES DANS LE DOMAINE DE LA NAVIGATION FLUVIALE. Revue Internationale du Droit des Gens I(II): (1962) |
| VINTL | _____ _____ PIRATERIA E DIRITTO DI ASILO. Storia e Politica II(2): (1963) |
| IIWQ | Sandler, Ross. REFUSE ACT OF 1899: KEY TO CLEAN WATER. American Bar Association Journal 58:468-471 (1972) |
| VOD | Sansom, R.L. OCEAN DUMPING CONTROLS. Marine Technology Society Journal 7(3):6-8 (1973) |
| VB | Santa-Pinter, J.J. LATIN AMERICAN COUNTRIES FACING THE PROBLEM OF TERRITORIAL WATERS. San Diego Law Review 8:606-620 (1971) |
| VINTL | Sarup, Amrit. TRANSIT TRADE OF LANDLOCKED NEPAL. International and Comparative Law Quarterly 21(2):287-306 (1972) |
| IIIF | S.A. TRAWLER MEN TO BENEFIT FROM STAND TAKEN BY OTHER STATES? South African Shipping News and Fishing Industry Review 28(7):67,69 (1973) |
| VB | Savasykov, P.V. LEGISLATION AND PRACTICE IN RUSSIA IN THE XIX CENTURY OF THE WIDTH OF TERRITORIAL WATERS. Vestnik Moskovskogo Pravo 6:69-75 (1973) |
| VOD | SAVING A DYING SEA? THE LONDON CONVENTION ON OCEAN DUMPING. Cornell International Law Journal 7:32-48 (1973) |
| IICONS | SAVING SAN FRANCISCO BAY: A CASE STUDY IN ENVIRONMENTAL LEGISLATION. Stanford Law Review :349-366 (1971) |
| IICONS | SAVING THE COAST: THE CALIFORNIA COASTAL ZONE CONSERVATION ACT OF 1972. Golden Gate Law Review 4:307-352 (1974) |
| IICONS | SAVING THE SEASHORE: MANAGEMENT PLANNING FOR THE COASTAL ZONE. Hastings Law Journal 25:191-211 (1973) |
| IIIFV&G | Saxon, D.R. KIND OF SHIPS PLANNED BY ENVIRONMENT CANADA 1972-78. Canadian Fisherman and Ocean Science 58:22-24 (1972) |
| IIIP | Scarratt, D.J., and V. Zitko. BUNKER C OIL IN SEDIMENTS AND BENTHIC ANIMALS FROM SHALLOW DEPTHS IN CHEDABUCTO BAY, N.S. Journal of the Canadian Fisheries Research Board 29:1347-1350 (1972) |
| VLOS | Scerni, M. LA NUOVA PROBLEMATICA DEL DIRITTO DEL MARE. Communità Internazionale 30:251-260 (1975) |

VINTL    Schaefer, Milner B. FREEDOM OF SCIENTIFIC RESEARCH AND EXPLORATION IN THE SEA. Stanford Journal of International Studies 4:46-70 (1969)

IIICONS   _____ _____ SOME RECENT DEVELOPMENTS CONCERNING FISHING AND THE CONSERVATION OF THE LIVING RESOURCES OF THE HIGH SEAS. San Diego Law Review 7:371-407 (1970)

IIE      Schell, Steven R. ESTUARIES OF OREGON - ECOSYSTEMS IN CRISIS, PROBLEMS AND LEGAL SOLUTIONS. The Environmental Lawyer 2:83-103 (1971)

VOD      Schenker, Michael S. SAVING A DYING SEA? THE LONDON CONVENTION ON OCEAN DUMPING. Cornell International Law Journal 7(1):32-48 (1973)

VENV     Schlesinger, James R. ENERGY, THE ENVIRONMENT AND SOCIETY. Atomic Energy Law Journal 14:3-13 (1972)

IIP&H    Schmid, R.C., et al. ENERGY NEEDS AND PORT GROWTH. World Dredging and Marine Construction 10(3):11-14 (1974)

VENV     Schneider, J. PROTECTION OF THE ENVIRONMENT AND WORLD PUBLIC ORDER: SOME RECENT DEVELOPMENTS. Mississippi Law Journal 45:1085-1124 (1975)

IIWQ     Schoenbaum, Thomas J. EFFICACY OF FEDERAL AND STATE CONTROL OF WATER POLLUTION IN INTRASTATE STREAMS. Arizona Law Review 14:1-38 (1972)

IICZM    _____ _____ THE MANAGEMENT OF LAND AND WATER USE IN THE COASTAL ZONE: A NEW LAW IS ENACTED IN NORTH CAROLINA. North Carolina Law Review 53(2):275-302 (1974)

IICZM    _____ _____ PUBLIC RIGHTS AND COASTAL ZONE MANAGEMENT. North Carolina Law Review 51(1):1-41 (1972)

IIIAFF   Scholes, William A. HARVESTING SEAWEED OFF AUSTRALIA. Ocean Industry 4:69-74 (1969)

IIIB     Schram, G.G. ICELAND'S 50-MILE FISHERIES ZONE. Ocean Management 2:127-138 (1974)

IIIF     _____ _____ PJODRETTARREGLUR UM VERND FISKIMIDA UTAN LANDHELGI. Timarit Loegfraedinga 1:1-20 (1968)

VOR      Schroth, Charles R. EXPLORACAO DOS OCEANOS: UNA NOVA FRONTEIRA INDUSTRIAL. Revista Nacional da Pesca 13(110):12-12 (1971)

IVDRIL   Schulze, H. DRILLING RENEWED IN THE GERMAN CONTINENTAL SHELF OF THE NORTH SEA. Marine Technology 6(1):1-8 (1975)

VP       Schuster Philip F., II. NUCLEAR SHIP POLLUTION: NATIONAL AND INTERNATIONAL REGULATION AND LIABILITY. Environmental Law 5:203-240 (1975)

VINTL    SCIENTISTS SEEK TO CLAIM COBB SEAMOUNT FOR U.S. Oceanology 3:17-18 (1968)

IVDRIL   Scoggins, Sue. OIL AND GAS DRILLING PROGRAMS - STRUCTURE AND REGULATION. George Washington Law Review 41:471-504 (1973)

| | |
|---|---|
| IIIF | Scott, A. FISHERIES, POLLUTION, AND CANADIAN-AMERICAN TRANSNATIONAL RELATIONS. *International Organization* 28:827-848 (1974) |
| IVMMR | Scott, John. NORTH SEA: RIGHT PLACE, RIGHT TIME. *Petroleum Engineer* 44(12):25-29 (1972) |
| IVDRIL | Scott, R.W. $500 MILLION COMMITTED FOR U.K. NORTH SEA EXPLORATORY DRILLING. *World Oil* 175(6):83-85 (1972) |
| IVMMR | _____ _____ THE NORTH SEA; OFFSHORE'S GREATEST VENTURE. *World Oil* 175:33-36,38,40,136,139 (1972) |
| IVOL | Scott, R.W., and R.E. Snyder. ACCORDING TO LOUISIANA GOVERNOR EDWIN W. EDWARDS... OPPOSITION TO OCS LEASING IS SINCERE, BUT MISGUIDED. *World Oil* 180:67-70 (1975) |
| VEZ | Scovazzi, T. LA ZONA ECONOMICA NEI LAVORI PER LA NUOVA CODIFICAZIONE DEL DIRITTO DEL MAR. *Rivista di Diritto Internazionale* 57:730-773 (1974) |
| VMT | Scoville, Herbert, Jr. MISSILE SUBMARINES AND NATURAL SECURITY. *Scientific American* 226(6): (1972) |
| VAC | SEABED ARMS LIMITATION TREATY: A SIGNIFICANT DEVELOPMENT IN ARMS CONTROL AND DISARMAMENT. *Journal of International Law and Economics* 6:157-174 (1971) |
| IVOSTR | SEAFLOOR COMPLETIONS HOLD THE KEY TO DEEP AREAS. *Ocean Industry* 8(2):77-86 (1973) |
| VOI | SEA-FLOOR PRODUCTION SYSTEMS. *Ocean Industry* 5:29-32 (1970) |
| VREFS | SEA GRANT. *Fish Boat* 19(4):26-27 (1974) |
| VREFS | SEA GRANT. *Fish Boat* 20(4):22-23 (1975) |
| IVOSTR | SEAL DEVELOPS A LOW COST SEAFLOOR COMPLETION SYSTEM FOR 100-450-FT. WATER. *Ocean Industry* 8(4):161-162 (1973) |
| IVP | Searle, W.F., Jr. TWO OIL SPILL CONTROL SYSTEMS TAILORED FOR SPECIFIC TASKS. *Ocean Industry* 5:45-49 (1970) |
| VOI | _____ _____ HOW DEEP SEA WORK CAPABILITY IS GROWING. *Ocean Industry* 4:36-38 (1969) |
| VENE | Sebo, S.A. OCEAN POWER. *Maritime Studies and Management* 2:202-214 (1975) |
| IVMMR | Seeparijadi, R.A., and Slocum, R.C. VAST GEOLOGIC BASINS ATTRACT INDONESIAN OIL EXPLORATION. *World Oil* 177(2):35-38 (1973) |
| IIIINTL | Selak, C. PROPOSED INTERNATIONAL CONVENTION FOR THE HIGH SEAS FISHERIES OF THE NORTH PACIFIC OCEAN. *American Journal of International Law* 46:323-330 (1952) |
| VINTL | Sepúlveda Amor, Bernando. DERECHO DEL MAR, APUNTES SOBRE EL SISTEMA LEGAL MEXICANO. *Foro International* XIII(2): (1972) |
| IIIFV&G | SERIES SHIPS FOR TUNA. *Fishing News International* 11(1):16-18 (1972) |

IVMMR    Setty, M.G.  MINERAL RESOURCES OF THE SEA.  Mahasagar Bulletin 5:81-91 (1972)

IIOSTR   Seymour, John L.  PRELIMINARY LEGAL CONSIDERATIONS IN DEVELOPING ARTIFICIAL REEFS.  Coastal Zone Management Journal 2(2):149-170 (1975)

VLOS     Shapley, D.  NOW, A DRAFT SEA LAW TREATY - BUT WHAT COMES AFTER.  Science 188(4191):918 (1975)

VOR      Shapley, Deborah.  OCEAN TECHNOLOGY; RACE TO SEABED WEALTH DISTURBS MORE THAN FISH.  Science 180:849-850,851,893 (1973)

VP       Share, Paul A.  POLLUTION OF THE GREAT LAKES: A STUDY OF INTERNATIONAL ENVIRONMENTAL CONTROL EFFORTS.  Wayne Law Review 19:165-179 (1972)

IVOL     Shavelson, J.  THE ADMINISTRATION OF OFFSHORE MINERAL LEASING STATUTES IN PACIFIC NORTHWEST (CALIFORNIA, OREGON, AND HAWAII.)  Natural Resources Lawyer 1(3):60-69 (1968)

VP       Sheaffer, John R.  POLLUTION CONTROL: WASTE WATER IRRIGATION.  De Paul Law Review 21:987-1007 (1972)

VENE     Sheets, Kenneth R.  IS OIL OFF EAST COAST ONE ANSWER TO FUEL SHORTAGE?  U.S. News and World Report 75:56-58 (1973)

VINTL    Sheikh, Ahmed.  PEOPLES' REPUBLIC OF CHINA AND INTERNATIONAL LAW.  The International Lawyer 7:770-787 (1973)

VP       SHELL SKIMMER EASES CLEANUP OF OIL SPILLS.  Oil and Gas Journal 70:106-106 (1972)

IIIB     Shenker, A.  FOREIGN FISHING IN PACIFIC NORTHWEST COASTAL WATERS.  Oregon Law Review 46:422-453 (1967)

IIP      Sheppard, C.R.C.  POLLUTION OF THE MEDITERRANEAN AROUND NAPLES.  Marine Pollution Bulletin 5:42-44 (1974)

VP       Sherrin, J.J.  INTERNATIONAL LAW AND CANADIAN ARCTIC POLLUTION CONTROL.  Albany Law Review 38:921-942 (1974)

IIP      Shinn, Clinton W.  FEDERAL GRANT PROGRAM TO AID CONSTRUCTION OF MUNICIPAL SEWAGE TREATMENT PLANTS: A SURVEY OF THE 1972 FWPCA AMENDMENTS.  Tulane Law Review 48:85-104 (1973)

IVOI     Short, Thomas E.  ESSO COMPUTERIZES BASS STRAIT PRODUCTION.  Petroleum Engineer 45(6):44-48 (1972)

IIIAFF   Shleser, Robert, and George Tchobanoglous.  THE AMERICAN LOBSTER AS A MODEL FOR THE CONTINUOUS PRODUCTION OF QUALITY SEAFOOD THROUGH AQUACULTURE.  Journal of the Marine Technology Society 8:4-8 (1974)

VENE     Shoupp, William E.  INVOLVING THE OCEANS IN SOLVING ENERGY PROBLEMS.  Journal of the Marine Technology Society 8:18-24 (1974)

VENV     Shuleikin, V.V.  VZAIMODEISTVIE ZVEN'EV V SISTEME "OKEAN-ATMOSFERA-MATERIKI".  Priroda (Moskva) 10:12-21 (1971)

VP          Shutler, N.D. POLLUTION OF THE SEA BY OIL. Houston Law Review 7(4): 415-441 (1970)

VOCET       Sigalove, Joel J., and Michael D. Pearlman. A CONTINUOUS OCEAN SAMPLING AND ANALYSIS SYSTEM. Undersea Technology 13:24-27 (1972)

VINTL       Shyam, M. INTERNATIONAL STRAITS AND OCEAN LAW. Indian Journal of International Law 15:17-76 (1975)

IVOCET      Silverman, Daniel. SEISMIC HOLOGRAPHY; OIL FINDING TOOL OF THE FUTURE? Ocean Industry 5:40-42 (1970)

VLOS        Simmonds, K.R. LAW OF THE SEA: THE SECOND GENEVA CONFERENCE. Law Journal 110:507-508 (1960)

VP          Simonov, A.I., et al. THE PRESENT STATE OF CHEMICAL WATER POLLUTION IN THE NORTH ATLANTIC. Meteorologiia i Gidrologiia 3:61-69 (1974)

VSUB        Sinclair, J.E. MOBILITY ON THE SEA FLOOR. Engineering 214:271-277 (1974)

IVMMR       600 MIO. T ERDOEL AUS DEM NORDSEEGRUND. Meerestechnik 4:207-210 (1973)

IVOSTR      643 PLATFORMS MAKE INDUSTRY'S CITY AT SEA. Offshore 33:91-92,96-98, 101 (1973)

VOR         LE SIXIEME CONTINENT: UN ESSAI D'INVENTAIRE DES RESSOURCES DES OCÉANS ET DES FONDS SOUS-MARINES. Problèmes Économiques 382:22-32 (1974)

IVOL        62 OFFSHORE LOUISIANA LEASE BIDS ARE ACCEPTED. World Oil 175(6):86-87 (1972)

VLOS        Skubiszewski, K. LA NATURE JURIDIQUE DE LA DÉCLARATION DES PRINCIPLES SUR LES FONDS MARINS. Annales d'Etudes Internationales 4:237-248 (1973)

VOD         Slansky, C.M., ed. PRINCIPLES FOR LIMITING THE INTRODUCTION OF RADIOACTIVE WASTES INTO THE SEA. Atomic Energy Review 9(4):853-868 (1971)

IIICONS     Sloan, Lucy. A BREAKTHROUGH IN INTERNATIONAL FISHERIES CONSERVATION. Journal of the Marine Technology Society 8:3-8 (1974)

VINTL       Slomanson, William R. FREE TRANSIT IN TERRITORIAL STRAITS: JURISDICTION ON EVEN KEEL? California Western International Law Journal 3:375-396 (1973)

IIIF        Slossom, P.W. FISHERMEN AND STATESMEN. Independant 81:462-463 (1915)

VLOS        Slouka, Zdenek. UNITED NATIONS AND THE DEEP OCEAN: FROM DATA TO NORMS. Syracuse Journal of International Law and Commerce 1:61-90 (1972)

IVOSTR      Small, S.W., et al. SUBMARINE PIPELINE SUPPORT BY MARINE SEDIMENTS. Journal of Petroleum Technology 24:317-322 (1972)

| | |
|---|---|
| VP | Smith, C.W. HIGHLIGHTS OF THE FEDERAL WATER POLLUTION CONTROL ACT OF 1972. Dickinson Law Review 77:459-491 (1973) |
| VORM | Smith, D. PIRATE BROADCASTING. Southern California Law Review 41:769-815 (1968) |
| IVINTL | Smith, D.N., and L.T. Wells, Jr. MINERAL AGREEMENTS IN THE DEVELOPING COUNTRIES: STRUCTURES AND SUBSTANCE. American Journal of International Law 69:560-590 (1975) |
| VORM | Smith, F.G.W. WHAT THE OCEAN MEANS TO MAN. American Scientist 50:16-19 (1972) |
| VOI | Smith, F.M. FINANCE AND ECONOMICS OF OFFSHORE OPERATIONS. World Oil 177(1):81-93 (1973) |
| VAC | Smith, G. AMBASSADOR SMITH PRESENTS U.S. VIEWS ON SEABED PROPOSAL AT EIGHTEEN-NATION DISARMAMENT CONFERENCE. U.S. Department of State Bulletin 60:333-337 (1969) |
| VOR | Smith, George P., II. APOSTROPHE TO A TROUBLED OCEAN. Indiana Legal Forum 5:267-299 (1972) |
| VENV | _____ _____ TOWARD AN INTERNATIONAL STANDARD OF ENVIRONMENT. Pepperdine Law Review 2:28-51 (1974) |
| VENV | Smith, J. Arthur, III. CURRENT DEVELOPMENTS IN ENVIRONMENTAL LAW. Illinois Bar Journal 20:323- (1973) |
| VAC | Smith, Jeffrey H. NATO NUCLEAR INFORMATION-SHARING ARRANGEMENTS AND THE NON-PROLIFERATION TREATY: COLLECTIVE DEFENSE CONFRONTS ARMS CONTROL. Atomic Energy Law Journal 13:331-370 (1972) |
| IIIAFF | Smith, J.O., et al. MARICULTURE: A NEW OCEAN USE. Georgia Journal of International and Comparative Law 4:307-342 (1974) |
| IISL | Smith, J. Owens, and Jack L. Sammons. PUBLIC RIGHTS IN GEORGIA'S TIDELANDS. Georgia Law Review 9:79-114 (1974) |
| IIP&H | Smith, L.L., Jr., and H.S. Marcus. DEEPWATER PORT CRISIS ON THE U.S. EAST COAST. Naval Engineers Journal 85(1):15-23 (1973) |
| IVMT | Smith, R.W. OCEANBORNE SHIPMENT OF PETROLEUM AND THE IMPACT OF STRAITS ON VLCC TRANSIT. Maritime Studies and Management 1:119-130 (1973) |
| IVMMR | Soerpajadi, R.A., and R.C. Slocum. VAST GEOLOGIC BASINS ATTRACT INDONESIAN OIL EXPLORATION. World Oil 177:80-83 (1973) |
| VLOS | Sohn, Louis B. THE COUNCIL OF AN INTERNATIONAL SEA-BED AUTHORITY. San Diego Law Review 9:404-431 (1972) |
| VINTL | _____ _____ A TRIBUNAL FOR THE SEA-BED OR THE OCEANS. Zeitschrift fur Ausländisches Offentliches Recht und Volkerrecht 32:253-264 (1972) |
| IIIP | Sokolova, N.V., and V.P. Parchevskii. LEAD-210 IN SOME AQUATIC FAUNA IN THE SEA OF OKHOTSK AND THE BERING SEA. Soviet Journal of Ecology 3:411-416 (1973) |

| | |
|---|---|
| IVOL | Solanas, Donald W. UPDATE - OUTER CONTINENTAL SHELF LEASE MANAGEMENT PROGRAM. Journal of Petroleum Technology 26:388-394 (1974) |
| IIIF | Solecki, J.J. NEW DEVELOPMENTS IN THE SOVIET UNION'S FISHING INDUSTRY. M.S.R.L. Bulletin 7(1): (1973) |
| VP | SOLID WASTE POLLUTION: CONTROL OF CONTAINER PACKAGING THROUGH TAXATION. Urban Law Annual 1973:387-395 (1973) |
| VOR | Sommereyns, R. DE DIEPE ZEEBODEN, HOOFD-BEKOMMERNIS VAN DE DERDE ZEERECHTCONFERENTIE VAN DE VERENIGDE NATIES. Nederlands Tijdschrift voor Internationaal Recht 18:299-342 (1971) |
| VOSTR | Soons, A.H.A. VOLKENRECHTELIJKE VRAGEN ROND HET PROJECT VOOR DE BOUW VAN EEN AFVALEILAND IN DE NOORDZEE. Nederlands Juristenblad 36:1009-1018 (1972) |
| IVMMR | Sorensen, P.E., and W.J. Mead. A COST-BENEFIT ANALYSIS OF OCEAN MINERAL RESOURCE DEVELOPMENT; THE CASE OF MANGANESE NODULES. American Journal of Economics and Sociology 50:1611-1620 (1968) |
| IVMMR | SOUTH AFRICA OIL SEARCH IS ACCELERATING RAPIDLY. World Oil 164:153-158 (1967) |
| IIP&H | SOUTH AFRICAN PORTS - HOW THEY COMPARE. South African Shipping News and Fishing Industry Review 28(2):25,27,29,31 (1973) |
| IIIFV&G | SOUTH AFRICA'S FIRST MARCO PURSE SEINER. South African Shipping News and Fishing Industry Review 27(4):46-47- (1972) |
| IIIFV&G | SOUTH AFRICA'S LARGEST TIMBER HULLED FISHING VESSEL? South African Shipping News and Fishing Industry Review 27(5):46-47,49 (1972) |
| IIP&H | SOUTHERN CALIFORNIA PORTS: AN ERA OF EXPANSION. World Ports 37:8, 10- (1975) |
| VOCET | SOVIET OCEANOGRAPHIC STUDIES, USSR. Okeanologiya 14(4): (1974) |
| VENV | SOVIET-U.S. ENVIRONMENTAL PROTECTION AGREEMENT. Natural Resources Journal 14:275-281 (1974) |
| IVMMR | SPANISH MEDITERRANEAN PLAY QUICKENS. Petroleum Engineer 45(7):99-100 (1972) |
| VMT | SPECULATION ON THE MILLION TON SHIP. Surveyor 7(1):12-15 (1973) |
| IIENV | Spencer, E.F., Jr., et al. THE STATE OF LOUISIANA SUPERPORT AUTHORITY ENVIRONMENTAL PROTECTION PLAN - OIL AND OYSTERS. Water Resources Bulletin 11(4):836-847 (1975) |
| VSG | Spilhaus, Athelstan. BIRTH OF SEA GRANT - LAND IS JUST AN ISLAND. American Geophysical Union 53(5):572-578 (1972) |
| VOR | Spong, William B., Jr. O MAR, NOVA FONTE DE RECURSOS. Revista Nacional da Pesca 12(96):14-15 (1970) |
| VMT | Spyrou, A.G. MOVING A MILLION TONS OF CRUDE OIL. Tanker and Bulk Carrier 19(9):3,5-6 (1973) |

VMT  Spyrou, A.G. ONE MILLION TON TANKER - THE ONASSIS GROUP VIEW. Marine Engineers Review :19-21 (1975)

IVOL  STAGE IS SET FOR FUTURE COOK INLET LEASES. Offshore 33(9):71-72 (1973)

VOR  Stang, David. THE DONNYBROOK FAIR OF THE OCEANS. San Diego Law Review 9:589-607 (1972)

VORM  _____ _____ OCEAN POLEMICS. India Quarterly 29:138-150 (1973)

VORM  _____ _____ POLITICAL COBWEBS BENEATH THE SEA. The International Lawyer 7:1-15 (1973)

VORM  _____ _____ THE WALLS BENEATH THE SEA. U.S. Naval Institute Proceedings 94:33-43 (March, 1968)

IISL  _____ _____ WET LAND: THE UNAVAILABLE RESOURCE OF THE OUTER CONTINENTAL SHELF. Journal of Law and Economic Development 2:153-189 (1968)

VOD  Staples, K.D. MARINE DISPOSAL OF EFFLUENT. Process Technology International 18:319-320 (1973)

IISL  STATE AND LOCAL WETLANDS REGULATION: THE PROBLEM OF TAKING WITHOUT JUST COMPENSATION. Virginia Law Review 58:876-906 (1972)

IVP  STATE PROTECTION FROM OIL SPILLS: ASKEW v. AMERICAN WATERWAYS OPERATORS, INC. (93 S.Ct. 1590). Environmental Law 4:433-443 (1974)

IVMMR  THE STATUS OF MINERAL RESOURCES ON THE OCEAN FLOOR. California Western Law Review :299-312 (1969)

IVOL  STATUTORY RELIEF FOR FAILURE TO RELEASE AN OIL AND GAS LEASE OF RECORD. Baylor Law Review 26:108-113 (1974)

IIDRIL  Stavland, A. REGULATIONS FOR MOBILE DRILLING PLATFORMS TO BE ISSUED BY THE MARITIME DIRECTORATE IN NORWAY AND OTHER REGULATORY AGENCIES. Northern Offshore 2(3):45,48 (1973)

VINTL  Staynov, P. ESTABLISHMENT OF A SPECIAL INTERNATIONAL STATUTE OF THE SEMI-ENCLOSED SEA. Trudove po Mezhdunarodno Pravo 2:29-40 (1974)

VP  Steele, J.H. POLLUTION STUDIES IN THE CLYDE SEA AREA. Marine Pollution Bulletin 4:153-157 (1973)

VOCET  Stefanov, Georgi. UNDERWATER RESEARCH IN THE BLACK SEA. Underwater Journal 4(6):249-251 (1972)

IVOI  Stentz, L.M. INSURANCE FIRM BALKS AT COSTLY OFFSHORE RISKS. World Oil 163:156-159 (1966)

IVM  Stevens, J.F. MINING THE ALASKAN SEAS. Ocean Industry 5:47-51 (1970)

IIICONS  Stevenson, C.H. PRESERVATION OF THE FISHERIES ON THE HIGH SEAS. Popular Science Monthly 76:389-395 (1910)

VLOS    Stevenson, John R. THE UNITED NATIONS CONFERENCE ON THE LAW OF THE SEAS HAS A BIG JOB - DRAFTING A CONSTITUTION FOR THE SEAS. American Bar Association Journal 61:185-190 (1975)

VLOS    _____ _____ WHO IS TO CONTROL THE OCEANS: U.S. POLICY AND THE 1973 LAW OF THE SEA CONFERENCE. International Lawyer 6:465-477 (1972)

VLOS    Stevenson, John R., and Bernard H. Oxman. THE PREPARATIONS FOR THE LAW OF THE SEA CONFERENCE. American Journal of International Law 68(1):1-32 (1974)

VLOS    _____ _____ THE THIRD UNITED NATIONS CONFERENCE ON THE LAW OF THE SEA: THE 1974 CARACAS SESSION. American Journal of International Law 69:1-30 (1975)

VLOS    _____ _____ THE THIRD UNITED NATIONS CONFERENCE ON THE LAW OF THE SEA: THE 1975 GENEVA SESSION. American Journal of International Law 69(4):763-797 (October, 1975)

IVOSTR  Stewart, J. KONSTRUKTIONSKRITERIEN FUER NORDSEE- OFFSHORE- ANLAGEN. Meerestechnik 4:131-133 (1973)

IIIFV&G Stewart, P.A.M. CATCH SELECTIVITY BY ELECTRICAL FISHING SYSTEMS. International Council for the Exploration of the Sea. Journal du Conseil 36:106-109 (1975)

VENV    STOCKHOLM CONFERENCE: A STEP TOWARD GLOBAL ENVIRONMENTAL COOPERATION AND INVOLVEMENT. Indiana Law Review 6:267-282 (1972)

IVDRIL  Stockton, Thomas R. DYNAMIC POSITIONING OF DEEP DRILLING VESSELS. Underwater Journal 4:228-234 (1972)

VAC     Stoever, W. "RACE" FOR THE SEABED: THE RIGHT TO EMPLACE MILITARY INSTALLATIONS ON THE DEEP OCEAN FLOOR. The International Lawyer 4:560-568 (1970)

IVOSTR  Stone, G. TRENDS IN DEEPWATER SUBSEA COMPLETION. Offshore Services 7(6):24-27 (1974)

IVOI    Stone, O. LEGAL ASPECTS OF OFFSHORE OIL AND GAS OPERATIONS. Natural Resources Journal 8:478-504 (1968)

VOR     _____ _____ RECENT LEGAL DEVELOPMENTS RELATING TO NATURAL RESOURCES OF THE MARINE ENVIRONMENT. Natural Resources Lawyer 2(1):26-46 (1969)

VB      _____ _____ SOME ASPECTS OF JURISDICTION OVER NATURAL RESOURCES UNDER THE OCEAN FLOOR. Natural Resources Lawyer 3(2):155-194 (1970)

VCS     _____ _____ UNITED STATES LEGISLATION RELATING TO THE CONTINENTAL SHELF. International and Comparative Law Quarterly 17:103-117 (1968)

VLOS    _____ _____ UNITED STATES DRAFT CONVENTION ON THE INTERNATIONAL SEABED AREA. Tulane Law Review 45:527-545 (1971)

VB      Stone, William. TERRITORIAL WATERS AND THE HIGH SEAS. Editorial Research Reports 2(13):673-690 (1955)

IIICONS   Straburzyński, A. CONSERVATION OF LIVING RESOURCES OF THE BALTIC SEA IN VIEW OF THE PROVISIONS OF THE GDAŃSK CONVENTION. Państwo i Prawo 29(5):68-75 (1974)

IIIEZ   _____ _____ EXCLUSIVE FISHERY ZONES: INTERNATIONAL AND POLISH PRACTICES. Polish Yearbook of International Law 3:257-272 (1970)

VB   _____ _____ THE EXPLOITATION OF NATURAL RESOURCES OF SEAS AND OCEANS BOTTOMS AND THE BOUNDARIES OF STATE JURISDICTION. Państwo i Prawo 26(12):1021-1030 (1971)

VLOS   _____ _____ L'ÉTENDUE TERRITORIALE DES DROITS DE L'ÉTAT MARITIME QUANT À L'UTILISATION DE LA MER ET DES TERRAINS SOUS-MARINS. Studia Prawnicze 38:35-66 (1973)

IIIB   _____ _____ THE POLISH ZONE OF SEA FISHING AND CONTEMPORARY INTERNATIONAL PRACTICE. Translation of Technika i Gospodarka Morska 29(7):305-307 (1970)

VOR   _____ _____ SOVEREIGN RIGHTS TO THE SEA-BED RESOURCES AND THE DECLARATION ON THE CONTINENTAL SHELF OF THE BALTIC SEA. Polish Yearbook of International Law 5:61-74 (1972/1973)

VENV   Strausberg, Gary I. NATIONAL ENVIRONMENTAL POLICY ACT AND THE AGENCY FOR INTERNATIONAL DEVELOPMENT. The International Lawyer 7:46-69 (1973)

IIIB   Strieker, G. AT SEA WITH THE 89th CONGRESS: THE UNITED STATES FISHERIES ZONE. Hastings Law Journal 18:937-957 (1967)

IVDRIL   SUB-ICE MAY AID OFFSHORE ARCTIC DRILLING. World Oil 175(5):71-72 (1972)

VMT   SUBMARINES: ACCEPTANCE AT LAST. Offshore Services 8(2):42-46,49 (1975)

VSUB   SUBMERSIBLE PROPOSED FOR DEEP-SEA TRENCHING. Oil and Gas Journal 70(29):89-89 (1972)

IVDRIL   SUBSEA ANCHOR DRILLING - A NEW CONCEPT. Ocean Industry 8(4):156-156 (1973)

VMT   Sudbury, J.D. SUBMERGED BARGES FOR ARCTIC TRANSPORTATION? Ocean Industry 8(3):22-24 (1973)

VINTL   Sulikowski, T. SOVIET OCEAN POLICY. Ocean Development and International Law 3:69-86,127-153 (1975)

VENV   Sullivan, James J., and H. Fernando Arias. CONCEPTS AND PRINCIPLES FOR ENVIRONMENTAL ECONOMICS. Environmental Affairs 2(3):597-613 (1972)

VLOS   SUMMARY OF DRAFT CONVENTION. U.S. Department of State Bulletin XLIII: 213-218 (August 24, 1970)

IVDRIL   Summer, M.N. NEW IDEAS FOR DRILLING OFFSHORE. World Oil 162:135-137 (1966)

| | |
|---|---|
| IICZM | Sunamura, T., and K. Horikawa. A STUDY USING AERIAL PHOTOGRAPHS OF THE EFFECT OF PROTECTIVE STRUCTURES ON COASTAL CLIFF EROSION. Coastal Engineering in Japan 15:105-111 (1972) |
| IIP&H | SUPERPORT PROPOSED FOR DELAWARE BAY. World Dredging and Marine Construction 8(13):79-79 (1972) |
| IIIFV&G | THE SUPERSEINERS KEEP COMING. Fish Boat 18(1):16-17 (1973) |
| IIP&H | SUPERTANKER DRY DOCK FOR CADIZ. Tanker and Bulk Carrier 20(14):27, 29 (1974) |
| VP | SUPREME COURT DECLINES ORIGINAL JURISDICTION IN LAKE ERIE POLLUTION CASE. University of Miami Law Review 25:794-799 (1971) |
| VENV | SURVEY OF ENVIRONMENTAL LEGISLATION. University of Miami Law Review 26:778-803 (1972) |
| VP | Sutton, Gary. POLLUTION PREVENTION IN THE ARCTIC - NATIONAL AND MULTINATIONAL APPROACHES COMPARED. Ottawa Law Review 5:32-64 (1971) |
| IIIP | Suzuki, Y., et al. CESIUM-137 CONTAMINATION OF MARINE FISHES FROM THE COASTS OF JAPAN. Journal of Radiation Research 14:382-391 (1973) |
| VCS | Sviridov, E.P. THE DIFFERENTIATION OF CONTINENTAL SHELF IN THE NORTH SEA. Sovetskoe Gosudarstov 10:106-110 (1974) |
| IIP | Swan, Peter N. AMERICAN WATERWAYS (AMERICAN WATERWAYS OPERATORS v. ASKEW, 335 F.Supp. 1241): FLORIDA OIL POLLUTION LEGISLATION MAKES IT OVER FIRST HURDLE. Journal of Maritime Law and Commerce 5:77-110 (1973) |
| VP | _____ _____ CHALLENGES TO FEDERALISM: STATE LEGISLATION CONCERNING MARINE OIL POLLUTION. Ecology Law Quarterly 2:437-470,801-836 (1972) |
| VP | _____ _____ INTERNATIONAL AND NATIONAL APPROACHES TO OIL POLLUTION RESPONSIBILITY: AN EMERGING REGIME FOR A GLOBAL PROBLEM. Oregon Law Review 50:504-598 (1971) |
| VP | _____ _____ MANAGEMENT OF HIGH-LEVEL RADIOACTIVE WASTES: THE AEC AND THE LEGAL PROCESS. Law and the Social Order 1973:263-311 (1973) |
| IICZM | Swanson, Gerald C. COASTAL ZONE MANAGEMENT FROM AN ADMINISTRATIVE PERSPECTIVE: A CASE STUDY OF THE SAN FRANCISCO BAY CONSERVATION AND DEVELOPMENT COMMISSION. Coastal Zone Management Journal 2(2):81-102 (1975) |
| IVOI | SWEDEN. Ocean Industry 9:83-84,87-89 (1974) |
| VCS | SWEDEN: CONTINENTAL SHELF. Departements Nytt 2:11-11 (1973) |
| IIIB | SWEDEN: FISHING LIMITS. Guardian :4 (May 9, 1973) |
| IIIB | SWEDEN: FISHING LIMITS. Svenska Dagbladet :7 (June 6, 1973) |
| VP | SWEDEN: POLLUTION. Svenska Dagbladet :19 (March 10, 1973) |
| IIIMM | SWEDEN: SEALS. Svenska Dagbladet :1 (June 5, 1973) |

| | |
|---|---|
| VMT | SWEDEN - USSR: MARITIME TRANSPORT. Svenska Dagbladet :17 (March 20, 1973) |
| VP | Sweeney, J. OIL POLLUTION OF THE OCEANS. Fordham Law Review 37:155-208 (1968) |
| IIP | Sweeney, J.C. ENVIRONMENTAL PROTECTION BY COASTAL STATES: THE PARADIGM FROM MARINE TRANSPORT OF PETROLEUM. Georgia Journal of International and Comparative Law 4:278-306 (1974) |
| VOR | Sweeney, R.J., et al. MARKET FAILURE, THE COMMON-POOL PROBLEM, AND OCEAN RESOURCE EXPLOITATION. Journal of Law and Economics 17:179-192 (1975) |
| VENE | Swidler, Joseph C. ROLE OF ENERGY CONSERVATION IN A NATIONAL ENERGY POLICY. Environmental Affairs 2:280- (1972) |
| IIIB | Swygard, Kline R. POLITICS OF THE NORTH PACIFIC FISHERIES WITH SPECIAL REFERENCE TO THE TWELVE MILE BILL. Washington Law Review 43:269-282 (1967) |
| VINTL | Syatauw, J.J.G. REVISITING THE ARCHIPELAGO - AN OLD CONCEPT GAINS NEW RESPECTABILITY. India Quarterly XXIX(2):104-119 (1973) |
| IIIP | Sylvester, J.R. POSSIBLE EFFECTS OF THERMAL EFFLUENTS ON FISH. A REVIEW. Environmental Pollution 3(3):205-215 (1972) |
| VINTL | Symmons, C.R. LEGAL ASPECTS OF THE ANGLO-IRISH DISPUTE OVER ROCKALL. Northern Ireland Legal Quarterly 26:65-93 (1975) |
| IVMMR | Symon, F.G. THE PROSPECTS FOR NORTH SEA NATURAL GAS. Northern Offshore 2(1):76- (1973) |
| VMT | Symonides, J. FREEDOM OF NAVIGATION IN SEA STRAITS. Sprawy Miedzynarodowe 4:49-61 (1975) |
| VINTL | _____ _____ LEGAL STATUS OF THE BALTIC STRAITS. Polish Yearbook of International Law 4:119-146 (1971) |
| IICZM | SYMPOSIUM. CALIFORNIA'S COASTLINE. California State Bar Journal 47:402-438 (1972) |
| VENV | SYMPOSIUM: HUMAN ENVIRONMENT; TOWARD AN INTERNATIONAL SOLUTION. Natural Resources Journal 12:187-194 (1972) |
| VENV | SYMPOSIUM: INTERNATIONAL ENVIRONMENTAL CONTROL. Stanford Journal of International Studies 8:1-153 (1973) |
| VLOS | SYMPOSIUM: LAW OF THE SEAS. Annual Issue. San Diego Law Review Vol. 7- 1970- |
| IVM | A SYMPOSIUM ON DEEP SEABED MINING. Virginia Journal of International Law 15(4):791-957 (1975) |
| VENV | SYMPOSIUM ON ENVIRONMENTAL LAW. Idaho Law Review 10:116p (1973) |
| VENV | SYMPOSIUM ON INTERNATIONAL PROTECTION OF THE ENVIRONMENT. POLLUTION: AN INTERNATIONAL PROBLEM NEEDING INTERNATIONAL SOLUTION. Texas International Law Journal 7:1-4 (1971) |

| | |
|---|---|
| VOR | SYMPOSIUM ON NATURAL RESOURCE PROPERTY RIGHTS. <u>Natural Resources Journal</u> 15:639-789 (October, 1975) |
| VP | SYMPOSIUM: RECENT ENVIRONMENTAL DEVELOPMENTS IN MARITIME AND OFF-SHORE ACTIVITIES. <u>Houston Law Review</u> 9:655-708 (1972) |
| VENE | SYMPOSIUM: THE NUCLEAR POWER PLANT LICENSING PROCESS. <u>William and Mary Law Review</u> 15:487-566 (1974) |
| IICONS | SYMPOSIUM: THE SAN FRANCISCO BAY AREA REGIONAL PROBLEMS AND SOLUTIONS. <u>California Law Review</u> 53:364-385 (1965) |
| VENE | SYMPOSIUM: U.S.-CANADIAN ENERGY RESOURCE DEVELOPMENT. <u>Case Western Reserve Journal of International Law</u> 5:36-85 (1972) |
| IIIF | Szuchiewicz, R. SALMON FISHING ACTIVATION IN THE BALTIC SEA. National Marine Fisheries Service, Division of Foreign Fisheries Trans. of <u>Biuletyn Zjednoezenia Gospodarki Rybnej</u> 7(1):21-25 (1970) |
| VLOS | Tabibi, A.H. THE RIGHT OF LAND-LOCKED COUNTRIES TO FREE ACCESS TO THE SEA. <u>Oesterreichische Zeitschrift fuer Oeffentliches Recht</u> 23: 117-146 (1972) |
| VLOS | Taft, George. THE THIRD U.N. LAW OF THE SEA CONFERENCE: MAJOR UNRESOLVED FISHERIES ISSUES. <u>Columbia Journal of Transnational Law</u> 14:112-117 (1975) |
| VMT | Taggart, R. A NEW APPROACH TO SUPERTANKER DESIGN. <u>Ocean Industry</u> 9:21-25 (1974) |
| VP | TANK VESSELS IN DOMESTIC TRADE: PROTECTION OF MARINE ENVIRONMENT: NOTICE OF PROPOSED RULEMAKING. <u>Federal Register</u> 39(126):24149-24157 (June 28, 1974) |
| IVMMR | Tarling, D.H. CONTINENTAL DRIFT AND RESERVES OF OIL AND NATURAL GAS. <u>Nature</u> 243:277-279 (1973) |
| VENV | Tarlock, A. Dan, et al. ENVIRONMENTAL REGULATION OF POWER PLANT SITING: EXISTING AND PROPOSED INSTITUTIONS. <u>Southern California Law Review</u> 45:502-569 (1972) |
| IVOL | TAX CONSEQUENCES AND DISTINCTIONS INVOLVED IN THE SALE OR LEASE OF OIL AND GAS INTERESTS. <u>Natural Resources Journal</u> 14:257-270 (1974) |
| VOR | TAXATION AS A TOOL OF NATURAL RESOURCE MANAGEMENT: OIL AS A CASE STUDY. <u>Ecology Law Quarterly</u> 1:749-772 (1971) |
| IVOI | Taylor, D.M. NEW CONCEPTS IN OFFSHORE PRODUCTION. <u>Ocean Industry</u> 4:66-70 (1969) |
| IVOI | \_\_\_\_\_ \_\_\_\_\_ OVERVIEW. <u>Ocean Industry</u> 8(2):61-63 (1973) |
| IVMMR | Taylor, Donald M. CONVERTING WORTHLESS NODULES TO VALUABLE ORE. <u>Ocean Industry</u> 6:27-28 (1971) |
| IVDRIL | \_\_\_\_\_ \_\_\_\_\_ HUMBLE'S SAFE APPROACH TO DEEP WATER DRILLING. <u>Ocean Industry</u> 6:20-22 (1971) |
| IVOI | \_\_\_\_\_ \_\_\_\_\_ NORTH SEA OVERVIEW. <u>Ocean Industry</u> 8:61-63 (1973) |

| | |
|---|---|
| VOR | Taylor, Donald M. POTENTIAL OF THE SEA; THE ECONOMY OF OCEAN RESOURCES. Ocean Industry 4:46-48 (1969) |
| IVDRIL | _____ _____ SEDCO 1972; FIRST OF A NEW GENERATION OF DRILLING RIGS. Ocean Industry 8:19-34 (1973) |
| IVMMR | Taylor, J. SETTLEMENT OF DISPUTE BETWEEN FEDERAL AND STATE GOVERNMENTS CONCERNING OFFSHORE PETROLEUM RESOURCES: ACCOMODATION OR ADJUDICATION? Harvard International Law Journal 11:358-399 (1970) |
| VP | Tearle, W.J. OIL POLLUTION FROM SHIPPING: THE INTERNATIONAL RESPONSE. University of Queensland Law Journal 7:303-310 (1971) |
| IIIFV&G | TECHNIQUES DE PECHE: NOUVELLES TECHNIQUES. France Peche 167:52,55 (1972) |
| IIIFV&G | TECHNOLOGIA SOFISTICADA PARA PRODUCAO PESQUEIRA. Revista Nacional da Pesca 13(110): (1971) |
| IISL | Teclaff, Ludwik A. COASTAL ZONE - CONTROL OVER ENCROACHMENTS INTO THE TIDEWATERS. Journal of Maritime Law 1(2):241-290 (1970) |
| VINTL | _____ _____ THE IMPACT OF ENVIRONMENTAL CONCERN ON THE DEVELOPMENT OF INTERNATIONAL LAW. Natural Resources Journal 13:177-390 (1973) |
| VP | _____ _____ INTERNATIONAL LAW AND THE PROTECTION OF THE OCEANS FROM POLLUTION. Fordham Law Review 40:529-564 (1972) |
| IIIB | _____ _____ JURISDICTION OVER OFFSHORE FISHERIES - HOW FAR INTO THE HIGH SEAS. Fordham Law Review 35:409-424 (1967) |
| IICONS | Teclaff, Ludwik A., and E. Teclaff. SAVING THE LAND-WATER EDGE FROM RECREATION, FOR RECREATION. Arizona Law Review 14:39-64 (1972) |
| IIIP | Tejam, B.M., and B.C. Haldar. A PRELIMINARY SURVEY OF MERCURY IN FISH FROM BOMBAY AND THANA ENVIRONMENT. Indian Journal of Environmental Health 17(1):9-16 (1975) |
| IICONS | Terich, Thomas A. THE RETREATING SHORE. Pacific Northwest Sea 8(3): 4-7 (1975) |
| IIP&H | TERMINAL FOR 540,000 DWT TANKERS. Offshore Services 7:56-56 (1974) |
| VB | Terr, Leonard B. THE DISTANCE PLUS JOINT DEVELOPMENT ZONE FORMULA: A PROPOSAL FOR THE SPEEDY AND PRACTICAL RESOLUTION OF THE EAST CHINA AND YELLOW SEA. Cornell International Law Journal 7:49-71 (1973) |
| VB | TERRITORIAL JURISDICTION - MASSACHUSETTS EXTENSION ACT - STATE LEGISLATURE EXTENDS JURISDICTION OF STATE COURTS TO 200 MILES AT SEA. Vanderbilt Journal of Transnational Law 5:490-496 (1972) |
| IVB | TERRITORIAL JURISDICTION - MINING THE DEEP SEABED - INTERNATIONAL PROBLEMS AND NATIONAL RESOLUTIONS. Vanderbilt Journal of Transnational Law 4:497-502 (1972) |
| VB | TERRITORIAL SEA (FRANCE). International and Comparative Law Quarterly 21(3):578 (1972) |
| VB | TERRITORIAL WATERS. Harvard International Law Journal 8:156-168 (1967) |

| | |
|---|---|
| IVOL | TEXAS LEASE SALE: INTERIOR TO OFFER 116 OFFSHORE TRACTS IN SPRING OF '73. Offshore 32(11):46-46 (1972) |
| IVOL | TEXAS OFFSHORE LEASE SALE MOVES ONE STEP NEARER TO REALIZATION. Offshore 33(2):46-47 (1973) |
| VORM | TEXT OF THE DECLARATION OF SANTO DOMINGO APPROVED BY THE MEETING OF MINISTERS OF THE SPECIALIZED CONFERENCE OF THE CARIBBEAN COUNTRIES ON PROBLEMS OF THE SEA, HELD ON 7 JUNE 1972. Indian Journal of International Law 13(1):117-120 (1973) |
| VP | Thacher, P.S. ASSESSMENT AND CONTROL OF MARINE POLLUTION: THE STOCKHOLM RECOMMENDATIONS AND THEIR EFFICACY. Stanford Journal of International Studies 8:79-98 (1973) |
| VLOS | _____ _____ U.S. REVIEWS WORK OF 2ND SESSION OF U.N. AD HOC COMMITTEE ON SEA-BED. U.S. Department of State Bulletin 59:150-153 (1968) |
| VP | THERMAL DISCHARGES: A LEGAL PROBLEM. Tennessee Law Review 38:369-390 (1971) |
| VLOS | THE THIRD UNITED NATIONS CONFERENCE ON THE LAW OF THE SEA AND AN ARCHIPELAGIC REGIME. San Diego Law Review 13(3):742-764 (1976) |
| VLOS | THE THIRD UNITED NATIONS CONFERENCE ON THE LAW OF THE SEA: THE 1974 CARACAS SESSION. American Journal of International Law 69:1-30 (1975) |
| IVOI | Thobe S. EAST CANADA CONTINUES TO LURE DRILLERS IN OFFSHORE WORK. Offshore 33(7):117-118,120 (1973) |
| IVDRIL | Thomas, F. NORTH SEA AND ITS ENVIRONS; LEGAL ASPECTS AND THE GRANTING OF DRILLING LICENSES. Geographical Review 56:12-39 (1966) |
| IVMMR | Thomas, J. OFF-SHORE MINERAL RESOURCES LEGISLATION. Australian Law Journal 38:408-417 (1965) |
| IVMMR | Thompson, A. AUSTRALIAN PETROLEUM LEGISLATION AND THE CANADIAN EXPERIENCE. Melbourne University Law Review 6:370-402 (1968) |
| IVMMR | _____ _____ AUSTRALIA'S OFF-SHORE PETROLEUM COMMON CODE. University of British Columbia Law Review 3:1-37 (1968) |
| VENV | Thompson, A.R. ARCTIC ENVIRONMENT AND LEGISLATION. Alberta Law Review 10:431- (1972) |
| VENE | _____ _____ A VIEW FROM THE NORTH. Case Western Reserve Journal of International Law 5:52-64 (1972) |
| VB | _____ _____ JURISDICTIONAL PROBLEM IN CANADA'S OFFSHORE. Alberta Law Review 11:431-469 (1973) |
| IVOI | _____ _____ LEGAL ASPECTS OF OFFSHORE OIL AND GAS OPERATIONS AND OTHER SELECTED MATTERS OF CURRENT INTEREST TO THE OIL AND GAS INDUSTRY. Jurisdictional Problems in Canada's Offshore. Alberta Law Review 11: (1973) |
| VP | Thompson, Andrew R. LEGAL RESPONSES TO POLLUTION PROBLEMS - THEIR STRENGTHS AND WEAKNESSES. Natural Resources Journal 12:227-241 (1972) |

| | |
|---|---|
| VOD | Thompson, W.J. SHIPBOARD WASTE TREATMENT. <u>Water Pollution Control</u> 72:545-559 (1973) |
| VMT | THOR: A TANKER CONVERTED INTO THE WORLD'S LARGEST OFFSHORE WORKSHOP. <u>Holland Shipbuilding</u> 23(3):198-202 (1974) |
| IIICONS | Thormodsson, J. SOME LEGAL ASPECTS OF THE CONSERVATION OF FISH STOCKS IN THE NORTHEAST ATLANTIC OCEAN. <u>Ulfljótur</u> 26:3-66 (1973) |
| IIIF | 338' TUNA RECEIVING VESSEL MAY HAVE IMPACT ON INDUSTRY. <u>National Fisherman</u> 53(2):B7 (1972) |
| VB | THREE-MILE LIMIT: ITS JURIDICAL STATUS. <u>Valparaiso University Law Review</u> 6:170-184 (1972) |
| IIIF | Tibaudin, R.J., et al. LA AFILACION PREVISIONAL EN LA ACTIVIDAD PESQUERA. <u>Legislación del Trabajo</u> 20:121-128 (1972) |
| IISL | TIDELAND OWNERSHIP - TIME FOR REFORM. <u>University of Cincinnati Law Review</u> 36:121-142 (1967) |
| IISL | TIDELAND TRUST: ECONOMIC CURRENTS IN A TRADITIONAL LEGAL DOCTRINE. <u>U.C.L.A. Law Review</u> 21:826-891 (1974) |
| IIIB | Tiewul, S.A. THE FISHERIES JURISDICTION CASES, 1973, AND THE GHOST OF REBUS SIC STANTIBUS. <u>New York University Journal of International Law and Politics</u> 6:455-472 (1973) |
| VINTL | _____ INTERNATIONAL LAW AND NUCLEAR TEST EXPLOSIONS ON THE HIGH SEAS. <u>Cornell International Law Journal</u> 8:45-70 (1974) |
| IIIINTL | _____ FISHERIES JURISDICTION CASES (1973) (UNITED KINGDOM v. ICELAND; FEDERAL REPUBLIC OF GERMANY v. ICELAND 1973 ICJ 3) AND THE GHOST OF REBUS SIC STANTIBUS. <u>New York University Journal of International Law and Politics</u> 6:455-672 (1973) |
| VP | Tihansky, D.P. INTERNATIONAL SCOPE OF MARINE POLLUTION DAMAGE. <u>Marine Pollution Bulletin</u> 4:149-152 (1973) |
| VOD | Timagenis, Gregory J. INTERNATIONAL CONTROL OF DUMPING AT SEA. <u>Anglo-American Law Review</u> 1973:157-187 |
| VORM | Timmermann, J.A., JR. COASTAL STATES ORGANIZATION: THE PAST AND FUTURE. <u>Coastal Zone Management Journal</u> 1:119-122 (1973) |
| VMT | Tocino, M.I. EL TRANSPORTE MARITIMO DE SUBSTANCIAS NUCLEARES. <u>Aquivoros do Ministério da Justiça</u> 29(122):134-141 (1972) |
| IVM | TO DRILL OR NOT TO DRILL. <u>BioScience</u> 24:393-395 (1974) |
| VOR | Tollison, Robert D., and Thomas D. Willett. MARKET FAILURE, THE COMMON-POOL PROBLEM, AND OCEAN RESOURCE EXPLOITATION. <u>Journal of Law and Economics</u> 17:179-192 (1974) |
| IIP&H | Tomczak, W. LES PORTS BRITANNIQUES ET L'ÉLARGISSEMENT DU MARCHE COMMUN. <u>Problemes Economiques</u> 1(348):3-7 (1973) |
| VP | TORREY CANYON: IT LOOKS BLACK. <u>Economist</u> 223:61-62 (1967) |

| | |
|---|---|
| VLOS | TOWARD A LEGAL REGIME FOR THE INTERNATIONAL SEABED: THE SOVIET UNION'S EVOLVING PERSPECTIVE. Virginia Journal of International Law 15:871-901 (1975) |
| IIIF | TOWARD A MODEL REGIONAL FISHERIES MANAGEMENT REGIME: AN IMMODEST PROPOSAL. Kansas Law Review 23:461-497 (1975) |
| VENE | TOWARD A RATIONAL FUTURE ENERGY POLICY. Natural Resources Journal 14:239-256 (1974) |
| VP | TOWARD A STATE REMEDY FOR OIL SPILL DAMAGES: AN INSURANCE APPROACH. New York University Law Review 47:60-82 (1972) |
| VOR | TOWARD PEACEFUL SETTLEMENT OF OCEAN SPACE DISPUTES: A WORKING PAPER. San Diego Law Review 11:733-755 (1974) |
| VOR | Traavik, Kim. THE CONQUERING OF INNER SPACE: RESOURCES AND CONFLICTS ON THE SEABED. Cooperation and Conflict 9:5-21 (1974) |
| VENV | Train, R.E. NEW APPROACH TO INTERNATIONAL ENVIRONMENTAL COOPERATION: THE NATO COMMITTEE ON THE CHALLENGES OF MODERN SOCIETY. University of Kansas Law Review 22:167-191 (1975) |
| VP | TRANSPORTATION AND STORAGE OF EXPLOSIVES OR OTHER DANGEROUS ARTICLES OR SUBSTANCES AND COMBUSTIBLE LIQUIDS ON BOARD VESSELS. Federal Register 38(7):1276-1277 (January 11, 1973) |
| IIIFV&G | TRAWLING IN A VICE. South African Shipping News and Fishing Industry Review 27(6):46-47 (1972) |
| IIIFV&G | TRAWLERS DESIGNED FOR GREENLAND. Fishing News International 11(1): 38-40 (1972) |
| IVB | Treby, E. THE ROLE OF THE POLITICAL IDIOM IN JURISDICTIONAL CONFLICTS OVER OFFSHORE OIL AND GAS. Journal of Maritime Law and Commerce 5:281-297 (1974) |
| IIIF | TRENDS IN AUSTRALIAN FISH MARKET PRICES. Australian Fisheries 31: 23-23 (1972) |
| IIIFP | TRENDS IN OVERSEAS TRADE IN MARINE PRODUCE. Australian Fisheries 36:24-28 (1973); 34:23-28 (1975) |
| IVOI | Trimble, N.F. BOATS HERALD THE BOOM OF OFFSHORE SCOTLAND. Offshore 35:96,98-99 (1975) |
| VP | TROUBLE WITH MERCURY: CAN DOMESTIC LAWS CONTAIN AN INTERNATIONAL THREAT? Cornell International Law Journal 5:219-241 (1972) |
| IIIFV&G | Trout, G.C. A DEEP-TRAWLING WINCH FOR CANADIAN FISHERIES RESEARCH. Ocean Engineering 2:117-122 (1972) |
| VP | Tubb, Maretta. CONTROL OF OIL SPILLS; RECENT TECHNICAL DEVELOPMENTS. Ocean Industry 5:48-51 (1970) |
| IVM | Tuerkheimer, F.M. COPPER MINING FROM UNDER LAKE SUPERIOR: THE LEGAL ASPECTS. Natural Resources Lawyer 7:137-155 (1974) |
| IIIFV&G | TUNA BOAT'S SINGLE CATCH BRINGS OWNER $750,000. Marine Engineering/Log 78(2):42-43 (1973) |

IIIINTL   TUNA EXAMPLE: IS THERE HOPE FOR INTERNATIONAL COOPERATION? San Diego Law Review 11:776-814 (1974)

IIIF   TUNA FISHING EXPANDS. Australian Fisheries 34(2):9-11 (1975)

VB   TWELVE MILE LIMIT. Egyptian Economic and Political Review 4:10-10 (1958)

IVOSTR   TWO CONDEEP PLATFORMS TO BE BUILT SIMULTANEOUSLY. Northern Offshore 3(4):135-136 (1974)

IIIEZ   THE 200-MILE EXCLUSIVE ECONOMIC ZONE: DEATH KNELL FOR THE AMERICAN TUNA INDUSTRY. San Diego Law Review 13(3):707-741 (1976)

IIIEZ   200-MILE LIMIT VS. SPECIES PLAN. Fish Boat 19(7):48-49 (1974)

VP   Tyler, R. METHODS FOR STATE LEGAL ENFORCEMENT OF AIR AND WATER POLLUTION LAWS. Texas Bar Journal 31:905-906 (1968)

IVMMR   Uchupi, E., and K.O. Emery. CARIBE'S OIL POTENTIAL IS BOUNDLESS Oil and Gas Journal 70:156-162 (1972)

VLOS   Udall, Stewart L. SOME SECOND THOUGHTS ON STOCKHOLM. American University Law Review 22:717-732 (1973)

IVOSTR   UNDERWATER STORAGE TANKS INTERCONNECTED QUICKLY. World Oil 177(1):119-121 (1973)

IIIFV&G   UNE USINE FLOTTANTE POUR LA PRODUCTION PORTUGAISE D'HUILE ET DE FARINE DE POISSON. France Peche 175:46-46 (1972)

IVOI   U.K. BLOCK 211 MAY SCORE THIRD STRIKE. Oil and Gas Journal 70(38):50,52 (1972)

IIIB   UNITED KINGDOM: FISHING LIMITS. Aftenposten :1-1 (November 27, 1973)

VP   UNITED KINGDOM: MARINE POLLUTION. Times :7-7 (November 8, 1973)

VP   UNITED KINGDOM: OIL POLLUTION. New Law Journal :1154 (December 28, 1972); :198 (March 1, 1973)

VOR   UNITED NATIONS AND RESOURCES OF THE DEEP OCEAN FLOOR; PROCEEDINGS OF THE AMERICAN SOCIETY OF INTERNATIONAL LAW. Syracuse Journal of International Law and Commerce 1:91-121 (1972)

VLOS   UN AND THE SEA. UNITAR News 6(1): (1975)

IVM   UNITED NATIONS CONFERENCE ON TRADE AND DEVELOPMENT: SEABED MINING. Bulletin of Legal Developments 17:8-9 (1973)

VT&L   UNITED NATIONS ENVIRONMENT PROGRAMME: FINAL ACT OF CONFERENCE ON THE PROTECTION OF THE MEDITERRANEAN SEA. (DONE AT BARCELONA, FEBRUARY 16, 1976). International Legal Materials XV(2):285-318 (March, 1976)

VLOS   UNITED NATIONS GENERAL ASSEMBLY RESOLUTION ON RESERVATION OF SEA-BED AND OCEAN FLOOR FOR PEACEFUL PURPOSES, DECEMBER 21, 1968. International Legal Materials 3:201-208 (1969)

| | |
|---|---|
| VLOS | UNITED NATIONS GENERAL ASSEMBLY ADOPTION OF FOUR DRAFT RESOLUTIONS ON RESERVATION OF THE SEA-BED FOR PEACEFUL PURPOSES AND THE USE OF ITS RESOURCES IN THE INTEREST OF MANKIND. U.N. Monthly Chronicle 6(1):56-62 (1969) |
| VLOS | UNITED NATIONS: LAW OF THE SEA. Bulletin of Legal Developments 18: 10-10 (1973) |
| VLOS | UNITED NATIONS: LAW OF THE SEA CONFERENCE. Aftenposten :15-15 (December 1, 1973); Times :9-9 (November 20, 1973) |
| VLOS | UNITED NATIONS: SEABED COMMITTEE. Times :4-4 (July 3, 1973) |
| VLOS | United Nations. Seabed Committee. THE STRUGGLE IN DEFENCE OF MARINE RIGHTS. Peking Review 16:9-12 (1973) |
| VLOS | U.N. SEEKS OCEAN FLOOR CONTROL. Oceanology International 3:17-17 (1968) |
| VLOS | UNITED NATIONS THIRD CONFERENCE ON THE LAW OF THE SEA: INFORMAL SINGLE NEGOTIATING TEXT ON SETTLEMENT OF DISPUTES. PART IV. A/CONF. 62/WP.9, JULY 21, 1975. International Legal Materials Current Documents XV(1):61-87 (January, 1976) |
| VP | UNITED STATES AND CANADIAN APPROACHES TO AIR POLLUTION CONTROL AND THE IMPLICATIONS FOR THE CONTROL OF TRANSBOUNDARY POLLUTION. Cornell International Law Journal 7:148-170 (1974) |
| IIIT&L | UNITED STATES AND POLAND SIGN NEW FISHERIES AGREEMENT. The Department of State Bulletin LXXIV (1907):66-68 (January 12, 1976) |
| IIOD | Updegraff, G. THE ECONOMICS OF SEWAGE DISPOSAL IN A COASTAL URBAN AREA - A CASE STUDY OF THE MONTEREY PENINSULA, CALIFORNIA. Natural Resources Journal 11(2):373-389 (1971) |
| IIIF | THE U.S. FISHERIES TODAY: U.S. LEGISLATORS DISCUSS THE PROBLEMS AND ISSUES FACING THE COMMERCIAL FISHING INDUSTRY AND THE EFFORTS THEY ARE MAKING TO SOLVE THEM. Fish Boat 19(4):11-12,15-17,54-61 (1974) |
| IVLOS | U.S. HITS MOVE TO GIVE U.N. CONTROL OF SUBSEA MINERALS. Oil and Gas Journal 65(39):77-77 (1967) |
| IIIF | THE U.S. FISHERIES TODAY. Fish Boat 18(3):13,15,50-53 (1973) |
| IIIF | U.S. PRODUCTION AND IMPORTS: AN APPARENT CONTINUATION OF A TREND. Fish Boat 19(4):20-21 (1974) |
| VAC | U.S. PROPOSAL PROHIBITING EMPLACEMENT OF NUCLEAR WEAPONS ON SEABED AND OCEAN FLOOR, SUBMITTED BY THE UNITED STATES AT THE EIGHTEEN-NATION DISARMAMENT CONFERENCE. International Legal Materials 8:667-670 (1969) |
| IIIF | U.S. SHRIMP IMPORTS REPORT. Fish Boat 17:47-50 (1972) |
| IIIF | U.S.A.: FISHERY LIMITS. Aftenposten :6 (March 14, 1973) |
| IIIB | U.S.A.: FISHING LIMITS. Bulletin of Legal Developments 2:15-15 (January 29, 1975) |

IIIF    USA-JAPAN: FISHERIES. <u>U.S. Department of State Bulletin</u> :718 (December 18, 1972)

IIIF    USA-KOREA: FISHERIES CO-OPERATION. <u>U.S. Department of State Bulletin</u> :742 (December 25, 1972)

VMLAD   U.S.A.: MARITIME LAW. <u>Bulletin of Legal Developments</u> 2:15-15 (January 29, 1975)

IIIF    USA-USSR: PACIFIC FISHING ACCORDS. <u>International Herald Tribune</u> :3 (February 23, 1973)

VMT     U.S.S.R.-FLAG VESSELS ARRIVING AT CUBAN AND NORTH VIETNAM PORTS. SUPPLEMENT TO LIST. <u>Federal Register</u> 38(24):3417-3418 (February 6, 1973)

VAC     U.S.S.R. PROPOSAL ON PROHIBITING USE OF SEABED AND OCEAN FLOOR FOR MILITARY PURPOSES, OFFERED AT THE CONFERENCE OF THE EIGHTEEN-NATION COMMITTEE ON DISARMAMENT. <u>International Legal Materials</u> 8:659-660 (1969)

IVMMR   Utton, A. INSTITUTIONAL ARRANGEMENTS FOR DEVELOPING NORTH SEA OIL AND GAS. <u>Virginia Journal of International Law</u> 9:66-81 (1968)

IVP     _____ _____ SURVEY OF NATIONAL LAWS ON THE CONTROL OF POLLUTION FROM OIL AND GAS OPERATIONS ON THE CONTINENTAL SHELF. <u>Columbia Journal of Transnational Law</u> 9:331-361 (1970)

VP      Utton, Albert E. ARCTIC WATERS POLLUTION PREVENTION ACT, AND THE RIGHT OF SELF-PROTECTION. <u>University of British Columbia Law Review</u> 7:221-234 (1972)

VP      _____ _____ INTERNATIONAL WATER QUALITY LAW. <u>Natural Resources Journal</u> 13:177-390 (1973)

VREFS   Vambery, Joseph T. THE LAW OF THE SEA: A SELECTIVE BIBLIOGRAPHY OF ARTICLES, DOCUMENTS AND MONOGRAPHS. <u>Columbia Journal of Transnational Law</u> 13:173-186 (1974)

VP      Vance, George P. CONTROL OF ARCTIC OIL SPILLS. <u>Ocean Industry</u> 6:14-17 (1971)

VCONS   Van Cleve, Richard. CONSERVATION AND FUTURE DEVELOPMENT OF WEST COAST MARINE RESOURCES. <u>California Academy of Sciences Proceedings</u> 28:425-437 (1956)

VLOS    van Panhuys, Haro F. IN SEARCH OF AN INTERNATIONAL LAW OF EMERGENCY - WITH SPECIFIC REFERENCE TO THE LAW OF THE SEA. <u>Netherlands Yearbook of International Law</u> :148-170 (1972)

VORM    van Panhuys, H., and M. Van Emde Boas. LEGAL ASPECTS OF PIRATE BROADCASTING: A DUTCH APPROACH. <u>American Journal of International Law</u> 60:303-341 (1966)

IIIAFF  Ván Someren, V.D. THE ARTIFICIAL CULTURE OF THE EDIBLE EAST AFRICAN OYSTER, CRASSOSTREA CUCULLATA (BORN). <u>East African Agriculture Journal</u> 25:245-250 (1960)

VINTL   Van Zwanenberg, Ann. INTERFERENCE WITH SHIPS ON THE HIGH SEAS. <u>International and Comparative Law Quarterly</u> 10(4):785-817 (1961)

IIIF    Vardtal, K. THE NORWEGIAN FISHING INDUSTRY. Holland Shipbuilding 23(3):208-209 (1974)

VLOS    Vargas Carreño, E. MAR TERRITORIAL Y MAR PATRIMONIAL. Revista Uruguaya de Derecho Internacional 2:67-82 (1973)

IVMMR   VAST N. SEA RESERVES YET TO BE FOUND. Oil and Gas Journal 70(49):33-33 (1972)

VB      Vázques Carrizosa, A. LA DOCTRINA COLOMBIANA DEL MAR TERRITORIAL Y LOS CRITERIOS DE AMERICANA LATINA. Foro Colombiano 8:363-381 (1973)

VP      Vernon, Manfred. THE NETHERLANDS AND ITS WATERS: A MAJOR PROBLEM FOR A SMALL AND CROWDED NATION. Environmental Affairs 2(1):250-270 (1972)

IVDRIL  Verschure, P.J.M. HOW LONG WILL OFFSHORE DRILLING BE AMERICAN-DOMINATED? Oil and Gas Journal 71:136-138,140-141 (1973)

IIP     VESSEL OWNER'S LIABILITY TO THE STATES FOR OIL POLLUTION DAMAGE. Environmental Affairs 2:562- (1972)

VLOS    Vieira, M.A. STATUS JURÍDICO DE LOS PAÍSES SIN LITORAL. Arquivos do Ministério da Justiça 32(134):11-21 (1975)

VLOS    VIEWS IN THE AMERICAS ON BASIC QUESTIONS RELEVANT TO THE LAW OF THE SEA DISCUSSION. Georgia Journal of International and Comparative Law 5:171-184 (1975)

VLOS    Vignes, D. LES COMMUNAUTÉS EUROPÉENNES ET LE DROIT DE LA MER. Revue du Marché Common 163:84-94 (1973)

VLOS    _____ ORGANISATION ET RÈGLEMENT INTÉRIEUR DE LA IIIE CONFERENCE SUR LE DROIT DE LA MER. Revue du Droit Public et La Science Politique en France et à l'Etranger :337-377 (1975)

VLOS    Vignes, Daniel. WILL THE THIRD CONFERENCE ON THE LAW OF THE SEA WORK ACCORDING TO THE CONSENSUS RULE? American Journal of International Law 69:119-129 (1975)

VP      Vaux, Walter G., et al. OIL SPILL TREATMENT WITH COMPOSTED DOMESTIC REFUSE. Compost Science 13:17-19 (1972)

IIIINTL Vilariño Pintos, E. LA LEGISLACIÓN INTERNA SOBRE PESCA MARÍTIMA Y EL DERECHO INTERNACIONAL. Boletín de Información 28(1004):3-17 (1974)

VINTL   Villagrán, Kramer. EL MAR PATRIMONIAL COMO BASE DEL CONSENSO REGIONAL: EL CASO DEL MAR CARIBE. Revista Uruguaya de Derecho Internacional 2:83-104 (1973)

VP      Villareal, Dewey R., Jr. PRACTICAL ASPECTS OF AN OIL POLLUTION CASE. Practical Lawyer 17(6):37-48 (1971)

VP      Vink, G.J. KOPER IN VIS. T.N.O.-Nieuws 27(9):493-496 (1972)

VMT     VITALITY OF THE NAVIGABILITY CRITERION IN THE ERA OF ENVIRONMENTALISM. Arkansas Law Review 25:250-287 (1971)

VLOS      Vitzthum, W.  AUF DEM WEEGE ZU EINEM NEUEN MEERESVOELKERRECHT. Jahrbuch fuer Internationales Recht 16:229-265 (1973)

VB        Voelkel, M.  LES LIGNES DE BASE DANS LE CONVENTION DE GENÈVE SUR LA MER TERRITORIALE.  Annuaire Français de Droit International 19:820-836 (1973)

IVOI      Von Hartz, H.E.  KAPITAL INVESTIONEN UND TECHNISCHER AUFWAND BEI DER ERSCHLIESSUNG EINES OFFSHOREOELFELDES IN DER NORDSEE (BEISPIEL FORTIES-FELD). Erdoel, Erdgas; Zeitschrift fuer Bohr und Foerder Technik 91(2):38-42 (1975)

IIIFV&G   VOSTOK'S DUAL PURPOSE CATCHER'S AT SEA.  World Fishing 21(4):44-44 (1972)

IIP       Waldichuk, M.  COASTAL MARINE POLLUTION AND FISH.  Ocean Management 2(1):1-60 (1974)

VP        _____ _____ IMCO INTERNATIONAL CONFERENCE ON MARINE POLLUTION, LONDON, GREAT BRITAIN, 8 OCTOBER - 2 NOVEMBER 1973.  Ocean Management 1:277-286 (1973)

VP        _____ _____ INTERNATIONAL APPROACH TO THE MARINE POLLUTION PROBLEM. Ocean Management 1:211-261 (1973)

VOCET     Walker, C.W.  JURISDICTIONAL PROBLEMS CREATED BY ARTIFICIAL ISLANDS. San Diego Law Review 10(3):638-663 (1973)

VOSTR     Walker, Craig W.  ARTIFICIAL ISLANDS.  San Diego Law Review 10:638-663 (1973)

VMT       Walker, J.M., and K.C. Scott.  THE NORTHWEST PASSAGE:  A MARINE HIGHWAY.  Weather 27(8):326-332 (1972)

IIIF      Walker, Richard K., and James L. McNish.  TOWARD A MODEL REGIONAL FISHERIES MANAGEMENT REGIME:  AN IMMODEST PROPOSAL.  University of Kansas Law Review 23:461-497 (1975)

VP        Walmsley, David J.  OIL POLLUTION PROBLEMS ARISING OUT OF EXPLOITATION OF THE CONTINENTAL SHELF:  THE SANTA BARBARA DISASTER.  San Diego Law Review 9:514-568 (1972)

VORM      Walsh, Donald.  SOME THOUGHTS ON NATIONAL OCEAN POLICY:  THE CRITICAL ISSUE.  San Diego Law Review 13(3):594-627 (1976)

VINTL     _____ _____ SOVEREIGNTY OVER THE SEA.  Pakistan Horizon 25:35-42 (1972)

VOCET     Walters, J.C.  THE SA NAVY'S HYDROGRAPHIC SURVEY SHIP PROTEA.  South African Shipping News and Fishing Industry Review 27(9):22-23,29 (1972)

IVM       Walthier, Thomas N.  CURRENT STATUS OF OCEAN MINING.  Mining Engineering 23:51-53 (1971)

IIP&H     Wanhill, S.R.C.  A STUDY IN PORT PLANNING:  THE EXAMPLE OF MINA ZAYED.  Maritime Studies and Management 2:48-55 (1974)

| | |
|---|---|
| IVMMR | Warbrick, C. OFF-SHORE PETROLEUM EXPLOITATION IN FEDERAL SYSTEMS: CANADIAN AND AUSTRALIAN ACTION. *International and Comparative Law Quarterly* 17:501-513 (1968) |
| IIP | Warner, D.G. OFFSHORE SAFETY AND POLLUTION CONTROL. *Oil and Gas Journal* 70:73-78 (1972) |
| VOR | Wassermann, U. PROSPECT FOR SEA-BED RESOURCES IN A RECESSION. *Journal of World Trade Law* 9:711-713 (1975) |
| VP | WASTE DISCHARGE PERMITS: NO DEFENSE TO WATER POLLUTION ACTIONS. *Environmental Law* 2:181-188 (1971) |
| VP | WATER POLLUTION IN LOUISIANA: AN ATTEMPT AT CONTROL. *Loyola Law Review* 18:734-745 (1971-1972) |
| VP | WATER POLLUTION: ROLE OF THE COURTS. *Washington University Law Quarterly* 1972:291-312 (1972) |
| IIWQ | WATER QUALITY CONTROL: FEDERAL WATER POLLUTION CONTROL ACT AMENDMENTS OF 1972. *Natural Resources Lawyer* 7:225-256 (1975) |
| IIWQ | WATER QUALITY STANDARDS OF THE 1972 FEDERAL WATER POLLUTION CONTROL ACT: PRODUCTIVE BUT UNREALISTIC. *Gonzaga Law Review* 10:165-180 (1974) |
| IIOD | Watling, L. EVALUATION OF SLUDGE DUMPING OFF DELAWARE BAY. *Marine Pollution Bulletin* 5:39-42 (1974) |
| IVOL | Watson, H.K. LOUISIANA DIRECT ACTION STATUTE INAPPLICABLE IN OUTER CONTINENTAL SHELF LANDS ACT CASE. *Journal of Maritime Law and Commerce* 5:135-139 (1973) |
| VOCET | Watt, D.C. GERMANY WANTS COOPERATION IN MARINE RESEARCH. *Offshore Services* 8(1):38,41 (1975) |
| IVOSTR | Webb, A.D. ZAKUM SUBSEA PRODUCTION IS ELECTRIC-POWERED. *Oil and Gas Journal* 71:142-144 (1973) |
| IIIAFF | Weeks, Ann. FISH CITIES; A NEW SCHOOL OF DESIGN. *NOAA* 2(2):25-29 (1972) |
| IVMMR | Weeks, L.G. OFFSHORE SUCCESSES RAISE FAR EAST/OCEANIA POTENTIAL. *World Oil* 176:87-88,92,94 (1973) |
| VOI | _____ _____ WORLD OFFSHORE SCENE IN RAPID CHANGE. *Oil and Gas Journal* 69:91-94,99 (1971) |
| VOI | Weichart, Guenter. THE NORTH SEA. *Environment* 16:29-33 (1974) |
| VP | _____ _____ POLLUTION OF THE NORTH SEA. *Ambio* 2:99-106 (1973) |
| VINTL | Weissberg, G. INTERNATIONAL LAW MEETS THE SHORT-TERM NATIONAL INTEREST: THE MALTESE PROPOSAL ON THE SEA-BED AND OCEAN FLOOR - ITS FATE IN TWO CITIES. *International and Comparative Law Quarterly* 18:41-102 (1969) |
| VP | Wellman, A.M. OIL FLOATING IN THE NORTHERN ATLANTIC. *Marine Pollution Bulletin* 4:190-191 (1973) |

IVDRIL   Wells, Michael J. NORWAY SLIPS INTO GEAR FOR OFFSHORE DRILLING. World Petroleum 37:22-26 (1966)

IVDRIL   Welter, Robert J. HOW TO BEST ACHIEVE THE FIVE TAX OBJECTIVES IN STRUCTURING AN OIL AND GAS DRILLING DEAL. Journal of Taxation 41: 38-45 (1974)

VP   Wenders, John T. POLLUTION CONTROL - USES OF CORRECTIVE TAXES RECONSIDERED. Natural Resources Journal 12:76-82 (1972)

IIIINTL   Wengler, W. DIE ISLAENDISCHE FISCHEREIVORBEHALTZONE VOR DEM INTERNATIONALEN GERICHTSHOF. Neue Juristische Wochenschrift 26:936-940 (1973)

VB   Wenk, Edward, Jr. COASTAL WATERS AND THE NATION. Civil Engineering 39:52-55 (1969)

VLOS   _____ \_\_\_\_\_ INTERNATIONAL INSTITUTIONS FOR RATIONAL MANAGEMENT OF OCEAN SPACE. Ocean Management 1:171-200 (1973)

VOR   _____ \_\_\_\_\_ THE PHYSICAL RESOURCES OF THE OCEAN. Scientific American 221:167-176 (1969)

VP   Wenner, Lettie M. ENFORCEMENT OF WATER POLLUTION CONTROL LAW. Law and Society Review 6:481-508 (1972)

VP   Wertenbaker, William. ANATOMY OF AN OIL SPILL. Journal of the Marine Technology Society 8:16-28 (1974)

IIIB   WEST GERMANY; FISHERY JURISDICTION. Financial Times :39-39 (September 5, 1972)

VMLAD   WEST GERMANY; SHIPPING LAW. Bundesgesetzblatt 1(56):966-966 (1972); Sammelblatt :1025-1025 (1972)

VLOS   West, Mary B., and B.H. Oxman. ISSUES TO BE RESOLVED IN THE SECOND SUBSTANTIVE SESSION IN THE THIRD UNITED NATIONS CONFERENCE ON THE LAW OF THE SEA. Columbia Journal of Transnational Law 14:87-101 (1975)

VOI   Westman, Walter E. DEVELOPMENT OFFSHORE. Ecology Today 2(2):11-13, 46 (1972)

IISL   WETLANDS' RELUCTANT CHAMPION: THE CORPS TAKES A FRESH LOOK AT "NAVIGABLE WATERS". Environmental Law 6:217-241 (1975)

IISL   WETLANDS STATUTES: REGULATION OR TAKING? Connecticut Law Review 5:64-99 (1972)

IIIENV   Wharam, A. ENVIRONMENT AND (THE) LAW. WEST GERMANY. SCANDINAVIA - FINLAND AND SWEDEN, NORWAY AND DENMARK. New Law Journal 122:875,921, 1043 (1972)

VINTL   WHAT DOES IT MEAN WHEN A STATE CLAIMS 200 MILES? Fish Boat 19(3): 19-19 (1974)

VOCET   WHAT WASHINGTON OCEANOGRAPHERS THINK ABOUT OCEANOGRAPHY IN WASHINGTON. Pacific Northwest Sea 4(2): (1971)

VOI   WHAT'S GOING ON OFFSHORE? Ocean Industry 4:12-14 (1969)

| | |
|---|---|
| VOCET | WHAT'S NEW IN MARINE EXPLORATION. World Oil 177(1):103,105-106 (1973) |
| IVREF | WHERE TO GO ... WHO TO CONTACT. Offshore Services 6(2):29-34,37-39 (1973) |
| VENV | White, Henry R. UNITED STATES ENVIRONMENTAL LAWS AND EXPLORATION AND PRODUCTION OPERATIONS. Alberta Law Review 13:1-17 (1975) (Petroleum law suppl.) |
| IICONS | Whitney, Mary C. FEDERAL RULE OF ACCRETION AND CALIFORNIA COASTAL PROTECTION. Southern California Law Review 48:1457-1476 (1975) |
| VENE | Whitney, Scott C. SITING OF ENERGY FACILITIES IN THE COASTAL ZONE - A CRITICAL REGULATORY HIATUS. William and Mary Law Review 16:805-822 (1975) |
| IVOL | Whitney, Steve. NIXON SELLS TOO SOON: THE UNDERSEA CHASE. Sierra Club Bulletin 59:15-16,22-23 (1974) |
| VINTL | WHO OWNS OCEAN'S WEALTH? Chemical Week 101:56-57 (October 14, 1967) |
| IVINTL | WHO OWNS THE MINERAL RIGHTS IN HUDSON BAY? Manitoba Law Journal 3:41-52 (1969) |
| VINTL | WHO OWNS THE OCEAN FLOOR? Chemical Week 101:5-5 (1967) |
| VINTL | WHO OWNS WHICH OCEAN? Science News 90:23-23 (July 9, 1966) |
| IVB | WHO SHOULD HAVE JURISDICTION OVER OFFSHORE MINERAL RESOURCES? Oil and Gas Journal 67:28-32 (1969) |
| IVOI | WHO SUPPLIES WHAT TO NORTH SEA DRILLING RIGS. Hydrospace 5(4):14-15 (1972) |
| IIOSTR | Wickizer, C.L. SUBSEA SYSTEM HAS STANDARD EQUIPMENT. Offshore 33(5):278- (1973) |
| VOR | Wiggins, J.R. U.S. SUGGESTS POSSIBLE STEPS BY U.N. TO PROMOTE PEACEFUL USES OF DEEP OCEAN FLOOR. U.S. Department of State Bulletin 59:554-558 (1968) |
| VSG | Wildman, R.D., and R.B. Abel. THE NATIONAL SEA GRANT PROGRAM. Coastal Zone Management Journal 1:129-131 (1973) |
| IVLOS | Wilke, H. DIE VERTRAEGE UEBER DIE ABGRENZUNG DES FESTLANDSOCKELS UNTER DER NORDSEE IN IHRER BEDEUTUNG FUER DIE WIRTSCHAFTLICHE NUTZUNG AUSBEUTBARER BODENSCHAETZE. Zeitschrift fuer Bergrecht 113:281-291 (1972) |
| IICZM | Wilkes, Daniel. CONSIDERATION OF ANTICIPATORY USES IN DECISIONS ON COASTAL DEVELOPMENT. San Diego Law Review 6:354-374 (1969) |
| VP | _____. CONSTITUTIONAL DILEMMAS POSED BY STATE POLICIES AGAINST MARINE POLLUTION - THE MAINE EXAMPLE. Maine Law Review 23:143-174 (1971) |
| VP | _____. INTERNATIONAL ADMINISTRATIVE DUE PROCESS AND CONTROL OF POLLUTION - THE CANADIAN ARCTIC EXAMPLE. Journal of Maritime Law 2:499-539 (1971) |

VLOS     Wilkes, Daniel. LAW OF THE SEA NEEDS FOR THE 1970'S. <u>San Diego Law Review</u> 8:453-458 (1971)

VOR     _____ _____ THE USE OF WORLD RESOURCES WITHOUT CONFLICT: MYTHS ABOUT THE TERRITORIAL SEA. <u>Wayne Law Review</u> 14:441-470 (1968)

VOR     Wilkey, M.R. DEEP OCEAN: ITS POTENTIAL MINERAL RESOURCES AND PROBLEMS. <u>The International Lawyer</u> 3:31-48 (1968)

IVMMR     WILL OFFSHORE BONANZA BY-PASS BRITAIN? <u>Dock and Harbour Authority</u> 53(630):477-480 (1973)

VLOS     Williams, J. LAW OF THE SEA: A PARALLEL FOR SPACE LAW. <u>Military Law Review</u> :155-172 (1963)

IICZM     Williams, S.J., and D.B. Duane. CONSTRUCTION IN THE COASTAL ZONE: A POTENTIAL USE OF WASTE MATERIALS. <u>Marine Geology</u> 18(1):1-15 (1975)

VENV     Willrich, Mason. ENERGY-ENVIRONMENT CONFLICT: SITING ELECTRIC POWER FACILITIES. <u>Virginia Law Review</u> 58:257-336 (1972)

IIDR     Wilmot, F. JAMAICA'S WATERFRONT, SUBURBS CREATED THROUGH DREDGING. <u>World Dredging and Marine Construction</u> 11(3):24-26 (1975)

VENE     Wilson, James E. POTENTIAL RESERVES OF DOMESTIC OIL AND GAS. <u>Journal of Petroleum Technology</u> 26:150-156 (1974)

VORM     Wilson, M. CONTINENTAL SHELF AND FOREIGN TAX CREDIT UNDER THE TAX REFORM ACT OF 1969. <u>Wayne Law Review</u> 16:1379-1403 (1970)

IVM     Wilson, T. HARNESSING SYSTEMS FOR UNDERSEA MINING. <u>Engineering and Mining Journal</u> 166:62-67 (1965)

IVM     _____ _____ OFFSHORE MINING PAVES THE WAY TO OCEAN MINERAL WEALTH. <u>Engineering and Mining Journal</u> 166:124-132 (1965)

IVMMR     _____ _____ OIL HUNTERS WILL HASTEN QUEST FOR MARINE RESERVES. <u>Offshore</u> 27(13):42-43 (1967)

IVM     _____ _____ UNDERSEA MINING; PROFILE OF A GROWING INDUSTRY. <u>Engineering Mining Journal</u> 166:82-88 (1965)

VLOS     Windeyer, V. KENNETH BAILEY MEMORIAL LECTURE: THE SEABED IN LAW. <u>Federal Law Review</u> 6(1):1-25 (1974)

IIIFV&G     Windley, David W., and Carmen J. Blondin. ISSUES RAISED BY THE ATTACHMENT OF THE SULEYMAN STAISKIY: SOVEREIGN IMMUNITY OF SOCIALIST FISHING VESSELS AND LIABILITY FOR DAMAGE TO FIXED FISHING GEAR BY VESSELS FISHING MOBILE GEAR. <u>Journal of Maritime Law and Commerce</u> 4(1):141-157 (1972)

IIP     Windom, Herbert L. UNCONFINED DUMPING OF DREDGE SPOIL SAID BETTER THAN DIKE METHOD. <u>Work Boat</u> 29:36,38,40,42 (1972)

VENV     Winter, Thomas C., Jr. THE NATIONAL ENVIRONMENTAL POLICY ACT AND ITS RELATION TO OFFSHORE AND MARITIME ACTIVITIES. <u>Houston Law Review</u> 9:700-708 (1972)

VENV     Winters, John M. ENVIRONMENTALLY SENSITIVE LAND USE REGULATION IN CALIFORNIA. <u>San Diego Law Review</u> 10:693-756 (1973)

| | |
|---|---|
| IIIF | WITHHELD FUNDS RESULT IN CURTAILED OR TERMINATED FISHERY PROGRAMS. Fish Boat 18(3):23-23 (1973) |
| VP | Wolf, P. de, and W.E. Lewis. EEN MEETNET VOOR ZWARE LANGS DE NEDER-LANDS KUST. T.N.O.- Nieuws 27(9):504-511 (1972) |
| VENV | Wolfrum, R. DER UMWELTSCHUTZ AUF HOHER SEE: INTERNATIONALE WIE NATIONALE MASSNAHMEN UND BESTREBUNGEN. Verfassung und Recht in Uebersee 8:201-219 (1975) |
| IIIF | Wollenberg, E. COLUMBIA RIVER FISH COMPACT. Oregon Law Review 13:88-167 (1939) |
| VP | Wolman, Abel. GLOBAL POLLUTION AND HUMAN RIGHTS. Natural Resources Journal 12:195-210 (1972) |
| VP | _____ _____ POLLUTION AS AN INTERNATIONAL ISSUE. Foreign Affairs 47:164-175 (1968) |
| VOR | Wong, Chung-ming. ECONOMIC DESALTING MOVES CLOSER TO REALITY. Undersea Technology 11:51-52 (1970) |
| VP | Wood, L.D. REQUIRING POLLUTERS TO PAY FOR AQUATIC NATURAL RESOURCES DESTROYED BY OIL POLLUTION. Natural Resources Lawyer 8:545-609 (1976) |
| VOD | Wood, Lance D. INTEGRATED INTERNATIONAL AND DOMESTIC APPROACH TO CIVIL LIABILITY FOR VESSEL-SOURCE OIL POLLUTION. Journal of Maritime Law 7:1-68 (1975) |
| IIIP | Woodin, Sarah A. EFFECT OF DIESEL OIL SPILLS ON INVERTEBRATES. Marine Pollution Bulletin 3(9):139-143 (1972) |
| VCS | Woodliffe, J. CONTINENTAL SHELF ACT, 1964 - A COMMENT. Solicitor's Journal 3:339-348 (1964) |
| IIIINTL | _____ _____ INSHORE FISHERIES AND INTERNATIONAL LAW. Law Journal 113:428-430 (1963) |
| VOR | Wooster, Warren S. THE OCEAN AND MAN; HOW CAN MEN OF ALL NATIONS STUDY AND EXPLOIT THE OCEAN FOR THEIR MUTUAL BENEFIT? Scientific American 221:218-220 (1969) |
| VB | _____ _____ SCIENTIFIC ASPECTS OF MARITIME SOVEREIGNTY CLAIMS. Ocean Development and International Law Journal 1:13-20 (1973) |
| IIIOI | WORLD FISH CATCH ROSE 10% IN 1970. Commercial Fisheries Review 34:34-35 (1972) |
| VINTL | WORLD OCEAN; A PLAN FOR INTERNATIONAL ACTION. Catholic University Law Review 18:491-523 (1969) |
| IIOSTR | WORLD'S BIGGEST, MOST EXPENSIVE OFFSHORE PLATFORM. Petroleum Engineer 44(12):42,46,53 (1972) |
| VP | WORLD'S LARGEST SLOP BARGE. Tanker and Bulk Carrier 19(9):9-9 (1973) |
| IVMMR | THE WORLDWIDE SEARCH FOR OIL. Business Week 2366:38-44 (February 3, 1975) |

| | |
|---|---|
| VP | Wright, C. OILSPILL CONCERN LEADS TO OIL CONTAINMENT DEVELOPMENTS. Offshore 33(2):60-61,63 (1973) |
| VP | _____ _____ RATING SYSTEM FOR SPILL CONTROL. World Ports 35:8-9 (1973) |
| IVOSTR | WRONGFUL DEATH - APPLICATION OF LAW OF THE COASTAL STATE TO TORTS OCCURRING ON OFFSHORE DRILLING PLATFORMS. Tulane Law Review 44:354-363 (1970) |
| IVMMR | Wu, Shu-Chuan, and Chieh Chu. USE OF DEEP SEA MANGANESE NODULES AS CATALYSTS FOR REDUCTION OF NITRIC OXIDE WITH AMMONIA. Atmospheric Environment 6(5):309-317 (1972) |
| IISL | Wulf, N. FREEZING THE BOUNDARY DIVIDING FEDERAL AND STATE INTERESTS IN OFFSHORE SUBMERGED LANDS. San Diego Law Review 8:584-605 (1971) |
| VP | Wulf, Norman A. CONTIGUOUS ZONES FOR POLLUTION CONTROL; ACTIONS TAKEN BY COASTAL STATES TO PREVENT OIL POLLUTION OF THE HIGH SEAS CONTIGUOUS TO THEIR TERRITORIAL SEAS. Journal of Maritime Law and Commerce 3:537-557 (1972) |
| VP | _____ _____ INTERNATIONAL CONTROL OF MARINE POLLUTION. JAG Journal XXV (3):93-100 (1971) |
| IIIF | Yablonskaya, E.A. ESTIMATION OF THE POTENTIAL FISH PRODUCTION OF SEA BASINS. Canada Fisheries Research Board Trans. of Trudy Vsesoyuznogo Nauchno-Issledovatel'skogo Instituta Morskogo Rynogo Khozyaistva i Okeanografii 71(2):75-82 (1970) |
| VLOS | Yamamoto, S. THE ABSTENTION PRINCIPLE AND ITS RELATION TO THE EVOLVING INTERNATIONAL LAW OF THE SEA. Washington Law Review 43:45-61 (1967) |
| VENV | Yannacone, Victor J., Jr. ENVIRONMENTAL LITIGATION. American Bar Association Section of Insurance, Negligence and Compensation Law 1971:320- (1971) |
| IICZM | Yorshis, S. APPRAISING OCEAN FRONT PROPERTY. Title News 47(11):8-13 (1968) |
| IIIOD | Young, D.L.K., and R.T. Barber. EFFECTS OF WASTE DUMPING IN NEW YORK BIGHT ON THE GROWTH OF NATURAL POPULATION OF PHYTOPLANKTON. Environmental Pollution 5:237-252 (1973) |
| IIIP | Young, David R., et al. MERCURY CONCENTRATIONS IN DATED VARVED MARINE SEDIMENTS COLLECTED OFF SOUTHERN CALIFORNIA. Nature 244:273-275 (1973) |
| VENV | Young, Harold W. POWER PLANT SITING AND THE ENVIRONMENT. Oklahoma Law Review 26:193-238 (1973) |
| IIIP | Young, J.S. A MARINE KILL IN NEW JERSEY COASTAL WATERS. Marine Pollution Bulletin 4(5):70-70 (1973) |
| VINTL | Young, R. LEGAL REGIME OF THE DEEP-SEA FLOOR. American Journal of International Law 62:641-653 (1968) |
| VB | _____ _____ OFFSHORE CLAIMS AND PROBLEMS IN THE NORTH SEA. American Journal of International Law 59:505-522 (1965) |

| | |
|---|---|
| IIIINTL | Young, Richard. SEDENTARY FISHERIES AND THE CONVENTION ON THE CONTINENTAL SHELF. <u>American Journal of International Law</u> 55:359-373 (1961) |
| VP | Young, Warren R. POSSIBLE SOLUTIONS TO OIL SPILLAGE, A GROWING PROBLEM. <u>Smithsonian</u> 1:19-27 (1970) |
| VLOS | Zacklin, R. AMERICA LATINA Y EL DESARROLLO DEL DERECHO DEL MAR. <u>Revista Uruguaya de Derecho Internacional</u> 2:9-32 (1973) |
| VLOS | Zacklin, Ralph. LATIN AMERICA AND THE DEVELOPMENT OF THE LAW OF THE SEA. <u>Annales d'Etudes Internationales</u> 4:31-54 (1973) |
| IVMT | Zannetos, Z.S. PERSISTENT ECONOMIC MISCONCEPTIONS IN THE TRANSPORTATION OF OIL BY SEA. <u>Maritime Studies and Management</u> 1:107-118 (1973) |
| IIICONS | Zaorski, R. PROBLEMS OF CONSERVATION OF LIVING RESOURCES OF THE BALTIC SEA. <u>Polish Yearbook of International Law</u> 3:39-51 (1970) |
| IICONS | Zubieta, Charles A. CALIFORNIA COASTAL ZONE CONSERVATION ACT OF 1972 (PROPOSITION 20) AND COMPARABLE LAND USE LIMITATIONS AFFECTING THE MINERAL INDUSTRY IN OTHER STATES. <u>Rocky Mountain Mineral Law Institute</u> 20:283-299 (1975) |
| IVOSTR | Zuidberg, H.M. SEACALF: A SUBMERSIBLE CONE-PENETROMETER RIG. <u>Marine Geotechnology: an International Journal of Seafloor Science and Engineering</u> 1(1):15-32 (1975) |
| IIENV | Zwicky, S., and J. Clark. ENVIRONMENTAL PROTECTION MOTIVATION IN COASTAL LAND-USE LEGISLATION. <u>Coastal Zone Management Journal</u> 1:103-108 (1973) |

APR 28 1977

Z
6464
M2
V65
v.2